1982 Supplement

**POLITICAL AND CIVIL RIGHTS
IN THE UNITED STATES**

WITHDRAWN FROM
MACALESTER COLLEGE
LIBRARY

EDITORIAL ADVISORY BOARD

Little, Brown and Company
Law Book Division

A. James Casner, *Chairman*
Austin Wakeman Scott Professor of Law, Emeritus
Harvard University

Francis A. Allen
Edson R. Sunderland Professor of Law
University of Michigan

Clark Byse
Byrne Professor of Administrative Law
Harvard University

Thomas Ehrlich
Provost and Professor of Law
University of Pennsylvania

Geoffrey C. Hazard, Jr.
John A. Garver Professor of Law
Yale University

Willis L. M. Reese
Charles Evans Hughes Professor of Law, Emeritus
Columbia University

Bernard Wolfman
Fessenden Professor of Law
Harvard University

1982 Supplement

Emerson, Haber, and Dorsen's
Political and Civil Rights
In the United States

Fourth Edition
Volume I

Norman Dorsen
Professor of Law
New York University

Paul Bender
Professor of Law
University of Pennsylvania

Burt Neuborne
Professor of Law
New York University

Joel Gora
Associate Professor of Law
Brooklyn Law School

Little, Brown and Company   Boston and Toronto

COPYRIGHT © 1982 by Norman Dorsen, Paul Bender, Burt Neuborne, and Joel Gora

All rights reserved. No part of this book may be reproduced in any form or by any electronic or mechanical means including information storage and retrieval systems without permission in writing from the publisher, except by a reviewer who may quote brief passages in a review.

Library of Congress Catalog Card No. 75-22786

ISBN 0-316-19052-7

FG

Published simultaneously in Canada
by Little, Brown & Company (Canada) Limited

PRINTED IN THE UNITED STATES OF AMERICA

Contents

Table of Cases	lx
Acknowledgments	xli

Chapter Two.   National Security   1

A.	Background of Laws on Treason, Rebellion, Insurrection, Espionage, Sabotage, and Similar Conduct	1
B.	Restrictions on Expression Which May Interfere with a War or Defense Effort	1
C.	Antisedition Laws and Similar Restrictions on Political Expression	2
D.	Denial of Privileges or Positions of Influence to Subversives	3
E.	Loyalty-Security Qualifications for Employment	4
[F.	Aliens and Citizenship]	4
F [G].	Legislative Investigations	5
G [H].	Surveillance and Other Forms of Police Action Interfering with Freedom of Political Expression	6
[I.	Inherent and Emergency Powers of the President and State Officials]	12

Chapter Three.   Government Secrecy and the Public's Right to Know   13

A.	The Development of a "Right to Know"	13
	Note — Freedom of Information Act Developments	19
B.	National Security Information: The Classification System	25
C.	Executive Privilege	32

Chapter Four.   Freedom of Expression in a Public Forum — First Amendment Relations in Public   35

Young v. American Mini Theatres, Inc.	*38*
FCC v. Pacifica Foundation	*38*

v

Chapter Five.   Administration of Justice   57

A [B]. The Protection of Confidential Sources in Judicial Proceedings   57
       Note — State Shield Laws   60
B [C]. Criticism of the Judicial Process   61
C [D]. Prejudicial Publicity and the Right to a Fair Trial 62
       Chandler v. Florida   *64*
       Note — Judicial Restrictive Orders   73
       Nebraska Press Assn. v. Stuart   *73*
       Richmond Newspapers, Inc. v. Virginia   *79*

Chapter Six.   Obscenity and "Offensive" Speech   89

  A. Obscenity   89
       Young v. American Mini Theatres, Inc.   *93*
  B. "Offensive" Speech   106
       Federal Communications Commission v. Pacifica Foundation   *107*

Chapter Seven.   Actions for Defamation and Invasion of Privacy   117

       Note — Group Libel   117
       Note — The Barr v. Mateo Privilege   117
       Note — Libel and the Speech or Debate Clause   117
       Note — The Constitutional Limitations ... Applicable ... to "Private" Defamation ...   127

Chapter Eight.   Commercial Speech   133

       Virginia State Board of Pharmacy v. Virginia Citizens Consumer Council   *133*
       Central Hudson Gas and Electric Corp. v. Public Service Commission of New York   *143*
       Note — Corporate Speech on Public Issues   153
       First National Bank of Boston v. Belloti   *153*

Chapter Nine.   Access to and Regulation of the Media   165

A [B]. The Press   165
B [C]. The Broadcast Media   166
       Note — FCC Regulation of the Broadcast Media: The Fairness Doctrine and Other Content Controls   167

Chapter Ten. Academic Freedom   **175**

    A. Introduction   175
    B. Freedom to Teach — Choice of Curriculum and Teaching Method   175
    C. Freedom of Speech — In the School or University   178
    D. Freedom of Speech — Outside the School or University   178
        Mt. Healthy City School District Board of Education v. Doyle   *178*
    E. The Right to Privacy and Individual Lifestyle   185
    F. Procedural Fairness   187
    G. Collective Bargaining   189
    H. The Rights of Students   190
        Board of Curators of the University of Missouri v. Horowitz   *190*

Chapter Eleven. The Right to Travel   **201**

    A. Domestic Travel   201
    B. International Travel   203

Chapter Twelve. Privacy   **207**

    A. Protected Private Activities: The Privacies of Life   207
        Carey v. Population Services International   *207*
    B. Informational Privacy   228
        Note — The Possibly Emerging Right of Informational Privacy   229
        Whalen v. Roe   *230*

Chapter Thirteen. The Right of Franchise   **237**

    A. Judicial Protection of the Right to Vote   237
    B. Judicial Protection of the Right to Run for Office   240
    C. Judicial Protection of the Right to Fair Representation   242
        Note — Federal Judicial Remedies for Violation of Franchise Rights   248
   [D]. Congressional Protection of the Franchise   248
        Note — Voting Rights Act Amendments of 1975   248
  D [E]. Regulation of the Electoral Process   249
        First National Bank of Boston v. Bellotti   *253*

Chapter Fourteen. Religious Freedom   **255**

    B. The Establishment Clause   255
        Stone v. Graham   *261*
    C. The "Free Exercise" of Religion   266

Chapter Fifteen. Individual Rights Within Private Associations 275

- A. Labor Unions — 275
  - *Abood v. Detroit Board of Education* — 276
- B. Professional, Trade, and Business Associations — 287
- C. Social and Athletic Clubs, Fraternities, and Religious Organizations — 290

Chapter Sixteen. The Rights of Groups with Diminished Constitutional Protection: Prisoners, Mental Patients, and Military Personnel 293

- A. Prisoners' Rights — 293
  - *Bounds v. Smith* — 293
  - *Jones v. North Carolina Prisoners' Labor Union, Inc.* — 297
  - *Hutto v. Finney* — 301
- B. Rights of Mental Patients — 314
- C. The Rights of Military Personnel — 317

Chapter Seventeen. The Constitutional Litigation Process 321

- A. The Doctrine of Standing — 321
  - Note — Supreme Court Standing Cases Since *Warth v. Seldin* — 321
- B. The Doctrines of Ripeness and Mootness — 329
  - *Franks v. Bowman* — 329
- C. The Doctrines of Immunity — 334
  - *Fitzpatrick v. Bitzer* — 338
- D. The Political Question Doctrine — 344
- E. Problems of Federal Jurisdiction and Federalism: Federal Jurisdiction over State Officials Alleged To Be Violating Federal Constitutional Rights — 345
  - *Monell v. Department of Social Services* — 345
  - *Parratt v. Taylor* — 353
  - *Paul v. Davis* — 361
  - Note — Jurisdiction over Supremacy Clause Cases — 380
  - *Carlson v. Green* — 380
  - *Examining Board of Engineers, Architects, and Surveyors v. Flores de Otero* — 391
  - *Allen v. McCurry* — 393
  - Note — Section 1983 Claims in State Court — 401

Table of Cases

(Principal cases in italics.)
Aafco Heating & Air Conditioning Co. v. Northwest Pubs., Inc., 127
Aberty v. Daniel, 401
Abood v. Detroit Bd. of Educ., 190, *276*
Abramovich v. Board of Educ., 189
Abu Eain v. Wilkes, 345
Ackley v. Maple Woodman Assocs., 379
ACLU v. New Jersey Election Law Enforcement Commn., 56
ACLU v. Tennessee, 377
Ad World, Inc. v. Township of Doylestown, 152
Addington v. Texas, 315, 316
AFL-CIO v. Federal Elections Commn., 253, 275
Aiello v. City of Wilmington, 351
Airport Bookstore, Inc. v. Jackson, 105
Akron Center for Reproductive Health v. City of Akron, 218
Alabama v. Davis, 332
Alaska Gay Coalition v. Sullivan, 166
Alaska v. Green, 341
Albright v. United States, 235
Aldinger v. Howard, 350
Alfred L. Snapp & Son, Inc. v. Puerto Rico, 325
Allen v. Austin, 240
Allen v. Board of Educ., 184, 241
Allen v. CIA, 21
Allen v. Ellisor, 239
Allen v. McCurry, 393, 398
Alma Socy., Inc. v. Mellon, 234
Alvey v. General Elec. Co., 284
Ambach v. Norwick, 175
American Benefit Life v. McIntyre, 122
American Fedn. of Govt. Employees v. Schlesinger, 235
American Future Sys. v. Pennsylvania State Univ., 198
American Intl. Group v. Islamic Rep. of Iran, 345
American Med. Assn. v. FTC, 15, 143

American Security Council Educ. Fund v. FCC, 167
Anderson v. Celebrezze, 240
Anderson v. City of Boston, 254
Anderson v. General Dynamics Convair Aerospace Div., 268, 269, 283
Andre v. Board of Trustees of Village of Maywood, 202
Andresen v. Maryland, 230
Andrews v. Ballard, 226
Andrews v. Chateau X, Inc., 103, 105
Angelico v. State of La., 56
Anton v. St. Louis Surburban Newspapers, 120
Application of A & M, 234
Arctic v. Loudoun Times Mirror, 123
Arnheiter v. Random House, 121
Arundar v. Dekalb Co., 197
Atlas Roofing Co. v. Occupational Safety & Health Review Commn., 377
Attorney General, In re, 31, 33
Aufiero v. Clarke, 250
Aumiller v. University of Del., 183
B, In re, 235
Babauer v. Woodcock, 275
Babbitt v. United Farm Workers, 243, 323, 329, 334, 393
Bachrach v. Secretary of Commonwealth, 240
Backus v. Chilivis, 401
Baez v. Department of Justice, 22
Bagby v. Beal, 376
Baird v. Department of Pub. Health, 219
Baker v. CIA, 21
Baker v. Detroit, 376
Baker v. McCollan, 370
Baker v. School Dist. of City of Allentown, 185
Baldridge v. Shapiro, 20
Baldwin v. Redwood City, 44, 252
Ball v. Board of Trustees of Kerrville, 186
Ball v. James, 237, 243
Banerjee v. Board of Trustees of Smith Coll., 178
Bang v. Chase, 253
Barbre v. Garland Independent School Dist., 183
Barnstone v. University of Houston, KUHT-TV, 173, 196
Barr v. Mateo, 117
Barrantine v. Arkansas Best Freight System, 400
Baskin v. Parker, 352
Bates v. State Bar of Az., 14, 42, 141, 328
Battle v. Anderson, 295

Baxter v. Palmigiano, 308, 333
Bayou Landing, Ltd. v. Watts, 39, 105
Bayside Enterprises v. Carson, 39
Beauharnais v. Illinois, 37
Beer v. United States, 243, 244
Bekins Moving & Storage Co., 284
Belcher v. Stengel, 372
Bell v. Wolfish, 295, 297, 304
Beller v. Middendorf, 220, 319
Bellotti v. Baird, 215, 392
Belluso v. Turner Commn. Corp., 253
Belo Broadcasting Corp. v. Clark, 19
Bennum v. Board of Governors of Rutgers, 399
Berg v. Clayton, 319
Berry v. Doles, 247
Bertot v. School Dist. No. 1, 183, 344
Beth Israel Hosp. v. NLRB, 47
Bicknell v. Vergennes Union High School, 175, 197
Bills v. Henderson, 310
Birnbaum v. United States, 9, 31, 344, 387
Birth Control Centers, Inc. v. Reizen, 219
Bishop v. Wood, 371
Bivens v. Six Unknown Fed. Narcs., 307, 371
Black Leadership Forum v. Hand, 37
Black Panther Party v. Smith, 31
Black v. Sheraton Corp., 33
Blameuser v. Andrews, 37
Blow v. Lascaris, 376
Blue Chip Stamps v. Manor Drug Store Co., 327
Blum v. Yaretsky, 373
Bly v. McLeod, 376
Board of Curators of Univ. of Missouri v. Horowitz, 190
Board of Educ. of Long Beach v. Jack M., 186
Board of Elections v. Libertarian Party, 241
Board of Regents v. Tomanio, 378
Board of Selectmen of Framingham v. Civil Serv. Commn., 223
Board of Trustees v. Holso, 401
Bob Jones Univ. v. United States, 198, 267
Boddicker v. Arizona State Dental Assn., 289
Bogen v. Doty, 264
Bohacs v. Reid, 401
Bono v. Saxbe, 303, 306
Bose v. Consumers Union, 123
Bossier City Med. Suite v. City of Bossier City, 219
Bounds v. Smith, 293

Boyd v. Shawnee Mission Pub. Schools, 375
Brady v. Patterson, 249
Branden v. Allen, 352
Brandon v. Board of Educ., 45, 198, 256, 271
Branti v. Finkel, 249
Branzburg v. Hayes, 18
Bread Political Action Comm. v. FEC, 254
Brewer v. Memphis Pub., 123
Brian W. v. Superior Court, 86
Brinke v. Crisp, 63
Briscoe v. Bell, 246
Briscoe v. Escalante, 242
Briscoe v. LaHue, 335
Brody v. Leamy, 401
Brookhaven Cable TV v. Kelly, 172
Browder v. Director, Dept. of Corrections, 398
Brown v. Bullard Independent School Dist., 183
Brown v. Dade Christian Schools, Inc., 198, 267
Brown v. General Servs. Admin., 388
Brown v. Glines, 28, 45, 318
Brown v. Hartlage, 41, 254
Brown v. Pritchess, 401
Brown v. Stackler, 377
Brown v. Stone, 198
Bruce v. Riddle, 336
Bruno & Stillman v. Globe Newspaper, 123, 125
Brunswick Corp. v. Pueblo Bowl-O-Mat, 327
Brush v. Pennsylvania State Univ., 198
Bryant v. Yellin, 323
Buckley v. Valeo, 28, 53, 56, 166, 250, 326
Buise v. Hudkins, 295
Burch v. Goodyear Tire & Rubber Co., 325
Burch v. Louisiana, 102
Burgin v. Henderson, 301
Burke v. Miller, 335
Burns v. Times Argus, 121
Burrell v. McCray, 389
Burrows v. Superior Court, 229
Bussie v. Larson, 124
Butz v. Economou, 117, 335, 337, 386
Byron, Harless, Inc. v. State, 235
C & C Plywood v. Hanson, 162
Cahill v. Hawaiian Paradise Pk. Corp., 127
Caldero v. Tribune Pub. Co., 57, 61
Calderon v. McGee, 247

xii

Califano v. Aznavorian, 203
Califano v. Jobst, 223
Califano v. Sanders, 387
California Bankers Assn. v. Schultz, 229
California Med. Assn. v. Federal Elec. Commn., 251
California v. Grace Brethren Church, 388, 390
Callahan v. Woods, 271
Calley v. Callaway, 64
Campbell v. Cauthron, 306
Campbell v. Seabury Press, 129
Cannon v. University of Chicago, 199, 327
Cantrell v. Vickers, 188
Caplan v. Bureau of Alcohol, Tobacco & Firearms, 21
Carchman v. Korman, 379
Carey v. Beans, 300
Carey v. Bert Randolph Sugar, 392
Carey v. Brown, 51, 324
Carey v. Piphus, 197, 374
Carey v. Population Servs. Intl. 14, 42, 106, 141, *207*, 328
Carlock v. Texas, 103
Carlson v. Green, 307, 378, *380*, 385
Carpagno v. Harris, 3
Carey v. White, 341
Carson v. Here's Johnny, 130
Carsten v. Psychologists Exam. Comm., 326
Carton v. Trustees of Tufts College, 178
Cary v. Board of Educ. of Adams-Arapahoe School Dist. 28-J, 175
Cary v. White, 342
Catalano v. Pechous, 119
Caulfield v. Board of Educ., 234
CBS, Inc. v. FCC, 167, 168, 253
CBS, Inc. v. Democratic Natl. Comm., 168
CBS, Inc. v. Young, 86
Central Hudson Gas & Elect. Corp. v. Public Serv. Commn. of New York, 14, 15, 42, *143*
Chadha v. Immigration & Naturalization Serv., 5
Chamberlain v. Brown, 401
Chancery Clerk of Chickausaw Co. v. Wallace, 316, 400
Chandler v. Florida, 18, *64*
Chandler v. Roudebush, 388
Chapadeau v. Utica Observer Dispatch, Inc., 127
Chapman v. Houston Welfare Rights Org., 379
Chappelle v. Greater Baton Rouge Airport Dist., 241, 243
Charles O. Finley & Co., Inc. v. Kuhn, 289
Charles v. Carey, 218

Charlton Co. Bd. of Educ. v. United States, 246
Chas. T. Main Intl., Inc. v. Khuzestan Water & Power Auth., 345
Chavis v. Rowe, 310
Cheyenne River Sioux Tribe v. Andrus, 237
Chiappe v. State Personnel Board, 223
Chicago v. Wilson, 221
Chicago Council of Lawyers v. Bauer, 86
Chicago Typographical Union No. 16 v. NLRB, 285
Chisholm v. FCC, 167
Choudhry v. Free, 243
Christianburg Garment Co. v. EEOC, 375, 377
Chrysler Corp. v. Brown, 20
Church of God v. Amarillo Ind. School Dist., 198
Church of Scientology of Cal. v. Simon, 2
Church of Scientology v. Cazares, 123
Church of Scientology v. Seigelman, 120
Cianci v. New Times, 126
Cibenko v. Worth Pub., Inc., 120
Cicero v. Ogliati, 324
Citizens Savings v. Califano, 386
Citizens Against Rent Control v. City of Berkeley, 252
Citizens Concerned for Separation of Church & State v. City & Co. of Denver, 261
Citizens for Jobs & Energy v. Fair Political Practices Comm., 252
Citizens for Parental Rights v. San Mateo Bd. of Educ., 197, 270
Civil Service Commn. v. Letter Carriers, 28
Clark v. Valeo, 254, 333
Clements v. Fashing, 241
Coastal State Gas Corp. v. Department of Energy, 22
Cobb v. Aytch, 310
Codd v. Velger, 187
Cofone v. Manson, 310
Colautti v. Franklin, 215, 329
Cole v. Erie Lackawanna Ry., 287
Cole v. Richardson, 28
Coleman v. Bradford, 105
Collin v. Smith, 36
Colorado v. New Horizons, 92
Columbus Educ. Assn. v. Columbus City School Dist., 189
Commercial Programming Unlimited v. Columbia Broadcasting Sys., Inc., 127
Commissioner of Int. Rev. v. Shapiro, 388
Committee Against Rent Control v. Berkeley, 166
Committee for GI Rights v. Calloway, 319
Committee for Pub. Educ. & Religious Liberty v. Regan, 257

Committee for Pub. Educ. v. Nyquist, 258
Committee to Defend Reproductive Rights v. Myers, 217
Common Cause v. Nuclear Regulatory Commn., 23
Common Cause v. Schmitt, 251
Commonwealth ex rel. Saunders v. Creamer, 401
Commonwealth v. Bonadio, 220, 221
Commonwealth v. Edelin, 215
Commonwealth v. Wadzinski, 121
Community Communications Co., Inc. v. City of Boulder, 172, 351
Community Serv. Broadcasting v. FCC, 173
Concerned Citizens v. Pine Creek Conservancy, 243
Concerned Jewish Youth v. McGuire, 43, 53
Connecticut v. Menillo, 214
Connecticut Bd. of Pardons v. Dumschat, 312
Connor v. Finch, 242, 243, 244, 248
Consolidated Edison Co. v. Public Serv. Commn., 14, 51, 161
Consumer Prods. Safety Commn. v. GTE Sylvania, 21
Cook v. Hudson, 186
Cooper v. General Dynamics, 268
Cooper v. Mitchell, 105
Cooper v. Ross, 187
Corbett v. Register Pub. Co., 127
Corning v. Village of Laurel Hollow, 352, 377
Cort v. Ash, 327
Cotton v. Lockhart, 306
Couch v. United States, 229
County of Imperial v. Munoz, 400
County of Los Angeles v. Davis, 332
Cox v. Cohn, 128
Craig v. Boren, 328, 332
Crain v. Krehbiel, 234
Cromwell Property Owners Assn. v. Toffolon, 255
Crooker v. Department of Justice, 376
Cruikshank v. United States, 10
Cruz v. Beto, 337
Cruz v. Hauk, 295
Culver v. Secretary of Air Force, 46
Cummins v. Parker Seal Co., 269
Curtis v. Loether, 378
Cuyler v. Adams, 310
Dale v. Cruikshank, 344
Dalehite v. United States, 344
Dalia v. United States, 7
Davis v. Duryea, 122
Davis v. Hubbard, 315

Davis v. Passman, 327, 385
Davis v. Paul, 235
Davis v. Smith, 306
Dean v. Timpson Indep. School Dist., 177
Debra P. v. Turlington, 197
Delaware Tribal Business Comm. v. Weeks, 344
Dellums v. Powell, 33, 42, 335
Democratic Party v. LaFollette, 239, 243
Dennis v. Sparks, 334
Department of St. v. Washington Post Co., 20
Deposit Guar. Natl. Bank v. Roper, 323, 333
Deroburt v. Gannet, 125
Dian v. United Steelworkers of America, 286
Dickey v. CBS, 119
Dike v. School Bd. of Orange County, 186, 225
DiLorenzo v. Carey, 189
District Attorney v. 3-Way Theaters Corp., 103
Dobbert v. State of Fla., 85
Dodrill v. Arkansas Democrat, 127
Dodson v. Polk Co., 336
Doe v. Carnright, 219
Doe v. Commonwealth's Attorney, 185, 221
Doe v. County of Suffolk, 335
Doe v. Irwin, 226
Doe v. Renfrow, 199, 372, 374
Doe v. Roe, 128
Doe v. Swinton, 370
Doherty v. Rutgers School of Law, 324
Dolter v. Wahlert High School, 266
Donohue v. Copiague Union School Dist., 177
Dorsey v. Solomon, 316
Dougherty County Bd. of Educ. v. White, 184, 245, 246
Downing v. Monitor Pub., 125
Draper v. United States Pipe & Foundry, 268
Driver v. Helms, 31
Dubree v. Association of Trial Lawyers of America, 129
Dudley v. Bell, 401
Duke Power Co. v. Carolina Envir. Study Group, 321, 328
Dunagin v. City of Oxford, Miss., 143, 165
Duplantier v. United States, 24, 235
Dupler v. Mansfield J., 120
DuPont v. Finkea, 234
Duquesne v. Sugarman, 220
Durham v. Brock, 143
E & B Enterprises v. City of University Park, 39

East Carroll Parish School Bd. v. Marshall, 243, 248
East Hartford Educ. Assn. v. Board of Educ., 178, 186
Eastex Inc. v. NLRB, 47
Eastlake v. Forest City Enterprises, 247
Echols v. Strickland, 351
Edwards v. National Audobon Socy., Inc., 126
Eikenberry v. Callahan, 380
Eisenstadt v. Baird, 221
Ellis v. Blum, 386
Ellis v. City of Chicago, 352
Elrod v. Burns, 190, 249, 344
Enonoto v. Cluchette, 308
Ensminger v. Commissioner, 224
Entertainment Concepts, Inc. v. Maciejewski, 39, 93
Environmental Protection Agency v. Brown, 332
Equifax Services, Inc. v. Cohen, 151
Estelle v. Gamble, 293, 307, 370
Estelle v. Williams, 42
Ettenson v. Dutchess Co. Med. Socy., 288
Evans v. Dillahunty, 312
Examining Bd. of Engrs., Archs., & Surveyors v. Flores De Otero, 391
Exon v. McCarthy, 240
Fadjo v. Coon, 234
Fair Assessment v. McNary, 389, 390
Falcon v. Alaska Pub. Offices Commn., 235
Familias Unidas v. Briscoe, 196, 338, 351, 376
Fantroy v. Greater St. Louis Labor Council, 378
Farber, Matter of, 60
Farmer v. Carpenter's Local 430, 388
Farmer v. United Brotherhood of Carpenters & Joiners of Am., Local 25, 118, 283, 284
FBI v. Abramson, 20
FCC v. Midwest Video Corp., 171
FCC v. National Citizens Comm. for Broadcasting, 170
FCC v. Pacifica Found., 38, 107, 168
FCC v. WNCN Listeners Guild, 171
Federal Elec. Commn. v. Central Long Is. Tax Reform Commn., 250
Federal Election Commn. v. CLITRIM, 56
Federal Election Commn. v. Democratic Senatorial Campaign Comm., 251
Federal Election Commn. v. Lance, 252
Federal Election Commn. v. Machinists Non-Partisan Pol. League, 250
Federal Election Commn. v. National Educ. Assn., 276
Federal Open Market Comm. v. Merrill, 19, 32

Federated Dept. Stores v. Moite, 400
Ferri v. Ackerman, 336
Fiedler v. Marumsco, 198
Fielder v. Bosshard, 308
Figueroa v. State, 343, 387
Filartiga v. Pena-Irala, 343
Finberg v. Sullivan, 332
Finley v. Murry, 335
Finnegan v. Leu, 285
First Natl. Bank of Boston v. Bellotti, 14, *153,* 166, 253, 328, 333
First Natl. Bank of Omaha v. Marquette Natl. Bank, 373
Fisher v. Reiser, 202
Fisher v. Shamburg, 379
Fisher v. United States, 229, 329
Fitzgerald v. Mountain Laurel Racing, Inc., 373
Fitzgerald v. Porter Memorial Hosp., 219
Fitzpatrick v. Bitzer, 338, 341, 375
Flagg Bros., Inc. v. Brooks, 243, 372
Flakes v. Percy, 314
Flemming v. Nestor, 3
Florey v. Sioux Falls School Dist., 198, 256
Florida Dept. of St. v. Treasure Salvors, Inc., 342
Florida Power & Light Co. v. International Brotherhood of Elec. Workers, Loc. 641, 285
Forsham v. Harris, 20
Forsher v. Bugliosi, 129
Foster v. Laredo Newspapers, Inc., 127
Fox v. City of LA, 261
Franklin v. White Egret Condos., Inc., 226
Franks v. Bowman, 329, 333
Fricke v. Lynch, 196
Friedman v. Rogers, 14, 42, 142, 323, 328
Furtado v. Bishop, 310, 376
Futrell v. Ahrens, 198
Gagnon v. Scarpelli, 311
Gaines v. Anderson, 256
Gambino v. Fairfax Co. School Board, 196
Gannett Co., Inc. v. DePasquale, 17, 56, 85
Garcia v. Uvalde Co., 245, 247
Garrity v. Gallen, 374
Garrity v. New Jersey, 222
Gary-Northwest Ind. Women's Servs. v. Orr, 218
Gaskill v. Specter, 335
Gates v. Collier, 340, 375
Gates v. Henderson, 399

Gavett v. Alexander, 281
Gay v. Williams, 127
Gay Activist Alliance v. Washington Metro. Area Transit Auth., 46
Gay Alliance of Students v. Matthews, 196
Gay Lib. v. University of Mo., 196
Gay Students v. Bonner, 196
Gaylor v. Tacoma School Dist. No. 10, 185
Gaylord v. Tacoma School Dist., 220
General Foods Corp. v. Massachusetts Dept. of Public Health, 400
General Motors Corp. v. Director of OSHA, 234
Genusa v. City of Peoria, 39
George v. Kay, 335
Gertz v. Robert Welch, 128
Gideon v. Alabama St. Ethics Commn., 235
Gilbert v. Allied Chem. Corp., 57
Gilfillan v. City of Phila., 261
Gillard v. Schmidt, 184
Gillespie v. Civiletti, 295
Gilmore v. Utah, 329
Gish v. Board of Educ. of Paramus, 220
Givhan v. Western Line Consol. School Dist., 183, 249
Gladstone Realtors v. Village of Bellwood, 326
Gleichenhaus v. Carlyle, 121
Globe Newspaper Co. v. Superior Court, 18
GM Leasing Co. v. United States, 386
Gobin v. Globe Pub. Co., 127
Goldberg v. Carey, 393
Goldblum v. NBC, 56
Golden Rule Ins. Co. v. Mathias, 373
Goldwater v. Carter, 345
Gomez v. Toledo, 337, 374, 387
Gordon v. Leeke, 295
Gordon, In re, 202
Gorman Towers v. Bogoslavsky, 336
Gotleib v. Delaware, 104
Goulden v. Oliver, 301
Grace v. Burger, 43
Grady, In re, 315
Graves v. Commissioner of Int. Rev., 271
Gray v. Udevitz, 122
Great American Fed. Sav. & Loan Assn. v. Novotny, 378
Greenberg v. Bolger, 240
Greenholtz v. Inmates, Nebraska Penal & Correction Complex, 311
Greer v. Spock, 28, 44, 317
Griffin v. Harris, 344

Griswold v. Connecticut, 14, 225
GTE Sylvania, Inc. v. Consumers Union, 21, 326
Gulf Oil Co. v. Bernard, 26, 86
Gunther v. Iowa State Men's Reformatory, 400
Gurmankin v. Costanzo, 188, 375
Hackbart v. Cincinnati Bengals, Inc., 290
Hague v. CIO, 43
Haig v. Agee, 30, 203
Halkin v. Helms, 31
Halkin, In re, 26, 31
Hall v. Tawney, 195
Halperin v. CIA, 323, 345
Halperin v. Department of St., 21
Halperin v. Kissinger, 8, 34
Hamilton v. Roth, 308
Hamling v. United States, 92
Hampton v. Hanrahan, 33, 376
Hampton v. United States, 11
H & L Messengers v. Brentwood, 152
Hanneman v. Breier, 282
Handy Andy, Inc., 284
Hanson v. Circuit Court, 398
Hardie v. Fong Eu, 252
Hardison v. Trans World Airlines, Inc., 269
Harless v. State, 235
Harlow v. Fitzgerald, 337, 386
Harman v. Daniels, 371
Harper v. Creer, 370
Harradine v. Board of Supervisors, 376
Harrah Independent School Dist. v. Martin, 188
Harrell v. Keohane, 295
Harrington v. Bush, 9
Harrington v. Vandalia-Bulter Bd. of Educ., 400
Harris v. McRae, 217, 328
Hart v. Edmiston, 99
Hart v. Playboy Enterprises, Inc., 118
Hart Bookstores v. Edmiston, 39
Hartford Accident Co. v. Hempstead, 352, 375
Hasting & Sons Pub. Co. v. City Treasurer, 235
Hathorn v. Lovorn, 245
Havens Realty v. Coleman, 326
Hawaii v. Standard Oil Co., 325
Hayden v. NSA, 31
Haymes v. Montayne, 310
Hays v. Wood, 235, 250

Hayward v. Procunier, 306
Heavey v. Chapman, 239
Heffron v. International Socy. for Krishna Consciousness, Inc., 44
Heggins v. City of Dallas, 246, 247
Henderson v. Kaulitz, 122
Henry v. First Natl. Bank of Clarksdale, 41
Herald Co. v. McNeal, 24, 393
Herbert v. Lando, 32, 57, 124, 126
Herron v. Koch, 246
Hickman v. Valley Local School Dist. Bd. of Educ., 189
Hildebrand v. Unemployment Ins. Appeals Bd., 268
Hillis v. Stephen F. Austin St. Univ., 183
Hills v. Gautreaux, 324
Hirschkopf v. Snead, 253
Hirych v. State, 401
H. L. v. Matheson, 215, 328
Hodel v. Virginia Surface Min. & Reclamation Assn., 323, 334
Hollenbaugh v. Carnegie Free Lib., 220
Holloway v. Wise, 246, 247
Holman v. Central Ark. Broadcasting Co., 128, 373
Holodnak v. Avco Corp., 282
Holt Civic Club v. City of Tuscaloosa, 237
Home Box Office v. Wilkinson, 172
Home Box Office, Inc. v. FCC, 172
Hop, In re, 314
Hotchner v. Castillo-Puche, 126
Houchins v. KQED, Inc., 16, 297
Howard v. Colorado Real Est. Commn., 290
Howe v. Smith, 310
Howell v. Woodlin School Dist. R-104, 189
Hudgens v. NLRB, 46, 47
Hudler v. Austin, 240
Hunt v. Nuclear Regulatory Commn., 23
Hunt v. Washington St. Adv. Commn. 325
Hunter v. Montgomery Co. Bd. of Educ., 199
Huntley v. Community School Bd. of Brooklyn, 187
Hutchinson v. Proxmire, 117, 120, 336
Hutto v. Finney, 301, 340, 341, 375
Hynes v. Mayor of Oradell, 49, 327
Illinois Brick Co. v. Illinois, 327
Illinois Migrant Council v. Campbell Soup Co., 48
Illinois Migrant Council v. Pilliod, 324
Illinois NORML v. Scott, 222
Illinois State Bd. of Elections v. Sangmeister, 242
Illinois State Board of Elections v. SWP, 241

Imbler v. Pachtman, 335
Ingraham v. Wright, 195, 371
Inmates of Alleghany Co. Jail v. Pierce, 306, 308
International Assn. of Machinists v. Street, 282
International Brotherhood of Elec. Workers v. Foust, 286
International Socy. for Krishna Consciousness v. Eaves, 45
International Socy. of Krishna Consciousness v. Rochford, 45
Irons v. Bell, 21
Irvin v. Dowd, 62
ISKCON v. New York, 43
Island Trees School Board v. Pico, 197
Jabara v. Kelley, 8
Jackson v. Virginia, 398
Jacobs v. Kunes, 223
Jacron Sales, Inc. v. Sindorf, 124, 127
Jaffee v. United States, 386
Jaggard v. Commissioner of Internal Revenue, 271
Jagnandan v. Giles, 341
Jago v. Van Curen, 313
James v. Benton, 335
James v. Board of Educ., 401
Janusaitis v. Middlebury Vol. Fire Dept., 373
J.B.K., Inc. v. Caron, 221
Jech v. Burch, 226
Jenoff v. Hearst, 122
John Donnelly & Sons v. Campbell, 151
Johnson v. GMC, 400
Johnson v. Kelly, 390
Jones v. Alfred H. Mayer Co., 225
Jones v. Diamond, 306
Jones v. Helms, 201
Jones v. Hildebrant, 378
Jones v. North Carolina Prisoners' Labor Union, Inc., 297
Jones v. Wolf, 260, 291, 345
Jordan v. Cagle, 183
Jordan v. Wolke, 305
Juidice v. Vail, 390
Kansas City v. Darby, 99
Kapp v. National Football League, 288
Karen v. Treen, 198, 256
Katz, In re, 268
Katz v. Superior Court, 268
Kay v. Federal Elec. Commn., 254
K.C.M. v. Alaska, 315
Kelley v. Johnson, 42, 186, 222

Kelsey v. Minnesota, 295
Kendall v. United Air Lines, Inc., 268
Kennedy for President Comm. v. FCC, 167, 253
Kenosha, City of, v. Bruno, 350
Kent v. Commissioner of Educ., 198, 256
Kent v. Dulles, 203
Kentucky St. Bd. v. Rudasill, 197
Kessler v. Assocs. Fin. Serv., 376
Key v. Doyle, 271
Kimble v. Swackhamer, 240
Kingsville Ind. School Dist. v. Cooper, 177
Kirkland v. New York St. Dept. of Correctional Servs., 376
Kissinger v. Halperin, 337
Kissinger v. Reporters Comm. for Freedom of the Press, 20
Kleindienst v. Mandel, 13, 16
Knight v. Carlson, 351
Knights of Ku Klux Klan v. East Baton Rouge Parish School Bd., 46
Koffler, In re, 151
Kops v. New York Tel. Co., 165
Kovacs v. Cooper, 54
Krause v. Rhodes, 41
Kremens v. Bartley, 332, 333
Kremer v. Chem. Constr. Corp., 399, 400
KSTP Television, In re Application of, 88
Kupau v. Yamamoto, 283
Labor Party v. Pomerleau, 54
Laclede Gas Co. v. Public Serv. Commn., 162
Ladoga Canning v. McKenzie, 103
Laird v. State, 222
Lake Country Estates, Inc. v. Tahoe Regional Planning Agency, 336, 341
Lakin v. United States, 89
Lamont v. Postmaster Gen., 13
Lamphere v. Brown Univ., 376
Landmark Communications Inc. v. Virginia, 15, 61, 129
Lane v. Williams, 333
Lange v. Nature Conservancy, Inc., 401
Lanner v. Wimmer, 256
Larkin v. Grendel's Den, 38
Larson v. Valente, 273, 323, 326
Laskarus v. Thornburgh, 341
Laski v. International Org. of Masters, Mates & Pilots, 283
Lawrence v. Moss, 121, 122
Lefkowitz v. Cunningham, 4, 239
Lehman v. Lycoming Co. Children's Servs. Agency, 399

Leibner v. Sharbaugh, 196
Leigh v. Olson, 218
Leite v. City of Providence, 352
Lemon v. Kurtzman, 175, 258, 260, 271
Lendall v. Jernigan, 240
Lesar v. Department of Justice, 21
Letelier v. Republic of Chile, 343
Let's Help Fla. v. McCrary, 252
Lewis v. Delaware St. Coll., 185
Lindsey v. Board of Regents of Univ. Sys. of Ga., 183
Linmark Assocs., Inc. v. Township of Willingboro, 14, 42, 141, 328
Lipscomb v. Wise, 323, 376
Littlefield v. Fort Dodge Messenger, 122
Lloyd Corp. v. Tanner, 46, 48
Lo-Ji Sales, Inc. v. New York, 103
Local 3489, United Steelworkers of Am., AFL-CIO v. Usery, 283
Lock v. Jenkins, 306
Loewen v. Turnipseed, 197
Long v. IRS, 21
Long v. United States, 39
Long Beach v. Bozek, 325
Longshoreman's & Warehouseman's Union, Local 13 v. NLRB, 285
Loretto v. Teleprompter Mahattan CATV Corp., 372
Lorillard v. Pons, 377
Los Angeles v. Davis, 332
Louisiana v. Short, 103
Louisiana v. Texas, 325
Louisiana v. Walden Books, 100
Louisiana v. Wrestle, Inc., 90, 101
Louisville Area Inter-Faith Comm. v. Nottingham Liquors, 390
Lovell v. Snow, 376
Loving v. Virginia, 223
Lugar v. Edmondson Oil Co., 373
Lux v. Board of Regents of New Mexico Highlands Univ., 183
Machinists v. OPEC, 343
Madison Joint School Dist. No. 8 v. Wisconsin Employment Relations Commn., 190
Maher v. Gagne, 375
Maher v. Roe, 217
Mahoning Women's Center v. Hunter, 219
Maine v. Thiboutot, 373, 374, 375, 379, 388, 401
Malerba v. Newsday, 122
Malnak v. Yogi, 266
Mandel v. Bradley, 241, 389
Manhattan St. Citizen's Group v. Bass, 239

Mapes v. United States, 224
Marathon Pipeline Co. v. Northern Pipeline Constr. Co., 327
Marchioro v. Chaney, 243
Marcoux v. Attorney Gen., 222
Margaret S. v. Edwards I, 218
Margoles v. United States, 63
Marks v. United States, 91
Marrapese v. Rhode Island, 341
Marriage of Schulke, In re, 264
Marsh v. Alabama, 14
Marshall v. District Unemployment Comp. Bd., 223
Marshall v. Edwards, 244
Marshall v. Local 1402, Intl. Longshoreman's Assn. of Tampa, Florida & Vicinity, 283
Marshall v. United States, 62
Martin Marietta Corp. v. Evening Star Newspaper Co., 123
Martin v. Bergland, 224
Martin v. Griffin TV, Inc., 127
Martin v. Merola, 335
Martin v. Struthers, 14
Martinez v. California, 343, 373, 401
Maryland Crystal v. Ramsden, 376
Maryland Pub. Interest Research Group v. Elkins, 196
Maryland v. Louisiana, 323, 325
Massachusetts v. Rosenberg, 101
Massachusetts v. Saxon Theatre, 100
Massachusetts v. Trainor, 102
Massachusetts v. 707 Main Corp., 102
Mathis v. Philadelphia Newspaper Co., 127
Matlovich v. Secretary of the Air Force, 319
Matthews v. Atlantic City, 241
Matthews v. Diaz, 388
Matthews v. Eldridge, 388
Matthews v. Weber, 388
Maxwell v. United Auto., Aerospace, & Agric. Implement Workers of Am., Loc. 1306, 282
Mayes v. Elrod, 351
Mayle v. Pennsylvania Dept. of Highways, 342
Mayola v. Alabama, 63
Mazzella v. Philadelphia Newspapers, 125
Mazzetti v. United States, 87
McAdams v. McSurely, 6
McCarthy v. Briscoe, 240
McCarthy v. FCC, 167
McCarthy v. Kirkpatrick, 240, 241

McCarthy v. Philadelphia Civil Serv. Commn., 202
McCarthy v. Tribbitt, 240
McClure v. Carter, 326
McCourt v. California Sports, Inc., 289
McCusker v. Valley News, 118, 122
McDaniel v. Essex Intl., Inc., 269, 283
McDaniel v. Paty, 240, 271
McDaniel v. Sanchez, 247
McElearney v. University of Illinois at Chicago Circle Campus, 187
McGill v. Board of Educ. of Pekin Elem. School Dist., 183
McGlyn v. New Jersey Pub. Broadcasting Auth., 253
McKenna v. Farge, 234
McKenna v. Peekskill Housing Auth., 225
McKinney v. Alabama, 102
McLain v. Meier, 241, 242
McLean v. Arkansas Bd. of Educ., 175, 196, 260
McNamara v. Moody, 377
McSurely v. McClellan, 5
Meachum v. Fano, 308, 311
Medico v. Times, 126
Meek v. Pittenger, 259
Megill v. Board of Regents, 183
Meltzer v. Board of Pub. Instr. of Orange Co., Florida, 256
Memphis Light, Gas & Water Div. v. Craft, 332
Memphis Pub. Co. v. Nichols, 127
Memphis Sheraton Corp. v. Kirkley, 377
Metpath v. Myers, 143
Metromedia, Inc. v. City of San Diego, 42, 44, 54, 151, 252
Meyer v. Nebraska, 224
Miami Herald Pub. Co. v. Tornillo, 165
Michaelson v. Booth, 240
Micklus v. Carlson, 310
Middendorf v. Henry, 319
Middlesex Co. Sewage Auth. v. National Sea Clammers Assn., 374
Middlesex Ethics Comm. v. Garden St. Bar Assn., 390
Millanhouse v. Murphy, 43
Miller v. California, 89
Miller v. Morris, 224
Miller v. Transamerican Press, 125
Millikan v. Board of Directors of Everett School Dist. No. 2, 177
Mills v. Baldwin, 261, 291
Mills v. Kingsport Times-News, 122, 127
Mills v. Rogers, 315
Milwaukee v. Illinois, 373
Minarcini v. Strongsville City School Dist., 175, 197

Minnesota 5th Cong. Dist. Ind. Rep. Party v. Minn., 240
Minnesota Civ. Liberties Union v. Roemer, 258
Minnesota Med. Assn. v. State, 234
Mississippi Gay Alliance v. Goudelock, 165, 196
Mississippi University for Women v. Hogarth, 199
Missouri Church of Scientology v. State Tax Commn., 266
Missouri v. All Star News Agency, 104
Mitchell v. Delaware, 100
Mitchell v. Hicks, 310
Mitchell v. NBC, Inc., 399
Mobil Oil v. Tully, 389
Mobile, City of, v. Bolden, 238, 243
Mobile Press Register v. Faulkner, 123, 124
Moe v. Secretary, 218
Moe v. The Confederated Salish & Kootenai Tribes, 388
Mogle v. Sevier Co. School Dist., 202
Molina v. Richardson, 386
Mondou v. New York, 401
Monell v. Department of Social Services, 345
Monroe v. Pape, 392
Montana v. United States, 400
Montanye v. Haymes, 309, 312
Moore v. Alameda Co., 350
Moore v. City of East Cleveland, 219
Moore v. Sims, 390
Morale v. Grigel, 199
Morgan v. State of Fl., 61
Morgan v. Winters 126
Morial v. Judiciary Commn. of Louisiana, 240
Moritt v. New York, 241
Morland v. Sprecher, 27
Morris v. Gressette, 246
Morrison v. Ayoob, 334
Moyer v. Phillips, 126
Mt. Healthy City School Dist. Bd. of Educ. v. Doyle, 178, 341, 351
Muir v. Alabama Educ. TV Commn., 173
Mullaney v. Woods, 271
Murphy v. Florida, 62
Murphy v. Hunt, 333
Murphy v. Mt. Carmel High School, 379
Myers v. Boton Magazine, 120
N.A. Cold Storage Co. v. County of Book, 351
NAACP v. Civiletti, 377
NAACP v. Claiborne Hardware, Inc., 41
Nader v. Allegheny Airlines, 334

Nader v. Baroody, 23
Nader v. Schaffer, 239
Naked City v. Chicago Sun-Times, 120
Nalley v. Douglas Co., 223
Natco Theatres v. Ratner, 106
National Assn. of Regulatory Util. Commrs. v. FCC, 172
National Citizens Comm. for Broadcasting v. FCC, 167
National Coalition for Pub. Educ. & Religious Liberty v. Harris, 259
National Right to Work Comm. v. FEC, 252
National Socialist Party v. Village of Skokie, 35
National Treasury Employees Union v. Department of Treasury, 377
NBC, In Re, 19
Nebraska ex rel Douglas v. Faith Baptist Church, 197
Nebraska Press Assn. v. Stuart, 26, *73,* 129, 332
Needleman v. Bohlen, 187
Neighborhood Dev. Corp. v. Advisory Comm. on Hist. Preservation, 328
Nelson v. Mustian, 223
Network Project v. Corporation for Pub. Broadcasting, 173
Nevada v. Hall, 342
New Jersey St. Chamber of Commerce v. New Jersey Elec. Commn., 250
New Jersey v. Portash, 323
New Jersey v. Schmid, 48, 196
New Jersey–Philadelphia Presbytery v. New Jersey, 197, 391
New Times, Inc. v. Arizona Bd. of Regents, 401
New York Civ. Liberties Union, Inc. v. Acito, 11, 56
New York Gaslight Club v. Carey, 375
New York St. Assn. for Retarded Children v. Carey, 314
New York St. Liquor Auth. v. Bellanca, 38, 90
New York v. Ferber, 100, 328
New York v. 11 Cornwell Co., 379
Newport v. Fact Concerts, Inc., 43, 352, 375
Niederhuber v. Camden Co. Voc. & Tech. School Dist. Bd. of Educ., 268
Nitzberg v. Parks, 195
Nixon v. Administrator, Gen. Serv. Admin., 33, 34, 233
Nixon v. Fitzgerald, 337, 387
Nixon v. Freeman, 34
Nixon v. Warner Communications, Inc., 34, 87, 129
NLRB v. International Longshoremen's & Warehousemen's Union, 287
NLRB v. Robbins Tire & Rubber Co., 19
NLRB v. Baptist Hosp., Inc., 47
NLRB v. Catholic Bishop of Chicago, 190, 265

Norris v. King, 129
North Haven Bd. of Educ. v. Bell, 199
Northend Cinema v. Seattle, 99
Nottelson v. A. O. Smith Corp., 269
Nyberg v. City of Va., 219
O'Brien v. Digrazzia, 235
Office of Communications, United Church of Christ v. FCC, 167
O'Hair v. Andrus, 261
Ohralik v. Ohio State Bar Assn., 14, 142, 377
Oklahoma Pub. Co. v. District Court, 85, 128
Oldham v. Ehrlich, 376
Olivia N. v. NBC, 40
Orazio v. Town of North Hempstead, 252
Orr v. Argus-Press, 119, 126
Orr v. Orr, 323, 326
Owen v. City of Independence, 337, 352, 374, 386
Owens v. Haas, 352
Palermo v. Warden, Green Haven St. Prison, 335
Palmer v. Board of Educ. of City of Chicago, 177, 197, 269
Parham v. J. L., 316
Parish of Jefferson v. Bayou Landing, Ltd., 103, 104
Parker v. Cook, 303
Parker v. Merlino, 247
Parklane Hosiery Co. v. Shore, 400
Parratt v. Taylor, 296, *353,* 370
Pasadena City Bd. of Educ. v. Spangler, 333
Paton v. LaPrade, 10, 379
Patsy v. Florida St. Bd. of Regents, 389
Paul v. Davis, 117, 187, 235, *361,* 371
Payton v. United States, 335
Peacock v. Guaranty Fed. Sav. & Loan Assn., 379
Peagler v. Phoenix Newspapers, Inc., 127
Peck v. United States, 373, 379
Peisner v. Detroit Free Press, Inc., 127
Pell v. Procunier, 297
Pennhurst St. School v. Halderman, 314
Pennington v. Chaffee, 61
Pennsylvania v. New Jersey, 325
Pennsylvania v. Porter, 325
Pennsylvania v. Wadzinski, 254
Penthouse v. McAuliffe, 100, 106
People v. Schmidt, 221
People v. Mobil Oil Corp., 143
People v. Onofre, 220

People v. Privitera, 226
People v. Sutherland, 53
Person v. New York Post Corp., 165
Petrey v. Flaugher, 222
Phaby v. KSD, 379
Philadelphia v. Washington Post Corp., 117, 325
Philips v. Bureau of Prisons, 300
Phillips v. Evening Star, 127
Pico v. Island Trees School District, 175
Pierce v. Society of Sisters, 224
Pinkus v. United States, 99
Piper v. Chris-Craft Indus., 327
Pittman v. Hutto, 300
Planned Parenthood Assn. v. Ashcroft, 218
Planned Parenthood League v. Bellotti, 218
Planned Parenthood of Central Missouri v. Danforth, 215, 233
Plante v. Gonzalez, 24, 234, 235, 250, 253
Plyer v. Doe, 198
Poelker v. Doe, 217
Police Dept. of Chicago v. Mosely, 51
Polk Co. v. Dodson, 336, 373
Pollard v. Cockrell, 234
Popow v. City of Margate, 352
Porter v. Guam Pub., 126
Post-Newsweek Stations, In re, 73
Powell v. Syracuse Univ., 178
Preast v. Cox, 300
Press v. Verran, 118
Press, In re, 288
Priest v. Secretary of the Navy, 39
Primus, In re, 14, 42, 142, 377
Princeton Univ. v. Schmid, 48, 196
Pring v. Penthouse, 122
Procunier v. Martinez, 13, 16, 393
Procunier v. Navarette, 295, 370
Protestant Episcopal Church in Diocese of LA v. Barker, 261
Prune Yard Shopping Center v. Robins, 42, 47, 372
Public Funds for Pub. Schools of NJ v. Byrne, 258
Public Media Center v. FCC, 167
Puerto Rico Intl. Airlines, Inc. v. Recio, 390
Pugliese v. Nelson, 310
Putnam v. Gerloff, 306
Quern v. Jordan, 341, 342
Quinlan, In re, 226, 270
Quinn v. Aetna Life Ins. Co., 162

Rakas v. Illinois, 329
Ramey v. Harber, 249
Ramirez v. County of Hudson, 401
Ramos v. Lamm, 295
Rankin v. Howard, 335
Ravin v. State, 221
Ray v. Turner, 21
Rebozo v. Washington Post, 121
Record Revolution No. 6, Inc., v. City of Parma, 143
Red Lion Broadcasting Co. v. FCC, 14, 171
Reese v. Danforth, 336
Reeves v. McConn, 115
Reeves Inc. v. Stake, 333
Regan v. Sullivan, 378
Reilly v. Sheet Metal Workers' Intl. Assn., 287
Reliance Ins. Co. v. Barron's, 58, 122
Remmers v. Brewer, 266
Rendall v. Baker-Kohn, 373
Rennie v. Klein, 315
Resetar v. Maryland St. Bd. of Educ., 178
Resnick v. East Brunswick Twp. Bd. of Educ., 257
Rhode Island Broadcasters v. Michaelson, 142
Rhodes v. Chapman, 305
Rhodes v. City of Wichita, 386
Rhodes v. Robinson, 295
Richards of Rockford, Inc. v. Pacific Gas & Elec. Co., 58
Richman v. Shevin, 253
Richmond, City of, v. United States, 244
Richmond Newspapers, Inc. v. Virginia, 17, 56, 79
Richter v. Dept. of Alcoholic Beverage Control, 90
Riegle v. Federal Open Market Comm., 326
Right to Read Defense Comm. v. School Comm., 197
Right to Choose v. Byrne, 217
Rinsley v. Brandt, 118
Ritter v. Mount St. Mary's Coll., 266
Rizzo v. Goode, 324, 352
R.M.J., In re, 15, 42, 142
Roadway Exp. v. Piper, 377
Roberts v. S. S. Kryiakovla D. Lemos, 376
Robertson v. Wegmann, 378
Robinson v. Bergstrom, 336
Rochester Gas & Elec. Corp. v. Public Serv. Commn., 162
Rodriguez v. Popular Democratic Party, 241
Roe v. Wade, 225
Roemer v. Board of Pub. Works of Md., 258

Roger B, In re, 19
Rogers v. Jinks, 165
Rogers v. Lodge, 238
Rogers v. Okin, 315
Rome, City of, v. United States, 245
Romeo v. Youngberg, 314
Rosanova v. Playboy Enterprises, 122
Rosario v. Amalgamated Ladies' Garment Cutters' Union, Local 10, 286
Rose v. Lundy, 400
Rose v. Mitchell, 398
Roseman v. Indiana Univ., 249
Rosewell v. LaSalle Natl. Bank, 389, 390
Ross v. Allen, 373
Rowan v. Post Office Dept., 52
Rowe v. Metz, 124
Rowe v. Tennessee, 373
Rucker v. Wilson, 391
Rudd v. Ray, 265
Ruiz v. Estelle, 295, 300, 304
Runyon v. McCrary, 186, 224
Rush v. Savchuck, 387
Rutherford v. United States, 226
Rutledge v. Liability Ins. Indus., 163
Sadowski v. Shevin, 252
Safeguard Mutual Ins. Co. v. Miller, 373
Sala v. County of Suffolk, 304
Salem Inn v. Frank, 90
Salinas v. Breier, 352
Salisbury v. List, 224
Salvail v. Nashua Bd. of Educ., 197
Santa Clara Pueblo v. Martinez, 343
San Juan Star Co., In re, 26
Santiago v. Clark, 290
Saxbe v. Washington Post Co., 297
Schachter v. Whalen, 234
Schad v. Borough of Mt. Ephraim, 38, 90, 99
Scheinberg v. Smith, 218
Scheuer v. Rhodes, 117, 337
Schiff v. Williams, 196
Schuman v. Muller, 391
Schuster v. Imperial Co. Mun. Court, 56
Schweiker v. Gray Panthers, 328
Scott v. Kentucky Parole Bd., 332
Scott v. Plante, 314, 315

Seatrain Shipbuilding Corp. v. Shell Oil Co., 326
Secretary of Pub. Welfare of Penn. v. Institutionalized Juveniles, 316
Secretary of the Navy v. Huff, 46, 318
Seegmiller v. KSL, 127
Sellars v. Procunier, 312, 335
Selzer v. Fleisher, 186
Sendak v. Arnold, 214
Serbian Eastern Orthodox Diocese for the US of Am. & Canada v. Milvojevich, 260, 290, 345
Severns v. Wilmington Med. Center, Inc., 226
Sewell v. Georgia, 104
Seyfried v. Walton, 197
Shabazz v. Barnauskas, 301
Shakman v. Democratic Org. of Cook Co., 250
Shangri-la v. Brennan, 99
Shannon v. HUD, 377
Shapiro v. Columbia Union Natl. Bank, 401
Shapiro v. Thompson, 201
Shepherd v. Trevina, 239
Sheppard v. De Kalb Co. Merit Council, 223
Sherrill v. Knight, 57
Shifrin v. Wilson, 324
Shuman v. City of Phila., 352
Signorelli v. Evans, 241
Silverman v. University of Colo., 401
Simon v. Eastern Ky. Welfare Rights Org., 322, 325
Simons v. Bellinger, 335
Simonson v. UPI, 118
Singleton v. Wulff, 328
Sinicropi v. Nassau Co., 400
Skehan v. Board of Trustees of Bloomsburg St. Coll., 188
Sladek v. Bensinger, 21
Smith v. Ambrogio, 351
Smith v. Daily Mail Pub. Co., 26, 84, 128
Smith v. Goguen, 53, 327
Smith v. Maryland, 229
Smith v. Nixon, 8
Smith v. Smith, 255
Smith v. United States, 99
Snepp v. United States, 204
Snyder v. Holy Cross Hosp., 270
Socialist Workers Party v. Attorney General, 31
Socialist Workers '74 Campaign Comm. v. Brown, 56
Society Hill Civic Assn. v. Harris, 400
Solery v. Tucker, 241

Southard v. Forbes, 124
South Ogden CVS Store, Inc. v. Ambach, 143
Southwestern Community Serv., Inc., 224
Spain v. Procunier, 306, 310
Spartacus Youth League v. Board of Trustees, 196
Spates v. Manson, 295
Spence v. Washington, 53
Splawn v. California, 89
Sprague v. Fitzpatrick, 249
Spring, In re, 227
Springfield School Dist. v. Pennsylvania Dept. of Educ., 255
St. Claire v. Cuyler, 301
Stafford v. Briggs, 31, 387
Stanley v. Georgia, 14, 92
Stansberry v. Holmes, 39
Star Distrib., Ltd. v. Marino, 337
State v. Boiardo, 60
State v. Chrisman, 221
State v. Ciuffini, 221
State v. Erickson, 221
State v. Green, 72
State v. Kells, 221
State v. Mitchell, 221
State v. Pilcher, 220
State v. Saunders, 220
State v. Vail, 221
State ex rel Dino, 86
State ex rel McCamik v. McCoy, 295
State of Cal. v. State of Ariz., 342
State of Mo. v. NOW, 41
State of Mo. ex rel Gore v. Woehner, 351
Staten v. Pittsburgh Housing Auth., 376
State School v. Halderman, 373
Steaks Unlimited v. Deaner, 123, 125
Stegmaier v. Trammel, 250
Stelling v. International Brotherhood of Elec. Workers, Loc. 1547, 284
Stencel Aero Engg. Corp. v. United States, 344
Sterling v. Cupp, 226, 304
Stevens v. Berger, 271
Stone v. Essex Co. Newspapers, Inc., 127
Stone v. Graham, 198, *261*
Stone v. Powell, 398, 399
Storar, In re, 227
Strauss Communications, Inc. v. FCC, 167

Street v. NBC, 122, 123
Stripling v. Literary Guild, 119, 120, 121
Student Members of Playcrafters v. Township of Teaneck, 198
Stump v. Sparkman, 315, 334
Sugarman v. Aero-Mexico, 343
Sullivan v. Meade Indep. School Dist. No. 101, 185
Sullivan v. Pennsylvania Dept. of Labor & Indus., 375
Sumner v. Mata, 398
Supreme Court of Va. v. Consumer's Union, 334, 336, 375
Sussli v. City of San Mateo, 44
Sutherland v. Illinois, 53
Suzuki v. Yuen, 316
Swain v. Pressley, 390
Swietlowich v. County of Buck, 376
Symm v. United States, 237
Symons v. Chrysler Corp. Loan Guar. Bd., 23
Taskett v. King Broadcasting Co., 127
Tatro v. Texas, 374
Tatum v. Morton, 43
Taxation With Representation v. IRS, 22
Taylor v. Kavanaugh, 335
Terry v. Adams, 242
Terry v. Kolski, 401
Testa v. Katt, 401
Teterud v. Burns, 301
Texas Women's Univ. v. Chayklintaste, 198
Themtron Prod., Inc. v. Hermansdorfer, 388
Theriault v. Silber, 265, 266
Thomas H. Maloney & Sons v. E. W. Scripps Co., 127
Thomas v. Collins, 14
Thomas v. Granville Bd. of Educ., 196
Thomas v. Review Bd. of Ind. Employment Sec. Div., 268
Thompson v. Board of Trustees, 198
Thorpe v. Duango School Dist., 401
Time, Inc. v. Firestone, 119, 120, 127, 128
Time, Inc. v. Hill, 119
Time, Inc. v. Pape, 119
Times v. Sullivan, 121, 126
Tincher v. Piasecki, 286
Tobeluk v. Lind, 401
Toll v. Moreno, 198
Torres v. Playboy Enterprises, Inc., 118
Town of Lockport v. Citizens for Community Action, 247
Township of Franklin v. Board of Educ. of the North Hunterdon Reg. High School, 243

Trachtman v. Anker, 196
Trafficante v. Metropolitan Life Ins. Co., 326
Trainor v. Hernandez, 390
Troman v. Wood, 127
Trotman v. Board of Trustees of Lincoln Univ., 184, 196
Tucker v. City of Montgomery Bd. of Commrs., 324
Tully v. Griffin, 388, 390
Tuma v. Idaho Bd. of Nursing, 290
Turner v. Air Transport Lodge 1894, 3, 284
Turner v. Raynes, 335
Turner v. Unification Church, 386
Turpin v. Mailet, 352, 386
Unidyne Corp. v. Government of Iran, 345
United Jewish Organizations of Williamsburgh, Inc. v. Carey, 244
United States v. Alberico, 63
United States v. AT&T, 6
United States v. Board of Commrs. of Sheffield, Ala., 246
United States v. Buttorff, 40
United States v. Capo, 63
United States v. Civella, 86
United States v. Criden, 19, 88
United States v. Defalco, 104
United States v. Dien, 33
United States v. Donovan, 7
United States v. Dost, 89, 102
United States v. Douglass, 45
United States v. Echols, 104
United States v. Ehrlichman, 8
United States v. Espinoza, 104
United States v. Georgia, 246, 247
United States v. Gillock, 336
United States v. Haldeman, 88
United States v. Helstoski, 336
United States v. Hernandez, 85
United States v. Herring, 63
United States v. ITT Rayonier, 400
United States v. Jenrette, 19
United States v. Johnson, 379
United States v. Kelner, 39
United States v. Lee, 271
United States v. Marcano-Garcia, 63
United States v. Mattson, 325
United States v. Middleton, 104
United States v. Miller, 228
United States v. Mississippi, 245

United States v. Moss, 40
United States v. Mowat, 45
United States v. Myers, 87
United States v. New York Tel., 7
United States v. Obscene Magazines, 103
United States v. Operating Engrs., 252
United States v. Orleans, 344
United States v. Payner, 329
United States v. Philadelphia, 325
United States v. Pinkus, 89, 103
United States v. Powell, 327
United States v. Powers, 85
United States v. Progressive, Inc., 26
United States v. Ramsey, 2
United States v. Reader's Digest, 143
United States v. Richards, 2
United States v. Salucci, 329
United States v. Sherman, 86
United States v. Sherwin, 104
United States v. Sioux Nation of Indians, 400
United States v. Solomon, 325
United States v. Steelhammer, 57
United States v. Testan, 344, 388
United States v. Texas, 392
United States v. Thompson, 63
United States v. Torch, 104
United States v. Trapnell, 63
United States v. Truong Dinh Hung, 8
United States v. Tupler, 104
United States v. Twigg, 12
United States v. Various Articles of Obscene Merchandise, 39, 100
United States v. Westinghouse Elec. Corp., 234
United States v. 2200 Paper Back Books, 102
United States ex rel Pulitzer Pub. Co., In re, 85
United States Knights of Ku Klux Klan v. East Baton Rouge School Bd., 377
United States Parole Commn. v. Geraghty, 326, 333
United States Postal Serv. v. Council of Greenburgh Civic Assns., 52
United Steelworkers v. Sadlowski, 284
Universal Amusement Co., Inc. v. Hofheinz, 337, 386
University of N.H. Ch. of the Am. Assn. of Univ. Prof. v. Haselton, 189
Uzzell v. Friday, 196
Valley Forge Christian Coll. v. Americans United for Separation of Church & State, 324

Vance v. Terrazas, 4
Vance v. Universal Amusement Co., Inc., 105
Vegod Corp. v. ABC, 123
Verrilli v. City of Concord, 44
Victor v. Brinkley, 187
Village of Arlington Heights v. Metropolitan Housing Corp., 323
Village of Schaumburg v. Citizens for a Better Environment, 50
Village of Skokie v. National Socialist Party, 36
Virgil v. Time, Inc., 130
Virginia Pharmacy Bd. v. Virginia Citizens Consumer Council, 13, 16
Virginia St. Bd. of Pharmacy v. Virginia Citizens Consumer Council, Inc., 133, 328
Vitek v. Jones, 313, 316, 332, 333
Voelker v. IRS, 22
Vorchheimer v. School Dist. of Phila., 198
Voswinkil v. City of Charlotte, 265
Vrazo, In re, 60
Wakinekona v. Olin, 310
Waldbaum v. Fairchild Pubs., 121
Walker v. Armco Steel Corp., 378
Walker v. Colorado Springs Sun, Inc., 127
Wallace v. House, 243
Walsh v. International Longshoremen's Assn., 400
Walsh v. Montgomery Co., 235
Walt Disney Prods. v. Shannon, 40
Ward v. Connor, 379
Ward v. Illinois, 89, 91
Warth v. Seldin, 322, 323, 325
Washington Mobilization Comm. v. Cullinane, 43
Washington Mobilization Comm. v. Jefferson, 43
Washington v. Davis, 370
Waste Mgmt. v. Fokakis, 398
Watson v. McGee, 370
Watt v. Energy Action Educ. Found., 325
Weatherford v. Bursey, 12, 33
Weaver v. Graham, 313
Weiler v. Carpenter, 151
Weinberger v. Catholic Action of Hawaii, 20
Weinberger v. Salfi, 388
Weiss v. Willow Tree Civic Assn., 378
Weissman v. CIA, 21
Welsh v. Likens, 314
Wendling v. Duluth, 105
Werbrouck v. United States, 63
West Gallery v. Salt Lake City, 105

West Va. St. Bd. of Educ. v. Barnette, 270
Western Corp. v. Kentucky, 104
Whalen v. Roe, 230, 235
White v. New Hampshire Dept. of Social Serv., 376
Widmar v. Vincent, 45, 198, 271
Wilder v. Berstein, 265
Wilder v. Sugarman, 265
Wilkes County v. United States, 245, 246
Williams v. Brown, 238
Williams v. Leeke, 295
Williams v. Shipping Corp. of India, 343
Williams v. Spencer, 196
Williams v. United States Dist. Court, 86
Williams v. Zbaraz, 217
Wilson v. California Health Facilities Commn., 234
Wilson v. Scripps-Howard, 126
Wilson v. Wilson, 202
Winpsinger v. Watson, 324
Wisconsin Socialist Workers Party 1976 Campaign Comm. v. McCann, 10
Wisconsin v. Constantineau, 392
Wisconsin v. Princess Cinema, 90
Wisconsin v. Yoder, 224
Wise v. Lipscomb, 242, 247
Withrow v. Larkin, 286
Wolman v. Walter, 257, 259
Wolston v. Reader's Digest Assn., 121
Women's Health Center v. Cohen, 218
Women's Med. Center v. Roberts, 328
Women's Serv. v. Throne, 218
Wood v. Strickland, 295
Woods v. Hamilton, 246
Woody v. City of West Miami, 351
Wool v. Hogan, 300
Wooley v. Maynard, 42, 270, 324, 399
Worldwide VW v. Woodson, 387
Worthington v. Wyoming, 343
Wright v. Chief of Transit Police, 45
Wright v. Regan, 323
Writers Guild of Am., West, Inc. v. FCC, 168
W. T. Grant Co., In re, 151
Wyche v. Madison Police Parish, 242
Wynn v. Scott, 234
Yiamouyiannis v. Consumers Union, 121

Yott v. North Am. Rockwell Corp., 269
Young v. American Mini Theaters, Inc., 38, *93*, 106, 327
Young v. Klutznick, 323
Young v. Toia, 401
Zablocki v. Redhail, 223, 324, 333
Zacchini v. Scripps-Howard Broadcasting Co., 119, 130

Acknowledgments

We wish to thank the following for their valuable research assistance in the preparation of this Supplement: at New York University School of Law, Gilda Brancato, Richard Schaeffer, M. Margaret Terry, Nancy Flickenger, and Bruce Saber; at Pennsylvania Law School, David Reed, Nancy L. Schultz, and Elaine M. Lustig; at Brooklyn Law School, Daniel Katz and Alice B. Newman.

We also wish to thank the following for their excellent secretarial and administrative skills: at New York University School of Law, Iris Ramer and Carole Sparkes; at Pennsylvania School of Law, Kathleen McClendon and Nancy Hirst.

Norman Dorsen
Paul Bender
Burt Neuborne
Joel Gora

Chapter Two
National Security

A. BACKGROUND OF LAWS ON TREASON, REBELLION, INSURRECTION, ESPIONAGE, SABOTAGE, AND SIMILAR CONDUCT

(page 48) [62]

NOTES

1. [continued] Recently enacted legislation in the national security area includes the Foreign Intelligence Surveillance Act of 1978, Pub. L. No. 95-511, 92 Stat. 1783 (1978); National Emergencies Act of 1977, Pub. L. No. 95-223, 91 Stat. 1625 (1977), amending the National Emergencies Act of 1976, Pub. L. No. 94-412, 90 Stat. 1255 (1976); Executive Order 12170, 44 Fed. Reg. 65729 (1979); Executive Order 12036 on United States Intelligence Activities, 43 Fed. Reg. 3674 (1978), as amended by Executive Order 12139, 44 Fed. Reg. 30311 (1979).

B. RESTRICTIONS ON EXPRESSION WHICH MAY INTERFERE WITH A WAR OR DEFENSE EFFORT

(page 54) [70]

NOTES

7. In Shaman, Revitalizing the Clear-and-Present Danger Test: Toward a Principled Interpretation of the First Amendment, 22 Vill. L. Rev. 60 (1976), the author proposes that use of a revitalized clear-and-present-danger test, with heightened emphasis on the "danger" element, would substantially increase First Amendment protection. See also Blasi, The Checking Value in First Amendment Theory, Samuel Pool Weaver Constitutional Law Series (Am. Bar Foundation, 1977).

(page 71) [87]

NOTES

2. [continued] See generally Church, Conspiracy Doctrine and Speech Offenses: A Reexamination of Yates v. United States From the Perspective of United States v. Spock, 60 Cornell L. Rev. 568 (1975).

C. ANTISEDITION LAWS AND SIMILAR RESTRICTIONS ON POLITICAL EXPRESSION

(page 90) [142]

NOTES

1. [continued] In upholding the statute authorizing customs officers to open sealed, incoming international mail if they have reasonable cause to suspect a customs law violation, the Supreme Court rejected the claim that such action impermissibly chills the exercise of free speech. "Here envelopes are opened at the border only when the customs officer has reason to believe they contain other than correspondence, while the reading of any correspondence inside the envelope is forbidden. Any 'chill' that might exist under these circumstances may fairly be considered not only 'minimal' but also wholly subjective." United States v. Ramsey, 431 U.S. 606 (1977). See also Church of Scientology of California v. Simon, 460 F. Supp. 56 (C.D. Cal. 1978) (three-judge court), summarily aff'd, sub nom. Church of Scientology of California v. Blumenthal, 441 U.S. 938 (1979) (upheld the constitutionality of statute prohibiting the importation of materials advocating treason or insurrection against the United States or forcible resistance to any law of the United States; court read the Brandenburg standard into the statute).

In United States v. Richards, 638 F.2d 765 (5th Cir.), cert. denied, 50 U.S.L.W. 3465 (1981), the court held this border search exception extends to mail delivered to addressee but not yet taken into private possession beyond the scrutiny of government officials.

(page 91) [143]

NOTE

See Note, Brandenburg v. Ohio: A Speech Test for All Seasons?, 43 U. Chi. L. Rev. 151 (1975).

(page 96) [150]

REFERENCES

For a discussion of surveillance by local Red Squads see Stickgold, Yesterday's Paranoia Is Today's Reality: Documentation of Police Surveillance of First Amendment Activity, 55 U. Det. J. of Urb. L. 877 (1978).

D. DENIAL OF PRIVILEGES OR POSITIONS OF INFLUENCE TO SUBVERSIVES

(page 114) [169]

NOTES

11. [continued] But see Turner v. Air Transport Lodge 1894, 590 F. 2d 409 (2d Cir.), cert. denied, 442 U.S. 919 (1979) (free speech provisions of the LMRDA prohibited union from expelling non-Communist Party member who espoused "communist" views in violation of the union constitution; there was no evidence that the union member's conduct caused any harm to the union or interfered with its contractual obligations).

(page 131) [189]

NOTES

5. In Carpagno v. Harris, 470 F. Supp. 219 (E.D. Ark. 1979), the court struck down an Arkansas bar admission question regarding membership in an organization that believes in or teaches the overthrow of the United States government by force or by any illegal or unconstitutional methods. The question ran afoul of the Constitution because it did not inquire whether the members knew of the organization's aims and had a specific intent to bring them about.

(page 131) [193]

NOTES

5. [continued] In a private letter ruling, 49 U.S.L.W. 2256 (1980), the Internal Revenue Service concluded that an arm of the United Church of Christ could distribute "report cards" on members of Congress without losing its tax-exempt status if they were sent only to members and

not targeted to election areas or timed to coincide with elections. This ruling was later issued as Rev. Rul. 80-282.

(page 132) [195]

NOTES

1. [continued] For an argument that the Supreme Court overrule Flemming v. Nestor or, alternatively, Congress repeal §202(n), see Legonsky, Suspending the Social Security Benefits of Deported Aliens: The Insult and the Injury, 5 Suffolk U.L. Rev. 1235 (1979).

E. LOYALTY-SECURITY QUALIFICATIONS FOR EMPLOYMENT

(page 135) [207]

NOTES

5. [continued] In Lefkowitz v. Cunningham, 431 U.S. 801 (1977), the Court held that the New York statute that subjects a political party officer to automatic removal from party office and disqualification for five years for refusing to sign a grand jury immunity waiver violates the Fifth and Fourteenth Amendments.

[F. ALIENS AND CITIZENSHIP]

[257]

[NOTES]

1. See Gardner, Due Process and Deportation: A Critical Examination of the Plenary Power and the Fundamental Fairness Doctrine, 8 Hastings Const. L.Q. 397 (1981).

[264]

[NOTES]

[6.] In Vance v. Terrazas, 444 U.S. 252 (1980), the Supreme Court upheld as constitutional §349(c) of the Immigration and Nationalization Act, 8 U.S.C. §1481(c). This section requires proof of an intentional expatriating act by only a preponderance of evidence and provides that all acts of expatriation, as denoted by §349(a)(2) of the Act, 8 U.S.C. §1481(a)(2), are presumed to be committed voluntarily. Concerning the evidentiary standard, the Court noted that expatriation proceedings are not criminal in nature and do not threaten a loss of liberty and, therefore, do not require the preponderance standard mandated in criminal and civil commitment contexts. The Court upheld the presumption of voluntariness, reasoning that the burden of proving that the voluntary act was performed with the intent to relinquish United States citizenship, a necessary element of proof, remained with the party claiming expatriation.

[7.] In Chadha v. Immigration and Naturalization Service, 634 F.2d 408 (9th Cir. 1980), the court held §244(c)(2) of the Immigration and Naturalization Act, 8 U.S.C. §1254(c)(2), permitting either the Senate or the House to override the Attorney General's decision to suspend deportation of aliens, to be unconstitutional under the separation of powers doctrine.

F [G]. LEGISLATIVE INVESTIGATIONS

(page 153) [267]

REFERENCES

For a general treatment of legislative investigations, see J. Hamilton, The Power to Probe: A Study of Congressional Investigations (1976).

(page 174) [289]

NOTES [REFERENCES]

8. [continued] See generally Sullivan, Kamin, Sussman, Zeisel & Stamler, The Case Against HUAC, 11 Harv. C.R.-C.L.L. Rev. 242 (1976) (documentation and analysis of the record of HUAC).

(page 177) [292]

NOTE

See generally Berger, Congressional Subpoenas to Executive Officials, 75 Colum. L. Rev. 865 (1975).

(page 178) [296]

NOTES

1. [continued] In McSurely v. McClellan, 553 F.2d 1277 (D.C. Cir. 1976) (en banc), cert. dismissed as improvidently granted sub nom.

McAdams v. McSurely, 438 U.S. 189 (1978), plaintiff brought a civil rights action for damages, alleging that a congressional investigator's transport and examination of materials that were previously illegally seized violated the Fourth Amendment. En banc, the District of Columbia Circuit, by an equally divided court, ruled that the Speech or Debate Clause does not protect a legislative employee from suit if unlawful means are used to implement an otherwise proper legislative investigation. See main volume, pages 173-174 [288], n.7. The court then remanded for district court determination the issue whether the Fourth Amendment was additionally violated by the investigator's subsequent examination.

(page 178) [297]

NOTES

2. [continued] In United States v. American Telephone & Telegraph Co., 551 F.2d 384 (D.C. Cir. 1976), cert. denied (1977), Congress had directed a subpoena to AT & T to disclose information about warrantless national security wiretaps. The court ruled, however, that AT & T was a mere stakeholder in the controversy; the Department of Justice, which sought an injunction against Congress, was deemed the interested party. The court then held that the possibility of a severe clash between the executive and legislative branches over issuance of the subpoena warranted judicial suggestion of compromise and pendente lite treatment of the injunctive action to allow further efforts at settlement. The compromise reached between Congress and the Executive is reported in United States v. AT & T Co., 567 F.2d (D.C. Cir. 1977).

G [H]. SURVEILLANCE AND OTHER FORMS OF POLICE ACTION INTERFERING WITH FREEDOM OF POLITICAL EXPRESSION

(page 184) [303]

NOTES

President Carter's Executive Order 12036 on United States Intelligence Activities, 43 Fed. Reg. 3674 (1978), as amended by Executive Order 12139, 44 Fed. Reg. 30311 (1979), governs conduct for federal agencies.

(page 185) [305]

NOTE

The Supreme Court confronted questions raised by covert entry to install otherwise legal electronic surveillance equipment in Dalia v. United States, 441 U.S. 238 (1979). In a 5-4 decision, the Court held that the Fourth Amendment does not prohibit per se a covert entry performed for that purpose; that Congress, in enacting Title III of the Omnibus Crime Control Act, clearly understood that it was conferring power upon the courts to authorize covert entries ancillary to their responsibility to review and approve surveillance applications under the statute; and that the Fourth Amendment does not require that a Title III surveillance order include a specific authorization to enter covertly the premises described in the order.

In United States v. New York Telephone, 434 U.S. 159 (1977), the Supreme Court found that Title III does not govern the authorization of pen registers because these records of phone numbers dialed do not acquire the contents of the communication.

In United States v. Donovan, 429 U.S. 413 (1977), the Court held that failure to comply with all the notice requirements of Title III of the Omnibus Crime Control Act does not render the wiretap illegal nor mandate suppression of wiretap evidence.

The Foreign Intelligence Surveillance Act of 1978, Pub. L. No. 95-511, 92 Stat. 1783 (1978), governs electronic surveillance for nondomestic national security. The statute permits the President to authorize surveillance without a court order for up to one year under certain prescribed circumstances: basically, for communications between foreign powers with no substantial likelihood that the surveillance will acquire the contents of a communication to which a United States citizen is a party. The Attorney General must certify that any such surveillance is in accordance with the Act and must transmit the certification under seal to the seven-judge special court established under the Act. A court order is required if communications of any United States person will be acquired. The Act also provides for a special three-judge appellate court and review by the Supreme Court if necessary.

See Note, Foreign Intelligence Surveillance Act of 1978, 13 Vand. Transnatl. L.J. 719 (1980).

(page 190) [310]

NOTES

[continued] The District of Columbia Circuit recently decided a trio of cases springing from the Nixon Administration's "national security" wiretaps. In Halperin v. Kissinger, 606 F.2d 1192 (D.C. Cir. 1979), aff'd by an equally divided court, 101 S. Ct. 3132 (1981) (per curiam), the court ruled that Title III of the Omnibus Crime Control Act applies to any electronic surveillance of the former National Security Counsel staff member that did not involve the primary purpose of protecting national security information against foreign intelligence activities. The award of only $1 nominal damages was reversed on the grounds that even if a constitutional violation inflicts only intangible injury, substantial compensation is still appropriate. The court of appeals also rejected the claims of absolute immunity raised by all the government officials involved, noting that "the President is the elected chief executive of our government, and not an omniscient leader cloaked in mystical powers." In Zweibon v. Mitchell, 606 F.2d 1172 (D.C. Cir. 1979), cert. denied, 101 S. Ct. 3147 (1981), the warrant requirement for domestic national security wiretaps was applied retroactively to a civil suit for damages brought by members of the Jewish Defense League against Attorney General Mitchell and 10 FBI agents. And in Smith v. Nixon, 606 F.2d 1183 (D.C. Cir. 1979), cert. denied, 101 S. Ct. 3147 (1981), the court ruled that Hedrick Smith, a New York Times reporter, had a valid cause of action against Nixon and other government officials under Title III for an illegal wiretap on his home phone. Because nothing in the record contradicted Smith's allegation that the wiretap was initiated to discover the sources of stories personally embarrassing to the Nixon Administration, Title III's national security clause did not apply.

See also United States v. Ehrlichman, 546 F.2d 910 (D.C. Cir. 1976), cert. denied, 429 U.S. 1120 (1977) (in upholding Ehrlichman's conviction for conspiracy to violate the civil rights of Daniel Ellsberg's psychiatrist, the court found the defendant's claim of a national security exemption to the Fourth Amendment was negated by absence of assertion of actual authorization by the President or the Attorney General); Clark v. United States, 481 F.Supp. 1086 (S.D.N.Y. 1979) (President is not immune to civil rights violations for surveillance program which was neither a function of his former office nor essential to the conduct of public business).

In United States v. Truong Dinh Hung, 629 F.2d 908 (4th Cir. 1980), cert filed, 50 U.S.L.W. 3280 (1981), the Fourth Circuit upheld defendants' convictions for espionage and espionage-related offenses, recognizing a foreign intelligence exception to the Fourth Amendment's warrant requirement. The court concluded that this exception must be limited to those situations in which the object of the search or surveillance is a foreign power, its agent or collaborators, and only when the surveillance is reasonable and is conducted "primarily" for foreign intelligence reasons. In accordance with the second limitation, the court upheld the district court's exclusion of evidence obtained subsequent to when the investigation became "primarily" criminal.

In Jabara v. Kelley, 476 F. Supp. 561 (E.D. Mich. 1979), the warrantless surveillance of plaintiff's communications and the transmission of summaries of their contents was held to violate the Fourth Amendment. The court found that the complainant was the target of surveillance and, absent proof that he or the domestic organization to which he belonged was a foreign agent, a warrant was required.

(page 190) [311]

REFERENCES

[3.] Recent literature on electronic surveillance is voluminous and includes Decker & Handler, Electronic Surveillance: Standards, Restrictions and Remedies, 12 Calif. W.L. Rev. 60 (1975); Donner, Electronic Surveillance: The National Security Game, 2 Civ. Lib. Rev. 15 (1975); Shattuck, National Security Wiretaps, 11 Crim. L. Bull. 7 (1975) (author explores governmental abuse of national security wiretaps, general opposition by the ACLU to electronic surveillance, and the need to impose legislative controls requiring wiretap specificity and minimization and providing effective sanctions); Note, Electronic Surveillance, Title III, and the Requirement of Necessity, 2 Hastings Const. L.Q. 571 (1975); Comment, Title III and National Security Surveillance, 56 B.U.L. Rev. 776 (1976); Comment, 45 Geo. Wash. L. Rev. 55 (1976); Comment, 28 Vand. L. Rev. 1135 (1975).

(page 197) [317]

NOTES

2. [continued] In Harrington v. Bush, 553 F.2d 190 (D.C. Cir. 1977), Judge Wilkey ruled that a United States Representative does not have standing to challenge the CIA's allegedly illegal domestic and foreign activities, including alleged use of secret funding, and reporting provisions in connection with those activities. The court found that Representative Harrington lacked "a distinct and palpable injury to himself" and that alleged CIA abuses did not affect the legal status of appropriations bills for which he had voted or would vote.

(page 197) [318]

NOTES

3. [continued] See Birnbaum v. United States, 588 F.2d 319 (2d Cir. 1978) (upheld state "intrusion of privacy" claim under Federal Tort Claims Act; rejected discretionary function exemption of general waiver of sovereign immunity because CIA's broad and indiscriminate inspec-

tion of private mail with a view to obtaining information on matters of domestic, as well as foreign concern, lay outside the CIA's charter which prohibits the CIA from exercising "internal security" functions); Cruikshank v. United States, 431 F. Supp. 1355 (D. Hawaii 1977) (government's motion to dismiss "invasion of privacy" claim arising from CIA's opening and photographing sealed first class letters mailed by plaintiff to colleagues in the Soviet Union; the government should not have the discretion to commit illegal acts whenever it pleases).

See generally Note, Governmental Investigations of the Exercise of First Amendment Rights: Citizens' Rights and Remedies, 60 Minn. L. Rev. 1257 (1976) (analyzes the role of the judiciary in remedying illegal governmental investigations of exercises of First Amendment rights).

(page 198) [318]

NOTES

5. [continued] On appeal in Paton v. La Prade, the Third Circuit ruled that plaintiff alleging a cognizable legal injury had standing to sue for expungement of the FBI records. 524 F.2d 862 (3d Cir. 1975). Judge Rosenn stated that, although the FBI alleged that the file had no pejorative connotations, the file's significance might not be correctly understood. Thus, since maintenance of the records could result in injuries and damages, expungement was warranted.

In Paton v. La Prade, 471 F. Supp. 166 (D.N.J. 1979), the court rejected defendants' claim that the investigation of the Socialist Workers Party and thus of plaintiff was part of a good faith criminal investigation. Although at various times 12 separate criminal statutes formed a basis for the investigation, "the thirty-six years of investigation produced no criminal indictments." Moreover, the court noted that once the FBI discovered that plaintiff was a high school student who contacted the SWP as part of a school project, the agent "should have contacted her parents and briefly and cordially explained the nature and purpose of this investigation. This would have removed the aura of mystery and surreptitiousness that the investigation created." Accordingly, plaintiff won her summary judgment motion on the unconstitutionality of the field investigation.

8. The Justice Department recently amended its regulations based on §524(b) of the Crime Control Act of 1973, which relate to the collection, storage, and dissemination of criminal history records. The amended regulations provide that (1) conviction data may be disseminated without limitation to criminal agencies, but (2) noncriminal access to such information must be expressly or impliedly authorized by statute, ordinance, executive order, court rule, or court order. 28 C.F.R. §20.21.

9. In Wisconsin Socialist Workers Party 1976 Campaign Committee

v. McCann, 433 F. Supp. 540 (E.D. Wis. 1977), the state was enjoined from requiring the SWP under its Campaign Finance Act to disclose the names of contributors and disbursement recipients; disclosure would subject the SWP to threats, harrassment, and reprisals from government officials and private parties. See also New York Civil Liberties Union, Inc. v. Acito, 459 F. Supp. 75 (1978) (New York referendum campaign disclosure statute declared unconstitutional on overbreadth and First Amendment grounds).

(page 200) [321]

NOTES

3. [continued] In Hampton v. United States, 425 U.S. 484 (1976), the Supreme Court confronted the issue left unresolved in Russell: whether and to what extent there remained due process limitations on entrapment — regardless of the defendant's predisposition. The defendant in Hampton was convicted of selling heroin supplied by a government informant. The defendant conceded his predisposition but contended that the government's outrageous conduct in supplying him with contraband violated due process. In a plurality opinion, Justices Rehnquist, Burger, and White rejected that contention and affirmed the conviction:

"The remedy of the criminal defendant with respect to the acts of Government agents, which, far from being resisted, are encouraged by him, lies solely in the defense of entrapment. But, as noted, petitioner's conceded predisposition rendered this defense unavailable to him. . . . The limitations of the Due Process Clause of the Fifth Amendment come into play only when the Government activity in question violates some protected right of the *defendant*. Here, as we have noted, the police, the Government informer, and the defendant acted in concert with one another. If the result of the governmental activity is to 'implant in the mind of an innocent person the disposition to commit the alleged offense and induce its commission . . . ,' the defendant is protected by the defense of entrapment. If the police engage in illegal activity in concert with a defendant beyond the scope of their duties the remedy lies, not in freeing the equally culpable defendant, but in prosecuting the police under the applicable provisions of state or federal law. . . ."

Justices Powell and Blackmun, concurring, concluded that the Russell case controlled the facts at bar but did not foreclose reliance in other cases on due process principles or on the Court's supervisory power to bar conviction if police conduct is outrageous. Justices Brennan, Stewart, and Marshall dissented, stating that the government involvement with the defendant was pervasive and exceeded permissible due process boundaries. Because of the Court's plurality opinion, the issue is left unsettled.

(page 201) [322]

NOTES

5. [continued] In Weatherford v. Bursey, 429 U.S. 545 (1977), a §1983 action brought against an undercover agent, the Supreme Court ruled that a criminal defendant is not denied effective assistance of counsel when an undercover agent meets with him and his counsel but does not communicate any information obtained at the meeting. The Court further emphasized that due process does not require that a prosecutor reveal before trial the names of undercover agents or witnesses who testify unfavorably to the defense.

6. In United States v. Twigg, 588 F.2d 373 (3d Cir. 1978), the "nature and extent of police involvement in [the] crime was so overreaching as to bar prosecution of [the] crime as a matter of due process." The government had supplied the defendants with rare chemicals essential to the manufacture of "speed," provided 20 percent of the necessary glassware, rented the farmhouse to be used as a laboratory, and made a deal with a chemical supply house so that defendants could buy other chemical supplies. Moreover, the government agent/informer was completely in charge of the entire laboratory; defendants' assistance was minor and under the specific direction of the government agent/informer.

[I. INHERENT AND EMERGENCY POWERS OF THE PRESIDENT AND STATE OFFICIALS]

[334]

The National Emergencies Act of 1976, Pub. L. No. 94-412, 90 Stat. 1255 (1976), as amended by the National Emergencies Act of 1977, Pub. L. No. 95-223, 91 Stat. 1625 (1977), authorizes the President to declare national emergencies. The Congress can terminate such emergency by concurrent resolution, and each House must meet within six months of the declaration to consider a vote on a concurrent resolution.

See generally, Goldstein, An American Gulag? Summary Arrest and Emergency Detention of Political Dissidents in the United States, 10 Colum. Human Rights 541 (1978-1979).

Chapter Three

Government Secrecy and the Public's Right to Know

A. THE DEVELOPMENT OF A "RIGHT TO KNOW"

(page 203) [344]

NOTE

[continued] In the last few years, the Supreme Court has wrestled frequently with the question of whether the public has a constitutional "right to know," and what that "right" requires.

First, in a series of cases extending First Amendment protection to "commercial speech," the Court has premised its rulings on the rights of the members of the public to receive ideas and information. The high water mark for this component of the right to know came in Virginia State Board of Pharmacy v. Virginia Citizens Consumer Council, 425 U.S. 748 (1976), where the Supreme Court held invalid a Virginia statute forbidding pharmacists' advertising of prescription drug prices. In recognizing the interests of the consumers of speech and information, the Court stated, 425 U.S. at 756-757:

"Freedom of speech presupposes a willing speaker. But where a speaker exists, as is the case here, the protection afforded is to the communication, to its source and to its recipients both. This is clear from the decided cases. In Lamont v. Postmaster General, 381 U.S. 301 (1965), the Court upheld the First Amendment rights of citizens to receive political publications sent from abroad. More recently, in Kleindienst v. Mandel, 408 U.S. 753, 762-763 (1972), we acknowledged that this Court has referred to a First Amendment right to 'receive information and ideas,' and that freedom of speech ' "necessarily protects the right to receive." ' And in Procunier v. Martinez, 416 U.S. 396, 408-409 (1974), where censorship of prison inmates' mail was under examination, we thought it unnecessary to assess the First Amendment rights of the inmates themselves, for it was reasoned that such censorship equally infringed the rights of noninmates to whom the correspondence was addressed. There are numerous other expressions to the same effect in the Court's decisions. See, e.g., Red Lion Broadcasting Co. v. FCC, 395 U.S. 367, 390 (1969); Stanley v. Georgia, 394 U.S. 557, 564 (1969); Griswold v. Connecticut, 381 U.S. 479, 482 (1965); Marsh v. Alabama, 326 U.S. 501, 505 (1946); Thomas v. Collins, 323 U.S. 516, 534 (1945); Martin v. Struthers, 319 U.S. 141 (1943). If there is a right to advertise, there is a reciprocal right to receive the advertising, and it may be asserted by these appellees."

The right to receive ideas and information has been recognized, explicitly or implicitly, in other recent decisions as well. See, e.g., Linmark Associates v. Town of Willingboro, 431 U.S. 85, 92-93 (1977) (invalidating ban on display of "For Sale" or "Sold" signs on residential property); Carey v. Population Services International, 431 U.S. 678, 700-701 (1977) (holding invalid a proscription on advertising of contraceptives); Bates v. State Bar of Arizona, 433 U.S. 350, 364 (1977) (overturning restrictions on advertising by lawyers and recognizing that the "listener's interest [in commercial information] is substantial: the consumer's concern for the free flow of commercial speech often may be far keener than his concern for urgent political dialogue." Ibid.); First National Bank of Boston v. Bellotti, 435 U.S. 765, 776-778 (1978) (corporations cannot be prohibited from spending corporate funds to communicate to the public on referenda issues; the "inherent worth of the speech in terms of its capacity for informing the public does not depend upon the identity of its source, whether corporation, association, union or individual." Id. at 777.); Consolidated Edison Co. v. Public Service Commission, 447 U.S. 530 (1980) (public service commission ban on the inclusion in monthly billing statements of inserts discussing controversial issues of public policy such as nuclear power held invalid, the Court noting the First Amendment's role in affording the public access to discussion, debate, information, and ideas); Central Hudson Gas and Electric Co. v. Public Service Commission, 447 U.S. 557 (1980) (voiding a commission prohibition on advertising that promotes the use of electricity, the Court observed that: "Even in monopoly markets, the suppression of advertising reduces the information available for consumer decisions and thereby defeats the purpose of the First Amendment." Id. at 567).

Though the Court has placed some limits on the protection afforded to commercial speech, see Friedman v. Rogers, 440 U.S. 1 (1979) (upholding restrictions on use of trade names by optometrist); compare Ohralik v. State Bar Association, 436 U.S. 447 (1978) (permitting broad regulation of overbearing attorney solicitation of personal injury suits) with In re Primus, 436 U.S. 412 (1978) (invalidating sanctions imposed on solicitation of public interest litigation) and In Re R.M.J., — U.S. —, 50 U.S.L.W. 4185 (Jan. 25, 1982) (broadly invalidating restrictions on lawyer advertising), the basic recognition of a First Amendment interest in receiving information has continued. See generally, Central Hudson Gas & Electric Corp. v. Public Service Commission, 447 U.S. 557 (1980). Similar *statutory* consumer rights issues were avoided by the Court in American Medical Association v. Federal Trade Commission, 638 F.2d 443 (2d Cir. 1980), aff'd by an equally divided Court, 50 U.S.L.W. 4313 (March 23, 1982), involving the validity under federal statutes of an FTC order preventing the AMA from restraining advertising by doctors; First Amendment issues were not squarely before the Court.

Literature on commercial speech and the right to know includes Rotunda, Commercial Speech Doctrine in the Supreme Court, 1976 U. Ill. L.F. 1080; Symposium, First Amendment and the Right to Know, 1976 Wash. U.L.Q. 1; Note, Professional Price Advertising Set Free? Consumers' "Right-to-Know" in Prescription Advertising, 8 Conn. L. Rev. 108 (1975); Note, The Right to Receive and the Commercial Speech Doctrine: New Constitutional Considerations, 63 Geo. L.J. 775 (1975), Baker, Commercial Speech: A Problem in the Theory of Freedom, 62 Iowa L. Rev. 1 (1976); Pitofsky, Beyond Nader: Consumer Protection and the Regulation of Advertising, 90 Harv. L. Rev. 661 (1977); Reich, Consumer Protection and the First Amendment: A Dilemma for the FTC? 61 Minn. L. Rev. 705 (1977); Note, The Constitutional Right to Know, 4 Hastings Const. L.Q. 109 (1977); see also: O'Brien, the First Amendment and the Public's "Right to Know," 7 Hast. Const. L.Q. 579 (1980); Baldasty & Simpson, The Deceptive "Right to Know": How Pessimism Rewrote The First Amendment, 56 Wash. L. Rev. 365 (1981). For an extensive treatment of commercial speech, see Chapter VIII, infra.

Second, the Court has also recognized the First Amendment importance of informing the public about the conduct and actions of governmental institutions, especially the courts. In Landmark Communications, Inc. v. Virginia, 435 U.S. 829 (1978), overturning the criminal conviction of a newspaper for publishing information about a confidential judicial misconduct investigation, the Court stated: "The operation of the Virginia Commission, no less than the operation of the judicial system itself, is a matter of public interest, necessarily engaging the attention of the news media. The article published by Landmark provided accurate factual information about a legislatively authorized inquiry pending before the Judicial Review and Inquiry Commission, and in so doing clearly served those interests in public scrutiny and discussion of governmental affairs which the First Amendment was adopted to protect." 435 U.S. at 839. Similarly, a year later, the Court acknowledged the same concerns in holding that a newspaper could not be punished for publishing the identity of a juvenile defendant, where the confidential information had been lawfully obtained. Smith v. Daily Mail Publishing Co., 443 U.S. 97 (1979).

Where the Court has had more difficulty, however, is on the issue of whether the First Amendment interest in the public's right to know requires or implies a right of access to information by the public at large or the press as its surrogate. For a time a plurality of the Court emphatically denied that the First Amendment required any such *constitutional* right of access to information about the way that government conducts its business. Instead, the Court had adopted Mr. Justice Stewart's pithy conclusion that "[t]he Constitution itself is neither a Freedom of Information Act nor an Official Secrets Act." Stewart, "Or of the Press," 26 Hastings L.J. 631, 636 (1975), quoted in Houchins v. KQED, Inc., 438 U.S. 1, 14 (1978).

In Houchins, a plurality opinion by Chief Justice Burger rejected the claim that news media representatives had any constitutional right of access, over and above that of other persons, to interview and film inmates in a county jail:

"The public importance of conditions in penal facilities and the media's role of providing information afford no basis for reading into the Constitution a right of the public or the media to enter these institutions, with camera equipment, and take moving and still pictures of inmates for broadcast purposes. This Court has never intimated a First Amendment guarantee of a right of access to all sources of information within government control. . . .

"The right to *receive* ideas and information is not the issue in this case. See, e.g., Virginia Pharmacy Board v. Virginia Citizens Consumer Council, 425 U.S. 748 (1976); Procunier v. Martinez, 416 U.S. [396, 408-409 (1974)]; Kleindienst v. Mandel, 408 U.S. 753, 762-763 (1972). The issue is a claimed special privilege of access which the Court rejected in Pell and Saxbe, a right which is not essential to guarantee the freedom to communicate or publish. . . .

"Neither the First Amendment nor the Fourteenth Amendment mandates a right of access to government information or sources of information within the government's control. . . . [U]ntil the political branches decree otherwise, as they are free to do, the media have no special right of access to the Alameda County Jail different from or greater than that accorded the public generally." 438 U.S. at 9-16.

As might be expected, Justice Stewart concurred in this reasoning: "The First and Fourteenth Amendments do not guarantee the public a right of access to information generated or controlled by government, nor do they guarantee the press any basic right of access superior to that of the public generally. The Constitution does no more than assure the public and the press equal access once government has opened its doors." Id. at 16. Justice Stewart believed, however, that the press is entitled to some limited form of access, as surrogate for the public, but that the access provided by the lower courts went beyond what the Constitution required. Id. at 16-19. The three dissenters, in an opinion by Justice Stevens, were of the view that the role of the First Amendment in our society imposed some obligation on government to facilitate press, and thereby public, access to information about the workings of government.

A year later, these same issues surfaced again, although in a slightly different context. In Gannett Co. v. DePasquale, 443 U.S. 368 (1979), the Court held that the press and public could be excluded from a pretrial suppression hearing in a murder case, where the parties requested a closed hearing. The bulk of the majority opinion analyzed the meaning of the Sixth Amendment "public trial" guarantee, concluding that, while there is an independent public interest in public trials, there is no constitutional right on the part of the public to attend trial or pre-trial proceedings. On the claim that the First Amendment supplies the press and public a right of access to pre-trial hearings, the majority held that, "even assuming, *arguendo,* that the First and Fourteenth Amendments may guarantee such access in some situations, a question we do not decide, . . ." the procedural opportunity afforded by the trial court for the press to contest the exclusion order, and the trial court's balancing of the interests at stake satisfied any First Amendment interests. Id. at 392.

In 1980, however, in a case directly involving the question of excluding the press and public from a criminal *trial,* a majority of the Court gave broad recognition to such a right of access. In Richmond Newspapers Inc. v. Commonwealth of Virginia, 448 U.S. 555 (1980), the Court held, 7-1, that the Constitution requires criminal trials be presumptively open to the press and public, and all or part of such a trial cannot be closed absent overriding countervailing interests. Although there was no opinion for the Court, the various majority justices all sounded the access to information theme and distinguished Gannett as involving the special case of pretrial hearings. Chief Justice Burger, pointing to the vital role of public trials in Anglo-American judicial traditions, found in that history support for a public right to attend trials and a press right to serve as "surrogates for the public":

"The Bill of Rights was enacted against the backdrop of the long history of trials being presumptively open. Public access to trials was then regarded as an important aspect of the process itself. . . . In guaranteeing freedoms such as those of speech and press, the First Amendment can be read as protecting the right of everyone to attend trials so as to give meaning to those explicit guarantees. . . . Free speech carries with it some freedom to listen. . . . What this means in the context of trials is that the First Amendment guarantees of speech and press, standing alone, prohibit government from summarily closing courtroom doors which had long been open to the public at the time that amendment was adopted....

"It is not crucial whether we describe this right to attend criminal trials to hear, see, and communicate observations concerning them as a 'right of access,'... or a 'right to gather information,' for we have recognized that 'without some protection for seeking out the news, freedom of the press could be eviscerated.' Branzburg v. Hayes, 408 U.S. 665, 681 (1972). The explicit, guaranteed rights to speak and to publish concerning what takes place at a trial would lose much meaning if access to observe the trial could, as it was here, be foreclosed arbitrarily." 448 U.S. at 575-576.

Justice Stevens, concurring, saw the ruling as a "watershed case," because the Court, for the first time, squarely held "that the acquisition of newsworthy matter" is entitled to constitutional protection. He observed: "Twice before, the Court has implied that any governmental restriction on access to information, no matter how severe and no matter how unjustified, would be constitutionally acceptable so long as it did not single out the press for special disabilities not applicable to the public at large.... Today, however, for the first time, the Court unequivocally holds that an arbitrary interference with access to important information is an abridgement of the freedoms of speech and of the press protected by the First Amendment." Id. at 582.

Similar reasons were given by the Court in Globe Newspaper Co. v. Superior Court, 50 U.S.L.W. 4759 (June 23, 1982) for invalidating a Massachusetts statute construed to bar the press and public from the courtroom in the trial of a rape or sexual abuse case during the testimony of any complainant who is a minor.

Although not directly involving a claimed First Amendment right to know, the Court's recent decision in Chandler v. Florida, — U.S. —, 66 L. Ed. 2d 740 (1981), unanimously ruling that the televising of criminal trials does not, per se, violate a defendant's constitutional rights, will further enhance access to information about criminal trials. The Chandler ruling clears the way for the various states to experiment with televising trials. For an argument that the First Amendment *requires* permitting the televising of public trials — a point not at issue in Chandler — see Zimmerman, Overcoming Future Shock: Estes Revisited Or A Modest Proposal for the Constitutional Protection of the News-Gathering Process, 1980 Duke L.J. 641 (1980). Finally, on this point, the recent ABSCAM and similar corruption prosecutions of public officials have produced interesting issues of press access to evidence introduced in judicial proceedings, namely, video tapes of Congressmen and others allegedly in the process of taking bribes. Avoiding First Amendment issues, the courts have tended to permit press access to the video tapes on the basis of a common law right to inspect and copy judicial records. See United States v. Myers, 635 F.2d 945 (2d Cir. 1980); In Re NBC

(United States v. Criden), 648 F.2d 814 (3rd Cir. 1981); In Re NBC (United States v. Jenrette), 653 F.2d 609 (D.C. Cir. 1981); but see Belo Broadcasting Corp. v. Clark, 654 F.2d 423 (5th Cir. 1981).

What the Court has thus done is to recognize the public's right to know, but more haltingly acknowledge the correlative right to gain access to the sources of news and information that would make such a right meaningful. The decisions in Richmond Newspapers and Chandler are clearly a move in the right direction. Whether they remain limited to the public's right to know about judicial proceedings remains to be seen.

Finally, for a rather poignant application of these principles, see In Re Roger B., 84 Ill. 2d 323, 418 N.E.2d 751 (1981), app. dismissed, 50 U.S.L.W. 3243 (Oct. 5, 1981), holding that, although the First Amendment protects the right to receive ideas and information, it does not guarantee a right of special access to information not available to the general public, and thus an adoptee's rights are not abridged by a statute that prevents his learning the identity of his natural parents.

(page 204) [387]

NOTE — FREEDOM OF INFORMATION ACT DEVELOPMENTS

Since the First Amendment has not yet become a Freedom of Information Act, the right of access to governmental information provided by the Act remains extremely important. The Supreme Court and the lower courts have been very busy in the FOIA area in the last few years.

1. The Court has recently decided several important cases construing various of the Act's exemptions from disclosure and the scope of the Act's coverage.

In NLRB v. Robbins Tire and Rubber Co., 437 U.S. 214 (1978), the Court held that the NLRB was not required to disclose, to the target of an unfair labor practice charge, the statement of witnesses in pending NLRB proceedings prior to the completion of the hearing. The Court ruled that such statements constituted "investigatory records" whose disclosure would "interfere with enforcement proceedings" within the meaning of Exemption 7(A) of the Act, 5 U.S.C. §552(b)(7)(A). Interpreting the legislative history of the 1974 amendment to exemption 7, the Court found a congressional concern to avoid disclosure of witness statements to agencies in ongoing investigations, including NLRB inquiries.

One year later, the Court had occasion to interpret Exemption 5 of the Act, which exempts from discovery "inter-agency or intra-agency memorandums or letters which would not be available by law to a party . . . in litigation with the agency. . . ." 5 U.S.C. §552(b)(5). In Federal Open Market Committee v. Merrill, 443 U.S. 340 (1979), the Court held that the practice of the Federal Reserve System's Committee of withholding from the public certain monetary policy directives during the month they are in effect, with subsequent publication in the Federal Register at the end of the month, is protected by Exemption 5, as incorporating a qualified privilege for confidential commercial information.

In both cases, the Court, though upholding an agency's claimed exemption from disclosure, has nevertheless interpreted the exemption at issue very narrowly.

Two more recent cases required the Court to deal with whether certain documents were covered by the Act at all. In Kissinger v. Reporters Committee for Freedom of the Press, 445 U.S. 136 (1980), the Court ruled that transcripts of Henry Kissinger's telephone conversations while he was National Security Advisor to the President were not within the Act's coverage. Similar transcripts of conversations made while Kissinger was Secretary of State were held unavailable because Kissinger removed them when he left office, and the State Department had no obligation to try to obtain them. Similarly, in Forsham v. Harris, 445 U.S. 169 (1980), the Department of HEW had funded a study by a private institute on various methods of treating diabetes. The Court ruled that this did not render the organization a federal "agency" for purposes of the Act, nor did it make the written data generated by the studies the equivalent of "agency records" for FOIA purposes.

Similarly, in two very recent cases the Court has denied FOIA disclosure because of the policies of other statutes and regulations. In Weinberger v. Catholic Action of Hawaii, — U.S. — , 50 U.S.L.W. 4027 (1981), the Court ruled that the existence of nuclear weapons storage facilities in Hawaii did not have to be disclosed because of the Act's Exemption 1 for national defense information. And in Baldridge v. Shapiro, — U.S. — , 50 U.S.L.W. 4227 (1982), the Court unanimously ruled that personal information gathered and explicitly safeguarded under the Census Act could not be disclosed under the FOIA.

Finally, the Court has decided two other important cases: FBI v. Abramson, 50 U.S.L.W. 4530 (May 24, 1982), upholding the application of Exemption 7 for law enforcement records to FBI reports given to the White House for political purposes, and Department of State v. Washington Post Co., 50 U.S.L.W. 4522 (May 17, 1982), invoking Exemption 6 as applied to State Department information about the U.S. citizenship of two individuals in Iran.

2. The Court has also been busy examining procedural issues under the Act. One important decision was the Court's ruling that so-called *reverse-FOIA* suits, whereby private parties seek to enjoin government from releasing, under the FOIA, information pertaining to them, will not lie under the Act. Chrysler Corp. v. Brown, 441 U.S. 281 (1979). The Court ruled that the Chrysler Corporation, which supplied to the Department of Defense information about its work force and affirmative

action programs as part of an equal employment contract compliance procedure, could not use the FOIA to prevent disclosure of such reports and information. Writing for the Court, Justice Rehnquist observed that the FOIA "is exclusively a disclosure statute" that is an attempt "to meet the demand for open government while preserving workable confidentiality in government decision-making." Id. at 282. The Act's limited exemptions from disclosure were designed to serve the agency's need, not the need of third parties who supply information.

Similarly, the Court has addressed the power of one federal court to interfere with an FOIA action pending in another court. In GTE Sylvania v. Consumer Union, 445 U.S. 375 (1980), involving complicated procedural issues under the Act, the Consumers Union had filed an FOIA suit against the Consumer Products Safety Commission to compel the release of reports on television-related accidents. In a separate federal action, Sylvania obtained an injunction to block the disclosure of the records. The Supreme Court held that the injunction rendered the records not obtainable under the Act because an agency under such a court order is not able to ignore that order and comply with the Act. See also the related matters in Consumer Products Safety Commission v. GTE Sylvania, 447 U.S. 102 (1980).

3. Recent lower court cases interpreting the FOIA include Weissman v. Central Intelligence Agency, 565 F.2d 692 (D.C. Cir. 1977) (statute requiring the CIA Director to protect intelligence sources and methods from disclosure is a statute within the meaning of Exemption 3; but materials compiled by the CIA in investigation of citizen considered for recruitment without his knowledge are not exempt as documents compiled for law enforcement purposes); Halperin v. Department of State, 565 F.2d 699 (D.C. Cir. 1977), cert. denied, 434 U.S. 1046 (1978) (deleted portions of transcript of "background" news conference by Secretary of State not "classified" and immune from disclosure within the meaning of Exemption 1, 5 U.S.C. §552(b)(1), but possibility of nondisclosure in interests of national security recognized); Baker v. Central Intelligence Agency, 580 F.2d 664 (D.C. Cir. 1978) (personnel and organizational information about CIA exempt from disclosure); Caplan v. Bureau of Alcohol, Tobacco and Firearms, 587 F.2d 544 (2d Cir. 1978) (pamphlet containing information on law enforcement techniques exempt from disclosure under Exemption 2 concerning "internal personnel rules and practices," 5 U.S.C. §552(b)(2)); Ray v. Turner, 587 F.2d 1187 (D.C. Cir. 1978) (extensive discussion outlining procedures to be used in FOIA cases involving national security issues); Irons v. Bell, 596 F.2d 468 (1st. Cir. 1979) (even if maintenance of records concerning activities protected by the First Amendment was illegal under the Privacy Act, the FOIA did not make such illegality grounds for disclosing such records if otherwise nondisclosable under law enforcement exemption); Sladek v. Bensinger, 605 F.2d 899 (5th Cir. 1979) (portions of Drug Enforcement Agency agents' manual describing pro-

cedures for handling informants and obtaining search warrants held not exempt from disclosure since not compiled in connection with specific investigation); Lesar v. Department of Justice, 636 F.2d 472 (D.C. Cir. 1980) (nondisclosure of FBI documents upheld under national defense exemption on basis of affidavit that disclosure would reveal intelligence source); Allen v. CIA, 636 F.2d 1287 (D.C. Cir. 1980) (documents containing filing and routing instructions for information concerning assassination of President Kennedy not exempt as claimed internal personnel, rules, and practices materials); Long v. IRS, 596 F.2d 362 (9th Cir. 1980) (taxpayer entitled to underlying electronic data from which statistical tabulations of Taxpayer Compliance Measurement Program are computed); Taxation With Representation v. IRS, 646 F.2d 666 (D.C. Cir. 1981) (IRS legal memoranda on revenue rulings and analysis of court decisions not exempt from disclosure as intra-agency memoranda); Coastal States Gas Corp. v. Department of Energy, 644 F.2d 969 (3d Cir. 1981) (agency's submission of grossly inadequate "Vaughn Index" of reasons for withholding portions of documents may warrant summary judgment); Baez v. Department of Justice, 662 F.2d 792 (D.C. Cir. 1981) (en banc) (costs may not be awarded against a bona fide requestor; ruling based on the Federal Rules of Appellate Procedure, not the FOIA); Voelker v. IRS, 646 F.2d 332 (8th Cir. 1981) (agency may not withhold information from a requestor's files on the ground that the information pertains to a third party).

4. Congress enacted certain procedural improvements for the FOIA. Pub. L. No. 95-454, 92 Stat. 1225 (Oct. 13, 1978). One requires agencies to promulgate regulations on fees charged to comply with FOIA requests. 5 U.S.C. §552(a)(4)(A). The other provides that disciplinary action may be taken against a federal official found to have acted "arbitrarily or capriciously" in withholding information requested under the Act. 5 U.S.C. §552(a)(4)(F).

The Reagan Administration has announced a new policy of defending all suits challenging an agency's refusal to grant an FOIA request unless the agency's refusal lacks a substantial legal basis or defense of the agency would risk an adverse impact on another agency's ability to protect important records. See Memorandum on FOIA, Office of the Attorney General, 49 U.S.L.W. 2711 (May 12, 1981). In addition, recent legislative proposals would severely restrict the Act's application to intelligence agencies.

[REFERENCES]

[4.] Commentary on the FOIA includes Clark, Holding Government Accountable: The Amended Freedom of Information Act, 84 Yale L.J. 741 (1975); Symposium, 1974 Amendments to the Freedom of Information Act, 25 Am. U.L. Rev. 1. (1975); Project, Government Information and the Rights of Citizens, 73 Mich. L. Rev. 971 (1975); Note, Discovery of Government Documents and the Official Information Privilege, 76 Colum. L. Rev. 142 (1976); Note, Judicial Review of Classified Documents: Amendments to the Freedom of Information Act, 12 Harv. J. Legis. 415 (1975); Note, National Security and the Public's Right to Know: A New Role for the Courts Under the Freedom of Information Act, 123 U. Pa. L. Rev. 1438 (1975); Note, National Security and the Amended Freedom of Information Act, 85 Yale L.J. 401 (1976); Note, Developments Under the FOIA — 1977, 1978 Duke L.J. 189 (1978); Fox & Weiss, The FOIA National Security Exemption and the New Executive Order, 37 Fed. B.J. (1978).

(page 204) [390]

NOTES

[continued] [3.] *Sunshine Laws.* In 1976, the Government in the Sunshine Act was enacted into federal law. Pub. L. No. 94-409, 90 Stat. 1241 (1976) (codified at 5 U.S.C. §552(b)). The policy of the statute is that: "... the public is entitled to the fullest information regarding the decision-making processes of the Federal Government. It is the purpose of this Act to provide the public with such information while protecting the rights of individuals and the ability of the Government to carry out its responsibilities." To effectuate this policy, the law provides that, except for enumerated exceptions, "every portion of every meeting of an agency shall be open to public observation." 5 U.S.C. §552(b). The exceptions are similar to those under the FOIA and include meetings (and information covered therein) which pertain to, inter alia, national security, internal personnel rules and practices, financial matters, private matters, and matters specifically exempted from disclosure by statute. Id. §552b(c).

For recent decisions under the Act, see: Common Cause v. Nuclear Regulatory Commission, — F.2d —, 50 U.S.L.W. 2529 (D.C. Cir., Feb. 26, 1982) (upholding access to transcripts of NRC budget meetings); Symons v. Chrysler Corp. Loan Guarantee Board, — F.2d —, 50 U.S.L.W. 2350 (D.C. Cir. 1981) (holding the Board not covered by the Act); Hunt v. Nuclear Regulatory Commission, 468 F. Supp. 817 (N.D. Okla. 1979) (Act does not cover boards or panels not composed of agency "members").

See also Nader v. Baroody, 396 F. Supp. 1231 (D.D.C. 1975) (biweekly informal White House meetings between executive department officials and business organizations or private groups do not constitute "advisory committee" meetings within meaning of the Federal Advisory Committee Act, 5 U.S.C. App. I, and thus need not comply with its open meetings requirements); Perritt & Wilkinson, Open Advisory Committees and the Political Process: The Federal Advisory Committee Act After Two Years, 63 Geo. L.J. 725 (1975).

REFERENCES

Comment, Fox, Government in the Sunshine Act, 1978 Ann. Survey Am. L. 305 (1978); Comment, The Federal "Government in the Sunshine Act": A Public Access Compromise, 29 U. Fla. L. Rev. 881 (Fall 1977); Comment, Government in the Sunshine Act: A Danger of Overexposure, 14 Harv. J. Legis. 620 (1977); Note, The Government in the Sunshine Act—An Overview, 1977 Duke L.J. 565 (1977).

State sunshine laws are common and are the subject of much legal commentary. See, e.g., Guy & McDonald, Government in the Sunshine: The Status of Open Meetings and Open Record Laws in North Dakota, 53 N.D.L. Rev. 51 (1976); Harper, Kansas Open Meetings Act of 1972, 43 J. Kan. B. Assn. 257 (1974); Lawrence, Interpreting North Carolina's Open-Meetings Law, 54 N.C.L. Rev. 777 (1976); Recchie, Government in the Sunshine: Open Meeting Legislation in Ohio, 37 Ohio St. L.J. 497 (1976); Note, Public Access to Governmental Records and Meetings in Arizona, 16 Ariz. L. Rev. 891 (1974); Note, Open Meeting Laws in Michigan, 53 J. Urban L. 532 (1976).

In an interesting recent case, a federal court held that the Missouri sunshine law, mandating closure of arrest records, did not violate the news media's right of access because the records were public for a period of time. See Herald v. MacNeil, 511 F. Supp. 269 (E.D. Mo. 1981).

Financial Disclosure Laws. In addition to the recent enactment of open meetings laws, many states have also enacted financial disclosure statutes, pursuant to which governmental officials are required to disclose their financial situation to the public. The movement for financial disclosure reached a high point when Congress enacted the Ethics in Government Act of 1978, Pub. L. No. 95-521, 92 Stat. 1824 et seq., U.S. Code Cong. & Ad. News 1824 (1978). The Act provides for detailed financial disclosure reports to be filed by high level officials of the legislative, executive, and judicial branches. In Duplantier v. United States, 606 F. 2d 654 (5th Cir. 1979), cert. denied, 49 U.S.L.W. 3493 (1980), a group of federal judges filed suit against the portion of the Act requiring disclosure by judges, contending that the Act's requirements violated constitutional separation of powers and constituted an invasion of privacy. The Fifth Circuit rejected both claims, reasoning that if Congress may direct a judge to disqualify himself because of financial interest, Congress can compel judges to disclose such interest; the privacy claim was rejected on the ground that financial privacy is not protected in this setting.

For a recent major decision upholding a Florida financial disclosure requirement challenged by several state legislators and helpfully gathering all of the lower court decisions on financial disclosure requirements, see Plante v. Gonzalez, 575 F.2d 1119 (5th Cir. 1978), cert. denied, 439 U.S. 1129 (1979).

B. NATIONAL SECURITY INFORMATION: THE CLASSIFICATION SYSTEM

(page 208)[349]

NOTES

1. [continued]

In 1978, President Carter promulgated a new Executive Order on classification and secrecy. Executive Order 12065, National Security Information (43 Fed. Reg. 28949). The new classification order was somewhat more restrictive of the government's power to classify information than the predecessor regulation, Executive Order 11652. It restricted the number of officials who may classify information, slightly tightened up the definitions of the kind of information which could be classified, provided procedures for declassification and review of declassification, and established an Information Security Oversight Office responsible for insuring compliance with the Order. Exempt from the Order was information covered by the Atomic Energy Act of 1954. The new Order provided that if there were "reasonable doubt which [classification] designation is appropriate, or whether the information should be classified at all, the less restrictive designation should be used, or the information should not be classified." Section 1-101. The Order defined the classification categories as follows:

"1-102. 'Top Secret' shall be applied only to information, the unauthorized disclosure of which reasonably could be expected to cause exceptionally grave damage to the national security.

"1-013. 'Secret' shall be applied only to information the unauthorized disclosure of which reasonably could be expected to cause serious damage to the national security.

"1-104. 'Confidential' shall be applied to information, the unauthorized disclosure of which reasonably could be expected to cause identifiable damage to the national security."

For an article discussing that Executive Order and its relationship to the FOIA, see Fox & Weiss, The FOIA National Security Exemption and The New Executive Order, 37 Fed. B.J. 1 (1978).

The Reagan Administration promulgated a new Executive Order that expanded the government's ability to classify documents as secret and thereby restrict public access to information. See In Re National Security Information, E.O. 12356, 8 Media L. Rptr. 1306 (April 2, 1982; effective Aug. 1, 1982).

(page 222) [363]

NOTES

1. [continued] For another major Supreme Court pronouncement on prior restraints, in the context of a judicial gag order against the press barring pre-trial publication of information about a sensational murder trial, see Nebraska Press Assn. v. Stuart, 427 U.S. 539 (1979), excerpted in Chapter V, Section C [D] infra. There is an interesting discussion of the question of the continued differentiation between prior restraint and subsequent punishment in Smith v. Daily Mail Pub. Co., 443 U.S. 97 (1979) (holding press cannot be criminally punished under juvenile delinquent confidentiality provision for publishing name of juvenile defendant). See generally, Barnett, The Puzzle of Prior Restraint, 29 Stan. L. Rev. 539 (1977). For an exhaustive opinion invalidating a gag order imposed, with respect to public discussion of discovery documents, on counsel and parties in a national security political surveillance case, see In re Halkin, 598 F.2d 176 (D.C. Cir. 1979). See also, In Re San Juan Star Co., 662 F.2d 108 (1st Cir. 1981). Finally, in Gulf Oil Co. v. Bernard, 452 U.S. 89, 68 L. Ed. 2d 693 (1981), the Court avoided a constitutional challenge to an order restricting communications to members of a class action suit by holding the gag order invalid under Rule 23 of the Federal Rules of Civil Procedure: " . . . the mere possibility of abuses does not justify routine adoption of a communications ban that interferes with the formation of a class or the prosecution of a class action in accordance with the Rules." 68 L. Ed. 2d at 705.

For a time, it appeared that the New York Times principles would receive a stiff test in a widely publicized case involving a magazine article entitled, "The H-Bomb Secret: How We Got It, Why We're Telling It." See United States v. Progressive, Inc., 467 F. Supp. 990 (W.D. Wis. 1979). In that case, the government obtained a preliminary injunction against a magazine's publishing an article containing information about the scientific principles underlying the making of a hydrogen bomb. Although the information for the article was obtained solely from material and sources in the public domain, the government's theory was that the assembling of the information in the article itself threatened the national security and required a prior restraint on publication. Since the government claimed that the publication of the information would violate the Atomic Energy Act of 1954, which is excluded from normal classification regulations, the fact of classification was not dispositive in the case. Although finding that the article did not provide a "do-it-yourself" guide to making a hydrogen bomb, the district court found that the concepts in the article "could accelerate the membership of a candidate nation in the thermonuclear club." 476 F. Supp. at 994. Based on its view that publication of the article might involve issues of national life or death and would likely violate the Atomic Energy Act, the district court concluded that a prior restraint was permissible: "In view of the showing of harm made by the United States, a preliminary injunction would be warranted even in the absence of statutory authorization because of the existence of the likelihood of direct, immediate and irreparable injury to our nation and its people. New York Times Co. v. United States . . . see also, Near v. Minnesota. . . ." 467 F. Supp. at 1000.

Subsequently, the district court refused to modify or vacate the preliminary injunction even after it appeared that the critical thermonuclear concepts in the article were also contained in two publicly available government documents in the library at Los Alamos. Thereafter, the Supreme Court denied a mandamus petition seeking to expedite the Seventh Circuit's hearing of the magazine's appeal from the preliminary injunction. See Morland v. Sprecher, 443 U.S. 709 (1979). Shortly following the appellate court argument, information comparable to that contained in the Progressive began to be published in other newspapers. After a brief attempt at a second restraining order, the government abandoned its efforts as futile, and dismissed the Progressive case. See 610 F.2d 819 (7th Cir. 1979). For scholarly commentary on the Progressive case, see Sobota, The Unexploded Bomb: The Progressive and Prior Restraint, 1980 S. Ill. U.L.J. 199 (1980); Cheh, The Progressive Case and the Atomic Energy Act: Waking to the Dangers of Government Information Controls, 48 Geo. Wash. L. Rev. 163 (1980); Scrimenti, A Journalist's View of the Progressive Case, 41 Ohio St. L.J. 1165 (1980); Note, 22 Wm. & Mary L. Rev. 141 (1980); see also: Symposium, Near v. Minnesota, 50th Anniversary, 66 Minn. L. Rev. 1 (1981).

(page 223) [364]

NOTES

2. [continued] The CIA Secrecy Agreement was finally before the Supreme Court in Snepp v. United States, 444 U.S. 507 (1980). Like Marchetti, the Snepp case involved a former CIA employee who wrote a book, Decent Interval, sharply criticizing the CIA's activities in Vietnam, particularly in connection with the U.S. withdrawal from the war. Snepp did not submit the manuscript for clearance, and the book was published before the government filed suit. Claiming a breach of the

secrecy agreement by failing to obtain prior permission and approval — though not claiming that the book disclosed any classified information — the government filed suit seeking a declaration that the agreement had been violated, damages for breach of contract, an injunction, and an accounting imposing a constructive trust over all revenues from the book. In an unusually caustic opinion, the District Court, after denying Snepp's request for a jury trial, granted all relief requested by the government. 456 F. Supp. 176. The Fourth Circuit affirmed the declaratory and injunctive relief but reversed the imposition of a constructive trust on the book's proceeds and remanded for a jury trial on awarding the United States anything more than nominal damages. The Court of Appeals upheld the secrecy agreement's requirement of prior submission of all materials, though noting that "manifestly the first amendment would not permit the CIA to withhold consent to publication except with respect to classified information not in the public domain." 595 F.2d 926, 932.

In a move that stunned most observers, the Supreme Court, without oral argument, summarily reversed, upholding the CIA Secrecy Agreement and permitting the "constructive trust" sanction against Snepp for violating that agreement. First, Snepp's claim that the agreement was an unenforceable prior restraint on speech was rejected in a footnote: "When Snepp accepted employment with the CIA, he voluntarily signed the agreement that expressly obligated him to submit any proposed publication for prior review. He does not claim that he executed this agreement under duress. Indeed, he voluntarily reaffirmed his obligation when he left the Agency. We agree with the Court of Appeals that Snepp's agreement is an 'entirely appropriate' exercise of the CIA Director's statutory mandate to 'protec[t] intelligence sources and methods from unauthorized disclosure,' 50 U.S.C. 403 (d)(3). Moreover, this court's cases make clear that — even in the absence of an express agreement — the CIA could have acted to protect substantial government interests by imposing reasonable restrictions on employee activities that in other contexts might be protected by the First Amendment. Civil Service Commn. v. Letter Carriers, 413 U.S. 548, 565 (1973); see Brown v. Glines, — U.S. — (1980); Buckley v. Valeo, 424 U.S. 1, 25-28 (1976); Greer v. Spock, 424 U.S. 828 (1976); id., at 844-848 (Powell, J., concurring); Cole v. Richardson, 405 U.S. 676 (1972). The Government has a compelling interest in protecting both the secrecy of information important to our national security and the appearance of confidentiality so essential to the effective operation of our foreign intelligence service. The agreement that Snepp signed is a reasonable means for protecting this vital interest." 444 U.S. at 509, n.3.

Turning to the validity of the constructive trust, the Court reasoned that Snepp's employment with the CIA "involved an extremely high degree of trust," that it included the specific duty not to publish information relating to the CIA without submission for prior clearance, and that he "deliberately and surreptitiously violated his obligation to submit all material for prepublication review." 444 U.S. at 511. Moreoever, the Court held, Snepp's breach of trust was not cured by the fact that none of the information published was, in fact, classified: ". . . a former intelligence agent's publication of unreviewed material relating to intelligence activities can be detrimental to vital national interests even if the published information is unclassified. When a former agent relies on his own judgment about what information is detrimental, he may reveal information that the CIA — with its broader understanding of what may expose classified information and classified sources — could have identified as harmful." 44 U.S. at 512.

Agreeing with the lower court's recognition that "Snepp's breach of his explicit obligation to submit his material — classified or not — for prepublication clearance has irreparably harmed the United States Government," the Court then addressed the issue of remedies. Since obtaining an award of damages might be difficult and proof might compromise "some of the very confidences that Snepp promised to protect," the Court found the constructive trust device preferable: "A constructive trust . . . protects both the Government and the former agent from unwarranted risks. This remedy is the natural and customary consequence of a breach of trust. It deals fairly with both parties by conforming relief to the dimensions of the wrong. If the agent secures prepublication clearance, he can publish with no fear of liability. If the agent publishes unreviewed material in violation of his fiduciary and contractual obligation, the trust remedy simply requires him to disgorge the benefits of his faithlessness. Since the remedy is swift and sure, it is tailored to deter those who would place sensitive information at risk. And since the remedy reaches only funds attributable to the breach, it cannot saddle the former agent with exemplary damages out of all proportion to his gain. The decision of the Court of Appeals would deprive the government of this equitable and effective means of protecting intelligence that may contribute to national security." 444 U.S. at 515.

The three dissenters charged the Court with disregarding "two venerable principles that favor a more conservative approach to this case," first, that equitable relief should not be granted unless the government could show that the remedy at law was inadequate, and second, that the "drastic new remedy has been fashioned to enforce a species of prior restraint on a citizen's right to criticize his government." 444 U.S. at 526.

Finally, as troubling as the result in the Snepp case were the Court's several suggestions that its newly created "fiduciary" duty with respect to confidential government information might be imposed on government employees whether or not they were subject to a Secrecy Agreement.

For law review commentary on the Snepp ruling see Note, 49 U. Cinn. L. Rev. 690 (1980); Note, 66 ABA J. 492 (1980).

The CIA Secrecy Agreement was tangentially before the Court in Haig v. Agee, 453 U.S. 280, 69 L. Ed. 2d 640 (1981), where the Court upheld the revocation of the passport of Philip Agee, a former CIA official who had revealed the identity of CIA agents abroad. Finding that Agee's activities "divulge classified information [and] violate Agee's express contract not to make any public statements about Agency matters without prior clearance by the Agency," the Court concluded that the Secretary of State had authority to revoke Agee's passport in order to protect against "serious damage to the national security or foreign policy of the United States." 69 L. Ed. 2d at 648-649. With respect to Agee's claim that the passport revocation violated his free speech rights, the Court observed:

"Assuming *arguendo* that First Amendment protections reach beyond our national boundaries, Agee's First Amendment claim has no foundation. The revocation of Agee's passport rests in part on the content of his speech: specifically, his repeated disclosures of intelligence operations and names of intelligence personnel. Long ago, however, this Court recognized that 'No one would question but that a government might prevent actual obstruction to its recruiting service or the publication of the sailing dates of transports or the number and location of troops.' Near v. Minnesota. . . . Agee's disclosures . . . have the declared purpose of obstructing intelligence operations and the recruiting of intelligence personnel. They are clearly not protected by the Constitution. The mere fact that Agee is also engaged in criticism of the Goverment does not render his conduct beyond the reach of the law.

To the extent the revocation of his passport operates to inhibit Agee, 'it is an inhibition of *action*,' rather than of speech. Zemel v. Rusk. . . . Agee is as free to criticize the United States Government as he was when he held a passport — always subject, of course, to express limits on certain rights by virtue of his contract with the Government. See Snepp v. United States." 69 L. Ed. 2d at 663.

For further discussion of Haig v. Agee, see Chapter XI, infra.

Finally, Congress has recently enacted legislation that would make it a crime to reveal the identity of intelligence agents or employees.

(page 224)[365]

NOTES

7. [continued] The Church Committee Report made public a great many of the political surveillance activities of the CIA and FBI, including warrantless wiretapping, electronic surveillance, mail covers, mail openings, burglaries, break-ins, and infiltration of lawful political activities.

See generally, Senate Select Committee to Study Government Operations with Respect to Intelligence Activities, Final Report, S. Rep. No. 94-755, 94th Cong., 1st Sess. (1976).

The revelations of wrongdoing by the CIA, FBI, and other national security agencies led to a number of cases seeking to enjoin the continuation of such activities and to compensate the groups and individuals whose political and privacy rights have been violated. The CIA mail-opening program, which involved the opening of over 200,000 pieces of mail between U.S. citizens and the Soviet Union over a twenty-year period, was involved in Birnbaum v. United States, 588 F.2d 319 (2d Cir. 1978) (upholding subject matter jurisdiction against the United States under the federal Tort Claims Act and sustaining monetary damages for persons whose mail was unlawfully opened but vacating an order requiring the government to write a letter of apology) and Driver v. Helms, 577 F.2d 147 (1st Cir. 1978), rev'd sub nom. Stafford v. Briggs, 444 U.S. 527 (1980) (nationwide jurisdiction not available for damage suits against federal officials responsible for mail opening programs). The FBI surveillance and disruption activities directed against the Socialist Workers Party are at issue in Socialist Workers Party v. Attorney General, 458 F. Supp. 895 (S.D.N.Y. 1978), vacated sub nom. In re Attorney General, 596 F.2d 58 (2d Cir. 1979), cert. denied, 444 U.S. 903 (1979) (order holding Attorney General in contempt of court for noncompliance with discovery orders held erroneous as too extreme a sanction). Finally, the surveillance activities of the CIA's "Operation Chaos," as well as the activities of the National Security Agency (NSA), are at issue in Halkin v. Helms, Civ. No. 76-1773 (D.D.C.), which has given rise to interlocutory appeals raising issues of considerable interest. See In Re Halkin, 598 F.2d 175 (D.C. Cir. 1978) (invalidating a gag order imposed on counsel and parties with respect to public discussion of government documents produced in discovery); Halkin v. Helms, 598 F.2d 1 (D.C. Cir. 1978) (broadly upholding state secrets privilege claimed by NSA as justification for refusing even to admit whether the plaintiffs' international communications had been monitored; approving ex parte in camera review of NSA's submissions). See also: Hayden v. NSA, 608 F.2d 1381 (D.C. Cir. 1979). Finally, a very recent decision will make it easier for victims of political surveillance and disruption to bring suit because the court limited the kind of discovery that can be directed against plaintiffs by governmental officials in such cases. See Black Panther Party v. Smith, 661 F.2d 1243 (D.C. Cir. 1981).

Revelations of government wrongdoing also led to a Presidential Executive Order on Intelligence Activities, Executive Order 12036 (Jan. 26, 1978), 43 Fed. Reg. 3674, sharply restricting the activities of intelligence agencies. The Reagan administration, however, has greatly eased those restrictions. See Executive Order 12333. Finally, in 1978, Congress enacted the Foreign Intelligence Surveillance Act, 50 U.S.C. §§1801 et seq., requiring warrants for most national security wiretaps and creating a special court to consider such applications.

(page 224) [365]

NOTES

9. See generally Katz, Government Information Leaks and the First Amendment, 64 Cal. L. Rev. 108 (1976); Murphy, Knowledge Is Power: Foreign Policy and Information Interchange Among Congress, the Executive Branch, and the Public, 49 Tul. L. Rev. 505 (1975); Note, Government Employee Disclosures of Agency Wrongdoing: Protecting the Right to Blow the Whistle, 42 U. Chi. L. Rev. 530 (1975).

10. In 1978, Congress passed the Civil Service Reform Act of 1978, Pub. L. No. 95-454, generally revising civil service employment procedures. One provision of the Act specifically states as follows: "The right of employees, individually or collectively, to petition Congress or a member of Congress, or to furnish information to either House of Congress, or to a committee or member thereof, may not be interfered with or denied." 5 U.S.C. §7211. This provision may provide some protection to future federal "whistle-blowers."

C. EXECUTIVE PRIVILEGE

(page 233) [375]

NOTES

2. [continued] For further debate and commentary on executive privilege, see Berger, Executive Privilege, Professor Rosenblum and the Higher Criticism, 1975 Duke L.J. 921 (1975); Clark, Executive Privilege: A Review of Berger, 8 Akron L. Rev. 324 (1975); Cox, Executive Privilege, 122 U. Pa. L. Rev. 1383 (1974); Symposium, United States v. Nixon: An Historical Perspective, 9 Loy. L. Rev. 11 (1975).

(page 234) [376]

NOTES

6. [continued] The Supreme Court has discussed the policies underlying the advice privilege in two cases slightly removed from the specific context of a formal assertion of executive privilege. See: Federal Open Market Committee v. Merrill, 443 U.S. 340, 359-360, (1979) (monthly monetary policy directives exempt from FOIA disclosure); Herbert v.

Lando, 441 U.S. 153, 173-174 (1979)(rejecting broad news media privilege to resist inquiry by defamation plaintiff into editorial processes that went into the story).

(page 235) [377]

NOTES

7. [continued] Recent cases involving claims dealing with aspects of executive privilege include Black v. Sheraton Corp., 564 F.2d 531, 541-547 (D.C. Cir. 1977) (damaged plaintiff not entitled to further discovery of FBI materials claimed to be protected by law enforcement informant privilege; in camera examination required); Black v. Sheraton Corp., 564 F.2d 550 (D. C. Cir. 1977) (informants' privilege protects identity of hotel employees who assisted FBI in conducting electronic surveillance); Dellums v. Powell, 561 F.2d 242 (D.C. Cir. 1977), cert. denied, 434 U.S. 880 (1977) (opportunity to establish attorney general's role in alleged substantial violation of constitutional rights during May Day antiwar demonstration outweighs presumption of executive privilege assumed to apply to tapes and transcripts of conversations of former president); In re Attorney General, 596 F.2d 58 (2d Cir. 1979) (District Court order holding Attorney General in contempt for refusing to permit discovery of identities of informants who infiltrated the Socialist Workers Party was improper; less drastic discovery sanctions must be considered first); see also Weatherford v. Bursey, 429 U.S. 545 (1977) (presence of police undercover agent among criminal defendant's associates and participation of informant in defense team meetings and discussions held not actionable absent evidence that informant's presence and activities had an actual impact on the conduct of the defense); Hampton v. Hanrahan, 600 F.2d 600 (7th Cir. 1979), modified, 446 U.S. 754 (1980)(in damage action for shooting death of Black Panther activist, serious controversy over existence of informant required that identity be disclosed); United States v. Dien, 609 F.2d 1038 (2d Cir. 1979) (presence of wife/informant at defense team meetings did not violate husband/defendant's rights since no information transmitted to government).

(page 235) [377]

NOTES

8. [continued] Even years after his resignation from office, former President Nixon continued to press his claims of executive privilege and personal privacy in the Supreme Court.

For example, in Nixon v. Administrator of General Services, 433 U.S. 425 (1977), the former president contended that the Presidential Recordings and Materials Act, which directs the GSA to hold and process Mr. Nixon's presidential papers and tapes, unconstitutionally invaded the executive sphere and infringed on executive privilege. The Court rejected the former president's claims. On the question of executive privilege, the Court found the safeguards provided by the Act adequate to protect presidential confidentiality and balanced the "minimal" intrusion into executive privilege that the Act allowed against the importance of the congressional purposes in preserving and maintaining access to Nixon's presidential materials. 433 U.S. at 446-456. See also, Nixon v. Freeman, — F.2d — , 50 U.S.L.W. 2479 (D.C. Cir. 1982).

In Nixon v. Warner Communications, Inc., 435 U.S. 589 (1978), the former President sought to resist media access to the tapes of White House conversations introduced into evidence in the Watergate trials. The ex-President argued that blanket release for reproduction by the media of all such conversations would, inter alia, breach executive privilege. The Court found it unnecessary to reach that issue, ruling that release of such materials should be governed by the rules and procedures set forth in the Presidential Recordings and Materials Act upheld in Nixon v. Administrator. Accordingly, the Court reversed a lower court decision permitting broad press access to the tapes and remanded for consideration of the issues under the Act.

In Halperin v. Kissinger, 606 F.2d 1192 (D.C. Cir. 1979), aff'd by an equally divided court, — U.S. — , 49 U.S.L.W. 4782 (June 22, 1981), the Court of Appeals held that the former President and his associates were not entitled to absolute immunity from an action in damages for the wiretapping of a former National Security Council staff member; only a qualified immunity is available: "Finally, we think the application of qualified immunity to defendant Nixon is mandated by our tradition of equal justice under law. The President is the elected chief executive of our government, not an omniscient leader cloaked in mystical powers." 606 F.2d at 1213. The Court also ruled that the evidence did not warrant dismissing former Secretary of State Kissinger as a defendant in the case. The Supreme Court, by a vote of 4-4, affirmed this ruling as to Nixon, Kissinger, and Mitchell.

However, the Court finally considered such similar issues in the case of Pentagon whistle-blower Ernest Fitzgerald, and the Court upheld the claims of absolute Presidential immunity from damage suits. See Nixon v. Fitzgerald, 50 U.S.L.W. 4797 (June 24, 1982); Harlow v. Fitzgerald, 50 U.S.L.W. 4815 (June 24, 1982).

Chapter Four

Freedom of Expression in a Public Forum — First Amendment Relations in Public

(page 236) [392]

Insert before Section A:

NOTE

The events surrounding the attempt of the Nazi National Socialist Party of America to march in the heavily Jewish Chicago suburb of Skokie, Illinois, placed the issues considered in this chapter on the front pages and editorial pages of our Nation's media in a way that few cases ever do. The "Skokie case" sparked a nationwide debate over the nature of our national commitment to free speech in a public forum. At the same time it challenged and strengthened the commitment of the American Civil Liberties Union to defend the peaceful expression of any political idea, no matter how abhorrent.

The Skokie case actually involved two related lawsuits. In April 1977, a state court judge entered an injunction prohibiting the Nazi party from holding a parade in Skokie, wearing the Nazi uniform, displaying the Swastika, or displaying other materials that would incite or promote hatred against persons of the Jewish faith or any other faith. Following Illinois State appellate court refusals to stay the injunction or expedite an appeal, the Supreme Court, per curiam, but by a divided 5 to 4 vote, reversed the denial of the stay and remanded the case to the Illinois courts for further proceedings. National Socialist Party v. Village of Skokie, 432 U.S. 43 (1977). On remand, the Illinois appellate court modified the injunction to permit only the ban on displaying the Swastika during any demonstration, parade or march in the Village, 51 Ill. App. 3d 279, 366 N.E.2d 347 (1977), and thereafter, the Illinois Supreme

Court invalidated that remaining portion of the injunction. Village of Skokie v. National Socialist Party, 69 Ill. 2d 605, 373 N.E.2d 21 (1978). The Illinois Supreme Court ruled that the public display of the Swastika neither came within the "fighting words" doctrine nor threatened a breach of the peace:

"The display of the Swastika, as offensive to the principles of a free nation as the memories it recalls may be, is symbolic political speech intended to convey to the public the belief of those who display it. It does not, in our opinion, fall within the definition of fighting words, and that doctrine cannot be used here to overcome the heavy presumption against the constitutional validity of a prior restraint.

"Nor can we find that the Swastika, while not representing fighting words, is nevertheless so offensive and peace threatening to the public that its display can be enjoined. We do not doubt that the sight of this symbol is abhorrent to the Jewish citizens of Skokie, and that the survivors of the Nazi persecutions, tormented by their recollections, may have strong feelings regarding its display. Yet it is entirely clear that this factor does not justify enjoining defendants' speech." 373 N.E.2d at 24. The Village did not seek Supreme Court review of this ruling.

The other Skokie case involved a federal court challenge to three ordinances enacted by the Village of Skokie in May 1977 a few days after the initial state trial court injunction against the Nazi march had been granted. See Collin v. Smith, 447 F. Supp. 676 (N.D. Ill. 1978), aff'd, 578 F.2d 1197 (7th Cir.), cert. denied, 439 U.S. 916. The first ordinance set up a comprehensive permit system for all parades or assemblies of more than fifty persons and required applicants to obtain $350,000 in liability and property insurance. A prerequisite for issuance of a permit was an official finding that the assembly will not "portray criminality, depravity or lack of virtue in, or incite violence, hatred, abuse or hostility toward a person or group of persons by reason of reference to religious, racial, ethnic, national or regional affiliation." See 578 F.2d at 1199. The second ordinance prohibited the dissemination of any material which "promotes and incites hatred against persons by reason of their race, national origin, or religion. . . ." Ibid. Finally, the third ordinance prohibited public demonstrations by members of political parties while wearing "military style" uniforms. The district court issued a comprehensive opinion holding the insurance ordinance to be an insuperable obstacle to speech, the permit ordinance an impermissible prior restraint, and the "inciting hatred" and "military style" uniform ordinances vague and overbroad. 447 F. Supp. at 684-700. On appeal, the Village conceded the invalidity of the insurance and uniform ordinances, and the basic question was the validity of prohibiting a march that would portray, promote, or incite racial or religious hatred. The Seventh Circuit held that the Nazi ideology or symbols could not be denied First Amendment protection on the ground that they were "false" and thereby lacked constitutional value. The Court further held that Beauharnais v. Illinois, 343 U.S. 250 (1952), could not sustain the ordinances because the Village conceded that violence would not ensue as a result of the march, and because the Court doubted the continued precedential vitality of Beauharnais. Finally, the Circuit Court rejected the claim that the proposed march would infringe the rights of a captive audience since the march would not occur in any residential areas. Recognizing the sensitivity of the issues in the case, the majority concluded its opinion as follows: "Although we would have thought it unnecessary to say so, it apparently deserves emphasis . . . that our *regret* at the use appellees plan to make of their rights is not in any sense an *apology* for upholding the First Amendment. The result we have reached is dictated by the fundamental proposition that if these civil rights are to remain vital for all, they must protect not only those society deems acceptable, but also those whose ideas it quite justifiably rejects and despises." 578 F.2d at 1210.

The Supreme Court denied certiorari, but Justice Blackmun, joined by Justice White, dissented:

"I therefore would grant certiorari in order to resolve any possible conflict that may exist between the ruling of the Seventh Circuit here and Beauharnais. I also feel that the present case affords the Court an opportunity to consider whether . . . there is no limit whatsoever to the exercise of free speech. There indeed may be no such limit, but when citizens assert, not casually but with deep conviction, that the proposed demonstration is scheduled at a place and in a manner that is taunting and overwhelmingly offensive to the citizens of that place, that assertion, uncomfortable though it may be for judges, deserves to be examined. It just might fall into the same category as one's 'right' to cry 'fire' in a crowded theater, for 'the character of every act depends upon the circumstances in which it is done.' Schenck v. United States. . . ." 439 U.S. at 919.

As a final postscript, it should be noted that the proposed Nazi march in Skokie never occurred. Having received legal vindication of their right to speak, the Nazis decided to hold a rally in Chicago instead. The agonizing controversy ended with the proverbial "whimper."

For a recent case involving associational rights of Nazis, see, Blameuser v. Andrews, 630 F.2d 538 (7th Cir. 1980) (Army's refusal to enroll Nazi in advanced ROTC program did not violate First Amendment); see also, Black Leadership Forum v. Hand, — F. Supp — (W.D.N.Y., Civ. 81-23E, Jan. 13, 1981) (denying injunction against Nazi demonstration scheduled to coincide with Martin Luther King's Birthday).

(page 237) [393]

Insert before NOTES [after ERZNOZNIK]:

YOUNG v. AMERICAN MINI THEATRES, INC.
427 U.S. 50, 96 S. Ct. 2440, 49 L. Ed. 2d 310 (1976)

[Young v. American Mini Theatres is set out in Chapter 6, Section A, infra.]

FCC v. PACIFICA FOUNDATION
438 U.S. 726, 98 S. Ct. 3026, 57 L. Ed. 2d 1073 (1978)

[FCC v. Pacifica Foundation is set out in Chapter 6, Section B, infra.]

NOTE

Another First Amendment challenge to a zoning ordinance was recently before the Court in Schad v. Borough of Mount Ephraim, 452 U.S. 61, 101 S. Ct. 2176 (1981), where a general zoning ordinance listing various "permitted uses" was applied to ban "live entertainment," including nude dancing, in the downtown area. After holding that nude "live entertainment" is protected by the First Amendment, the Court then rejected the various justifications offered to sustain the ordinance, finding no showing that live entertainment presented unusual or unique problems that would justify singling out such activity for particular treatment or that any such problems could not be handled by a more narrowly drawn regulation.

The Court distinguished Young v. American Mini Theatres, Inc., as involving only a minimal burden on protected speech, taking the form of dispersal rather than prohibition, and based on specific municipal findings that the concentration of adult movie theaters lead to neighborhood deterioration. But see New York State Liquor Authority v. Bellanca, — U.S. —, 101 S.Ct. 2599 (1981) (per curiam) ("The State's power to ban the sale of alcoholic beverages entirely includes the lesser power to ban the sale of liquor on premises where topless dancing occurs. . . . Whatever artistic or communicative value may attach to topless dancing is overcome by the State's exercise of its broad powers arising under the Twenty-first Amendment." Id. at 2601.)

Similar issues will be before the Court in Larkin v. Grendel's Den, No. 81-878, prob. juris. noted, 50 U.S.L.W. 3547 (Jan 11, 1982), involving the validity of a Massachusetts statute that allows churches to veto the operation of a bar within a short distance of the church. The First Circuit, en banc, held the statute violated the Establishment Clause. See 662 F.2d 102.

For pre-Schad cases involving the validity of ordinances patterned after the Detroit Scheme upheld in Young, see: Bayou Landing, Ltd. v. Watts, 563 F.2d 1172 (5th Cir. 1977), cert. denied, 439 U.S. 818 (1978) (invalid); Hart Bookstores v. Edmiston, 612 F.2d 821 (4th Cir. 1979) (valid); Stansberry v. Holmes, 613 F.2d 1285 (5th Cir. 1980) (invalid); Genusa v. City of Peoria, 619 F.2d 1203 (7th Cir. 1980) (partly valid); Entertainment Concepts v. Maciejewski, 631 F.2d 497 (7th Cir. 1980) (invalid); E and B Enterprises v. City of University Park, 449 F. Supp. 695 (N.D. Tex. 1977) (invalid); Bayside Enterprises v. Carson, 450 F. Supp. 696 (M.D. Fla. 1978) (invalid).

(page 243) [399]

NOTES

5. [continued] In Priest v. Secretary of the Navy, 570 F.2d 1013 (D.C. Cir. 1977), the Court refused to set aside the court martial conviction of a former Navy seaman who had distributed a newsletter that, in sharp terms, urged violent resistance to the draft and the military.

6. [continued] In United States v. Kelner, 534 F.2d 1020 (2d Cir.), cert. denied, 429 U.S. 1022 (1976), the Court of Appeals upheld the conviction of a member of the Jewish Defense League who, at a publicly held and televised press conference, "threatened" to assassinate Yasser Arafat, head of the PLO. The court held that the question of whether the statements were "mere political hyperbole" or manifested an express intent to carry out the threat was properly left to the jury. With respect to the First Amendment claim, the court stated: "So long as the threat on its face and in the circumstances in which it is made is so unequivocal, unconditional, immediate and specific as to the person threatened, as to convey a gravity of purpose and imminent prospect of execution, the statute may properly be applied. This clarification of the scope of 18 U.S.C. §875(c) is . . . consistent with a rational approach to First Amendment construction which provides for governmental authority in instances of inchoate conduct, where a communication has become 'so interlocked with violent conduct as to constitute for all practical purposes part of the [proscribed] action itself.' T. Emerson, [The System of Freedom of Expression] at 329." 534 F.2d at 1027.

(page 244) [400]

NOTES

1. [continued] In one of the proposals to revise the Federal Criminal Code, a provision has been added to the bill, section 3311 of S. 1437, which would limit venue in obscenity/conspiracy cases to those districts in which a "substantial portion of the conspiracy occurred." See also, United States v. Various Articles of Obscene Merchandise, 562 F.2d 185 (2d Cir. 1977), cert. denied sub nom. Long v. United States, 436 U.S.

931 (1978) (in federal civil forfeiture action, venue is permissible in district of entry of allegedly obscene materials shipped from abroad, even though district is remote from addressee).

(page 245) [401]

NOTES

5. [continued] In United States v. Buttorff, 572 F.2d 619 (8th Cir), cert denied, 437 U.S. 906 (1978), the court upheld a conviction for aiding and abetting tax evasion where the defendants, tax protesters, at public meetings had asserted the unconstitutionality of the graduated income tax and recommended that the members of the audience file false and fraudulent income tax returns and withholding certificates. The court stated: "Although the speeches here do not incite the type of imminent lawless activity referred to in criminal syndicalism cases, the defendants did go beyond mere advocacy of tax reform. They explained how to avoid withholding and their speeches and explanations incited several individuals to activity that violated federal law and had the potential of substantially hindering the administration of the revenue." Id. at 624. See also United States v. Moss, 604 F.2d 569 (8th Cir. 1979).

Similar attempts to impose *civil* liability on speakers who allegedly "planted" destructive ideas in people's minds have generally been rejected. See Zamora v. CBS, 480 F. Supp. 199 (S.D. Fla. 1979) (convicted juvenile murder defendant's claim that his crime was caused by exposure to violence on television held not to state a cause of action because, by virtue of First Amendment, network owed youth no duty of care in this regard); Walt Disney Productions v. Shannon, 247 Ga. 402, 276 S.E.2d 580 (1981) (television show's directions for simulating sound of explosion, when followed in a way that injured plaintiff child, failed to present clear and present danger of injury); Olivia N. v. NBC, — Cal. App. 3d — , 50 U.S.L.W. 2379 (Cal. Ct. App. 1981) (suit for injury to minor in manner similar to that presented in television drama).

(page 245) [401]

NOTES

6. In recent years, efforts have been made to utilize civil analogues to conspiracy laws in order to prevent public speech. The NAACP has been involved in extended litigation stemming from an antitrust suit filed against it in Mississippi state courts. The theory of the suit is that the NAACP's organization of economic boycotts of business establishments to protest racial discrimination violated the state's antitrust laws.

In 1976, the state trial court granted an injunction against the NAACP boycott and awarded the merchants damages of $1.25 million. Thereafter the Fifth Circuit affirmed a preliminary injunction against enforcement of the state court judgment pending appeals through the Mississippi courts. Henry v. First National Bank of Clarksdale, 595 F.2d 291 (5th Cir. 1979). The appeals court found that the plaintiffs were likely to prevail on their ultimate argument that laws regulating economic activity, boycotts, and restraints of trade cannot be applied to boycotts that are "intimately bound up with political speech and unrelated to any economic interests." Id. at 304. Although the Mississippi Supreme Court upheld liability for damages and sustained the injunction against the boycott, see NAACP v. Claiborne Hardware, Inc., 393 So. 2d 1290 (1981), the Supreme Court reversed. 50 U.S.L.W. 5122 (July 2, 1982).

The same principle was also recently applied to dismiss a suit filed by the state of Missouri against the National Organization for Women claiming that the "ERA Boycott" of conventions and meetings in states that have not ratified the Equal Rights Amendment is a conspiracy in restraint of trade under the Sherman and Clayton Acts. In State of Missouri v. National Organization for Women, 467 F. Supp. 289 (W.D. Mo. 1979), the district court ruled that the ERA boycott is "essentially political" and not validly subject to the antitrust laws. The Eighth Circuit affirmed, 620 F.2d 1301, reasoning that such laws were intended to reach economic competitors ". . . and not non-competitors motivated socially or politically in connection with legislation." Id. at 1309. "We hold that NOW's boycott activities are privileged on the basis of the First Amendment right to petition, and the Supreme Court's recognition of that important right when it collides with the commercial effects of trade restraints." Id. at 1319.

Very similar issues were before the Court in Brown v. Hartlage, 50 U.S.L.W. 4359 (April 5, 1982). There, the lower courts upheld a statute providing for the disqualification of any political candidate who promised to support any measure in consideration for the vote in an election. The candidate had promised to reduce his own salary if elected. The Supreme Court reversed.

(page 254) [410]

NOTES

2. [continued] In Krause v. Rhodes, 570 F.2d 563 (6th Cir. 1977), cert. denied, 435 U.S. 924 (1978), the damage suit arising out of events at Kent State, the Sixth Circuit held that the banning and dispersal of assemblies on the campus was justified in light of the violence, disorder, and vandalism that had occurred in the preceding days.

(page 256) [412]

NOTES

8. In Wooley v. Maynard, 430 U.S. 705 (1977), the Court recognized a right to refrain from public expression with which one disagrees. In Maynard, a Jehovah's Witness refused to display the motto "Live Free or Die" on his New Hampshire license plate. Chief Justice Burger, writing for the Court, ruled that New Hampshire could not compel its citizens to express an idea with which they disagreed. See also, Estelle v. Williams, 425 U.S. 501 (1976) (recognizing right to be tried in civilian clothing rather than in prison garb); but see, Kelley v. Johnson, 425 U.S. 238 (1976) (upholding hair length requirements for policemen). More recently, however, the Court rejected a Wooley v. Maynard claim made by the owner of a California shopping center required by state law to permit leafletters to exercise free speech rights on shopping center property. See Prune Yard Shopping Center v. Robins, 447 U.S. 74 (1980). The Court distinguished the license plate case on the grounds that (1) the shopping center owner had opened the property to the public, (2) the state had not dictated that a particular message be displayed on private property, and (3) the owner could easily disavow sponsorship of or support for the leafletters' message. (For further discussion of Prune Yard see, infra, p. 47).

9. For cases discussing the extent of protection to be afforded to the public expression of information of a commercial nature, see Linmark Associates, Inc. v. Township of Willingboro, 431 U.S. 85 (1977) ("For Sale" signs); Carey v. Population Services, International, 431 U.S. 678 (1977) (contraceptive advertising); Bates v. State Bar of Arizona, 433 U.S. 350 (1977) (attorney newspaper advertising); In Re Primus, 436 U.S. 412 (1978) (face-to-face attorney solicitation); Friedman v. Rogers, 440 U.S. 1 (1979) (optometrists' trade names); Central Hudson v. Public Service Commission, 447 U.S. 557 (1980) (promotional advertising by utilities); Metromedia, Inc. v. City of San Diego, 453 U.S. 490, 101 S. Ct. 2882 (1981) (regulation of advertising on billboards); In Re R.M.J., — U.S. —, 50 U.S.L.W. 4185 (Jan. 25, 1982) (attorney advertising). For further discussion of these issues, see Chapter VIII, infra.

(page 259) [415]

NOTES

1. [continued] In Dellums v. Powell, 566 F.2d 167 (D.C. Cir. 1977), cert. denied, 438 U.S. 976 (1978), involving class damage claims by May Day demonstrators arrested on the steps of the Capitol, the court of appeals ruled that the arrests clearly violated primary First Amendment rights: "The demonstration, the picket line, and the myriad other forms of protest which abound in our society each offer peculiarly important

opportunities in which speakers may at once persuade, accuse and seek sympathy or political support, all in a manner likely to be noticed. Loss of such opportunity is surely not insignificant." 566 F.2d at 195. The Court ruled, however, that the jury award of $10,000 per demonstrator was "extravagant," remanding the case for reconsideration of damages. More recently, the D.C. Circuit ruled that former Attorney General Mitchell had absolute prosecutorial immunity from suit to the extent his activities involved initiating prosecutions, see Dellums v. Powell, 660 F.2d 802 (D.C. Cir. 1981). See also Tatum v. Morton, 562 F.2d 1279 (D.C. Cir. 1977) (district court award of damages to persons arrested for Quaker vigil on sidewalk in front of White House held too limited). In Washington Mobilization Committee v. Cullinane, 566 F.2d 107 (D.C. Cir. 1977), however, the court upheld the general validity of Washington, D.C., crowd control statutes, uthorizing the arrest of demonstrators who crossed police lines or failed to move on when ordered to do so. See also, Washington Mobilization Committee v. Jefferson, 617 F.2d 848 (D.C. Cir. 1980) (refusing to re-open issues in case); Concerned Jewish Youth v. McGuire, 621 F.2d 471 (2d Cir. 1980) (upholding severe police restrictions on location and number of demonstrators near Soviet Mission to U.N. in Manhattan and limitations on use of sound equipment; revised guidelines were promulgated in a related case, Millanhouse v. Murphy, — N.Y.S.2d — (Sup. Ct. N.Y. Co. 1980) (app. pending)); ISKCON v. New York, 501 F. Supp 684 (S.D.N.Y. 1980) (upholding ban on ISKCON proselytizing and solicitation activities on sidewalks adjacent to U.N. Building). Finally, the D.C. Circuit has recently invalidated a federal statute prohibiting all demonstrations in the United States Supreme Court building or on the adjacent sidewalks. See Grace v. Burger, 665 F.2d 1193 (D.C. Cir. 1981), prob. juris. noted, 50 U.S.L.W. 3998.01 (June 21, 1982).

In a related development, the Supreme Court has recently made it more difficult for victims of First Amendment violations to vindicate their rights. In City of Newport v. Fact Concerts, 101 S. Ct. 2748 (1981) the Court ruled that municipalities are wholly immune from awards of punitive damages in Section 1983 actions. In that case, the Court reached out to overturn a jury verdict of $275,000 punitive damages against a city whose officials had cancelled a license for a rock concert at the last minute because of a change in musical format.

For an interesting reminiscence on Hague v. CIO by one of the participants, see Gibbons, Hague v. CIO: A Retrospective, 52 N.Y.U.L. Rev. 731 (1977).

(page 260) [416]

NOTES

3. [continued] In recent years, a number of cases have dealt with municipal efforts to limit the size, number and location of political signs

and posters. See Baldwin v. Redwood City, 540 F.2d 1360 (9th Cir. 1976), cert. denied, 431 U.S. 913 (1977); Verrilli v. City of Concord, 548 F.2d 262 (9th Cir. 1977); Sussli v. City of San Mateo, 120 Cal. App. 3d 1 (1st Dist. Ct. App. 1981); see generally, Note, Architecture, Aesthetic Zoning and The First Amendment, 28 Stan. L. Rev. 179 (1975). Much of the analysis in these cases has been superceded by the Supreme Court's recent decision in the billboard case, Metromedia, Inc. v. City of San Diego, 453 U.S. 490 (1981), discussed infra at p. 54.

(page 264) [420]

Insert before Notes:

See discussion of Greer v. Spock, 424 U.S. 828 (1976), Chapter 16, Section C, infra.

The Court confronted classic "time, place and manner" problems in its recent decision in Heffron v. International Society for Krishna Consciousness, Inc., 452 U.S. 640 (1981). The issue was whether the operators of a state fair could require a religious organization that wished to distribute and sell religious literature and solicit donations at the fair to do so only at an assigned booth or location within the fairgrounds. The Court, 5-4, upheld the restriction. Broadly reviewing its rules on the protection of religious solicitation and the permissibility of reasonable time, place, and manner restrictions, the Court was obviously impressed by the fact that the "booth only" rule was content-neutral and had been evenhandedly applied. Turning to whether the rule served a "significant governmental interest" in the "orderly movement of the crowd" at the fair, the Court indicated that the significance of those interests had to be "assessed in light of the characteristic nature and function of the particular forum involved." Based on that perspective, the Court questioned the analogy between fairgrounds and city streets: "... there are significant differences between a street and the fairgrounds. A street is continually open, often uncongested, and constitutes not only a necessary conduit in the daily affairs of a locality's citizens, but also a place where people may enjoy the open air or the company of friends and neighbors in a relaxed environment. The Minnesota Fair ... is a temporary event attracting great numbers of visitors who come to the event for a short period to see and experience the host of exhibits and attractions at the Fair. The flow of the crowd and demands of safety are more pressing in the context of the Fair." Id. at 2566. Accordingly, the Court concluded that the state's interest in confining distribution, selling, and fund solicitation to fixed locations served a substantial state interest. Finding that less drastic alternatives would be insufficient to achieve that interest and noting that "alternative forums" for the group's expression existed, the Court upheld the restriction as consistent with the "limited public forum" nature of the state fair.

More recently, on a related issue, the Court held that a public university could not deny religious groups the right to use its facilities for their activities where such facilities were available to comparable nonreligious groups. In Widmar v. Vincent, 50 U.S.L.W. 4062 (1981), the Court reasoned that religious groups are entitled to the same free speech access to a public forum as anyone else; nor would it violate the Establishment Clause for the university to permit such access. By contrast, in Brandon v. Board of Education, 635 F.2d 971 (2d Cir. 1980), the Second Circuit held it permissible for a high school to refuse to allow a voluntarily formed prayer group to use school facilities, noting: "... the students' free speech and associational rights cognizable in a public forum, are severely circumscribed by the Establishment Clause in the public school setting." Id. at 980.

(page 265) [421]

NOTES

2. [continued] For recent cases involving speech activities in public transportation facilities, see Wright v. Chief of Transit Police, 558 F.2d 67 (2d Cir. 1977) (complete ban on subway distribution of political newspaper is impermissible absent proof that reasonable regulation of such activity not possible); International Society for Krishna Consciousness v. Rochford, 585 F.2d 263 (7th Cir. 1978) (invalidating airport regulations restricting sale of literature and solicitation of contributions, and limiting solicitation to one-half hour and one person at a time but upholding (1) exclusion of activities from security areas, captive audience areas, and limited space areas, (2) allocating space on a first-come-first-served basis, and (3) prohibiting activity during any "emergency"); International Society for Krishna Consciousness v. Eaves, 601 F.2d 809 (5th Cir. 1980) (upholding requirement that religious solicitation at Atlanta airport be conducted only in designated booths). The Krishna Consciousness group has challenged similar restrictions at numerous airports throughout the country.

(page 265) [421]

NOTES

3. [continued] Following Greer v. Spock, the Ninth Circuit upheld a number of criminal convictions of people who went upon various military installations to engage in protest activity. See United States v. Douglass, 579 F.2d 545 (9th Cir. 1978) (protest at naval submarine base); United States v. Mowat, 582 F.2d 1194 (9th Cir.), cert. denied, 439 U.S. 967 (1978) (protest at Hawaiian island used by military for bombing

targets). In Brown v. Glines, 444 U.S. 348 (1980), the Court addressed the free speech rights of military personnel, holding that Air Force regulations that require prior command approval to circulate petitions on military installations do not violate the First Amendment or the special statute, 10 U.S.C. §1034, protecting the right of military personnel to communicate with members of Congress. See also Secretary of the Navy v. Huff, 444 U.S. 453 (1980) (same). For further discussion of these cases, see Chapter XVI, Section C, infra. Finally, in Culver v. Secretary of Air Force, 559 F.2d 622 (D.C. Cir. 1977), the court of appeals upheld an Air Force regulation banning off-duty military personnel from engaging in any "demonstration" while stationed in a foreign country, thus sustaining the court martial conviction of an officer who organized and participated in an antiwar march to Hyde Park in London.

(page 265) [421]

NOTES

4. [continued] See also, Knights of Ku Klux Klan v. East Baton Rouge Parish School Board, 578 F.2d 1122 (5th Cir. 1978) (KKK cannot be denied use of public school facilities previously made available to other outside groups, board has thus created public forum and could not deny its use absent showing of imminent danger of violence); Gay Activist Alliance v. Washington Metropolitan Area Transit Authority, — F. Supp. — ,48 U.S.L.W. 2053 (D.D.C. 1979) (transit authority's refusal to accept advertisement submitted by gay rights organization while accepting other ads espousing controversial political and social causes violates public forum equal access principles).

(page 273) [429]

Insert before Note 1:

NOTE

In 1976, the Court continued its retreat from constitutional protection of speech activities on privately owned premises or property. Since Lloyd Corp. v. Tanner had severely restricted non-labor-related picketing and leafletting on privately owned shopping center premises, one focus of litigation shifted to the protections afforded to labor-related speech activities under the National Labor Relations Act.

The first major case was Hudgens v. NLRB, 424 U.S. 507 (1976), which involved peaceful primary type labor picketing within the confines of a large, privately owned shopping center in the suburbs of Atlanta, Georgia. The labor dispute involved employees of a shoe company warehouse, and the shopping center picketing was directed at a company retail outlet. The NLRB had concluded that the threat to arrest the pickets for trespass violated the NLRA. Looking back past Logan Valley Plaza to Marsh v. Alabama, the Court reasoned that if the shopping center in Logan Valley had really been viewed as the functional equivalent of a municipality, then the content-related distinctions drawn in Logan Valley would have been impermissible. Accordingly, the Court reasoned, Logan Valley was really a Lloyd v. Tanner case and "did not survive the court's decision in the Lloyd case." Id. at 518. Finding that Lloyd controlled and that the Atlanta shopping center was "private property," the Court concluded that "under the present state of the law the constitutional guarantee of free expression has no part to play in a case such as this." Id. at 521. Turning to the issues under the NLRA, the Court concluded that further consideration of the proper accommodation of union members' rights "and private property rights" was required, and a remand to the Board was directed. Dissenting, Justice Marshall contended that Logan Valley and Lloyd Corp. were reconcilable, given the different nature of the relationship between the speech engaged in and the facility utilized. The dissent concluded as follows:

"In the final analysis, The Court's rejection of any role for the First Amendment in the privately owned shopping center stems, I believe, from an overly formalistic view of the relationship between the institution of private ownership of property and the First Amendment's guarantee of freedom of speech.... [P]roperty that is privately owned is not always held for private use, and when a property owner opens his property to public use the force of those values diminishes.... [T]he shopping center owner has assumed the traditional role of the state in its control of historical First Amendment forums. Lloyd and Logan Valley recognized the vital role the First Amendment has to play in such cases, and I believe that this Court errs when it holds otherwise." Id. at 542-543.

As it has turned out, however, the protections of the NLRA have served as a limited safety valve for the pressures of speech activity denied constitutional status by Hudgens v. NLRB. In three recent post-Hudgens cases, the Court has used the Act to afford significant statutory protection to free speech in the work place. See: Beth Israel Hospital v. NLRB, 437 U.S. 483 (1978); Eastex Inc. v. NLRB, 437 U.S. 556 (1978); NLRB v. Baptist Hospital, Inc., 442 U.S. 773 (1979).

In 1980, the Court permitted the opening of another safety valve to the Hudgens ruling, namely, the use of *state* law rather than the First Amendment to safeguard free speech rights on the premises of privately owned shopping centers. See Prune Yard Shopping Center v. Robins, 447 U.S. 74 (1980). In that case, the California Supreme Court had held that the state constitution's free speech protections gave demonstrators the right to solicit petition signatures and distribute literature superior to the owner's rights to ban such activity from his premises. The U.S. Supreme Court unanimously affirmed. Finding that Lloyd Corp. v. Tanner had only held that there was no *First Amendment* right to enter a shopping center to engage in speech activities, Justice Rehnquist agreed that Lloyd did not ". . . limit the authority of the state to exercise its police power or its sovereign right to adopt in its own constitution individual liberties more expansive than those conferred by the Federal Constitution. . . . It is, of course, well-established that a state in the exercise of its police powers may adopt reasonable restrictions on private property so long as the restrictions do not amount to a taking without just compensation or contravene any other federal constitutional provision." 447 U.S. at 81. Accordingly, the Court then addressed whether the state rights California had given the demonstrators constituted a "taking" or a "deprivation" of the shopping center owner's property rights and found no violation since the literal "taking" of the owner's traditional property right to exclude demonstrators from a shopping center otherwise generally open to the public had an insignificant impact on "the value or use of [the] property as a shopping center." Id. at 83. Finally, the Court rejected the owner's First Amendment claims that he was improperly being compelled by the state to use his property as a forum for the speech of others.

In Prune Yard, there were a number of concurring opinions emphasizing the narrowness of the Court's ruling in terms of state-created free speech rights, exercised on shopping center premises open to the general public, as opposed to other kinds of privately owned property, with no strong record showing that the owner took particular issue with the demonstrators' message. The precise reach of the Prune Yard principle was to have been tested, however, in a case involving not a shopping center but a private educational institution, namely, Princeton University. In New Jersey v. Schmid, 84 N.J. 535, 423 A.2d 615 (1980), dismissed as moot sub nom. Princeton University v. Schmid, — U.S. —, 50 U.S.L.W. 4159 (Jan. 13, 1982), a sharply divided New Jersey Supreme Court, following the lead of the California court in Prune Yard, had ruled that the State Constitution's free speech guarantees permitted the exercise of limited free speech rights on private university property and thus invalidated the trespass conviction of a person who entered the Princeton campus to hand out political leaflets. The Supreme Court, following argument, dismissed the appeal for mootness because Princeton had changed its regulation.

(page 274) [430]

NOTES

2. [continued] In Illinois Migrant Council v. Campbell Soup Co., 574 F.2d 374 (7th Cir. 1978), the Seventh Circuit ruled that a Campbell

Soup Company mushroom farm was not the functional equivalent of a company town, and thus farm workers' union organizers had no right of access to the premises.

(page 275) [431]

NOTE

5. In a number of cases since 1976, the Court has considered restrictions on the ability of speakers to communicate with homeowners and residential dwellers. In these cases, the Court has broadly recognized the right of government to protect individuals in their homes from crime, undue annoyance, fraud, and invasion of privacy by regulation of solicitation, canvassing, and other efforts to speak to people in their homes. The Court, however, has invalidated most of the regulations at issue because of the imprecision with which such goals were sought to be achieved.

The first case, Hynes v. Mayor of Oradell, 425 U.S. 610 (1976), involved a classic method of regulating door-to-door canvassing and solicitation: requiring advance notice to the police. Under the scheme, while door-to-door solicitors had to apply for and obtain a police permit prior to solicitation, "any person desiring to canvass, solicit or call from house to house for a recognized charitable . . . or political campaign or cause" had to give advance notice to the police "in writing for identification only." The latter requirement was challenged by a local political candidate, and the Court ultimately invalidated that portion of the ordinance on vagueness grounds, for failing adequately to specify who was covered and what the "identification" requirement entailed. En route to that holding, however, Chief Justice Burger, re-affirming older precedent, observed that ". . . the Court has consistently recognized a municipality's power to protect its citizens from crime and undue annoyance by regulating soliciting and canvassing. A narrowly drawn ordinance, that does not vest in municipal officers the undefined power to determine what messages residents will hear, may serve these important purposes without running afoul of the First Amendment." Id. at 616-617. "There is, of course, no absolute right under the Federal Constitution to enter on the private premises of another and knock on a door for any purpose, and the police power permits reasonable regulation for public safety. We cannot say . . . that door-to-door canvassing and solicitation are immune from regulation under the state's police power, whether the purpose of the regulation is to protect from danger or to protect the peaceful enjoyment of the home." Id. at 619. These broad remarks prompted a concurrence by Justice Brennan who objected to the suggestion that "vagueness defects aside, an ordinance of this kind would ordinarily withstand constitutional attack. . . . I believe that such ordinances must encounter substantial First Amendment barriers besides vagueness. . . ." Id. at 623. In his view, "door-to-door solicitation and canvassing is a method of communication essential to the preservation of our free society . . ." and identification requirements chill and burden such free expression.

Similar issues were before the Court again in Village of Schaumburg v. Citizens for a Better Environment, 444 U.S. 620 (1980). There a local ordinance required that a permit be obtained by any "charitable organization" intending to solicit contributions door-to-door or on the public streets of the town. Prerequisite to obtaining such a permit was a showing that at least 75 percent of the proceeds must be used for "charitable purposes," defined to exclude solicitation expenses, salaries, overhead, and other administrative expenses. The requirement was challenged by a bona fide environmental rights group denied a permit because it spent more than half its proceeds on employee salaries and expenses. In addressing the issues raised, the Court extensively surveyed its prior decision concerning solicitation of funds and canvassing and summed up the rules as follows:

"Prior authorities, therefore, clearly establish that charitable appeals for funds, on the street or door to door, involve a variety of speech interests — communication of information, the dissemination and propagation of views and ideas, and the advocacy of causes — that are within the protection of the First Amendment. Soliciting financial support is undoubtedly subject to reasonable regulation but the latter must be undertaken with due regard for the reality that solicitation is characteristically intertwined with informative and perhaps persuasive speech seeking support for particular causes or for particular views on economic, political or social issues, and for the reality that without solicitation the flow of such information and advocacy would likely cease. Canvassers in such contexts are necessarily more than solicitors for money. Furthermore, because charitable solicitation does more than inform private economic decisions and is not primarily concerned with providing information about the characteristics and costs of goods and services, it has not been dealt with in our cases as a variety of purely commercial speech." 444 U.S. at 632.

Turning to the 75 percent requirement, the Court found that, given its effect on advocacy and issue organizations, it was "a direct and substantial limitation on protected activity that cannot be sustained unless it serves a sufficiently strong, subordinating interest that the Village is entitled to protect." Id. at 636. While acknowledging the "substantial governmental interests in protecting the public from fraud, crime and undue annoyance . . . they are only peripherally promoted by the 75 percent requirement and could be sufficiently served by measures less destructive of First Amendment interests." Id.

A few months later, the Court considered two other kinds of restrictions on communicating with people in their homes. In Carey v. Brown, 447 U.S. 455 (1980), an Illinois statute barred all residential picketing, except picketing "of a place of employment involved in a labor dispute." The statute was challenged by a civil rights group prosecuted for holding a demonstration on the public sidewalk in front of the home of the Mayor of Chicago. Writing for the Court, Justice Brennan had little difficulty in concluding that in exempting residential labor picketing from the statutory ban Illinois had engaged in precisely the kind of content discrimination condemned in Police Department of Chicago v. Mosley, 408 U.S. 92 (1972), namely, making the "permissibility of residential picketing . . . dependent solely on the nature of the message being conveyed." 447 U.S. at 461. Since the content-based distinction between labor and nonlabor picketing had no bearing on protection of or intrusion on residential privacy, the Court determined that the Mosley principles had been violated. In doing so, however, the Court emphasized that a content-*neutral* protection of residential privacy would be viewed much differently:

"We are not to be understood to imply, however, that residential picketing is beyond the reach of uniform and nondiscriminatory regulation. . . . Preserving the sanctity of the home, the one retreat to which men and women can repair to escape from the tribulations of their daily pursuits, is surely an important value. Our decisions reflect no lack of solicitude for the right of an individual 'to be let alone' in the privacy of the home. . . . The State's interest in protecting the well-being, tranquility, and privacy of the home is certainly of the highest order in a free and civilized society." 447 U.S. at 470-471. Three dissenters would have gone further, however, to hold that "[a]n absolute ban on picketing at residences used solely for residential purposes permissibly furthers the State interest in protecting residential privacy. The State could certainly conclude that the presence of even a solitary picket in front of a residence is an intolerable intrusion on residential privacy." Id at 478.

Privacy of the home was also one of the asserted justifications for the public service commission ban on "bill inserts" discussing controversial questions of public policy, which was at issue in Consolidated Edison Co. v. Public Service Commission, 447 U.S. 530 (1980). The Commission claimed that prohibiting utility companies from including literature on nuclear power in monthly billing statements was a justifiable protection of the privacy and sensibilities of consumers who would find the messages offensive. The Court rejected the claim, finding that the assault on privacy was far from "intolerable" since the customer "may escape exposure to objectionable material simply by transferring the bill insert from envelope to wastebasket." Id. at 542. Moreover, "[e]ven if there were a compelling state interest in protecting consumers against overly intrusive bill inserts, it is possible that the state could achieve its goal simply by requiring [the utility] to stop sending bill inserts to the homes of objecting customers. See Rowan v. Post Office Department [397 U.S 728 (1970)]...." Id. at n.11.

In each of these four cases, the Court invalidated the particular restriction on the speaker's ability to communicate to residential dwellers but indicated that the home remains strongly insulated against crime, fraud, and undue annoyance generated by speech activities. In the final case in the sequence, the speaker wishing to communicate to a residence did not prevail. But the speaker's claim was rejected not in the interests of residential privacy and security but, rather, to safeguard the federal government's paramount proprietary interests in the postal system, even where the recipient of the message welcomes the communication.

In United States Postal Service v. Council of Greenburgh Civic Associations, 101 S. Ct. 2676 (1981), a group of community activists challenged a federal postal statute that prevented them from putting notices and pamphlets in people's mailboxes without paying postage, thus inhibiting their ability to communicate with residents in their town. After examining the history of the federal postal power, including the broad authority to regulate the use of "authorized depositories," i.e., mailboxes, Justice Rehnquist, for the Court, rejected the argument that government approval of use of a mailbox transforms it into "a 'public forum' of some limited nature to which the First Amendment guarantees access to all comers.... [I]t is difficult to accept appellees' assertion that because it may be somewhat more efficient to place their messages in letter boxes there is a First Amendment right to do so." 101 S. Ct. at 2684. Analogizing mailboxes to other kinds of government property, the Court observed that "... The First Amendment does not guarantee access to property simply because it is owned or controlled by the government". Id, at 2685. Justice Rehnquist then observed:

"This Court has not hesitated in the past to hold invalid laws which ... granted too much discretion to public officials as to who might and who might not solicit individual homeowners, or which too broadly inhibited the access of persons to traditional First Amendment forums such as the public streets and parks.... But it is a giant leap from the traditional 'soap box' to the letter box designated as an authorized depository of the United States mails, and we do not believe the First Amendment requires us to make that leap." Id. at 2685-2686. Accordingly, having concluded that a mailbox is not a "public forum," the Court felt no need to inquire whether the challenged restriction was reasonable.

Justice Marshall, dissenting, observed: "I would adhere to our usual analysis which looks to whether the exercise of a First Amendment right is burdened by the challenged governmental action, and then upholds that action only where it is necessary to advance a substantial and legitimate governmental interest. In my view, the statute criminalizing the placement of hand-delivered civic association notices in letter boxes fails this test." Id. at 2696. Finally, Justice Stevens found the statute unconstitutional by viewing it from the vantage point not of the speaker, but of the listener: "If the [mailbox] owner welcomes messages from his neighbors, from the local community organization, or even from the newly-arrived entrepreneur passing out free coupons, it is presumptively unreasonable to interfere with his ability to receive such communications. The nationwide criminal statute at issue here deprives millions of homeowners of the legal right to make a simple decision affecting their ability to receive communications from others." Id. at 2697.

(page 280) [436]

NOTES

3. [continued] The Supreme Court in the Sutherland case may have finally resolved, in a summary way, the constitutionality of flag burning statutes. Following the 1974 remand for reconsideration in light of Spence v. Washington and Smith v. Goguen, the Illinois Appellate Court adhered to its earlier application of the O'Brien test and concluded that the statute served "a valid governmental interest unrelated to expression — that is, the prevention of breaches of the peace and the preservation of public order." People v. Sutherland, 29 Ill. App. 3d 199, 329 N.E.2d 820, 821 (3d Dist. 1975). Following denial of review by the Illinois Supreme Court, the defendants once again appealed to the U.S. Supreme Court. This time, by a vote of 6-3, the Court dismissed the appeal "for want of a substantial federal question." Sutherland v. Illinois, 425 U.S. 947 (1976).

(page 283) [439]

NOTES

5. In U.S. Labor Party v. Pomerleau, 557 F.2d 410 (4th Cir. 1977), the Court of Appeals invalidated a Baltimore noise control ordinance, as applied to amplifiers used by political party street speakers, because of the highly arbitrary way in which the prohibited decibel levels were ascertained in any given case. More recently, in Concerned Jewish Youth v. MacGuire, 621 F.2d 471 (2d Cir. 1980), the Second Circuit upheld restrictions on use of sound devices by demonstrators near the Soviet Mission to the U.N.

In Buckley v. Valeo, 424 U.S. 1 (1976), the Court rejected an attempt to analogize the sound truck cases to sustain ceilings on political campaign expenditures. In effect, the Court held that the financial amplification of speech facilitated by campaign expenditures could not be limited by the Kovacs principle: "The . . . appellees argue that just as the decibels emitted by a sound truck can be regulated . . . the Act may restrict the volume of dollars in political campaigns without impermissibly restricting freedom of speech. . . . This comparison underscores a fundamental misconception. The decibel restriction upheld in Kovacs limited the *manner* of operating a sound truck, but not the *extent* of its proper use. By contrast, the Act's dollar ceilings restrict the extent of the reasonable use of virtually every means of communicating information." 424 U.S. at 18 n.17.

6. In recent years, many state and local governments have used their zoning and police powers to prohibit off-site advertising billboards, that is, billboards not located on the premises of the person or firm whose advertising appears in them. These prohibitions, designed to further environmental and aesthetic goals, have a direct effect on a medium of communication frequently used for political speech.

In 1981, the Supreme Court addressed these issues in Metromedia, Inc. v. City of San Diego, 453 U.S. 490, 101 S. Ct. 2882 (1981). The decision struck down the ordinance at issue, but there was no opinion of the Court although there was considerable common ground among the Justices.

The San Diego ordinance prohibited any billboard except those coming within two kinds of exceptions: (1) on-site, i.e., relating to the premises, and (2) those in a specific list of exempted categories. The precise nature of the on-site exemption was unclear, but Justice White's plurality opinion assumed that "on-site commercial advertising is permitted, but other commercial advertising and noncommercial communications using fixed-structure signs are everywhere forbidden unless permitted by one of the specified exceptions." 101 S. Ct. at 2886. The scheme was challenged by outdoor advertising companies.

The Court first noted that billboards are "a well established medium of communication, used to convey a broad range of different kinds of messages." Id. at 2887. But, because of their nature, billboards, "like other media of communication, combine communicative and non-communicative aspects. As with other media, the government has legitimate interest in controlling the noncommunicative aspects of the medium, Kovacs v. Cooper . . . but the First and Fourteenth Amendments foreclose a similar interest in controlling the communicative aspects. Because regulation of the noncommunicative aspects of a medium often impinges to some degree on the communicative aspects, it has been necessary for the courts to reconcile the government's regulatory interests with the individual's right to expression." Id. at 2890.

The Court next addressed the ordinance's prohibition of all commercial billboards except those that were "on-site." Drawing upon the distinctions between commercial and noncommercial speech and the "lesser" protection given the former, the plurality concluded that it was permissible for a city to ban all off-site commercial advertising on billboards; the "city's land-use interests" and concerns with traffic safety and the appearance of the city were deemed sufficient to outweigh "the commercial interests of those seeking to purvey goods and services within the city." Id. at 2895. The defects in the ordinance, however, were that it (1) permitted on-site commercial billboards while prohibiting on-site *or* off-site noncommercial messages, and (2) exempted a wide variety of noncommercial messages from this prohibition. With respect to the ordinance's preference for commercial speech, Justice White observed: "Insofar as the city tolerates billboards at all, it cannot choose to limit their content to commercial messages; the city may not conclude that the communication of commercial information concerning goods and services connected with a particular site is of greater value than the communication of noncommercial messages." Id. at 2895.

Similarly, permitting some kinds of noncommercial billboards by granting various content-based exemptions while prohibiting other messages offended the principle that a city "may not choose the appropriate subjects for public discourse. . . . Because some non-commercial messages may be conveyed on billboards . . . San Diego must similarly allow billboards conveying other noncommercial messages. . . ." Id. at 2896. Finally, the plurality rejected the claim that the ordinance was a valid "time, place and manner" restriction, noting that it did not ban all billboards, but rather "distinguishes in several ways between permissible and impermissible signs at a particular location by reference to their content. Whether or not these distinctions are themselves constitutional, they take the regulation out of the domain of time, place and manner restrictions." Id. at 2897.

In Justice Brennan's view, however, the practical effect of the ordinance was "to eliminate the billboard as an effective medium of communication for the speaker" who wants to express political and social messages. Id. at 2901. So characterized, the ban was invalid not because of the exceptions to it, but because the prohibition was an unjustified restriction on an important medium of communication.

By contrast, Chief Justice Burger's sharp dissent found the ordinance well within traditional municipal power over traffic safety and aesthetic zoning and not violative of any recognized First Amendment protections. Justice Rehnquist's dissent was characteristically direct: ". . . The aesthetic justification alone is sufficient to sustain a total prohibition of billboards within a community." Id. at 2924. Finally, Justice Stevens' dissent also agreed that a city, in order to protect urban and property values, could "entirely ban one medium of communication," id. at 2924, and found it ironic that the plurality invalidated the ordinance "because it does not abridge enough speech."

Despite the plethora of approaches and opinions, at least seven justices would clearly permit a broad and content-neutral prohibition of billboards as a method of communication.

(page 295) [451]

NOTES

5. The Walker doctrine has caused difficult problems in another context, namely, preserving the right of the media to report information about an ongoing judicial proceeding in the face of a gag order against publication. For recent cases discussing this problem see: Goldblum v. NBC, 584 F.2d 907 (9th Cir. 1978); Angelico v. State of Louisiana, 593 F.2d 585 (5th Cir. 1979). See also Richmond Newspapers v. Commonwealth of Virginia, 444 U.S. 896 (1980); Gannett Co. v. De Pasquale, 443 U.S. 368 (1979).

(page 301) [457]

NOTES

1. [continued] In Buckley v. Valeo, 424 U.S. 1 (1976), the disclosure requirements of the Federal Election Campaign Act were sustained as a facial matter. The Court noted, however, that controversial organizations would qualify for judicial exemption if they could demonstrate that compulsory identification of their supporters would be likely to inhibit their activities. For recent cases dealing with the claim that disclosure of contributors would inhibit political or issue advocacy see: Federal Election Commission v. CLITRIM, 616 F.2d 45 (2d Cir. 1980) (en banc); NYCLU v. Acito, 459 F. Supp. 75 (S.D.N.Y. 1978); ACLU v. New Jersey Election Law Enforcement Commission, 509 F. Supp. 1123 (D.N.J. 1981) (three-judge court). Finally, a California appellate court recently applied the Talley principles to invalidate a statute prohibiting anonymous campaign donations, see Schuster v. Imperial County Municipal Court, 109 Cal. App. 3d 887, 167 Cal. Rptr. 447 (4th Dist. 1981).

These issues will be considered by the Court again in Socialist Workers '74 Campaign Committee v. Brown, — F. Supp. — (S.D. Ohio 1981), prob. juris. noted, 50 U.S.L.W. 3479 (Dec. 14, 1981), where a three-judge court ruled that the Ohio Socialist Workers Party campaign committee had made a sufficient showing of potential harm so as to warrant a constitutional exemption from disclosing campaign contributors.

Chapter Five
Administration of Justice

A [B]. THE PROTECTION OF CONFIDENTIAL SOURCES IN JUDICIAL PROCEEDINGS

(page 310) [471]

NOTES

2. [continued] A First Amendment privilege against revealing confidential sources in federal litigation is recognized by some courts but not by all. See Gilbert v. Allied Chemical Corp., 411 F. Supp. 505 (E.D. Va. 1976) (privilege granted to nonparty journalist absent a showing that the only practical access to crucial information is through the journalist's sources; Branzburg limited to grand jury subpoenas). But see United States v. Steelhammer, 539 F.2d 373 (4th Cir. 1976), rev'd en banc, 561 F.2d 539 (4th Cir. 1977) upheld contempt convictions of reporters who refused to testify about union rally they attended but vacated the unserved sentences because the underlying proceeding had been terminated); Caldero v. Tribune Publishing Co., 98 Idaho 288, 562 P.2d 791 (1977), cert. denied, 434 U.S. 930 (1978) (court read Branzburg to afford no First Amendment journalist's privilege in civil action, unless harrassment is demonstrated). See also Sherrill v. Knight, 569 F.2d 124 (D.C. Cir. 1977) (secret service ordered to devise and implement general standards for issuance or denial of White House press credentials and to provide procedural safeguards).

(page 311) [471]

NOTES

4. [continued] In Herbert v. Lando, 441 U.S. 153 (1979), the Supreme Court found that the First Amendment does not bar a public figure libel

plaintiff from discovering the thoughts and editorial processes of members of the press where relevant evidence would be produced. Justice White, writing for the six-judge majority, noted that "[c]ourts have traditionally admitted any direct or indirect evidence relevant to the state of mind of the defendant. The rules are applicable to the press and to other defendants alike, and it is evident that the courts across the country have been accepting evidence going to the editorial processes of the media without constitutional objections." Justice White rejected the claim that the disclosure of editorial processes would "chill" those processes; the press would be inhibited only from publishing falsehoods. The Court also rejected the argument that the high costs of pre-trial discovery 1 54would intimidate the news media and lead to self-censorship. Justices would intimidate the news media and lead to self-censorship. Justices Brennan, Stewart and Marshall filed a dissent.

See also Reliance Insurance Co. v. Barron's, 428 F. Supp. 200 (S.D.N.Y. 1977) (rule disfavoring prior restraints permits journalist/defendant to use nonpublic material produced in discovery proceedings by corporation prosecuting libel suit).

(page 311) [472]

NOTE

5. [continued] See generally Note, Newsman's Privilege After Branzburg: The Case for a Federal Shield Law, 24 U.C.L.A.L. Rev. 160 (1976).

(page 313) [474]

NOTES

7. [continued] In Richards of Rockford, Inc. v. Pacific Gas & Electric Co., 71 F.R.D. 388 (N.D. Cal. 1976), Judge Renfrew upheld a scholar's privilege against testifying in a civil defamation and breach of contract action. The court found that a strong public interest in maintaining the research of its scholars, much of which depends upon pledges of confidentiality, outweighs the litigant's and the public's interest in fair resolution of civil disputes. Although this ruling was not constitutionally based, but rather was grounded in the broad discretion of the trial judge to supervise the course of discovery, Judge Renfrew followed the guidelines used in journalist's privilege cases in weighing the interests at stake. He noted, for example, that this proceeding was civil, that the professor was not a party, and that the information sought was largely supplementary. Hence he ruled that, on balance, the scholar's privilege should prevail.

8. A fragmented Supreme Court rejected another press claim for special protection from law enforcement demands for information in

Zurcher v. Stanford Daily, 436 U.S. 519 (1978). The Stanford Daily claimed that the First Amendment entitled the media to special safeguards before a search warrant could be issued against them. In rejecting the claim, Justice White's plurality opinion contained only one sentence suggesting that First Amendment considerations be taken into account in applying Fourth Amendment search warrant criteria in the media context: "[Prior cases insist] that courts apply the warrant requirements with particular exactitude when First Amendment interests would be endangered by the search." Justic Powell's concurrence, in contrast, elaborated the relevance of First Amendment concerns. He stated, for example: "This is not to say that a warrant which would be sufficient to support the search of an apartment or an automobile necessarily would be reasonable in supporting the search of a newspaper office. . . . While there is no justification for the establishment of a separate Fourth Amendment procedure for the press, a magistrate asked to issue a warrant for the search of press offices can and should take cognizance of the independent values protected by the First Amendment — such as those highlighted by Mr. Justice Stewart — when he weighs such factors." And he added in a footnote that his Branzburg concurrence, like the concurring opinion here, may properly be read as supporting the view "that under the warrant requirement of the Fourth Amendment, the magistrate should consider the values of a free press as well as the societal interest in enforcing the criminal laws."

On October 13, 1980, Congress passed the Privacy Protection Act of 1980, 42 U.S.C. 2000aa (Supp. 1974-1980), to "lessen greatly the threat that Stanford Daily poses to the vigorous exercise of First Amendment rights." The Act protects a journalist's work product from searches and seizures by federal, state, and local police in pursuit of a criminal investigation unless the journalist himself is a suspect or there is danger of death or serious bodily harm. Non-work product material is also protected, except when the journalist is a suspect; a life is in danger; notice pursuant to a subpoena would result in the destruction, alteration, or concealment of the materials; or such materials have not been produced in response to a court order directing compliance with a subpoena and either all appellate remedies have been exhausted or delay would threaten the interests of justice.

See Comment, The Constitutionality of Congressional Legislation to Overrule Zurcher v. Stanford Daily, 71 J. Crim. L. & Criminology 147 (1980) (questions the constitutional validity of proposed privacy protection legislation); Zurcher v. Stanford Daily: The Legislative Debate, 17 Harv. J. Legis. 152 (1980); Teeter & Singer, Search Warrants in Newsrooms: Some Aspects of the Impact of Zurcher v. The Stanford Daily, 67 Ky. L. J. 847 (1979); The Theory of Probable Cause and Searches of Innocent Persons: The Fourth Amendment and Stanford Daily, 25 U.C.L.A.L. Rev. 1445 (1978).

REFERENCES

Legal commentary on the protection of confidential sources includes Annot., Privilege of Newsgatherer Against Disclosure of Confidential Sources or Information, 99 A.L.R.3d 37 (1980); Note, The Right of Sources — The Critical Element in the Clash over Reporter's Privileges, 88 Yale L.J. 1202 (1979); Goodale, Branzburg v. Hayes and the Developing Qualified Privilege for Newsmen, 26 Hastings L.J. 709 (1975) (explores civil and criminal case law and expresses the need for high court articulation of the scope of the journalist's privilege); Symposium, Governmental Suppression of the Media, 29 U. Miami L. Rev. 446 (1975); Note, Newsgathering: Second-Class Right Among First Amendment Freedoms, 53 Tex. L. Rev. 1440 (1975); Note, Right of the Press to Gather Information After Branzburg and Pell, 124 U. Pa. L. Rev. 166 (1975) Cf. Note, The Right to Record and Broadcast Public Legislative Proceedings, 42 U. Chi. L. Rev. 356 (1975). See also Note, Search Warrants and Journalists' Confidential Information, 25 Amer. U.L. Rev. 938 (1976); Note, Search and Seizure of the Media: A Statutory, Fourth Amendment and First Amendment Analysis, 28 Stan. L. Rev. 957 (1976) (develops a constitutional and statutory attack on a recent government mode of acquiring information from reporters — the search warrant).

(page 315) [476]

NOTE — STATE SHIELD LAWS

[continued] In Matter of Farber, 78 N.J. 259, 394 A.2d 330, cert. denied, 439 U.S. 997 (1978), the New Jersey Supreme Court found Branzburg controlling in determining that a newspaper and its reporter have no First Amendment right to refuse to produce documents in response to a murder defendant's subpoenas duces tecum. Farber and the New York Times had argued that producing the documents would impair the gathering and dissemination of news by causing confidential sources to clam up. The court refused to consider the argument. "[W]e do no weighing or balancing of societal interests in reaching our determination that the First Amendment does not afford appellants the privilege they claim. The weighing and balancing have been done by a higher court." The New Jersey Supreme Court also rejected appellants' claim to protection under the New Jersey shield law.

Other recent cases include State v. Boiardo, 82 N.J. 446, 414 A.2d 14 (N.J. 1980) (trial court erred in requiring reporter to produce letter as defendant failed to prove that information contained therein was not available through less intrusive sources); In re Vrazo, 176 N.J. Super. 455, 423 A.2d 695 (N.J. Super. Law Div. 1980) (reporter's observations of fraud did not fall within the "eyewitness" exception to the state shield law for acts involving physical violence or property damage); Pennington v. Chaffee, 224 Kan. 573, 581 P.2d 812 (1978), cert. denied, 440 U.S. 929 (1979) (recognized qualified reporter's privilege but found that murder defendant's right to a fair trial outweighed reporter's privilege to conceal the name of source who claimed that a prosecution witness had threatened to kill the victim); Zelenka v. Wisconsin, 83 Wis. 2d 601, 266 N.W.2d 279 (1978) (no error in trial court's refusal to require reporter to reveal source when defendant presented only a mere suggestion that the information might lead to an entrapment defense); Morgan v. State of Florida, 337 So. 2d 951 (Fla. 1976) (journalist's privilege and the public interest in access to anonymous information deemed to outweigh government interest in compelling disclosure before grand jury investigation of prior grand jury leaks); Caldero v. Tribune Publishing Co., 98 Idaho 288, 562 P.2d 791, cert. denied 434 U.S. 930 (1977) (upheld contempt conviction for reporter refusing to testify in libel action, and read Branzburg to afford neither an absolute nor a qualified privilege except in harrassment cases).

B [C]. CRITICISM OF THE JUDICIAL PROCESS

(page 322) [484]

NOTES

4. [6.] In Landmark Communications, Inc. v. Virginia, 435 U.S. 829 (1978), the Supreme Court held that a state statute enacted to protect the confidentiality of investigations into judicial behavior could not be invoked to punish nonparticipants in the proceedings for divulging information. Landmark, a newspaper publisher, had printed an accurate report of a pending inquiry by the Virginia Judicial Inquiry and Review Commission and had identified the state judge whose conduct was being investigated. The state statute declared that information before the Commission was confidential and made disclosure a crime. Chief Justice Burger's majority opinion held that Landmark's conviction violated the First Amendment. Though the Chief Justice refused to adopt the publisher's "categorical" argument that "truthful reporting about officials [is] always" protected by First Amendment, he concluded that the information lay near "the core of the First Amendment" and that the "interests advanced by the imposition of criminal sanctions [were] insufficient to justify the actual and potential encroachments on freedom of speech and of the press." In the majority's view, then, "criminal punishment of third persons who are strangers to the inquiry, including news media, for divulging or publishing truthful information" regardless the Commission's "confidential proceedings" was impermissible.

The Chief Justice noted that the operation of judicial review commissions, like the operation of the judicial system itself, is a matter of public interest. He conceded that the State's interests in maintaining confidentiality were "legitimate," but he insisted that they were not "sufficient to justify the subsequent punishment of speech at issue here." The asserted interests were promoting efficient Commission proceedings, protecting the reputation of Virginia judges, and maintaining the institutional integrity of its courts. In the course of his discussion, the Chief Justice commented that "injury to official reputation is an insufficient reason 'for repressing speech that would otherwise be free.' "

In the concluding portion of his opinion, Chief Justice Burger repudiated the highest state court's reliance on the clear and present danger test. The Chief Justice stated: "We question the relevance of that standard here; moreover we cannot accept the mechanical application of the test which led [the state] court to its conclusion. . . . Properly applied, the test requires a court to make its own inquiry into the imminence and magnitude of the danger said to flow from a particular utterance and then to balance the character of the evil, as well as its likelihood, against the need for free and unfettered expression. The possibility that other methods will serve the State's interest should also be weighed." The Chief Justice insisted that the clear and present danger test had not been met here any more than in the earlier, contempt of court cases.

C [D]. PREJUDICIAL PUBLICITY AND THE RIGHT TO A FAIR TRIAL

(page 327) [498]

NOTES

2. [continued] In Murphy v. Florida, 421 U.S. 794 (1975), the Supreme Court rejected petitioner's claim that he had been denied a fair trial because members of the jury had learned from news accounts about a prior felony conviction and/or certain facts about the crime with which he was charged. Petitioner argued that the principles underlying Marshall v. United States, 360 U.S. 310 (1959), should apply to state criminal convictions: persons who have learned from news sources of a defendant's prior criminal record are presumed to be prejudiced. Justice Marshall, writing for the majority, rejected the argument, applying instead the fundamental fairness standard of Irvin v. Dowd, 366 U.S. 717 (1961). "The constitutional standard of fairness requires that a defendant have 'a panel of impartial, "indifferent" jurors.' Qualified jurors need not, however, be totally ignorant of the facts and issues involved. . . . 'It is

sufficient if the juror can set aside his impression or opinion and render a verdict based on the evidence presented in court.' " (Citations omitted.) Petitioner's trial met this constitutional standard. The Court found that while some of the jurors were familiar with the petitioner or his past, none displayed that actual predisposition against him that would have rendered his trial unfair. The Court discounted the concession of one juror in response to a "leading and hypothetical question," that his prior impression of petitioner would dispose him to convict. "We cannot attach great significance to this statement, however, in light of the leading nature of counsel's questions and the juror's other testimony indicating that he had no deep impression of petitioner at all." Justice Marshall also emphasized that the petitioner's trial did not take place in a generally inflammatory atmosphere. The "offending" publicity occurred seven months before the jury was selected and only 20 of the 78 persons questioned were excused because they indicated an opinion as to petitioner's guilt. Thus, petitioner failed "to show that the setting of the trial was inherently prejudicial or that the jury selection process of which he complains permits an inference of actual prejudice."

Other recent decisions rejecting a claim of prejudicial publicity include United States v. Thompson, 624 F.2d 819 (6th Cir. 1980) (no showing that jurors affected); Mayola v. Alabama, 623 F.2d 992 (5th Cir. 1980) (same); United States v. Marcano-Garcia, 622 F.2d 12 (1st Cir. 1980) (publicity consisted entirely of objective stories); United States v. Alberico, 604 F.2d 1315 (10th Cir.), cert. denied, 444 U.S. 992 (1979) (publicity consisted of videotapes previously shown to jurors; no showing that jurors exposed to publicity; defendant acknowledged guilt).

3. [continued] See United States v. Herring, 568 F.2d 1099 (5th Cir. 1978) (court overturned the defendant's drug conviction because of the trial court's failure to take such precautionary measures in the face of presumptively prejudicial publicity about a death threat made to Greg Allman, a primary prosecution witness, the day after he testified against his former road manager; the jury had not been sequestered and the trial judge denied the defendant's request to voir dire the jury on the potential prejudice created by the banner-headlined article in the city's leading morning paper).

Courts have relied on the procedures outlined in Margoles v. United States, 407 F.2d 727 (7th Cir. 1969), with varying degrees of success. See, e.g., United States v. Trapnell, 638 F.2d 1016 (7th Cir. 1980) (trial court's vigorous voir dire examination of jurors and careful instructions insufficient); Brinke v. Crisp, 608 F.2d 839 (10th Cir. 1979), cert. denied, 444 U.S. 1047 (1980) (voir dire and instructions sufficient); United States v. Capo, 595 F.2d 1086 (5th Cir. 1979), cert. denied, 444 U.S. 1012 (1980) (same); Werbrouck v. United States, 589 F.2d 273 (7th Cir. 1978), cert. denied, 440 U.S. 962 (1979) (rejected defendant's claim that the exclusion of 23 potential jurors who had been exposed to pretrial publicity resulted in the exclusion of a geographic group from the jury thereby denying defendant his right to a jury reflecting a representative cross-section of the community).

5. In Calley v. Callaway, 519 F.2d 184 (5th Cir. 1975) (en banc) (8-5 decision), cert. denied, 425 U.S. 911 (1976), the court upheld the murder conviction of Lieutenant William Calley by a military tribunal for his actions during the 1968 My Lai massacre. Lieutenant Calley had challenged the conviction on grounds of inherent and actual prejudice resulting from massive pre-trial publicity. Judge Ainsworth first noted that the legal standards for determining that an unfair trial resulted from publicity are the same in military and nonmilitary settings. He then stated that the acknowledged massive publicity was not inherently prejudicial because much of it consisted of objective factual statements rather than vitriolic attacks. Furthermore, some coverage was favorable to Calley, and the public held no single sentiment about the case. Additionally, Judge Ainsworth found that the record revealed no actual prejudice: the voir dire was sensitively conducted, no juror had prejudged Calley's guilt, the jurors had combat experience and knew the rigors of warfare, the military court exerted its best efforts to control publicity, and a long period of time had passed between the publicity and the trial.

(page 332) [503]

After first Note 3 add:

CHANDLER v. FLORIDA
449 U.S. 560 (1981)

CHIEF JUSTICE BURGER delivered the opinion of the Court.

The question presented on this appeal is whether, consistent with constitutional guarantees, a state may provide for radio, television, and still photographic coverage of a criminal trial for public broadcast, notwithstanding the objection of the accused.

I

A

Background. Over the past 50 years, some criminal cases characterized as "sensational" have been subjected to extensive coverage by news media, sometimes seriously interfering with the conduct of the proceedings and creating a setting wholly inappropriate for the administration of justice. Judges, lawyers, and others soon became concerned, and in 1937, after study, the American Bar Association House of Delegates adopted Judicial Canon 35, declaring that all photographic and broadcast coverage of courtroom proceedings should be prohibited. In 1952, the House of Delegates amended Canon 35 to proscribe television coverage as well. 77 A.B.A. Rep. 610-611 (1952). The Canon's proscription was reaffirmed in 1972 when the Code of Judicial Conduct replaced the Canons of Judicial Ethics and Canon 3A(7) superseded Canon 35. E. Thode, Reporter's Notes to Code of Judicial Conduct 56-59 (1973). Cf. Fed. Rule Crim. Proc. 53. A majority of the states, including Florida, adopted the substance of the ABA provision and its amendments. In Florida, the rule was embodied in Canon 3A(7) of the Florida Code of Judicial Conduct.

In February 1978, the American Bar Association Committee on Fair Trial–Free Press proposed revised standards. These included a provision permitting courtroom coverage by the electronic media under conditions to be established by local rule and under the control of the trial judge, but only if such coverage was carried out unobtrusively and without affecting the conduct of the trial. The revision was endorsed by the ABA's Standing Committee on Standards for Criminal Justice and by its Committee on Criminal Justice and the Media, but it was rejected by the House of Delegates on February 12, 1979. 65 A.B.A.J. 304 (1979).

In 1978, based upon its own study of the matter, the Conference of State Chief Justices, by a vote of 44 to 1, approved a resolution to allow the highest court of each state to promulgate standards and guidelines regulating radio, television, and other photographic coverage of court proceedings.

The Florida Program. In January 1975, while these developments were unfolding, the Post-Newsweek Stations of Florida petitioned the Supreme Court of Florida urging a change in Florida's Canon 3A(7). In April 1975, the court invited presentations in the nature of a rulemaking proceeding, and, in January 1976, announced an experimental program for televising one civil and one criminal trial under specific guidelines. Petition of Post-Newsweek Stations, Florida, Inc., 327 So. 2d 1. These initial guidelines required the consent of all parties. It developed, however, that in practice such consent could not be obtained. The Florida Supreme Court then supplemented its order and established a new 1-year pilot program during which the electronic media were permitted to cover all judicial proceedings in Florida without reference to the consent of participants, subject to detailed standards with respect to technology and the conduct of operators. In re Petition of Post-Newsweek Stations, Florida, Inc., 347 So. 2d 402 (1977). The experiment began in July 1977 and continued through June 1978.

When the pilot program ended, the Florida Supreme Court received and reviewed briefs, reports, letters of comment, and studies. It conducted its own survey of attorneys, witnesses, jurors, and court personnel through the Office of the State Court Coordinator. A separate survey was taken of judges by the Florida Conference of Circuit Judges. The court also studied the experience of 6 States that had, by 1979, adopted rules relating to electronic coverage of trials, as well as that of the 10 other States that, like Florida, were experimenting with such coverage.[6]

Following its review of this material, the Florida Supreme Court concluded "that on balance there [was] more to be gained than lost by permitting electronic media coverage of judicial proceedings subject to standards for such coverage."In re Petition of Post-Newsweek Stations, Florida, Inc., 370 So. 2d 764, 780 (1979). The Florida court was of the view that because of the significant effect of the courts on the day-to-day lives of the citizenry, it was essential that the people have confidence in the process. It felt that broadcast coverage of trials would contribute to wider public acceptance and understanding of decisions. Ibid. Consequently, after revising the 1977 guidelines to reflect its evaluation of the pilot program, the Florida Supreme Court promulgated a revised Canon 3A(7). Id., at 781. The Canon provides:

"Subject at all times to the authority of the presiding judge to (i) control the conduct of proceedings before the court, (ii) ensure decorum and prevent distractions, and (iii) ensure the fair administration of justice in the pending cause, electronic media and still photography coverage of public judicial proceedings in the appellate and trial courts of this state shall be allowed in accordance with standards of conduct and technology promulgated by the Supreme Court of Florida." Ibid.

The implementing guidelines specify in detail the kind of electronic equipment to be used and the manner of its use. Id., at 778-779, 783-784....

In July 1977, appellants were charged with conspiracy to commit burglary, grand larceny, and possession of burglary tools. The counts covered breaking and entering a well-known Miami Beach restaurant....

By pretrial motion, counsel for the appellants sought to have experimental Canon 3A(7) declared unconstitutional on its face and as applied. The trial court denied relief but certified the issue to the Florida Supreme Court. However, the Supreme Court declined to rule on the question, on the ground that it was not directly relevant to the criminal charges against the appellants. State v. Granger, 352 So. 2d 175 (1977).

After several additional fruitless attempts by the appellants to prevent electronic coverage of the trial, the jury was selected. At voir dire, the appellants' counsel asked each prospective juror whether he or she would be able to be "fair and impartial" despite the presence of a television camera during some, or all, of the trial. Each juror selected re-

---

6. The number of states permitting electronic coverage of judicial proceedings has grown larger since 1979. As of October 1980, 19 States permitted coverage of trial and appellate courts, 3 permitted coverage of trial courts only, 6 permitted appellate court coverage only, and the court systems of 12 other States were studying the issue. Brief for the Radio Television News Directors Association et al. as Amici Curiae. On November 10, 1980, the Maryland Court of Appeals authorized an 18-month experiment with broadcast coverage of both trial and appellate court proceedings. 49 U.S.L.W. 2335 (1980).

sponded that such coverage would not affect his or her consideration in any way. A television camera recorded the voir dire.

A defense motion to sequester the jury because of the television coverage was denied by the trial judge. However, the court instructed the jury not to watch or read anything about the case in the media and suggested that jurors "avoid the local news and watch only the national news on television." App. 13. . . .

A television camera was in place for one entire afternoon, during which the State presented the testimony of Sion, its chief witness.[7] No camera was present for the presentation of any part of the case for the defense. The camera returned to cover closing arguments. Only 2 minutes and 55 seconds of the trial below were broadcast — and those depicted only the prosecution's side of the case.

The jury returned a guilty verdict on all counts. Appellants moved for a new trial, claiming that because of the television coverage, they had been denied a fair and impartial trial. No evidence of specific prejudice was tendered.

The Florida District Court of Appeal affirmed the convictions. . . .

The Florida Supreme Court denied review, holding that the appeal, which was limited to a challenge to Canon 3A(7), was moot by reason of its decision in In re Petition of Post-Newsweek Stations, Florida, Inc., 370 So. 2d 764 (1979), rendered shortly after the decision of the District Court of Appeal.

II

At the outset, it is important to note that in promulgating the revised Canon 3A(7), the Florida Supreme Court pointedly rejected any state or federal constitutional right of access on the part of photographers or the broadcast media to televise or electronically record and thereafter disseminate court proceedings. [See Nixon v. Warner Communications, Inc., 435 U.S. 589 (1978).] . . .

The Florida Supreme Court predicated the revised Canon 3A(7) upon its supervisory authority over the Florida courts, and not upon any constitutional imperative. Hence, we have before us only the limited question of the Florida Supreme Courts's authority to promulgate the Canon for the trial of cases in Florida courts. . . .

III

Appellants rely chiefly on Estes v. Texas, 381 U.S. 532 (1965), and Chief Justice Warren's separate concurring opinion in that case. They

[7]. At one point during Sion's testimony, the judge interrupted the examination and admonished a cameraman to discontinue a movement that the judge apparently found distracting. App. 15. Otherwise, the prescribed procedures appear to have been followed, and no other untoward events occurred.

argue that the televising of criminal trials is inherently a denial of due process, and they read *Estes* as announcing a per se constitutional rule to that effect.... If appellants' reading of Estes were correct, we would be obliged to apply that holding and reverse the judgment under review.

The six separate opinions in Estes must be examined carefully to evaluate the claim that it represents a per se constitutional rule forbidding all electronic coverage. Chief Justice Warren and Justices Douglas and Goldberg joined Justice Clark's opinion announcing the judgment, thereby creating only a plurality. Justice Harlan provided the fifth vote necessary in support of the judgment. In a separate opinion, he pointedly limited his concurrence:

"I concur in the opinion of the Court, subject, however, to the reservations and only to the extent indicated in this opinion." Id., at 587. A careful analysis of Justice Harlan's opinion is therefore fundamental to an understanding of the ultimate holding of Estes.

Justice Harlan began by observing that the question of the constitutional permissibility of televised trials was one fraught with unusual difficulty:

"... My conclusion is that there is no constitutional requirement that television be allowed in the courtroom, *and, at least as to a notorious criminal trial such as this one, the considerations against allowing television in the courtroom so far outweigh the countervailing factors advanced in its support as to require a holding that what was done in this case infringed the fundamental right to a fair trial* assured by the Due Process Clause of the Fourteenth Amendment." Ibid. (emphasis added).

He then proceeded to catalog what he perceived as the inherent dangers of televised trials. "In the context of a trial of intense public interest, there is certainly a strong possibility that the timid or reluctant witness, for whom a court appearance even at its traditional best is a harrowing affair, will become more timid or reluctant when he finds that he will also be appearing before a 'hidden audience' of unknown but large dimensions. There is certainly a strong possibility that the 'cocky' witness having a thirst for the limelight will become more 'cocky' under the influence of television. And who can say that the juror who is gratified by having been chosen for a front-line case, an ambitious prosecutor, a publicity-minded defense attorney, and even a conscientious judge will not stray, albeit unconsciously, from doing what 'comes naturally' into pluming themselves for a satisfactory television 'performance'?" Id., at 591. Justice Harlan faced squarely the reality that these possibilities carry "grave potentialities for distorting the integrity of the judicial process."... The "countervailing factors" alluded to by Justice Harlan were, as here, the educational and informational value to the public.

Justice Stewart, joined by Justices Black, Brennan, and White in dissent, concluded that no prejudice had been shown and that Estes' Fourteenth Amendment rights had not been violated. While expressing reservations not unlike those of Justice Harlan and those of Chief Justice Warren, the dissent expressed unwillingness to "escalate this personal view into a per se constitutional rule." Id., at 601. The four dissenters disagreed both with the per se rule embodied in the plurality opinion of Justice Clark and with the judgment of the Court that "the *circumstances of [that]* trial led to a denial of [Estes'] Fourteenth Amendment rights." Ibid. (emphasis added).

[I]t is fair to say that Justice Harlan viewed the holding as limited to the proposition that "*what was done in this case* infringed the fundamental right to a fair trial assured by the Due Process Clause of the Fourteenth Amendment," id., 587 (emphasis added). . . . Justice Harlan's opinion, upon which analysis of the constitutional holding of Estes turns, must be read as defining the scope of that holding; we conclude that Estes is not to be read as announcing a constitutional rule barring still photographic, radio, and television coverage in all cases and under all circumstances.[8]

IV

Since we are satisfied that Estes did not announce a constitutional rule that all photographic or broadcast coverage of criminal trials is inherently a denial of due process, we turn to consideration, as a matter of first impression, of the appellants' suggestion that we now promulgate such a per se rule.

A

Any criminal case that generates a great deal of publicity presents some risks that the publicity may compromise the right of the defendant to a fair trial. Trial courts must be especially vigilant to guard against any impairment of the defendant's right to a verdict based solely upon the evidence and the relevant law. Over the years, courts have developed a range of curative devices to prevent publicity about a trial from infecting jury deliberations. See, e.g., Nebraska Press Assn. v. Stuart, 427 U.S. 539, 563-565 (1976).

An absolute constitutional ban on broadcast coverage of trials cannot be justified simply because there is a danger that, in some cases, prej-

---

8. Our subsequent cases have so read Estes. In Sheppard v. Maxwell, 384 U.S. 333, 352 (1966), the Court noted Estes as an instance where the "totality of circumstances" led to a denial of due process. In Murphy v. Florida, 421 U.S. 794, 798 (1975), we described it as "a state-court conviction obtained in a trial atmosphere that had been utterly corrupted by press coverage." And, in Nebraska Press Assn. v. Stuart, 427 U.S. 539, 552 (1976), we depicted Estes as a trial lacking in due process where "the volume of trial publicity, the judge's failure to control the proceedings, and the telecast of a hearing and of the trial itself" prevented a sober search for the truth. . . .

udicial broadcast accounts of pretrial and trial events may impair the ability of jurors to decide the issue of guilt or innocence uninfluenced by extraneous matter. . . .

B

... Not unimportant to the position asserted by Florida and other states is the change in television technology since 1962, when Estes was tried. It is urged, and some empirical data are presented,[11] that many of the negative factors found in Estes — cumbersome equipment, cables, distracting lighting, numerous camera technicians — are less substantial factors today than they were at that time.

It is also significant that safeguards have been built into the experimental programs in state courts, and into the Florida program, to avoid some of the most egregious problems envisioned by the six opinions in the Estes case. Florida admonishes its courts to take special pains to protect certain witnesses — for example, children, victims of sex crimes, some informants, and even the very timid witness or party — from the glare of publicity and the tensions of being "on camera." In re Petition of Post-Newsweek Stations, Florida, Inc. 370 So. 2d, at 779.

... Inherent in electronic coverage of a trial is the risk that the very awareness by the accused of the coverage and the contemplated broadcast may adversely affect the conduct of the participants and the fairness of the trial, yet leave no evidence of how the conduct or the trial's fairness was affected. Given this danger, it is significant that Florida requires that objections of the accused to coverage be heard and considered on the record by the trial court. See, e.g., Green v. State, 377 So. 2d 193, 201 (Fla. App. 1979). In addition to providing a record for appellate review, a pretrial hearing enables a defendant to advance the basis of his objection to broadcast coverage and allows the trial court to define the steps necessary to minimize or eliminate the risks of prejudice to the accused. Experiments such as the one presented here may well

---

11. Considerable attention is devoted by the parties to experiments and surveys dealing with the impact of electronic coverage on the participants in a trial other than the defendant himself. The Florida pilot program itself was a type of study, and its results were collected in a postprogram survey of participants. While the data thus far assembled are cause for some optimism about the ability of states to minimize the problems that potentially inhere in electronic coverage of trials, even the Florida Supreme Court conceded the data were "limited," In re Petition of Post-Newsweek Stations, Florida, Inc., 370 So. 2d 764, 781 (1979), and "non-scientific," id., at 768. Still, it is noteworthy that the data now available do not support the proposition that, in every case and in all circumstances, electronic coverage creates a significant adverse effect upon the participants in trials — at least not one uniquely associated with electronic coverage as opposed to more traditional forms of coverage. Further research may change the picture. At the moment, however, there is no unimpeachable empirical support for the thesis that the presence of the electronic media, ipso facto, interferes with trial proceedings.

increase the number of appeals by adding a new basis for claims to reverse, but this is a risk Florida has chosen to take after preliminary experimentation. Here, the record does not indicate that appellants requested an evidentiary hearing to show adverse impact or injury. Nor does the record reveal anything more than generalized allegations of prejudice.

Nonetheless, it is clear that the general issue of the psychological impact of broadcast coverage upon the participants in a trial, and particularly upon the defendant, is still a subject of sharp debate — as the amici briefs of the American College of Trial Lawyers, and others of the trial bar in opposition to Florida's experiment demonstrate. These amici state the view that the concerns expressed by the concurring opinions in Estes, see Part III, supra, have been borne out by actual experience. Comprehensive empirical data are still not available — at least on some aspects of the problem....

Whatever may be the "mischievous potentialities [of broadcast coverage] for intruding upon the detached atmosphere which should always surround the judicial process," Estes v. Texas, 381 U.S., at 587, at present no one has been able to present empirical data sufficient to establish that the mere presence of the broadcast media inherently has an adverse effect on that process. See n.11, supra....

Amici members of the defense bar, see n.10, supra, vigorously contend that displaying the accused on television is in itself a denial of due process. Brief for the California State Public Defenders Association et al., as Amici Curiae 5-10. This was a source of concern to Chief Justice Warren and Justice Harlan in Estes: that coverage of select cases "singles out certain defendants and subjects them to trials under prejudicial conditions not experienced by others." 381 U.S., at 565 (Warren, C.J., concurring). Selection of which trials, or parts of trials, to broadcast will inevitably be made not by judges but by the media, and will be governed by such factors as the nature of the crime and the status and position of the accused — or of the victim; the effect may be to titillate rather than to educate and inform. The unanswered question is whether electronic coverage will bring public humiliation upon the accused with such randomness that it will evoke due process concerns by being "unusual in the same way that being struck by lightning" is "unusual." Furman v. Georgia, 408 U.S. 238, 309 (1972) (Stewart, J., concurring)....

The concurring opinion of Chief Justice Warren joined by Justices Douglas and Goldberg in Estes can fairly be read as viewing the very broadcast of some trials as potentially a form of punishment in itself — a punishment before guilt. This concern is far from trivial. But, whether coverage of a few trials will, in practice, be the equivalent of a "Yankee Stadium" setting — which Justice Harlan likened to the public pillory long abandoned as a barbaric perversion of decent justice — must also await the continuing experimentation.

D

To say that the appellants have not demonstrated that broadcast coverage is inherently a denial of due process is not to say that the appellants were in fact accorded all of the protections of due process in their trial. As noted earlier, a defendant has the right on review to show that the media's coverage of his case — printed or broadcast — compromised the ability of the jury to judge him fairly. Alternatively, a defendant might show the broadcast coverage of his particular case had an adverse impact on the trial participants sufficient to constitute a denial of due process. Neither showing was made in this case.

To demonstrate prejudice in a specific case a defendant must show something more than juror awareness that the trial is such as to attract the attention of broadcasters. Murphy v. Florida, 421 U.S. 794, 800 (1975). No doubt the very presence of a camera in the courtroom made the jurors aware that the trial was thought to be of sufficient interest to the public to warrant coverage. Jurors, forbidden to watch all broadcasts, would have had no way of knowing that only fleeting seconds of the proceeding would be reproduced. But the appellants have not attempted to show with any specificity that the presence of cameras impaired the ability of the jurors to decide the case on only the evidence before them or that their trial was affected adversely by the impact of any of the participants of the presence of cameras and the prospect of broadcast.

Although not essential to our holding, we note that at voir dire, the jurors were asked if the presence of the camera would in any way compromise their ability to consider the case. Each answered that the camera would not prevent him or her from considering the case solely on the merits. App. 8-12. The trial court instructed the jurors not to watch television accounts of the trial, id., at 13-14, and the appellants do not contend that any juror violated this instruction. The appellants have offered no evidence that any participant in this case was affected by the presence of cameras. In short, there is no showing that the trial was compromised by television coverage, as was the case in Estes. . . .

In this setting, because this Court has no supervisory authority over state courts, our review is confined to whether there is a constitutional violation. We hold that the Constitution does not prohibit a state from experimenting with the program authorized by revised Canon 3A(7).

Affirmed.

JUSTICE STEVENS took no part in the decision of this case.

[JUSTICES STEWART and WHITE concurred separately in the result but expressed the belief that Estes announced a per se prohibition and should therefore be overruled.]

NOTES

1. In a post-Chandler case, State v. Green, 395 So. 2d 532 (Fla. 1981),

the Florida Supreme Court upheld the exclusion of electronic media coverage when such would have rendered an otherwise competent defendant incompetent to stand trial. The Court found that the exclusion met the "qualitatively different" test enunciated in In re Post-Newsweek Stations, 370 So. 2d 764 (Fla. 1979): electronic media would have a substantial effect on the defendant which would be qualitatively different from the effect on members of the public in general and from the effect of other media coverage.

2. For a state-by-state summary of court rules or statutes allowing broadcast coverage of court proceedings see News Media and the Law, June-July 1981, at 45. See generally Zimmerman, Overcoming Future Shock: Estes Revisited, or a Modest Proposal for the Constitutional Protection of the News-Gathering Process, 1980 Duke L.J. 641 (1980).

NOTE — JUDICIAL RESTRICTIVE ORDERS

NEBRASKA PRESS ASSN. v. STUART
427 U.S. 539 (1976)

Mr. CHIEF JUSTICE BURGER delivered the opinion of the Court.

The respondent State District Judge entered an order restraining the petitioners from publishing or broadcasting accounts of confessions or admissions made by the accused or facts "strongly implicative" of the accused in a widely reported murder of six persons. We granted certiorari to decide whether the entry of such an order on the showing made before the state court violated the constitutional guarantee of freedom of the press.

I

[Six members of a family in a small Nebraska town were murdered, attracting widespread local, regional, and national media coverage. Three days after the crime and two days after the defendant, Erwin Charles Simants, was arrested and arraigned, the County Attorney and Simants' attorney, joined in asking the County Court for a restrictive order relating to "matters that may or may not be publicly reported or disclosed to the public" because of the likelihood that prejudicial pretrial publicity would make it difficult to impanel an impartial jury and tend to prevent a fair trial.]

The County Court granted the prosecutor's motion for a restrictive order and entered it the next day, October 22. The order prohibited everyone in attendance from "releas[ing] or authoriz[ing] the release for public dissemination in any form or manner whatsoever any testimony given or evidence adduced"; the order also required members of the press to observe the Nebraska Bar-Press Guidelines.[1] ...

The Nebraska Supreme Court ... modified the District Court's order to accommodate the defendant's right to a fair trial and the petitioners' interest in reporting pretrial events. The order as modified prohibited reporting of only three matters: (a) the existence and nature of any confessions or admissions made by the defendant to law enforcement officers; (b) any confessions or admissions made to any third parties, except members of the press; and (c) other facts "strongly implicative" of the accused. The Nebraska Supreme Court did not rely on the Nebraska Bar-Press Guidelines. ...

We granted certiorari to address the important issues raised by the District Court order as modified by the Nebraska Supreme Court, but we denied the motion to expedite review or to stay entirely the order of the State District Court pending Simants' trial. 423 U.S. 1027 (1975). We are informed by the parties that since we granted certiorari, Simants has been convicted of murder and sentenced to death. His appeal is pending in the Nebraska Supreme Court. [The Court first determined that the case was not mooted by the expiration of the restrictive order, since the controversy between the parties was "capable of repetition, yet evading review."]

V

... [P]rior restraints on speech and publication are the most serious and the least tolerable infringement on First Amendment rights. A criminal penalty or a judgment in a defamation case is subject to the whole panoply of protections afforded by deferring the impact of the judgment until all avenues of appellate review have been exhausted. Only after judgment has become final, correct or otherwise, does the law's sanction become fully operative.

A prior restraint, by contrast and by definition, has an immediate and irreversible sanction. If it can be said that a threat of criminal or civil sanctions after publication "chills" speech, prior restraint "freezes" it at least for the time. ...

The authors of the Bill of Rights did not undertake to assign priorities

---

1. These Guidelines are voluntary standards adopted by members of the state bar and news media to deal with the reporting of crimes and criminal trials. They outlined the matters of fact that may appropriately be reported, and also list what items are not generally appropriate for reporting, including: confessions, opinions on guilt or innocence, statements that would influence the outcome of a trial, the results of tests or examinations, comments on the credibility of witnesses, and evidence presented in the jury's absence. The publication of an accused's criminal record should, under the Guidelines, be "considered very carefully." The Guidelines also set out standards for taking and publishing photographs, and set up a joint bar-press committee to foster cooperation in resolving particular problems that emerge.

as between First Amendment and Sixth Amendment rights, ranking one as superior to the other. In this case, the petitioners would have us declare the right of an accused subordinate to their right to publish in all circumstances. But if the authors of these guarantees, fully aware of the potential conflicts between them, were unwilling or unable to resolve the issue by assigning to one priority over the other, it is not for us to rewrite the Constitution by undertaking what they declined to do. It is unnecessary, after nearly two centuries, to establish a priority applicable in all circumstances. Yet it is nonetheless clear that the barriers to prior restraint remain high unless we are to abandon what the Court has said for nearly a quarter of our national existence and implied throughout all of it. The history of even wartime suspension of categorical guarantees, such as habeas corpus or the right to trial by civilian courts, see Ex parte Milligan, 4 Wall. 2 (1867), cautions against suspending explicit guarantees. . . .

VI

We turn now to the record in this case to determine whether, as Learned Hand put it, "the gravity of the 'evil,' discounted by its improbability, justifies such invasion of free speech as is necessary to avoid the danger." United States v. Dennis, 183 F.2d 201, 212 (CA2 1950), aff'd, 341 U.S. 494 (1951); see also L. Hand, The Bill of Rights 58-61 (1958). To do so, we must examine the evidence before the trial judge when the order was entered to determine: (a) the nature and extent of pretrial news coverage; (b) whether other measures would be likely to mitigate the effects of unrestrained pretrial publicity; and (c) how effectively a restraining order would operate to prevent the threatened danger. The precise terms of the restraining order are also important. We must then consider whether the record supports the entry of a prior restraint on publication, one of the most extraordinary remedies known to our jurisprudence.

A

. . . Our review of the pretrial record persuades us that the trial judge was justified in concluding that there would be intense and pervasive pretrial publicity concerning this case. He could also reasonably conclude, based on common human experience, that publicity might impair the defendant's right to a fair trail. He did not purport to say more, for he found only "a clear and present danger that pre-trial publicity *could* impinge upon the defendant's right to a fair trial." (Emphasis added.) His conclusion as to the impact of such publicity on prospective jurors was of necessity speculative, dealing as he was with factors unknown and unknowable.

B

We find little in the record that goes to another aspect of our task, determining whether measures short of an order restraining all publication would have insured the defendant a fair trial. Although the entry of the order might be read as judicial determination that other measures would not suffice, the trial court made no express findings to that effect; the Nebraska Supreme Court referred to the issue only by implication. . . .

Most of the alternatives to prior restraint of publication in these circumstances were discussed with obvious approval in Sheppard v. Maxwell, 384 U.S., at 357-362: (a) change of trial venue to a place less exposed to the intense publicity that seemed imminent in Lincoln County; (b) postponement of the trial to allow public attention to subside; (c) searching questioning of prospective jurors, as Mr. Chief Justice Marshall used in the Burr case, to screen out those with fixed opinions as to guilt or innocence; (d) the use of emphatic and clear instructions on the sworn duty of each juror to decide the issues only on evidence presented in open court. Sequestration of jurors is, of course, always available. Although that measure insulates jurors only after they are sworn, it also enhances the likelihood of dissipating the impact of pretrial publicity and emphasizes the elements of the jurors' oaths. . . .

We have noted earlier that pretrial publicity, even if pervasive and concentrated, cannot be regarded as leading automatically and in every kind of criminal case to an unfair trial. The decided cases "cannot be made to stand for the proposition that juror exposure to information about a state defendant's prior convictions or to news accounts of the crime with which he is charged alone presumptively deprives the defendant of due process." Murphy v. Florida, 421 U.S., at 799. . . .

We have therefore examined this record to determine the probable efficacy of the measures short of prior restraint on the press and speech. There is no finding that alternative measures would not have protected Simants' rights, and the Nebraska Supreme Court did no more than imply that such measures might not be adequate. Moreover, the record is lacking in evidence to support such a finding.

C

We must also assess the probable efficacy of prior restraint on publication as a workable method of protecting Simants' right to a fair trial, and we cannot ignore the reality of the problems of managing and enforcing pretrial restraining orders. [The limited jurisdiction of the trial court, the difficulty in predicting what information would prejudice jurors, and the court's inability to prevent the small town residents from gossiping about the case would all undermine the effectiveness of the prior restraint.]

Given these practical problems, it is far from clear that prior restraint on publication would have protected Simants' rights.

D

[The court relied on two other features of the case to conclude that the restraining order was not supportable: (1) the order prohibiting the news media from reporting evidence introduced in an open preliminary hearing, and (2) the part of the order restricting the publication of information "implicative" of the accused's guilt was too vague and too broad to survive the scrutiny given to restraints on First Amendment rights.]

E

The record demonstrates, as the Nebraska courts held, that there was indeed a risk that pretrial news accounts, true or false, would have some adverse impact on the attitudes of those who might be called as jurors. But on the record now before us it is not clear that further publicity, unchecked, would so distort the views of potential jurors that 12 could not be found who would, under proper instructions, fulfill their sworn duty to render a just verdict exclusively on the evidence presented in open court. We cannot say on this record that alternatives to a prior restraint on petitioners would not have sufficiently mitigated the adverse effects of pretrial publicity so as to make prior restraint unnecessary. Nor can we conclude that the restraining order actually entered would serve its intended purpose. Reasonable minds can have few doubts about the gravity of the evil pretrial publicity can work, but the probability that it would do so here was not demonstrated with the degree of certainty our cases on prior restraint require.

Of necessity our holding is confined to the record before us. But our conclusion is not simply a result of assessing the adequacy of the showing made in this case; it results in part from the problems inherent in meeting the heavy burden of demonstrating, in advance of trial, that without prior restraint a fair trial will be denied.... However difficult it may be, we need not rule out the possibility of showing the kind of threat to fair trial rights that would possess the requisite degree of certainty to justify restraints. This Court has frequently denied that First Amendment rights are absolute and has consistently rejected the proposition that a prior restraint can never be employed....

Mr. JUSTICE BRENNAN, with whom Mr. JUSTICE STEWART and Mr. JUSTICE MARSHALL join, concurring in the judgment.

... The right to a fair trial by a jury of one's peers is unquestionably one of the most precious and sacred safeguards enshrined in the Bill of Rights. I would hold, however, that resort to prior restraints on the freedom of the press is a constitutionally impermissible method for enforcing that right; judges have at their disposal a broad spectrum of devices for ensuring that fundamental fairness is accorded the accused without necessitating so drastic an incursion on the equally fundamental and salutary constitutional mandate that discussion of public affairs in a free society cannot depend on the preliminary grace of judicial censors....

III

I unreservedly agree with Mr. Justice Black that "free speech and fair trials are two of the most cherished policies of our civilization, and it would be a trying task to choose between them." Bridges v. California, 314 U.S., at 260. But I would reject the notion that a choice is necessary, that there is an inherent conflict that cannot be resolved without essentially abrogating one right or the other. To hold that courts cannot impose any prior restraints on the reporting of or commentary upon information revealed in open court proceedings, disclosed in public documents, or divulged by other sources with respect to the criminal justice system is not, I must emphasize, to countenance the sacrifice of precious Sixth Amendment rights on the altar of the First Amendment. For although there may in some instances be tension between uninhibited and robust reporting by the press and fair trials for criminal defendants, judges possess adequate tools short of injunctions against reporting for relieving that tension....

There is, beyond peradventure, a clear and substantial damage to freedom of the press whenever even a temporary restraint is imposed on reporting of material concerning the operations of the criminal justice system, an institution of such pervasive influence in our constitutional scheme. And the necessary impact of reporting even confessions can never be so direct, immediate, and irreparable that I would give credence to any notion that prior restraints may be imposed on that rationale. It may be that such incriminating material would be of such slight news value or so inflammatory in particular cases that responsible organs of the media, in an exercise of self restraint, would choose not to publicize that material, and not make the judicial task of safeguarding precious rights of criminal defendants more difficult. Voluntary codes such as the Nebraska Bar-Press Guidelines are a commendable acknowledgment by the media that constitutional prerogatives bring enormous responsibilities, and I would encourage continuation of such voluntary cooperative efforts between the bar and the media. However, the press may be arrogant, tyrannical, abusive, and sensationalist, just as it may be incisive, probing, and informative. But at least in the context of prior restraints on publication, the decision of what, when, and how to publish is for editors, not judges.... Every restrictive order imposed on the press in this case was accordingly an unconstitutional prior restraint on the freedom of the press, and I would therefore reverse the judgment of the Nebraska Supreme Court and remand for further proceedings not inconsistent with this opinion.

[In his concurrence, Justice White expressed doubts that prior restraints of press trial coverage are ever justifiable. He declined to announce such a rule in this case, however, preferring to wait until "the federal courts and ourselves have been exposed to a broader spectrum of cases presenting similar issues."

[Justice Powell also concurred and announced his criteria for imposing prior restraints to preserve a defendant's right to a fair trial. There must be a showing that: (1) a clear threat to a fair trial is posed by the actual publicity to be restrained, (2) no less restrictive alternatives are available, and (3) previous publicity or publicity from unrestrained sources will not render the restraint inefficacious.

[Justice Stevens, in his concurrence, agreed with Brennan's reasoning but refused to commit himself to absolute protection against prior restraints "no matter how shabby or illegal the means by which the information was obtained, no matter how serious an intrusion on privacy might be involved...." However, Stevens indicated that, if ever required to face the issue squarely, he may well accept Brennan's ultimate conclusion.]

NOTE

See Symposium, Nebraska Press Association v. Stuart, 29 Stan. L. Rev. 383 (1977). See generally Rendleman, Free Press — Fair Trial: Restrictive Orders After Nebraska Press, 67 Ky. L.J. 867 (1979).

RICHMOND NEWSPAPERS, INC. v. VIRGINIA
448 U.S. 555 (1980)

Mr. CHIEF JUSTICE BURGER announced the judgment of the Court and delivered an opinion, in which Mr. JUSTICE WHITE and Mr. JUSTICE STEVENS joined....

II

We begin consideration of this case by noting that the precise issue presented here has not previously been before this Court for decision. In Gannett Co. v. DePasquale, supra, the Court was not required to decide whether a right of access to *trials*, as distingushed from hearings on *pre*trial motions, was constitutionally guaranteed. The Court held that the Sixth Amendment's guarantee to the accused of a public trial gave neither the public nor the press an enforceable right of access to a *pre*trial suppression hearing. One concurring opinion specifically emphasized that "a hearing on a motion before trial to suppress evidence is not a *trial*. . . ." 443 U.S., at 394 (Burger, C.J., concurring). Moreover, the Court did not decide whether the First and Fourteenth Amendments guarantee a right of the public to attend trials, id., at 392, and n.24; nor did the dissenting opinion reach this issue. Id., at 447 (opinion of Blackmun, J.).

. . . [H]ere for the first time the Court is asked to decide whether a criminal trial itself may be closed to the public upon the unopposed request of a defendant, without any demonstration that closure is required to protect the defendant's superior right to a fair trial, or that some other overriding consideration requires closure.

A

The origins of the proceeding which has become the modern criminal trial in Anglo-American justice can be traced back beyond reliable historical records. We need not here review all details of its development, but a summary of that history is instructive. What is significant for present purposes is that throughout its evolution, the trial has been open to all who cared to observe. . . .

C

From this unbroken, uncontradicted history, supported by reasons as valid today as in centuries past, we are bound to conclude that a presumption of openness inheres in the very nature of a criminal trial under our system of justice. . . .

Despite the history of criminal trials being presumptively open since long before the Constitution, the State presses its contention that neither the Constitution nor the Bill of Rights contains any provision which by its terms guarantees to the public the right to attend criminal trials. Standing alone, this is correct, but there remains the question whether, absent an explicit provision, the Constitution affords protection against exclusion of the public from criminal trials.

III

A

The First Amendment, in conjunction with the Fourteenth, prohibits governments from "abridging the freedom of speech, or of the press; or the right of the people peaceably to assemble, and to petition the Government for a redress of grievances." These expressly guaranteed freedoms share a common core purpose of assuring freedom of communication on matters relating to the functioning of government. Plainly it would be difficult to single out any aspect of government of higher concern and importance to the people than the manner in which criminal trials are conducted; as we have shown, recognition of this pervades the centuries-old history of open trials and the opinions of this Court.

... The explicit, guaranteed rights to speak and to publish concerning what takes place at a trial would lose much meaning if access to observe the trial could, as it was here, be foreclosed arbitrarily.[12]

B

The right of access to places traditionally open to the public, as criminal trials have long been, may be seen as assured by the amalgam of the First Amendment guarantees of speech and press; and their affinity to the right of assembly is not without relevance. From the outset, the right of assembly was regarded not only as an independent right but also as a catalyst to augment the free exercise of the other First Amendment rights with which it was deliberately linked by the draftsmen. ... [A] trial courtroom also is a public place where the people generally — and representatives of the media — have a right to be present, and where their presence historically has been thought to enhance the integrity and quality of what takes place.

C

The State argues that the Constitution nowhere spells out a guarantee for the right of the public to attend trials, and that accordingly no such right is protected. ...

But arguments such as the State makes have not precluded recognition of important rights not enumerated. Notwithstanding the appropriate caution against reading into the Constitution rights not explicitly defined, the Court has acknowledged that certain unarticulated rights are implicit in enumerated guarantees. For example, the rights of association and of privacy, the right to be presumed innocent and the right to be judged by a standard of proof beyond a reasonable doubt in a criminal trial, as well as the right to travel, appear nowhere in the Constitution or Bill of Rights. Yet these important but unarticulated rights have nonetheless been found to share constitutional protection in common with explicit guarantees. The concerns expressed by Madison and others have thus been resolved; fundamental rights, even though not expressly guaranteed, have been recognized by the Court as indispensable to the enjoyment of rights explicitly defined.

12. That the right to attend may be exercised by people less frequently today when information as to trials generally reaches them by way of print and electronic media in no way alters the basic right. Instead of relying on personal observation or reports from neighbors as in the past, most people receive information concerning trials through the media whose representatives "are entitled to the same rights [to attend trials] as the general public." Estes v. Texas, supra, at 540.

We hold that the right to attend criminal trials[17] is implicit in the guarantees of the First Amendment; without the freedom to attend such trials, which people have exercised for centuries, important aspects of freedom of speech and "of the press could be eviscerated." Branzburg supra, at 681.

D

Having concluded there was a guaranteed right of the public under the First and Fourteenth Amendments to attend the trial of Stevenson's case, we return to the closure order challenged by appellants. The Court in Gannett, supra, made clear that although the Sixth Amendment guarantees the accused a right to a public trial, it does not give a right to a private trial. 443 U.S., at 382. Despite the fact that this was the fourth trial of the accused, the trial judge made no findings to support closure; no inquiry was made as to whether alternative solutions would have met the need to ensure fairness; there was no recognition of any right under the Constitution for the public or press to attend the trial. In contrast to the pretrial proceeding dealt with in Gannett, supra, there exist in the context of the trial itself various tested alternatives to satisfy the constitutional demands of fairness. See, e.g., Nebraska Press Association v. Stuart, 427 U.S., at 563-565; Sheppard v. Maxwell, 384 U.S., at 357-362. There was no suggestion that any problems with witnesses could not have been dealt with by their exclusion from the courtroom or their sequestration during the trial. See Sheppard v. Maxwell, 384 U.S., at 359. Nor is there anything to indicate that sequestration of the jurors would not have guarded against their being subjected to any improper information. All of the alternatives admittedly present difficulties for trial courts, but none of the factors relied on here was beyond the realm of the manageable. Absent an overriding interest articulated in findings, the trial of a criminal case must be open to the public.[18] Accordingly, the judgment under review is

17. Whether the public has a right to attend trials of civil cases is a question not raised by this case, but we note that historically both civil and criminal trials have been presumptively open.

18. We have no occasion here to define the circumstances in which all or parts of a criminal trial may be closed to the public, cf., e.g., 6 J. Wigmore, Evidence §1835 (Chadbourn rev. 1976), but our holding today does not mean that the First Amendment rights of the public and representatives of the press are absolute. Just as a government may impose reasonable time, place, and manner restrictions upon the use of its streets in the interest of such objectives as the free flow of traffic, see, e.g., Cox v. New Hampshire, 312 U.S. 569 (1941), so may a trial judge, in the interest of the fair administration of justice, impose reasonable limitations on access to a trial. "[T]he question in a particular case is whether that control is exerted so as not to deny or unwarrantedly abridge... the opportunities for the communication of thought and the discussion of public questions immemorially associated with resort to public places." Id., at 574.

Reversed.

Mr. JUSTICE POWELL took no part in the consideration or decision of this case.

[JUSTICES WHITE and STEVENS concurred separately.]

[Mr. JUSTICE BRENNAN, with whom Mr. JUSTICE MARSHALL joined, concurred in the judgment but would have held the statute itself unconstitutional. He argued that agreement of the trial judge and parties cannot alone close a trial to the public and that the statute conferred unfettered discretion on the trial judge.]

Mr. JUSTICE BLACKMUN, concurring in the judgment.

My opinion and vote in partial dissent last Term in Gannett Co. v. DePasquale, 443 U.S. 368, 406 (1979), compels my vote to reverse the judgment of the Supreme Court of Virginia. . . .

II

The Court's ultimate ruling in Gannett, with such clarification as is provided by the opinions in this case today, apparently is now to the effect that there is no *Sixth* Amendment right on the part of the public — or the press — to an open hearing on a motion to suppress. I, of course, continue to believe that Gannett was in error, both in its interpretation of the Sixth Amendment generally, and in its application to the suppression hearing, for I remain convinced that the right to a public trial is to be found where the Constitution explicitly placed it — in the Sixth Amendment.

The Court, however, has eschewed the Sixth Amendment route. The plurality turns to other possible constitutional sources and invokes a veritable potpourri of them — the speech clause of the First Amendment, the press clause, the assembly clause, the Ninth Amendment, and a cluster of penumbral guarantees recognized in past decisions. . . .

Having said all this, and with the Sixth Amendment set to one side in this case, I am driven to conclude, as a secondary position, that the First Amendment must provide some measure of protection for public access to the trial. The opinion in partial dissent in Gannett explained that the public has an intense need and a deserved right to know about the administration of justice in general; about the prosecution of local crimes in particular; about the conduct of the judge, the prosecutor, defense counsel, police officers, other public servants, and all the actors in the judicial arena; and about the trial itself. See 443 U.S., at 413, and n.2, 414, 428-429, 448. See also Cox Broadcasting Corp. v. Cohn, 420 U.S. 469, 492 (1975). It is clear and obvious to me, on the approach the Court has chosen to take, that, by closing this criminal trial, the trial judge abridged these First Amendment interests of the public.

I also would reverse, and I join the judgment of the Court.

Mr. JUSTICE REHNQUIST, dissenting.

... For the reasons stated in my separate concurrence in Gannett Co., Inc. v. DePasquale, 443 U.S. 368, 403 (1979), I do not believe that either the First or Sixth Amendments, as made applicable to the States by the Fourteenth, require that a State's reasons for denying public access to a trial, where both the prosecuting attorney and the defendant have consented to an order of closure approved by the judge, are subject to any additional constitutional review at our hands. And I most certainly do not believe that the Ninth Amendment confers upon us any such power to review orders of state trial judges closing trials in such situations. ...

NOTE

For an early commentary on the Richmond case, see Richmond Newspapers, Inc. v. Virginia: A Demarcation of Access, 34 U. Miami L. Rev. 936 (1980).

In Globe Newspaper Co. v. Superior Court, 50 U.S.L.W. 4759 (1982), the Supreme Court invalidated a Massachusetts statute requiring the closure of sexual assault trials during testimony of complainants who are minors. The Court held the statute violated the First Amendment, which requires that any such restriction on access to criminal trials be necessitated by a compelling state interest and narrowly tailored to serve that interest.

(page 335) [506]

NOTES

8. [continued] In Smith v. Daily Mail Publishing Co., 443 U.S. 97 (1979), the Supreme Court held that the state cannot, consistent with the First and Fourteenth Amendments, punish the truthful publication of an alleged juvenile delinquent's name lawfully obtained by a newspaper. Only a "state interest of the highest order" can justify such punishment of truthful information in the public domain and the state's interest in protecting the anonymity of juvenile offenders does not rise to that level. Moreover, the statute, which applies only to newspapers and not to the electronic media, does not accomplish its stated purposes. Finally, there is no evidence to demonstrate that the imposition of criminal penalties is necessary to protect the confidentiality of juvenile proceedings. Justice Rehnquist concurred in the judgment on the ground that "[i]t is difficult to take very seriously West Virginia's asserted need to protect the anonymity of its youthful offenders when it permits other, equally, if not more, effective means of mass communication to distribute this information without fear of punishment."

In Oklahoma Publishing Co. v. District Court, 430 U.S. 308 (1977), the Court unanimously and summarily set aside a state court pretrial order enjoining members of the news media from publishing the name or picture of a juvenile involved in a pending delinquent proceeding. The reporters had obtained the information at an earlier detention hearing which could have been closed under state law, but had not been. See also Dobbert v. State of Florida, 328 So. 2d 433 (Fla. 1976), aff'd, 432 U.S. 982 (1977).

8. [continued] In Gannett Co., Inc. v. DePasquale, 443 U.S. 368 (1979), the Supreme Court held that neither the press nor the general public has an independent constitutional right of access to a pre-trial suppression hearing when the accused, the prosecutor, and the trial judge all have agreed to the closure of that proceeding in order to assure a fair trial. Justice Stewart, writing for the five-judge majority, found that the Sixth Amendment guarantee of a public trial is for the benefit of the defendant alone; the public interest in public trials is fully protected by the participants in the litigation. The majority noted that historically pretrial proceedings, because of a concern for a fair trial, were never characterized by the same degree of openness as actual trials. Moreover, even if the Sixth and Fourteenth Amendments may guarantee a right of public access, this putative right was given all appropriate deference by the state court. Although the petitioner's reporter did not object when defendants made the closure motion, the newspaper was given an opportunity to be heard. The court concluded that the defendant's right to a fair trial outweighed the "constitutional rights of the press and the public." Moreover, the denial of press access was only temporary; once the danger of prejudice had dissipated, a transcript of the suppression hearing was made available to the press. Justice Blackmun, joined by Justices Brennan, Marshall, and White, dissented on the grounds that the Sixth Amendment establishes public and press right of access to a pretrial proceeding.

For discussion and summary of gag orders issued in the wake of Gannett, see, New Media and the Law, June-July, 1981, at 52; Public Access to Pretrial Criminal Hearings: The Use of Closure Orders After Gannett v. DePasquale, 44 Albany L. Rev. 455 (1980).

See In re United States ex rel. Pulitzer Pub. Co., 635 F.2d 676 (8th Cir. 1980) (in-chambers voir dire of jurors inappropriate in light of Richmond v. Virginia); United States v. Powers, 622 F.2d 317 (8th Cir.), cert. denied, 449 U.S. 837 (1980) (upheld refusal to exclude public from trial in absence of prosecutorial consent, or evidence of physical danger for which closure was the only effective protection); United States v. Hernandez, 608 F.2d 741 (9th Cir. 1979) (upheld exclusion of public from courtroom during testimony of informant and during evidentiary hearing to protect witness from physical danger); United States v. Civella, 493 F. Supp. 786 (W.D. Mo. 1980) (no closure of pre-trial hearings to news media as no proof that alternatives were inadequate, or of risk of prejudicial publicity); State in Interest of Dino, 359 So. 2d 586 (La. 1978), cert. denied, 439 U.S. 1047 (1978) (striking down statute providing for private juvenile proceedings in so far as it prohibits the juvenile from electing public trial in proceeding based on criminal charges which would entitle an adult accused to have his trial conducted in public); Brian W. v. Superior Court, 20 Cal. 3d 618, 574 P.2d 788, 143 Cal. Rptr. 717 (1978) (when past media coverage relating to a case has been neither excessive nor sensational and the jury pool in the jurisdiction is large, trial court did not err in refusing to bar press representatives from a juvenile fitness hearing; adequate safeguards are available, should they be necessary, to protect the defendant's rights if he is certified to adult court).

(page 335) [507]

NOTES

9. [continued] In Gulf Oil v. Bernard, 49 U.S.L.W. 4604 (1981), the Supreme Court upheld the Fifth Circuit decision setting aside an order prohibiting the parties and their counsel from communicating with potential class members without court approval. The Court found that the district court had abused its discretion in failing to weigh competing factors before issuing the gag order.

For recent circuit court decisions invalidating broad gag orders restricting comment by lawyers or parties see, e.g., Williams v. United States District Court, 658 F.2d 430 (6th Cir.), cert. denied, 50 U.S.L.W. 3487 (1981) (local district court rule prohibiting communications between party or his attorney and potential class members without prior court approval); Chicago Council of Lawyers v. Bauer, 522 F.2d 242 (7th Cir. 1975), cert. denied, 427 U.S. 912 (1976) (federal district court rules for criminal cases and ABA canon for civil cases that ban commentary by counsel that is reasonably likely to interfere with fair trial); CBS, Inc. v. Young, 522 F.2d 234 (6th Cir. 1975) (per curiam) (restrictive order in civil case dealing with Kent State killings, which prohibited discussion by parties, "relatives, close friends, and associates" with the press).

In United States v. Sherman, 581 F.2d 1358 (9th Cir. 1978), the court overturned the trial judge's order restricting everyone, including the media, from speaking to the jury which had convicted two members of the George Jackson Brigade, a revolutionary organizaton, of bank robbery. The court of appeals found that enabling them to serve on future panels and protecting them from harrassment could not justify the potential First Amendment infringements made by the post-verdict order.

See also, Note, Gag Orders on Criminal Defendants, 27 Hastings L.J.

1369 (1976) (author argues that no legal justification exists to limit defendant's First Amendment right to speak freely; furthermore, even if a justification is established, current procedural and substantive standards are inadequate).

(page 336) [507]

NOTES

11. [continued] In Mazzetti v. United States, 518 F.2d 781 (10th Cir. 1975), the court upheld a contempt conviction of a photographer for taking pictures of federal prisoners in prohibited areas of a courthouse and environs. The court held that the rule was not overbroad nor an improper restraint of First Amendment rights. Rather, because the journalist's activity purportedly presented an immediate threat to the judicial process, the rule was deemed a reasonable effectuation of the due process guarantee of fair trial.

(page 337) [508]

NOTES

13. [14.] In Nixon v. Warner Communications, Inc. 435 U.S. 589 (1978), the Supreme Court upheld the refusal to grant television networks access to the Nixon tapes. The Court found that the lower court had the responsibility to exercise an informed discretion as to release of the tapes, with sensitive appreciation of the circumstances that had led to their production, and such responsibility did not permit copying upon demand. Moreover, Congress had through the Presidential Recordings Act created an administrative procedure for processing and releasing the President's materials, including the tapes, to the public. Finally, the Court found that the common law right of access to judicial records, the First Amendment free press guarantee, and the Sixth Amendment public trial guarantee did not provide the press with a right of access to the tape recordings.

In two recent ABSCAM cases, courts of appeals have allowed the release for network broadcasting of videotapes admitted into evidence. The Second Circuit, in United States v. Myers, 635 F.2d 945 (2d Cir. 1980), upheld the district court's release of the tapes, reasoning that even though the prosecution was still in progress and jurors had not yet been selected to try related indictments of the defendants, the possibility of impinging on a fair trial was speculative and could be prevented by other, less restrictive means. The Third Circuit, in United States v. Criden, 648 F.2d 814 (3d Cir. 1981), reversed the district court's denial of network access, arguing that the strong presumption of release, founded on serving public awareness and "catharsis," was not rebutted by fears that rebroadcast publicity would jeopardize a fair trial and serve as enhanced punishment.

Compare In re Application of KSTP Television, 504 F. Supp. 360 (D. Minn. 1980) (distinguished Nixon and Myers in that videotapes made by kidnapper of the abduction and rape of the victim would serve no public interest and would impinge on the privacy of the victim).

(page 337) [509]

[REFERENCES]

[7.] See generally Apfel, Gag Orders, Exlusionary Orders, and Protective Orders: Expanding the Use of Preventive Remedies to Safeguard a Criminal Defendant's Right to a Fair Trial, 29 Am. U.L. Rev. 439 (1980); Note, Trial Secrecy and the First Amendment Right of Public Access to Judicial Proceedings, 91 Harv. L. Rev. 1899 (1978): Project, Law and the Media (Free Press – Fair Trial), 20 St. Louis U.L.J. 610, 640-642 (1976); Note, Gag Order Protection for Civil Trials, 64 Geo. L.J. 967 (1976); Comment, Gagging the Press in Criminal Trials, 10 Harv. C.R.-C.L.L. Rev. 608 (1975) (author attempts to provide framework for issuance of gag order and proposes a balancing test which gives latitude to press and demands that danger of prejudice be imminent, that gag order be narrowly drawn and that due process protections be strictly enforced).

(page 338) [510]

NOTE

2. [continued] Watergate principals Haldeman, Ehrlichman, and Mitchell lost their combined appeal to have their convictions overturned. United States v. Haldeman, 559 F.2d 31 (D.C. Cir. 1977) (en banc), cert. denied, 431 U.S. 933 (1977) (Watergate publicity held not so prejudicial as to require venue change before impaneling jury; a presumption of prejudice was inapplicable). See generally Note, Prejudicial Publicity in Trials of Public Officials, 85 Yale L.J. 123 (1975).

Chapter Six
Obscenity and "Offensive" Speech

A. OBSCENITY

(page 356) [528]

NOTES

4. [end of first paragraph continued] Pandering instructions were again approved in Splawn v. California, 431 U.S. 595 (1977), and United States v. Pinkus, 436 U.S. 293 (1978). The Court in Splawn cited Ginzburg and Hamling for the proposition that "as a matter of First Amendment obscenity law, evidence of pandering to prurient interests in the creation, promotion or dissemination of material is relevant in determining whether the material is obscene." For a recent court of appeals decision approving pandering instructions, see United States v. Dost, 575 F.2d 1303 (10th Cir. 1978).

(page 357) [529]

NOTES

5. [continued] For an application of the narrower form of the Mishkin holding see, e.g., Lakin v. United States, 363 A.2d 990 (D.C. App. 1976).

In Ward v. Illinois, 431 U.S. 767 (1977), the Court applied Mishkin to affirm a holding of obscenity with regard to sado-masochistic materials, even though such materials were not among the examples given in Miller v. California of the kinds of patently offensive sexually explicit representations that may be prohibited as obscene. The Miller examples " 'were not intended to be exhaustive.' . . . If the Mishkin publications remain unprotected, surely those before us today deal with a category of sexual conduct which, if obscenely described, may be proscribed by state law." See also Pinkus v. United States, 436 U.S. 293 (1978), which repeats the broader view of the Mishkin rule reflected in Hamling.

(page 359) [531]

NOTES

9. [continued] Recent cases involving challenges to obscenity statutes on vagueness grounds include Louisiana v. Wrestle, Inc., 360 So. 2d 831 (La. 1978) (statute upheld) and Wisconsin v. Princess Cinema, 292 N.W.2d 807 (Wisc. 1980) (statute held facially vague and overbroad).

(page 363) [535]

NOTES

15. [insert in first paragraph after LaRue] See also Richter v. Dept. of Alcoholic Beverage Control, 559 F.2d 1168 (9th Cir. 1977).

[end of first paragraph continued] The decision in Salem Inn v. Frank was affirmed on both grounds. 522 F.2d 1045 (2d Cir. 1975). Because the ordinance did not limit itself to establishments serving liquor, it was not valid under the Twenty-first Amendment. The court held that topless dancing involves a "modicum of expression" and the ordinance was thus subject to strict scrutiny.

[insert after last paragraph] In New York State Liquor Authority v. Bellanca, 101 S. Ct. 2599 (1981), the Court relied on Doran and LaRue to uphold a statute prohibiting topless dancing in an establishment licensed by the State to serve liquor. The Court's per curiam opinion stated that "[w]hatever artistic or communicative value may attach to topless dancing is overcome by the State's exercise of its broad powers arising under the Twenty-first Amendment." Justice Stevens dissented. However, in Schad v. Borough of Mount Ephraim, 101 S. Ct. 2176 (1981), the Court struck down a zoning ordinance that prohibited live entertainment, including nude dancing. Noting that the ordinance prohibited "a wide range of expression that has long been held to be within the protections of the First and Fourteenth Amendment[s]," Justice White's opinion for the Court held that the borough had "not adequately justified its substantial restriction of protected activity." Neither the borough's asserted plan to create a commercial area catering only to the immediate needs of its residents nor its attempt to avoid problems such as parking that may be associated with live entertainment withstood scrutiny. Moreover, the ordinance could not be upheld as a "time, place and manner restriction," since no alternative channels of communication were available within the borough. Justice Stevens concurred; Chief Justice Burger and Justice Rehnquist dissented.

(page 395) [567]

NOTE

3.(a) [continued]

In Ward v. Illinois, 431 U.S. 767 (1977), the Supreme Court upheld a pre-Miller state conviction (affirmed by the state appellate courts after Miller) under an Illinois statute that defined a thing as obscene if "its predominant appeal is to prurient interest, that is a shameful or morbid interest in nudity, sex or excretion, and if it goes substantially beyond customary limits of candor in description or representation of such matters." The prosecution involved sado-masochistic materials. Justice White's opinion for the Court held "wholly without merit" the claim that the state had failed to comply with the Miller requirement that patently offensive sexual depictions be specifically defined by state law. Rather the Court held that the Illinois Supreme Court had complied with Miller in 1974 by construing its statute to incorporate part (b) of the Miller guidelines. There was "no reason to doubt" that the Illinois court thus meant to "adopt the Miller examples, which gave substantive meaning to part (b) by indicating the kinds of materials within its reach." The state court had thus done "surely as much as this Court did in its post-Miller constructions of federal obscenity statutes." And "even if this were not the case," appellant had "ample guidance from the Illinois Supreme Court that his conduct did not conform to Illinois law" since sado-masochistic materials similar to those involved in Ward had been held to violate the Illinois statute prior to the sale for which Ward was prosecuted.

Justice Stevens, joined by Justices Brennan, Stewart, and Marshall, dissented: "Today, the Court silently abandons one of the cornerstones of the Miller test announced so forcefully just five years ago." Although the Illinois Supreme Court had made clear that its statute covered all the Miller examples, it had not made clear that its statute was limited to those examples, or to any other specifically defined category. "One of the strongest arguments against regulating obscenity through criminal law is the inherent vagueness of the obscenity concept. The specificity requirement as described in Miller held out the promise of a principled effort to respond to that argument. By abandoning that effort today, the Court withdraws the cornerstone of the Miller structure and, undoubtedly, hastens its ultimate downfall."

3(b). [continued]

In Marks v. United States, 430 U.S. 188 (1977), the Supreme Court reversed and remanded the conviction in United States v. Marks, noted in the main volume. Petitioner in Marks had been convicted, after Miller, for pre-Miller conduct. The district court instructed the jury under the

Miller standards. After holding that the plurality opinion in Memoirs v. Massachusetts provided the "governing standards" of obscenity prior to Miller, and that Miller's "serious literary, artistic, political, or scientific value" test "expanded criminal liability" as compared with the Memoirs plurality's "utterly without redeeming social value" test, Justice Powell's opinion for the Court concluded "that the Due Process Clause precludes the application to petitioners of the standards announced in Miller ... to the extent that those standards may impose criminal liability for conduct not punishable under Memoirs. Specifically ... petitioners ... are entitled to jury instructions requiring the jury to acquit unless it finds that the materials are 'utterly without redeeming social value.' At the same time we reaffirm our holding in Hamling v. United States, 418 U.S. at 102, that 'any constitutional principle enunciated in Miller which would serve to benefit petitioners must be applied in their case.'" The Court rejected the suggestion that the court of appeals' conclusion on appeal that the materials were obscene under both Memoirs and Miller could save the conviction. The court of appeals' determination was "not an adequate substitute for the decision in the first instance of a properly instructed jury, as to this important element of the offense."

Justices Brennan, Stewart, and Marshall agreed with the Court's holding as to retro-activity, but dissented from the remand for a new trial in light of their view that general obscenity statutes are constitutionally overbroad. Justice Stevens also dissented from the remand: "There are three reasons which, in combination, persuade me that this criminal prosecution is constitutionally impermissible. First ... [h]owever distasteful these materials are to some of us, they are nevertheless a form of communication and entertainment acceptable to a substantial segment of society.... Second, the statute is predicated on the somewhat illogical premise that a person may be prosecuted criminally for providing another with material he has a constitutional right to possess. See Stanley v. Georgia, 394 U.S. 557. Third, the present constitutional standards ... are so intolerably vague that evenhanded enforcement of the law is a virtual impossibility."

(page 396) [568]

7. For an interesting example of statutory interpretation under Miller, see Colorado v. New Horizons, 616 P.2d 106 (Colo. 1980) (obscenity statute excluding printed or written matter invalidated as precluding satisfaction of the "taken as a whole" standard).

(page 397) [569]

Insert at end of Note on Variable Obscenity:

YOUNG v. AMERICAN MINI THEATRES, INC.
427 U.S. 50, 96 S. Ct. 2440, 49 L. Ed. 2d 310 (1976)

Mr. JUSTICE STEVENS delivered the opinion of the Court.*

Zoning ordinances adopted by the city of Detroit differentiate between motion picture theaters which exhibit sexually explicit "adult" movies and those which do not. The principal question presented by this case is whether that statutory classification is unconstitutional because it is based on the content of communication protected by the First Amendment.

Effective November 2, 1972, Detroit adopted the ordinances challenged in this litigation. Instead of concentrating "adult" theaters in limited zones, these ordinances require that such theaters be dispersed. Specifically, an adult theater may not be located within 1,000 feet of any two other "regulated uses" or within 500 feet of a residential area. The term "regulated uses" includes 10 different kinds of establishments [e.g., adult bookstores, bars, and hotels] in addition to adult theaters.

The classification of a theater as "adult" is expressly predicated on the character of the motion pictures which it exhibits. If the theater is used to present "material distinguished or characterized by an emphasis on matter depicting, describing or relating to 'Specified Sexual Activities' or 'Specified Anatomical Areas,' " it is an adult establishment.

The 1972 ordinances were amendments to an "Anti-Skid Row Ordinance" which had been adopted 10 years earlier. At that time the Detroit Common Council made a finding that some uses of property are especially injurious to a neighborhood when they are concentrated in limited areas. The decision to add adult motion picture theaters and adult book stores to the list of businesses which, apart from a special waiver, could not be located within 1,000 feet of two other "regulated uses," was, in part, a response to the significant growth in the number of such establishments. In the opinion of urban planners and real estate experts who supported the ordinances, the location of several such businesses in the same neighborhood tends to attract an undesirable quantity and quality of transients, adversely affects property values, causes an increase in crime, especially prostitution, and encourages residents and businesses to move elsewhere.

Respondents are the operators of two adult motion picture theaters. One, the Nortown, was an established theater which began to exhibit adult films in March 1973. The other, the Pussy Cat, was a corner gas station which was converted into a "mini theater," but denied a certificate of occupancy because of its plan to exhibit adult films. Both theaters

---

*Part III of this opinion is joined by only The Chief Justice, Mr. Justice White, and Mr. Justice Rehnquist.

were located within 1,000 feet of two other regulated uses and the Pussy Cat was less than 500 feet from a residential area. The respondents brought two separate actions against appropriate city officials, seeking a declaratory judgment that the ordinances were unconstitutional and an injunction against their enforcement. . . .

The District Court granted defendants' motion for summary judgment [373 F. Supp. 363]. . . .

The Court of Appeals reversed. American Mini Theatres, Inc. v. Gribbs, 518 F.2d 1014 (CA6 1975). . . .

II

. . . The ordinances are not challenged on the ground that they impose a limit on the total number of adult theaters which may operate in the city of Detroit. There is no claim that distributors or exhibitors of adult films are denied access to the market or, conversely, that the viewing public is unable to satisfy its appetite for sexually explicit fare. Viewed as an entity, the market for this commodity is essentially unrestrained.

It is true, however, that adult films may only be exhibited commercially in licensed theaters. But that is also true of all motion pictures. . . . The mere fact that the commercial exploitation of material protected by the First Amendment is subject to zoning and other licensing requirements is not a sufficient reason for invalidating these ordinances.

Putting to one side for the moment the fact that adult motion picture theaters must satisfy a locational restriction not applicable to other theaters, we are also persuaded that the 1,000-foot restriction does not, in itself, create an impermissible restraint on protected communication. The city's interest in planning and regulating the use of property for commercial purposes is clearly adequate to support that kind of restriction applicable to all theaters within the city limits. In short, apart from the fact that the ordinances treat adult theaters differently from other theaters and the fact that the classification is predicated on the content of material shown in the respective theaters, the regulation of the place where such films may be exhibited does not offend the First Amendment.[18] . . .

III[a]

A remark attributed to Voltaire characterizes our zealous adherence to the principle that the government may not tell the citizen what he

18. Reasonable regulations of the time, place, and manner of protected speech, where those regulations are necessary to further significant governmental interests, are permitted by the First Amendment. . . .

a. This part of the Young opinion was joined in by only four Justices. See n.* at the beginning of Justice Stevens' opinion.

may or may not say. Referring to a suggestion that the violent overthrow of tyranny might be legitimate, he said: "I disapprove of what you say, but I will defend to the death your right to say it." The essence of that comment has been repeated time after time in our decisions invalidating attempts by the government to impose selective controls upon the dissemination of ideas. . . . As we said in [Police Dept. of Chicago v.] Mosley [, 408 U.S. 92, at 95-96]:

". . . [A]bove all else, the First Amendment means that government has no power to restrict expression because of its message, its ideas, its subject matter, or its content. . . ."

This statement, and others to the same effect, read literally and without regard for the facts of the case in which it was made, would absolutely preclude any regulation of expressive activity predicated in whole or in part on the content of the communication. But we learned long ago that broad statements of principle, no matter how correct in the context in which they are made, are sometimes qualified by contrary decisions before the absolute limit of the stated principle is reached. . . .

The question whether speech is, or is not, protected by the First Amendment often depends on the content of the speech. Thus, the line between permissible advocacy and impermissible incitation to the crime or violence depends, not merely on the setting in which the speech occurs, but also on exactly what the speaker had to say. . . .

Even within the area of protected speech, a difference in content may require a different governmental response. In New York Times Co. v. Sullivan, 376 U.S. 254, we recognized that the First Amendment places limitations on the States' power to enforce their libel laws. . . .

We have recently held that the First Amendment affords some protection to commercial speech. We have also made it clear, however, that the content of a particular advertisement may determine the extent of its protection. . . .

More directly in point are opinions dealing with the question whether the First Amendment prohibits the State and Federal Governments from wholly suppressing sexually oriented materials on the basis of their "obscene character." . . .

Such a line may be drawn on the basis of content without violating the government's paramount obligation of neutrality in its regulation of protected communication. For the regulation of the places where sexually explicit films may be exhibited is unaffected by whatever social, political, or philosophical message a film may be intended to communicate; whether a motion picture ridicules or characterizes one point of view or another, the effect of the ordinances is exactly the same.

Moreover, even though we recognize that the First Amendment will not tolerate the total suppression of erotic materials that have some arguably artistic value, it is manifest that society's interest in protecting this type of expression is of a wholly different, and lesser, magnitude than the interest in untrammeled political debate that inspired Voltaire's immortal comment. Whether political oratory or philosophical discussion moves us to applaud or to despise what is said, every schoolchild can understand why our duty to defend the right to speak remains the same. But few of us would march our sons and daughters off to war to preserve the citizen's right to see "Specified Sexual Activities" exhibited in the theaters of our choice. Even though the First Amendment protects communication in this area from total suppression, we hold that the State may legitimately use the content of these materials as the basis for placing them in a different classification from other motion pictures.

The remaining question is whether the line drawn by these ordinances is justified by the city's interest in preserving the character of its neighborhoods.... The record discloses a factual basis for the Common Council's conclusion that this kind of restriction will have the desired effect.[34] It is not our function to appraise the wisdom of its decision to require adult theaters to be separated rather than concentrated in the same areas. In either event, the city's interest in attempting to preserve the quality of urban life is one that must be accorded high respect. Moreover, the city must be allowed a reasonable opportunity to experiment with solutions to admittedly serious problems.

Since what is ultimately at stake is nothing more than a limitation on the place where adult films may be exhibited,[35] even though the determination of whether a particular film fits that characterization turns on the nature of its content, we conclude that the city's interest in the present and future character of its neighborhoods adequately supports its classification of motion pictures....

Mr. JUSTICE POWELL, concurring.

Although I agree with much of what is said in the Court's opinion, and concur in Parts I and II, my approach to the resolution of this case is sufficiently different to prompt me to write separately. I view the case as presenting an example of innovative land-use regulation, implicating First Amendment concerns only incidentally and to a limited extent....

34. The City Council's determination was that a concentration of "adult movie theaters causes the area to deteriorate and become a focus of crime, effects which are not attributable to theaters showing other types of films. It is this secondary effect which these zoning ordinances attempt to avoid, not the dissemination of "offensive" speech. In contrast, in Erznoznik v. City of Jacksonville, 422 U.S. 205, the justifications offered by the city rested primarily on the city's interest in protecting its citizens from exposure to unwanted, "offensive" speech. The only secondary effect relied on to support that ordinance was the impact on traffic—an effect which might be caused by a distracting open-air movie even if it did not exhibit nudity.

35. The situation would be quite different if the ordinance had the effect of suppressing, or greatly restricting access to, lawful speech. Here, however, the District Court specifically found that "[t]he Ordinances do not affect the operation of existing establishments but only the location of new ones. There are myriad locations in the City of Detroit which must be over 1000 feet from existing regulated establishments. This burden on First Amendment rights is slight." 373 F. Supp., at 370....

... [I]t is clear beyond question that the Detroit Common Council had broad regulatory power to deal with the problem that prompted enactment of the Anti-Skid Row Ordinance....

The inquiry for First Amendment purposes is not concerned with economic impact; rather, it looks only to the effect of this ordinance upon freedom of expression. This prompts essentially two inquiries: (i) Does the ordinance impose any content limitation on the creators of adult movies or their ability to make them available to whom they desire, and (ii) does it restrict in any significant way the viewing of these movies by those who desire to see them? On the record in this case, these inquiries must be answered in the negative. At most the impact of the ordinance on these interests is incidental and minimal....

In these circumstances, it is appropriate to analyze the permissibility of Detroit's action under the four-part test of United States v. O'Brien, 391 U.S. 367, 377 (1968). Under that test, a governmental regulation is sufficiently justified, despite its incidental impact upon First Amendment interests, "if it is within the constitutional power of the Government; if it furthers an important or substantial governmental interest; if the governmental interest is unrelated to the suppression of free expression; and if the incidental restriction on ... First Amendment freedoms is no greater than is essential to the furtherance of that interest."...

There is, as noted earlier, no question that the ordinance was within the power of the Detroit Common Council to enact.... Nor is there doubt that the interests furthered by this ordinance are both important and substantial....

The third and fourth tests of O'Brien also are met on this record. It is clear both from the chronology and from the facts that Detroit has not embarked on an effort to suppress free expression.... Nor is there reason to question that the degree of incidental encroachment upon such expression was the minimum necessary to further the purpose of the ordinance. The evidence presented to the Common Council indicated that the urban deterioration was threatened, not by the concentration of *all* movie theaters with other "regulated uses," but only by a concentration of those that elected to specialize in adult movies. The case would present a different situation had Detroit brought within the ordinance types of theaters that had not been shown to contribute to the deterioration of surrounding areas....

Mr. JUSTICE STEWART, with whom Mr. JUSTICE BRENNAN, Mr. JUSTICE MARSHALL, and Mr. JUSTICE BLACKMUN join, dissenting....

This case does not involve a simple zoning ordinance, or a content-neutral time, place, and manner restriction, or a regulation of obscene expression or other speech that is entitled to less than the full protection of the First Amendment. The kind of expression at issue here is no doubt objectionable to some, but that fact does not diminish its protected status....

What this case does involve is the constitutional permissibility of selective interference with protected speech whose content is thought to produce distasteful effects. It is elementary that a prime function of the First Amendment is to guard against just such interference. By refusing to invalidate Detroit's ordinance the Court rides roughshod over cardinal principles of First Amendment law, which require that time, place, and manner regulation that affect protected expression be content neutral except in the limited context of a captive or juvenile audience. In place of these principles the Court invokes a concept wholly alien to the First Amendment. Since "few of us would march our sons and daughters off to war to preserve the citizen's right to see 'Specified Sexual Activities' exhibited in the theaters of our choice," the Court implies that these films are not entitled to the full protection of the Constitution. This stands "Voltaire's immortal comment" on its head. For if the guarantees of the First Amendment were reserved for expression that more than a "few of us" would take up arms to defend, then the right of free expression would be defined and circumscribed by current popular opinion. The guarantees of the Bill of Rights were designed to protect against precisely such majoritarian limitations on individual liberty.

The fact that the "offensive" speech here may not address "Important" topics — "ideas of social and political significance," in the Court's terminology — does not mean that it is less worthy of constitutional protection. "Wholly neutral futilities ... come under the protection of free speech as fully as do Keats' poems or Donne's sermons." Winters v. New York, 333 U.S. 507, 528 (Frankfurter, J., dissenting); accord, Cohen v. California, [403 U.S. 15], at 25. Moreover, in the absence of a judicial determination of obscenity, it is by no means clear that the speech is not "important" even on the Court's terms. "[S]ex and obscenity are not synonymous.... The portrayal of sex, e.g., in art, literature and scientific works, is not itself sufficient reason to deny material the constitutional protection of freedom of speech and press. Sex, a great and mysterious motive force in human life, has indisputably been a subject of absorbing interest to mankind through the ages; it is one of the vital problems of human interest and public concern." Roth v. United States, 354 U.S. 476, 487 (footnotes omitted). See also Kingsley Pictures Corp. v. Regents, supra, at 688-689.

I can only interpret today's decision as an aberration. The Court is undoubtedly sympathetic, as am I, to the well-intentioned efforts of Detroit to "clean up" its streets and prevent the proliferation of "skid rows." But it is in those instances where protected speech grates most unpleasantly against the sensibilities that judicial vigilance must be at its height....

[Dissenting opinion by Mr. JUSTICE BLACKMUN, joined by JUSTICES BRENNAN, STEWART, and MARSHALL, is omitted.]

NOTES

1. Examples of ordinances upheld under Young v. Mini-Theatres include Northend Cinema v. Seattle, 585 P.2d 1153 (Wash. 1978) (restriction of adult theatres to certain locales); Hart v. Edmisten 612 F.2d 821 (4th Cir. 1979) (prohibition of more than one adult establishment in the same building); and Shangri-la v. Brennan, 483 F. Supp. 281, (E.D. Wis. 1980) (prohibition of adult bookstores and theatres within 1000 feet of similar businesses). For an example of a zoning ordinance struck down in partial reliance on Young see Entertainment Concepts, Inc. v. Maciejewski, 631 F.2d. 497 (7th Cir. 1980)

2. Young was distinguished in Schad v. Borough of Mount Ephraim, 101 S. Ct. 2176 (1981), summarized at page 90, supra.

(page 401) [573]

NOTES

4. Smith v. United States, 431 U.S. 291 (1977), affirmed a federal mailing prosecution for an intrastate mailing to adults in Iowa. Iowa did not have a general obscenity statute (and prohibited localities from having such provisions) but prohibited only the dissemination of obscene materials to minors. The Supreme Court held that the fact that defendant's conduct thus did not violate state law was not conclusive on the issue of contemporary community standards in the federal prosecution. That question was to be decided by the jurors, "in accordance with their own understanding of the tolerance of the average person in their community." Justices Brennan, Stewart, Marshall, and Stevens dissented.

5. The question of the make-up of the relevant community was addressed by the Supreme Court in Pinkus v. United States, 436 U.S. 293 (1978). Chief Justice Burger's opinion held that children are not part of the "community" by whose standards obscenity is to be judged; that "sensitive persons" may, however, be included in the relevant community; and that an instruction on prurient appeal to deviant groups may be included as part of an instruction pertaining to appeal to the average person where the materials support such a charge.

6. In Kansas City v. Darby, 544 S.W.2d 529 (1976), appeal dismissed, 431 U.S. 935 (1977), the Missouri Supreme Court held (1) that the Kansas City Municipal Court could not constitutionally hear obscenity cases because no jury trial is provided in that court, and (2) that this deficiency is not cured by the availability of a trial de novo as of right before a jury in the circuit court. Rather, the Miller and Hamling decisions require a jury trial in the first instance and preclude any restriction of free expression by a judge prior to a jury determination of obscenity.

(page 403) [575]

NOTES

1.a. [continued] In Penthouse v. McAuliffe, 610 F.2d 1353 (5th Cir. 1980), the court read Miller to require consideration of the interrelationship between a magazine's basic editorial philosophy and its feature articles, rather than merely an article-by-article analysis. Applying this standard, the court reversed a lower court decision and found Penthouse and Oui magazines to be obscene.

(page 404) [576]

NOTES

2. [continued] In Penthouse v. McAuliffe, supra, the court found Playboy magazine not to be obscene under Miller. In United States v. Various Articles of Obscene Merchandise, 600 F.2d 394 (2d Cir. 1979), the court held that the place and manner in which allegedly obscene materials are to be used are not proper subjects of inquiry in determining patent offensiveness.

Interesting state court applications of the Miller standard include Louisiana v. Walden Books, 386 So. 2d 342 (La. 1980) (issue of Penthouse magazine not obscene, despite its appeal to purient interest, in light of its articles on subjects of important and current concern); Mitchell v. Delaware, 6 Media L. Rptr. 1988 (Del. 1980) (magazine devoted to transvestism, which contained patently offensive photographs of sexual conduct, found to have serious political and scientific value in facilitating communication among persons who share common and lawful sexual habits); and Massachusetts v. Saxon Theatre, 6 Media L. Rptr. 1979 (Mass., Mun. Ct. 1980) (film Caligula not obscene, even though it appeals to prurient interest, depicts sexual conduct in a patently offensive manner, and lacks serious literacy, artistic, and scientific value, because not shown to lack serious political value).

(page 405) [577]

Insert after Note 3.

NOTE — CHILD PORNOGRAPHY

In New York v. Ferber, 50 U.S.L.W. 5077 (July 2, 1982), the Supreme Court held that "child pornography," i.e., "works that *visually* depict sexual conduct by children below a specified age," is "a category of material outside the protection of the First Amendment." The Court upheld a New York statute making it a crime to distribute material depicting sexual performances by children.

[579]

[REFERENCES]

F. Schauer, The Law of Obscenity (1976); Schauer, Obscenity and the Conflict of Laws, 77 W. Va. L. Rev. 377 (1975); Schauer, Speech and "Speech" — Obscenity and "Obscenity": An Exercise in the Interpretation of Constitutional Language, 67 Geo. L.J. 899 (1979); Rosenblum, The Judicial Politics of Obscenity, 3 Pepperdine L. Rev. 377 (1975); Diel & Salinger, Demon Rum and the Dirty Dance: Reconsidering Government Regulation of Live Sex Entertainment After California v. LaRue, 1975 Wis. L. Rev. 161; Note, Community Standards Class Actions, and Obscenity Under Miller v. California, 88 Harv. L. Rev. 1838 (1975); Leventhal, Project: An Empirical Inquiry Into the Effects of Miller v. California on the Control of Obscenity, 52 N.Y.U.L. Rev. 810 (1977); Waples & White, Choice of Community Standards in Federal Obscenity Proceedings: The Role of the Constitution and the Common Law, 64 Va. L. Rev. 399 (1978); Symposium: Obscenity and the First Amendment, 7 Cap. L. Rev. 519 (1978); Daniels, the Supreme Court and Obscenity: An Exercise in Empirical Constitutional Policy-Making, 17 San Diego L. Rev. 757 (1980); Farber, Content Regulation and the First Amendment: A Revisionist View, 68 Geo. L.J. 727 (1980); Stone, Restrictions of Speech Because of its Content: The Peculiar Case of Subject-Matter Restrictions, 46 U. Chi. L. Rev. 81 (1978); Note, Young v. American Mini-Theatres, Inc.: Creating Levels of Protected Speech, 4 Hastings Const. L.Q. 321 (1977); Garvey, Children and the First Amendment, 57 Tex. L. Rev. 321 (1979).

(page 408) [582]

NOTES

1. [continued] Recent cases relying on Mishkin and Hamling include Massachusetts v. Rosenberg, 5 Media L. Rptr. 2339 (Mass. 1979) (reversing conviction of variety store owner for sale of Hustler magazine due to lack of evidence of his knowledge of the magazine's contents); and Louisiana v. Wrestle, Inc., 360 So. 2d 831 (La. 1978) (upholding conviction of corporate president for showing obscene films since his local residence and participation in building the peep-show booths gave him "reason to know" the nature of the films being shown).

(page 409) [583]

NOTES

3. [continued] The Alabama decision in McKinney was reversed by a unanimous Supreme Court in McKinney v. Alabama, 424 U.S. 669 (1976). Justice Rehnquist's opinion for the Court held that petitioner had not had a constitutionally adequate opportunity to litigate the obscenity of the magazine in question: "Nonparties like petitioner may assess quite differently the strength of their constitutional claims and may, of course, have very different views regarding the desirability of disseminating particular materials. We think they must be given the opportunity to make these assessments themselves, as well as the chance to litigate the issues if they so choose."

In Burch v. Louisiana, 441 U.S. 130 (1979), the Supreme Court held that a conviction by a nonunanimous six-person jury in a state criminal trial violates the defendant's right to a jury trial in an obscenity prosecution.

(page 412) [586]

NOTES

5. [continued] Lower courts have taken varying views on the necessity and desirability of expert testimony in obscenity cases. See, e.g., Massachusetts v. 707 Main Corp., 357 N.E.2d 753 (Mass. 1976) (expert testimony admissible, especially on the question of serious literary, artistic, political, or scientific value, because cultural, ideological, and scientific values are not necessarily within the understanding of the trier of fact); Massachusetts v. Trainor, 374 N.E.2d 1216 (Mass. 1978) (expert testimony on question of what is obscene admissible or excludable in judge's discretion, but it would be a rare case in which such testimony should be excluded on the ground that it would not be helpful to the trier of fact; similarly, a properly conducted public opinion survey should be admitted); United States v. 2200 Paper Back Books, 565 F.2d 566 (9th Cir. 1977) (while allegedly obscene materials themselves are the best evidence of what they represent, in-court viewing of allegedly pornographic movies and occasional observations of bookstores with questionable material will not alone form an adequate basis for jury to establish community standards — such information must come either from prior knowledge of the trier of fact or be supplied by expert witnesses); United States v. Dost, 575 F. 2d 1303 (10th Cir. 1978) (testimony of expert witnesses and clinical psychologists, together with photographs, created an issue of fact and sustained a jury determination of obscenity.)

Lower courts have also differed on the importance of public opinion in assessing community standards. See, e.g., Carlock v. Texas, 609 S.W.2d 787 (Crim. App. 1980) (trial court erred in excluding from evidence a public opinion survey dealing with community views regarding obscenity); Louisiana v. Short, 368 So. 2d 1079 (La. Sup. Ct. 1979) (trial court's failure to admit lay opinion testimony concerning the availability of explicit sexual material is not reversible error, although such evidence is admissible and relevant).

With regard to comparative materials, United States v. Obscene Magazines, 541 F.2d 810 (9th Cir. 1976), affirmed finding of nonobscenity "as a matter of law" that followed the district judge's determination that the exhibits in question were no worse than photographs found in magazines for sale in the city. The government had taken the position that the exhibits spoke for themselves and that no evidence of community standards was necessary. See also United States v. Pinkus, 436 U.S. 293 (1978).

(page 415) [589]

NOTES

1. [continued] Recent lower court decisions have continued to impose narrow limits on injunctions against the distribution of obscene materials. See, e.g., District Attorney v. 3-Way Theaters Corp., 357 N.E.2d 747 (Mass. 1976); Parish of Jefferson v. Bayou Landing, Ltd., 350 So. 2d 158 (La. 1977); Andrews v. Chateau X, Inc., 250 S.E.2d 603 (N.C. 1979); Ladoga Canning v. McKenzie, 370 So.2d 1137 (Fla. 1979).

(page 417) [591]

NOTES

2(d). [continued] In Lo-Ji Sales, Inc. v. New York, 442 U.S. 319 (1979), the Court ruled that Heller did not permit a town justice to abandon his neutral role and "telescope" the processes of application for and the issuance and execution of a warrant by participating in an open-ended search. A search warrant issued on the basis of two allegedly obscene films was used to seize over 800 items in a six-hour search conducted by eleven law enforcement officials, including the justice.

Recent lower court decisions on the question of the degree to which the issuing magistrate must be familiar with the allegedly obscene materials before a warrant may issue include Parish of Jefferson v. Bayou Landing, Ltd., 350 So. 2d 158 (La. 1977) (search warrant defective where no indication that any books purchased by police officers had been scrutinized by issuing magistrate); United States v. Tupler, 564 F.2d 1294 (9th Cir. 1977) (magistrate must base evaluation of probable cause on direct evidence of contents or at least a fair sample of the material); Western Corp. v. Kentucky, 558 S.W.2d 605 (Ky. 1977) (seizure upheld where magistrate viewed a public showing of the film and then issued written authority to a police officer present to seize the film; United States v. Defalco, 509 F. Supp. 127 (S.D. Fla. 1981) (evidence suppressed where warrant issued solely on the basis of grand jury indictment for conspiracy to commit interstate transportation of obscene material). Other courts have held that an affidavit giving detailed descriptions of the contents of films or magazines, plus underlying facts from which the magistrate could independently find probable cause of obscenity, is sufficient. See United States v. Sherwin, 572 F.2d 196 (9th Cir. 1977); United States v. Middleton, 599 F. 2d 1349 (5th Cir. 1979); United States v. Espinoza, 641 F.2d 153 (4th Cir. 1981); cf. Gotleib v. Delaware, 5 Media L. Rptr. 1818 (Del. 1979) (warrantless police seizure of film, based solely upon officer's observations and absent evidence of exigent circumstances, is unlawful).

With regard to what materials may be seized in the execution of a properly issued warrant, see Parish of Jefferson v. Bayou Landing, Ltd., supra (police restricted in execution of warrant to specific materials determined by the magistrate to be probably obscene); United States v. Sherwin, supra (seizure of magazines not identified in warrant not proper under "nexus" or "plain view" exceptions to general Fourth Amendment restrictions, since those exceptions are not applicable when the materials seized are arguably protected by the First Amendment); Sewell v. Georgia, 238 Ga. 495 (1977), appeal dismissed, 435 U.S. 982 (1978) (seizure of material on sale in a glass case came with "plain view" doctrine.) The seizure of business records and documents relating to the transportation or sale of unspecified "obscene" materials has been upheld under a lower standard of probable cause than that required to seize allegedly obscene material itself. See United States v. Torch, 609 F. 2d 1088 (4th Cir. 1979); United States v. Espinoza, 641 F.2d. 153 (4th Cir. 1981).

With regard to the requirement of a pre-trial adversarial hearing on the question of probable cause, see United States v. Echols, 577 F.2d 308 (5th Cir. 1978) (where defendant failed to exercise his right to a pre-trial adversarial hearing, a 497-day lapse between seizure of allegedly obscene films and trial at which judicial determination of obscenity would be made is constitutional); Missouri v. All Star News Agency, 580 S.W.2d 245 (Mo. 1979) (police seizure, pursuant to statute, of 1000 films and 13,000 magazines from a wholesale distributor, after notice to the distributor but before an adversarial hearing, was an unconstitutional prior restraint).

(page 419) [593]

NOTES

3. [continued] Recent decisions continue to cast doubt on the viability of nuisance statutes as an effective means of dealing with obscenity. The Supreme Court struck down a Texas obscenity-nuisance statute in Vance v. Universal Amusement Co., Inc., 445 U.S. 308 (1980), on the grounds that it was unconstitutional insofar as it authorized an injunction against the future exhibition of unnamed films and that it failed to provide required procedural safeguards, including a provision for prompt and final adjudication on the merits. The Court noted that the restraint on exhibition of films that had not been finally adjudicated to be obscene constituted a "more onerous and more objectionable [prior restraint] than the threat of criminal sanctions after a film has been exhibited, since nonobscenity would be a defense to any criminal prosecution." Compare Andrews v. Chateau X, Inc., — S.E.2d — (N.C. 1981), aff'g, 250 S.E.2d 603 (N.C. 1979), where the court distinguished Vance to uphold a North Carolina moral nuisance statute which authorized temporary injunctions against future exhibition of allegedly obscene films. Since the procedural safeguard of nonobscenity as a defense in any contempt proceeding was provided for by statute, the prior restraint was held to be no more onerous than a post-exhibition criminal sanction.

In Cooper v. Mitchell Bros.' Santa Ana Theater, 102 S. Ct. 172 (1982), the Court held that a state need not employ a reasonable doubt standard on the issue of obscenity in a civil nuisance abatement suit.

(page 423) [597]

NOTES

3. [continued] Aspects of licensing procedures remain a matter of constitutional controversy. See Airport Bookstore, Inc. v. Jackson, 248 S.E.2d 623 (Ga. 1978) (upholding a licensing system); West Gallery v. Salt Lake City, 586 P.2d 429 (Utah 1978) (upholding procedure for suspension of theatre license for past violation of obscenity ordinance); Bayou Landing, Ltd. v. Watts, 563 F.2d 1172 (5th Cir. 1977) (invalidating a city ordinance that withheld an occupancy permit from an "adult" bookstore); Coleman v. Bradford, 233 S.E.2d 764 (Ga. 1977) (invalidating an ordinance imposing an annual license fee on movie houses that exhibited nonobscene "X-rated" films); Wendling v. Duluth, 495 F. Supp. 1380 (D. Minn. 1980) (invalidating an ordinance that used annual adult bookstore license fees to finance enforcement of a separate

obscenity statute); Natco Theatres v. Ratner, 463 F. Supp. 1124 (S.D.N.Y. 1979) (invalidating an ordinance that denied licenses to theater owners who had been convicted of certain criminal offenses, including some unrelated to theater operation).

(page 439) [613]

NOTES

2. [continued] In Penthouse v. McAuliffe, 610 F.2d 1353 (5th Cir. 1980), the court found that a Georgia sheriff's obscenity law enforcement program, which included harassment and warrantless arrests, constituted an informal system of prior restraint under Bantam Books.

[614]

REFERENCES

Edelstein & Mott, Collateral Problems in Obscenity Regulation: A Uniform Approach to Prior Restraints, Community Standards, a Judgment Preclusion, 7 Seton Hall L. Rev. 161 (1975); Hogue, Regulating Obscenity Through the Power to Define and Abate Nuisances, 14 Wake Forest L. Rev. 1 (1978); Rendleman, Civilizing Pornography: The Case for an Exclusive Obscenity Nuisance Statute, 44 U. Chi. L. Rev. 509 (1977).

B. "OFFENSIVE" SPEECH

(page 468) [644]

NOTES

3. The Erznoznik case was distinguished by the Supreme Court in Young v. American Mini-Theatres, Inc., 427 U.S. 50 (1976), set out at page 93 supra.
4. In Carey v. Population Services International, 431 U.S. 678 (1977), set out at page 207, infra, the Court held that the principle of Cohen v. California precluded the contention that a ban on any advertisement of contraceptives was justified because such advertisements "would be offensive and embarrassing to those exposed to them."

(page 471) [646]

Insert after Note:

FEDERAL COMMUNICATIONS COMMISSION v. PACIFICA FOUNDATION

438 U.S. 726 (1978)

Mr. JUSTICE STEVENS delivered the opinion of the Court (Parts I, II, III, and IV-C) and an opinion in which THE CHIEF JUSTICE and Mr. JUSTICE REHNQUIST joined (Parts IV-A and IV-B).

This case requires that we decide whether the Federal Communications Commission has any power to regulate a radio broadcast that is indecent but not obscene.

A satiric humorist named George Carlin recorded a 12-minute monologue entitled "Filthy Words" before a live audience in a California theater. He began by referring to his thoughts about "the words you couldn't say on the public, ah, airwaves, um, the ones you definitely wouldn't say, ever." He proceeded to list those words and repeat them over and over again in a variety of colloquialisms.* . . .

At about 2 o'clock in the afternoon on Tuesday, October 30, 1973, a New York radio station, owned by respondent Pacifica Foundation, broadcast the "Filthy Words" monologue. A few weeks later a man, who stated that he had heard the broadcast while driving with his young son, wrote a letter complaining to the Commission. . . .

The complaint was forwarded to the station for comment. In its response, Pacifica explained that the monologue had been played during a program about contemporary society's attitude toward language and that, immediately before its broadcast, listeners had been advised that it included "sensitive language which might be regarded as offensive to some." . . . Pacifica stated that it was not aware of any other complaints about the broadcast.

On February 21, 1975, the Commission issued a declaratory order granting the complaint and holding that Pacifica "could have been the subject of administrative sanctions." 56 F.C.C.2d 94, 99. The Commission did not impose formal sanctions, but it did state that the order would be "associated with the station's license file, and in the event that subsequent complaints are received, the Commission will then decide whether it should utilize any of the available sanctions it has been granted by Congress." . . .

---

*The five page transcript of the "Filthy Words" monologue, appended to the opinion of the Court, begins as follows: "Okay, I was thinking one night about the words you couldn't say on the public, ah, airwaves, um, the ones you definitely wouldn't say, ever . . . [B]astard you can say, and hell or damn so I have to figure out which ones you couldn't ever and it came down to seven but the list is open to amendment, and in fact, has been changed, uh, by now, ha, a lot of people pointed things out to me and I noticed some myself. The original seven words were, shit, piss, fuck, cunt, cocksucker, motherfucker and tits. Those are the ones that will curve your spine, grow hair on your hands and (laughter) maybe even bring us, God help us, peace without honor (laughter) um, and a bourbon. (laughter) . . ." [Eds.]

The Commission characterized the language used in the Carlin monologue as "patently offensive," though not necessarily obscene, and expressed the opinion that it should be regulated by principles analogous to those found in the law of nuisance where the "law generally speaks to *channeling* behavior more than actually prohibiting it. . . . [T]he concept of 'indecent' is intimately connected with the exposure of children to language that describes, in terms patently offensive as measured by contemporary community standards for the broadcast medium, sexual or excretory activities and organs, at times of the day when there is a reasonable risk that children may be in the audience." 56 F.C.C.2d, at 98. . . .

After the order issued, the Commission was asked to clarify its opinion by ruling that the broadcast of indecent words as part of a live newscast would not be prohibited. The Commission issued another opinion in which it pointed out that it "never intended to place an absolute prohibition on the broadcast of this type of language, but rather sought to channel it to times of day when children most likely would not be exposed to it" 59 F.C.C.2d 892 (1976). . . .

The United States Court of Appeals for the District of Columbia Circuit reversed with each of the three judges on the panel writing separately. 556 F.2d 9. . . .

[Part I of Justice Stevens' opinion found the administrative action to be an adjudication "issued in a specific factual context" rather than formal rulemaking, and stated that "the focus of our review must be on the Commission's determination that the Carlin monologue was indecent as broadcast." In Part II, he concluded that the statutory prohibition against FCC "censorship" was not intended to apply to subsequent review of completed broadcasts or to regulation of obscene, indecent, or profane broadcasts. In Part III, he agreed with the FCC's conclusion that Carlin's monologue was "indecent" within the meaning of the governing statute, 18 U.S.C. §1464. In Part IV-A, Justice Stevens addressed the first of two constitutional arguments before the Court by declining to rule that the FCC order was impermissibly overbroad and would therefore exert a chilling effect on constitutionally protected speech. He then turned to the central First Amendment questions:]

IV

B

When the issue is narrowed to the facts of this case, the question is whether the First Amendment denies government any power to restrict the public broadcast of indecent language in any circumstances. For if the government has any such power, this was an appropriate occasion for its exercise.

The words of the Carlin monologue are unquestionable "speech" within the meaning of the First Amendment. It is equally clear that the Commission's objections to the broadcast were based in part on its content. The order must therefore fall if, as Pacifica argues, the First Amendment prohibits all governmental regulation that depends on the content of speech. Our past cases demonstrate, however, that no such absolute rule is mandated by the Constitution. . . .

The question in this case is whether a broadcast of patently offensive words dealing with sex and excretion may be regulated because of its content. Obscene materials have been denied the protection of the First Amendment because their content is so offensive to contemporary moral standards. Roth v. United States, 354 U.S. 476. But the fact that society may find speech offensive is not a sufficient reason for suppressing it. Indeed, if it is the speaker's opinion that gives offense, that consequence is a reason for according it constitutional protection. For it is a central tenet of the First Amendment that the government must remain neutral in the marketplace of ideas. If there were any reason to believe that the Commission's characterization of the Carlin monologue as offensive could be traced to its political content — or even to the fact that it satirized contemporary attitudes about four-letter words — First Amendment protection might be required. But that is simply not this case. These words offend for the same reasons that obscenity offends. . . .

Although these words ordinarily lack literary, political, or scientific value, they are not entirely outside the protection of the First Amendment. Some uses of even the most offensive words are unquestionably protected. See, e.g., Hess v. Indiana, 414 U.S. 105. Indeed, we may assume, arguendo, that this monologue would be protected in other contexts. Nonetheless, the constitutional protection accorded to a communication containing such patently offensive sexual and excretory language need not be the same in every context. . . .

In this case it is undisputed that the content of Pacifica's broadcast was "vulgar," "offensive," and "shocking." Because content of that character is not entitled to absolute constitutional protection under all circumstances, we must consider its context in order to determine whether the Commission's action was constitutionally permissible.

C

We have long recognized that each medium of expression presents special First Amendment problems. . . . And of all forms of communication, it is broadcasting that has received the most limited First Amendment protection. . . .

. . . [T]he broadcast media have established a uniquely pervasive presence in the lives of all Americans. Patently offensive, indecent material presented over the airwaves confronts the citizen, not only in public, but also in the privacy of the home, where the individual's right to be left alone plainly outweighs the First Amendment rights of an intruder. Rowan v. Post Office Dept., 397 U.S. 728. Because the broadcast audience is constantly tuning in and out, prior warnings cannot completely protect the listener or viewer from unexpected program content. To say that one may avoid further offense by turning off the radio when he hears indecent language is like saying that the remedy for an assault, is to run away after the first blow. One may hang up on an indecent phone call, but that option does not give the caller a constitutional immunity or avoid a harm that has already taken place.

[B]roadcasting [also] is uniquely accessible to children, even those too young to read. Although [the] written message [in Cohen v. California] might have been incomprehensible to a first grader, Pacifica's broadcast could have enlarged a child's vocabulary in an instant.... We held in Ginsberg v. New York, 390 U.S. 629, that the government's interest in the "well-being of its youth" and in supporting "parents' claim to authority in their own household" justified the regulation of otherwise protected expression.... The ease with which children may obtain access to broadcast material, coupled with the concerns recognized in Ginsberg [v. New York, 390 U.S. 629, at p. 530 of the main volume] amply justify special treatment of indecent broadcasting.[28]

It is appropriate, in conclusion, to emphasize the narrowness of our holding. This case does not involve a two-way radio conversation between a cab driver and a dispatcher, or a telecast of an Elizabethan comedy. We have not decided that an occasional expletive in either setting would justify any sanction or, indeed, that this broadcast would justify a criminal prosecution. The Commission's decision rested entirely on a nuisance rationale under which context is all-important. The concept requires consideration of a host of variables. The time of day was emphasized by the Commission. The content of the program in which the language is used will also affect the composition of the audience, and differences between radio, television, and perhaps closed-circuit transmissions, may also be relevant. As Mr. Justice Sutherland wrote, a "nuisance may be merely a right thing in the wrong place — like a pig in the parlor instead of the barnyard." Euclid v. Ambler Realty Co., 272 U.S. 365, 388. We simply hold that when the Commission finds that a

---

28. The Commission's action does not by any means reduce adults to hearing only what is fit for children. Cf. Butler v. Michigan, 352 U.S. 380, 383. Adults who feel the need may purchase tapes and records or go to theaters and nightclubs to hear these words. In fact, the Commission has not unequivocally closed even broadcasting to speech of this sort; whether broadcast audiences in the late evening contain so few children that playing this monologue would be permissible is an issue neither the Commission nor this Court has decided.

pig has entered the parlor, the exercise of its regulatory power does not depend on proof that the pig is obscene.

The judgment of the Court of Appeals is reversed.

Mr. JUSTICE POWELL, with whom Mr. JUSTICE BLACKMUN joins, concurring in part and concurring in the judgment.

I join Parts I, II, III, and IV-C of Mr. JUSTICE STEVENS' opinion. . . .

Because I do not subscribe to all that is said in Part IV, however, I state my views separately.

I

I do not think Carlin, consistently with the First Amendment, could be punished for delivering the same monologue to a live audience composed of adults who, knowing what to expect, chose to attend his performance. See Brown v. Oklahoma, 408 U.S. 914 (1972) (Powell, J., concurring in result). And I would assume that an adult could not constitutionally be prohibited from purchasing a recording or transcript of the monologue and playing or reading it in the privacy of his own home. Cf. Stanley v. Georgia, 394 U.S. 557 (1969).

But it also is true that the language employed is, to most people, vulgar and offensive. It was chosen specifically for this quality, and it was repeated over and over as a sort of verbal shock treatment. . . .

The issue, however, is whether the Commission may impose civil sanctions on a licensee radio station for broadcasting the monologue at two o'clock in the afternoon. The Commission's primary concern was to prevent the broadcast from reaching the ears of unsupervised children who were likely to be in the audience at that hour. . . .

The Court has recognized society's right to "adopt more stringent controls on communicative materials available to youths than on those available to adults." Erznoznik v. Jacksonville, 422 U.S. 205, 212 (1975). . . . [S]ociety may prevent the general dissemination of such speech to children, leaving to parents the decision as to what speech of this kind their children shall hear and repeat. . . . The Commission properly held that the speech from which society may attempt to shield its children is not limited to that which appeals to the youthful prurient interest. The language involved in this case is as potentially degrading and harmful to children as representations of many erotic acts.

In most instances, the dissemination of this kind of speech to children may be limited without also limiting willing adults' access to it. . . . The difficulty is that such a physical separation of the audience cannot be accomplished in the broadcast media. . . . This, as the Court emphasizes, is one of the distinctions between broadcast and other media to which we often have adverted as justifying a different treatment of the broadcast media for First Amendment purposes.... In my view, the Commission was entitled to give substantial weight to this difference in reacing its decision in this case.

A second difference, not with relevance, is that broadcasting — unlike most other forms of communication — comes directly into the home, the one place where people ordinarily have the right not to be assaulted by uninvited and offensive sights and sounds.... The Commission also was entitled to give this factor appropriate weight in the circumstances of the instant case....

II

As the foregoing demonstrates, my views are generally in accord with what is said in Part IV-C of Mr. Justice Stevens' opinion.... I do not join Part IV-B, however, because I do not subscribe to the theory that the Justices of this Court are free generally to decide on the basis of its content which speech protected by the First Amendment is most "valuable" and hence deserving of the most protection, and which is less "valuable" and hence deserving of less protection. In my view, the result in this case does not turn on whether Carlin's monologue, viewed as a whole, or the words that constitute it, have more or less "value" than a candidate's campaign speech. This is a judgment for each person to make, not one for the judges to impose upon him....

Mr. JUSTICE BRENNAN, with whom Mr. JUSTICE MARSHALL joins, dissenting.

I agree with Mr. Justice Stewart that... the word "indecent" in 18 U.S.C. §1464 (1976 ed.) must be construed to prohibit only obscene speech. I would, therefore, normally refrain from expressing my views on any constitutional issues implicated in this case. However, I find the Court's misapplication of fundamental First Amendment principles so patent, and its attempt to impose *its* notions of propriety on the whole of the American people so misguided, that I am unable to remain silent.

I

For the second time in two years, see Young v. American Mini Theatres, 427 U.S. 50 (1976), the Court refuses to embrace the notion, completely antithetical to basic First Amendment values, that the degree of protection the First Amendment affords protected speech varies with the social value ascribed to that speech by five Members of this Court.... Moreover, as do all parties, all Members of the Court agree that the Carlin monologue aired by Station WBAI does not fall within one of the categories of speech, such as "fighting words," Chaplinsky v. New Hampshire, 315 U.S. 568 (1942), or obscenity, Roth v. United

States, 354 U.S. 476 (1957), that is totally without First Amendment protection. . . . Yet . . . a majority of the Court nevertheless finds that, on the facts of this case, the FCC is not constitutionally barred from imposing sanctions on Pacifica for its airing of the Carlin monologue. This majority apparently believes that the FCC's disapproval of Pacifica's afternoon broadcast of Carlin's "Dirty Words" recording is a permissible time, place, and manner regulation. Kovacs v. Cooper, 336 U.S. 77 (1949). Both the opinion of my Brother Stevens and the opinion of my Brother Powell rely principally on two factors in reaching this conclusion: (1) the capacity of a radio broadcast to intrude into the unwilling listener's home, and (2) the presence of children in the listening audience. Dispassionate analysis, removed from individual notions as to what is proper and what is not, starkly reveals that these justifications, whether individually or together, simply do not support even the professedly moderate degree of governmental homogenization of radio communications — if, indeed, such homogenization can ever be moderate given the pre-eminent status of the right of free speech in our constitutional scheme — that the Court today permits.

A

. . . I am in wholehearted agreement with my Brethren that an individual's right "to be let alone" when engaged in private activity within the confines of his own home is encompassed within the "substantial privacy interests" to which Mr. Justice Harlan referred in Cohen v. California, and is entitled to the greatest solicitude. Stanley v. Georgia, 394 U.S. 557 (1969). However, I believe that an individual's actions in switching on and listening to communications transmitted over the public airways and directed to the public at large do not implicate fundamental privacy interests, even when engaged in within the home. Instead, because the radio is undeniably a public medium, these actions are more properly viewed as a decision to take part, if only as a listener, in an ongoing public discourse. . . .

. . . Whatever the minimal discomfort suffered by a listener who inadvertently tunes into a program he finds offensive during the brief interval before he can simply extend his arm and switch stations or flick the "off" button, it is surely worth the candle to preserve the broadcaster's right to send, and the right to those interested to receive, a message entitled to full First Amendment protection. To reach a contrary balance, as does the Court, is clearly to follow Mr. Justice Stevens' reliance on animal metaphors "to burn the house to roast the pig." Butler v. Michigan, 352 U.S. 380, 383 (1957).

The Court's balance, of necessity, fails to accord proper weight to the interests of listeners who wish to hear broadcasts the FCC deems offensive. It permits majoritarian tastes completely to preclude a protected message from entering the homes of a receptive, unoffended minority. . . .

B

Most parents will undoubtedly find understandable as well as commendable the Court's sympathy with the FCC's desire to prevent offensive broadcasts from reaching the ears of unsupervised children. Unfortunately, the facial appeal of this justification for radio censorship masks its constitutional insufficiency. Although the government unquestionably has a special interest in the well-being of children and consequently "can adopt more stringent controls on communicative materials available to youths than on those available to adults," Erznoznik v. Jacksonville, 422 U.S. 205, 212 (1975) . . . the Court has accounted for this societal interest by adopting a "variable obscenity" standard that permits the prurient appeal of material available to children to be assessed in terms of the sexual interests of minors. Ginsberg v. New York, 390 U.S. 629 (1968). . . .

Because the Carlin monologue is obviously not an erotic appeal to the prurient interests of children, the Court, for the first time, allows the government to prevent minors from gaining access to materials that are not obscene, and are therefore protected, as to them. This result violates in spades the principle of Butler v. Michigan, [main volume page 350 [522] note 1]. . . . Where, as here, the government may not prevent the exposure of minors to the suppressed material, the principle of Butler applies a fortiori. . . .

In concluding that the presence of children in the listening audience provides an adequate basis for the FCC to impose sanctions for Pacifica's broadcast of the Carlin monologue, the opinions of my Brother Powell and my Brother Stevens both stress the time-honored right of a parent to raise his child as he sees fit — a right this Court has consistently been vigilant to protect. See Wisconsin v. Yoder, 406 U.S. 205 (1972); Pierce v. Society of Sisters, 268 U.S. 510 (1925). Yet this principle supports a result directly contrary to that reached by the Court. Yoder and Pierce hold that parents, *not* the government, have the right to make certain decisions regarding the upbringing of their children. As surprising as it may be to individual Members of the Court, some parents may actually find Mr. Carlin's unabashed attitude towards the seven "dirty words" healthy, and deem it desirable to expose their children to the manner in which Mr. Carlin defuses the taboo surrounding the words. Such parents may constitute a minority of the American public, but the absence of great numbers willing to exercise the right to raise their children in this fashion does not alter the right's nature or its existence. Only the Court's regrettable decision does that.

C

... For my own part, even accepting that this case is limited to its facts, I would place the responsibility and the right to weed worthless and offensive communications from the public airways where it belongs and where, until today, it resided: in a public free to choose those communications worthy of its attention from a marketplace unsullied by the censor's hand....

III

It is quite evident that I find the Court's attempt to unstitch the warp and woof of First Amendment law in an effort to reshape its fabric to cover the patently wrong result the Court reaches in this case dangerous as well as lamentable. Yet there runs throughout the opinions of my Brothers Powell and Stevens another vein I find equally disturbing: a depressing inability to appreciate that in our land of cultural pluralism, there are many who think, act, and talk differently from the Members of this Court, and who do not share their fragile sensibilities. It is only an acute ethnocentric myopia that enables the Court to approve the censorship of communications solely because of the words they contain.

Today's decision will thus have its greatest impact on broadcasters desiring to reach, and listening audiences composed of, persons who do not share the Court's view as to which words or expressions are acceptable and who, for a variety of reasons, including a conscious desire to flout majoritarian conventions, express themselves using words that may be regarded as offensive by those from different socio-economic backgrounds. The words that the Court and the Commission find so unpalatable may be the stuff of everyday conversations in some, if not many, of the innumerable subcultures that compose this Nation.... In this context, the Court's decision may be seen for what, in the broader perspective, it really is: another of the dominant culture's inevitable efforts to force those groups who do not share its mores to conform to its way of thinking, acting, and speaking. See Moore v. East Cleveland, 431 U.S. 494, 506-511 (1977) (Brennan, J., concurring)....

Mr. JUSTICE STEWART, with whom Mr. JUSTICE BRENNAN, Mr. JUSTICE WHITE, and Mr. JUSTICE MARSHALL join, dissenting....

The statute pursuant to which the Commission acted, 18 U.S.C. §1464 (1976 ed.), makes it a federal offense to utter "any obscene, indecent, or profane language by means of radio communication." The Commission held, and the Court today agrees, that "indecent" is a broader concept than "obscene" as the latter term was defined in Miller v. California, 413 U.S. 15, because language can be "indecent" although it has social, political, or artistic value and lacks prurient appeal. 56 F.C.C.2d, at 97-98. But this construction of §1464, while perhaps plausible, is by no means compelled. To the contrary, I think that "indecent" should properly be read as meaning no more than "obscene." Since the Carlin monologue concededly was not "obscene," I believe that the Commission lacked statutory authority to ban it. Under this construction of the statute, it is unnecessary to address the difficult and important issue of the Commission's constitutional power to prohibit speech that would be constitutionally protected outside the context of electronic broadcasting. . . .

NOTE

1. In Reeves v. McConn, 638 F.2d 762 (5th Cir. 1981), the court extended the reasoning of Pacifica to uphold a statute prohibiting amplification of "obscene or slanderous" sound, holding that the word "obscene" was not unconstitutionally vague in the context of broadcast speech, where the power to regulate was thought to be much broader than in the area of printed speech.

[646]

[REFERENCES]

[continued] Bonnicksen, Obscenity Reconsidered: Bringing Broadcasting into the Mainstream Commentary, 14 Val. U.L. Rev. 261 (1980); Glasser & Jassem, Indecent Broadcasts and the Listener's Right of Privacy, 24 J. Broadcast. 285 (1980); Note, "Filthy Words", the First Amendment and the Broadcast Media, 78 Colum. L. Rev. 164 (1978); Note, Sticks and Stones May Break My Bones . . . FCC v. Pacifica Foundation (The Seven Dirty Words Case), 3 Glendale L. Rev. 192 (1979); Note, Regulating Indecent Speech: A New Attack on the First Amendment, 41 U. Pitt. L. Rev. 321 (1980); Note, Regulating Broadcast Obscenity, 6 Va. L. Rev. 579 (1975).

Chapter Seven

Actions for Defamation and Invasion of Privacy

(Page 483) [658]

NOTE — GROUP LIBEL

[continued] See also, Philadelphia v. Washington Post, 482 F. Supp. 897 (E.D. Pa. 1979) (governmental entities cannot maintain libel actions).

(page 485) [660]

NOTE — THE BARR v. MATEO PRIVILEGE

[continued] In Paul v. Davis, 424 U.S. 693 (1976), the Court held that a defamatory police circular, erroneously describing plaintiff as "an active shoplifter," did not deprive him of "liberty" or "property" within the meaning of the Due Process Clause, and so did not give rise to a cause of action against police officials under 42 U.S.C. §1983.

In Butz v. Economou, 438 U.S. 478 (1978), the Court modified the absolute privilege language of Barr v. Mateo and held that, except for certain quasi-judicial and prosecutorial officers (who enjoy absolute immunity), federal executive officials generally, like state officials under Scheuer v. Rhodes, 416 U.S. 232 (1974), enjoy only a qualified immunity when they commit constitutional violations in the exercise of their official responsibilities. See Chapter XVII.

NOTE — LIBEL AND THE SPEECH OR DEBATE CLAUSE

In Hutchinson v. Proxmire, 443 U.S.111 (1979), the Court addressed the extent to which the Speech or Debate Clause of the Constitution immunizes federal legislators from libel actions. The case involved Senator William Proximire's "Golden Fleece" of the month award for wasteful federal spending. Proxmire gave the award in 1975 to federal agencies that had funded studies by Hutchinson, a scientist who was performing behavioral research on monkeys. In addition to presenting the award in a speech published in the Congressional Record, the Senator incorporated portions of the allegedly defamatory speech into a news release sent to newsmen, referred to the award in a newsletter sent to 100,000 constituents, made reference to Hutchinson's research on a television interview program, and had a member of his staff telephone the federal agencies that were responsible for the federal grants to discuss Hutchinson's research with them. The Court held that the Speech or Debate Clause immunity, although applicable to speeches made on the floor of Congress, did not extend to newsletters and press releases because neither "was 'essential to the deliberations of the Senate' and neither was part of the deliberative process." The Court also held that the Speech or Debate Clause does not cover telephone calls by legislators to executive agencies intended to influence the conduct of those agencies. Chief Justice Burger wrote the opinon for the Court; Justice Brennan dissented.

(page 487) [662]

NOTES

3 [continued] In Farmer v. United Brotherhood of Carpenters and Joiners of America, Local 25, 430 U.S. 290 (1977), the Court held that the NLRA does not preempt state law actions for "intentional infliction of emotional distress."

(page 488) [664]

NOTES

4. [continued] Recent cases finding public/official status under Rosenblatt include Rinsley v. Brandt, 6 Media L. Rptr. 1222 (D. Kan. 1980) (psychiatrist/director of state hospital); Press v. Verran, 569 S.W.2d 435 (Tenn. 1978) (social worker); Torres v. Playboy Enterprises, Inc., 7 Media L. Rptr. 1182 (S.D. Tex. 1980) (federal customs inspector); Simonson v. UPI, 500 F. Supp. 1261 (E.D. Wis. 1980) (county juvenile court judge). But see McCusker v. Valley News, 428 A.2d 493 (N.H. 1981) (appointed deputy sheriff not a public official for purposes of maintaining a libel action).

Cases addressing the continued public/official status of former employees for alleged defamation involving their official conduct include Hart v. Playboy Enterprises, Inc., 5 Media L. Rptr. 1811 (D. Kan. 1979) (federal narcotics agent whose employment had terminated six years earlier held to be a public official); Stripling v. Literary Guild, 5 Media L. Rptr. 1958 (W.D. Tex. 1979) (former chief investigator of the House Committee on Un-American Activities held to be a public official despite the passage of 30 years).

(page 490) [665]

NOTES

5. [continued] The Court refused to apply the Time, Inc. v. Hill standard to a non-false light privacy case in Zacchini v. Scripps-Howard Broadcasting Co., 433 U.S. 562 (1977), see page 130 infra.

(page 492) [668]

NOTES

8. [continued] In Dickey v. CBS, 583 F.2d 1221 (3d Cir. 1978), the court ruled that evidence showing inadequate investigation by a television station prior to airing a taped interview in which a congressman accused plaintiff of accepting bribes was not sufficient to establish reckless disregard. Compare Catalano v. Pechous, 83 Ill. 2d 146 (1980), where a city clerk's statement charging city aldermen with accepting bribes, which was made without documentary evidence, personal knowledge, or attempt to verify, and was based only on "inference," was held to have been made with reckless disregard for its truth or falsity.

(page 494) [670]

NOTES

12. [continued] In Time, Inc. v. Firestone, 424 U.S. 448 (1976), the Court restricted the rule of Time, Inc. v. Pape to those cases where actual malice is the applicable standard of care. Lower courts have continued to apply the Pape rule in such cases. See, e.g., Orr v. Argus-Press, 586 F.2d 1108 (6th Cir. 1978).

(page 511) [687]

NOTES

1. [continued] Relying on the Gertz language that "[u]nder the First Amendment there is no such thing as a false idea," lower courts have consistently held that statements of "opinion" cannot form the basis of

a libel action. See, e.g., Naked City v. Chicago Sun-Times, 77 Ill. App. 3d 188 (1979) (article and editorial describing nudist camp's "Mr. and Mrs. Nude Teeny Bopper" pageant as pornography); Church of Scientology v. Siegelman, 475 F. Supp. 950 (S.D.N.Y. 1979) (book author's characterization of the methods and practices used by controversial religious movement); Stripling v. Literary Guild, 5 Media L. Rptr. 1958 (W.D. Tex. 1979) (statements regarding plaintiff's official role in the "red-baiting, blacklisting McCarthy years"); Myers v. Boston Magazine, 6 Media L. Rptr. 1241 (Mass. 1980) humorous "best and worst" magazine article rating TV sports announcer as the "worst" in Boston); Anton v. St. Louis Suburban Newspapers, 598 S.W.2d 493 (Mo. Ct. App. 1980)(editorial referring to attorney's "sleazy sleight of hand" in connection with a membership change in fire district's board of directors); Cibenko v. Worth Publishers, Inc., 510 F. Supp. 761 (D.N.J. 1981) (sociology textbook photograph of white policeman prodding black man with nightstick in order to keep him from falling asleep in a public place, with caption asking whether policeman would do the same if man were well-dressed, middle-aged, and white).

(page 512) [688]

NOTES

2. [continued] Similar to the statute struck down in Tornillo are "retraction" statutes, which require publication of a retraction upon showing of a defamatory falsehood. In Dupler v. Mansfield Journal, 64 Ohio St. 2d 116 (1980), the court held that evidence of a newspaper's noncompliance with a state retraction statute cannot be evidence of actual malice, since such conduct would occur after publication of the allegedly libelous statements.

(page 512) [688]

NOTE

1. [insert at beginning of note] The Supreme Court has decided three public figure cases since the main volume was published. In Time, Inc. v. Firestone, 424 U.S. 448 (1976), the Court held that a prominent socialite, involved in a celebrated divorce, who had held conferences about the divorce proceedings, was not a public figure. The Court emphasized that the plaintiff "did not assume any role of special prominence in the affairs of society ... nor did she thrust herself into the forefront of any particular public controversy in order to influence the resolution of any issues involved in it." In Hutchinson v. Proxmire, 443 U.S. 111 (1979), the Court held that a scientist who had received federal

grant monies to conduct research studies was not a public figure. Once again the Court emphasized that he had not thrust himself into any public controversy, except that generated by the alleged libel. Hutchinson also noted in dictum that the category of public officials "cannot be thought to include all public employees." Finally, Wolston v. Reader's Digest Association, 443 U.S. 157 (1979), involved a plaintiff (the nephew of a convicted Soviet spy) who had been subpoenaed by a grand jury in 1958 and had failed to respond. He received a contempt citation and substantial newspaper coverage at the time. The Court held that these occurrences did not make him a public figure, since his involvement in these matters was not a "voluntary" engagement in matters of public concern. Rather, Wolston's involvement was the result of being "dragged into" the issues.

(page 514) [690]

NOTES

1.a.(1) [continued] In Commonwealth v. Wadzinski, 422 A.2d 124 (Pa. 1980), the court held that a state may apply its general laws of defamation to a political campaign speech as long as such laws comport with the actual malice standard of Times v. Sullivan. Additional instances in which the Times v. Sullivan standards have been deemed applicable because of voluntary involvement in political affairs include Stripling v. Literary Guild, 5 Media L. Rptr. 1958 (W.D. Tex. 1979) (former chief investigator of the House Committee on Un-American Activities); Gleichenhaus v. Carlyle, 597 P.2d 611 (Kan. 1979) (real estate appraiser who received appraisal contracts from city and contributed to mayor's re-election campaign); Rebozo v. Washington Post, 637 F.2d 375 (5th Cir. 1981) (close friend of President who was actively involved in re-election campaign and offered advice on financial as well as nonfinancial matters); Burns v. Times Argus, 7 Media L. Rptr. 1212 (Vt. 1981) (wife of lieutenant governor who was involved in his gubernatorial campaign).But see Lawrence v. Moss, 639 F.2d 634 (10th Cir 1981) (U.S. Senatorial candidate's campaign aide whose duties were primarily administrative not a public figure).

1.a.(2) [continued] Additional examples of deliberate involvement in issues of public concern include Arnheiter v. Random House, 578 F.2d 804 (9th Cir. 1978)(former naval officer removed from command during the Vietnam War who sought to reverse his removal by arousing public sentiment); Yiamouyiannis v. Consumers Union, 619 F.2d 932 (2d Cir. 1980) (plaintiff whose articles, speeches, testimony, and active involvement thrust him into the forefront of a public controversy over fluoridation of water supplies); Waldbaum v. Fairchild Publications, 627 F.2d 1287 (D.C. Cir. 1980) (president of consumer cooperative who, by involvement in public controversies concerning marketing policies, attempted to influence the policies of firms in the supermarket business); Street v. NBC, 645 F.2d 1227 (6th Cir. 1981) (major witness in highly publicized rape prosecution who used her access to the media to promote her version of the events); Henderson v. Kaulitz, 6 Media L. Rptr. 2409 (6th Cir. 1981) (high school student senate president who intentionally thrust himself into controversy between school board and students over a local drug counseling center). But see Littlefield v. Fort Dodge Messenger, 614 F. 2d 581 (8th Cir. 1980) (attorney subjected to disciplinary proceedings based on misdemeanor conviction not a public figure despite substantial public interest in proceedings).

(page 515) [691]

NOTES

1.a.(3) [continued] Additional occupations which have been held to confer public figure status are: mob associate, Rosanova v. Playboy Enterprises, 580 F.2d 859 (5th Cir. 1978), and policeman, Gray v. Udevitz, 5 Media L. Rptr. 1412 (D. Wyo. 1979); Malerba v. Newsday, 4 Media L. Rptr. 1110 (N.Y. App. Div. 1978). Positions that, by themselves, have been held not to make one a public figure include U.S. senatorial campaign aide, Lawrence v. Moss, 639 F.2d 634 (10th Cir. 1981); appointed deputy sheriff, McCusker v. Valley News, 428 A.2d 493 (N.H. 1981); "Miss Wyoming," Pring v. Penthouse, 7 Media L. Rptr. 1101 (D. Wyo. 1981); undercover police informant, Jenoff v. Hearst, 644 F.2d 1004 (4th Cir. 1981).

1.a.(4) [continued] A murder defendant who assumed no prominence beyond being charged with homicide was held not to be a public figure in Mills v. Kingsport Times-News, 475 F. Supp. 1005 (W.D. Va. 1979). But see Davis v. Duryea, 4 Media L. Rptr. 1746 (N.Y. Sup. Ct. 1978), where an indicted murder suspect shown on television behind a political candidate during his anticrime campaign was held to be a public figure.

(page 516) [692]

NOTES

1.a.(6) [continued] Corporations have been subjected to much the same type of scrutiny as individuals in determining whether they merit public figure status in libel actions. Cases holding corporations to be public figures (and the factors relied upon) include Reliance Insurance Co. v. Barron's, 442 F. Supp. 1341 (S.D.N.Y. 1977); (size of assets and interest surrounding recent $50 million public stock offering); American Benefit Life v. McIntyre, 375 So. 2d 239 (Ala. 1979) (insurance business's close governmental regulation and powerful societal influence); Church of Scientology v. Cazares, 638 F.2d 1272 (5th Cir. 1981) (world-wide religious movement); Steaks Unlimited v. Deaner, 623 F.2d 264 (3d Cir. 1980) (meat company's intensive advertising campaign and continuing access to media); Bose v. Consumers Union, 508 F. Supp. 1249 (D. Mass. 1981) (extensive advertisements and active solicitation of reviews concerning innovative loudspeaker system). Bose is noteworthy in another sense because the court there applied the actual malice standard in a product disparagement action rather than the more traditional action alleging defamation of the corporation itself. For a statement of the proposition that corporations are always public figures unless the matter publicized is of no legitimate public interest, see Martin Marietta Corp. v. Evening Star Newspaper Co., 417 F. Supp. 947 (D.D.C. 1976). But see Vegod Corp. v. ABC, 603 P.2d 14 (Cal. 1979) (corporation that conducted a closeout sale for a "landmark" San Francisco department store not a public figure by virtue of doing business with parties to a public controversy or by advertising its services); Bruno & Stillman v. Globe Newspaper, 633 F.2d 583 (1st Cir. 1980) successful corporation recognized in its field is not a public figure unless "thrust into vortex" of public controversy); Arctic v. Loudoun Times Mirror, 624 F.2d 518 (4th Cir. 1980) (historical and archaelogical research corporation employed as consultant and which exercised no judgment or discretion regarding the project not a public figure).

(page 516) [692]

NOTES

1.a.(7) *Continued public figure status.* Despite the possibility that passage of time may deprive one of public figure status, lower courts have generally held to the contrary. See Mobile Press Register v. Faulkner, 372 So. 2d 1282 (Ala. 1979) (21-year lapse for former mayor, state senator and unsuccessful gubernatorial candidate); Brewer v. Memphis Publishing, 626 F.2d 1238 (5th Cir. 1980) (23-year lapse for former entertainer and one-time girlfriend of Elvis Presley); Street v. NBC, 645 F.2d 1227 (6th Cir. 1981) (major witness in 1930's rape prosecution of Scottsboro boys).

(page 517) [693]

NOTES

2. [insert before 2.a.] For a recent case on the use of summary judgment procedures to implement First Amendment protections for def

amation defendants, see Southard v. Forbes, 588 F.2d 140 (5th Cir. 1979). See also Herbert v. Lando, 441 U.S. 153 (1979), discussed infra.

(page 518) [694]

NOTES

2a. [continued] The Times malice standard is occasionally confused with malice in the sense of ill will or evil intent, which is immaterial in this context. See Mobile Press Register v. Faulkner, 372 So. 2d 1282 (Ala. 1979).

It has been contended that Gertz affords constitutional protection only to media defendants. Under this approach, statements made by private individuals have been held to fall outside the Constitution and within full state control. See Rowe v. Metz, 579 P.2d 83 (Colo. 1978), Wheeler v. Green, 593 P.2d 777 (Ore. 1979). This position has been rejected and the actual malice standard applied in Bussie v. Larson, 501 F. Supp. 1107 (M.D. La. 1980), and Jacron Sales v. Sindorf, 350 A.2d 688 (Md. 1975).

(page 521) [697]

NOTES

3. [continued] In Herbert v. Lando, 441 U.S. 153 (1979), a retired army officer sued a television network, two of its employees, and a magazine for allegedly falsely portraying him in a television program as a liar in making charges in 1969-1970 that his superiors had covered up war crimes reports in Vietnam. Plaintiff conceded that he was a public figure who had to establish actual malice in order to recover. In preparing for trial, plaintiff deposed Lando, the producer and editor of the television program ("Sixty Minutes"), and sought to ask him questions about the preparation of the program. These questions related to Lando's state of mind at that time regarding the veracity of sources and reports used on the program. The district court held the discovery permissible as relevant to the claim of malice, but a divided panel of the court of appeals reversed on the ground that First Amendment protection for editorial processes gave Lando an absolute privilege to refuse to respond to inquiries about his thoughts, opinions, and conclusions relating to material gathered by him, and about his conversations with editorial colleagues. 585 F.2d 974 (2d Cir. 1977). The Supreme Court reversed the court of appeals. Justice White's opinion for the Court relied primarily on the view that according an absolute privilege to the editorial process of a media defendant in a libel case "would substantially

enhance the burden of proving actual malice, contrary to the expectations of the New York Times, Butts and similar cases." With regard to the alleged "chilling effect" on the press of inquiries like plaintiff's, the Court said that "our cases necessarily contemplate examination of the editorial process to prove the necessary awareness of probable falsehood, and if indirect proof of this element does not stifle truthful publication and is consistent with the First Amendment, as respondents seem to concede, we do not understand how direct inquiry with respect to the ultimate issue would be substantially more suspect." Excessive burdens on the press from discovery can be prevented by "what in fact and in law are ample powers of the district judge to prevent abuse."

Justice Powell joined the Court's opinion "on my understanding that . . . the District Court must ensure that the values protected by the First Amendment, though entitled to no constitutional privilege in a case of this kind, are weighed carefully in striking a proper balance." Justice Brennan dissented in part: "I would hold . . . that the First Amendment requires predecisional communication among editors to be protected by an editorial privilege, but that this privilege must yield if a public figure plaintiff is able to demonstrate to the prima facie satisfaction of a trial judge that the libel in question constitutes defamatory falsehood." Justices Stewart and Marshall also dissented, Justice Stewart on the ground that " 'actual malice' has nothing to do with hostility or ill will" so that "the question 'why' is totally irrelevant"; Justice Marshall on the ground that discovery of the substance of "editorial conversation" should be foreclosed.

In applying Herbert, courts have generally held that, in order to justify a claim for disclosure, a plaintiff must show that: (1) his claim has merit, (2) the desired information would be relevant and necessary in establishing a jury question regarding actual malice, and (3) the information sought is not available from alternative sources. See Miller v. Transamerican Press, 621 F.2d 721 (5th Cir. 1980); Bruno and Stillman v. Globe Newspaper, 633 F.2d 583 (1st Cir. 1980); Deroburt v. Gannet, 6 Media L. Rptr. 2473 (D. Hawaii 1981).

Once disclosure is ordered, a refusal to provide the information has been held to require the application of a presumption that the newspaper had no source for its allegedly libelous article. Downing v. Monitor Publishing, 415 A.2d 683 (N.H. 1980).

Herbert has been distinguished in cases interpreting Pennsylvania's shield law, which provides almost absolute protection against disclosure of a reporter's sources. See Mazzella v. Philadelphia Newspapers, 479 F. Supp. 523 (E.D.N.Y. 1979); Steaks Unlimited v. Deaner, 623 F.2d 264 (3d Cir. 1980). The court in Deaner read Herbert to allow states to establish a privilege against state-of-mind discovery, and paid deference to the legislative determination to favor protection of news sources above facilitating remedies for defamation.

(page 522) [698]

NOTES

4. [continued] On the media as a "conduit" for defamatory statements of others, see also Orr v. Argus-Press, 586 F.2d 1108 (6th Cir. 1978); Edwards v. National Audubon Society, Inc., 556 F.2d 113 (2d Cir. 1977). In Hotchner v. Castillo-Puche, 551 F.2d 910 (2d Cir. 1977), the court held that the malice of a publishing company itself, rather than a non-employee author, is the relevant factor under Times v. Sullivan. In Porter v. Guam Publications, 643 F.2d 615 (9th Cir. 1981), the court found no malice in a newspaper's accurate report of the contents of a broadcast daily police bulletin that was based upon false charges made by a complainant.

(page 522) [698]

NOTES

5. [continued] In Herbert v. Lando, supra, the Court noted the effect of decisions such as Times v. Sullivan and Gertz in shifting the burden of proving falsity from the defendant to the plaintiff: "In years gone by, plaintiffs made out a prima facie case by proving the damaging publication. Truth and privilege were defenses. . . . The plaintiff's burden is now considerably expanded. In every or almost every case, the plaintiff must focus on the editorial process and prove a false publication attended by some degree of culpability on the part of the publisher." Lower courts have generally followed this approach. See Cianci v. New Times, 639 F.2d 54 (2d Cir. 1980); Morgan v. Winters, 594 P.2d 1220 (Okla. 1979) (any presumption of actual malice based on a ruling that material is libelous per se is unconstitutional); Wilson v. Scripps-Howard, 7 Media L. Rptr. 1169 (6th Cir. 1981) (common law's placement of the burden of proving truth on the defendant permits imposition of liability without fault contrary to Gertz). But at least one state — Pennsylvania — still appears to place the burden of proving truth on the defendant, see Steaks Unlimited v. Deaner, 623 F.2d 264 (3d Cir. 1980); Medico v. Time, 643 F.2d 134 (3d Cir. 1981), although this rule seems of extremely questionable constitutionality after Gertz. See Medico v. Time, supra, 643 F.2d at 146 n.40; Moyer v. Phillips, 341 A.2d 441, 447 (Pa. 1975) (Roberts, J. concurring) But cf. Eaton, The American Law of Defamation through Gertz v. Robert Welch, Inc. and Beyond: An Analytical Primer, 61 Va. L. Rev. 1349, 1381-1386, 1429 (1976) (Gertz tolerates common law rule of presuming falsity of defamatory publication and placing burden of proving truth on defendant).

(page 522) [698]

FOOTNOTE H

[continued] The Court appeared to adopt Justice Powell's position on this issue in Time, Inc. v. Firestone, 424 U.S. 448 (1976), where, in a private defamation case, it observed that "demonstration that an article was true would seem to preclude finding the publisher at fault."

(page 526) [702]

NOTE — THE CONSTITUTIONAL LIMITATIONS ... APPLICABLE ... TO "PRIVATE" DEFAMATION ...

[continued] Since the Gertz decision, fifteen state courts have adopted a negligence standard for private defamation actions. See Peagler v. Phoenix Newspapers, Inc., 560 P.2d 1216 (Ariz. 1977); Dodrill v. Arkansas Democrat, 590 S.W.2d 840 (Ark. 1979); Corbett v. Register Publishing Co., 356 A.2d 472 (Conn. Super. Ct. 1975); Phillips v. Evening Star, 424 A.2d 94 (D.C. Ct. App. 1980); Cahill v. Hawaiian Paradise Park Corp., 543 P.2d 1356 (Hawaii 1975); Troman v. Wood, 340 N.E. 2d 292 (Ill. 1976); Gobin v. Globe Publishing Co., 531 P.2d 76 (Kan. 1975); Jacron Sales Inc. v. Sindorf, 350 A.2d 688 (Md. 1976); Stone v. Essex County Newspapers, Inc., 330 N.E.2d 161 (Mass. 1975); Thomas H. Maloney & Sons, Inc. v. E. W. Scripps Co., 334 N.E.2d 494 (Ohio 1974); Martin v. Griffin Television, Inc., 549 P.2d 85 (Okla. 1976); Memphis Publishing Co. v. Nichols, 569 S.W.2d 412 (Tenn. 1978); Foster v. Laredo Newspapers, Inc. 541 S.W.2d 809 (Tex. 1976); Seegmiller v. KSL, 626 P.2d 968 (Utah 1981); Taskett v. King Broadcasting Co., 546 P.2d 81 (Wash. 1976). See also Mills v. Kingsport Times-News, 475 F. Supp. 1005 (W.D. Va. 1979); Mathis v. Philadelphia Newspaper Co., 445 F. Supp. 406 (E.D. Pa. 1978) (federal courts exercising diversity jurisdiction). Four states have adopted an actual malice standard, thus equating public figure and nonpublic figure defamation actions. Walker v. Colorado Springs Sun, Inc., 538 P.2d 181 (Colo. 1976); Aafco Heating & Air Conditioning Co. v. Northwest Publications, Inc., 321 N.E.2d 580 (Ind. Ct. App. 1975); Peisner v. Detroit Free Press, Inc., 266 N.W.2d 693 (Mich. Ct. App. 1975); Commercial Programming Unlimited v. Columbia Broadcasting Systems, Inc., 367 N.Y.S.2d 986 (1975). See also Gay v. Williams, 486 F. Supp. 12 (Alaska 1979) (federal court exercising diversity jurisdiction). One state has adopted a "gross negligence" standard. Chapadeau v. Utica Observer Dispatch, Inc., 38 N.Y.2d 196, 341 N.E.2d 569 (1975). The Restatement of Torts (Second) adopts the Gertz principle without selecting a particular standard of care. Restatement of Torts (Second) §580B (1976). See Collins & Dushal, The Reaction of

State Courts to Gertz v. Robert Welch, 28 Case W. Res. L. Rev. 306 (1978).

In Time, Inc. v. Firestone, 424 U.S. 448 (1976), the Court had its first post-Gertz opportunity to elaborate on the meaning of the Gertz "fault" and evidence of "actual injury" requirements. Justice Rehnquist's opinion for the Court seemed to play down both requirements, thus perhaps making recovery for private defamation plaintiffs easier than might have appeared from Gertz itself. As to actual injury, the Firestone opinion rejected the contention that "the only compensable injury in a defamation case is that which may be done to one's reputation." Rather, states could base awards "on elements other than injury to reputation." In Firestone, plaintiff has apparently withdrawn her claim of reputational injury; a jury verdict of $100,000 was permitted, however, based on proof of plaintiff's "anxiety and concern" over the falsehood and plaintiff's "fear that her young son would be adversely affected . . . when he grew older." As to fault, that issue was not submitted to the jury in Firestone because Florida law did not require a finding of fault at the time of trial. The Supreme Court held, however, that "[n]othing in the Constitution requires that assessment of fault in a civil case tried in a state court be made by a jury, nor is there any prohibition against such a finding being made in the first instance by an appellate, rather than a trial court." There was not, however, a sufficiently clear appellate court finding of fault in Firestone to warrant affirmance, and the issue was remanded. The evidence of fault in Firestone was extremely thin. Defendant (Time Magazine) had reported that plaintiff had been found guilty of adultery in divorce proceedings (a conclusion supported by language in the divorce court's opinion). Knowledge of the intricacies of Florida law would have revealed, however, that plaintiff could not have been formally found to have committed adultery because she received an award of alimony, and such an award could not, under Florida law, be made to an adulterous wife. Justice Rehnquist's opinion for the Court nevertheless observed that "[i]t may well be" that Time's account "was the product of some fault on its part." For proceedings on remand in Firestone see 332 So. 2d 68 (Fla. 1976).

(page 540) [716]

NOTES

1. [continued] In Doe v. Roe, 93 Misc. 2d 201 (N.Y. Sup. Ct. 1977), the Doe plaintiff recovered both damages and a permanent injunction.

Cox v. Cohn was invoked by the Supreme Court in Oklahoma Publishing Co. v. District Court, 430 U.S. 308 (1977). An eleven-year-old boy had been charged with murder in delinquency proceedings. Although an Oklahoma statute provided that juvenile proceedings were to be held in private, reporters were present during a pre-trial detention hearing that took place three days after the murder. Petitioner's reporter learned the name of the boy at the hearing, and petitioner's photographer took his picture as he was being escorted from the courthouse after the hearing. The name and picture were published. Subsequently, at a closed arraignment hearing, the judge enjoined publication of the name and picture. The Supreme Court held this "gag" order unconstitutional, relying on Cox and Nebraska Press Assn. v. Stewart, 427 U.S. 539 (1976).

See also Landmark Communications, Inc. v. Virginia, 435 U.S. 829 (1978), holding unconstitutional a state statute that made it a crime to divulge the name of a judge currently under investigation by a judicial inquiry commission: "Criminal punishment of third persons who are strangers to the inquiry, including news media, for divulging or publishing truthful information" regarding "confidential proceedings" was not permissible. And see Smith v. Daily Mail Publishing Co., 443 U.S. 97 (1979), striking down a West Virginia statute that made it a crime for a newspaper to publish the name of a juvenile offender without the court's permission.

Lower courts that have relied on Cox v. Cohn in ruling for defendants include Holman v. Central Arkansas Broadcasting, 610 F.2d 542 (8th Cir. 1979) (broadcast of tape recording of attorney's "boisterous complaints" during his arrest for drunken driving); Dubree v. Association of Trial Lawyers of America, 6 Media L. Rptr. 1158 (D. Vt. 1980) (publication of report of lawsuit based on official court records); Campbell v. Seabury Press, 614 F.2d 395 (5th Cir. 1980) (references to wife of major characer in book, which were of public interest and limited to the period of their marriage); Forsher v. Bugliosi, 27 Cal. 3d 792 (1980) (book's mention of plaintiff's minor role in disappearance of attorney handling Charles Manson murder case).

Cox v. Cohn was distinguished by the Supreme Court in Nixon v. Warner Communications, 435 U.S. 589 (1978), where the Court held that the district court had not abused its discretion by refusing to release the Watergate tapes for copying by the media. The Cox right, said the Court, was preserved by the freedom of the media to publish the tapes as they were introduced into evidence in the courtroom.

In Time v. Firestone, supra, the Court declined to extend the "public records" privilege recognized in Cox to protect false or inaccurate reports of published judicial proceedings.

(page 541) [717]

NOTES

2. [continued] In Norris v. King, 355 So. 2d 1035 (La. App. 1978), it was held that a convicted thief could maintain an action for invasion

of privacy against a store owner who had posted accurate pictures of the thief taken by an automatic camera during a robbery of the store. The pictures were posted, along with the thief's name and disparaging remarks about his abilities as a criminal. See also Virgil v. Time, Inc., 527 F.2d 1122 (D.C. Cir. 1975), cert. denied, 425 U.S. 998 (1976) (publication of true private facts not protected by First Amendment unless they are of legitimate concern to the public rather than "a morbid and sensational prying into private lives for its own sake.")

(page 541) [717]

NOTES

4. [continued] In Zacchini v. Scripps-Howard Broadcasting Co., 433 U.S. 562 (1977), the Supreme Court held that a state right of publicity may in some circumstances override the ordinarily applicable constitutional privilege of the press to broadcast true information about matters of public interest. Zacchini was an entertainer at a county fair whose entire fifteen-second "human cannonball" performance was video-taped and broadcast on a TV news program. He brought an action against the TV station under Ohio law for damages for unlawful appropriation of his professional property. The Ohio Supreme Court reversed the trial court's grant of summary judgment for defendants in an opinion that appeared to hold the TV station's conduct privileged under the First and Fourteenth Amendments. In an opinion by Justice White, the U.S. Supreme Court reversed. The Court held that the protection extended to the press by the First Amendment in defamation cases did not mandate a similar media privilege to televise a performer's entire act without his consent since the interests sought to be protected in the two situations were entirely different. The "right to publicity" in a case like Zacchini, said the Court, protects the performer's proprietary interest in a manner analogous to the protection constitutionally provided by patent and copyright laws. Justice Powell, joined by Justices Brennan and Marshall, dissented.

In Carson v. Here's Johnny, 498 F. Supp. 71 (E.D. Mich. 1980), the court relied on Zacchini in holding that a portable toilet company's use of the trade name "Here's Johnny" did not constitute an appropriation of Carson's right to publicity, due to the lack of any specific identification of the entertainer by the company.

[720]

[REFERENCES]

[continued] On defamation since Gertz, see Ashdown, Gertz & Firestone: A Study in Constitutional Policy-Making, 61 Minn. L. Rev. 645

(1977); Bezanson, Herbert v. Lando, Editorial Judgment, and Freedom of the Press: An Essay, 1978 U. Ill. L.F. 605 (1978); Eaton, The American Law of Defamation Through Gertz v. Robert Welch, Inc., and Beyond: An Analytical Primer, 61 Va. L. Rev. 1349 (1975); Frakt, Defamation Since Gertz v. Robert Welch, Inc.: The Emerging Common Law, 10 Rut-Cam. L.J. 519 (1979); Goldberg, The First Amendment and Its Protections, 8 Hastings Const. L.Q. 5 (1980); Green, Political Freedom of the Press and the Libel Problem, 56 Tex. L. Rev. 341 (1978); Hill, Defamation and Privacy Under the First Amendment, 76 Colum. L. Rev. 1205 (1976); Ingber, Defamation: A Contest Between Reason and Decency, 65 Va. L. Rev. 785 (1979); Keeton, Defamation and Freedom of the Press, 51 Tex. L. Rev. 1221 (1976); Kulzick & Hogue, Chilled Bird: Freedom of Expression in the Eighties, 14 Loy. L.A.L. Rev. 57 (1980); LaRue, Living with Gertz: A Practical Look at Constitutional Libel Standards, 67 Va. L. Rev. 287 (1981); Mertz, Constitutional Limitations on Libel Actions, 28 Baylor L. Rev. 79 (1976); C. Morris, Modern Defamation Law (1978); Oakes, Proof of Actual Malice in Defamation Actions: An Unsolved Dilemma, 7 Hofstra L. Rev. 655 (1979); Robertson, Defamation and the First Amendment: In Praise of Gertz v. Robert Welch, Inc., 54 Tex. L. Rev. 199 (1976); Rosenberg, The New Law of Political Libel: A Historical Perspective, 28 Rutgers L. Rev. 1141 (1975); R. Sack, Libel, Slander, and Related Problems (1980); Schaefer, Defamation and the First Amendment, 52 U. Colo. L. Rev. 1 (1980); Shiffrin, Defamatory Non-Media Speech and First Amendment Methodology, 25 U.C.L.A.L. Rev. 915 (1978); Silver, Libel, the "Higher Truths" of Art, and the First Amendment, 126 U. Pa. L. Rev. 1065 (1978); K. Sowle, Defamation and the First Amendment: The Case for a Constitutional Privilege of Fair Report, 54 N.Y.U.L. Rev. 469 (1979); Stevens, Performing Artists as "Public Figures": The Implications of Gertz v. Robert Welch, Inc., 6 Performing Arts L. Rev. 3 (1975); Wade, The Communicative Torts and the First Amendment, 48 Miss. L.J. 671 (1977); Yasser, Defamation As a Constitutional Tort: With Actual Malice For All, 12 Tulsa L.J. 601 (1977); Comment, Constitutional Privilege to Republish Defamation, 77 Colum. L. Rev. 1266 (1977); Comment, Gertz and Public Figure Doctrine Revisited, 54 Tul. L. Rev. 1053 (1980); Comment, The Involuntary Public Figure Class of Gertz v. Robert Welch: Dead or Merely Dormant?, 14 U. Mich. J.L. Ref. 71 (1980); Note, Defamation, Privacy and the First Amendment, 1976 Duke L.J. 1016; Note, Corporate Defamation and Product Disparagement: Narrowing the Analogy to Personal Defamation, 75 Colum. L. Rev. 963 (1975); Note, In Defense of Truth in Defamation Law, 88 Yale L.J. 1735 (1979).

On actions for invasion of privacy, see Christie, Injury to Reputation and the Constitution: Confusion Amid Conflicting Approaches, 75 Mich. L. Rev. 43 (1976); Felcher & Rubin, Privacy, Publicity, and the Portrayal of Real People by the Media, 88 Yale L.J. 1577 (1979); Ferber, Beating

Bad Press: Protecting the California Criminal Defendant from Adverse Publicity, 10 U.S.F.L. Rev. 391 (1976); Phillips, Defamation, Invasion of Privacy and the Constitutional Standard of Care, 16 Santa Clara L. Rev. 77 (1975); Posner, The Right of Privacy, 12 Ga. L. Rev. 393 (1978); Woito & McNulty, Privacy Disclosure Tort and the First Amendment: Should the Community Decide Newsworthiness?, 64 Iowa L. Rev. 185 (1979); Comment, An Accommodation of Privacy Interests and First Amendment Rights in Public Disclosure Cases, 124 U. Pa. L. Rev. 1385 (1976).

On testimonial privilege and publicity, see Compton, Increasing Press Protection from Libel Through a New Public Official Standard: Herbert v. Lando Revisited, 15 Suffolk U.L. Rev. 79 (1981); Reese & Leiwant, Testimonial Privileges and Conflict of Laws, 86 Law & Contemp. Problems 85 (1977); Sterk, Testimonial Privileges: An Analysis of Horizontal Choice of Law Problems, 61 Minn. L. Rev. 461 (1977); Shielding Editorial Conversations from Discovery: The Relationship Between Herbert v. Lando and Oregon's Shield Law, 59 Ore. L. Rev. 477 (1981); Sims, Right of Publicity: Survivability Reconsidered, 49 Fordham L. Rev. 453 (1981).

Chapter Eight
Commercial Speech

(page 573) [752]

Insert text after Notes [References]

Since publication of the main volume, the Supreme Court has decided several important cases that have significantly elaborated upon the First Amendment protection applicable to commercial advertising and similar activity:

VIRGINIA STATE BOARD OF PHARMACY v.
VIRGINIA CITIZENS CONSUMER COUNCIL, INC.
425 U.S. 748 (1976)

Mr. JUSTICE BLACKMUN delivered the opinion of the Court.

The plaintiff-appellees in this case attack, as violative of the First and Fourteenth Amendments, that portion of §54-524.35 of Va. Code Ann. (1974), which provides that a pharmacist licensed in Virginia is guilty of unprofessional conduct if he "(3) publishes, advertises or promotes, directly or indirectly, in any manner whatsoever, any amount, price, fee, premium, discount, rebate or credit terms . . . for any drugs which may be dispensed only by prescription." The three-judge District Court declared the quoted portion of the statute "void and of no effect," and enjoined the defendant-appellants, the Virginia State Board of Pharmacy and the individual members of that Board, from enforcing it. 373 F. Supp. 683 (ED Va. 1974). . . .

Inasmuch as only a licensed pharmacist may dispense prescription drugs in Virginia, . . . advertising or other affirmative dissemination of prescription drug price information is effectively forbidden in the State [by §54-524.35.] . . . The prohibition does not extend to nonprescription drugs, but neither is it confined to prescriptions that the pharmacist compounds himself. Indeed, about 95% of all prescriptions now are filled with dosage forms prepared by the pharmaceutical manufacturer....

The present... attack on the statute is one made not by one directly subject to its prohibition, that is, a pharmacist, but by prescription drug consumers who claim that they would greatly benefit if the prohibition were lifted and advertising freely allowed.... Their claim is that the First Amendment entitles the user of prescription drugs to receive information that pharmacists wish to communicate to them through advertising and other promotional means, concerning the prices of such drugs.

Certainly that information may be of value. [It was stipulated, for example, that drug prices in Virginia may vary by as much as 650% within the same locality.]....

The question first arises whether, even assuming that First Amendment protection attaches to the flow of drug price information, it is a protection enjoyed by the appellees as recipients of the information, and not solely, if at all, by the advertisers themselves who seek to disseminate that information.

Freedom of speech presupposes a willing speaker. But where a speaker exists, as is the case here, the protection afforded is to the communication, to its source and to its recipients both.... If there is a right to advertise, there is a reciprocal right to receive the advertising, and it may be asserted by these appellees.

The appellants contend that the advertisement of prescription drug prices is outside the protection of the First Amendment because it is "commercial speech." There can be no question that in past decisions the Court has given some indication that commercial speech is unprotected....

[However, last] Term, in Bigelow v. Virginia, the notion of unprotected "commercial speech" all but passed from the scene....

Some fragment of hope for the continuing validity of a "commercial speech" exception arguably might have persisted because of the subject matter of the advertisement in Bigelow [the availability of legal abortions.] Indeed, we observed [in Bigelow]: "We need not decide in this case the precise extent to which the First Amendment permits regulation of advertising that is related to activities the State may legitimately regulate or even prohibit."

Here, in contrast, the question whether there is a First Amendment exception for "commercial speech" is squarely before us. Our pharmacist does not wish to editorialize on any subject, cultural, philosophical, or political. He does not wish to report any particularly newsworthy fact, or to make generalized observations even about commercial matters. The "idea" he wishes to communicate is simply this: "I will sell you the X prescription drug at the Y price." Our question, then... is whether speech which does "no more than propose a commercial transaction,"

Pittsburgh Press Co. v. Human Relations Comm'n, 413 U.S., at 385, is so removed from any "exposition of ideas," Chaplinsky v. New Hampshire, 315 U.S. 568, 572 (1942), and from " 'truth, science, morality, and arts in general, in its diffusion of liberal sentiments on the administration of Government,' " Roth v. United States, 354 U.S. 476, 484 (1957), that it lacks all protection. Our answer is that it is not.

Focusing first on the individual parties to the transaction that is proposed in the commercial advertisement, we may assume that the advertiser's interest is a purely economic one. That hardly disqualifies him from protection under the First Amendment. . . .

As to the particular consumer's interest in the free flow of commercial information, that interest may be as keen, if not keener by far, than his interest in the day's most urgent political debate. . . . When drug prices vary as strikingly as they do, information as to who is charging what becomes more than a convenience. It could mean the alleviation of physical pain or the enjoyment of basic necessities.

Generalizing, society also may have a strong interest in the free flow of commercial information. Even an individual advertisement, though entirely "commercial," may be of general public interest. . . . Obviously, not all commercial messages contain the same or even a very great public interest element. There are few to which such an element, however, could not be added. Our pharmacist, for example, could cast himself as a commentator on store-to-store disparities in drug prices, giving his own and those of a competitor as proof. We see little point in requiring him to do so, and little difference if he does not.

Moreover, there is another consideration that suggests that no line between publicly "interesting" or "important" commercial advertising and the opposite kind could ever be drawn. Advertising, however tasteless and excessive it sometimes may seem, is nonetheless dissemination of information as to who is producing and selling what product, for what reason, and at what price. So long as we preserve a predominantly free enterprise economy, the allocation of our resources in large measure will be made through numerous private economic decisions. It is a matter of public interest that those decisions, in the aggregate, be intelligent and well informed. To this end, the free flow of commercial information is indispensable. . . . And if it is indispensable to the proper allocation of resources in a free enterprise system, it is also indispensable to the formation of intelligent opinions as to how that system ought to be regulated or altered. Therefore, even if the First Amendment were thought to be primarily an instrument to enlighten public decisionmaking in a democracy, we could not say that the free flow of information does not serve that goal.

Arrayed against these substantial individual and societal interests are a number of justifications for the advertising ban. These have to do principally with maintaining a high degree of professionalism on the part of licensed pharmacists. Indisputably, the State has a strong interest in maintaining that professionalism....

Price advertising, it is argued, will place in jeopardy the pharmacist's expertise and, with it, the customer's health. It is claimed that the aggressive price competition that will result from unlimited advertising will make it impossible for the pharmacist to supply professional services in the compounding, handling, and dispensing of prescription drugs....

The strength of these proffered justifications is greatly undermined by the fact that high professional standards, to a substantial extent, are guaranteed by the close regulation to which pharmacists in Virginia are subject.... At the same time, we cannot discount the Board's justifications entirely. The Court regarded justifications of this type sufficient to sustain the advertising bans challenged on due process and equal protection grounds in Head v. New Mexico Board, [374 U.S. 424 (1963) (optometrists' services)]; Williamson v. Lee Optical Co., [348 U.S. 483 (1955) (eyeglass frames)]; and Semler v. Dental Examiners, [294 U.S. 608 (1935) (dentists' services)].

The challenge now made, however, is based on the First Amendment. This casts the Board's justifications in a different light, for on close inspection it is seen that the State's protectiveness of its citizens rests in large measure on the advantages of their being kept in ignorance....

It appears to be feared that if the pharmacist who wishes to provide low cost, and assertedly low quality, services is permitted to advertise, he will be taken up on his offer by too many unwitting customers. They will choose the low-cost, low-quality service and drive the "professional" pharmacist out of business.... [T]his is not in their best interests, and . . . can be avoided if they are not permitted to know who is charging what.

There is, of course, an alternative to this highly paternalistic approach. That alternative is to assume that this information is not in itself harmful, that people will perceive their own best interests if only they are well enough informed, and that the best means to that end is to open the channels of communication rather than to close them. If they are truly open, nothing prevents the "professional" pharmacist from marketing his own assertedly superior product, and contrasting it with that of the low-cost, high-volume prescription drug retailer. But the choice among these alternative approaches is not ours to make or the Virginia General Assembly's. It is precisely this kind of choice, between the dangers of suppressing information, and the dangers of its misuse if it is freely available, that the First Amendment makes for us. Virginia is free to require whatever professional standards it wishes of its pharmacists; it may subsidize them or protect them from competition in other ways.... But it may not do so by keeping the public in ignorance of the entirely lawful terms that competing pharmacists are offering. In this sense, the justifications Virginia has offered for suppressing the flow of prescription drug price information, far from persuading us that the flow is not protected by the First Amendment, have reinforced our view that it is. We so hold. . . .

In concluding that commercial speech, like other varieties, is protected, we of course do not hold that it can never be regulated in any way. Some forms of commercial speech regulation are surely permissible. We mention a few only to make clear that they are not before us and therefore are not foreclosed by this case.

There is no claim, for example, that the prohibition on prescription drug price advertising is a mere time, place, and manner restriction. We have often approved restrictions of that kind provided that they are justified without reference to the content of the regulated speech, that they serve a significant governmental interest, and that in so doing they leave open ample alternative channels for communication of the information. . . . Whatever may be the proper bounds of time, place, and manner restrictions on commercial speech, they are plainly exceeded by this Virginia statute, which singles out speech of a particular content and seeks to prevent its dissemination completely.

Nor is there any claim that prescription drug price advertisements are forbidden because they are false or misleading in any way. Untruthful speech, commercial or otherwise, has never been protected for its own sake. . . . Obviously, much commercial speech is not provably false, or even wholly false, but only deceptive or misleading. We foresee no obstacle to a State's dealing effectively with this problem.[24] The First Amendment, as we construe it today, does not prohibit the State from insuring that the stream of commercial information flow cleanly as well as freely. . . .

Also, there is no claim that the transactions proposed in the forbidden advertisements are themselves illegal in any way. . . . Finally, the special

24. In concluding that commercial speech enjoys First Amendment protection, we have not held that it is wholly undifferentiable from other forms. There are commonsense differences between speech that does "no more than propose a commercial transaction," and other varieties. Even if the differences do not justify the conclusion that commercial speech is valueless, and thus subject to complete suppression by the State, they nonetheless suggest that a different degree of protection is necessary to insure that the flow of truthful and legitimate commercial information is unimpaired. The truth of commercial speech, for example, may be more easily verifiable by its disseminator than, let us say, news reporting or political commentary, in that ordinarily the advertiser seeks to disseminate information about a specific product or service that he himself provides and presumably knows more about than anyone else. Also, commercial speech may be more durable than other kinds. Since advertising is the sine qua non of commercial profits, there is litttle likelihood of its being chilled by proper regulation and forgone entirely.

Attributes such as these, the greater objectivity and hardiness of commercial speech, may make it less necessary to tolerate inaccurate statements for fear of silencing the speaker. . . . They may also make it appropriate to require that a commercial message appear in such a form, or include such additional information, warnings, and disclaimers, as are necessary to prevent its being deceptive. . . .

problems of the electronic broadcast media are likewise not in this case....

What is at issue is whether a State may completely suppress the dissemination of concededly truthful information about entirely lawful activity, fearful of that information's effect upon its disseminators and its recipients. Reserving other questions,[25] we conclude that the answer to this one is in the negative.

The judgment of the District Court is affirmed....

Mr. JUSTICE STEVENS took no part in the consideration or decision of this case.

Mr. CHIEF JUSTICE BURGER, concurring....

Our decision today ... deals largely with the State's power to prohibit pharmacists from advertising the retail price of *prepackaged drugs*. As the Court notes, quite different factors would govern were we faced with a law regulating or even prohibiting advertising by the traditional learned professions of medicine or law.... Attorneys and physicians are engaged *primarily* in providing services in which professional judgment is a large component, a matter very different from the retail *sale* of labeled drugs already prepared by others.

... I think it important to note also that the advertisement of professional services carries with it quite different risks from the advertisement of standard products....

I doubt that we know enough about evaluating the quality of medical and legal services to know which claims of superiority are "misleading" and which are justifiable. Nor am I sure that even advertising the price of certain professional services is not inherently misleading, since what the professional must do will vary greatly in individual cases. It is important to note that the Court wisely leaves these issues to another day.

Mr. JUSTICE STEWART, concurring....

Today the Court ... holds that a communication which does no more than propose a commercial transaction is not "wholly outside the protection of the First Amendment." ... But since it is a cardinal principle of the First Amendment that "government has no power to restrict expression because of its message, its ideas, its subject matter, or its content," the Court's decision calls into immediate question the constitutional legitimacy of every state and federal law regulating false or deceptive advertising. I write separately to explain why I think today's decision does not preclude such governmental regulation.

---

25. We stress that we have considered in this case the regulation of commercial advertising by pharmacists. Although we express no opinion as to other professions, the distinctions, historical and functional, between professions, may require consideration of quite different factors. Physicians and lawyers, for example, do not dispense standardized products: they render professional *services* of almost infinite variety and nature, with the consequent enhanced possibility for confusion and deception if they were to undertake certain kinds of advertising.

The Court's determination that commercial advertising of the kind at issue here is not "wholly outside the protection of" the First Amendment indicates by its very phrasing that there are important differences between commercial price and product advertising, on the one hand, and ideological communication on the other.... Ideological expression, be it oral, literary, pictorial, or theatrical, is integrally related to the exposition of thought — thought that may shape our concepts of the whole universe of man. Although such expression may convey factual information relevant to social and individual decisionmaking, it is protected by the Constitution, whether or not it contains factual representations and even if it includes inaccurate assertions of fact. Indeed, disregard of the "truth" may be employed to give force to the underlying idea expressed by the speaker....

Commercial price and product advertising differs markedly from ideological expression because it is confined to the promotion of specific goods or services.... Since the factual claims contained in commercial price or product advertisements relate to tangible goods or services, they may be tested empirically and corrected to reflect the truth without in any manner jeopardizing the free dissemination of thought. Indeed, the elimination of false and deceptive claims serves to promote the one facet of commercial price and product advertising that warrants First Amendment protection — its contribution to the flow of accurate and reliable information relevant to public and private decisionmaking.

Mr. JUSTICE REHNQUIST, dissenting.

The logical consequences of the Court's decision in this case, a decision which elevates commercial intercourse between a seller hawking his wares and a buyer seeking to strike a bargain to the same plane as has been previously reserved for the free marketplace of ideas, are far reaching indeed. Under the Court's opinion the way will be open not only for dissemination of price information but for active promotion of prescription drugs, liquor, cigarettes, and other products the use of which it has previously been thought desirable to discourage. Now, however, such promotion is protected by the First Amendment so long as it is not misleading or does not promote an illegal product or enterprise....

... [T]he issue on the merits is ... whether appellee consumers may override the legislative determination that pharmacists should not advertise even though the pharmacists themselves do not object. In deciding that they may do so, the Court necessarily adopts a rule which cannot be limited merely to dissemination of price alone, and which cannot possibly be confined to pharmacists but must likewise extend to lawyers, doctors, and all other professions.

The Court speaks of the consumer's interest in the free flow of commercial information, particularly in the case of the poor, the sick, and the aged. It goes on to observe that "society also may have a strong interest in the free flow of commercial information." One need not disagree with either of these statements in order to feel that they should presumptively be the concern of the Virginia Legislature, which sits to balance these and other claims in the process of making laws such as the one here under attack. The Court speaks of the importance in a "predominantly free enterprise economy" of intelligent and well-informed decisions as to allocation of resources. While there is again much to be said for the Court's observation as a matter of desirable public policy, there is certainly nothing in the United States Constitution which requires the Virginia Legislature to hew to the teachings of Adam Smith in its legislative decisions regulating the pharmacy profession. . . .

There are undoubted difficulties with an effort to draw a bright line between "commercial speech" on the one hand and "protected speech" on the other, and the Court does better to face up to these difficulties than to attempt to hide them under labels. In this case, however, the Court has unfortunately substituted for the wavering line previously thought to exist between commercial speech and protected speech a no more satisfactory line of its own — that between "truthful" commercial speech, on the one hand, and that which is "false and misleading" on the other. . . .

Unless the State can show that . . . advertisements are either actually untruthful or misleading, it presumably is not free to restrict in any way commercial efforts on the part of those who profit from the sale of prescription drugs to put them in the widest possible circulation. But such a line simply makes no allowance whatever for what appears to have been a considered legislative judgment in most States that while prescription drugs are a necessary and vital part of medical care and treatment, there are sufficient dangers attending their widespread use that they simply may not be promoted in the same manner as hair creams, deodorants, and toothpaste. The very real dangers that general advertising for such drugs might create in terms of encouraging, even though not sanctioning, illicit use of them by individuals for whom they have not been prescribed, or by generating patient pressure upon physicians to prescribe them, are simply not dealt with in the Court's opinion. . . .

Both Congress and state legislatures have by law sharply limited the permissible dissemination of information about some commodities because of the potential harm resulting from those commodities, even though they were not thought to be sufficiently demonstrably harmful to warrant outright prohibition of their sale. Current prohibitions on television advertising of liquor and cigarettes are prominent in this category, but apparently under the Court's holding so long as the advertisements are not deceptive they may no longer be prohibited.

This case presents a fairly typical First Amendment problem — that of balancing interests in individual free speech against public welfare determinations embodied in a legislative enactment. . . .

Here the rights of the appellees seem to me to be marginal at best. There is no ideological content to the information which they seek and it is freely available to them. . . . On the other hand, the societal interest against the promotion of drug use for every ill, real or imaginary, seems to me extremely strong. I do not believe that the First Amendment mandates the Court's "open door policy" toward such commercial advertising.

NOTES

1. In Carey v. Population Services International, 431 U.S. 678 (1977), at p. 207 infra, the Court relied on Virginia Pharmacy to invalidate a New York statute prohibiting any advertisement or display of contraceptives.

2. In Linmark Associates, Inc. v. Township of Willingboro, 431 U.S. 85 (1977), the Court unanimously invalidated a municipal ordinance that, in the Court's words, prohibited "the posting of 'For Sale' or 'Sold' signs when the municipality acts to stem what it perceives as the flight of white homeowners from a racially integrated community." Justice Marshall wrote the Court's opinion. Although there could be "no question about the importance" of the governmental objective served by the ordinance, the record, said the Court, "demonstrates that respondents failed to establish that this ordinance is needed to assure that Willingboro remains an integrated community." The evidence did not establish that "For Sale" signs were a major cause of panic selling or public concern over sales. More basically, "[i]f dissemination of this information can be restricted, then every locality in the country can suppress any facts that reflect poorly on the locality, so long as a plausible claim can be made that disclosure would cause the recipients of the information to act 'irrationally.' Virginia Pharmacy denies government such sweeping powers."

3. In four cases dealing with lawyer advertising and solicitation, the Court has begun to spell out First Amendment limits on the regulation of professional advertising and solicitation. The first of these cases, Bates v. State Bar of Arizona, 433 U.S. 350 (1977), extended constitutional protection to lawyers' price advertising of legal services. Justice Blackmun's opinion for the Court observed that this result "might be said to flow a fortiori" from Virginia Pharmacy. (But see footnote 25 of his Virginia Pharmacy opinion, supra). The Court was persuaded that none of the proffered governmental justifications for prohibition (adverse effect on professionalism; the alleged inherently misleading nature of attorney advertising; effect on the administration of justice; economic effects; effects on the quality of legal services; and the difficulties of enforcing limited regulations on advertising) "rises to the level of an

acceptable reason for suppression of all advertising by attorneys." Chief Justice Burger dissented in part, as did Justices Powell and Stewart. Justice Rehnquist dissented.

In a pair of cases decided together, Ohralik v. Ohio State Bar Assn., 436 U.S. 447 (1978), and In re Primus, 436 U.S. 412 (1978), the Court then turned to regulations dealing with attorneys' solicitation of clients. Ohralik involved a lawyer who was suspended for soliciting business from two teenage girls who had just been injured in an automobile accident. Primus involved the imposition of disciplinary sanctions on an ACLU-cooperating lawyer who offered legal assistance to a woman who had been sterilized as a condition of receiving public medical assistance. Justice Powell wrote the Court's opinions in both cases. In Ohralik, he upheld the lawyer's suspension for violating anti-solicitation rules: "In-person solicitation by a lawyer of remunerative employment is a business transaction in which speech is an essential but subordinate component . . . [and is therefore] only marginally affected with First Amendment concerns." Because the situation involved actions that were "inherently conducive to overreaching and other forms of misconduct," the State acted properly in asserting its "strong interest in adopting and enforcing rules of conduct designed to protect the public from harmful solicitation by lawyers whom it has licensed." In Primus, on the other hand, the lawyer's public reprimand was set aside because "her actions were undertaken to express personal political beliefs and to advance the civil-liberties objectives of the ACLU, rather than to derive financial gain." Because of these political and associational interests, "a state must regulate with significantly greater precision" than when mere "commercial transaction[s]" were at stake. In order to impose discipline, the state would have to show, not merely the "potential danger" that sufficed in Ohralik, but that "undue influence, overreaching, misrepresentation, or invasion of privacy actually occurred in this case." Justice Rehnquist dissented in Primus.

Finally, in In Matter of R.M.J., 102 S. Ct. 929 (1982), the Court unanimously reversed a state disbarment decision based on the violation of lawyers' advertising rules held to be unconstitutionally restrictive. Invalidated were rules limiting advertisable specialities, forbidding the listing of jurisdiction where a lawyer is licensed, forbidding of advertisement of membership in the U.S. Supreme Court bar, and prohibiting mail advertisements to persons other than lawyers, clients, friends, and relatives.

4. In Friedman v. Rogers, 440 U.S. 1 (1979), the Court distinguished Bates and Virginia Pharmacy in upholding a Texas statute prohibiting the practice of optometry under a trade name.

5. Lower court cases applying Virginia Pharmacy and Bates to strike down advertising bans include Rhode Island Broadcasters v. Michaelson, 4 Med. L. Rptr. 2224 (D.R.I. 1978) (income tax return preparation

services); Metpath v. Myers, 462 F. Supp. 1104 (N.D. Cal. 1978) (clinical laboratories); People v. Mobil Oil Corp., 397 N.E.2d 724 (N.Y. 1979); South Ogden CVS Store, Inc. v. Ambach, 493 F. Supp. 374 (S.D.N.Y. 1980) (pharmacies); Durham v. Brock, 498 F. Supp. 213 (M.D. Tenn. 1980) (lawyers); American Medical Assn. v. FTC, 638 F.2d 443 (2d Cir. 1980) (doctors).

6. Virginia Pharmacy indicates that commercial advertising may be prohibited as part of the regulation of unlawful activity. For recent applications of this principle see Dunagin v. City of Oxford, 489 F. Supp. 763 (N.D. Miss. 1980) (liquor); Record Revolution No. 6, Inc. v. City of Parma, 492 F. Supp. 1157 (N.D. Ohio 1980), vacated and remanded, 101 S. Ct. 2998 (1981) (drug paraphernalia); United States v. Reader's Digest, 494 F. Supp. 770 (D. Del. 1980) (sweepstakes prizes).

CENTRAL HUDSON GAS AND ELECTRIC CORP. v. PUBLIC SERVICE COMMISSION OF NEW YORK
447 U.S. 557 (1980)

Mr. JUSTICE POWELL delivered the opinion of the Court.

This case presents the question whether a regulation of the Public Service Commission of the State of New York violates the First and Fourteenth Amendments because it completely bans promotional advertising by an electrical utility.

I

[The Commission first instituted its ban in 1973 in response to a severe fuel shortage and then extended it in 1977, after the shortage had eased. The Commission divided advertising expenses into two broad categories: promotional — advertising intended to stimulate the purchase of utility services; and institutional and informational — a broad category inclusive of all advertising not clearly intended to promote sales. All promotional advertising was banned as being "contrary to the national policy of conserving energy."

Central Hudson challenged the ban in state court, arguing that the Commission had restrained commercial speech in violation of the First and Fourteenth Amendments. The Commission's order was upheld by the trial and intermediate appellate courts, and the New York Court of Appeals affirmed.]

II

The Commission's order restricts only commercial speech, that is, expression related solely to the economic interests of the speaker and its audience.... The First Amendment, as applied to the States through the Fourteenth Amendment, protects commercial speech from unwarranted governmental regulation.... Commercial expression not only serves the economic interest of the speaker, but also assists consumers and furthers the societal interest in the fullest possible dissemination of information. In applying the First Amendment to this area, we have rejected the "highly paternalistic" view that government has complete power to suppress or regulate commercial speech.... Even when advertising communicates only an incomplete version of the relevant facts, the First Amendment presumes that some accurate information is better than no information at all....

Nevertheless, our decisions have recognized "the 'commonsense' distinction between speech proposing a commercial transaction, which occurs in an area traditionally subject to government regulation, and other varieties of speech." Ohralik v. Ohio State Bar Assn., 436 U.S. 447, 455-456 (1978).... The Constitution therefore accords a lesser protection to commercial speech than to other constitutionally guaranteed expression. The protection available for particular commercial expression turns on the nature both of the expression and of the governmental interests served by its regulation.

The First Amendment's concern for commercial speech is based on the informational function of advertising.... Consequently, there can be no constitutional objection to the suppression of commercial messages that do not accurately inform the public about lawful activity. The government may ban forms of communication more likely to deceive the public than to inform it, Friedman v. Rogers, ... Ohralik v. Ohio State Bar Assn. ... or ... commercial speech related to illegal activity, Pittsburgh Press Co. v. Human Relations Comm'n, 413 U.S. 376, 388 (1973).[6]

If the communication is neither misleading nor related to unlawful activity, the government's power is more circumscribed. The State must assert a substantial interest to be achieved by restrictions on commercial speech. Moreover, the regulatory technique must be in proportion to that interest. The limitation on expression must be designed carefully to achieve the State's goal. Compliance with this requirement may be measured by two criteria. First, the restriction must directly advance the state interest involved; the regulation may not be sustained if it provides only ineffective or remote support for the government's purpose. Sec-

---

6. In most other contexts, the First Amendment prohibits regulation based on the content of the message.... Two features of commercial speech permit regulation of its content. First, commercial speakers have extensive knowledge of both the market and their products. Thus, they are well situated to evaluate the accuracy of their messages and the lawfulness of the underlying activity.... In addition, commercial speech, the offspring of economic self-interest, is a hardy breed of expression that is not "particularly susceptible to being crushed by overbroad regulation." [Bates v. State Bar of Arizona.]

ond, if the governmental interest could be served as well by a more limited restriction on commercial speech, the excessive restrictions cannot survive.

Under the first criterion, the Court has declined to uphold regulations that only indirectly advance the state interest involved. In both Bates and Virginia Pharmacy Board, the Court concluded that an advertising ban could not be imposed to protect the ethical or performance standards of a profession. . . .

The second criterion recognizes that the First Amendment mandates that speech restrictions be "narrowly drawn." In re Primus. . . . The regulatory technique may extend only as far as the interest it serves. The State cannot regulate speech that poses no danger to the asserted state interest . . . nor can it completely suppress information when narrower restrictions on expression would serve its interest as well. . . .[9]

In commercial speech cases, then, a four-part analysis has developed. At the outset, we must determine whether the expression is protected by the First Amendment. For commercial speech to come within that provision, it at least must concern lawful activity and not be misleading. Next, we ask whether the asserted governmental interest is substantial. If both inquiries yield positive answers, we must determine whether the regulation directly advances the governmental interest asserted, and whether it is not more extensive than is necessary to serve that interest.

III

We now apply this four-step analysis for commercial speech to the Commission's arguments in support of its ban on promotional advertising.

A

The Commission does not claim that the expression at issue either is inaccurate or relates to unlawful activity. Yet the New York Court of Appeals questioned whether Central Hudson's advertising is protected commercial speech. Because appellant holds a monopoly over the sale of electricity in its service area, the state court suggested that the Commission's order restricts no commercial speech of any worth. The court stated that advertising in a "noncompetitive market" could not improve the decisionmaking of consumers. The court saw no constitutional prob-

---

9. We review with special care regulations that entirely suppress commercial speech in order to pursue a nonspeech-related policy. In those circumstances, a ban on speech could screen from public view the underlying governmental policy. . . . Indeed, in recent years this Court has not approved a blanket ban on commercial speech unless the expression itself was flawed in some way, either because it was deceptive or related to unlawful activity.

lem with barring commercial speech that it viewed as conveying little useful information.

This reasoning falls short of establishing that appellant's advertising is not commercial speech protected by the First Amendment. Monopoly over the supply of a product provides no protection from competition with substitutes for that product. . . . For consumers in those competitive markets, advertising by utilities is just as valuable as advertising by unregulated firms.

Even in monopoly markets, the suppression of advertising reduces the information available for consumer decisions and thereby defeats the purpose of the First Amendment. . . . [A] monopoly enterprise legitimately may wish to inform the public that it has developed new services or terms of doing business. A consumer may need information to aid his decision whether or not to use the monopoly service at all, or how much of the service he should purchase. In the absence of factors that would distort the decision to advertise, we may assume that the willingness of a business to promote its products reflects a belief that consumers are interested in the advertising. . . .

B

The Commission offers two state interests as justifications for the ban on promotional advertising. . . . The Commission argues, and the New York court agreed, that the State's interest in conserving energy is sufficient to support suppression of advertising designed to increase consumption of electricity. . . . Plainly, . . . the state interest asserted is substantial.

The Commission also argues that promotional advertising will aggravate inequities caused by the failure to base the utilities' rates on marginal cost. . . . The choice among rate structures involves difficult and important questions of economic supply and distributional fairness. The State's concern that rates be fair and efficient represents a clear and substantial governmental interest.

C

Next, we focus on the relationship between the State's interests and the advertising ban. Under this criterion, the Commission's laudable concern over the equity and efficiency of appellant's rates does not provide a constitutionally adequate reason for restricting protected speech. The link between the advertising prohibition and appellant's rate structure is, at most, tenuous. . . .

In contrast, the State's interest in energy conservation is directly advanced by the Commission order at issue here. There is an immediate connection between advertising and demand for electricity. . . .

D

We come finally to the critical inquiry in this case: whether the Commission's complete suppression of speech ordinarily protected by the First Amendment is no more extensive than necessary to further the State's interest in energy conservation. The Commission's order reaches all promotional advertising, regardless of the impact of the touted service on overall energy use. But the energy conservation rationale, as important as it is, cannot justify suppressing information about electric devices or services that would cause no net increase in total energy use. In addition, no showing has been made that a more limited restriction on the content of promotional advertising would not serve adequately the State's interests. . . .

The Commission's order prevents appellant from promoting electric services that would reduce energy use by diverting demand from less efficient sources, or that would consume roughly the same amount of energy as do alternative sources. In neither situation would the utility's advertising endanger conservation or mislead the public. To the extent that the Commission's order suppresses speech that in no way impairs the State's interest in energy conservation, the Commission's order violates the First and Fourteenth Amendments and must be invalidated.

The Commission also has not demonstrated that its interest in conservation cannot be protected adequately by more limited regulation of appellant's commercial expression. To further its policy of conservation, the Commission could attempt to restrict the format and content of Central Hudson's advertising. It might, for example, require that the advertisements include information about the relative efficiency and expense of the offered service, both under current conditions and for the foreseeable future. . . .[13] In the absence of a showing that more limited speech regulation would be ineffective, we cannot approve the complete suppression of Central Hudson's advertising. . . .

[An opinion by Mr. Justice Brennan, concurring the judgment, is omitted.]

Mr. JUSTICE BLACKMUN, with whom Mr. JUSTICE BRENNAN joins, concurring in the judgment.

I agree with the Court that the Public Service Commission's ban on promotional adertising of electricity by public utilities is inconsistent with the First and Fourteenth Amendments. I concur only in the Court's

---

13. The Commission also might consider a system of previewing advertising campaigns to insure that they will not defeat conservation policy. . . . We have observed that commercial speech is such a sturdy brand of expression that traditional prior restraint doctrine may not apply to it. Virginia Pharmacy Board v. Virginia Citizens Consumer Council, 425 U.S., at 771-772, n.24. And in other areas of speech regulation, such as obscenity, we have recognized that a prescreening arrangement can pass constitutional muster if it includes adequate procedural safeguards. Freedman v. Maryland, 380 U.S. 51 (1965).

judgment, however, because I believe the test now evolved and applied by the Court is not consistent with our prior cases and does not provide adequate protection for truthful, nonmisleading, noncoercive commercial speech.

The Court asserts that "a four-part analysis has developed" from our decisions concerning commercial speech.... I agree with the Court that this level of intermediate scrutiny is appropriate for a restraint on commercial speech designed to protect consumers from misleading or coercive speech, or a regulation related to the time, place, or manner of commercial speech. I do not agree, however, that the Court's four-part test is the proper one to be applied when a State seeks to suppress information about a product in order to manipulate a private economic decision that the State cannot or has not regulated or outlawed directly.

Since the Court, without citing empirical data or other authority, finds a "direct link" between advertising and energy consumption, it leaves open the possibility that the State may suppress advertising of electricity in order to lessen demand for electricity. I, of course, agree with the Court that, in today's world, energy conservation is a goal of paramount national and local importance. I disagree with the Court, however, when it says that suppression of speech may be a permissible means to achieve that goal....

I seriously doubt whether suppression of information concerning the availability and price of a legally offered product is ever a permissible way for the State to "dampen" demand for or use of the product. Even though "commercial" speech is involved, such a regulatory measure strikes at the heart of the First Amendment. This is because it is a covert attempt by the State to manipulate the choices of its citizens, not by persuasion or direct regulation, but by depriving the public of the information needed to make a free choice....

If the First Amendment guarantee means anything, it means that, absent clear and present danger, government has no power to restrict expression because of the effect its message is likely to have on the public.... Our cases indicate that this guarantee applies even to commercial speech. In Virginia Pharmacy Board v. Virginia Consumer Council... [we] did not analyze the State's interests to determine whether they were "substantial." Nor did the opinion analyze the ban on speech to determine whether it "directly advance[d]"... these goals. We also did not inquire whether a "more limited regulation of... commercial expression"... would adequately serve the State's interests. Rather, we held that the State "may *not* [pursue its goals] by keeping the public in ignorance." 425 U.S., at 770. (Emphasis supplied.)

Until today, this principle has governed.... Linmark Associates, Inc. v. Willingboro, 431 U.S. 85 (1977)....

Our prior references to the "'commonsense differences'" between commercial speech and other speech "'suggest that a different degree of protection is necessary to insure that the flow of truthful and legitimate commercial information is unimpaired.' " Virginia Pharmacy Board. We have not suggested that the "commonsense differences" between commercial speech and other speech justify relaxed scrutiny of restraints that suppress truthful, nondeceptive, noncoercive commercial speech. . . .

Mr. JUSTICE STEVENS, with whom Mr. JUSTICE BRENNAN joins, concurring in the judgment.

Because "commercial speech" is afforded less constitutional protection than other forms of speech, it is important that the commercial speech concept not be defined too broadly lest speech deserving of greater constitutional protection be inadvertently suppressed. The issue in this case is whether New York's prohibition on the promotion of the use of electricity through advertising is a ban on nothing but commercial speech.

In my judgment one of the two definitions the Court uses in addressing that issue is too broad and the other may be somewhat too narrow. The Court first describes commercial speech as "expression related solely to the economic interests of the speaker and its audience." Although it is not entirely clear whether this definition uses the subject matter of the speech or the motivation of the speaker as the limiting factor, it seems clear to me that it encompasses speech that is entitled to the maximum protection afforded by the First Amendment. Neither a labor leader's exhortation to strike, nor an economist's dissertation on the money supply, should receive any lesser protection because the subject matter concerns only the economic interests of the audience. Nor should the economic motivation of a speaker qualify his constitutional protection; even Shakespeare may have been motivated by the prospect of pecuniary reward. Thus, the Court's first definition of commerical speech is unquestionably too broad. The Court's second definition refers to " 'speech proposing a commercial transaction.' " . . . Whatever the precise contours of the concept, and perhaps it is too early to enunciate an exact formulation, I am persuaded that it should not include the entire range of communication that is embraced within the term "promotional advertising."

This case involves a governmental regulation that completely bans promotional advertising by an electric utility. This ban encompasses a great deal more than mere proposals to engage in certain kinds of commercial transactions. It prohibits all advocacy of the immediate or future use of electricity. It curtails expression by an informed and interested group of persons of their point of view on questions relating to the production and consumption of electrical energy—questions frequently discussed and debated by our political leaders. For example, an electric company's advocacy of the use of electric heat for environmental reasons, as opposed to wood-burning stoves, would seem to fall squarely within New York's promotional advertising ban and also within the bounds of maximum First Amendment protection. The breadth of the ban thus exceeds the boundaries of the commercial speech concept, however that concept may be defined.

The justification for the regulation is nothing more than the expressed fear that the audience may find the utility's message persuasive. Without the aid of any coercion, deception, or misinformation, truthful communication may persuade some citizens to consume more electricity than they otherwise would. I assume that such a consequence would be undesirable and that government may therefore prohibit and punish the unnecessary or excessive use of electricity. But if the perceived harm associated with greater electrical usage is not sufficiently serious to justify direct regulation, surely it does not constitute the kind of clear and present danger that can justify the suppression of speech.

... I concur in the result because I do not consider this to be a "commercial speech" case. Accordingly, I see no need to decide whether the Court's four-part analysis adequately protects commercial speech—as properly defined—in the face of a blanket ban of the sort involved in this case.

Mr. JUSTICE REHNQUIST, dissenting. . . .

... I disagree with the Court's conclusion that the speech of a state-created monopoly, which is the subject of a comprehensive regulatory scheme, is entitled to protection under the First Amendment. I also think that the Court errs here in failing to recognize that the state law is most accurately viewed as an economic regulation and that the speech involved (if it falls within the scope of the First Amendment at all) occupies a significantly more subordinate position in the hierarchy of First Amendment values than the Court gives it today. Finally, the Court in reaching its decision improperly substitutes its own judgment for that of the State in deciding how a proper ban on promotional advertising should be drafted. . . . [T]he Court adopts as its final part of a four-part test a "no more extensive than necessary" analysis that will unduly impair a state legislature's ability to adopt legislation reasonably designed to promote interests that have always been rightly thought to be of great importance to the State. . . .

I remain of the view that the Court unlocked a Pandora's Box when it "elevated" commercial speech to the level of traditional political speech by according it First Amendment protection in Virginia Pharmacy Board v. Virginia Citizens Consumer Council. . . . The line between "commercial speech," and the kind of speech that those who drafted the First Amendment had in mind, may not be a technically or intellectually easy one to draw, but it surely produced far fewer problems than has the development of judicial doctrine in this area since Virginia Pharmacy Board. For in the world of political advocacy and *its* marketplace of ideas, there is no such thing as a "fraudulent" idea: there may be useless proposals, totally unworkable schemes, as well as very sound proposals that will receive the imprimatur of the "marketplace of ideas" through our majoritarian system of election and representative government. The free flow of information is important in this context not because it will lead to the discovery of any objective "truth," but because it is essential to our system of self-government.

The notion that more speech is the remedy to expose falsehood and fallacies is wholly out of place in the commercial bazaar, where if applied logically the remedy of one who was defrauded would be merely a statement, available upon request, reciting the Latin maxim "*caveat emptor.*" But since "fraudulent speech" in this area is to be remediable under Virginia Pharmacy Board, . . . the remedy of one defrauded is a lawsuit or an agency proceeding based on common-law notions of fraud that are separated by a world of difference from the realm of politics and government. What time, legal decisions, and common sense have so widely severed, I declined to join in Virginia Pharmacy Board, and regret now to see the Court reaping the seeds that it there sowed. For in a democracy, the economic is subordinate to the political, a lesson that our ancestors learned long ago, and that our descendants will undoubtedly have to relearn many years hence. . . .

NOTES

1. In Metromedia v. City of San Diego, 101 S. Ct. 2882 (1981), the Court struck down an antibillboard ordinance as it applied to noncommercial speech. However, the Court relied on Central Hudson to uphold the ordinance insofar as it regulated commercial advertising, reiterating that "[t]he constitution . . . accords a lesser protection to commercial speech than to other constitutionally guaranteed expression." In reaching this conclusion, Justice White's opinion for the Court held that the ordinance's regulation of commercial advertisements satisfied the third part of the Central Hudson test by directly advancing governmental interests in traffic safety and the appearance of the city. To the same effect, see John Donnelly & Sons v. Campbell, 639 F.2d 6 (1st Cir. 1980), aff'd, 101 S. Ct. 3151 (1981).

2. Lower courts have applied Central Hudson in a variety of contexts similar to those involving reliance on Virginia Pharmacy. Advertising bans have been struck down in Equifax Services, Inc. v. Cohen, 420 A.2d 189 (Me. 1980) (consumer credit information); In re Koffler, 412 N.E.2d 927 (N.Y. 1980) (lawyer advertising by direct mail to potential clients); Weiler v. Carpenter, 507 F. Supp. 837 (D.N.M. 1981) (drug paraphernalia). On the other hand, restraint of commercial speech was upheld under the Central Hudson test in In re W.T. Grant Co., 1980-2 Fed. Sec. L. Rep. (CCH) ¶97,636 (S.D.N.Y. 1980) (dissemination of

allegedly misleading proxy solicitation to debentureholders), and in Ad World, Inc. v. Twp. of Doylestown, 510 F. Supp. 851 (E.D. Pa. 1981) (prohibition on unsolicited house-to-house distribution of free community newspaper). But see H & L Messengers v. Brentwood, 577 S.W.2d 444 (Tenn. 1979) (striking down a restriction on the unsolicited distribution of handbills based on their commercial content). The Ad World decision, supra, was reversed by the court of appeals, — F.2d — (3d Cir., Feb. 5, 1982), the court holding that the newspaper there (a 16-page tabloid primarily consisting of ads but containing a few pages of editorial and feature material) was fully protected, rather than commercial, speech.

[752]

[REFERENCES]

Alexander & Farber, Commercial Speech and First Amendment Theory: A Critical Exchange, 75 Nw. U.L. Rev. 307 (1980); Baker, Commercial Speech: A Problem in the Theory of Freedom, 62 Iowa L. Rev. 1 (1976); Elman, New Constitutional Right to Advertise, 64 A.B.A.J. 206 (1978); Emerson, First Amendment Doctrine and the Burger Court, 68 Calif. L. Rev. 422 (1980); Farber, Content Regulation and the First Amendment: A Revisionist View, 68 Geo. L.J. 727 (1980); Farber, Commercial Speech and First Amendment Theory, 74 Nw. U.L. Rev. 372 (1979); Hellman, Oklahoma Supreme Court's Rules on Lawyer Advertising: Some Practical, Legal and Policy Questions, 31 Okla. L. Rev. 509 (1978); Jackson and Jeffries, Commercial Speech: Economic Due Process and the First Amendment, 65 Va. L. Rev. 1 (1979); Knapp, Commercial Speech, the Federal Trade Commission and the First Amendment, 9 Mem. St. U. L. Rev. 1 (1978); Meiklejohn, Commercial Speech and the First Amendment, 13 Cal. W.L. Rev. 430 (1977); Reich, Consumer Protection and the First Amendment: A Dilemma for the F.T.C.?, 61 Minn. L. Rev. 705 (1977); Reich, Preventing Deception in Commercial Speech, 54 N.Y.U.L. Rev. 775 (1979); Rotunda, The Commercial Speech Doctrine in the Supreme Court, 1976 U. Ill. L.F. 1080 (1976); Schiro, Commercial Speech: The Demise of a Chimera, 1976 Sup. Ct. Rev. 45 (1976); Sims, Lawyer Solicitation Rules, 7 Litigation 22 (1981); Comment, Metromedia, Inc. v. City of San Diego: Aesthetics, the First Amendment, and the Realities of Billboard Control, 9 Ecology L.Q. 295 (1981); Comment, The New Commercial Speech Doctrine and Broadcast Advertising, 14 Harv. C.R.–C.L.L. Rev. 385 (1979).

(page 573) [752]

Add new Section:

CORPORATE SPEECH ON PUBLIC ISSUES

FIRST NATIONAL BANK OF BOSTON v. BELLOTTI
435 U.S. 765 (1978)

Mr. JUSTICE POWELL delivered the opinion of the Court.

In sustaining a state criminal statute that forbids certain expenditures by banks and business corporations for the purpose of influencing the vote on referendum proposals, the Massachusetts Supreme Judicial Court held that the First Amendment rights of a corporation are limited to issues that materially affect its business, property, or assets. The court rejected appellants' claim that the statute abridges freedom of speech in violation of the First and Fourteenth Amendments. The issue presented in this context is one of first impression in this Court.... We now reverse.

I

The statute at issue, Mass. Gen. Laws Ann., ch. 55, §8 (West Supp. 1977), prohibits appellants, two national banking associations, and three business corporations, from making contributions or expenditures "for the purpose of ... influencing or affecting the vote on any question submitted to the voters, other than one materially affecting any of the property, business or assets of the corporation." The statute further specifies that "[n]o question submitted to the voters solely concerning the taxation of the income, property or transactions of individuals shall be deemed materially to affect the property, business or assets of the corporation." A corporation that violates §8 may receive a maximum fine of $50,000; a corporate officer, director, or agent who violates the section may receive a maximum fine of $10,000 or imprisonment for up to one year, or both.

Appellants wanted to spend money to publicize their views on a proposed constitutional amendment that was to be submitted to the voters as a ballot question at a general election on November 2, 1976. The amendment would have permitted the legislature to impose a graduated tax on the income of individuals. After appellee, the Attorney General of Massachusetts, informed appellants that he intended to enforce §8 against them, they brought this action seeking to have the statute declared unconstitutional....

III

The court below framed the principal question in this case as whether and to what extent corporations have First Amendment rights. We believe that the court posed the wrong question. The Constitution often protects interests broader than those of the party seeking their vindication. The First Amendment, in particular, serves significant societal interests. The proper question therefore is not whether corporations "have" First Amendments rights and, if so, whether they are coextensive with those of natural persons. Instead, the question must be whether §8 abridges expression that the First Amendment was meant to protect. We hold that it does.

A

The speech proposed by appellants is at the heart of the First Amendment's protection. . . .

. . . In appellants' view, the enactment of a graduated personal income tax, as proposed to be authorized by constitutional amendment, would have a seriously adverse effect on the economy of the State. The importance of the referendum issue to the people and government of Massachusetts is not disputed. Its merits, however, are the subject of sharp disagreement.

. . . If the speakers here were not corporations, no one would suggest that the State could silence their proposed speech. It is the type of speech indispensable to decisionmaking in a democracy, and this is no less true because the speech comes from a corporation rather than an individual. The inherent worth of the speech in terms of its capacity for informing the public does not depend upon the identity of its source, whether corporation, association, union, or individual.

The court below nevertheless held that corporate speech is protected by the First Amendment only when it pertains directly to the corporation's business interests. In deciding whether this novel and restrictive gloss on the First Amendment comports with the Constitution and the precedents of this Court, we need not survey the outer boundaries of the Amendment's protection of corporate speech, or address the abstract question whether corporations have the full measure of rights that individuals enjoy under the First Amendment. The question in this case, simply put, is whether the corporate identity of the speaker deprives this proposed speech of what otherwise would be its clear entitlement to protection. . . .

C

We . . . find no support in the First or Fourteenth Amendment, or in the decisions of this Court, for the proposition that speech that otherwise would be within the protection of the First Amendment loses that protection simply because its source is a corporation that cannot prove, to the satisfaction of a court, a material effect on its business or property. The "materially affecting" requirement is not an identification of the boundaries of corporate speech etched by the Constitution itself. Rather, it amounts to an impermissible legislative prohibition of speech based on the identity of the interests that spokesmen may represent in public debate over controversial issues and a requirement that the speaker have a sufficiently great interest in the subject to justify communication.

Section 8 permits a corporation to communicate to the public its views on certain referendum subjects — those materially affecting its business — but not others. It also singles out one kind of ballot question — individual taxation — as a subject about which corporations may never make their ideas public. . . .

In the realm of protected speech, the legislature is constitutionally disqualified from dictating the subjects about which persons may speak and the speakers who may address a public issue. Police Dept. of Chicago v. Mosley, 408 U.S. 92, 96 (1972). If a legislature may direct business corporations to "stick to business," it also may limit other corporations — religious, charitable, or civic — to their respective "business" when addressing the public. Such power in government to channel the expression of views is unacceptable under the First Amendment. Especially where, as here, the legislature's suppression of speech suggests an attempt to give one side of a debatable public question an advantage in expressing its views to the people, the First Amendment is plainly offended. Yet the State contends that its action is necessitated by governmental interests of the highest order. . . .

IV

The constitutionality of §8's prohibition of the "exposition of ideas" by corporations turns on whether it can survive the exacting scrutiny necessitated by a state-imposed restriction of freedom of speech. Especially where, as here, a prohibition is directed at speech itself, and the speech is intimately related to the process of governing, "the State may prevail only upon showing a subordinating interest which is compelling," . . . "and the burden is on the government to show the existence of such an interest." . . . Even then, the State must employ means "closely drawn to avoid unnecessary abridgment. . . ."

. . . Appellee . . . advances two principal justifications for the prohibition of corporate speech. The first is the State's interest in sustaining the active role of the individual citizen in the electoral process and thereby preventing diminution of the citizen's confidence in government. The second is the interest in protecting the rights of shareholders whose views differ from those expressed by management on behalf of the corporation. . . .

A

Preserving the integrity of the electoral process, preventing corruption, and "sustain[ing] the active, alert responsibility of the individual citizen in a democracy for the wise conduct of government" are interests of the highest importance.... Preservation of the individual citizen's confidence in government is equally important....

Appellee advances a number of arguments in support of his view that these interests are endangered by corporate participation in discussion of a referendum issue. They hinge upon the assumption that such participation would exert an undue influence on the outcome of a referendum vote, and — in the end — destroy the confidence of the people in the democratic process and the integrity of government. According to appellee, corporations are wealthy and powerful and their views may drown out other points of view. If appellee's arguments were supported by record or legislative findings that corporate advocacy threatened imminently to undermine democratic processes, thereby denigrating rather than serving First Amendment interests, these arguments would merit our consideration.... But there has been no showing that the relative voice of corporations has been overwhelming or even significant in influencing referenda in Massachusetts, or that there has been any threat to the confidence of the citizenry in government....

Nor are appellee's arguments inherently persuasive or supported by the precedents of this Court. Referenda are held on issues, not candidates for public office. The risk of corruption perceived in cases involving candidate elections ... simply is not present in a popular vote on a public issue. To be sure, corporate advertising may influence the outcome of the vote; this would be its purpose. But the fact that advocacy may persuade the electorate is hardly a reason to suppress it.... Moreover, the people in our democracy are entrusted with the responsibility for judging and evaluating the relative merits of conflicting arguments. They may consider, in making their judgment, the source and credibility of the advocate.

B

Finally, appellee argues that §8 protects corporate shareholders, an interest that is both legitimate and traditionally within the province of state law. The statute is said to serve this interest by preventing the use of corporate resources in furtherance of views with which some shareholders may disagree. This purpose is belied, however, by the provisions of the statute, which are both underinclusive and overinclusive.

The underinclusiveness of the statute is self-evident. Corporate expenditures with respect to a referendum are prohibited, while corporate activity with respect to the passage or defeat of legislation is permitted, even though corporations may engage in lobbying more often than they take positions on ballot questions submitted to the voters. Nor does §8 prohibit a corporation from expressing its views, by the expenditure of corporate funds, on any public issue until it becomes the subject of a referendum, though the displeasure of disapproving shareholders is unlikely to be any less. . . .

Nor is the fact that §8 is limited to banks and business corporations without relevance. Excluded from its provisions and criminal sanctions are entities or organized groups in which numbers of persons may hold an interest or membership, and which often have resources comparable to those of large corporations. . . . Thus the exclusion of Massachusetts business trusts, real estate investment trusts, labor unions, and other associations undermines the plausibility of the State's purported concern for the persons who happen to be shareholders in the banks and corporations covered by §8.

The overinclusiveness of the statute is demonstrated by the fact that §8 would prohibit a corporation from supporting or opposing a referendum proposal even if its shareholders unanimously authorized the contribution or expenditure. . . .

V

Because that portion of §8 challenged by appellants prohibits protected speech in a manner unjustified by a compelling state interest, it must be invalidated.

Mr. CHIEF JUSTICE BURGER, concurring. . . .

A disquieting aspect of Massachusetts' position is that it may carry the risk of impinging on the First Amendment rights of those who employ the corporate form — as most do — to carry on the business of mass communications, particularly the large media conglomerates. This is so because of the difficulty, and perhaps impossibility, of distinguishing, either as a matter of fact or constitutional law, media corporations from corporations such as the appellants in this case.

Making traditional use of the corporate form, some media enterprises have amassed vast wealth and power and conduct many activities, some directly related — and some not — to their publishing and broadcasting activities. . . .

In terms of "unfair advantage in the political process" and "corporate domination of the electoral process," it could be argued that such media conglomerates . . . pose a much more realistic threat to valid interests than do appellants and similar entities not regular concerned with shaping popular opinion on public issues. . . .

In terms of Massachusetts' other concern, the interests of minority shareholders, I perceive no basis for saying that the managers and directors of the media conglomerates are more or less sensitive to the views and desires of minority shareholders than are corporate officers generally.... Thus, no factual distinction has been identified as yet that would justify government restraints on the right of appellants to express their views without, at the same time, opening the door to similar restraints on media conglomerates with their vastly greater influence.

... [T]hose who view the Press Clause as somehow conferring special and extraordinary privileges or status on the "institutional press" — which are not extended to those who wish to express ideas other than by publishing a newspaper — might perceive no danger to institutional media corporations flowing from the position asserted by Massachusetts.... The Court has not yet squarely resolved whether the Press Clause confers upon the "institutional press" any freedom from government restraint not enjoyed by all others.

I perceive two fundamental difficulties with a narrow reading of the Press Clause. First, although certainty on this point is not possible, the history of the Clause does not suggest that the authors contemplated a "special" or "institutional" privilege....

To conclude that the Framers did not intend to limit the freedom of the press to one select group is not necessarily to suggest that the Press Clause is redundant. The Speech Clause standing alone may be viewed as a protection of the liberty to express ideas and beliefs, while the Press Clause focuses specifically on the liberty to disseminate expression broadly and "comprehends every sort of publication which affords a vehicle of information and opinion."... The liberty encompassed by the Press Clause, although complementary to and a natural extension of Speech Clause liberty, merited special mention simply because it had been more often the object of official restraints....

The second fundamental difficulty with interpreting the Press Clause as conferring special status on a limited group is one of definition.... The very task of including some entities within the "institutional press" while excluding others, whether undertaken by legislature, court, or administrative agency, is reminiscent of the abhorred licensing system of Tudor and Stuart England — a system the First Amendment was intended to ban from this country....

In short, the First Amendment does not "belong" to any definable category of persons or entities: It belongs to all who exercise its freedoms.

Mr. JUSTICE WHITE, with whom Mr. JUSTICE BRENNAN and Mr. JUSTICE MARSHALL join, dissenting....

By holding that Massachusetts may not prohibit corporate expenditures or contributions made in connection with referenda involving issues having no material connection with the corporate business, the Court not only invalidates a statute which has been on the books in one form or another for many years, but also casts considerable doubt upon the constitutionality of legislation passed by some 31 States restricting corporate political activity, as well as upon the Federal Corrupt Practices Act. 2 U.S.C. §441b (1976 ed.). The Court's fundamental error is its failure to realize that the state regulatory interests in terms of which the alleged curtailment of First Amendment rights accomplished by the statute must be evaluated are themselves derived from the first Amendment. . . .

There is now little doubt that corporate communications come within the scope of the First Amendment. This, however, is merely the starting point of analysis, because an examination of the First Amendment values that corporate expression furthers and the threat to the functioning of a free society it is capable of posing reveals that it is not fungible with communications emanating from individuals and is subject to restrictions which individual expression is not. Indeed, what some have considered to be the principal function of the First Amendment, the use of communication as a means of self-expression, self-realization, and self-fulfillment, is not at all furthered by corporate speech. . . .

Of course, it may be assumed that corporate investors are united by a desire to make money, for the value of their investment to increase. Since even communications which have no purpose other than that of enriching the communicator have some First Amendment protection, activities such as advertising and other communications integrally related to the operation of the corporation's business may be viewed as a means of furthering the desires of individual shareholders. This unanimity of purpose breaks down, however, when corporations make expenditures or undertake activities designed to influence the opinion or votes of the general public on political and social issues that have no material connection with or effect upon their business, property, or assets. . . .

The self-expression of the communicator is not the only value encompassed by the First Amendment. One of its functions, often referred to as the right to hear or receive information, is to protect the interchange of ideas. Any communication of ideas, and consequently any expenditure of funds which makes the communication of ideas possible, it can be argued, furthers the purposes of the First Amendment. This proposition does not establish, however, that the right of the general public to receive communications financed by means of corporate expenditures is of the same dimension as that to hear other forms of expression. In the first place, as discussed supra, corporate expenditures designed to further political causes lack the connection with individual self-expression which is one of the principal justifications for the constitutional protection of speech provided by the First Amendment. Ideas which are not a product of individual choice are entitled to less First Amendment protection. Secondly, the restriction of corporate speech concerned with political matters impinges much less severely upon the availability of ideas to the general public than do restrictions upon individual speech. Even the complete curtailment of corporate communications concerning political or ideological questions not integral to day-to-day business functions would leave individuals, including corporate shareholders, employees, and customers, free to communicate their thoughts.

It bears emphasis here that the Massachusetts statute forbids the expenditure of corporate funds in connection with referenda but in no way forbids the board of directors of a corporation from formulating and making public what it represents as the views of the corporation even though the subject addressed has no material effect whatsoever on the business of the corporation. These views could be publicized at the individual expense of the officers, directors, stockholders, or anyone else interested in circulating corporate view on matters irrelevant to its business.

The governmental interest in regulating corporate political communications, especially those relating to electoral matters, also raises considerations which differ significantly from those governing the regulation of individual speech. . . . [T]he interest of Massachusetts and the many other States which have restricted corporate political activity . . . is not one of equalizing the resources of opposing candidates or opposing positions, but rather of preventing institutions which have been permitted to amass wealth as a result of special advantages extended by the State for certain economic purposes from using that wealth to acquire an unfair advantage in the political process, especially where, as here, the issue involved has no material connection with the business of the corporation. The State need not permit its own creation to consume it. . . .

This Nation has for many years recognized the need for measures designed to prevent corporate domination of the political process. The Corrupt Practices Act, first enacted in 1907, has consistently barred corporate contributions in connection with federal elections. This Court has repeatedly recognized that one of the principal purposes of this prohibition is "to avoid the deleterious influences on federal elections resulting from the use of money by those who exercise control over large aggregations of capital.". . . Although this Court has never adjudicated the constitutionality of the Act, there is no suggestion in its cases construing it, cited supra, that this purpose is in any sense illegitimate or deserving of other than the utmost respect; indeed, the thrust of its opinions, until today, has been to the contrary. . . .

There is an additional overriding interest related to the prevention of corporate domination which is substantially advanced by Massachusetts' restrictions upon corporate contributions: assuring that shareholders are not compelled to support and financially further beliefs with which they disagree where, as is the case here, the issue involved does not materially affect the business, property, or other affairs of the corporation. . . . Massachusetts has chosen to forbid corporate management from spending corporate funds in referenda elections absent some demonstrable effect of the issue on the economic life of the company. In short, corporate management may not use corporate monies to promote what does not further corporate affairs but what in the last analysis are the purely personal views of the management, individually or as a group. . . .

In my view, the interests in protecting a system of freedom of expression . . . are sufficient to justify any incremental curtailment in the volume of expression which the Massachusetts statute might produce. I would hold that apart from corporate activities . . . which are integrally related to corporate business operations, a State may prohibit corporate expenditures for political or ideological purposes. There can be no doubt that corporate expenditures in connection with referenda immaterial to corporate business affairs fall clearly into the category of corporate activities which may be barred. The electoral process, of course, is the essence of our democracy. It is an arena in which the public interest in preventing corporate domination and the coerced support by shareholders of causes with which they disagree is at its strongest and any claim that corporate expenditures are integral to the economic functioning of the corporation is at its weakest.

Mr. JUSTICE REHNQUIST, dissenting. . . .

. . . A State grants to a business corporation the blessings of potentially perpetual life and limited liability to enhance its efficiency as an economic entity. . . .

I can see no basis for concluding that the liberty of a corporation to engage in political activity with regard to matters having no material effect on its business is necessarily incidental to the purposes for which the Commonwealth permitted these corporations to be organized or admitted within its boundaries. . .

It is true, as the Court points out, that recent decisions of this Court have emphasized the interest of the public in receiving the information offered by the speaker seeking protection. The free flow of information is in no way diminished by the Commonwealth's decision to permit the operation of business corporations with limited rights of political expression. All natural persons, who owe their existence to a higher sovereign than the Commonwealth, remain as free as before to engage in political activity. . . .

NOTES

1. Following Bellotti, courts have extended constitutional protection to corporate speech in various settings. In Consolidated Edison Co. v.

Public Service Commn., 447 U.S. 530 (1980), the Supreme Court struck down an order of the New York Public Service Commission prohibiting the inclusion with monthly electric bills of inserts that discussed "political matters, including the desirability of future development of nuclear power." The order was issued after the utility had included pro-nuclear inserts in its bills and the Commission had denied a request by the Natural Resources Defense Council to order the utility to include opposing views with its bills. The state's highest court upheld the order. In reversing, Justice Powell's opinion for the Court concluded that the ban could not be upheld as "(i) a reasonable time, place or manner restriction, (ii) a permissible subject-matter regulation, or (iii) a narrowly tailored means of serving a compelling state interest." The Court stated that "time, place and manner regulations must be 'applicable to all speech irrespective of content.'" Because the Commission had "undertaken to suppress certain bill inserts precisely because they address[ed] controversial issues of public policy . . . [t]he Commission's own rationale demonstrate[d] that its action [could not] be upheld as a content-neutral time, place, or manner regulation." Nor could the ban on all bill inserts regardless of content be upheld as a valid subject-matter regulation, since "[t]he First Amendment's hostility to content-based regulation extends not only to restrictions on particular viewpoints, but also to prohibition of public discussion of an entire topic." Finally, the order could not be upheld as a precisely drawn means of serving a compelling state interest. The intrusiveness of a bill insert was found insufficient to justify the Commission's interest in protecting the utility customers' privacy, the primary ground relied upon by the lower court in upholding the ban. Justices Marshall and Stevens concurred separately; Justices Blackmun and Rehnquist dissented.

See also, C & C Plywood v. Hanson, 583 F.2d 421, (9th Cir. 1980), where the court applied Bellotti to invalidate a Montana statute that prohibited corporate contributions to promote or defeat any ballot issue. See, however, Rochester Gas & Electric Corp. v. Public Service Commn., 413 N.E.2d 359 (N.Y. 1980), in which the New York Court of Appeals held that the utility had no First Amendment right to have its ratepayers bear the expense of informational advertising where that advertising was not necessary to furnishing utility services. To the same effect is State ex rel. Laclede Gas Co. v. Public Service Commn., 600 S.W.2d 222 (Mo. App. 1980).

2. In Quinn v. Aetna Life Insurance Co., 616 F.2d 38 (2d Cir. 1980), a plaintiff in a pending personal injury action sued for an injunction forbidding publication by the insurance company of advertisements attacking an alleged trend toward excessive damage awards in tort cases. Plaintiff alleged that such advertisements violated state laws against false advertising and jury tampering. The court affirmed the district court's

denial of injunctive relief, stating that the corporate speech in question was entitled to full First Amendment protection. To the same effect is Rutledge v. Liability Insurance Industry, 487 F. Supp. 5 (W.D. La. 1979).

[REFERENCES]

Bolton, Constitutional Limitations on Restricting Corporate and Union Political Speech, 22 Ariz. L. Rev. 373 (1980); Budde, The Practical Role of Corporate PACs in the Political Process, 22 Ariz. L. Rev. 427 (1980); Hart & Shore, Corporate Spending on State and Local Referendums: First National Bank of Boston v. Bellotti, 22 Corp. Prac. Comment. 524 (1981); Kiley, PACing the Burger Court: The Corporate Right to Speak and the Public Right to Hear After First National Bank v. Bellotti, 22 Ariz. L. Rev. 427 (1980); Mayton, Politics, Money, Coercion, and the Problem with Corporate PACs, 29 Emory L.J. (1980); Miller, On Politics, Democracy, and the First Amendment: A Comment on First National Bank v. Bellotti, 38 Wash. Lee L. Rev. 21 (1981); Nicholson, Constitutionality of the Federal Restrictions on Corporate and Union Campaign Contributions and Expenditures, 65 Corn. L. Rev. 945 (1980); Rome & Roberts, Bellotti and the First Amendment: A New Era in Corporate Speech, 3 Corp. L. Rev. 28 (1980); Schaefer, The First Amendment, Media Conglomerates and "Business" Corporations: Can Corporations Safely Involve Themselves in the Political Process?, 55 St. John's L. Rev. 1 (1980); Vandegrift, The Corporate Political Action Committee, 55 N.Y.U.L. Rev. 422 (1980).

Chapter Nine

Access To and Regulation of the Media

A [B]. THE PRESS

(page 580) [766]

NOTES

3. [continued] In Person v. New York Post Corp., 427 F. Supp. 1297 (E.D.N.Y. 1977), aff'd without opinion, 573 F.2d 1294 (2d Cir.), the court held there was no right of access to newspapers to publish "tombstone" advertisements announcing securities offerings. See also: Rogers v. Jinks, —F.2d—, 7 Media L. Reptr. 1293 (9th Cir. 1981) (no right of access to newspaper for articles on public referendum issue).

4. [continued] The court in Mississippi Gay Alliance v. Goudelock, 536 F.2d 1073 (5th Cir. 1976), cert. denied, 430 U.S. 982 (1977), declined to find state action in a rejection of a Gay Alliance advertisement by a state university student newspaper that was funded by the university but run entirely by students. In addition, referring to Miami Herald Publishing Co. v. Tornillo, 418 U.S. 241 (1974), the court found the editorial discretion of the students to be protected by the First Amendment. See also: Dunagin v. City of Oxford, Mississippi, 489 F. Supp. 763 (N.D. Miss. 1980) (upholding city ban on liquor advertisements in university newspaper).

In Kops v. New York Telephone Co., 456 F. Supp. 1090 (S.D.N.Y. 1978), aff'd, 603 F.2d 213 (2d Cir. 1979), the court held that the refusal of the telephone company to accept a Bates-type legal clinic advertisement for placement in the Yellow Pages did not constitute state action sufficient to implicate any right of access.

Finally, however, the Alaska Supreme Court ruled that a municipality, which prepared and published a city services guide that included descriptions of the services provided by political and public interest organizations, had thereby created a public forum and could not deny a listing to a gay rights organization. See Alaska Gay Coalition v. Sullivan, 578 P.2d 951 (Sup. Ct. 1978).

(page 586) [771]

Insert before Note 1.

NOTE

The kinds of concerns about access of different points of view into the market place of ideas which underlay the right of access claims rejected in Tornillo were considered by the Court in three related cases dealing with equal access of political ideas. In Buckley v. Valeo, 424 U.S. 1 (1976), the Court invalidated campaign expenditure controls that sought to equalize the amount of money that federal candidates could spend on their campaigns, rejecting, as "wholly foreign to the First Amendment," the concept that government may restrict the speech of some elements of our society in order to enhance the relative voice of others. Id. at 48-49. The Court did, however, uphold provisions providing for the public financing, in equal amounts, of the presidential campaigns of major party candidates. In 1978, the equal access question arose in the context of restrictions on corporate spending to lobby the public and influence the outcome of referenda campaigns. In First National Bank of Boston v. Bellotti, 435 U.S. 765 (1978), a 5-4 majority rejected the claim that such corporate spending to promote corporate views would have a disproportionate and distorting impact on the debate before the electorate, or that such impact, if proven, would justify restricting such corporate speech. 435 U.S. at 786-792. Finally, in Committee Against Rent Control v. Berkeley,—U.S.—, 50 U.S.L.W. 4071 (1981), the Court invalidated limitations on contributions to committees supporting or opposing ballot questions.

(page 588) [774]

NOTES [References]

4. For additional discussion of the access question, see B. Schmidt, Freedom of the Press v. Public Access (1976); Bollinger, Freedom of the Press and Public Access: Toward A Theory of Partial Regulation of the Mass Media, 75 Mich. L. Rev. 1 (1976).

B [C]. THE BROADCAST MEDIA

(page 595) [793]

Insert before CBS decision:

NOTE — FCC REGULATION OF THE BROADCAST MEDIA: THE FAIRNESS DOCTRINE AND OTHER CONTENT CONTROLS

In recent years the courts, particularly the District of Columbia Circuit, have continued to wrestle with the tension, imbedded in the Fairness Doctrine, between editorial discretion and public access to a range of ideas and information. As Judge Skelly Wright aptly put it, despite Red Lion, ". . . important constitutional questions continue to haunt this area of the law. The [fairness] doctrine and the [personal attack] rule do, after all, involve the Government to a significant degree in policing the content of communication. . . . The abiding First Amendment difficulties, however, along with an appreciation of Congress' intent in enacting the Communication Act, have engendered an important corollary: The licensee is to have the maximum editorial freedom consistent with its position as public trustee of a portion of the air waves." Strauss Communications, Inc. v. FCC, 530 F.2d 1001, 1008 (D.C. Cir. 1976). In Strauss, the application of the "personal attack" rule, providing the subject of the attack an opportunity to respond, was narrowed, the Court holding that a licensee radio station should be found in violation of the personal attack rule only when the licensee has acted unreasonably or in bad faith. The Court reasoned that, in order to protect the licensee's First Amendment rights, the FCC should allow the licensee the maximum editorial freedom consistent with its role as a trustee of a portion of the airwaves.

For other illustrative cases, see: National Citizens Committee for Broadcasting v. FCC, 567 F.2d 1095 (D.C. Cir. 1977), cert. denied, 436 U.S. 926 (1978) (upholding the FCC's retreat from applying fairness doctrine principles to commercial advertisements); Public Media Center v. FCC, 587 F.2d 1322 (D.C. Cir. 1978) (whether fairness doctrine applies to nuclear power utility company advertisements); American Security Council Education Fund v. FCC, 607 F.2d 438 (D.C. Cir. 1979)(en banc), cert. denied, 444 U.S. 1013 (1980) (whether CBS News gave unbalanced "dovish" news coverage to "national security" issues).

In the related area of the political candidate "equal time" requirement of 315(a) of the Act, several decisions have permitted a general narrowing of the range of situations in which the equal time requirements apply by expanding the concept of bona fide news events exempt from the requirement. See: McCarthy v. FCC, 45 U.S.L.W. 3535 (D.C. Cir. 1976), cert. denied, 430 U.S. 955 (1977); Chisholm v. FCC, 538 F.2d 349 (D.C. Cir.), cert. denied, 429 U.S. 890 (1976); Office of Communications, United Church of Christ v. FCC, 590 F.2d 1062 (D.C. Cir. 1978); Kennedy for President Committee v. FCC, 636 F.2d 432 (D.C. Cir. 1980).

Most importantly, in CBS v. FCC, 453 U.S. 367, 101 S. Ct. 2913 (1981), the Court recognized and upheld a statutorily created limited right of access by federal candidates to purchase radio or television time. This new and significant decision is discussed following this note. See generally: Note, The Right of "Reasonable Access" for Federal Political Candidates Under Section 312(a)(7) of The Communications Act, 78 Colum. L. Rev. 1287 (1978).

Finally, in terms of direct Commission attempts to regulate the content of programming, the recent record of judicial response is a poor one.

In Writers Guild of America, West, Inc. v. FCC, 423 F. Supp. 1064 (C.D. Cal. 1976), the district court found that the Commission had improperly engaged in an informal campaign to pressure the network into adopting "family hour" viewing rules. Such coercive government activity was found to violate the First Amendment. In a potentially far-reaching decision, the court also held the networks liable for damages claimed by independent producers harmed by adoption of the family hour rules. Unfortunately, however, the Ninth Circuit vacated the lower court ruling on the ground that the "serious issues" should first have been addressed by the Commission, before a broad judicial remedy was fashioned. 609 F.2d 355 (9th Cir. 1979).

Similarly, the Commission's prohibition of the radio broadcast of a satirical monologue containing seven "offensive" words, based on the need to protect the sensibilities of children and others in the audience, was upheld by the Supreme Court in FCC v. Pacifica Foundation, 438 U.S. 726 (1978). For a general discussion of these and other issues, see Student Symposium, Communications Regulation, 69 Calif. L. Rev. 442 (1981).

(page 605) [803]

NOTE

3.a. *The second CBS case.* Almost a decade after its 1973 holding that there was no right of editorial access to the electronic media, the Supreme Court considered the validity of a more focused, statutorily based right of access prevailed. The 6-3 decision in CBS Inc. v. FCC, 453 U.S. 367, 101 S. Ct. 2813 (1981), arose out of the efforts of President Carter's campaign committee to secure 30 minutes of time on the three major networks early in December 1979 for a program announcing the President's candidacy for re-election and presenting his administration's record. All three networks declined to provide the time. The committee filed a complaint with the FCC charging that the networks' refusal contravened a statutory requirement (47 U.S.C. §312(a)(7)) that directs licensees "to allow reasonable access to or to permit purchase of reasonable amounts of time for the use of a broadcasting station by a legally qualified candidate for federal elective office on behalf of his candidacy." The Commission agreed, and the networks sought review of this determination in the courts.

Most of Chief Justice Burger's opinion for the Court is devoted to the history, purpose, and interpretation of §312(a)(7). The Court held that the section did, indeed, create "an affirmative promptly enforceable right of reasonable access to the use of broadcast stations for individual candidates seeking federal elective office." 101 S. Ct. at 2820. Moreover, this right was distinct from the equal time requirement of section 315(a): ". . . the legislative history supports the plain meaning of the statute that individual candidates for federal elective office have a right of reasonable access to the use of stations for paid political broadcasts on behalf of their candidacies, without reference to whether an opponent has secured time." Id. at 2823.

Lastly, the Court addressed the networks' argument, based on the first CBS decision, that section 312(a)(7) as implemented "violates the First Amendment rights of broadcasters by unduly circumscribing their editorial discretion." Id. at 2829. While acknowledging the importance of the "widest jounalistic freedom" for broadcasters, the Court observed, emphatically quoting from Red Lion, that *"[i]t is the right of viewers and listeners, not the right of the broadcasters which is paramount."* Ibid. Moreover, "[t]he First Amendment interests of candidates and voters, as well as broadcasters, are implicated by §312(a)(7) . . . [which] makes a significant contribution to freedom of expression by enhancing the ability of candidates to present, and the public to receive, information necessary for the effective operation of the democratic process." Id. at 2830. The Court's opinion concluded as follows:

"Petitioners are correct that the Court has never approved a *general* right of access to the media. See, e.g., FCC v. Midwest Video Corp., 440 U.S. 689 (1979); Miami Herald Publishing Co. v. Tornillo, 418 U.S. 241 (1974); CBS, Inc. v. Democratic National Committee, supra. Nor do we do so today. Section 312(a)(7) creates a *limited* right to reasonable access that pertains only to legally qualified federal candidates and may be invoked by them only for the purpose of advancing their candidacies once a campaign has commenced. The Commission has stated that, in enforcing the statute, it will 'provide leeway to broadcasters and not merely attempt de novo to determine the reasonableness of their judgments. . . .' If broadcasters have considered the relevant factors in good faith, the Commission will uphold their decisions. Further, §312(a)(7) does not impair the discretion of broadcasters to present their views on any issue or to carry any particular type of programming.

"Section 312(a)(7) represents an effort by Congress to assure that an important resource—the airwaves—will be used in the public interest. We hold that the statutory right of access, as defined by the Commission and applied in these cases, properly balances the First Amendment rights of federal candidates, the public, and broadcasters." Id. at 2830. Three dissenting justices insisted that the "limited" right of access applied by the Commission and approved by the Court was far less limited than the Court suggested and far more sweeping than the Congress intended.

The second CBS decision is thus a considerable victory for access advocates.

3.b. *Access and cross-ownership.* Structural changes in the broadcast and news media industry have the potential for increasing — or decreasing — public access to air time. To deal with this problem, the FCC promulgated cross-ownership rules that generally forbid future formation of jointly owned newspaper-broadcast station combinations in the same city, and require divestiture of existing combinations in certain circumstances. Those rules were unanimously upheld by the Court in FCC v. National Citizens Committee for Broadcasting, 436 U.S. 775 (1978). The targets of those rules contended that they exceeded the Commission's statutory authority and violated the First and Fifth Amendment rights of newspaper owners.

Addressing the claim that the rules violated the First Amendment rights of newspaper owners, the Court reiterated the Red Lion proposition that there is no "unabridgeable First Amendment right to broadcast comparable to the right of every individual to speak, write or publish," 395 U.S. at 388, and that the power of government that flows from the need to regulate use of the broadcast spectrum continues to serve as the valid predicate for a policy of promoting diversification in the mass media, 436 U.S. at 799. Similarly, the Court reaffirmed the continued distinction between the permissibility of access and diversification regulation of the broadcast media and the impermissibility of comparable regulation of the print media. Finally, the Court rejected the contention that "the regulations unconstitutionally condition receipt of a broadcast license upon forfeiture of the right to publish a newspaper." 436 U.S. at 800. The Court distinguished various unconstitutional conditions cases on the ground that in those cases ". . . denial of a benefit had the affect of abridging freedom of expression, since the denial was based solely on the content of constitutionally protected speech. . . . Here the regulations are not content related; moreover, their purpose and effect is to promote free speech, not to restrict it." Id. at 801.

3.c. *Access and program format.* Another access problem arises when a broadcast outlet with a distinct programming format, e.g., classical music, is to be sold to a new licensee who intends to eliminate that format completely and replace it with more "popular" programming. The net effect will be a contraction in the available viewing or listening fare. Access advocates contended that, when applying the statutory "public interest, convenience and necessity" standard to approve a radio license transfer or renewal, the Commission must consider anticipated changes in entertainment programming when ruling on the application. The Commission disagreed and so did the Supreme Court. See FCC v. WNCN Listeners Guild, 450 U.S. 582, 101 S. Ct. 1266 (1981). The Court addressed the access advocates' First Amendment claims as follows:

"Respondents contend that . . . the Policy Statement conflicts with the First Amendment rights of listeners 'to receive suitable access to social political, aesthetic, moral, and other ideas and experience.' Red Lion Broadcasting Co. v. FCC, 395 U.S. 367, 390 (1969). Red Lion held that the Commission's 'fairness doctrine' was consistent with the public-interest standard of the Communications Act and did not violate the First Amendment, but rather enhanced First Amendment values by promoting 'the presentation of vigorous debate of controversial issues of importance and concern to the public.' 395 U.S., at 385. Although observing that the interests of the people as a whole were promoted by debate of public issues on the radio, we did not imply that the First Amendment grants individual listeners the right to have the Commission review the abandonment of their favorite entertainment programs. The Commission seeks to further the interests of the listening public as a whole by relying on market forces to promote diversity in radio entertainment formats and to satisfy the entertainment preferences of radio listeners. This policy does not conflict with the First Amendment." 101 S. Ct. at 1279.

In this regard, it should be noted that the Commission recently "deregulated" almost all programming requirements imposed on radio stations relating to (1) nonentertainment programs, (2) permissible number of commercial minutes per hour, and (3) program logging rules. See Amendment to FCC Rules and Regulations, 46 Fed. Reg. 13888 (Feb. 24, 1981), 49 U.S.L.W. 2588. Similarly, the House Subcommittee on Telecommunications, Consumer Protection, and Finance, formerly chaired by Congressman Van Deerlin, has been engaged in an extensive investigation looking toward "deregulation" of television.

(page 606) [804]

NOTES

4. [continued]
The courts continue to be extremely active in overseeing governmental policy toward the development and expansion of cable television.

In 1979 the Court dealt with FCC cable television "public access" rules in FCC v. Midwest Video, 440 U.S. 689 (1979). Beginning in 1972, the Commission promulgated rules requiring cable operators to develop at least a 20-channel capacity and to dedicate four of those channels for public, governmental, educational, and leased access, respectively. In 1976, however, the Commission modified the rules in certain ways favorable to cable operators. The respective FCC Orders were challenged in court by cable operators, claiming that they went too far, and public interest groups such as the ACLU, contending that the orders did not go far enough to insure public access to cable television.

The Eighth Circuit, agreeing completely with the cable operators, held that the regulations were not "reasonably ancillary" to the commission's statutory jurisdiction over broadcasting, that they improperly sought to impose common carrier status and obligations on the operators and that they presented severe First Amendment problems of governmental interference with editorial discretion.

The Supreme Court, 6-3, affirmed, holding that the FCC actions exceeded and were in contravention of its statutory authority: "With its access rules . . . the Commission has transferred control of the content of access cable channels from cable operators to members of the public who wish to communicate by the cable medium. Effectively, the Commission has relegated cable systems, pro tanto, to common-carrier status. . . . Congress has restricted the Commission's ability to advance objectives associated with public access at the expense of the journalistic freedom of persons engaged in broadcasting. . . .

"The exercise of jurisdiction in Midwest Video, it has been said, 'strain[ed] the outer limits' of Commission authority. 406 U.S., at 676 (Burger, C.J., concurring). In light of the hesitancy with which Congress approached the access issue in the broadcast area, and in view of its outright rejection of a broad right of public access on a common-carrier basis, we are constrained to hold that the Commission exceeded those limits in promulgating its access rules. The Commission may not regulate cable systems as common carriers, just as it may not impose such obligations on television broadcasters. We think authority to compel cable operators to provide common carriage of public-originated transmissions must come specifically from Congress." Id. at 707-709.

For cases dealing with the extent to which local government may regulate cable television free from federal pre-emption or First Amendment restraints, see: Community Communications Co., Inc. v. City of Boulder, — U.S. — , 50 U.S.L.W. 4144 (Jan. 13, 1982)(municipal regulation of cable operators not exempt from federal antitrust laws); National Association of Regulatory Utility Commissioners v. FCC, 533 F.2d 601 (D.C. Cir. 1976); Brookhaven Cable TV. v. Kelly, 573 F.2d 765 (2d Cir. 1978); Community Communications Co., Inc. v. City of Boulder, — F.2d — , 50 U.S.L.W. 2200 (10th Cir. 1981); Home Box Office v. Wilkinson, — F. Supp. — , 50 U.S.L.W. 2476 (D. Utah 1982).

For a case invalidating broad FCC restrictions on pay television, see Home Box Office, Inc., v. FCC, 567 F.2d 9 (D.C. Cir.), cert. denied, 434 U.S. 829 (1977).

5. The development and encouragement of public television contains great potential for expanding public access to broadcasting. One of the problems, however, is the inherent capacity for censorship and repression that can be exercised by public and quasi-public institutions which control the activities of public television. In two cases, the courts have expressed a sensitivity to the dangers of governmental censorship in this area. In The Network Project v. Corporation for Public Broadcasting, 561 F.2d 963 (D.C. Cir. 1977), cert. denied, 434 U.S. 1068 (1978), the court ruled that public television producers and viewers, claiming that the elimination of funding for controversial programs and the practice of pre-screening of such programs constituted prohibited censorship, stated a valid cognizable claim for violation of constitutional rights. Similarly, in Community Service Broadcasting v. FCC, 593 F.2d 1102 (D.C. Cir. 1978) (en banc), the court ruled unconstitutional a statutory requirement that noncommercial educational television stations receiving public funds must retain for 60 days and make available on demand tapes of any program "in which any issue of public importance is discussed." The court, in an extensive discussion of the role and potential of public television, was quick to notice the censorship possibilities inherent in such a retention requirement: "We hold that Section 399(b) of the Communications Act places substantial burdens on non-commercial educational broadcasters and presents the risk of direct governmental interference in program content. Since no substantial governmental interest has been shown on the other side of the constitutional balance, the statute and rules at issue are unconstitutional." 593 F.2d at 1105.

For two cases involving extremely interesting issues of access and censorship in the public television setting, see: Barnstone v. University of Houston, KUHT-TV, 660 F.2d 137 (5th Cir. 1981) and Muir v. Alabama Educational Television Commission, 656 F.2d 1012 (5th Cir. 1981). Both cases deal with viewer challenges to the decision of certain stations to not show the controversial program "Death of a Princess" dealing with the execution for adultery of a young woman from a royal Saudi Arabian family. The Fifth Circuit has set the cases for en banc consideration.

Chapter Ten
Academic Freedom

A. INTRODUCTION

(page 607) [805]

See generally Project, Education and the Law: State Interests and Individual Rights, 74 Mich L. Rev.1373, 1420 (1976).

B. FREEDOM TO TEACH — CHOICE OF CURRICULUM AND TEACHING METHOD

(page 616) [814]

NOTES

3. In Ambach v. Norwick, 441 U.S. 68 (1979), the Supreme Court held that a state can validly forbid permanent certification as a public school teacher of an alien who does not express an intention to become a United States citizen. Justice Powell, writing for the five-judge majority, found that teaching in public schools constitutes a governmental function. Public school teachers are responsible for "developing students' attitudes toward government and understanding of the role of citizens in our society" through both the presentation of course materials and the examples they set. Accordingly, the Court evaluated this alienage classification under the rational basis test and found that the statute barring aliens from permanent certification did bear a rational relationship to a legitimate state interest. Justice Blackmun, joined by Justices Brennan, Marshall, and Stevens, dissented. Blackmun could discern no principled difference between teaching in a public school and the practice of law; aliens, of course, cannot validly be barred from the practice of law.

For an early discussion of Ambach v. Norwick, see Order, Are Aliens Still a Suspect Class After Norwick?, 11 Colum. Human Rights L. Rev. 227 (1979).

(page 621) [820]

NOTES

2. [continued] In McLean v. Arkansas Board of Education, 529 F. Supp. 1255 (E.D. Ark. 1982), the court held that an Arkansas statute mandating that public schools give balanced treatment to creation science and to evolution science violated the Establishment Clause. The court found that creation science is religion, not a science, and that it has no educational merit. Therefore, the statute failed all three prongs of the test enuciated in Lemon v. Kurtzman, 403 U.S. 602 (1971) (see Chapter XIV): that it have a secular purpose, not have the primary effect of the advancement of religion, and not foster excessive governmental entanglement.

3. [continued] School board removal of books from school libraries and classrooms and of courses from school curricula have generally been upheld when not caused by political or ideological motivation. See, e.g., Bicknell v. Vergennes Union High School Board of Directors, 638 F.2d 438 (2d Cir. 1980); Zykan v. Warsaw Community School Corporation, 631 F.2d 1300 (7th Cir. 1980). In Board of Education, Island Trees Union Free School District v. Pico, 50 U.S.L.W. 4831 (1982), the Supreme Court ruled that books may not be removed from school libraries if the purpose of the removal is to reinforce political orthodoxy. The case was remanded in trial on the issue of purpose.

In Minarcini v. Strongsville City School District, 541 F.2d 577 (6th Cir. 1976), another "book banning" case, a public high school board refused to approve the use of certain family recommended textbooks, including Catch-22, by Joseph Heller, and novels by Kurt Vonnegut. In addition, the board ordered the removal of these books from the school library. The Sixth Circuit ruled that the board's refusal to approve the textbooks was a constitutionally valid exercise of its statutory power to select and purchase textbooks. However, the court held that teachers' classroom commentary on these books was protected by the teachers' right of academic freedom and by the students' right to receive information. The court also ruled that the removal of the books from the school library, based on allegedly objectionable content, unconstitutionally interfered with students' First Amendment rights. Students' rights in this area are discussed in Section H, infra.

In Cary v. Board of Education of the Adams-Arapahoe School District 28-J, 427 F. Supp. 945 (D. Colo. 1977), aff'd, 598 F.2d 535 (10th Cir. 1979), the court took a different tack from that of Minarcini and stated that the teacher's selection of books as material for an elective course falls within the protection of academic freedom. The teacher's bargaining contract with the school district, however, gave the board the right to determine the "techniques, methods, and means of teaching." Hence, the court upheld the school board's ban of ten books from use in class assignments.

For other cases delimiting constitutional school board control over curricula and teaching methods, see Kingsville Independent School District v. Cooper, 611 F.2d 1109 (5th Cir. 1980) (nonrenewal of untenured teacher's contract for classroom discussions violated the first amendment; Palmer v. Board of Education of Chicago, 603 F.2d 1271 (7th Cir. 1979), cert. denied, 444 U.S. 1026 (1980) (public school teacher's religious-based refusal to teach patriotic matters was counterbalanced by the state's compelling interest); Dean v. Timpson Independent School District, 486 F. Supp. 302 (E.D. Tex. 1979) (introduction of survey into class that offended community beliefs but did not disrupt the operation of the school could not be the basis for discharge); Millikan v. Board of Directors of Everett School District No. 2, 93 Wash. 2d 522, 611 P.2d 414 (1980) (en banc) (upheld school board requirement that teachers teach in conventional manner and not team-teach).

For a view that the Constitution does not afford teachers a right to choose what to teach, see Goldstein, The Asserted Constitutional Right of Public School Teachers to Determine What They Teach, 124 U. Pa. L. Rev. 1293, 1355-1356 (1976) ("Neither sound constitutional analysis nor authoritative precedent support a federal constitutional right of teachers to determine what they teach contrary to the desires of school authorities superior to teachers within the state-sanctioned chain of command. The cases involving restrictions on teachers' rights of curricular control are often erroneously viewed as censorship cases when the real issue is who should make curricular choices given the fact that someone has to make the choices.") See also Hirschoff, Parents and the Public School Curriculum: Is there a Right to Have One's Child Excused From Objectionable Instruction? 50 S. Cal. L. Rev. 871 (1977); Censoring the School Library: Do Students Have a Right to Read? 10 Conn. L. Rev. 747 (1978).

(page 622) [821]

NOTES

5. [continued] In Donahue v. Copiague Union School District, 47 N.Y.2d 440 (1979), the New York Court of Appeals refused to recognize either a common law or constitutional cause of action for "educational malpractice" because it would involve excessive court intervention into school affairs. "Recognition in the courts of this cause of action would constitute blatant interference with the responsibility for the administration lodged by constitution and statute in school administrative agencies."

This judicial reluctance to intervene in academic affairs has sometimes resulted in minimal scrutiny of college and university employment decisions challenged under Title VII of the 1964 Civil Rights Act. Judge Moore rejected this anti-interventionist stance in Powell v. Syracuse University, 580 F.2d 1150 (2d Cir. 1978), cert. denied, 439 U.S. 1075 (1979): "It might be said that far from taking an anti-interventionist position, [in enacting Title VII], Congress had instructed courts to be particularly sensitive to evidence of academic bias.... Courts, then, must steer a careful course between excessive intervention in the affairs of the university and the unwarranted tolerance of unlawful behavior. Faro [502 F.2d 1229 (2d Cir. 1974)] does not, and was never intended to, indicate that academic freedom embraces the freedom to discriminate."

But see Banerjee v. Board of Trustees of Smith College, [1981] 25 Fair Empl. Prac. Cas. (Lab. Rel. Rep.) 1073 (1st Cir. Apr. 21, 1981); Carton v. Trustees of Tufts College, [1981] 25 Fair Empl. Prac. Cas. (Lab. Rel. Rep.) 1114 (1st Cir. Feb. 20 1981). See generally Yurko, Judicial Recognition of Academic Collective Interests: A New Approach to Faculty Title VII Litigation, 60 B.U.L. Rev. 473 (1980); Note, Academic Freedom and Federal Regulation of University Hiring, 92 Harv. L. Rev. 879 (1979).

C. FREEDOM OF SPEECH — IN THE SCHOOL OR UNIVERSITY

(page 628) [827]

NOTES

8. See East Hartford Education Association v. Board of Education, 562 F.2d 838, rev'd on rehearing en banc, 562 F.2d 856 (2d Cir. 1977) (rejected teacher's claim that his refusal to wear a tie in his English class consitituted protected "symbolic speech"); Resetar v. Maryland State Board of Education, 399 A.2d 225 (Md. Ct. App. 1979), cert. denied, 444 U.S. 838 (1979) (upheld dismissal of teacher with history of intemperate conduct for calling his students "jungle bunnies").

D. FREEDOM OF SPEECH — OUTSIDE THE SCHOOL OR UNIVERSITY

(page 637) [837]

*MT. HEALTHY CITY SCHOOL DISTRICT
BOARD OF EDUCATION v. DOYLE*
429 U.S. 274 (1977)

Mr. JUSTICE REHNQUIST delivered the opinion of the Court. Respondent Doyle sued petitioner Mt. Healthy Board of Education in the United States District Court for the Southern District of Ohio. Doyle claimed that the Board's refusal to renew his contract in 1971 violated his rights under the First and Fourteenth Amendments to the United States Constitution. After a bench trial the District Court held that Doyle was entitled to reinstatement with back pay. The Court of Appeals for the Sixth Circuit affirmed the judgment, and we granted the Board's petition for certiorari to consider an admixture of jurisdictional and constitutional claims. . . .

IV

Having concluded that respondent's complaint sufficiently pleaded jurisdiction under 28 U.S.C. §1331, that the Board has failed to preserve the issue whether that complaint stated a claim upon which relief could be granted against the Board, and that the Board is not immune from suit under the Eleventh Amendment, we now proceed to consider the merits of respondent's claim under the First and Fourteenth Amendments.

Doyle was first employed by the Board in 1966. He worked under one-year contracts for the first three years, and under a two-year contract from 1969 to 1971. In 1969 he was elected president of the Teachers' Association, in which position he worked to expand the subjects of direct negotiation between the Association and the Board of Education. During Doyle's one-year term as president of the Association, and during the succeeding year when he served on its executive committee, there was apparently some tension in relations between the Board and the Association.

Beginning early in 1970, Doyle was involved in several incidents not directly connected with his role in the Teachers' Association. In one instance, he engaged in an argument with another teacher which culminated in the other teacher's slapping him. Doyle subsequently refused to accept an apology and insisted upon some punishment for the other teacher. His persistence in the matter resulted in the suspension of both teachers for one day, which was followed by a walkout by a number of other teachers, which in turn resulted in the lifting of the suspensions.

On other occasions, Doyle got into an argument with employees of the school cafeteria over the amount of spaghetti which had been served him; referred to students, in connection with a disciplinary complaint, as "sons of bitches"; and made an obscene gesture to two girls in connection with their failure to obey commands made in his capacity as cafeteria supervisor. Chronologically the last in the series of incidents which respondent was involved in during his employment by the Board was a telephone call by him to a local radio station. It was the Board's consideration of this incident which the court below found to be a violation of the First and Fourteenth Amendments.

In February of 1971, the principal circulated to various teachers a memorandum relating to teacher dress and appearance, which was apparently prompted by the view of some in the administration that there was a relationship between teacher appearance and public support for bond issues. Doyle's response to the receipt of the memorandum — on a subject which he apparently understood was to be settled by joint teacher-administration action — was to convey the substance of the memorandum to a disc jockey at WSAI, a Cincinnati radio station, who promptly announced the adoption of the dress code as a news item. Doyle subsequently apologized to the principal, conceding that he should have made some prior communication of his criticism to the school administration.

Approximately one month later the superintendent made his customary annual recommendations to the Board as to the rehiring of nontenured teachers. He recommended that Doyle not be rehired. The same recommendation was made with respect to nine other teachers in the district, and in all instances, including Doyle's, the recommendation was adopted by the Board. Shortly after being notified of this decision, respondent requested a statement of reasons for the Board's actions. He received a statement citing "a notable lack of tact in handling professional matters which leaves much doubt as to your sincerity in establishing good school relationships." That general statement was followed by references to the radio station incident and to the obscene gesture incident.

The District Court found that all of these incidents had in fact occurred. It concluded that respondent Doyles's telephone call to the radio station was "clearly protected by the First Amendment," and that because it had played a "substantial part" in the decision of the Board not to renew Doyle's employment, he was entitled to reinstatement with backpay.... The District Court did not expressly state what test it was applying in determining that the incident in question involved conduct protected by the First Amendment, but simply held that the communication to the radio station was such conduct. The Court of Appeals affirmed in a brief per curiam opinion.

Doyle's claims under the First and Fourteenth Amendments are not defeated by the fact that he did not have tenure. Even though he could have been discharged for no reason whatever, and had no constitutional right to a hearing prior to the decision not to rehire him, ... he may nonetheless establish a claim to reinstatement if the decision not to rehire him was made by reason of his exercise of constitutionally protected First Amendment freedoms....

That question of whether speech or a government employee is constitutionally protected expression necessarily entails striking "a balance between the interests of the teacher, as a citizen, in commenting upon matters of public concern and the interest of the State as an employer, in promoting the efficiency of the public services it performs through its employees." ... There is no suggestion by the Board that Doyle violated any established policy, or that its reaction to his communication to the radio station was anything more than an ad hoc response to Doyle's action in making the memorandum public. We therefore accept the District Court's finding that the communication was protected by the First and Fourteenth Amendments. We are not, however, entirely in agreement with that court's manner of reasoning from this finding to the conclusion that Doyle is entitled to reinstatement with backpay.

The District Court made the following "conclusions" on this aspect of the case: "(1) If a non-permissible reason, e.g., exercise of First Amendment rights, played a substantial part in the decision not to renew — even in the face of other permissible grounds — the decision may not stand (citations omitted).

"(2) A non-permissible reason did play a substantial part. That is clear from the letter of the Superintendent immediately following the Board's decision, which stated two reasons — the one, the conversation with the radio station clearly protected by the First Amendment. A court may not engage in any limitation of First Amendment rights based on 'tact' — that is not to say that 'tactfulness' is irrelevant to other issues in this case." ...

At the same time, though, it stated that "in fact, as this Court sees it and finds, both the Board and the Superintendent were faced with a situation in which there did exist in fact reason . . . independent of any First Amendment rights or exercise thereof, to not extend tenure." . . .

Since respondent Doyle had no tenure, and there was therefore not even a state law requirement of "cause" or "reason" before a decision could be made not to renew his employment, it is not clear what the District Court meant by this latter statement. Clearly the Board legally could have dismissed respondent had the radio station incident never come to its attention. One plausible meaning of the court's statement is that the Board and the Superintendent not only could, but in fact would have reached that decision had not the constitutionally protected incident of the telephone call to the radio station occurred. We are thus brought to the issue whether, even if that were the case, the fact that the protected conduct played a "substantial part" in the actual decision not to renew would necessarily amount to a constitutional violation justifying remedial action. We think that it would not.

A rule of causation which focuses solely on whether protected conduct played a part, "substantial" or otherwise, in a decision not to rehire, could place an employee in a better position as a result of the exercise of constitutionally protected conduct than he would have occupied had he done nothing. The difficulty with the rule enunciated by the District Court is that it would require reinstatement in cases where a dramatic and perhaps abrasive incident is inevitably on the minds of those responsible for the decision to rehire, and does indeed play a part in that decision — even if the same decision would would have been reached had the incident not occurred. The constitutional principle at stake is sufficiently vindicated if such an employee is placed in no worse a position than if he had not engaged in the conduct. A borderline or marginal candidate should not have the employment question resolved against him because of constitutionally protected conduct. But that same candidate ought not be be able, by engaging in such conduct, to prevent his employer from assessing his performance record and reaching a decision not to rehire on the basis of that record, simply because the protected conduct makes the employer more certain of the correctness of its decision.

This is especially true where, as the District Court observed was the case here, the current decision to rehire will accord "tenure." The long term consequences of an award of tenure are of great moment both to the employee and to the employer. They are too significant for us to hold that the Board in this case would be precluded, because it considered constitutionally protected conduct in deciding not to rehire Doyle, from attempting to prove to a trier of fact that quite apart from such conduct Doyle's record was such that he would not have been rehired in any event.

In other areas of constitutional law, the Court has found it necessary to formulate a test of causation which distinguishes between a result caused by a constitutional violation and one not so caused....

... [T]he proper test to apply in the present context is one which likewise protects against the invasion of constitutional rights without commanding undesirable consequences not necessary to the assurance of those rights.

Initially, in this case, the burden was properly placed upon respondent to show that his conduct was constitutionally protected, and that this conduct was a "substantial factor"— or to put it in other words, that it was a "motivating factor" in the Board's decision not to rehire him. Respondent having carried that burden, however, the District Court should have gone on to determine whether the Board and shown by a preponderance of the evidence that it would have reached the same decision as to respondent's reemployment even in the absence of the protected conduct.

We cannot tell from the District Court opinion and conclusions, nor from the opinion of the Court of Appeals affirming the judgment of the District Court, what conclusion those courts would have reached had they applied this test. The judgment of the Court of Appeals is therefore vacated, and the case remanded for further proceedings consistent with this opinion.

For discussion of the Mt. Healthy case see Gee, Teacher Dismissal: A view From Mt. Healthy, 2 B.Y.U.L. Rev. 255 (1980).

(page 638) [837]

NOTES

1. [continued] In Givhan v. Western Line Consolidated School District, 439 U.S. 410 (1979), a unanimous Supreme Court held that the First Amendment protects a teacher from being dismissed for the private expression of opinions to her principal. "The First Amendment forbids abridgement of 'freedom of speech.' Neither the Amendment itself nor our decisions indicate that this freedom is lost to the public employee who arranges to communicate privately with his employer rather than to spread his views before the public." The Court remanded the case to determine whether, under the Mt. Healthy standard, plaintiff would have been rehired but for her criticism of school policies that she conceived to be racially discriminatory in purpose or effect.

For recent decisions protecting teachers from administrative reprisals for their exercise of free speech see, e.g., Brown v. Bullard Independent School District, 640 F.2d 651 (5th Cir. 1979), cert. denied, 50 U.S.L.W. 3246 (1981)(private conversations with principal, superintendant, and trustees, and speech at faculty meeting); Lindsey v. Board of Regents of University System of Georgia, 607 F.2d 672 (5th Cir. 1979) (distribution of questionnaire to faculty); McGill v. Board of Education of Pekin Elementary School District #108, 602 F.2d 774 (7th Cir. 1979) (statements in teachers' lounge and at school board meeting favoring master collective bargaining contract); Bertot v. School District No. 1, 522 F.2d 1171 (10th Cir. 1975) (teacher's activities with underground newspaper held protected where actions in question did not impede classroom performance nor interfere with school operations); Hillis v. Stephen F. Austin State University, 486 F. Supp. 663 (E.D. Tex. 1980) (criticism of directives from department head requiring teacher to carry student on class roll and give her a "B" for the course); Jordan v. Cagle, 474 F. Supp. 1198 (N.D. Miss. 1979), aff'd mem., 620 F.2d 298 (5th Cir. 1980) (public criticism of superintendant and school board for changing regulation allowing teachers to work at election booths); Aumiller v. University of Delaware, 434 F. Supp. 1273 (D. Del. 1977) (published interviews on the subject of his homosexuality). Compare Barbre v. Garland Independent School District, 474 F. Supp. 687 (N.D. Tex. 1979) (nontenured teacher's aide's speech at board meeting was not of "public concern"); Lux v. Board of Regents of New Mexico Highlands University, 622 P.2d 266 (N. Mex. Ct. App. 1980) (remarks did not constitute protected free speech because they did not "serve to foster rational discourse, exchange of ideas, and meaningful discussion about a matter of legitimate public interest").

2. [continued] See Megill v. Board of Regents, 541 F.2d 1073 (5th Cir. 1976) (upheld failure to grant tenure to professor who had made

false and misleading public statements about university and its president, used profanity, and disrupted a meeting).

(page 638) [838]

NOTES

3. [continued] But see Trotman v. Board of Trustees of Lincoln University, 635 F.2d 216 (3d Cir. 1980), cert. denied, 101 S. Ct. 2320 (1981) (criticism of university via speech and picketing constituted protected action.

(page 639) [838]

NOTES

4. [continued] In Dougherty County, Ga., Board of Education v. White, 439 U.S. 32 (1978), the Supreme Court, by a 5-4 vote, found that the Voting Rights Act of 1965 applied to a board of education requirement that its employees take unpaid leaves of absence while campaigning for elective office, and thus it required the board to seek prior approval of the rule from the Attorney General. In his majority opinion, Justice Marshall found that the rule qualified as a "standard, practice, or procedure with regard to voting" because it imposed substantial economic disincentives on employees who wish to seek elective office, burdened the entry into elective campaigns, and, concomitantly, limited the choices available to Dougherty County voters. And the circumstances surrounding the enactment of the rule suggested that it had the potential for discrimination: respondent was the first black in the county ever to run for office; the rule was enacted one month after he announced his candidacy; and the leave was contingent on announced candidacy rather than absence from school. Finally, the court found that the board of education qualified as a political subdivision for purposes of the Voting Rights Act.

See Allen v. Board of Education of Jefferson County, 584 S.W.2d 408 (Ky. App. 1979) (holding unconstitutional school board policy imposing mandatory leaves of absence for teachers running for office: no determination whether such would adversely affect their performance of duties).

6. The Fourth Amendment protects a high school guidance counselor from the after-hours search of his desk by a school board member in search of evidence the counselor had drawn a political cartoon uncomplimentary of the board of education. Gillard v. Schmidt, 579 F.2d 825 (3d Cir. 1978). In reversing the district court, the Third Circuit found that a guidance counselor, charged with maintaining sensitive student

records, at least in the absence of an accepted practice or regulation to the contrary, enjoys a reasonable expectation of privacy in his school desk.

E. THE RIGHT TO PRIVACY AND INDIVIDUAL LIFESTYLE

(page 646) [846]

NOTES

2. [continued] See Baker v. School District of City of Allentown, 371 A.2d 1028 (Pa. Commw. Ct. 1977) (in upholding teacher's "immorality" dismissal for pleading nolo contendere of federal offense of operating an illegal gambling business, court rejected claims that gambling did not offend community moral standards and that the immorality standard is unconstitutionally vague); Sullivan v. Meade Independent School District No. 101, 530 F.2d 799 (8th Cir. 1976) (upheld dismissal of §1983 action for damages challenging discharge of unmarried elementary school teacher for cohabitation).

(page 647) [846]

NOTES

3. [continued] See Gaylord v. Tacoma School District No. 10, 88 Wash. 2d 286, 559 P.2d 1340 (1977) (en banc), cert. denied, 434 U.S. 879 (1977) (public school teacher's status as known homosexual justified dismissal for immorality).
In Doe v. Commonwealth's Attorney, 425 U.S. 901 (1976), aff'g, 403 F. Supp. 1199 (E.D. Va. 1975) (three-judge court), the Supreme Court summarily affirmed the dismissal of a challenge to Virginia's criminal sodomy law by consenting adult homosexuals. The district court limited the right of privacy to marriage and family matters and, under a rational basis test, upheld as legitimate the state's interest in promoting "morality and decency."
See Free Speech Rights of Homosexual Teachers, 80 Colum. L. Rev. 1513 (1980); Gay Teachers: A Disteemed Minority in an Overly Esteemed Profession, 9 Rvt.-Cam. L. J. 399 (1978).

(page 647) [847]

NOTES

4. [continued] See Lewis v. Delaware State College, 455 F. Supp. 239 (D. Del. 1978) (granted preliminary injunction to director of women's

residence halls whose contract was not renewed because she had recently given birth to an illegitimate child); Board of Education of Long Beach v. Jack M., 19 Cal. 3d 691, 566 P.2d 602, 139 Cal. Rptr. 700 (1977) (evidence supported findings that teacher's arrest for lewd conduct in a public place did not render him unfit to teach and did not demonstrate unfitness to teach per se).

5. [continued] But cf. Kelly v. Johnson, 425 U.S. 238 (1976). In Kelly, the Court upheld a regulation which limited the length of police officers' hair. The applicability of this ruling to teachers and other public employees is unclear; the Court stressed the need for "discipline" and "uniformity" in the police force and left unanswered the question whether a citizen has a Fourteenth Amendment due process interest in her or his personal appearance.

See also Ball v. Board of Trustees of Kerrville, 584 F.2d 684 (5th Cir. 1978), cert. denied, 440 U.S. 972 (1979) (sustained lower court's dismissal of §1983 claim that untenured teacher's Fourteenth Amendment rights were violated when he was dismissed for failure to shave beard; plaintiff's "wholly insubstantial and frivolous" claim did not raise a substantial federal question); East Hartford Education Association v. Board of Education, 562 F.2d 838, rev'd on rehearing en banc, 562 F.2d 856 (2d Cir. 1977) (rejected teacher's claim that dress code requiring him to wear a tie in class violated the Fourteenth Amendment; the school board's interest in promoting respect for authority and traditional values as well as discipline outweighted plaintiff's "liberty" interest).

(page 648) [847]

NOTES

8. In Cook v. Hudson, 429 U.S. 165 (1976) (per curiam), the question arose whether a school board may dismiss a teacher who sent her or his children to a private racially segregated school. The Supreme Court dismissed the writ of certiorari in this case as improvidently granted, since such schools are now illegal. See also Runyon v. McCrary, 427 U.S. 160 (1976) (private, racially segregated nonsectarian schools violate 42 U.S.C. §1981).

9. In Dike v. School Board of Orange County, 650 F.2d 783 (5th Cir. 1981), the Court of Appeals held that a school teacher's desire to breastfeed a child was entitled to constitutional protection. In reversing the lower court's dismissal of teacher's complaint, the Fifth Circuit found that further inquiry was necessary to determine whether the school board's interest was strong enough to warrant interference with complainant's right to privacy.

10. In Selzer v. Fleisher, 629 F.2d 809 (2d Cir. 1980), cert. denied, 101 S. Ct. 2046 (1981), the Court of Appeals held that denial of tenure

and promotion to a professor because of his contacts with the CIA would violate his freedom of expression and association. The court remanded the case to the district court to determine whether complainant's contacts were the basis of the education board's actions. See Cooper v. Ross, 472 F. Supp. 802 (E.D. Ark. 1979) (decision not to reappoint untenured professor because of his affiliation with the Progressive Labor Party and his open acknowledgement of communist beliefs violated the first amendment).

F. PROCEDURAL FAIRNESS

(page 656) [856]

NOTES

2. [continued] In Paul v. Davis, 424 U.S. 693 (1976), excerpted in Chapter XVII, infra, the Court held that loss of reputation does not constitute a liberty or property interest protected under the Due Process Clause. And in Codd v. Velger, 429 U.S. 624 (1977) (per curiam), the Court held that a nontenured employee has no due process right to a hearing before dismissal unless the employee challenges the truth of the information on which the dismissal was based, since the purpose of the hearing can only be to clear the employee's name, not to defend a property interest.

Lower courts, however, have distinguished a mere unprotected interest in reputation from an impairment of future employment opportunities. In Huntley v. Community School Board of Brooklyn, 543 F.2d 979 (2d Cir. 1976), cert. denied, 430 U.S. 929 (1977), the Second Circuit held that the termination of an untenured school principal, during which charges of incompetence were publicly announced and recorded, impaired his property interest in future government employment and therefore required application of procedural safeguards.

See also McElearney v. University of Illinois at Chicago Circle Campus, 612 F.2d 285 (7th Cir. 1979) (no liberty or property interest). But see Victor v. Brinkley, 476 F. Supp. 888 (E.D. Mass. 1979) (suspension because of alleged sexual improprieties with students implicated professor's liberty).

(page 657) [857]

NOTES

4. [continued] For recent decisions recognizing a property interest and therefore requiring due process protection see Needleman v. Boh-

len, 602 F.2d 1 (1st Cir. 1979) (due process afforded by full notice of charges, opportunity to answer in writing, and full access to files); Cantrell v. Vickers, 495 F. Supp. 195 (N.D. Miss. 1980) (removal without hearing by impartial tribune violated due process).

(page 658) [858]

NOTES

5. [continued] See Skehan v. Board of Trustees of Bloomsburg State College, 590 F.2d 470 (3d Cir. 1978), cert. denied, 442 U.S. 832 (1979) (college's Statement of Policy for Continuous Employment and Academic Freedom was source of nontenured teacher's contractual right to due process hearing).

(page 659) [859]

NOTES

11. [continued] See generally Note, Dismissing Tenured Faculty: A Proposed Standard, 54 N.Y.U.L. Rev. 827 (1979); Note, Due Process Rights of Public Employees, 50 N.Y.U.L. Rev. 310 (1975).

12. Nontenured teachers and applicants may be afforded due process protection under an irrebuttable presumption doctrine. In Gurmankin v. Costanzo, 556 F.2d 184 (3d Cir. 1977), cert. denied, 101 S. Ct. 1375 (1981), Judge Gibbons held that the Philadelphia school policy that disallowed otherwise qualified blind applicants from taking a teacher's qualifying examination violated due process by creating an irrebuttable presumption that blindness equals incompetency.

(page 662) [862]

For a general discussion of tenure, see Matheson, Judicial Enforcement of Academic Tenure: An Examination, 50 Wash. L. Rev. 597 (1975).

(page 666) [866]

NOTES

1. [continued] The Fourteenth Amendment provides tenured teachers with the right to a due process hearing, but it does not give them a substantive due process right not to be discharged. In Harrah Independent School District v. Martin, 440 U.S. 194 (1979) (per curiam), the Supreme Court reversed the Tenth Circuit's finding that a tenured teacher's rights were violated by her dismissal for failure to comply with

the board's continuing education requirements. She received procedural due process. And, her dismissal was not so arbitrary as to offend "notions of fairness" generally held.

See generally Rosenberger & Plimpton, Teacher Incompetence and the Courts, 4 J.L. & Educ. 469 (1975).

(page 666) [867]

NOTES

2. [continued] See Howell v. Woodlin School District R-104, 198 Colo. 40, 596 P.2d 56 (1979) (en banc) (holding statute permitting termination without hearing when predicated on justifiable decrease in the number of positions unconstitutional as applied: no hearing to determine justifiable basis); Abramovich v. Board of Education, 46 N.Y.2d 450, 414 N.Y.S.2d 109, cert. denied, 444 U.S. 845 (1979) (public policy does not prohibit a tenured teacher's waiver of statutory due process rights when that waiver is freely, knowingly, and openly arrived at, without taint of coercion or duress).

(page 668) [869]

NOTES

3. [continued] See DiLorenzo v. Carey, 62 App. Div. 2d 583 (4th Dept.), app. dismissed, 45 N.Y.2d 382, 381 N.E.2d 610, 409 N.Y.S.2d 212 (1978), cert. denied, 440 U.S. 914 (1979) (tenured professor validly waived constitutional rights to hearing prior to dismissal by agreeing to be bound by collective bargaining agreement that provided for grievance procedure resolution of such disputes).

G. COLLECTIVE BARGAINING

(page 670) [871]

NOTES

1. [continued] Recent decisions finding education board action predicated on teacher's union activities unconstitutional include Columbus Education Association v. Columbus City School District, 623 F.2d 1155 (6th Cir. 1980); Hickman v. Valley Local School District Board of Education, 619 F.2d 606 (6th Cir. 1980).

But see University of New Hampshire Chapter of the American Association of University Professors v. Haselton, 397 F. Supp. 107 (D.N.H.

1975) (three-judge court). In Haselton, the court upheld against equal protection and First Amendment challenges a statute which denied collective bargaining rights to state university academic employees. The court ruled that the First Amendment right to organize collectively is not infringed because academic employees are still free to unionize, although the state has no constitutional obligation to respond.

(page 671) [872]

NOTES

6. In City of Madison Joint School District No. 8 v. Wisconsin Employment Relations Commission, 429 U.S. 167 (1976), the Court held that the First Amendment protected the right of a teacher to speak against an agency shop at a public school board meeting. The Court denied that the board's permitting the teacher to speak constituted an unfair labor practice or that an abridgement of speech was necessary in this case to avoid disruption in labor-management relations.

7. In Abood v. Detroit Board of Education, 431 U.S. 209 (1977), excerpted in Chapter XV, infra, the Court upheld statutorily mandated agency shop clauses for public school teachers against charges that they violated rights of speech or association. The Court noted that any differences between the public and private sectors for collective bargaining purposes did not translate into differences in First Amendment protections. Hence, agency shop clauses, previously held valid for private employees, could also apply to public employees. The Court held, however, that fees collected by unions from objecting, nonunion members for political and ideological purposes unrelated to collective bargaining violated the First and Fourteenth Amendments. Relying on Elrod v. Burns, 427 U.S. 347 (1976), excerped in Chapter XI, Section E, supra, the Court reasoned that beliefs must be shaped by individual conscience rather than coerced by the state as a condition of employment.

8. The National Labor Relations Board lacks the authority to assert jurisdiction over labor disputes in schools operated by religious groups. NLRB v. Catholic Bishop of Chicago, 440 U.S. 490 (1979).

H. THE RIGHTS OF STUDENTS

(page 678) [879]

BOARD OF CURATORS OF
THE UNIVERSITY OF MISSOURI v. HOROWITZ
435 U.S. 78 (1978)

Mr. JUSTICE REHNQUIST delivered the opinion of the Court. Respondent, a student at the University of Missouri-Kansas City Medical School, was dismissed by petitioner officials of the school during her final year of study for failure to meet academic standards. Respondent sued petitioners under 42 U.S.C. §1983 in the United States District Court for the Western District of Missouri alleging, among other constitutional violations, that petitioners had not accorded her procedural due process prior to her dismissal. . . .

Respondent was admitted with advanced standing to the Medical School in the fall of 1971. During the final years of a student's education at the school, the student is required to pursue in "rotational units" academic and clinical studies pertaining to various medical disciplines such as obstetrics-gynecology, pediatrics, and surgery. Each student's academic performance at the school is evaluated on a periodic basis by the Council on Evaluation, a body composed of both faculty and students, which can recommend various actions including probation and dismissal. The recommendations of the Council are reviewed by the Coordinating Committee, a body composed solely of faculty members, and must ultimately be approved by the Dean. Students are not typically allowed to appear before either the Council or the Coordinating Committee on the occasion of their review of the student's academic performance.

In the spring of respondent's first year of study, several faculty members expressed dissatisfaction with her clinical performance during a pediatrics rotation. The faculty members noted that respondent's "performance was below that of her peers in all clinical patient-oriented settings," that she was erratic in her attendance at clinical sessions, and that she lacked a critical concern for personal hygiene. Upon the recommendation of the Council on Evaluation, respondent was advanced to her second and final year on a probationary basis.

Faculty dissatisfaction with respondent's clinical performance continued during the following year. For example, respondent's docent, or faculty adviser, rated her clinical skills as "unsatisfactory." In the middle of the year, the Council again reviewed respondent's academic progress and concluded that respondent should not be considered for graduation in June of that year; furthermore, the Council recommended that absent "radical improvement," respondent be dropped from the school.

Respondent was permitted to take a set of oral and practical examinations as an "appeal" of the decision not to permit her to graduate. Pursuant to this "appeal," respondent spent a substantial portion of time with seven practicing physicians in the area who enjoyed a good reputation among their peers. The physicians were asked to recommend whether respondent should be allowed to graduate on schedule and, if not, whether she should be dropped immediately or allowed to remain on probation. Only two of the doctors recommended that respondent be graduated on schedule. Of the other five, two recommended that she be immediately dropped from the school. The remaining three recommended that she not be allowed to graduate in June and be continued on probation pending further reports on her clinical progress. Upon receipt of these recommendations, the Council on Evaluation reaffirmed its prior position.

The Council met again in mid-May to consider whether respondent should be allowed to remain in school beyond June of that year. Noting that the report on respondent's recent surgery rotation rated her performance as "low-satisfactory," the Council unanimously recommended that "barring receipt of any reports that Miss Horowitz has improved radically, [she] not be allowed to re-enroll in the . . . School of Medicine." The Council delayed making its recommendation official until receiving reports on other rotations; when a report on respondent's emergency rotation also turned out to be negative, the Council unanimously reaffirmed its recommendation that respondent be dropped from the school. The Coordinating Committee and the Dean approved the recommendation and notified respondent, who appealed the decision in writing to the University's Provost for Health Sciences. The Provost sustained the school's actions after reviewing the record compiled during the earlier proceedings.

To be entitled to the procedural protections of the Fourteenth Amendment, respondent must in a case such as this demonstrate that her dismissal from the school deprived her of either a "liberty" or a "property" interest. Respondent has never alleged that she was deprived of a property interest. Because property interests are creatures of state law, Perry v. Sindermann, 408 U.S. 593, 599-603 (1972), respondent would have been required to show at trial that her seat at Medical School was a "property" interest recognized by Missouri state law. Instead, respondent argued that her dismissal deprived her of "liberty" by substantially impairing her opportunities to continue her medical education or to return to employment in a medically related field. . . .

We need not decide, however, whether respondent's dismissal deprived her of a liberty interest in pursuing a medical career. Nor need we decide whether respondent's dismissal infringed any other interest constitutionally protected against deprivation without procedural due process. Assuming the existence of a liberty or property interest, respondent has been awarded at least as much due process as the Fourteenth Amendment requires. The school fully informed respondent of the faculty's dissatisfaction with her clinical progress and the danger that this posed to timely graduation and continued enrollment. The ultimate decision to dismiss respondent was careful and deliberate. These procedures were sufficient under the Due Process Clause of the Fourteenth Amendment. We agree with the District Court that respondent "was afforded full procedural due process by the [school]. In fact, the Court is of the opinion, and so finds, that the school went beyond [constitutionally required] procedural due process by affording [respondent] the opportunity to be examined by seven independent physicians in order to be absolutely certain that their grading of the [respondent] in her medical skills was correct." App 47.

In Goss v. Lopez, 419 U.S. 565 (1975), we held that due process requires, in connection with the suspension of a student from public school for disciplinary reasons, "that the student be given oral or written notice of the charges against him and, if he denies them, an explanation of the evidence the authorities have and an opportunity to present his side of the story." Id., at 581. The Court of Appeals apparently read Goss as requiring some type of formal hearing at which respondent could defend her academic ability and performance. All that Goss required was an "informal give-and-take" between the student and the administrative body dismissing him that would, at least, give the student "the opportunity to characterize his conduct and put it in what he deems the proper context." Id., at 584. But we have frequently emphasized that "[t]he very nature of due process negates any context of flexible procedures universally applicable to every imaginable situation." Cafeteria Workers v. McElroy, 367 U.S. 886, 895 (1961). The need for flexibility is well illustrated by the significant difference between the failure of a student to meet academic standards and the violation by a student of valid rules of conduct. This difference calls for far less stringent procedural requirements in the case of an academic dismissal.[3]

Since the issue first arose 50 years ago, state and lower federal courts have recognized that there are distinct differences between decisions to suspend or dismiss a student for disciplinary purposes and similar actions taken for academic reasons which may call for hearings in connection with the former but not the latter. . . .

Until the instant decision by the Court of Appeals for the Eighth Circuit, the Courts of Appeals were also unanimous in concluding that dismissals for academic (as opposed to disciplinary) cause do not necessitate a hearing before the school's decisionmaking body. . . .

These prior decisions of state and federal courts, over a period of 60 years, unanimously holding that formal hearings before decisionmaking bodies need not be held in the case of academic dismissals, cannot be rejected lightly.

Reason, furthermore, clearly supports the perception of these deci-

3. We fully recognize that the deprivation to which respondent was subjected — dismissal from a graduate medical school — was more severe than the 10-day suspension to which the high school students were subjected in Goss. And a relevant factor in determining the nature of the requisite due process is "the private interest that [was] affected by the official action." Mathews v. Eldridge, 424 U.S. 319, 335 (1976). But the severity of the deprivation is only one of several factors that must be weighed in deciding the exact due process owed. Ibid. We conclude that considering all relevant factors, including the evaluative nature of the inquiry and the significant and historically supported interest of the school in preserving its present framework for academic evaluations, a hearing is not required by the Due Process Clause of the Fourteenth Amendment.

sions. A school is an academic institution, not a courtroom or administrative hearing room. In Goss, this Court felt that suspensions of students for disciplinary reasons have a sufficient resemblance to traditional judicial and administrative factfinding to call for a "hearing" before the relevant school authority.... Even in the context of a school disciplinary proceeding, however, the Court stopped short of requiring a *formal* hearing since "further formalizing the suspension process and escalating its formality and adversary nature may not only make it too costly as a regular disciplinary tool but also destroy its effectiveness as a part of the teaching process." Id., at 583.

Academic evaluations of a student, in contrast to disciplinary determinations, bear little resemblance to the judicial and administrative factfinding proceedings to which we have traditionally attached a full-hearing requirement. In Goss, the school's decision to suspend the students rested on factual conclusions that the individual students had participated in demonstrations that had disrupted class, attacked a police officer, or caused physical damage to school property. The requirement of a hearing, where the student could present his side of the factual issue, could under such circumstances "provide a meaningful hedge against erroneous action." Ibid. The decision to dismiss respondent, by comparison, rested on the academic judgment of school officials that she did not have the necessary clinical ability to perform adequately as a medical doctor and was making insufficient progress toward that goal. Such a judgment is by its nature more subjective and evaluative than the typical factual questions presented in the average disciplinary decision. Like the decision of an individual professor as to the proper grade for a student in his course, the determination whether to dismiss a student for academic reasons requires an expert evaluation of cumulative information and is not readily adapted to the procedural tools of judicial or administrative decisionmaking....

We decline to further enlarge the judicial presence in the academic community and thereby risk deterioration of many beneficial aspects of the faculty-student relationship....

In reversing the District Court on procedural due process grounds, the Court of Appeals expressly failed to "reach the substantive due process ground advanced by Horowitz." 538 F.2d, at 1321 n.5. Respondent urges that we remand the cause to the Court of Appeals for consideration of this additional claim. In this regard, a number of lower courts have implied in dictum that academic dismissals from state institutions can be enjoined if "shown to be clearly arbitrary or capricious." Mahavongsanan v. Hall, 529 F.2d, at 449. See Gaspar v. Bruton, 513 F.2d, at 850, and citations therein. Even assuming that the courts can review under such a standard an academic decision of a public educational institution, we agree with the District Court that no showing of arbitrariness or capriciousness has been made in this case. Courts are particularly ill-equipped to evaluate academic performance. The factors discussed in Part II with respect to procedural due process speak a fortiori here and warn against any such judicial intrusion into academic decisionmaking.

[The separate opinions of Justices Powell, White, and Marshall are omitted.]

NOTE

1. Horowitz declined to expand the procedural due process rights of students to areas of academic rather than disciplinary concern. In Ingraham v. Wright, 430 U.S. 651 (1977), moreover, the Court refused to recognize a right to a hearing prior to the imposition of corporal punishment. Justice Powell, writing for a divided Court, held that the possibility of a post-beating hearing in state court in connection with a tort action constituted sufficient due process to satisfy the Fourteenth Amendment. Moreover, he ruled, the Eighth Amendment guarantee against "cruel and unusual punishment" did not apply to school children, but only to persons punitively incarcerated after trial. Thus, he held, actions alleging excessive corporal punishment of students do not give rise to a cause of action under §1983.

After Ingraham, no procedural formalities are required prior to administering corporal punishment in a school setting — as long as a state judicial procedure exists that permits post-punishment vindication of the student's state law rights. Thus, federal due process protection may continue to be required, even after Ingraham, wherever state process is not adequate. Whether a facially adequate state process can be attacked as inadequate in fact has not yet been decided. However, Justice Powell's majority opinion appears to assume the existence of a state remedy adequate in practice as well as in theory.

Ingraham rejects the notion that students are protected from excessive corporal punishment by the Eighth Amendment. However, if the Due Process clause is read to provide "substantive" protection of a student's "liberty" interest in freedom from excessive beatings, allegations of excessive corporal punishment should give rise to an identical §1983 cause of action sounding in substantive due process, instead of the Eighth Amendment. See Hall v. Tawney, 621 F.2d 607 (4th Cir. 1980) (recognizing substantive due process claim for excessive beating of student). Thus, as Justice White suggests in dissent, Ingraham may be nothing more than a lesson in pleading. The majority explicitly declined to decide whether a claim of excessive corporal punishment would give rise to a substantive due process cause of action.

2. Although after Ingraham students can be beaten, they retain the right to publish newspapers. In Nitzberg v. Parks, 525 F.2d 378 (4th

Cir. 1975), a regulation banning distribution of student newspapers that tracked the language of Tinker was declared unconstitutionally vague. See also, Schiff v. Williams, 519 F.2d 257 (5th Cir. 1975) (reinstating student editors removed for content); Gambino v. Fairfax Co. School Board, 429 F. Supp. 731 (E.D. Va.), aff'd, 564 F.2d 157 (4th Cir. 1977) (regulation of junior high school newspaper invalid); Leibner v. Sharbaugh, 429 F. Supp. 744 (E.D. Va. 1977) (same). In Mississippi Gay Alliance v. Goudelock, 536 F.2d 1073 (5th Cir. 1976), cert. denied, 430 U.S. 982 (1977), the Fifth Circuit ruled that the editors of a school newspaper could reject an advertisement by a homosexual group. In Thomas v. Granville Board of Education, 607 F.2d 1043 (2d Cir. 1979), disciplinary action taken in connection with the publication of an off-campus newspaper was reversed. The right to leaflet on campus was upheld in New Jersey v. Schmid, 423 A.2d 615 (1980), app. dism. for mootness, sub nom. Princeton Univ. v. Schmid, 50 U.S.L.W. 4159 (1982). (New Jersey Constitution guaranties access to private campus) and Spartacus Youth League v. Board of Trustees, 502 F. Supp. 789 (N.D. Ill. 1980) (striking down prohibition on leafletting not sponsored by registered student organization). In Trachtman v. Anker, 563 F.2d 512 (2d Cir. 1977), the court upheld a ban on a student questionnaire and article surveying student attitudes toward sex. Similarly, in Williams v. Spencer, 622 F.2d 1200 (4th Cir. 1980), a ban on a student newspaper that included an advertisement for drug paraphernalia was upheld.

In a related context, a state-owned educational television station was barred from censoring program content in Barnstone v. University of Houston, 514 F. Supp. 670 (S.D. Tex. 1980). The order was, however, stayed by the Fifth Circuit. Barnstone v. University of Houston, 446 U.S. 1318 (1980). See also, Trotman v. Board of Trustees of Lincoln University, 635 F.2d 216 (3d Cir. 1980) (protecting faculty right to criticize administration), and Uzzell v. Friday, 625 F.2d 1117 (4th Cir. 1981) (remanding benign quota in student government for hearing on necessity).

3. Student associational rights were upheld in Gay Alliance of Students v. Matthews, 544 F.2d 162 (4th Cir. 1976), when the refusal of a state university to recognize a homosexual group was declared unconstitutional. See also, Gay Lib v. University of Missouri, 558 F.2d 848 (8th Cir. 1977) (same). But see, Maryland Public Interest Research Group v. Elkins, 565 F.2d 864 (4th Cir. 1977) (sustaining a restriction forbidding a student organization to finance litigation.) In Fricke v. Lynch, 491 F. Supp. 381 (D.R.I. 1980), a ban on homosexual dating at a school dance was overturned. See also, Gay Students v. Bonner, 509 F.2d 652 (1st Cir. 1974). In Familias Unidas v. Briscoe, 619 F.2d (5th Cir. 1980), the court invalidated a law mandating the disclosure of the membership lists of parents' organizations critical of the school board.

4. Attempts by pressure groups to dictate the content of the curric-

ulum and the choice of teaching materials have increased dramatically in recent years. In Island Trees School Board v. Pico, 50 U.S.L.W. 4831 (1982), the Court ruled that books may not be removed from school libraries if the purpose of the removal is to reinforce political orthodoxy. The case was remanded for a trial on the issue of purpose. In Mclean v. Arkansas Board of Education, 529 F.Supp 1255 (D. Ark. 1981), a statute requiring "balanced treatment" of creationism and evolution was struck down on Establishment Clause grounds. In Minarcini v. Strongville City School District, 541 F.2d 577 (6th Cir. 1976), the forced removal of controversial books from a school library was deemed an unconstitutional abridgement of student's rights. See also, Salvail v. Nashua Board of Education, 469 F. Supp. 1269 (D.N.H. 1979) (Ms. Magazine ordered returned to school library); Right to Read Defense Committee v. School Committee, 454 F. Supp. 703 (D. Mass. 1978) (ordering books reinstated); Loewen v. Turnipseed, 488 F. Supp. 1138 (N.D. Miss. 1980) (overturning textbook ban without justification). Courts have upheld board action in Palmer v. Chicago Board of Education, 603 F.2d 1271 (7th Cir. 1979) (Jehovah's Witness fired for refusing to teach patriotism in kindergarten); Zykan v. Warsaw Community College, 631 F.2d 1300 (7th Cir. 1980) (removal of teachers and books for socio-political reasons upheld); Bicknell v. Vergennes Union High School, 475 F. Supp. 615 (D. Vt. 1980), aff'd, 638 F.2d 438 (2d Cir. 1981) (removal of books upheld); Seyfried v. Walton, 512 F. Supp. 235 (D. Del. 1981) (decision not to produce Pippin as school production because too "sexy" upheld). In Citizens for Parental Rights v. San Mateo County Board of Education, 134 Cal. Rptr. 68 (1975), app. dismissed, 425 U.S. 908 (1976), the court ruled that sex education classes did not violate the rights of students.

In Arundar v. De Kalb County, 620 F.2d 493 (5th Cir. 1980), a challenge to a curricular decision was dismissed with the observation that students lack a property interest in a particular course of study.

5. Challenges by fundamentalist schools to general state control over curriculum and licensing occurred in Kentucky State Board v. Rudasill, 589 S.W.2d 877 (Ky. 1979) (overturning Kentucky's regulations as too strict) and Nebraska ex rel. Douglas v. Faith Baptist Church, 301 N.W. 2d 571 (Neb. Sup. Ct. 1981) (upholding Nebraska's regulations). See also New Jersey–Philadelphia Presbytery v. New Jersey State Board of Higher Education, 49 U.S.L.W. 2674 (3d Cir. 1981). In Debra P. v. Turlington, 474 F. Supp. 244 (M.D. Fla. 1981), a certification examination covering material not taught in the curriculum was enjoined.

6. In Carey v. Piphus, 435 U.S. 247 (1978), the Court ruled that students suspended in violation of their procedural due process rights were not entitled to substantial damages unless they could prove actual damages as a consequence of the failure to hold a hearing.

7. Regulations prohibiting dormitory visits by persons of the opposite sex were upheld in Futrell v. Ahrens, 540 P.2d 214 (N.M. Sup. Ct. 1975).

See also, Texas Women's University v. Chayklintaste, 530 S.W.2d 927 (Tex. Sup. Ct. 1975) (upholding rule requiring all students under 23 to live on campus). In Bob Jones University v. United States, 639 F.2d 147 (4th Cir. 1980), the court affirmed the denial of tax deductible status to a university that prohibits interracial dating. The Supreme Court will review the Bob Jones case during the 1982-1983 term. However, the abandonment by the government of its traditional opposition to tax exemptions for segregated academies raises potential mootness issues. See also, Brown v. Dade Christian School, 556 F.2d 310 (4th Cir. 1977); Fiedler v. Marumsco, 486 F. Supp. 960 (E.D. Va. 1979) (recognizing §1981 cause of action for expulsion for interracial dating). See also, Thompson v. Board of Trustees, 627 P.2d 1229 (Mont. 1981) (invalidating rules against spouses working in same school system).

In Brush v. Penn. State University, 414 A.2d 48 (1980), rules barring all canvassing in student dormitories in the absence of a vote in its favor or an invitation by a resident were upheld. In American Future Systems v. Penn. State University, 618 F.2d 252 (3d Cir. 1979), a ban on commercial solicitation on campus was upheld in connection with the sale of merchandise. However, the demonstration of merchandise unaccompanied by on-campus sales was permitted.

8. In Stone v. Graham, 101 S. Ct. 192 (1980), the display of the Ten Commandments in public school classrooms was deemed unconstitutional on Establishment Clause grounds. In Widmar v. Vincent, 50 U.S.L.W. 4062 (1981), the Court ruled that facilities at a state university must be made equally available to groups seeking to use them for religious as well as for secular purposes. An attempt by a student group to hold a voluntary prayer meeting before school was upheld in Karen B. Treen, 49 U.S.L.W. 2471 (E.D. La. 1980). Prior to Widmar similar requests were denied in Brandon v. Guilderland Central School District, 635 F.2d 971 (2d Cir. 1980), and Kent v. Commissioner of Education, — F. Supp. — (D. Mass. 1979). In Florey v. Sioux Falls High School, 619 F.2d 1311 (8th Cir. 1980), studying the significance of religious holidays as part of the curriculum was upheld. See also Student Members of Playcrafters v. Township of Teaneck, 424 A.2d 1192 (N.J. Super. Ct. 1981) (upholding ban on extra-curricular activities on Friday night and Saturday and Sunday mornings). In Church of God v. Amarillo Ind. School District, 511 F. Supp. 613 (N.D. Tex. 1981), a policy of recognizing not more than two religious holidays each year was deemed a violation of the Free Exercise clause. However, in Brown v. Stone, 48 U.S.L.W. 2459 (Miss. 1981), a religiously based exemption from a compulsory vaccination law was deemed to violate the Establishment Clause.

9. In Vorchheimer v. School District of Philadelphia, 430 U.S. 703 (1977), an equally divided Supreme Court affirmed a Third Circuit decision upholding the separate but equal doctrine in the context of sexually segregated schools. However, in Mississippi University for

Women v. Hogarth, 50 U.S.L.W. 5068 (1982), a ban on male students at a state nursing school was invalidated. In Cannon v. University of Chicago, 441 U.S. 677 (1979), the Court recognized a private cause of action for the violation of Title IX. In North Haven Board of Education v. Bell, 50 U.S.L.W. 4501 (1982), the Court ruled that Title IX bars discrimination in employment by educational entities receiving federal funds.

10. In Morale v. Grigel, 422 F. Supp. 988, 997 (D.N.H. 1976), nonconsensual searches of student dormitories were deemed a violation of the Fourth Amendment. In Doe v. Renfrow, 631 F.2d 91 (8th Cir. 1980), the nude search of a 13-year-old girl merely because a dog trained to detect drugs reacted to her was the basis of a §1983 damage award.

11. Jurisdictions have systematically declined to recognize a cause of action for educational malpractice. E.g., Hunter v. Montgomery County Board of Education, 425 A.2d 681 (Md. 1981).

12. In Plyler v. Doe, 50 U.S.L.W. 4650 (1982), the Court invalidated a Texas statute which barred the children of illegal aliens from attending public school. In Troll v. Moreno, 50 U.S.L.W. 4889 (1982), a Maryland regulation which denied resident tuition status to the children of aliens possessing G-4 visas (issued in connection with employment by an international organization) was invalidated.

Chapter Eleven
The Right to Travel

A. DOMESTIC TRAVEL

[895]

[REFERENCES]

Comments, Baker, A Strict Scrutiny of the Right to Travel, 22 U.C.L.A.L. Rev. 1129 (1975); The Right to Travel: Judicial Curiosity or Practical Tool?, 52 J. Urban L. 749 (1975).

(page 698) [899]

Insert before Note 1:

NOTE

A right to travel claim was made and rejected in an unusual context in Jones v. Helms, 452 U.S. 412, 69 L. Ed. 2d 118 (1981). The case involved a Georgia statute that makes it a misdemeanor for a parent to willfully abandon a child but elevates the crime to a felony if the parent commits the offense and thereafter leaves the State of Georgia. The defendant left Georgia after his misdemeanor guilty plea, and, as a consequence, he was subjected to enhanced punishment. The claim that the statute impairs the fundamental right of a Georgia resident to leave the state was rejected. The Court distinguished its prior cases upholding the right to travel, such as Shapiro v. Thompson, 394 U.S. 618 (1970), on the ground "the statute at issue imposed a burden on the exercise of the right to travel by citizens whose right to travel had not been qualified in any way. In contrast, in this case, appellee's criminal conduct within the State of Georgia necessarily qualified his right thereafter freely to travel interstate." 69 L. Ed 2d at 126. Finally, the Court found that Georgia had a legitimate reason to deter faithless parents from leaving the state in order more readily to enforce their parental obligations.

(page 710) [911]

NOTES

1.f. [continued] In In Re Gordon, 48 N.Y.2d 266 (1979), the court invalidated, on Privileges and Immunities grounds, a requirement that bar applicants reside in New York six months prior to application for admission.

(page 714) [915]

NOTES

2.a. [continued] In McCarthy v. Philadelphia Civil Service Commission, 424 U.S. 645 (1976) (per curiam), the Court, 6-3, summarily upheld a continuing residency requirement imposed on municipal employees that requires them to be and remain residents of the city. For cases following McCarthy, see: Mogle v. Sevier County School District, 540 F.2d 478 (10th Cir. 1976); Andre v. Board of Trustees of Village of Maywood, 561 F.2d 48 (7th Cir. 1977); Fisher v. Reiser, 610 F.2d 629 (9th Cir. 1979).

(page 715) [916]

NOTES

2.b. [continued] In Wilson v. Wilson, 430 U.S. 925 (1977), the Supreme Court summarily affirmed a district court decision upholding Oregon's requirement that applicants for admission to the Oregon bar state their intention to be residents of the state at the time they are admitted. The district court had found no infringement of the right to travel because an applicant remained free to travel to or reside in any state prior to becoming a member of the Oregon bar. 416 F. Supp. 984 (D. Ore. 1976).

[917]

[REFERENCES]

Boone, Durational Residency Requirements: The Alaskan Experience, 6 U.C.L.A.-Alaska L. Rev. 50 (1976).

[921]

[REFERENCES]

Carmichael, Land Use Controls and the Right to Travel, 6 Cum. L. Rev. 541 (1976).

B. INTERNATIONAL TRAVEL

(page 723) [925]

NOTES

10. In Califano v. Aznavorian, 439 U.S. 170 (1978), the Court upheld, as against a right to travel challenge, a provision of the Social Security Act that withholds Supplemental Security Income benefits for the needy, aged, blind, and disabled for any month that the recipient spends entirely outside the U.S. and for 30 days thereafter. Justice Stewart's opinion for the Court observed that legislation allegedly infringing on the right to travel abroad "is not to be judged by the same standard applied to laws that penalize the [virtually unqualified] right of interstate travel." Moreover, the statute at issue here "does not have nearly so direct an impact on the freedom to travel internationally as occurred in the Kent, Aptheker, or Zemel cases [all in the main volume] . . . [but] merely withdraws a governmental benefit during and shortly after an extended absence from the country." Unless such a limitation is wholly irrational "it is constitutional despite its incidental effect on international travel." The statutory justification of preserving benefits for residents, though perhaps not "compelling," was sufficient under this test. Justices Marshall and Brennan concurred in the result.

(page 723) [926]

Insert after Notes [References]:

The broad question at issue in Kent v. Dulles, 357 U.S. 116 (1958), and Zemel v. Rusk, 381 U.S. 1 (1965) — the power of the President to restrict the right to travel on grounds not explicitly sanctioned by Congress — was again before the Court in Haig v. Agee, 453 U.S. 280, 69 L. Ed. 2d 640 (1981). The case involved the revocation of the passport of ex-CIA official Philip Agee on the ground that his activities abroad, particularly his actions in identifying CIA personnel operating in various foreign countries, were causing or were likely to cause "serious damage to the national security or foreign policy of the United States." Lower courts had agreed with Agee's contention that the regulation which allowed passport revocation on that ground had not been authorized by Congress, either expressly or impliedly. The Supreme Court, 7-2, reversed.

Most of Chief Justice Burger's opinion addressed the question of statutory authority in the absence of explicit statutory direction. The Court found that "[t]he history of passport controls since the earliest days of the Republic shows congressional recognition of Executive authority to withhold passports on the basis of substantial reasons of national security and foreign policy." 69 L. Ed. 2d at 653. Nor did it matter that the Executive had exercised such a power on rare and infrequent occasions; implicit congressional approval could be shown by legislative acquiescence to repeated Executive claims that it possessed such power: "The exercise of a power emerges only in relation to a factual situation, and the continued validity of the power is not diluted simply because there is no need to use it." Id. at 659. Thus, the regulations were found consonant with the wishes of Congress.

The Court also rejected Agee's constitutional claims. His right to travel argument was dismissed on the ground that the freedom to travel abroad by use of a passport "is subordinate to national security and foreign policy considerations; as such, it is subject to reasonable governmental regulation." Id. at 661. Finding that Agee's activities abroad threatened such interests, the Court concluded that the revocation of his passport was justifiable. Finally, the First Amendment argument, that the passport was revoked because Agee had engaged in protected speech, was rejected: "Agee's disclosures, among other things, have the declared purpose of obstructive intelligence operations and the recruiting of intelligence personnel. They are clearly not protected by the Constitution. The mere fact that Agee is also engaged in criticism of the Government does not render his conduct beyond the reach of the law.

"To the extent the revocation of his passport operates to inhibit Agee, 'it is an inhibition of *action*,' rather than of speech. Zemel, 381 U.S., at 16-17 (emphasis supplied). Agee is as free to criticize the United States Government as he was when he held a passport — always subject, of course, to express limits on certain rights by virtue of his contract with the Government. See Snepp v. United States, . . ." 69 L. Ed. 2d at 663.

Justice Brennan, joined by Justice Marshall, dissented. In his view, the Court's approach to congressional approval was a departure from established analysis: ". . . clearly neither Zemel nor Kent holds that a long-standing Executive *policy* or *construction* is sufficient proof that Congress has implicitly authorized the Secretary's action. The cases hold that an administrative *practice* must be demonstrated; in fact, Kent unequivocally states that mere *contruction* by the Executive — no matter how longstanding and consistent — is *not* sufficient." Id. at 666-667. Justice Brennan's dissent concluded as follows: "I suspect that this case is a prime example of the adage that 'bad facts make bad law.' Philip

Agee is hardly a model representative of our Nation. And the Executive Branch has attempted to use one of the only means at its disposal, revocation of a passport, to stop respondent's damaging statements. But just as the Constitution protects both popular and unpopular speech, it likewise protects both popular and unpopular travelers. And it is important to remember that this decision applies not only to Philip Agee, whose activities could be perceived as harming the national security, but also to other citizens who may merely disagree with Government foreign policy and express their views.

"The Constitution allocates the lawmaking function to Congress, and I fear that today's decision has handed over too much of that function to the Executive. In permitting the Secretary to stop this unpopular traveler and critic of the CIA, the Court professes to rely on, but in fact departs from, the two precedents in the passport regulation area, Zemel and Kent. Of course it is always easier to fit oneself within the safe haven of stare decisis than boldly to overrule precedents of several decades' standing. Because I find myself unable to reconcile those cases with the decision in this case, however, and because I disagree with the Court's sub silentio overruling of those cases, I dissent." Id. at 669-670.

Chapter Twelve

Privacy

A. PROTECTED PRIVATE ACTIVITIES: THE PRIVACIES OF LIFE

(page 754) [957]

Insert at end of Note 1:

CAREY v. POPULATION SERVICES INTERNATIONAL
431 U.S. 678

Mr. JUSTICE BRENNAN delivered the opinion of the Court (Parts I, II, III, and V) together with an opinion (Part IV), in which Mr. JUSTICE STEWART, Mr. JUSTICE MARSHALL, and Mr. JUSTICE BLACKMUN joined.

Under New York Education Law §6811(8) it is a crime (1) for any person to sell or distribute any contraceptive of any kind to a minor under the age of 16 years; (2) for anyone other than a licensed pharmacist to distribute contraceptives to persons over 16; and (3) for anyone, including licensed pharmacists, to advertise or display contraceptives. A three judge District Court for the Southern District of New York declared §6811(8) unconstitutional in its entirety under the First and Fourteenth Amendments of the Federal Constitution insofar as it applies to nonprescription contraceptives, and enjoined its enforcement as so applied. 398 F. Supp. 321 (1975). . . . We affirm. . . .

II

Although "[t]he Constitution does not explicitly mention any right of privacy," the Court has recognized that one aspect of the "liberty" protected by the Due Process Clause of the Fourteenth Amendment is "a right of personal privacy, or a guarantee of certain areas or zones of privacy." Roe v. Wade. This right of personal privacy includes "the interest in independence in making certain kinds of decisions." Whalen v. Roe, [infra]. . . .

The decision whether or not to beget or bear a child is at the very heart of this cluster of constitutionally protected choices. . . . [I]n a field that by definition concerns the most intimate of human activities and relationships, decisions whether to accomplish or to prevent conception are among the most private and sensitive. . . .

That the constitutionally protected right of privacy extends to an individual's liberty to make choices regarding contraception does not, however, automatically invalidate every state regulation in this area. The business of manufacturing and selling contraceptives may be regulated in ways that do not infringe protected individual choices. And even a burdensome regulation may be validated by a sufficiently compelling state interest. . . . "Compelling" is of course the key word; where a decision as fundamental as that whether to bear or beget a child is involved, regulations imposing a burden on it may be justified only by compelling state interests, and must be narrowly drawn to express only those interests. . . .

III

We consider first the . . . restriction on access to contraceptives created by §6811(8)'s prohibition of the distribution of nonmedical contraceptives to adults except through licensed pharmacists.

Appellants argue that this Court has not accorded a "right of access to contraceptives" the status of a fundamental aspect of personal liberty. They emphasize that Griswold v. Connecticut struck down a state prohibition of the *use* of contraceptives, and so had no occasion to discuss laws "regulating their manufacture or sale." Eisenstadt v. Baird was decided under the Equal Protection Clause, holding that "whatever the rights of the individual to access to contraceptives may be, the rights must be the same for the unmarried and the married alike." Thus appellants argue that neither case should be treated as reflecting upon the State's power to limit or prohibit distribution of contraceptives to any persons, married or unmarried. . . .

The fatal fallacy in this argument is that it overlooks the underlying premise of those decisions that the Constitution protects "the right of the individual . . . to be free from unwarranted governmental intrusion into . . . the decision whether to bear or beget a child." Eisenstadt v. Baird. Read in light of its progeny, the teaching of Griswold is that the Constitution protects individual decisions in matters of childbearing from unjustified intrusion by the State.

Restrictions on the distribution of contraceptives clearly burden the freedom to make such decisions. . . .

An instructive analogy is found in decisions after Roe v. Wade, supra, that held unconstitutional statutes that did not prohibit abortions outright but limited in a variety of ways a woman's access to them.... The significance of these cases is that they establish that the same test must be applied to state regulations that burden an individual's right to decide to prevent conception or terminate pregnancy by substantially limiting access to the means of effectuating that decision as is applied to state statutes that prohibit the decision entirely....

There remains the inquiry whether the provision serves a compelling state interest.... Appellants argue that the limitation of retail sales of nonmedical contraceptives to pharmacists (1) expresses "a proper concern that young people not sell contraceptive products"; (2) "allows purchasers to inquire as to the relative qualities of the varying products and prevents anyone from tampering with them"; and (3) facilitates enforcement of the other provisions of the statute. The first hardly can justify the statute's incursion into constitutionally protected rights, and in any event the statute is obviously not substantially related to any goal of preventing young people from selling contraceptives. Nor is the statute designed to serve as a quality control device. Nothing in the record suggests that pharmacists are particularly qualified to give advice on the merits of different nonmedical contraceptives, or that such advice is more necessary to the purchaser of contraceptive products than to consumers of other nonprescription items. Why pharmacists are better able or more inclined than other retailers to prevent tampering with prepackaged products, or, if they are, why contraceptives are singled out for this special protection, is also unexplained.[11] As to ease of enforcement, the prospect of additional administrative inconvenience has not been thought to justify invasion of fundamental constitutional rights....

IV[12]

The District Court also held unconstitutional, as applied to nonprescription contraceptives, the provision of §6811(8) prohibiting the distribution of contraceptives to those under 16 years of age. Appellants contend that this provision of the statute is constitutionally permissible as a regulation of the morality of minors, in furtherance of the State's policy against promiscuous sexual intercourse among the young.

The question of the extent of state power to regulate conduct of minors not constitutionally regulable when committed by adults is a vexing one, perhaps not susceptible to precise answer....

Of particular significance to the decision of this case, the right to

---

11. We express no opinion on, for example, restrictions on the distribution of contraceptives through vending machines, which are not before us in this case.
12. This part of the opinion expresses the views of Justices Brennan, Stewart, Marshall, and Blackmun.

privacy in connection with decisions affecting procreation extends to minors as well as to adults. Planned Parenthood of Central Missouri v. Danforth [infra]. . . . State restrictions inhibiting privacy rights of minors are valid only if they serve "any significant state interest . . . that is not present in the case of an adult."[15]

Since the State may not impose a blanket prohibition, or even a blanket requirement of parental consent, on the choice of a minor to terminate her pregnancy, the constitutionality of a blanket prohibition of the distribution of contraceptives to minors is a fortiori foreclosed. . . .

Appellants argue, however, that significant state interests are served by restricting minors' access to contraceptives, because free availability to minors of contraceptives would lead to increased sexual activity among the young in violation of the policy of New York to discourage such behavior.[17] The argument is that minors' sexual activity may be deterred by increasing the hazards attendant on it. The same argument, however, would support a ban on abortions for minors, or indeed support a prohibition on abortions, or access to contraceptives, for the unmarried, whose sexual activity is also against the public policy of many States. Yet, in each of these areas, the Court has rejected the argument, noting in Roe v. Wade, that "no court or commentator has taken the argument seriously." The reason for this unanimous rejection was stated in Eisenstadt v. Baird: "It would be plainly unreasonable to assume that [the state] has prescribed pregnancy and the birth of an unwanted child [or the physical and psychological dangers of an abortion] as punishment for fornication." We remain reluctant to attribute any such "scheme of values" to the State.

Moreover, there is substantial reason for doubt whether limiting access to contraceptives will in fact substantially discourage early sexual behavior. . . .

[W]hen a State, as here, burdens the exercise of a fundamental right, its attempt to justify that burden as a rational means for the accomplish-

15. The test is apparently less rigorous than the "compelling state interest" test applied to restrictions on the privacy rights of adults. Such lesser scrutiny is appropriate both because of the State's greater latitude to regulate the conduct of children. . . . and because the right of privacy implicated here is "the interest in independence in making certain kinds of decisions," . . . and the law has generally regarded minors as having a lesser capability for making important decisions. . . .

17. Appellees argue that the State's policy to discourage sexual activity of minors is itself unconstitutional, for the reason that the right to privacy comprehends a right of minors as well as adults to engage in private consensual sexual behavior. We observe that the Court has not definitively answered the difficult question whether and to what extent the Constitution prohibits state statutes regulating such behavior among adults. . . . But whatever the answer to that question, Ginsberg v. New York, 390 U.S. 629 (1968), indicates that in the area of sexual mores, as in other areas, the scope of permissible state regulation is broader as to minors than as to adults. In any event, it is unnecessary to pass upon this contention of appellees, and our decision proceeds on the assumption that the Constitution does not bar state regulation of the sexual behavior of minors.

ment of some significant State policy requires more than a bare assertion, based on a conceded complete absence of supporting evidence, that the burden is connected to such a policy. . . .

V

The District Court's holding that the prohibition of any "advertisement or display" of contraceptives is unconstitutional was clearly correct. . . . [T]he statute challenged here seeks to suppress completely any information about the availability and price of contraceptives. . . .

Appellants contend that advertisements of contraceptive products would be offensive and embarrassing to those exposed to them, and that permitting them would legitimize sexual activity of young people. But these are classically not justifications validating the suppression of expression protected by the First Amendment. . . . As for the possible "legitimation" of illicit sexual behavior, whatever might be the case if the advertisements directly incited illicit sexual activity among the young, none of the advertisements in this record can even remotely be characterized as "directed to inciting or producing imminent lawless action and . . . likely to incite or produce such action." Brandenburg v. Ohio, 395 U.S. 44, 47 (1969). . . .

The Chief Justice dissents.

Mr. JUSTICE WHITE, concurring in part and concurring in the result in part.

I join Parts I, III and V of the Court's opinion and concur in the result with respect to Part IV.

Although I saw no reason in Eisenstadt v. Baird, to reach "the novel constitutional question whether a State may restrict or forbid the distribution of contraceptives to the unmarried," four of the seven Justices participating in that case held that in this respect the rights of unmarried persons were equal to those of the married. Given Eisenstadt and given the decision of the Court in the abortion case, Roe v. Wade, the result reached by the Court in Part III of its opinion appears warranted. I do not regard the opinion, however, as declaring unconstitutional any state law forbidding extramarital sexual relations. On this assumption I join Part III.

I concur in the result in Part IV primarily because the State has not demonstrated that the prohibition against distribution of contraceptives to minors measurably contributes to the deterrent purposes which the State advances as justification for the restriction. Again, however, the legality of state laws forbidding premarital intercourse is not at issue here: and, with Justice Stevens, "I would describe as 'frivolous' appellee's argument that a minor has the constitutional right to put contraceptives to their intended use, notwithstanding the combined objection of both parents and the State."

In joining Part V of the Court's opinion, I should also say that I agree with the views of Mr. Justice Stevens expressed in . . . his concurring opinion.

Mr. JUSTICE POWELL, concurring in part and concurring in the judgment....

... In my view, the extraordinary protection the Court would give to all personal decisions in matter of sex is neither required by the Constitution nor supported by our prior decisions....

... Neither our precedents nor sound principles of constitutional analysis require state legislation to meet the exacting compelling state interest standard whenever it implicates sexual freedom. In my view, those cases make clear that that standard has been invoked only when the state regulation entirely frustrates or heavily burdens the exercise of constitutional rights in this area....

There is also no justification for subjecting restrictions on the sexual activity of the young to heightened judicial review. Under our prior cases, the States have broad latitude to legislate with respect to adolescents.... [T]he relevant question in any case where state laws impinge on the freedom of action of young people in sexual matters is whether the restriction rationally serves valid state interests.... [T]he New York provision is defective in two respects. First, it infringes the privacy interests of married females between the ages of 14 and 16 . . . in that it prohibits the distribution of contraceptives to such females except by a physician. In authorizing marriage at that age, the State also sanctions sexual intercourse between partners and expressly recognizes that once the marriage relationship exists the husband and wife are presumed to possess the requisite understanding and maturity to make decisions concerning sex and procreation. Consequently, the State interest that justifies a requirement of prior counseling with respect to minors in general simply is inapplicable with respect to minors for whom the State has affirmatively approved marriage.

Second, this provision prohibits parents from distributing contraceptives to their children, a restriction that unjustifiably interferes with parental interests in rearing their children....

But in my view there is considerably more room for state regulation in this area than would be permissible under the Court's opinion. It seems clear to me, for example, that the State would further a constitutionally permissible end if it encouraged adolescents to seek the advice and guidance of their parents before deciding whether to engage in sexual intercourse....

New York also makes it a crime for anyone other than a licensed pharmacist to sell or distribute contraceptives to adults and to minors over the age 15.... Restricting the kinds of retail outlets that may distribute contraceptives may well be justified, but the present statute works a significant invasion of the constitutionally protected privacy decisions concerning sexual relations. By requiring individuals to buy contraceptives over the counter, the statute heavily burdens constitutionally protected freedom.

I also agree with the Court that New York cannot lawfully prohibit all "advertisement or display" of contraceptives. But it seems to me that the Court's opinion may be read too broadly. . . . I see no reason to cast any doubt on the authority of the State to impose carefully tailored restrictions designed to serve legitimate governmental concerns as to the effect of commercial advertising on the young.

Mr. JUSTICE STEVENS, concurring in part and concurring in the judgment. . . .

There are two reasons why I do not join Part IV [of Justice Brennan's opinion]. First, the holding in Planned Parenthood of Missouri v. Danforth, that a minor's decision to abort her pregnancy may not be conditioned on parental consent, is not dispositive here. The options available to the already pregnant minor are fundamentally different from those available to nonpregnant minors. The former must bear a child unless she aborts; but persons in the latter category can and generally will avoid childbearing by abstention. Consequently, even if I had joined that part of Planned Parenthood, I could not agree that the Constitution provides the same measure of protection to the minor's right to use contraceptives as to the pregnant female's right to abort.

Second, I would not leave open the question whether there is a significant state interest in discouraging sexual activity among unmarried persons under 16 years of age. Indeed, I would describe as "frivolous" appellee's argument that a minor has the constitutional right to put contraceptives to their intended use, notwithstanding the combined objection of both parents and the State". . . .

Common sense indicates that many young people will engage in sexual activity regardless of what the New York Legislature does; and further, that the incidence of venereal disease and premarital pregnancy is affected by the availability or unavailability of contraceptives. Although young persons, theoretically may avoid those harms by practicing total abstention, inevitably many will not. The statutory prohibition denies them and their parents a choice which, if available, would reduce their exposure to disease or unwanted pregnancy.

The State's asserted justification is a desire to inhibit sexual conduct by minors under 16. It does not seriously contend that if contraceptives are available, significant numbers of minors who now abstain from sex will cease abstaining because they will not longer fear pregnancy or disease. Rather its central argument is that the statute has the important *symbolic* effect of communicating disapproval of sexual activity by minors. In essence, therefore, the statute is defended as a form of propaganda, rather than a regulation of behavior.

Although the State may properly perform a teaching function, it seems to me that an attempt to persuade by inflicting harm on the listener is an unacceptable means of conveying a message that is otherwise legitimate. The propaganda technique used in this case significantly increases the risk of unwanted pregnancy and venereal disease. It is as though a State decided to dramatize its disapproval of motorcycles by forbidding the use of safety helmets. One need not posit a constitutional right to ride a motorcycle to characterize such a restriction as irrational and perverse.

Even as a regulation of behavior, such a statute would be defective. Assuming that the State could impose a uniform sanction upon young persons who risk self-inflicted harm by operating motorcycles, or by engaging in sexual activity, surely that sanction could not take the form of deliberately injuring the cyclist or infecting the promiscuous child. If such punishment may not be administered deliberately, after trial and a finding of guilt, it manifestly cannot be imposed by a legislature, indiscriminately and at random. This kind of government-mandated harm is, in my judgment, appropriately characterized as a deprivation of liberty without due process of law....

Mr. JUSTICE REHNQUIST, dissenting....

...The Court holds that New York may not use its police power to legislate in the interests of its concept of the public morality as it pertains to minors. The Court's denial of a power so fundamental to self-government must, in the long run, prove to be but a temporary departure from a wise and heretofore settled course of adjudication to the contrary....

(page 781) [984]

NOTES

6. *Supreme Court abortion decisions after Roe and Doe.*

a. In Connecticut v. Menillo, 423 U.S. 9 (1975), the Court held, per curiam, that states may constitutionally prohibit abortions by nonphysicians. However, in Sendak v. Arnold, 429 U.S. 968 (1976), the Court summarily affirmed a decision, 416 F. Supp. 22 (S.D. Ind. 1976), holding unconstitutional a statute requiring first trimester abortions to be performed in a hospital or a "licensed health facility." Justices White, Burger, and Rehnquist dissented, relying on Menillo.

See also Franklin v. Fitzpatrick, 428 U.S. 901 (1976), summarily affirming a district court decision (401 F. Supp. 554 (E.D. Pa. 1975)), upholding the constitutionality of requirements that women give informed prior written consent for abortions, that aborted fetuses be disposed of in a "humane" fashion, that abortions be performed only after a determination of pregnancy, and that abortions be performed only by physicians in facilities approved by the Department of Health; and holding unconstitutional parental and spousal consent requirements.

b. In Planned Parenthood of Central Missouri v. Danforth, 428 U.S. 52 (1976), the Court, in an opinion by Justice Blackmun, resolved a number of right-to-abortion issues raised by a comprehensive Missouri abortion statute enacted after the Roe and Doe decisions.

(i) *Defining viability.* The Court upheld a definition of "viability" as "that stage of fetal development when the life of the unborn child may be continued indefinitely outside the womb by natural or artificial life-supportive systems." This definition properly reflected the fact that "[t]he time when viability is achieved may vary with each pregnancy, and the determination of whether a particular fetus is viable is, and must be, a matter for the judgment of the responsible attending physician." A "specified number of weeks in pregnancy" need not be fixed by statute as the point of viability. Compare Colautti v. Franklin, 439 U.S. 379 (1979), holding unconstitutionally vague a Pennsylvania definition of viability in a statute imposing liability for a physician's failure to attempt to preserve the life of an aborted fetus. In this connection see Commonwealth v. Edelin, 359 N.E.2d 4 (Mass. 1976) (insufficient evidence of wanton and reckless conduct by physician after birth to support a conviction for manslaughter for death of aborted fetus).

(ii) *The woman's consent.* The court upheld a requirement that a woman seeking an abortion give prior written consent to the procedure.

(iii) *Spousal consent.* The Court struck down a requirement of spousal consent (a question reserved in Roe and Doe): "Since the state cannot regulate or proscribe abortion during the first stage [of pregnancy] . . . the state cannot delegate authority to any particular person, even the spouse, to prevent abortion during that same period."

(iv) *Parental consent.* The Court also struck down a parental consent requirement for abortions by unmarried women under 18: "Any independent interest the parent may have . . . is no more weighty than the right to privacy of the competent minor mature enough to have become pregnant."

(v) The Court also struct down a prohibition on the use of saline amniocentesis as an abortion technique, upheld certain recordkeeping requirements, and invalidated the imposition of criminal civil liability on physicians who failed to attempt to preserve the life of all aborted fetuses, including those aborted before viability. See also Colautti v. Franklin, supra.

c. Abortion consent requirements for minors were reconsidered by the Court in Bellotti v. Baird, 443 U.S. 622 (1979), and H. L. v. Matheson, 101 S. Ct. 1164 (1981). In Bellotti the Court struck down a Massachusetts statute requiring parental or judicial consent before an abortion could be performed on any unmarried minor. The minor was required to obtain the consent of both parents; if they refused a state judge could authorize the abortion "for good cause shown." Although only Justice White voted to uphold the requirement, there was no opinion for the Court. Justice Stevens, joined by Justices Brennan, Marshall and Blackmun, thought that the case was governed by Roe and Danforth since, in all situations under the statute, "the minor's decision to secure an abortion is subject to an absolute third-party veto." Justice Powell, joined by the Chief Justice and Justices Stewart and Rehnquist, appeared to agree that an absolute third-party veto for all minors would be unconstitutional; they also appeared to agree that a requirement of parental consultation in all cases would be unconstitutional. These four Justices, however, sought to set out guidelines that *would* permit a third-party veto or require parental consultation for minors not sufficiently "mature" or "well informed" to make the abortion decision on their own. In their view, a valid minors-abortion statute would provide every minor with "the opportunity . . . to go directly to a court without first consulting or notifying her parents. If she satisfies the court that she is mature and well-informed enough to make intelligently the abortion decision on her own, the court must authorize her to act without parental consultation or consent." Even if she fails to satisfy the court as to her maturity, she must "be permitted to show that an abortion nevertheless would be in her best interest. If the court is persuaded that it is, the court must authorize the abortion." However, if the court is persuaded neither that the minor is sufficiently mature nor that the abortion is in her best interest, "it may decline to sanction the operation." In addition, these Justices thought that a court could require parental consultation by an immature minor prior to making its decision about the minor's best interest.

In Matheson the Court considered the constitutionality of a Utah statute that required a physician to "notify, if possible" the parents of all dependent, unmarried minors prior to performing abortions on them. The statute was challenged as overbroad on its face under prior decisions, since it "can be construed to apply to all unmarried minor girls, including those who are mature and emancipated." Chief Justice Burger's opinion for the Court refused to reach this question since appellant, an unmarried girl of 15 who lived at home and was dependent on her parents, "did not allege or proffer any evidence that either she or any member of her class is mature or emancipated." As applied to such a minor, the parental notice requirement was constitutional because it "plainly serves important state interests, is narrowly drawn to protect only those interests, and does not violate any guarantees of the Constitution." The Court relied on Justice Powell's opinion in Bellotti, supra, and the fact that "[t]he Utah statute gives neither parents nor judges a veto power over the minor's abortion decision." Justice Powell, joined by Justice Stewart, joined the Court's opinion "on the understanding that it leaves open the question whether [the statute] unconstitutionally burdens the right of a mature minor or a minor whose best interests would not be served by parental notification." Justice Stevens concurred in the judgment, finding the Utah statute constitutional as applied to *all* unmarried minors. In his opinion, "the special importance of a young woman's abortion decision" gives a state an interest in ensuring that she receive "appropriate consultation," including "parental advice." Justice Marshall, joined by Justices Brennan and Blackmun, dissented. They recognized the "traditional responsibility" of parents "to guide their children's development, especially in personal and moral concerns." However, "the Utah notice requirement is not necessary to assure parents this traditional child-rearing role, [while] it burdens the minor's fundamental right to choose with her physician whether to terminate her pregnancy."

d. *Abortion funding.* In Maher v. Roe, 432 U.S. 464 (1977) (in main Vol. II, Ch. XX, Sec. A-2), the Court held that the Constitution is not violated by a state's refusal to use its Medicaid program to pay for nonmedically necessary abortions for indigent women while funding other medical expenses for indigents including those for pregnancy and childbirth. Justice Powell's opinion for the Court held that the refusal to fund nontherapeutic abortions did not "impinge on the fundamental right recognized in Roe" because that refusal, given the fact that the state was not constitutionally obligated to fund abortions, did not place "substantial state-created obstacles in the pregnant woman's path to an abortion." The Court applied an equal protection analysis. It detected neither a "suspect" classification nor a "penalty" on a constitutional right, and therefore applied a "rationality" test. This test was satisfied, the Court held, because the funding scheme was related to the "constitutionally permissible" state purpose of "encouraging childbirth." Justices Brennan, Marshall and Blackmun dissented. See also Poelker v. Doe, 432 U.S. 519 (1977), decided on the same day as Maher and holding that a city hospital's refusal to perform abortions is not a violation of the equal protection clause.

Three years later, in Harris v. McRae, 448 U.S. 297 (1980), and Williams v. Zbaraz, 448 U.S. 358 (1980), the Court refused to distinguish Maher, which had dealt only with *non*therapeutic abortions; instead, it used the Maher analysis to uphold federal and state refusals to fund most medically *necessary* abortions as well. (These funding restrictions were imposed pursuant to the so-called Hyde Amendment to federal appropriations legislation, enacted annually by Congress between 1976 and 1980). Justice Stewart wrote the Court's opinions in both cases. Justices Brennan, Marshall, Blackmun, and Stevens dissented.

Despite these Supreme Court decisions, state courts in three states have recently held that abortion funding restrictions violate state constitutional principles. See Committee to Defend Reproductive Rights v. Myers, 625 P.2d 779 (Cal. 1981); Right to Choose v. Byrne, 165 N.J.

Super. 443 (1979) (appeal pending); Moe v. Secretary, 417 N.E.2d 387 (Mass. 1981). Since abortion funding cases are treated by the Court as principally raising equal protection rather than privacy or substantive due process issues, they are discussed primarily in main Vol. II, Ch. XX, Sec. A-2 and Ch. XXXV, Sec. E.

7. *Recent lower court decisions dealing with abortion regulations.* In the wake of Roe, and undoubtedly encouraged to some extent by the Supreme Court's subsequent decisions in Bellotti and the abortion funding cases, supra, a number of states and localities have recently enacted comprehensive abortion-control legislation (sometimes referred to as "Akron-type statutes, see Akron Center for Reproductive Health v. City of Akron, infra). These statutes, which often are premised on legislative findings that the fetus is a "human life" from the time of conception, appear in some respects designed to place substantial obstacles in the way of abortions while stopping short of actually imposing legal prohibitions prior to viability. Among the provisions typically contained in these statutes are: mandatory waiting periods of 24 or 48 hours; informed written consent requirements; requirements that physicians personally convey information to women about the alternatives to abortion and about possible medical consequences of abortion; requirements that women seeking abortions be shown color photographs of fetuses at various stages of development and of aborted fetuses; prohibitions of abortions not deemed "necessary" in the clinical judgment of the physician; parental or judicial consent or notice provisions for minors; spousal consent or notice provisions for married women; requirements that post-first-trimester abortions be performed in hospitals; requirements for "humane" disposal of and pathology reports upon fetal remains; funding limitations; prohibitions of abortions in state or city hospitals or clinics; statutory or administrative definitions of viability; and required efforts to preserve the lives of fetuses who are born alive. Many of these provisions, including the mandatory waiting period and the requirements of display of fetal photographs, have been held unconstitutional in serveral recent court of appeals decisions. See Charles v. Carey, 627 F.2d 772 (7th Cir. 1980); Planned Parenthood League v. Bellotti, 641 F.2d 1006 (1st Cir. 1981); Women's Services v. Throne, 636 F.2d 206 (8th Cir. 1980); Akron Center for Reproductive Health, Inc. v. City of Akron, 651 F.2d 1198 (6th Cir. 1981); Planned Parenthood Assn. v. Ashcroft, — F.2d — (8th Cir. 1981). To the same effect is Margaret S. v. Edwards I, 488 F. Supp. 181 (E.D. La. 1980) (appeal moot because of repeal of statute). See also, Women's Health Center v. Cohen, 477 F. Supp. 542 (D. Maine 1979); Leigh v. Olson, 497 F. Supp. 1340 (D.N.D. 1980). Other recent lower court abortion regulation decisions on issues not yet authoritatively settled by the Supreme Court include: Scheinberg v. Smith, 482 F. Supp. 529 (S.D. Fla. 1979) (spousal notice provision invalid); Gary-Northwest Indiana Women's Services v. Orr, 496 F. Supp.

894 (N.D. Ind. 1980), summarily affirmed, 101 S. Ct. 2012 (1981) (upholding requirement that all post-first-trimester abortions be performed in hospitals); Mahoning Women's Center v. Hunter, 610 F.2d 456 (6th Cir. 1979) (invalidating ordinance imposing costly medical and building code regulations on clinics performing first-trimester abortions); Birth Control Centers, Inc. v. Reizen, 508 F. Supp. 1366 (E.D. Mich. 1981) (invalidating aspects of regulation of abortion clinics); Baird v. Department of Public Health, 599 F.2d 1098 (1st Cir. 1979) (upholding Massachusetts clinic license law as applied to ambulatory health care center performing first-trimester abortions); Bossier City Medical Suite v. City of Bossier City, 483 F. Supp. 633 (W.D. La. 1980) (upholding application to abortion clinic of zoning restriction on performance of major surgery); and Nyberg v. City of Virginia, — F. Supp. — (D. Minn. 1980), and Doe v. Carnright, — F. Supp. — (D. Ind. 1980) (holding unconstitutional prohibitions on city hospitals performing abortions where other facilities are not available).

(page 785) [988]

NOTES

4. [continued] Cf. Fitzgerald v. Porter Memorial Hospital, 523 F.2d 716 (7th Cir. 1975), cert. denied, 425 U.S. 916 (1976), where plaintiff couples, who had been trained in the Lamaze method of childbirth (which requires participation of the husband during labor and delivery), claimed that a public hospital policy excluding everyone but medical and nursing personnel from the delivery room violated their right to privacy. The Court (Stevens, J.) held that "deciding the question whether the child shall be born is of a different magnitude from deciding where, by whom, and by what method he or she shall be delivered. We are not persuaded that the married partners' special interest in their child gives them any greater right to determine the procedures to be followed at birth than that possessed by other individuals in need of extraordinary medical assistance."

(page 798) [1001]

NOTE

[continued] Belle Terre was distinguished by a Court plurality in Moore v. City of East Cleveland, 431 U.S. 494 (1977). In Moore the Court held unconstitutional an East Cleveland ordinance that limited occupancy of a dwelling unit to members of a single family and that defined "family" so as to prohibit appellant, a grandmother, from living with her son, his child, and another grandchild, neither of whose parents

219

lived in the unit. Justice Powell's plurality opinion (joined by Justices Brennan, Marshall and Blackmun) found "one overriding fact [that] set this case apart from Belle Terre. The ordinance there affected only unrelated individuals... East Cleveland, in contrast, has chosen to regulate the occupancy of its housing by slicing deeply into the family itself.... When a city undertakes such intrusive regulation of the family... the usual judicial deference to the legislature is inappropriate." Justice Stevens concurred in the judgment on the ground that the ordinance was an impermissible restriction "on appellant's right to use her own property as she sees fit." Justices Burger, Stewart, Rehnquist, and White dissented. On the right of members of a family to live together, see also Duquesne v. Sugarman, 566 F.2d 817 (2d Cir. 1977).

(page 807) [1010]

NOTE

1.a. [continued] See also Hollenbaugh v. Carnegie Free Library, 436 F. Supp. 1338 (W.D. Pa. 1977), affirmed, 578 F.2d 1374 (3d Cir. 1978), cert. denied, 439 U.S. 1052 (Marshall, J., dissenting) (library employees fired for living together); Beller v. Middendorf, 632 F.2d 788 (9th Cir. 1980) (upholding Navy regulations requiring discharge of persons engaging in homosexual activities); Gaylord v. Tacoma School Dist., 559 P.2d 1340 (Wash. 1977) (allowing school board to presume homosexual to be "immoral" and thus unfit to teach); Gish v. Board of Educ. of Paramus, 366 A.2d 1337 (1976) (upholding the discharge of public school teacher who refused to undergo a psychiatric exam after becoming active in gay rights organization).

(page 809) [1012]

NOTE

1.d. [continued] Since publication of the main volume, several cases have held criminal prohibitions on consensual sexual conduct between unmarried adults to be unconstitutional. In State v. Saunders, 381 A.2d 333 (N.J. 1977), the court held a state fornication law unconstitutional as an invasion of privacy. See also Commonwealth v. Bonadio, 490 Pa. 91, 415 A.2d 47 (1980), using the equal protection clause to strike down a statute prohibiting oral or anal intercourse between unmarried persons. The criterion of marriage was held not to be related to the purpose of the statute. And see People v. Onofre, 51 N.Y.2d 476, 415 N.E.2d 936 (1980) (statute criminalizing consensual sodomy or deviate intercourse between unmarried persons unconstitutional under privacy and equal protection concepts). To the same effect are State v. Pilcher, 242

N.W.2d 348 (Iowa), and State v. Ciuffini, 164 N.J. Super. 145, 395 A.2d 904. But cf. J. B. K., Inc. v. Caron, 600 F.2d 710 (8th Cir. 1979), which, in denying a request by a massage parlor for a preliminary injunction against enforcement of the state's prostitution law, held that privacy rights do not encompass "commercialized sexual activities."

In Doe v. Commonwealth's Attorney, 425 U.S. 901 (1976), the Supreme Court summarily affirmed, without opinion, a district court decision upholding Virginia's criminal sodomy statute as applied to consensual acts between homosexual males. The district court majority, 403 F. Supp. 1199, viewed Griswold as limited to marital and familial privacy. Judge Merhige, dissenting, found the marital-nonmarital distinction "unsupportable" in view of Eisenstadt v. Baird. But see State v. Ciuffini, supra, 395 A.2d 904 (N.J. 1978) (refusing to follow Doe and holding that the right of privacy forbids criminalization of consensual homosexual activities). To the same effect are People v. Onofre and other cases, supra, holding regulations on consensual adult sexual activity unconstitutional.

(page 809) [1012]

NOTE

1.e. [continued] Commonwealth v. Bonadio, supra, 415 A.2d 47 (Pa. 1980), struck down a statute prohibiting "deviant" sexual activity, even though the activity in that case occured in a performance on stage. An interesting case in a closely related area is City of Chicago v. Wilson, 75 Ill. 2d 525, 389 N.E.2d 522 (1978), holding unconstitutional an ordinance prohibiting the wearing of clothes of the opposite sex with intent to conceal one's gender. Two men wearing women's clothes had been arrested emerging from a restaurant. The court said that one's choice of appearance is not a fundamental right but held that the City had offered no plausible governmental justification for the ordinance.

(page 812) [1015]

NOTE

2. [continued] Ravin v. State is reported at 537 P.2d 494 (Alaska 1975). The Ravin decision, striking down state marijuana use laws, was based on the Alaska Constitution. The Alaska Supreme Court subsequently distinguished cocaine laws in State v. Erickson, 574 P.2d 1 (1978). Other states have continued to reject privacy challenges to marijuana laws. See State v. Mitchell, 563 S.W.2d 18 (Mo. 1978); State v. Vail, 274 N.W.2d 127 (Minn. 1979); State v. Kells, 259 N.W.2d 19 (Neb. 1977); People v. Schmidt, 272 N.W.2d 732 (Mich. 1978); State v. Chrisman,

364 So. 2d 906 (Ala. 1978); Laird v. State, 342 So. 2d 962 (Fla. 1977); Marcoux v. Attorney General, 375 N.E.2d 688 (Mass. 1978); Illinois NORML v. Scott, 383 N.E.2d 1330 (Ill. 1978). And see, Petrey v. Flaugher, 505 F. Supp. 1087 (E.D. Ky. 1981) (upholding expulsion of high school student for smoking marijuana in school).

(page 813) [1016]

NOTE

3.a. [continued] In Kelley v. Johnson, 425 U.S. 238 (1976), the Supreme Court rejected an attack on regulations that limited the length and style of hair, sideburns, and mustaches that could be worn by policemen and that also prohibited policemen from wearing beards and goatees (except for medical reasons) and wigs (except for cosmetic reasons). Justice Rehnquist's opinion for the court found the case distinguishable from previous decisions like Roe, Griswold, Eisenstadt, Stanley, and Meyer, that had "involved a substantial claim of infringement on the individual's freedom of choice with respect to certain basic matters of procreation, marriage and family life." The Court nevertheless assumed "for purposes of deciding this case," that "the citizenry at large has some sort of 'liberty' interest within the Fourteenth Amendment in matters of personal appearance." This assumption, however, was "insufficient to carry the day for [the plaintiff's] claim" since plaintiff "has sought the protection of the Fourteenth Amendment, not as a member of the citizenry at large, but . . . as an employee of the police force. . . ." Although the " 'unique judicial deference' accorded by the judiciary to regulation of members of the military" was "inapplicable," "[c]hoice of organization, dress, and equipment for law enforcement personnel is a decision entitled to the same sort of presumption of legislative validity as are state choices designed to promote other aims within the cognizance of the State's police power." Thus, the applicable test was not whether the state could establish a "genuine public need" for the regulation (as the court of appeals below had held) but whether plaintiff could "demonstrate that there is no rational connection between the regulation . . . and the promotion of safety of persons and property." The Court thought it "so clear" that such a rational connection existed that plaintiff's complaint should have been dismissed: "The overwhelming majority of state and local police . . . are uniformed. . . . [S]imilarity in appearance of police officers is desirable. This choice may be based on a desire to make police officers readily recognizable to the members of the public, or a desire for the esprit de corps which such similarity is felt to inculcate within the police force itself. Either one is a sufficiently rational justification . . . to defeat [plaintiff's] claim. . . ." Language in Garrity v. New Jersey, 385 U.S. 493, 500 (1967), that "policemen, like teachers and lawyers, are not relegated to a watered-down version of constitutional rights . . . certainly . . . cannot be taken to suggest that the claim of a member of a uniformed civilian service based on the 'liberty' interest protected by the Fourteenth Amendment must necessarily be treated for constitutional purposes the same as a similar claim by a member of the general public."

Justice Stevens did not participate in Kelley. Justice Powell concurred in the Court's opinion, finding in it "no negative implication . . . with respect to a liberty interest within the Fourteenth Amendment as to matters of personal appearance." Weighing the competing interests, however, "justifies the application of a reasonable regulation to a uniformed police force that would be an impermissible intrusion upon liberty in a different context." Justice Marshall, joined by Justice Brennan, dissented: "While fully accepting the aims of 'identifiability' and maintenance of esprit de corps, I find no rational relationship between the challenged regulation and these goals."

Lower court opinions applying Kelley to uphold hair or beard regulations include: Marshall v. District Unemployment Comp. Bd., 377 A.2d 429 (D.C. 1977) (police); Board of Selectmen of Framingham v. Civil Service Commn., 387 N.E.2d 1198 (Mass. App. 1979) (police); Sheppard v. De Kalb County Merit Council, 240 S.E.2d 316 (Ga. 1977) (firemen); Jacobs v. Kunes, 541 F.2d 222 (9th Cir. 1976) (employees of county assessor's office); Chiappe v. State Personnel Board, 622 P.2d 527 (Colo. 1981) (food service employees at the University of Colorado). Cf. Nelson v. Mustian, 502 F. Supp. 698 (N.D. Fla. 1980) (nurse has no privacy right to wear unlimited number of rings). But see Nalley v. Douglas County, 498 F. Supp. 1228 (N.D. Ga. 1980) (county regulations prohibiting employees from wearing beards unconstitutional as applied to employee of road department).

(page 815) [1017]

NOTE

4. [continued] In Zablocki v. Redhail, 434 U.S. 374 (1978), relying in part on Loving v. Virginia, 388 U.S. 1 (1967), the Court stated that the right to marry was "part of the fundamental 'right of privacy' implicit in the Fourteenth Amendment's Due Process Clause." Justice Marshall's opinion for the Court then used the Equal Protection Clause to strike down a Wisconsin statute that prohibited persons with an obligation to support minor children not in their custody to marry without court approval. Justice Rehnquist dissented. Earlier in the same term, in Califano v. Jobst, 434 U.S. 47 (1977), the Court had unanimously upheld Social Security Act provisions that provided for termination of disability benefits when a person receiving benefits married a person not entitled

to benefits. The Court in Zablocki distinguished Jobst on the ground that the statute there "placed no direct legal obstacle in the path of persons desiring to get married." Zablocki was followed in Miller v. Morris, 386 N.E. 2d 1203 (Ind. 1979), which involved a similar restriction. For cases reaching results similar to that in Jobst, see Mapes v. United States, 576 F.2d 896 (Ct. Cl. 1978) (higher federal income tax for married persons filing jointly as compared with single taxpayers does not infringe on the right to marry); Southwestern Community Services, Inc., 462 F. Supp. 297 (W. Va. 1978) (OEO anti-nepotism instruction does not infringe on the right to marry); Martin v. Bergland, 639 F.2d 647 (10th Cir. 1981) (Department of Agriculture rule that husband and wife are a single person for purposes of statute limiting farm program payments to $20,000 per person is not an unconstitutional burden on the freedom to marry under Zablocki); Ensminger v. Commissioner, 610 F.2d 189 (4th Cir. 1979) (Internal Revenue Code provision that individual is not a member of taxpayer's household if the relationship violates local law applied to woman cohabiting with taxpayer does not burden fundamental rights under Zablocki). But see, Salisbury v. List, 501 F. Supp. 105 (D. Nev. 1980) (Nevada prison rules allowing Director of Prisons to permit inmate marriage only when marriage would have a constructive effect on both parties unconstitutionally interferes with right to marry).

(page 815) [1018]

NOTES

5b. [continued] In Runyon v. McCrary, 427 U.S. 160 (1976), the Court held that a private school's refusal to admit black students violates 42 U.S.C. §1981, which provides that "All persons ... shall have the same right in every State ... to make and enforce contracts ... as is enjoyed by white citizens." Justice Stewart's opinion for the Court rejected arguments that §1981, as thus construed, violated privacy type rights:

"1. *Freedom of Association*. ... [I]t may be assumed that parents have a First Amendment right to send their children to educational institutions that promote the belief that racial segregation is desirable, and that the children have an equal right to attend such institutions. But it does not follow that the *practice* of excluding racial minorities from such institutions is also protected by the same principle." In any event, "there is no showing that discontinuance of [the] discriminatory admission practices would inhibit in any way the teaching in these schools of any ideas or dogma.

"2. Parental Rights. ... It is clear that the present application of §1981 infringes no parental right recognized in Meyer [v. Nebraska], Pierce [v. Society of Sisters, or Wisconsin v.] Yoder. ... No challenge is made to the petitioner schools' right to operate or the right of parents to send their children to a particular private school rather than a public school. Nor do these cases involve a challenge to the subject matter which is taught at any private school. Thus, the [schools] remain presumptively free to inculcate whatever values and standards they deem desirable. Meyer and its progeny entitle them to no more.

"3. *The Right of Privacy.* . . . While the application of §1981 to the conduct at issue here — a private school's adherence to a racially discriminatory admissions policy — does not represent governmental intrusion into the privacy of the home or a similarly intimate setting, it does implicate parental interests. These interests are related to the procreative rights protected in Roe v. Wade and Griswold v. Connecticut. A person's decision whether to bear a child and a parent's decision concerning the manner in which his child is to be educated may fairly be characterized as exercises of familial rights and responsibilities. But it does not follow that because government is largely or even entirely precluded from regulating the child-bearing decision, it is similarly restricted by the Constitution from regulating the implementation of parental decisions concerning a child's education.

"The Court has repeatedly stressed that while parents have a constituitional right to send their children to private schools and a constitutional right to select private schools that offer specialized instruction, they have no constitutional right to provide their children with private school education unfettered by reasonable government regulation. . . .

"Section 1981, as applied to the conduct at issue here, constitutes an exercise of federal legislative power under §2 of the Thirteenth Amendment fully consistent with Meyer, Pierce, and the cases that followed in their wake. . . . The prohibition of racial discrimination that interferes with the making and enforcement of contracts for private educational services furthers goals closely analogous to those served by §1981's elimination of racial discrimination in the making of private employment contracts and, more generally, by [42 U.S.C.] §1982's guarantee that 'a dollar in the hands of a Negro will purchase the same things as a dollar in the hands of a white man.' Jones v. Alfred H. Mayer Co., [392 U.S.] at 443." Justice White joined by Justice Rehnquist, dissented on the ground that 42 U.S.C. §1981 should not be construed as being applicable to private conduct.

Interesting recent lower court cases considering privacy claims of various kinds include the following: Dike v. School Board, 650 F.2d 783 (5th Cir. 1981) (school teacher's desire to breast-feed her child during lunch period is "a communion between mother and child" entitled to protection of a "close scrutiny" test under Griswold and Zablocki); McKenna v. Peekskill Housing Authority, 497 F. Supp. 1217 (S.D.N.Y. 1980), aff'd in part and rev'd in part, 647 F.2d 332 (2d Cir. 1981) (upholding rule that tenants in state-funded housing project must obtain prior approval for and register overnight guests); Andrews v. Ballard, 498 F. Supp. 1038 (S.D. Tex. 1980) (statute limiting practice of acupuncture to licensed physicians burdens right to obtain treatment and is unsupported by a compelling interest); Jech v. Burch, 466 F. Supp. 714 (D. Hawaii 1979) (striking down state law forbidding parents from giving children a surname "fuscd" out of parents' surnames); Doe v. Irwin, 615 F.2d 1162 (6th Cir. 1980) (family planning center's distribution of contraceptives to unemancipated minors without notice to their parents does not infringe constitutional rights of parents); Franklin v. White Egret Condominium, Inc., 358 So. 2d 1084 (Fla. Dist. Ct. App. 1978) (unconstitutional for court to enforce condominium article prohibiting children under twelve years of age from residing on premises); cf. Sterling v. Cupp, 625 P.2d 123 (Ore. 1981) (state constitutional privacy principles prohibit prison guards of the opposite sex from conducting patdowns or frisks on prisoners' anal-genital areas unless necessary in view of particular immediate circumstances).

Several cases have rejected privacy claims made against regulations restricting or prohibiting the distribution of laetrile as a treatment for cancer. See, e.g., People v. Privitera, 153 Cal. Rptr. 431, 591 P.2d 919 (1979); Rutherford v. United States, 616 F.2d 445 (10th Cir. 1980) (on remand from decison of Supreme Court, 442 U.S. 544 (1979), that held that the federal Food, Drug and Cosmetic Act prohibits interstate shipment of laetrile even to terminally ill cancer patients).

(page 815) [1018]

NOTE

5.c. [continued] In In re Quinlan, 70 N.J. 10, 355 A.2d 647 (1976), the father of a twenty-two-year-old woman in a chronic vegetative state appealed the denial by the New Jersey Superior Court, 348 A.2d 801 (1975), of his petition for guardianship and the power to authorize discontinuance of all extraordinary means of sustaining life. The New Jersey Supreme Court reversed, holding that the right of privacy is "broad enough to encompass a patient's decision to decline medical treatment under certain circumstances," and that the right of an incompetent patient in this regard can be asserted by a guardian. The court held that the guardian's decision to terminate life-sustaining procedures should be confirmed by an Ethics Committee of the hospital and that, if the Committee finds that there is no reasonable possibilty of return to a cognitive sapient state, the life-support system could be withdrawn without fear of civil or criminal liability. Cases similar to Quinlan include: Severns v. Wilmington Medical Center, Inc., 421 A.2d 1334 (Del. 1980) (husband, as guardian of comatose wife, has standing to invoke her privacy rights and apply for an order authorizing removal of life-sustaining supports); In re Storar, 438 N.Y.S.2d 266 (1981), affirming 426 N.Y.S.2d 517 (App. Div. 1980) (right to privacy "encompasses the freedom of the terminally ill but competent individual . . . to forgo medical treatment and allow the natural processes of death to follow their inevitable course.") In re Spring, 405 N.E.2d 115 (Mass. 1980) (affirming probate court order permitting wife and son to terminate hemodialysis treatment with physician's agreement).

[1023]

[REFERENCES]

See generally Lackland, Toward Creating a Philosophy of Fundamental Human Rights, 6 Colum. Hum. Rts. L. Rev. 473 (1974-1975); Bostwick, A Taxonomy of Privacy: Repose, Sanctuary and Intimate Decision, 64 Calif. L. Rev. 1447 (1976); Levy, Privacy Revisited: The Downfall of Griswold, 12 U. Rich. L. Rev. 627 (1978); Toward a Constitutional Theory of Individuality: The Privacy Opinions of Justice Douglas, 87 Yale L.J. 1579 (1978); Gerety, Redefining Privacy, 12 Harv. Civ. Rts. Civ. Lib. L. Rev. 233 (1977); Ely, on Discovering Fundamental Values, 92 Harv. L. Rev. 5 (1978); Karst, The Freedom of Intimate Association, 89 Yale L.J. 624 (1980).

On the right to an abortion: Dellapenna, The Supreme Court on Abortion, 6 Colum. Hum. Rts. L. Rev. 379 (1974-1975); Lee & Paxman, Pregnancy and Abortion in Adolescence, 6 Colum. Hum. Rts. L. Rev. 307 (1974-1975); Pilpil & Patton, Abortion, Conscience, and the Constitution, 6 Colum. Hum. Rts. L. Rev. 279 (1974-1975); Perry, Abortion, the Public Morals and the Police Power, 23 U.C.L.A.L. Rev. 689 (1976); Comment, Medical Responsibility for Fetal Survival Under Roe and Doe, 10 Harv. Civ. Rts. Civ. Lib. L. Rev. 444 (1975).

On the abortion funding decisions: Hardy, Privacy and Public Funding, 18 Ariz. L. Rev. 903 (1976); Perry, Why the Supreme Court Was Plainly Wrong in the Hyde Amendment Case, 32 Stan. L. Rev. 1113 (1980); Goldstein, A critique of the Abortion Funding Decisions, 8 Hastings Const. L.Q. 313 (1980); Note, Abortion, Medicaid and Constitution, 54 N.Y.U.L. Rev. 120 (1979).

On euthanasia and the right to die: Brown & Truitt, Euthanasia and the Right to Die, 3 Ohio N.U.L. Rev. 615 (1976); Delgado, Euthanasia Reconsidered, 17 Ariz. L. Rev. 474 (1975); Steele & Hill, A Plea for the Legal Right to Die, 20 Okla. L. Rev. 328 (1976); Collester, A Prosecutorial View of the Quinlan Case, 30 Rutgers L. Rev. 304 (1977); Kutner, Due Process for Death With Dignity, 54 Ind. L. J. 201 (1978); Richards, Constitutional Privacy, the Right to Die and the Meaning of Life, 22 Wm. & Mary L. Rev. 327 (1981).

On other aspects of the right to privacy: Note, The Right to Wear a Traditional Indian Hair Style, 4 Am. Indian L. Rev. 105; Hunter & Polikoff, Custody Rights of Lesbian Mothers, 25 Buffalo L. Rev. 691 (1976); Note, The Avowed Lesbian Mother and Her Right to Child Custody, 12 San Diego L. Rev. 799 (1975); Wilkinson & White, Constitutional Protection for Personal Life-Styles, 62 Cornell L. Rev. 563 (1977); Hindes, Morality Enforcement through the Criminal Law and the Modern Doctrine of Substantive Due Process, 126 U. Pa. L. Rev. 344 (1977); Richards, Unnatural Acts and the Constitutional Right to Privacy, 45 Fordham L. Rev. 1281 (1977); Richards, Sexual Autonomy and the Constitutional Right to Privacy, 30 Hastings L.J. 957 (1979); Note, Laetrile: Statutory and Constitutional Limitations on the Regulation of Ineffective Drugs, 127 U. Pa. L. Rev. 233 (1978); Von Biegel, The Criminalization of Private Homosexual Acts, 6 Hum. Rts. 23 (1977); Burt, The Constitution of the Family, 1979 Sup. Ct. Rev. 329; Madison, Marital and Nonmarital Relationships; The Right to Alternative Lifestyles, 11 Colum. Hum. Rts. L. Rev. 189 (1979-1980); Developments in the Law, The Constitution and the Family, 93 Harv. L. Rev. 1156 (1980).

B. INFORMATIONAL PRIVACY

(page 834) [1038]

NOTES

4. [continued] The court of appeals decision in Miller was reversed by the Supreme Court. United States v. Miller, 425 U.S. 435 (1976). Justice Powell's opinion for the Court held that the court below had erred in assuming that the defendant depositor "had the necessary Fourth Amendment interest." Defendant could assert "neither ownership nor possession" of the subpoenaed copies of his checks; "[i]nstead, these are the business records of the banks." Moreover, "[e]ven if we direct our attention to the original checks and deposit slips, rather than to the microfilm copies actually viewed and obtained by means of the subpoena, we perceive no legitimate 'expectation of privacy' in their contents.... The checks are not confidential communications but negotiable instruments to be used in commercial transactions.... All of the documents obtained ... contain only information voluntarily conveyed to the banks.... The Court has held repeatedly that the Fourth Amendment does not prohibit the obtaining of information revealed to a third party and conveyed by him to Government authorities, even if the information is revealed on the assumption that it will be used only for a limited purpose and the confidence placed in the third party will not be betrayed...."

The analysis in Miller was not changed "by the mandate of the Bank

Secrecy Act that records of depositors' transactions be maintained by banks" (a question that had been expressly reserved in California Bankers Assn. v. Shultz): "[E]ven if the banks could be said to have been acting solely as Government agents in transcribing the necessary information and complying without protest [or notification to the depositor] with the requirements of the subpoenas, there would be no intrusion upon the depositors' Fourth Amendment rights." Banks traditionally kept records of their depositors' accounts; thus the Bank Secrecy Act, by requiring that such records be kept, was "not a novel means designed to circumvent established Fourth Amendment rights." Justices Brennan and Marshall dissented, Justice Brennan stating his agreement with Burrows v. Superior Court (in main volume page (835) [1039], footnote a).

See also Smith v. Maryland, 442 U.S. 735 (1979), holding that the installation and use by the telephone company, at police request, of a "pen register" — a device used to record the telephone numbers dialed from an individual's telephone — was not a search within the meaning of the Fourth Amendment. Justice Blackmun's opinion for the Court relied on the "expectation of privacy" holding of Miller. Justices Brennan, Stewart and Marshall dissented.

(page 835) [1038]

NOTE — THE POSSIBLY EMERGING RIGHT OF INFORMATIONAL PRIVACY

Insert after second paragraph:
In two recent cases, the Supreme Court has reinforced Fifth Amendment doctrines that limit the usefulness of that Amendment in protecting informational privacy:

a. Fisher v. United States, 425 U.S. 391 (1976), involved a taxpayer who, after being interviewed by an IRS agent and informed that he was under investigation, obtained from his accountant the working papers used by the accountant in preparing taxpayer's income tax returns, and then transferred those papers to an attorney he had retained to assist him during the IRS investigation. When the IRS learned of this, it served the attorney with a summons requiring production of the accountant's workpapers; the attorney declined to comply, based on (1) the Fifth Amendment, and (2) the taxpayer's attorney-client privilege.

The Supreme Court, in an opinion by Justice White, rejected the view that the taxpayer's Fifth Amendment privilege was violated by the enforcement of the summons against his attorney. The Court relied on Couch v. United States, 409 U.S. 322 (1973), which had held that a documentary summons served on an accountant, requiring production of taxpayer's own records that were temporarily in the accountant's possession, could be enforced without violating the taxpayer's privilege against self-incrimination. In Fisher, as in Couch, "the ingredient of personal compulsion against an accused is lacking." Nor was the taxpayer's expectation of privacy in transferring the papers to attorney Fisher of great importance: "We cannot cut the Fifth Amendment completely loose from the moorings of its language, and make it serve as a general protector of privacy — a word not mentioned in its text and a concept directly addressed in the Fourth Amendment." Finally, the Court indicated that the attorney-client privilege *would* justify an attorney's refusal to comply with a summons demanding papers if the papers were such that, had the client retained them, they could not have been obtained directly from him by reason of the Fifth Amendment. The taxpayer in Fisher, however, could assert no Fifth Amendment privilege were such a summons directed to him. The Fifth Amendment applies only when a person is compelled to make a *testimonial* communication that is incriminating. The mere act of producing the accountant's workpapers (however incriminating they might be) would not amount to incriminating testimony by the client within the protection of the Fifth Amendment.

b. Andresen v. Maryland, 427 U.S. 463 (1976), involved a search by state investigators of Andresen's law office. The search was carried out pursuant to a valid search warrant, some of the papers seized were introduced at trial, and Andresen was convicted for his part in fraudulent land transactions. The Supreme Court affirmed, holding that no compulsion, within the meaning of the Fifth Amendment, is brought to bear upon a defendant whose business records are seized by law enforcement personnel and introduced at his trial. Justices Brennan and Marshall dissented.

(page 839) [1042]

Insert after Note 1.a.:

WHALEN v. ROE
429 U.S. 589

Mr. JUSTICE STEVENS delivered the opinion of the Court.

The constitutional question presented is whether the State of New York may record, in a centralized computer file, the names and addresses of all persons who have obtained, pursuant to a doctor's prescription, certain drugs for which there is both a lawful and an unlawful market.

The District Court enjoined enforcement of the portions of the New York State Controlled Substances Act of 1972, which require such recording, on the ground that they violate appellees' constitutionally protected rights of privacy. We ... reverse. ...

The ... New York statute classifies potentially harmful drugs in five schedules. Drugs, such as heroin, which are highly abused and have no recognized medical use, are in Schedule I; they cannot be prescribed. Schedules II through V include drugs which have a progressively lower potential for abuse but also have a recognized medical use. Our concern is limited to Schedule II, which includes the most dangerous of the legitimate drugs.[8]

With an exception for emergencies, the Act requires that all prescriptions for Schedule II drugs be prepared by the physician in triplicate on an official form. The completed form identifies the prescribing physician, the dispensing pharmacy, the drug and dosage, and the name, address and age of the patient. One copy of the form is retained by the physician, the second by the pharmacist, and the third is forwarded to the New York State Department of Health in Albany. A prescription made on an official form may not exceed a 30-day supply, and may not be refilled.

The District Court found that about 100,000 Schedule II prescription forms are delivered to a receiving room at the Department of Health in Albany each month. They are sorted, coded, and logged and then taken to another room where the data on the forms is recorded on magnetic tapes for processing by a computer. Thereafter, the forms are returned to the receiving room to be retained in a vault for a five-year period and then destroyed as required by the statute. The receiving room is surrounded by a locked wire fence and protected by an alarm system. The computer tapes containing the prescription data are kept in a locked cabinet. When the tapes are used, the computer is run "off-line," which means that no terminal outside of the computer room can read or record any information. Public disclosure of the identity of patients is expressly prohibited by the statute and by a Department of Health regulation. Wilful violation of these prohibitions is a crime punishable by up to one year in prison and a $2000 fine. At the time of trial there were 17 Department of Health employees with access to the files; in addition, there were 24 investigators with authority to investigate cases of over-dispensing which might be identified by the computer. Twenty months after the effective date of the Act, the computerized data had only been used in two investigations involving alleged over-use by specific patients.

A few days before the Act became effective, this litigation was commenced by a group of patients regularly receiving prescriptions for

8. These include opium and opium derivatives, cocaine, methadone, amphetamines and methaqualone. . . . These drugs have accepted uses in the amelioration of pain and in the treatment of epilepsy, narcolepsy, hyperkinesia, schizo-affective disorders, and migraine headaches.

Schedule II drugs, by doctors who prescribe such drugs, and by two associations of physicians.... Appellees offered evidence tending to prove that persons in need of treatment with Schedule II drugs will from time to time decline such treatment because of their fear that the misuse of the computerized data will cause them to be stigmatized as "drug addicts."...

The New York statute challenged in this case represents a considered attempt to deal with a problem [of vital local concern]. It is manifestly the product of an orderly and rational legislative decision.... There surely was nothing unreasonable in the assumption that the patient identification requirement might aid in the enforcement of laws designed to minimize the misuse of dangerous drugs. For the requirement could reasonably be expected to have a deterrent effect on potential violators as well as to aid in the detection or investigation of specific instances of apparent abuse. At the very least, it would seem clear that the state's vital interest in controlling the distribution of dangerous drugs would support a decision to experiment with new techniques for control....

Appellees contend that the statute invades a constitutionally protected "zone of privacy." The cases sometimes characterized as protecting "privacy" have in fact involved at least two different kinds of interests. One is the individual interest in avoiding disclosure of personal matters, and another is the interest in independence in making certain kinds of important decisions....

We are persuaded, however, that the New York program does not, on its face, pose a sufficiently grievous threat to either interest to establish a constitutional violation....

... There is no support in the record ... for an assumption that the security provisions of the statute will be administered improperly. And the remote possibility that judicial supervision of the evidentiary use of particular items of stored information will provide inadequate protection against unwarranted disclosures is surely not a sufficient reason for invalidating the entire patient identification program.

Even without public disclosure, it is, of course, true that private information must be disclosed to the authorized employees of the New York Department of Health.... Unquestionably, some individuals' concern for their own privacy may lead them to avoid or to postpone needed medical attention. Nevertheless, disclosures of private medical information to doctors, to hospital personnel, to insurance companies, and to public health agencies are often an essential part of modern medical practice even when the disclosure may reflect unfavorably on the character of the patient. Requiring such disclosures to representatives of the State having responsibility for the health of the community, does not automatically amount to an impermissible invasion of privacy.

Appellees also argue, however, that even if unwarranted disclosures do not actually occur, the knowledge that the information is readily available in a computerized file creates a genuine concern that causes some persons to decline needed medication. The record supports the conclusion that some use of Schedule II drugs has been discouraged by that concern; it also is clear, however, that about 100,000 prescriptions for such drugs were being filled each month prior to the entry of the District Court's injunction. Clearly, therefore, the statute did not deprive the public of access to the drugs.

Nor can it be said that any individual has been deprived of the right to decide independently, with the advice of his physician, to acquire and to use needed medication. Although the State no doubt could prohibit entirely the use of particular Schedule II drugs, it has not done so. This case is therefore unlike those in which the Court held that a total prohibition of certain conduct was an impermissible deprivation of liberty....

... We are not unaware of the threat to privacy implicit in the accumulation of vast amounts of personal information in computerized data banks or other massive government files.... The right to collect and use such data for public purposes is typically accompanied by a concomitant statutory or regulatory duty to avoid unwarranted disclosures. Recognizing that in some circumstances that duty arguably has its roots in the Constitution, nevertheless New York's statutory scheme, and its implementing administrative procedures, evidence a proper concern with, and protection of, the individual's interest in privacy. We therefore need not, and do not, decide any question which might be presented by the unwarranted disclosure of accumulated private data — whether intentional or unintentional — or by a system that did not contain comparable security provisions....

[concurring opinions by Justices Brennan and Stewart omitted.]

NOTES

1. In Planned Parenthood of Central Missouri v. Danforth, supra, the Supreme Court rejected a challenge to Missouri's statutory requirement that extensive records be maintained by physicians and health facilities as to all abortions, including first trimester abortions. Justice Blackmun's opinion noted, however, that the Missouri scheme "perhaps approach[ed] impermissible limits."

2. In Nixon v. Administrator, General Services Admin., 433 U.S. 425 (1977), the Court held that the Presidential Recordings and Materials Act, 44 U.S.C. §2107, requiring that Presidential materials and tapes be handed over to the Administrator of the General Services Administration, did not violate President Nixon's informational privacy rights. Nixon had a legitimate expectation of privacy with regard to the personal

communications contained within the vast amount of materials in question, but the screening process established by the law, regulations controlling access to the papers, and the small amount of private material in the mass of public material, made the Act's provisions a minimal and justifiable intrusion.

3. Since Whalen, several lower courts have addressed similar issues with similar results. See Caulfield v. Board of Education, 583 F.2d 605 (2d Cir. 1978) (ethnic background questions as part of a plan to end segregation in teacher assignments a justifiable intrusion into privacy); Schachter v. Whalen, 581 F.2d 35 (2d Cir. 1978) (medical conduct board subpoena of records of patients using laetrile does not violate Whalen where a coding system is employed to protect confidentiality); McKenna v. Farge, 451 F. Supp. 1355 (D.N.J. 1978) (psychological tests to applicants for fireman constituted a justified intrusion into privacy); DuPont v. Finkea, 442 F. Supp. 821 (D.W. Va. 1977) (tumor registry); Crain v. Krehbiel, 443 F. Supp. 202 (N.D. Cal. 1977) (drug enforcement agency's threats to reveal informant's drug involvement unless informant cooperated not a violation of privacy rights); Pollard v. Cockrell, 578 F.2d 1002 (5th Cir. 1978) (ordinance requiring massage parlors to keep appointment books listing names and addresses of clients a justifiable intrusion under Whalen). The Pollard case suggested the applicability of a "rational relationship" test under Whalen. But see Plante v. Gonzalez, 575 F.2d 1119 (5th Cir. 1978), indicating greater scrutiny under a "balancing" test. See also, Wilson v. California Health Facilities Commn., 167 Cal. Rptr. 801 (1980) (zone of privacy under Whalen not invaded by statute requiring public disclosure of detailed financial statements of health care facilities); General Motors Corp. v. Director of OSHA, 636 F.2d 163 (6th Cir. 1980) (OSHA subpoena for medical records as part of research study does not violate Whalen); Minnesota Medical Assn. v. State, 274 N.W.2d 84 (Minn. 1978) (refusing to enjoin publication of names of doctors, clinics, and hospitals performing abortions for persons on medical assistance. An especially interesting case involving a claim of a right of access to allegedly private information is Alma Society, Inc. v. Mellon, 601 F.2d 1225 (2d Cir. 1979) (upholding N.Y. statute sealing adoption records against challenge by adult adoptees who wish to learn names of their natural parents).

Cases upholding informational privacy claims after Whalen include: Wynn v. Scott, 449 F. Supp. 1302 (N.D. Ill. 1978) (state law requiring the listing in vital statistics of names of women obtaining abortions after 20 weeks of pregnancy constitutes an invasion of women's privacy rights); United States v. Westinghouse Electric Corp., 638 F.2d 570 (3d Cir. 1980) (employee medical records within zone of privacy under Whalen); Application of A and M, 61 App. Div. 2d 426, 403 N.Y.S.2d 375 (4th Dept. 1978) (some communications between parents and minor child within context of family relationship constitutionally protected from grand jury subpoena into arson allegedly caused by child); Fadjo

v. Coon, 633 F.2d 1172 (5th Cir. 1981) (informational privacy rights violated if prosecutor obtained private information in confidence in the course of a murder investigation and subsequently revealed it to credit investigators); In re B, 394 A.2d 419 (Pa. 1978) (state and federal constitutions prohibit doctors from being compelled to disclose records of in-patient psychiatric treatment to juvenile court seeking information regarding mother's treatment); Byron, Harless, Inc. v. State, 360 So. 2d 83 (Fla. Dist. Ct. of App. 1978) (disclosure of psychologists' reports in search for managing director of public authority would violate applicants' privacy rights); cf. Albright v. United States, 631 F.2d 915 (D.C. Cir. 1980) (federal Privacy Act does not permit Social Security Administration to keep videotape records of employee complaints about work-related grievances since complaints are exercise of First Amendment rights); Falcon v. Alaska Public Offices Commn., 570 P.2d 469 (Alaska 1977) (Alaska constitution violated by conflict of interest law when applied to require reporting of names of patients of psychiatrists and psychologists and of physicians treating sex problems or venereal disease).

Laws requiring public officials to disclose sources of income and financial holdings have generally been upheld after Whalen. See Plante v. Gonzalez, 575 F.2d 1119 (5th Cir. 1978); Duplantier v. United States, 606 F.2d 654 (5th Cir. 1979); Opinion of the Justices, 376 N.E.2d 810 (Mass. 1978); Harless v. State, 360 So. 2d 83 (Fla. 1978); Hasting & Sons Publishing Co. v. City Treasurer, 375 N.E.2d 299 (Mass. 1978); Hays v. Wood, 78 Cal. App. 3d 351, 144 Cal. Reptr. 456 (1978); Gideon v. Alabama State Ethics Commn., 379 So. 2d 570 (Ala. 1980); see also, O'Brien v. Digrazzia, 544 F.2d 543 (1st Cir. 1976); Walsh v. Montgomery County, 424 U.S. 901 (1976), dismissing the appeal from 336 A.2d 97 (Md. 1975). But see American Federation of Government Employees v. Schlesinger, 443 F. Supp. 431 (1978) (Department of Energy questionnaire to employees designed to reveal holdings in energy related businesses violates privacy rights).

(839) [1043]

NOTES

1.b. [Add to second paragraph] In Whalen v. Roe, supra, the Supreme Court reversed the decision of the district court, on remand, holding the state law unconstitutional.

(844) [1048]

NOTES

2. [penultimate paragraph continued] The Supreme Court reversed the court of appeals decision in Davis v. Paul. See Paul v. Davis, 424

U.S. 639 (1976). Justice Rehnquist's opinion for the Court responded to plaintiff's informational privacy claim as follows:

"While there is no 'right of privacy' found in any specific guarantee of the Constitution, the Court has recognized that 'zones of privacy' may be created by more specific constitutional guarantees and thereby impose limits upon government power. . . .

Respondent's case, however, comes within none of these areas. He does not seek to suppress evidence seized in the course of an unreasonable search. . . . And our other 'right of privacy' cases, while defying categorical description, deal generally with substantive aspects of the Fourteenth Amendment. . . .

"Respondent's claim is far afield from this line of decisions. He claims constitutional protection against the disclosure of the fact of his arrest on a shoplifting charge. His claim is based, not upon any challenge to the State's ability to restrict his freedom of action in a sphere contended to be 'private,' but instead on a claim that the State may not publicize a record of an official act such as an arrest. None of our substantive privacy decisions hold this or anything like this, and we decline to enlarge them in this manner." Justices Brennan and Marshall dissented.

[1052]

[REFERENCES]

On informational privacy generally, see Government Information and the Rights of Citizens, 73 Mich. L. Rev. 971 (1975); Hanus & Relyea, A Policy Assessment of the Privacy Act of 1974, 25 Am. U.L. Rev. 555 (1976); Swan, Privacy and Record Keeping: Remedies for the Misuse of Accurate Information, 54 N.C.L. Rev. 585 (1976); Comment, Barber, The California Public Records Act: the Public's Right of Access to Governmental Information, 7 Pac. L.J. 105 (1976).

On the right to privacy and records such as arrest records, student records, and medical records, see Smith, The Public Dissemination of Arrest Records and the Right to Reputation: The Effect of Paul v. Davis on Individual Rights, 5 Am. J. Crim. L. 72 (1977); Cudlipp, The Family Educational Rights and Privacy Act Two Years Later, 11 U. Rich. L. Rev. 33 (1976); Medical Data Privacy, 25 Buffalo L. Rev. 491 (1976); Smith, Constitutional Privacy in Psychotherapy, 49 Geo. Wash. L. Rev. 1 (1980); Note, Federal Protection of Employment Record Privacy, 18 Harv. J. Legis. 207 (1981).

Chapter Thirteen

The Right of Franchise

A. JUDICIAL PROTECTION OF THE RIGHT TO VOTE

(page 868) [1074]

NOTES

2.a. In Cheyenne River Sioux Tribe v. Andrus, 566 F.2d 1085 (8th Cir. 1977), the 8th Circuit ruled that the provisions of the Twenty-Sixth Amendment superseded tribal voting age limitations if the tribe elected to proceed pursuant to the Indian Reorganization Act.

(page 871) [1076]

NOTES

2.f. In Holt Civic Club v. City of Tuscaloosa, 439 U.S. 60 (1978), the Court upheld the constitutionality of denying the vote to residents of contiguous suburbs falling within the police and fire jurisdiction of a municipality. The Court rejected the notion that a right to vote was triggered by the imposition of police and fire jurisdiction over a given area, pointing out that laws inevitably have an effect on nonresidents. The dissenters argued that by imposing police and fire jurisdiction over an area the city had de facto annexed it. In Ball v. James, 101 S. Ct. 1811 (1981), a sharply divided Court sustained an Arizona law that permitted landowners to vote according to their acreage in a water conservation district election, despite the district's role as a major supplier of electricity and water to Phoenix.

In Symm v. United States, 99 S. Ct. 1006 (1979), aff'g 445 F. Supp. 1245 (S.D. Tex. 1978), the court affirmed an injunction aimed at a questionnaire which subjected college students to a searching investigation of domicile. The court noted that the questionnaire was part of a discriminatory policy designed to prevent college students (who were predominantly black) from voting in the town elections.

In City of Mobile v. Bolden, 446 U.S. 55 (1980), a deeply divided Court upheld multimember districting against Fourteenth and Fifteenth Amendment challenges, holding that a multimember district was valid unless plaintiffs "prove that the disputed plan was conceived or operated as a purposeful device to further racial discrimination." See also Williams v. Brown, 446 U.S. 236 (1980). The plurality ruled that a challenge by a racial minority to a multimember district, whether premised on the Fourteenth or Fifteenth Amendments, could succeed only if the plaintiffs established an intent to use the multimember districting device to disenfranchise the racial minority. Moreover, the plurality apparently ruled that the effect of a multimember scheme, while some evidence of discriminatory intent, was not sufficient to justify a finding of such intent. The plurality remanded to the district court for specific findings on the issue of purposeful discrimination. Justices Marshall and Brennan dissented, arguing that, when the allocation of fundamental rights was at stake, a scheme's discriminatory effect was sufficient to invalidate it. Justices Blackmun, White, Brennan, and Marshall also argued that even if discriminatory intent were a necessary element, the effect of the scheme, coupled with certain aspects of its administration, justified the district court's finding that discriminatory purpose existed. Justice Blackmun concurred in the remand, however, since he believed the remedial decree to have been unnecessarily broad. Since Justices Marshall, Brennan, White, and Blackmun seem prepared to apply a relatively relaxed standard of proof on the issue of discriminatory purpose, while Chief Justice Burger and Justices Stewart, Powell, and Rehnquist appear to demand some direct evidence of purposeful discrimination, Justice Stevens holds the balance of power. Unfortunately, his position is not promising. According to Justice Stevens, even a finding of some purposeful discrimination will not invalidate a multimember scheme that is otherwise supported by substantial policies. Central to Justice Stevens' thesis is his insistence that a single standard govern all challenges to multimember districting, whether or not the challenger is a member of a racial minority.

In Rogers v. Lodge, 50 U.S.L.W. 5041 (1982), Chief Justice Burger and Justice O'Connor joined Justices Marshall, Brennen, Blackmun, and White in affirming a finding that proscribed intent existed in maintaining an at large system of government. The relaxed standard of proof endorsed in Rogers coupled with the passage of the amended Voting Rights Act, which adopts an "effect" as opposed to an "intent" standard, dramatically reduces the practical effect of City of Mobile v. Bolden.

(page 872) [1078]

2.f.(2) [continued] Americans residing abroad have been provided substantial federal voting guarantees by The Overseas Citizen's Voting

Rights Act of 1975. 42 U.S.C. §1973dd. However, their right to vote in state and local elections continues to turn on the vagaries of local domicil law.

In Democratic Party v. LaFollette, 101 S. Ct. 1010 (1981), the Court ruled that delegates to a political party nominating convention who were selected pursuant to a primary open to nonmembers of the party cannot be bound to follow the results of the primary in violation of party rules. In Heavey v. Chapman, 611 P.2d 1256 (Wash. Sup. Ct. 1980), the constitutionality of an open primary was sustained. Conversely, in Nader v. Schaffer, 417 F. Supp. 837 (D. Conn. 1976), the court once again sustained the constitutionality of primaries open only to members of the political party in question. The court rejected plaintiff's argument that "closed" primaries discriminated against independent voters by freezing them out of the nominating process. In Lefkowitz v. Cunningham, 431 U.S. 801 (1977), the Court invalidated a statute mandating the removal of a party official from office as a penalty for claiming the Fifth Amendment.

(page 874) [1080]

NOTES

2.i. [continued] In Shepherd v. Trevina, 575 F.2d 1110 (5th Cir. 1978), the Fifth Circuit ruled that although a state possessed the power to disenfranchise felons, it could not draw irrational distinctions among ex-felons for voting purposes. However, the court found that a Texas law that banned federal felons from voting, while permitting Texas felons to regain voting rights, was rationally related to the advancement of a legitimate state purpose and, thus, valid. In Allen v. Ellisor, 664 F.2d 391 (4th Cir. 1980), the court sustained the validity of South Carolina's felon disenfranchisement statute. See also, Manhattan State Citizen's Group v. Bass, 524 F. Supp. 1270 (S.D.N.Y. 1981) (invalidating ban on voting by persons committed to mental institutions who have not been adjudicated "incompetent").

(page 875) [1081]

NOTES

2.k. [continued] Michigan has enacted a registration provision which authorizes high school officials to enroll qualified students as they attain voting age. On the other hand, Ohio voters have repealed Ohio's mail registration statute by referendum. The Federal Election Campaign Act, discussed infra, permits corporations and labor unions to sponsor voter registration drives and to distribute voter registration material, including mail registration material.

In Michaelson v. Booth, 437 F. Supp. 439 (D.R.I. 1977), the court enjoined the holding of an election on a Jewish holiday.

In Kimble v. Swackhamer, 584 P.2d 161 (1978), Nevada's decision to hold a nonbinding preference referendum on the ERA was held to be consistent with Article V.

B. JUDICIAL PROTECTION OF THE RIGHT TO RUN FOR OFFICE

(page 886) [1092]

NOTES

1. [continued] The right of an independent to run for office and to appear on the ballot was recognized in McCarthy v. Briscoe, 429 U.S. 1317 (1976) (independent candidacy for Presidency upheld); McCarthy v. Tribbitt, 421 F. Supp. 1193 (D. Del. 1976) (same); McCarthy v. Kirkpatrick, 420 F. Supp. 366 (W.D. Mo. 1976) (same); Exon v. McCarthy, 429 U.S. 972 (1976) (same). See also, Lendall v. Jernigan, 424 F. Supp. 951 (E.D. Ark. 1977) (requirement that independent candidate for governor secure signatures equal to 10 percent of last election invalid). In Hudler v. Austin, 419 F. Supp. 1002 (E.D. Mich. 1976), aff'd sub nom. Allen v. Austin, 430 U.S. 924 (1977), the court sustained a requirement that a new political party poll .3 percent of the vote at an open primary in order to obtain a place on the ballot.

In Greenberg v. Bolger, 497 F. Supp. 756 (E.D.N.Y. 1980), the court invalidated a postal rate structure that favored the major parties. In Bachrach v. Secretary of Commonwealth, 415 N.E.2d 832 (Mass. Sup. Ct. 1980), a provision barring the use of the term *Independent* on the ballot was invalidated. However, in Minnesota 5th Congressional District Independent Republican Party v. Minnesota, 295 N.W.2d 650 (Minn. Sup. Ct. 1979), a law forbidding independents from receiving aid from a political party was upheld. See also, Anderson v. Celbrezze, 664 F.2d 554 (6th Cir. 1981) (upholding Ohio law requiring Independents to announce by March, although major parties need not hold primary until August). The Supreme Court has scheduled argument in Anderson early in the 1982 term.

In McDaniel v. Paty, 435 U.S. 618 (1978), the Court upheld the right of a clergyman to run for office by invalidating a Tennessee prohibition on a clergyman serving as a delegate to a constitutional convention. The majority of the Court analyzed the Tennessee prohibition as an interference with the free exercise of religion. Justice White approached the issue as a deprivation of the right to vote.

In Morial v. Judiciary Commission of Louisiana, 565 F.2d 295 (5th

Cir. 1977), the Fifth Circuit upheld the constitutionality of a Louisiana requirement that a sitting judge resign in order to seek elective office.

See also, Signorelli v. Evans, 657 F.2d 853 (2d Cir. 1980) (upholding requirement that state judge resign to run for Congress). In Clements v. Fashing, 50 U.S.L.W. 4869 (1982), the Court upheld a Texas statute which provided for the automatic resignation of certain officials to serve out their terms of office before running for any other office. In Allen v. Board of Education, 584 S.W.2d 408 (Ky. App. 1979), a requirement that school board employees take a mandatory leave if they run for office was struck down. In Rodriguez v. Popular Democratic Party, 50 U.S.L.W. 4869 (1982), the Court upheld a statute delegating the power to fill a vacancy to the political party to which the incumbent had belonged.

(page 888) [1094]

NOTES

2.d. [continued] In Chappelle v. Greater Baton Rouge Airport District, 431 U.S. 159 (1977), a requirement that appointed officials own property in the parish in which they serve was invalidated.

See also, Matthews v. Atlantic City, 417 A.2d 1011 (N.J. 1980) (invalidating durational residency requirement on Equal Protection grounds).

(page 890) [1096]

NOTES

2.g. [continued] In Illinois State Board of Elections v. SWP, 440 U.S. 173 (1979), the Court invalidated an Illinois provision that required minor parties to secure more signatures to get on the ballot in Chicago than to get on the ballot statewide. The Court ruled that the Chicago ballot access requirement advanced no rational purpose.

In McLain v. Meier, 612 F.2d 349 (8th Cir. 1979), North Dakota's minor party ballot access law that required 15,000 signatures (3.3 percent) 90 days before the primary and 150 days before the general election was invalidated.

In McCarthy v. Kirkpatrick, 420 F. Supp. 366 (W.D. Mo. 1976), an independent candidate filing requirement 188 days before the election was invalidated. See also, Solery v. Tucker, 399 F. Supp. 1258 (E.D. Pa. 1975), aff'd, 424 U.S. 959 (1976). However, in Mandel v. Bradley, 432 U.S. 173 (1977), the Court vacated a District Court decision invalidating a requirement that an independent candidate submit petitions 70 days before primary day containing signatures equal to 3 percent of the vote. In Morritt v. New York, — F. Supp. — (S.D.N.Y. 1978), the court sus tained a New York provision requiring a candidate for statewide office to secure 20,000 signatures, with at least 100 from one half the state's Congressional Districts.

In Illinois State Board of Elections v. Sangmeister, 565 F.2d 460 (7th Cir. 1977), the practice of permitting election clerks to list their own party first on the ballot was invalidated. However, in Board of Elections v. Libertarian Party, 591 F.2d 23 (7th Cir. 1979) the court upheld a practice of listing major parties first.

See also, McLain v. Meier, 612 F.2d 349 (8th Cir. 1979) (invalidating incumbent-first rule but upholding bloc listing of independents).

C. JUDICIAL PROTECTION OF THE RIGHT TO FAIR REPRESENTATION

(page 902) [1108]

NOTES

2. [continued] In Connor v. Finch, 431 U.S. 407 (1977), a judicially promulgated reapportionment plan for the Mississippi legislature exhibiting population variations of from 16-19 percent was invalidated by the Supreme Court. The Court declined to accept the desire to adhere to county lines as a sufficient justification for substantial population deviations. The Court, once again, noted that stricter standards govern a judicially imposed reapportionment scheme that would govern a legislative scheme. Thus, it is unclear whether a plan similar to the plan invalidated in Connor would survive scrutiny if it had been legislatively promulgated. In Briscoe v. Escalante, 435 U.S. 901 (1978), a judicially promulgated plan with a 7.7 percent population deviation was set aside in favor of an equally practical plan with only a 2.2 percent deviation. In Wise v. Lipscomb, 437 U.S. 535 (1978), the Court ruled that a plan promulgated by the legislature in response to a judicial invalidation of the preexisting scheme remains a legislative plan for the purposes of reviewing standards even though it is subsequently adopted by the court. In Wyche v. Madison Police Parish, 635 F.2d 1151 (5th Cir. 1980), the court noted that a judicially proposed plan was not required to achieve a racial proportional representation as long as it was fair.

In Marchioro v. Chaney, 442 U.S. 191 (1979), the Court declined to invalidate a malapportioned party central committee despite its role in the nominating process because the statute did not mandate that nominations be made by the central committee. It is difficult to reconcile the Court's refusal in Marchioro to review a "permissive" nominating process which allegedly violates the equal protection clause with the Court's vigorous protection of black voting rights in Terry v. Adams, 345 U.S.

461 (1953). Marchioro is symptomatic of a narrow view of state action that may be re-emerging on the Court. Compare, Flagg Bros., Inc. v. Brooks, 436 U.S. 149 (1978), and Babbitt v. United Farm Workers, 442 U.S. 289 (1979), with Marchioro v. Chaney, 442 U.S. 191 (1979).

See also, Democratic Party v. LaFollette, 101 S. Ct. 1010 (1980) (upholding internal party rules refusing to give binding effect to open primaries). The Court has agreed to hear a claim of political gerrymandering in connection with the reapportionment of the New Jersey Congressional delegation during the 1982 Term.

(page 905) [1111]

NOTES

1. [continued] In Ball v. James, 101 S. Ct. 1811 (1980), the Court read Salyer broadly and ruled that the one man – one vote principle did not apply to an Arizona water district that supplied electricity and water to one half of the state. However, in Choudhry v. Free, 131 Cal. Rptr. 654, 552 P.2d 438 (1976), the California Supreme Court read Salyer narrowly and ruled that irrigation districts were not limited-purpose governmental units. Similarly, in Township of Franklin v. Board of Education of the North Hunterdon Regional High School, 74 N.J. 345, 378 A.2d 218 (1977), school boards were deemed covered by the one person–one vote doctrine. In Chappelle v. Greater Baton Rouge Airport District, 431 U.S. 159 (1977), a property qualification for service as an appointee of the Airport District was invalidated.

(page 906) [1112]

In Concerned Citizens v. Pine Creek Conservancy, 46 U.S.L.W. 3734 (1978), the court reaffirmed that judicial elections are not subject to the one person — one vote principle.

(page 912) [1118]

NOTES

3. [continued] In East Carroll Parish School Board v. Marshall, 424 U.S. 636 (1976), the Court reiterated its reluctance to approve judicially promulgated reapportionment plans utilizing multimember districts. See also, Wallace v. House, 538 F.2d 1138 (5th Cir. 1976). However, in Beer v. United States, 425 U.S. 130 (1976), a partial multimember councilmanic system for New Orleans was approved despite a challenge under the Voting Rights Act. Voting Rights Act cases are discussed infra. In City of Mobile v. Bolden 446 U.S. 55 (1980), the Court ruled that

multimember districting does not violate the Fourteenth and Fifteenth Amendments in the absence of an intent to disenfranchise a submerged racial minority. The impact of at large districting on racial minorities was noted in Connor v. Finch, 431 U.S. 407 (1977), when the Court applauded the end of multimember districting in Mississippi.

(page 918) [1124]

NOTES

1. [continued] The extent to which a jurisdiction may engage in benign racial gerrymandering to assure adequate minority representation was considered by the Court in United Jewish Organizations of Williamsburgh, Inc. v. Carey, 430 U.S. 144 (1977). In UJO v. Carey, New York's first attempt to re-district Kings County had been rejected by the Attorney General under the pre-clearance mechanism of the Voting Rights Act, discussed infra. A second reapportionment attempt, aimed at assuring a strong black majority in the 14th Congressional District, was challenged by Jewish voters who were adversely affected by the new district lines. The Court, struggling for a rationale, upheld the benign racial gerrymander as a good faith attempt to comply with the Voting Rights Act. The extent of permissible benign racial gerrymandering is discussed in Marshall v. Edwards, 582 F.2d 927 (5th Cir. 1978).

(page 919) [1125]

NOTES

2. [continued] In Connor v. Finch, 431 U.S. 407 (1977), Justice Stewart implied that whenever a reapportionment plan appears to depart from principles of contiguity and numerical equality to the detriment of minority voters, an inference of purposeful racial gerrymandering may arise. Accordingly, whenever a departure occurs which may be detrimental to minority voters, it must be clearly shown to have been motivated by nonracial factors.

In Beer v. United States, 425 U.S. 130 (1976), the Court continued to construe the substantive reach of Section 5 narrowly. In City of Richmond v. United States, 422 U.S. 358 (1975), the Court had upheld an annexation which transformed Richmond from a city having a black voting majority to a city in which blacks were a voting minority. In Beer, the Court was confronted with a New Orleans councilmanic apportionment which diluted the potential black vote. Justice Stewart, writing for the Court, ruled that as long as blacks were better off under the new plan than they had been under the old plan, Section 5 pre-clearance could not be refused, even though alternative plans existed which would be more likely to enhance minority political power. Thus, Beer establishes a "non-retrogression" principles that forbids clearance for election law changes that leave blacks worse off than before but that requires Section 5 clearance so long as the plan incrementally improves the lot of minority voters. Of course, the resulting plan remains subject to review under constitutional standards. By adopting a "non-retrogression" reading of Section 5, rather than a "best possible alternative" reading, the Court has deprived the Attorney General of substantial leverage in negotiating with subdivisions seeking pre-clearance. Under Beer's nonretrogression principles, it is doubtful whether the initial apportionment plan in UJO v. Carey, supra, could have been denied pre-clearance. In United States v. Mississippi, 444 U.S. 1050 (1980), the Court suggested that the measuring point for the nonretrogression text was the last legislative plan rather than a more favorable judicially imposed interim plan.

In City of Rome v. United States, 446 U.S. 156 (1980), the Supreme Court reaffirmed the constitutionality of the "effect" standard of the pre-clearance provisions of the Voting Rights Act. Specifically, the Court held that although the Fourteenth and Fifteenth Amendments prohibit only purposeful discrimination, Congress could condition pre-clearance on either the purpose or the effect of the challenged act. In addition, the Court held that once a state is brought within the coverage of the pre-clearance provisions of the Voting Rights Act, political subdivisions of the State may not secure an exemption from pre-clearance merely by demonstrating the absence of discrimination in that subdivision. Finally, the Rome Court ruled that the 60-day time limit within which the Attorney General must grant or deny pre-clearance begins running anew each time the entity seeking pre-clearance submits additional information. In Garcia v. Uvalde County, 439 U.S. 1059 (1979), aff'g without opinion, 455 F. Supp. 101 (W.D. Tex. 1978), the Court upheld a ruling that once an applicant for pre-clearance informs the Attorney General that no additional data exists, the Attorney General must act in 60 days or pre-clearance will be deemed granted. In Dougherty County Board of Education v. White, 439 U.S. 32 (1978), the Court ruled that once a subdivision (such as a county) becomes subject to pre-clearance, all entities located within the county (such as school boards) become subject to pre-clearance, despite the fact that they do not conduct voter registration. Thus, a change in Board of Education leave policy for teachers seeking public office was deemed subject to pre-clearance because the Board was located in a political entity subject to pre-clearance. In Wilkes County v. United States, 439 U.S. 999 (1980), aff'g without opinion, 450 F. Supp. 1171 (D.D.C. 1979), the Court affirmed a ruling that the burden of proof rests with the applicant for pre-clearance on both the purpose and effect of the act in question. In Hathorn

v. Lovorn, 50 U.S.L.W. 4664 (1982), the Court ruled that state courts asked to implement a new provision of state law are empowered to determine whether pre-clearance was required.

In Holloway v. Wise, 439 U.S. 1110 (1979), the Court affirmed without opinion a ruling of the district court of the Middle District of Georgia that a denial of pre-clearance blocks the affected change from going into effect. Finally, in United States v. Georgia, 436 U.S. 941 (1978), the Court appeared to approve a pre-clearance submission procedure pursuant to which Georgia submitted its entire Election Code to the Attorney General, with a blanket request for pre-clearance of all changes. See generally, MacCoon, The Enforcement of the Pre-clearance Requirement of Section 5 of the VRA of 1965, 29 Catholic U.L. Rev. 107 (1979), and Berry and Dye, The Discriminatory Effect of At-Large Elections, 7 Fla. State L. Rev. 85 (1979).

For a representative lower court application of the pre-clearance provisions, see, Heggins v. City of Dallas, 469 F. Supp. 739 (N.D. Tex. 1979) (pre-clearance required for change in power and status of at-large representatives; injunction granted against election until approval granted). But see, Charlton County Board of Education v. United States, 459 F. Supp. 530 (D.D.C. 1978) (injunction denied because of eleventh-hour nature of case); Woods v. Hamilton, 473 F. Supp. 641 (D.S.C. 1979) (failure of Attorney General to interpose objection grants pre-clearance).

See also, Herron v. Koch, 523 F. Supp. 167 (E.D.N.Y. 1981) (enjoining New York City's 1981 City Council elections for failure to secure pre-clearance of reapportionment and modification of election districts).

3. In Briscoe v. Bell, 432 U.S. 404 (1977), the Court ruled that the decision of the Attorney General that a state falls within the language minority provisions of the Voting Rights Act of 1975 is not subject to judicial review. Similarly, in Morris v. Gressette, 432 U.S. 491 (1977), the Court held that the failure of the Attorney General to interpose an objection to a proposed law under Section 5 of the Voting Rights Act was not subject to judicial review.

4. Despite the narrow construction of the substantive reach of Section 5, the courts have continued to construe its procedural applicability very broadly. In United States v. Board of Commissioners of Sheffield, Alabama, 435 U.S. 110 (1978), and Dougherty County Board of Education v. White, 439 U.S. 32 (1979), the Court ruled that once a subdivision becomes subject to pre-clearance, all political entities within that subdivision seeking to amend a law or practice affecting voting must seek pre-clearance, even if they have never conducted voter registration. Thus once a county becomes subject to the Voting Rights Act, school boards located within the county may not require employees to take an unpaid leave of absence before running for office without first obtaining pre-clearance.

5. In Wilkes County v. United States, 450 Supp. 1171 (D.D.C. 1978),

aff'd. 439 U.S. 999 (1979), the court noted the burden of proof which rests on a subdivision seeking pre-clearance. In Garcia v. Uvalde County, 439 U.S. 1059 (1979), the Court noted that the Attorney General must respond to a request for pre-clearance within 60 days. The court declined to permit the Attorney General to toll the 60 days by repeated demands for more information. Once a covered subdivision informs the Attorney General that no additional information exists, the 60-day period may not be tolled. In United States v. Georgia, 436 U.S. 941 (1978), the Court upheld a submission procedure pursuant to which Georgia submitted its entire election code to the Attorney General with a blanket request for pre-clearance of all changes. Once pre-clearance is denied, it blocks the affected change from going into effect, together with any other changes which are closely-bound up with the challenged provision. Holloway v. Wise, 439 U.S. 1110 (1979). In McDaniel v. Sanchez, 448 U.S. 1318 (1980), the Court ruled that a legislatively proposed reapportionment plan enacted to replace one that had been judicially invalidated, which is approved by the court, must also be submitted for pre-clearance.

In Calderon v. McGee, 589 F.2d 909 (5th Cir. 1979), the Fifth Circuit held that failure by the Attorney General to object to a judicially promulgated plan did not constitute pre-clearance. Once a legislative plan is promulgated, even under judicial pressure, it must receive Section 5 pre-clearance. See, e.g., Wise v. Lipscomb, 437 U.S. 535 (1978). The complex question of whether a plan is judicial or legislative and the differing standards applicable to each may be charted through Wise v. Lipscomb, 437 U.S. 535 (1978), on remand, sub nom., Lipscomb v. Wise, 583 F.2d 212 (5th Cir. 1978); related proceeding sub nom., Heggins v. City of Dallas, 469 F. Supp. 739 (N.D. Tex. 1979). See also, Calderon v. McGee, 589 F.2d 909 (5th Cir. 1979).

6. A court may set aside an election held under provisions which failed to receive pre-clearance. However, courts have been reluctant to do so when the impact of the challenged provision was slight and no intent to avoid the Voting Rights Act appeared to have existed. Berry v. Doles, 438 U.S. 190 (1978).

Insert before d. Refusal to Seat Duly Elected Representatives:

In City of Eastlake v. Forest City Enterprises, 426 U.S. 668 (1976), the Court sustained the validity of a provision requiring zoning variances to be approved in a super-majority (55 percent) referendum. Moreover, in Town of Lockport v. Citizens for Community Action, 430 U.S. 259 (1977), the Court reversed the District Court and upheld a dual majority scheme, requiring separate ratification by rural and urban voters of a suggested change in the structure of local government affecting each group. See also, Parker v. Merlino, 646 F.2d 848 (3d Cir. 1981) (upholding cloture procedure in legislature).

(page 921) [1127]

NOTE — FEDERAL JUDICIAL REMEDIES FOR VIOLATION OF FRANCHISE RIGHTS

[continued] It is now clear that reapportionment plans promulgated by a court will be reviewed more closely by the Supreme Court than would a legislatively promulgated scheme. The existence of multimember districts or substantial population deviations, even if explained by weighty local considerations, will probably doom a judicially promulgated plan. E.g., Connor v. Finch, 431 U.S. 407 (1977) (16-19 percent deviation invalid, even though necessary in order to adhere to county lines); East Carroll Parish School Board v. Marshall, 424 U.S. 636 (1976) (multimember districts in judicially promulgated plan invalid).

Moreover, in Connor v. Finch, (1977), the Court admonished judges engaged in the promulgation of reapportionment plans to avoid even the appearance of unfairness to minority voters.

[D]. CONGRESSIONAL PROTECTION OF THE FRANCHISE

(page 921) [1143]

NOTE — VOTING RIGHTS ACT AMENDMENTS OF 1975

1. The Voting Rights Act amendments of 1975 provide substantial protection to language minorities by requiring bi-lingual elections in any jurisdiction in which a language minority (a) constitutes 5 percent of the population and (b) has a literacy rate lower than the general population. A listing of the areas designated by the Attorney General as falling within the bi-lingual election provisions of the 1975 Act is found in 42 Fed. Reg. 35971 (July 13, 1977).

2. In addition to providing for bi-lingual elections, the 1975 Act expanded the pre-clearance coverage of the Act by broadening the definition of "test of device" to include the holding of English language elections in jurisdictions with a 5 percent language minority in 1972. If such a jurisdiction exhibited a sub-50 percent turnout in 1972, it would fall under Section 5.

As of July 1, 1977, the following subdivisions, including all political entities located within the covered subdivision, must obtain pre-clearance of any change in law or practice affecting voting or running for office: *Alabama, Alaska, Arizona,*; four counties in *California* — Kings, Merced, Monterey, and Yuba; one county in *Colorado* — El Paso; five counties in *Florida* — Collier, Hardee, Hendry, Hillsborough, and Monroe; *Georgia*; one county in *Hawaii* — Honolulu; one county in *Idaho* —

Elmore; *Louisiana*; eighteen towns in *Maine* — Beddington, Carroll Plantation, Caswell Plantation, Charleston, Chelsea, Connor Unorganized Territory, Cutler, Limestone, Ludlow, Nashville Plantation, New Gloucester, Reed Plantation, Winter Harbor, and Woodland; nine towns in *Massachusetts* — Amherst, Ayer, Belchertown, Bourne, Harvard, Sandwich, Shirley, Sunderland, and Wrentham; ten towns in *New Hampshire* — Antrim, Benton, Boscawen, Millsfield Township, Newington, Pinkhams Grant, Rindge, Stewartstown, Stratford, and Unity; two townships in *Michigan* — Clyde and Buena Vista; *Mississippi*; three counties in *New York* — Bronx, Kings, and New York; 40 counties in *North Carolina* — Anson, Beaufort, Bertie, Bladen, Camden, Caswell, Chowen, Cleveland, Craven, Cumberland, Edgecomb, Franklin, Gatson, Gates, Granville, Greene, Guilford, Halifax, Harnett, Hertford, Hoke, Lee, Lenoir, Martin, Nash, Northhampton, Orslow, Pasquotank, Perquamins, Person, Pitt, Robeson, Rockingham, Scotland, Union, Vance, Wake, Washington, Wayne, and Wilson; two counties in *Oklahoma* — Choctaw and McCurtain; *South Carolina*; two counties in *South Dakota* — Shannon and Todd; *Virginia*; and *Texas*.

3. The Voting Rights Act has been re-enacted and extended to forbid electoral practices having the "effect" of denying the right to vote. In return for the expansion of its substantive coverage, the pre-clearance mechanism has been modified to permit covered subdivisions to "bail out" by demonstrating good faith effort to deal with past discrimination.

D[E]. REGULATION OF THE ELECTORAL PROCESS

(page 931) [1152]

NOTES

2. [continued] In Givhan v. Western Line Consolidated School District, 439 U.S. 410 (1979), the Court recognized that the First Amendment protected the private expression of views to a superior. However, although such private expression is entitled to First Amendment protection, the employee nevertheless risks dismissal if his or her expression destroys the ability to work with the superior. E.g., Roseman v. Indiana University, 520 F.2d 1364 (3d Cir. 1975); Sprague v. Fitzpatrick, 546 F.2d 560 (3d Cir. 1976).

In Elrod v. Burns, 427 U.S. 347 (1976), the Court invalidated patronage dismissals as a violation of associational rights. In Branti v. Finkel, 445 U.S. 507 (1980), the Court applied Elrod to bar the patronage dismissals of assistant county public defenders. See also, Brady v. Patterson, 515 F. Supp. 695 (N.D.N.Y. 1980) (employees whose terms have expired but who have been permitted to remain as holdovers entitled to Elrod protection). However, in Stegmaier v. Trammel, 597 F.2d 1027 (5th Cir. 1979), a Deputy County Clerk was deemed to be a policymaking position and, thus, exempt from Elrod. In Aufiero v. Clarke, 639 F.2d 49 (1st Cir. 1981), Elrod was deemed not to apply to actions taken prior to its announcement. See also, Ramey v. Harber, 599 F.2d 753 (4th Cir. 1978). In Shakman v. Democratic Org. of Cook County, 508 F. Supp. 1059 (N.D. Ill. 1979), the court ruled that patronage hiring practices provided an unfair advantage to the major political parties and discriminated against independents.

(page 934) [1157]

1. [continued] In Plante v. Gonzalez, 575 F.2d 1119 (5th Cir. 1978), Judge Wisdom recognized the existence of a constitutional right of privacy, but held that the state's interest in restoring faith in the electoral process justified a broad Florida statute requiring financial disclosure by candidates. Judge Wisdom's opinion collects the cases discussing the constitutionality of campaign disclosure laws. Recent cases involving disclosure requirements in connection with election campaigns include: Hays v. Wood, 603 P.2d 19 (1979) (rules requiring disclosure by lawyer and broker officials struck down because more stringent than other officials); Federal Election Commission v. Central Long Island Tax Reform Commission, 616 F.2d 45 (2d Cir. 1980) (John Birch Society pamphlet attacking tax consequences of Congressman's voting record does not fall within disclosure requirements of Act); New Jersey State Chamber of Commerce v. New Jersey Election Commission, 411 A.2d 168 (1980) (New Jersey disclosure law valid if restrictively construed to cover only substantial sums, direct contacts, and intentional acts). Federal Elections Commn. v. Machinists Non-Partisan Political League, — F.2d — (D.C. Cir. 1981) (Draft Kennedy Committee not subject to disclosure rules as long as Kennedy not yet a candidate).

(page 936) [1158]

In Buckley v. Valeo, 424 U.S. 1 (1976), the Court considered the constitutionality of the Federal Election Campaign Act. Drawing an analytically questionable line between "expenditures," which the Court treated as direct First Amendment activity, and "contributions," which the Court treated as indirect activity subject to governmental regulation, the Court:

(1) sustained the constitutionality of the Act's $1,000 limit on contributions to a given candidate for federal office in connection with a given election. A primary and general election are treated as two elections for the purpose of computing the ceiling;

(2) sustained the constitutionality of an aggregate ceiling of $25,000 in contributions to all candidates for federal office in any calendar year;

(3) sustained the constitutionality of a disclosure requirement in connection with all contributions or expenditures in excess of $10. Under current guidelines, however, only contributions in excess of $50 need be disclosed and the information is not made public unless the contributions exceed $100. Expenditures under $100 need not be reported;

(4) sustained the public financing of the Presidential election;

(5) invalidated the limitations on campaign expenditures imposed by the Act;

(6) invalidated the limitation on personal expenditures contained in the Act; and

(7) invalidated the exotic makeup of the Federal Election Commission.

NOTES

1. After Buckley, an individual may not contribute more than $1,000 to a federal candidate but may expend an unlimited amount of his own funds on a candidates behalf, as long as the expenditure is not under the candidate's direction and control. Moreover, an individual may contribute to an independent political committee that is not connected to the candidate's campaign.

In California Medical Association v. Federal Elections Commission, 101 S. Ct. 2712 (1981), the Court sustained a $5,000 ceiling on contributions to a multicandidate committee.

A candidate may continue to spend unlimited amounts of his personal funds on the election. See also, Common Cause v. Schmitt, 50 U.S.L.W. 4168 (1982) (invalidation of ceiling on expenditures by unauthorized Committee affirmed by equally divided Court); FEC v. Democratic Senatorial Campaign Committee, 50 U.S.L.W. 4001 (1981) (state and local committee designation of national committee as agent for expenditure purposes valid). See generally, Neuborne and Eisenberg, The Rights of Candidates and Voters (2d ed. 1979).

2. The Act provides for the public funding of Presidential campaigns. No provision is made for the funding of House or Senate campaigns. If a candidate for President elects to receive public funding, he subjects himself to a $50,000 personal expenditure ceiling and a campaign expenditure ceiling of $10 million for the primaries and $20 million for the general election. Expenditures on a candidate's behalf by persons and groups acting wholly independently of the campaign are not counted toward the expenditure ceiling. In order to qualify for a $20 million general election grant, a candidate must be the nominee of a political party which polled more than 25 percent of the vote in the last Presidential election. In order to qualify for the $5 million primary matching subsidy, a Presidential candidate must raise $100,000 (at least $5,000 in 20 states) in contributions of not more than $250. Once the

$100,000 is raised, a primary candidate becomes eligible for matching grants up to the $10,000,000 ceiling. Only the first $250 of any contribution is eligible for matching.

3. Candidates of parties which polled from 5 to 25 percent receive a pro rata general election grant based on the party's showing at the last election. Only three minor party candidates had polled 5 percent of the vote in this century: Eugene Debs (1900, 1908), Theodore Roosevelt (1912), and Robert LaFollette (1924). Candidates of parties polling less than 5 percent of the vote in the last Presidential election get no subsidy. However, if they poll more than 5 percent of the vote, they receive a retroactive subsidy. No provision is made for the payment of subsidies to independent candidates. The treatment of minor parties was sustained by the Court in Buckley. The campaign of John Anderson polled 6 percent of the vote in the 1980 Presidential election thus qualifying him for a post-election subsidy.

4. The Buckley court upheld the stringent disclosure requirements of the Act, even as applied to controversial minor parties. However, the Court held that if a party demonstrated that it was sufficiently controversial, it could receive a judicial exemption from disclosure to protect the anonymity of its adherents. The Socialist Workers Party has obtained such an exemption through 1982.

5. In the wake of Buckley, spending ceilings in political campaigns were invalidated in Hardie v. Fong Eu, 134 Cal. Rptr. 201, 556 P.2d 301 (1976), and Citizens for Jobs and Energy v. Fair Political Practices Committee, 16 Cal. 3d 671 (1976). See also, Sadowski v. Shevin, 345 So. 2d 330 (1977) (invalidating ban on advertising prior to qualification as candidate as a disguised expenditure ceiling). The right to display political posters was upheld in Baldwin v. Redwood City, 540 F.2d 1360 (9th Cir. 1976) (regulation of size of posters valid but ban on number of posters invalid as a disguised expenditure ceiling), and Orazio v. Town of North Hempstead, 426 F. Supp. 1144 (E.D.N.Y. 1977) (ban on political posters prior to six weeks before election invalid). For the right to display political billboards, see, Metromedia, Inc. v. City of San Diego, 101 S. Ct. 2882 (1981).

Contribution ceilings in connection with issue-oriented referenda were invalidated in Citizens Against Rent Control v. City of Berkeley, 50 U.S.L.W. 4071 (1982) ($250 ceiling) and Let's Help Florida v. McCrary, 621 F.2d 195 (5th Cir. 1980). See also National Right to Work Committee v. FEC, 50 U.S.L.W. 2163 (D.C. Cir. 1981) (contributors to non-stock-corporations deemed members for purposes of permitting solicitation of "member" only). In Federal Elections Commission v. Lance, 635 F.2d 1132 (5th Cir. 1980), the court treated bank loans that were not made in the ordinary course of business as improper corporate campaign contributions. See also, United States v. Operating Engineers, 638 F.2d 1161 (9th Cir. 1979) (Attorney General may prosecute without exhausting administrative sanctions); AFL-CIO v. Federal Elections Commn., 628 F.2d 97 (D.C. Cir. 1980) (no civil penalty for innocent error).

6. In Plante v. Gonzalez, 575 F.2d 1119 (5th Cir. 1978) a broad candidate financial disclosure law was upheld. Judge Wisdom's decision exhaustively canvasses the authorities. In Richman v. Shevin, 354 So. 2d 1200 (1977), the court sustained a contribution ceiling on gifts to an escrow fund to support all judicial candidates. In Bang v. Chase, 442 F. Supp. 758 (D. Minn. 1977), a tax check off device for financing the electoral process was sustained.

7. In CBS Inc. v. FCC, 101 S. Ct. 936 (1981), the Court sustained an FCC rule requiring broadcasters to sell time to candidates. However, in Kennedy for President Committee v. FCC, 636 F.2d 432 (D.C. Cir. 1980), the court ruled that a Presidential news conference did not trigger either the equal time or fairness doctrines. See also, Hirschkopf v. Snead, 475 F. Supp. 59 (E.D. Va. 1979). In Belluso v. Turner Commission Corp., 633 F.2d 393 (5th Cir. 1980), the court declined to recognize a private cause of action for violation of the equal time doctrine. See also, McGlyn v. New Jersey Public Broadcasting Authority, 50 U.S.L.W. 2308 (N.J. 1981) (upholding stringent state rules requiring balance in coverage of the election by state owned television station, but permitting station to broadcast statements of "leading" candidates).

(page 935) [1158]

FIRST NATIONAL BANK OF BOSTON v. BELLOTTI
435 U.S. 765 (1978)

[Reproduced supra in Chapter 8.]

NOTES

1. Despite First Natl. Bank of Boston v. Bellotti, the prohibition on corporate and union campaign contributions to federal elections continues to be enforced. However, the 1979 Act permits corporations and labor unions to establish voluntary, segregated funds (called Political Action Committees or PACs) for the purpose of making campaign contributions to federal candidates. Generally, corporate PACs may solicit funds from shareholders, executives, and administrative personnel; while union PACs may solicit from members. Employees may be solicited twice yearly by a corporate PAC, but the identity of all employee-contributors must be kept secret from the corporation. PACs may make contributions to campaigns (subject to the $1,000 ceiling or, if the PAC qualifies, a $5,000 ceiling) or may operate as independent committees

with no limits on expenditures. See, Kay v. FEC, 7 Media L. Rptr. 1474 (D.C. Cir. 1981) (newspaper's publication of comparative chart of candidates' positions is a news story, not a corporate campaign contribution).

2. In Anderson v. City of Boston, 380 N.E.2d 628, app. dism., 439 U.S. 1389 (1979), a state law barring Boston from expending funds on a referendum was sustained as necessary to protect dissenting taxpayers.

3. The Federal Election Campaign Act has spawned a bewildering array of regulations administered by the Federal Election Commission, which was reconstituted after its initial mode of appointment was invalidated in Buckley. The Commission issues interpretive rulings and regulations. In Clark v. Valeo, 559 F.2d 642 (D.D.C.), aff'd, 431 U.S. 950 (1977), the courts declined on ripeness grounds to pass on the constitutionality of the power of a single House of Congress to veto an FEC regulation. A valuable research tool in coping with the Act is The Campaign Law Reporter (Washington, D.C.). The Commission's current regulations are set forth in 11 C.F.R. The Commission also issues advisory opinions at the request of a candidate or any political committee. The advisory opinions are available from the Public Records Division of the Federal Election Commission. In Bread Political Action Committee v. FEC, 50 U.S.L.W. 4291 (1982), the Court read section 310(a) of the Act narrowly, and excluded trade associations from invoking expedited review mechanisms.

(page 942) [1164]

In Pennsylvania v. Wadzinski, 422 A.2d 124 (Pa. Sup. Ct. 1980), the court invalidated a prohibition on campaign charges made on the eve of an election. In Brown v. Hartlege, 50 U.S.L.W. 4359 (1982), the Court invalidated a statute which forbade a candidate from promising to lower his salary if elected. The Court resolved that the State interest in assuring equal access to office by rich and poor candidates could be served by prohibiting a diminution in salary during a term office.

Chapter Fourteen
Religious Freedom

B. THE ESTABLISHMENT CLAUSE

(page 953) [1177]

NOTES

6. [continued] Cromwell Property Owners Assn. v. Toffolon, 495 F. Supp. 915 (D. Conn. 1979) (upheld law authorizing partial reimbursement for transportation of students to private religious schools in a contiguous district); Springfield School District v. Pennsylvania Dept. of Education, 397 A.2d 1154 (Pa.), appeal dismissed, 443 U.S. 901 (1979) (upheld law requiring school districts to provide free transportation to students attending private nonprofit schools located within ten miles of the district).

(page 958) [1183]

NOTES

4. [continued] On appeal in Smith v. Smith, the Fourth Circuit reversed the district court decision and upheld the released-time program. 523 F.2d 121 (4th Cir. 1975). The program was conducted as follows: the religious organization did not enter the school to solicit students but contacted them by mail and then enrolled them from cards deposited by students at the public school; public school officials did not encourage attendance at the program but coordinated schedules with the religious officials to allow attendance. The Fourth Circuit, per Judge Winter, found that Zorach v. Clauson, 343 U.S. 306 (1952), was still viable authority and was indistinguishable from the instant case. Judge Winter noted three important common factors in Zorach and Smith: (1) the religious instruction program was not conducted in the public school,

(2) the program did not involve expenditure of public funds, (3) the public school did not promote the program.

See also, Lanner v. Wimmer, 463 F. Supp. 867 (N.D. Utah 1978) (struck down that part of a released-time program granting state credit for Old and New Testament courses because such were not planned and not taught strictly from historical, literary, or comparative viewpoints but were geared toward reinforcing religious beliefs).

(page 975) [1200]

NOTES

3. [continued] See Meltzer v. Board of Public Instruction of Orange County, Florida, 548 F.2d 559 (5th Cir. 1977), aff'd in part, rev'd in part on rehearing en banc, 577 F.2d 311 (5th Cir. 1978) (reversed district court and invalidated school board policy providing for morning meditation, opportunity for prayers, and Bible reading; affirmed by equally divided vote the district court's refusal to strike down guidelines for Bible distribution on school property and its dismissal, for lack of a case or controversy, of the challenge to a statute requiring teachers to inculcate Christian virtues "by precept and example").

5. [continued] See Gaines v. Anderson, 421 F. Supp. 337 (D. Mass. 1976) (opening each school day with a minute of silence for prayer or meditation offends neither the Establishment Clause nor the Free Exercise Clause).

In Karen v. Treen, 653 F.2d 897 (5th Cir.), cert. filed, 50 U.S.L.W. 3489 (1981), the court invalidated the Louisiana voluntary school prayer law enabling school boards to authorize that the teacher or a student volunteer lead the class in prayer. The court held that prayer is necessarily religious and the statute lacked a secular purpose and that these constitutional infirmities were not cured by the school board resolution requiring written parental permission for student participants and permitting nonparticipants to either sit silently in class or remain outside the classroom during the minute of prayer. See Kent v. Commissioner of Education, 402 N.E.2d 1340 (Mass. 1980) (invalidated Massachusetts voluntary school prayer law). See also Brandon v. Board of Education of Guilderland Central School District, 487 F. Supp. 1219 (N.D.N.Y.), aff'd, 635 F.2d 971 (2d Cir. 1980) (upheld school board refusal to permit high school student group to hold prayer meetings on school premises immediately before the school day commenced).

(page 976) [1201]

NOTES

6. [continued] See Florey v. Sioux Falls School District, 464 F. Supp. 911 (D.S.D. 1979), aff'd, 619 F.2d 1311 (8th Cir.), cert. denied, 449 U.S.

987 (1980) (upheld school board policy permitting the observance of holidays having both a religious and secular basis and the accompanying use of religious symbols, art, music, literature, and drama provided such have a secular focus).

(page 976) [1201]

NOTES

8. In Resnick v. East Brunswick Township Board of Education, 77 N.J. 88, 389 A.2d 944 (1978), the court found that a public school could permit the temporary use of its facilities during nonschool hours by religious groups for religious services and classes without violating the First Amendment. The incidental expenses of wear and tear on school property were not a public expense primarily for the benefit of religion. And the scheduling of religious events by school personnel and the storage of religious artifacts and books in school closets did not impermissibly entangle the school with religion. The court cautioned, however, that the use must be temporary; prolonged use of school facilities by a congregation without evidence of immediate intent to construct or purchase its own building would be impermissible.

In Committee for Public Education and Religious Liberty v. Regan, 444 U.S. 646 (1980), the Court upheld a New York law authorizing direct payments to nonpublic sectarian schools for complying with state-mandated attendance, testing, and reporting requirements. The New York law, unlike the Ohio statute upheld in Wolman v. Walter, 433 U.S. 229 (1977), provided that nonpublic school personnel grade two of the three tests administered and authorized a direct cash reimbursement. The Court nevertheless held Wolman controlling, finding that these distinguishing factors neither had the primary effect of advancing religion nor constituted excessive government entanglement. The tests at issue addressed only a secular academic matter and consisted largely of objective multiple choice questions. Furthermore, even though some of the tests may include an essay question, state review procedures constituted a sufficient safeguard. Therefore, the school did not control the content of the test or its results. Second, the Court concluded that no constitutional distinction could be drawn between paying the nonpublic school to do the grading and paying state employees or some independent service to perform that task; the grading function and its effect would be the same regardless of who performed it.

Justices Blackmun, Brennan, and Marshall dissented. They agreed that Wolman controlled but found that the distinguishing provisions at issue mandated an opposite result. Wolman did not sanction direct financial aid to sectarian schools, which has the primary effect of advancing religion, and the New York system of reimbursement required ongoing surveillance and therefore constituted excessive government entanglement. Justice Stewart, filing a separate dissent, argued that the Court should abandon all efforts to justify subsidies to nonpublic schools.

(page 995) [1221]

NOTES

3. [continued] Committee for Public Education v. Nyquist, 413 U.S. 756 (1973), is discussed in Comment, 50 Wash. L. Rev. 653 (1975).

(page 1000) [1225]

NOTES

11. [continued] Compare Public Funds for Public Schools of New Jersey v. Byrne, 590 F.2d 514 (3d Cir.), summarily aff'd, 442 U.S. 907 (1979) (invalidated New Jersey's $1,000.00 state income tax exemption for each child attending nonpublic elementary or secondary schools) with Minnesota Civil Liberties Union v. Roemer, 452 F. Supp. 1316 (D. Minn. 1978) (upheld Minnesota's $700.00 exemption for the tuition, transportation, and secular books of each child attending public or private elementary or secondary schools). See also IRS Revenue Ruling 79-99 (March 18, 1979) (disallowing deduction under I.R.C. §170 for the amount of taxpayer's contribution to religious society equal to the fair market value of child's education provided by the society's school).

(page 1000) [1226]

NOTES

13. [continued] In Roemer v. Board of Public Works of Maryland, 426 U.S. 736 (1976), plaintiffs challenged a Maryland statute that authorized payments of state funds to any private institution of higher learning except those awarding only seminarian or theological degrees. The aid consisted of annual subsidies that were based on the number of nontheological students and that were to be used for nonsectarian purposes. Each year the recipient institution reported and identified its expenditures, subject to verification.

Justice Blackmun, speaking for a plurality of three Justices, declared the program constitutional. Employing the three-pronged test of Lemon v. Kurtzman, 403 U.S. 602 (1971), he stated that the recipient colleges were not "pervasively sectarian," nor was the aid directed to religious purposes; hence the statute did not have a primary effect of advancing religion. Justice Blackmun found more troublesome the contention that the verification-of-expenses requirement constituted an excessive entanglement. He concluded, however, that contacts between the state and the schools were not excessive, and on-site inspections were unnecessary. Justices White and Rehnquist concurred narrowly, stating that the constitutional inquiry in Establishment Clause cases should embrace only the first two tiers of Lemon's test: secular purpose and primary effect. Justices Stewart, Stevens, Brennan, and Marshall dissented.

As evidenced by Roemer, the boundaries of permissible state aid to religious institutions remain unsettled, and litigation on this issue is frequent. In Wolman v. Walter, 433 U.S. 229 (1977), the Court upheld the provisions of an Ohio statute authorizing the state to supply nonpublic school pupils with books, standardized testing, diagnostic services, and therapeutic and remedial services. But the Court struck down provisions for supplying instructional materials and equipment and field trip services, refusing to accept the suggestion that such expensive equipment as weather forecasting charts, lunar models, and fossil collections supplied to the school was merely loaned to the pupils. Although the Court went beyond earlier decisions to the extent of allowing the state to bear the cost of administering state-prepared tests in purely secular subjects in nonpublic schools, the Court reemphasized the principle that public funds may not be used to finance educational services in religious schools.

For a critical look at Meek v. Pittenger, 421 U.S. 349 (1975), an economic analysis of aid to parochial schools, and the view that an absolute ban on meaningful aid is counterproductive to First Amendment values, see Nowak. The Supreme Court, the Religion Clauses, and the Nationalization of Education, 70 Nw. L. Rev. 883 (1976).

For an excellent analysis of the Burger Court's decisions in the area of church-state relations, see Kirby, Everson to Meek and Roemer: From Separation to Détente in Church-State Relations, 55 N.C.L. Rev. 563 (1977).

(page 1001) [1228]

NOTES

5. [continued] See National Coalition for Public Education and Religious Liberty v. Harris, 489 F. Supp. 1248 (S.D.N.Y.), appeal dismissed, 449 U.S. 808 (1980) (New York allowed to appropriate funds under Title I for the remedial education of parochial school students by public school teachers on the premises of parochial schools during regular school hours).

(page 1002) [1229]

NOTES

1. [continued] In McLean v. Arkansas Board of Education, 529 F. Supp. 1255 (E.D. Ark. 1982), the court held that an Arkansas statute mandating that public schools give balanced treatment to creation science and to evolution science violated the Establishment Clause. The court found that creation science is religion, not a science, and that it has no educational merit. Therefore, the statute failed all three prongs of the test enunciated in Lemon v. Kurtzman, 403 U.S. 602 (1971): that it have a secular purpose, not have the primary effect of the advancement of religion, and not foster excessive governmental entanglement.

(page 1004) [1230]

NOTES

2. [continued] The Supreme Court emphatically reaffirmed that the judiciary must not interfere in matters of ecclesiastical polity in Serbian Eastern Orthodox Diocese for the United States of America and Canada v. Milivojevick, 426 U.S. 696 (1976), discussed in Chapter XV, infra. There, a bishop was defrocked during a complex dispute over control of a Church diocese. The bishop alleged that the defrockment proceedings were procedurally and substantially defective under internal court rules. The Supreme Court refused to hear the claim, holding that review would constitute the adjudication of essentially religious controversies, in violation of the First Amendment. The Court did not rely on a "fraud, collusion or arbitrariness" exception to the rule that tribunals must recognize the finality of religious decisions; nor did the Court view this as a property dispute cognizable by courts under neutral principles.

The Court did confront a dispute over the ownership of local church property in Jones v. Wold, 443 U.S. 595 (1979), when it once again emphasized that courts may resolve such disputes only through the application of "neutral principles of law." Here, the dispute was between the majority faction of a local congregation that had seceded from the Presbyterian Church of the United States (PCUS) and the minority group that remained affiliated with the PCUS. The Court vacated and remanded to the Georgia Supreme Court to determine whether under Georgia law the process of identifying the faction that represents a local church involves considerations of religious doctrine and polity. Thus, if Georgia law provides that the identity of the local church here is to be determined according to the laws and regulations of the PCUS, then the First Amendment requires that the Georgia courts give deference to the presbyterial commission's determination as to which faction represents the true congregation.

See Protestant Episcopal Church in Diocese of Los Angeles v. Barker, 115 Cal. App. 3d 599 (Cal. Ct. App.) cert. denied, 50 U.S.L.W. 3248 (1981) (no implied trust under California law, and, therefore, local churches that have seceded from national church may keep church property, absent an express trust).

In Mills v. Baldwin, 377 So. 2d 971 (Fla. 1979), cert. denied, 446 U.S. 983 (1980), the Florida Supreme Court held, in light of Jones v. Wolf, that when the majority of a local church withdrew from the national religious organization with which it had been affiliated and which had hierarchial rather than congregational structure, ownership of property of the local church remained with the minority loyal to the national organization.

For a comprehensive discussion of the "neutral principles" approach to church property disputes, see Adams and Hanlon, Jones v. Wolf: Church Autonomy and the Religion Clauses of the First Amendment, 128 U. Pa. L. Rev. 1291 (1980).

(page 1004) [1231]

NOTES

3. [continued] See Citizens Concerned for Separation of Church and State v. City and County of Denver, 481 F. Supp. 522 (D. Colo. 1979) (action of city in erecting, maintaining, and displaying a nativity scene on public property violated the establishment clause), dismissed on jurisdictional grounds, 628 F.2d 1289 (10th Cir. 1980), cert. denied, 101 S. Ct. 3114 (1981); Fox v. City of Los Angeles, 22 Cal. 3d 792, 587 P.2d 663, 150 Cal. Rptr. 867 (1978) (California Constitution prohibits the city from displaying the Latin cross on the city hall tower during Christian holidays). Compare Gilfillan v. City of Philadelphia, 480 F. Supp. 1161 (E.D. Pa. 1979), aff'd, 637 F.2d 924 (3d Cir. 1980), cert. denied, 101 S. Ct. 2322 (1981) (certain city expenditures in connection with Pope John Paul II's visit violated the establishment clause) with O'Hair v. Andrus, 613 F.2d 631 (D.C. Cir. 1979) (denied constitutional challenge to city's provision of police, fences, and utilities for the Pope's visit).

STONE v. GRAHAM
449 U.S. 39

Per Curiam.
A Kentucky statute requires the posting of a copy of the Ten Commandments, purchased with private contributions, on the wall of each

public classroom in the State.[1] Petitioners, claiming that this statute violates the Establishment and Free Exercise Clauses of the First Amendment, sought an injunction against its enforcement. The state trial court upheld the statute, finding that its "avowed purpose" was "secular and not religious," and that the statute would "neither advance or inhibit any religion or religious group" nor involve the State excessively in religious matters. App. to Pet. for Cert. 38-39. The Supreme Court of the Commonwealth of Kentucky affirmed by an equally divided court. 599 S.W.2d 157 (1980). We reverse.

This Court has announced a three-part test for determining whether a challenged state statute is permissible under the Establishment Clause of the United States Constitution: "First, the statute must have a secular legislative purpose; second, its principal or primary effect must be one that neither advances nor inhibits religion . . . ; finally the statute must not foster 'an excessive government entanglement with religion.' " Lemon v. Kurtzman, 403 U.S. 602, 612-613 (1971) (citations omitted). If a statute violates any of these three principles, it must be struck down under the Establishment Clause. We conclude that Kentucky's statute requiring the posting of the Ten Commandments in public school rooms has no secular legislative purpose, and is therefore unconstitutional.

The Commonwealth insists that the statute in question serves a secular legislative purpose, observing that the legislature required the following notation in small print at the bottom of each display of the Ten Commandments: "The secular application of the Ten Commandments is clearly seen in its adoption as the fundamental legal code of Western Civilization and the Common Law of the United States." 1978 Ky. Acts, ch. 436, §1 (effective June 17, 1978), Ky. Rev. Stat. §158.178 (1980).

The trial court found the "avowed" purpose of the statute to be secular, even as it labeled the statutory declaration "self-serving." App. to Pet. for Cert. 37. Under this Court's rulings, however, such an "avowed" secular purpose is not sufficient to avoid conflict with the First Amendment. In Abington School District v. Schempp, 374 U.S. 203 (1963), this

---

1. The statute provides in its entirety:

"(1) It shall be the duty of the superintendent of public instruction, provided sufficient funds are available as provided in subsection (3) of this Section, to ensure that a durable, permanent copy of the Ten Commandments shall be displayed on a wall in each public elementary and secondary school classroom in the Commonwealth. The copy shall be sixteen (16) inches wide by twenty (20) inches high.

"(2) In small print below the last commandment shall appear a notation concerning the purpose of the display, as follows: 'The secular application of the Ten Commandments is clearly seen in its adoption as the fundamental legal code of Western Civilization and the Common Law of the United States.'

"(3) The copies required by this Act shall be purchased with funds made available through voluntary contributions made to the state treasurer for the purposes of this Act." 1978 Ky. Acts, ch. 436, §1 (effective June 17, 1978), Ky. Rev. Stat. §158.178 (1980).

Court held unconstitutional the daily reading of Bible verses and the Lord's Prayer in the public schools, despite the school district's assertion of such secular purposes as "the promotion of moral values, the contradiction to the materialistic trends of our times, the perpetuation of our institutions and the teaching of literature." Id., at 223.

The pre-eminent purpose for posting the Ten Commandments on schoolroom walls is plainly religious in nature. The Ten Commandments are undeniably a sacred text in the Jewish and Christian faiths,[3] and no legislative recitation of a supposed secular purpose can blind us to that fact. The Commandments do not confine themselves to arguably secular matters, such as honoring one's parents, killing or murder, adultery, stealing, false witness, and covetousness. See Exodus 20:12-17; Deuteronomy 5:16-21. Rather, the first part of the Commandments concerns the religious duties of believers: worshipping the Lord God alone, avoiding idolatry, not using the Lord's name in vain, and observing the Sabbath Day. See Exodus 20:1-11; Deuteronomy 5:6-15.

This is not a case in which the Ten Commandments are integrated into the school curriculum, where the Bible may constitutionally be used in an appropriate study of history, civilization, ethics, comparative religion, or the like. Abington School District v. Schempp, supra, at 225. Posting of religious texts on the wall serves no such educational function. If the posted copies of the Ten Commandments are to have any effect at all, it will be to induce the schoolchildren to read, meditate upon, perhaps to venerate and obey, the Commandments. However desirable this might be as a matter of private devotion, it is not a permissible state objective under the Establishment Clause.

It does not matter that the posted copies of the Ten Commandments are financed by voluntary private contributions, for the mere posting of the copies under the auspices of the legislature provides the "official support of the State . . . Government" that the Establishment Clause prohibits. 374 U.S., at 222; se Engel v. Vitale, 370 U.S. 421, 431 (1962).[4] Nor is it significant that the Bible verses involved in this case are merely posted on the wall, rather than read aloud as in Schempp and Engel, for "it is no defense to urge that the religious practices here may be relatively minor encroachments on the First Amendment." Abington School District v. Schempp, supra, at 225. We conclude that Ky. Rev. Stat. §158.178 (1980) violates the first part of the Lemon v. Kurtzman test, and thus the Establishment Clause of the Constitution.

3. As this Court commented in Abington School District v. Schempp, supra, at 224, "Surely the place of the Bible as an instrument of religion cannot be gainsaid. . . ."

4. Moreover, while the actual copies of the Ten Commandments were purchased through private contributions, the State nevertheless expended public money in administering the statute. For example, the statute requires that the state treasurer serve as a collecting agent for the contributions. Ky. Rev. Stat. §158.178(3)(1980).

The petition for a writ of certiorari is granted, and the judgment below is reversed.

It is so ordered.

The CHIEF JUSTICE and JUSTICE BLACKMUN dissent. They would grant certiorari and give this case plenary consideration.

JUSTICE STEWART dissents from this summary reversal of the courts of Kentucky, which, so far as appears, applied wholly correct constitutional criteria in reaching their decisions.

JUSTICE REHNQUIST, dissented:

... The Court's summary rejection of a secular purpose articulated by the legislature and confirmed by the state court is without precedent in Establishment Clause jurisprudence. This Court regularly looks to legislative articulations of a statute's purpose in Establishment Clause cases and accords such pronouncements the deference they are due.... The fact that the asserted secular purpose may overlap with what some may see as a religious objective does not render it unconstitutional....

The Court rejects the secular purpose articulated by the State because the Decalogue "is undeniably a sacred text." It is equally undeniable, however, as the elected representatives of Kentucky determined, that the Ten Commandments have had a significant impact on the development of secular legal codes of the western world.... Certainly the State was permitted to conclude that a document with such secular significance should be placed before its students, with an appropriate statement of the document's secular import....

The Establishment Clause does not require that the public sector be insulated from all things which may have a religious significance or origin....

(page 1005) [1231]

NOTES

4. [continued] See in re Marriage of Schulke, 579 P.2d 90 (Colo. Ct. App. 1978), cert. denied, 439 U.S.861 (1978) (consideration during divorce proceedings of custody investigation prepared by Catholic Community Services did not violate husband's First Amendment rights; there was no evidence that the Roman Catholic Church favors awarding custody to mothers in general and no evidence of religious bias in this particular report).

5. [continued] See Bogen v. Doty, 456 F. Supp. 983 (D. Mont. 1978), aff'd, 598 F.2d 1110 (8th Cir. 1979) (First Amendment not violated by the policy of opening the public meetings of the county board of commissioners with a prayer delivered by invited clergy).

(page 1005) [1232]

NOTES

7. [continued] See, Theriault v. Silber, 547 F.2d 1279 (5th Cir. 1977), cert. denied, 434 U.S. 871 (1978) (employment of chaplains in federal prisons did not violate the First Amendment); Rudd v. Ray, 248 N.W.2d 125 (Iowa 1976) (same for Iowa state prisons). See also, Voswinkil v. City of Charlotte, 495 F. Supp. 588 (W.D.N.C. 1980) (voided agreement between city and Providence Baptist Church that the church would provide a minister to serve as the full-time police chaplain).

(page 1006) [1233]

NOTES

8. [continued] In Wilder v. Bernstein, 499 F. Supp. 980 (S.D.N.Y. 1980), the district court again confronted a challenge on establishment grounds to the New York foster care sysem. At the time the action was brought, the court had yet to issue a final order with respect to the merits of Wilder v. Sugarman, 385 F. Supp. 1013 (S.D.N.Y. 1974) (Wilder I). Therefore, with the agreement of the parties, the court issued an order dismissing Wilder I without prejudice under the conditions (1) that all discovery from Wilder I not be challengeable solely on the basis that it had not been produced or obtained in the present action, and (2) that the opinion in Wilder I upholding the facial validity of the New York laws be adopted by the court on the basis of stare decisis. In accordance with this order, the district court granted defendants' motion to dismiss plaintiffs' claim challenging the facial validity of the New York statutory scheme and denied defendant's motion to dismiss plaintiffs' complaint regarding the constitutionality of the laws as applied. The case is still in discovery.

(page 1007) [1233]

NOTES

10. In NLRB v. Catholic Bishop of Chicago, 440 U.S. 490 (1979), the Supreme Court held that the National Labor Relations Board lacks the authority to assert jurisdiction over labor disputes in schools operated by religious groups. While the five-judge majority relied on the National Labor Relations Act for its decision, the Court was clearly concerned that the NLRB, in its resolution of labor-management disputes, would necessarily entangle itself in the religious mission of the schools. "It is not only the conclusions that may be reached by the Board which may

impinge on rights guaranteed by the Religion Clauses, but the very process of inquiry leading to findings and conclusions." As a result of these potential First Amendment problems, the Court looked for, and did not find, a clear expression of an affirmative Congressional intention that teachers in church-operated schools should be covered by the Act. Justice Brennan, joined by Justices Marshall, White, and Blackmun, dissented, disputing both the Court's conclusion and the principle of statutory construction by which it was reached.

See Ritter v. Mount St. Mary's College, 495 F. Supp. 724 (D. Md. 1980) (neither Equal Pay Act nor Age Discrimination Act expresses a clear affirmative intention to include within their scope religious non-profit educational institutions); Dolter v. Wahlert High School, 483 F. Supp. 266 (N.D. Iowa 1980) (Congress intended Title VII of the Civil Rights Act to cover sectarian schools).

For a discussion of NLRB v. Catholic Bishop of Chicago, see, Durso and Brice, NLRB v. The Catholic Bishop of Chicago: Government Regulation Versus First Amendment Religious Freedoms, 24 St. Louis U.L.J. 295 (1980).

C. THE "FREE EXERCISE" OF RELIGION

(page 1008) [1234]

NOTE

Recent cases confronting the need for a definition of religion have surfaced in the context of the prison group called Church of the New Song. See, e.g., Theriault v. Silber, 547 F.2d 1279 (5th Cir. 1977), cert. denied, 434 U.S. 871 (1978); Remmers v. Brewer, 529 F.2d 656 (8th Cir. 1976). Other nonconventional, arguably religious, groups have caused the courts to re-examine the parameters of "religion." See, e.g., Missouri Church of Scientology v. State Tax Commn., 560 S.W.2d 837 (Mo. Sup. Ct. 1978), appeal dismissed, 439 U.S. 803 (1978) (Scientology does not constitute religion for purposes of exemption from the state ad valorem tax; Scientology is applied philosophy rather than religion because it does not involve a belief in a Supreme Being); Malnak v. Yogi, 440 F. Supp. 1284 (D.N.J. 1978), aff'd, 592 F.2d 197 (3d Cir. 1979) (the teaching of the Science of Creative Intelligence/Transcendental Meditation as an elective in public secondary schools violates the Establishment Clause because it has the primary effect of advancing religion and religious concepts). For a general discussion, see, Note, Toward a Constitutional Definition of Religion, 91 Harv. L. Rev. 1056 (1978).

(page 1012) [1239]

NOTES

4. [continued] In Brown v. Dade Christian Schools, Inc., 556 F.2d 310 (5th Cir. 1977), cert. denied, 434 U.S. 1063 (1978), the court of appeals confronted the clash between the Free Exercise Clause and §1981. Two black children and their parents sought to have the children admitted to a church-operated school that barred blacks. The school claimed that segregation was a tenet of religious faith protected by the First Amendment. In a 5-2-6 decision, the Fifth Circuit enjoined the school from refusing to enroll the students because of their race. The plurality examined the expressions of religious belief formulated by the school and its affiliated church and the development of the school's segregation policy. It concluded that segregation was not the exercise of religion but a social or philosophical policy unprotected by the First Amendment. Judge Goldberg, in a special concurrence, concluded that the school's segregation policy was religious albeit a "very minor" part of the religion. However, the school's free exercise interest in preventing interracial schooling and marriage was outweighed by the compelling governmental interest in eradicating some of the badges and indicia of slavery. Chief Judge Brown joined in Goldberg's conclusion that the governmental interest in desegregation outweighed the First Amendment claim, if any, of the school. The five-judge dissent concluded that the school's segregation policy was protected by the Free Exercise clause and voted to remand the case to the district court on the balancing issue. Judge Coleman, in a separate opinion, insisted that no court should have the power to compel the admission of a student to a church-operated school.

In Bob Jones University v. United States, 639 F.2d 147 (4th Cir. 1980), cert. granted, 50 U.S.L.W. 3278 (1981), the court of appeals held that the Internal Revenue Service had the statutory authority to revoke the tax-exempt status of a religious university for prohibiting interracial dating and having previously excluded unmarried blacks. Though these policies were based on the religious belief of nonmiscegenation, the court found that the IRS action did not violate the First Amendment: it was predicated on a compelling governmental interest in eliminating racial discrimination in education and did not prevent the university from teaching the Scriptural doctrine of nonmiscegenation or its students from adhering to their personal beliefs in not dating or marrying outside their race.

5. The Free Exercise Clause has also been called into play by parents' efforts to deprogram their adult children who belong to so-called religious cults. A California trial court, after an adversary hearing, granted parents temporary conservatorships over five adult members of Rev-

erend Sun Myung Moon's Unification Church so that they could be deprogrammed. In re Katz, No. 216828 (San Francisco County Superior Court, March 24, 1977), rev'd sub nom., Katz v. Superior Court, 73 Cal. App. 3d 952, 141 Cal. Rptr. 234 (Ct. App. 1977). The appellate court reversed on both statutory and constitutional grounds. The court concluded that the First Amendment rights of the converts were violated by the appointment of conservators over their persons. The Katz case is discussed in Note, Conservatorships and Religious Cults: Divining a Theory of Free Exercise, 53 N.Y.U.L. Rev. 1247 (1978) (proposing that absent proof of physical or mental coercion — that is, proof that the proposed conservatees' involvement in the sect was nonconsensual — or a showing of harm to innocent third parties, there is no state interest that can be allowed to overbear their right to practice their religion); see also, Note, People v. Religious Cults: Legal Guidelines for Criminal Activities, Tort Liability and Parental Remedies, 11 Suffolk L. Rev. 1025 (1977).

(page 1022) [1249]

NOTES

1. [continued] In Thomas v. Review Board of Indiana Employment Security Division, 101 S. Ct. 1425 (1981), the Court rejected an attack on Sherbert v. Verner and held that Indiana's denial of unemployment benefits to claimant, who terminated his job because his religious beliefs forbade direct participation in the production of armaments, violated the Free Exercise Clause. Reversing the Indiana Supreme Court, the Court cautioned that a reviewing court in this context should not dissect the claimant's religious beliefs but determine merely whether there was an appropriate finding that an individual rejected work because of an honest conviction that his religion forbade it.

See also, Hildebrand v. Unemployment Ins. Appeals Board 10 Cal. 3d 765, 566 P.2d 1297, 140 Cal. Rptr. 151 (1977), cert. denied, 434 U.S. 1068 (1978). (Sherbert v. Verner distinguished; unemployment benefits validly denied to Sabbatarian who left job for religious reasons; plaintiff knew when she took the job that Saturday work was required).

Constructions of the 1972 Amendment to Title VII requiring "reasonable accommodation" of an employee's religious practices are found in Cooper v. General Dynamics, 533 F.2d 163 (5th Cir. 1976); Draper v. United States Pipe and Foundry, 527 F.2d 515 (6th Cir. 1975), cert. denied, 433 U.S. 908 (1976); Niederhuber v. Camden County Voc. & Tech. School Dist. Board of Ed., 495 F. Supp. 273 (D.N.J. 1980); Kendall v. United Air Lines, Inc., 494 F. Supp. 1380 (N.D. Ill. 1980).

Federal courts are divided over whether Title VII's accommodation clause constitutes an unlawful establishment of religion. Compare Anderson v. General Dynamics Convair Aerospace Div., 648 F.2d 1247 (9th Cir.) (no violation), cert. denied, 50 U.S.L.W. 3376 (1981); Cummins v. Parker Seal Co., 516 F.2d 544 (6th Cir. 1975) (same), aff'd by an equally divided court, 429 U.S. 65 (1976) (per curiam); Hardison v. Trans World Airlines, Inc., 527 F.2d 33 (8th Cir. 1975) (same), aff'd, 643 F.2d 445 (7th Cir.), cert. denied, 50 U.S.L.W. 3376 (1981); Nottelson v. A.O. Smith Corp., 489 F. Supp. 94 (E.D. Wisc. 1980) (same) with Yott v. North American Rockwell Corp., 428 F. Supp. 763 (C.D. Cal. 1977) (violation). In reviewing the Hardison decision, the Supreme Court did not rule on the question of constitutionality, finding that the employer had made reasonable efforts to accommodate the employee's religious needs. 432 U.S. 63 (1977). Similarly, in its review of Yott, the court of appeals affirmed the district court decision that the employee could not be reasonably accommodated and therefore never reached the constitutional issue. 602 F.2d 904 (9th Cir. 1979), cert. denied, 445 U.S. 928 (1980). See Retter, The Rise and Fall of Title VII's Requirement of Reasonable Accomodation for Religious Employees, II Colum. Hum. Rts. L. Rev. 63 (1979); Comment, 62 Va. L. Rev. 237 (1976).

2. [continued] But in McDaniel v. Essex International, Inc., 571 F.2d 338 (6th Cir. 1978), a Seventh Day Adventist, whose faith forbade her from joining a union and paying dues, was fired for violating the union security clause. Before her termination, plaintiff offered to contribute an equivalent amount to a nonsectarian charity chosen by the union and the employer but received no response. And, during trial, she offered to pay an amount equal to that percentage of the union budget used for purposes that did not violate her religion, with the remainder going to charity. The Sixth Circuit reversed the district court's summary judgment for the defendants and remanded to determine whether a reasonable accommodation to plaintiff's religious beliefs could be made without undue hardship to the union and the employer. See also, Anderson v. General Dynamics Convair Aerospace Division, 589 F.2d 397 (9th Cir. 1978) (union and employer were not relieved of duty to accommodate plaintiff's religious beliefs by plaintiff's payment of equivalent amount to charity of his own choice rather than to union for charitable purposes).

(page 1029) [1256]

NOTES

4. [continued] See Palmer v. Board of Ed. of City of Chicago, 603 F.2d 1271 (7th Cir. 1979), cert. denied, 444 U.S. 1026 (1980) (because of compelling state interest, public school teachers are not free to disregard the prescribed curriculum concerning patriotic matters notwithstanding that adherence thereto may conflict with religious principles);

Citizens for Parental Rights v. San Mateo County Board of Education, 51 Cal. App. 3d 1, 124 Cal. Rptr. 68 (1975), appeal dismissed, 425 U.S. 908 (1976) (public school family and sex education program education program held not to violate rights of free exercise, privacy, due process, or equal protection).

6. In Wooley v. Maynard, 430 U.S. 705 (1977), the Court invalidated a statute that imposed criminal sanctions against persons who covered the motto "Live Free or Die" on their automobile license plates. Plaintiffs, who were Jehovah's Witnesses, challenged the statute as repugnant to their moral, religious, and political beliefs. Although the Court invalidated the statute on free speech grounds, Chief Justice Burger's opinion evinced strong religious overtones:

"We are ... thus faced with the question of whether the State may constitutionally require an individual to participate in the dissemination of an ideological message by displaying it on his private property in a manner and for the express purpose that it be observed and read by the public. We hold that the State may not do so.

"We begin with the proposition that the right of freedom of thought protected by First Amendment against state action includes both the right to speak freely and the right to refrain from speaking at all. See West Virginia State Board of Education v. Barnette, 319 U.S. 624, 633-634, 645 (1943). A system which secures the right to proselytize religious, political, and ideological causes must also guarantee the concomitant right to decline to foster such concepts. The right to speak and the right to refrain from speaking are complementary components of the broader concept of "individual freedom of mind...."

(page 1031) [1258]

NOTES

1.c. [continued] See Snyder v. Holy Cross Hospital, 30 Md. App. 317, 352 A.2d 334 (1976) (performance of state-required autopsy on eighteen-year-old son of Orthodox Jewish father does not violate Free Exercise Clause).

1.d. [continued] The New Jersey Supreme Court unanimously found that the constitutional right of privacy — rather than the Free Exercise Clause — encompasses a "right to die" in certain carefully circumscribed circumstances. In Matter of Quinlan 70 N.J. 10, 355 A.2d 647 (1976). In rejecting the Free Exercise claim, the court held that "ranged against the State's interest in the preservation of life, the impingement of religious belief, much less religious 'neutrality' as here, does not reflect a constitutional question, in the circumstances at least of the case presently before the Court. Moreover, ... we do not recognize an independent parental right of religious freedom to support the relief requested." See, e.g., Riga, Euthanasia, The Right to Die and Privacy: Observations on Some Recent Cases, 11 Lincoln L. Rev. 109 (1980); Note, The Legal Aspects of the Right to Die: Before and After the Quinlan Decision, 65 Ky. L.J. 823 (1977).

(page 1034) [1261]

NOTES

4. [continued] In Widmar v. Vincent, 50 U.S.L.W. 4062 (1981), the Supreme Court held a public university regulation prohibiting the use of university facilities for religious worship or teaching violative of the Free Exercise and Free Speech clauses. The Court rejected the university's Establishment Clause defense, finding that an "equal access" policy would satisfy the three-pronged "compatibility" test enunciated in Lemon v. Kurtzman, 403 U.S. 602 (1971), by (1) serving a secular purpose, (2) not having the primary effect of advancement of religion, and (3) not fostering excessive governmental entanglement.

After summarily addressing the first and third prongs, the Court reasoned that equal access would provide only incidental benefits to religion because (1) the forum would be available to a broad spectrum of nonreligious as well as religious speakers, and (2) "an open forum in a public university does not confer any imprimatur of State approval on religious sects or practices." The Court concluded that the university policy would not transgress the Establishment clause and that a discriminatory exclusion based on religious content was not sufficiently justified by a compelling state interest.

Compare Brandon v. Board of Education of Guilderland Central School District, 487 F. Supp. 1219 (N.D.N.Y. 1980), aff'd, 635 F.2d 971 (2d Cir. 1980) (school board may refuse to permit high school group to hold prayer meetings because alternative locations are available to accommodate the group's religious expression).

(page 1034) [1262]

NOTES

5. [continued] In United States v. Lee, 50 U.S.L.W. 4201 (1982), the Court ruled that members of the Old Order Amish Church who operate businesses must pay social security and unemployment taxes despite their religious belief that paying taxes is a sin. The Court took account of the conflict between the Amish faith and taxes but concluded that because "mandatory participation is indispensible to the fiscal vitality" of the social security system, the limitation on religious liberty was justified by an overriding governmental interest.

In Jaggard v. Commissioner of Internal Revenue, 582 F.2d 1189 (8th Cir. 1978), cert. denied, 440 U.S. 913 (1979), the court denied the taxpayer's claim to a religious exemption from the federal self-employment tax. Taxpayer failed to qualify because he did not belong to a religious faith that opposes accceptance of the benefits of any private or public insurance as an established tenet, reasonably provides for its dependent members, and has been in existence at all times since December 31, 1950. In another tax case involving the First Amendment, Quakers adhering to the principle of total nonviolence claimed a "war tax credit" on 50 percent of their tax due in 1973. The Sixth Circuit rejected their claim that paying taxes for the Vietnam war violated their free exercise of religion. Graves v. Commissioner of Internal Revenue, 579 F.2d 392 (6th Cir. 1978), cert. denied, 440 U.S. 946 (1979).

(page 1036) [1263]

NOTES

6.f. *Social security numbers.* In Callahan v. Woods, 658 F.2d 679 (9th Cir. 1981), the court held that plaintiff's objection to the requirement that he take a social security number for his daughter on the basis that the numbers are the "mark of the beast" was sincerely held and rooted in religious belief, and it was therefore the government's burden to show a compelling interest in making the numbers a prerequisite for Aid to Families with Dependent Children benefits. The court remanded the case for the trial court to determine the extent to which plaintiff's beliefs were burdened, whether the government's interest was compelling, and whether that interest could be accommodated by less restrictive means.

Courts have differed in deciding the issues remanded in Callahan. Compare Stevens v. Berger, 428 F. Supp. 896 (E.D.N.Y. 1977) (government must devise alternative) and Mullaney v. Woods, 97 Cal. App. 3d 710 (Cal. Ct. App. 1979) (government interest compelling and unachievable by other means).

6.g. *Mortmain statutes.* In Key v. Doyle, 365 A.2d 621 (D.C. Ct. App. 1976), app. dismissed, 434 U.S. 59 (1978), a mortmain statute, which invalidated any bequest to a cleric or religious organization if made within 30 days of a testator's death, was invalidated on equal protection and due process grounds. Chief Judge Reilly, concurring, stated that the statute interfered with the free exercise of religion.

(page 1036) [1264]

NOTES

8. In McDaniel v. Paty, 435 U.S. 618 (1978), the Court held unconstitutional a Tennessee statute declaring that ministers and priests were

ineligible for legislative office. The provision had been invoked by a candidate for delegate to a state constitutional convention to bar her opponent, a Baptist minister, from the ballot. While the Court's decision was unanimous, the Justices differed widely about the appropriate rationale. Chief Justice Burger, joined by Justices Powell, Rehnquist, and Stevens, found that the barrier was subject to strict scrutiny under Sherbert v. Verner and Wisconsin v. Yoder because it interfered with the minister's "right to the free exercise of religion." The Chief Justice rejected the state's contention that it was preventing the establishment of religion because Tennessee had "failed to demonstrate that its views of the dangers of clergy participation in the political process have not lost whatever validity they may once have enjoyed."

Justice Brennan, joined by Justice Marshall, concurred in the judgment but found that different reasons supported the Free Exercise violation and that the Establishment Clause was violated as well. Justice Brennan insisted that, under Sherbert, the Tennessee provision "imposed an unconstitutional penalty upon appellant's exercise of his religious faith." Moreover, the Justice found that the Establishment Clause was violated because "government may not use religion as a basis of classification for the imposition of duties, penalties, privileges or benefits" except in those limited situations in which the purpose is to accommodate traditions of religious liberty. He concluded that: "The Establishment Clause [is] a shield against any attempt by government to inhibit religion as it has done here. It may not be used as a sword to justify repression of religion or its adherents from any aspect of public life." 435 U.S. at 641. In Larson v. Valente, 50 U.S.L.W. 4411 (1982), the Supreme Court held violative of the Establishment Clause a Minnesota charitable contributions statute that exempted from registration and reporting religious organizations that solicit less than 50 percent of their funds from nonmembers. Because the statute granted denominational preferences, it was subject to strict scrutiny, a test appellants failed to satisfy.

Chapter Fifteen
Individual Rights Within Private Associations

A. LABOR UNIONS

(page 1060) [1290]

NOTES

3. [continued] In American Federation of Labor and Congress of Industrial Organizations v. Federal Election Commission, 628 F.2d 97 (D.C. Cir.), cert. denied, 449 U.S. 982 (1980), the union was prohibited from transferring funds from its education fund, which was used for nonpartisan voter registration and communications with union members, to its political contributions committee, which was permitted to make direct contributions to candidates for federal elective office. Though the funds that be legally contributed to political campaigns were generally segregated, the court held that no part of such monies should even be temporarily commingled with involuntary dues monies.

(page 1061) [1290]

NOTES

5. [continued] For a discussion of Buckley, see also, Note, Television and Radio Commentators' Freedom of Speech Not Infringed By Dues Requirement of Union Shop Agreement, 3 Fordham Urb. L.J. (1974-1975).

7. In Babauer v. Woodcock, 594 F.2d 662 (8th Cir.) cert. denied, 440 U.S. 841 (1979), union members unsuccessfully challenged the UAW's contribution of Community Action Program funds to controversial political, social, and civic organizations totally unrelated to the union's interest. The court of appeals rejected the members' claims that union

officials had violated their fiduciary duty under Section 501 of the Landrum-Griffin Act because the funds were spent under a valid provision in the union constitution: to engage in "activities to improve the economic and social conditions of UAW members and their families and to promote the general welfare and democratic way of life for all people."

See also, Federal Election Commission v. National Education Association, 457 F. Supp. 1102 (D.D.C. 1978) ("reverse check-off" system, whereby $1 contribution to union's "voluntary" political action fund was automatically deducted from member's paychecks unless he made a separate written request, violated the Federal Election Campaign Act because it resulted in some unknowing and therefore involuntary contributions). For a critical analysis of the federal Election Commission case see Note, Reverse Political Checkoff Per Se Illegal as Violation of Federal Election Campaign Act, 2 U.S.C. §4416, 1980 B.Y.L. Rev. 403 (1980).

ABOOD v. DETROIT BOARD OF EDUCATION
431 U.S. 209

Mr. JUSTICE STEWART delivered the opinion of the Court.

The State of Michigan has enacted legislation authorizing a system for union representation of local governmental employees. A union and a local government employer are specifically permitted to agree to an "agency shop" arrangement, whereby every employee represented by a union — even though not a union member — must pay to the union, as a condition of employment, a service fee equal in amount to union dues. The issue before us is whether this arrangement violates the constituitional rights of government employees who object to public sector unions as such or to various union activities financed by the compulsory service fees....

Consideration of the question whether an agency shop provision in a collective-bargaining agreement covering governmental employees is, as such, constitutionally valid must begin with two cases in this Court that on their face go far towards resolving the issue. The cases are Railway Employe[e]s Department v. Hanson, [351 U.S. 225], supra, and International Association of Machinists v. Street, 367 U.S. 740....

The designation of a union as exclusive representative carries with it great responsibilities. The tasks of negotiating and administering a collective-bargaining agreement and representing the interests of employees in settling disputes and processing grievances are continuing and difficult ones. They often entail expenditure of much time and money.... The services of lawyers, expert negotiators, economists, and a research staff, as well as general administrative pesonnel, may be required. Moreover, in carrying out these duties, the union is obliged "fairly and equitably to represent all employees, ... union and nonunion," within the relevant unit.... A union-shop arrangement has been thought to distribute fairly the cost of these activities among those who benefit, and it counteracts the incentive that employees might otherwise have to become "free riders" — to refuse to contribute to the union while obtaining benefits of union representation that necessarily accrue to all employees....

To compel employees financially to support their collective bargaining representative has an impact upon their First Amendment interests. An employee may very well have ideological objections to a wide variety of activities undertaken by the union in its role as exclusive representative. His moral or religious views about the desirability of abortion may not square with the union's policy in negotiating a medical benefits plan. ... To be required to help finance the union as a collective-bargaining agent might well be thought, therefore, to interfere in some way with an employee's freedom to associate for the advancement of ideas, or to refrain from doing so, as he sees fit. But the judgment clearly made in Hanson and Street is that such interference as exists is constitutionally justified by the legislative assessment of the important contribution of the union shop to the system of labor relations established by Congress. . . .

B

The National Labor Relations Act leaves regulation of the labor relations of state and local governments to the States. See 29 U.S.C. §152(2). Michigan has chosen to establish for local government units a regulatory scheme which, altough not identical in every respect to the NLRA or RLA, is broadly modeled after federal law. . . .

Several aspects of Michigan law that mirror provisions of the Railway Labor Act are of particular importance here. A union that obtains the support of a majority of employees in the appropriate bargaining unit is designated the exclusive representative of those employees. Mich. Comp. Laws §423.211. A union so designated is under a duty of fair representation to all employees in the unit, whether or not union members. . . . And in carrying out all of its various responsibilities, a recognized union may seek to have an agency-shop clause included in a collective-bargaining agreement. . . .

Our province is not to judge the wisdom of Michigan's decision to authorize the agency shop in public employment. Rather, it is to adjudicate the contitutionality of that decision. The same important government interests recognized in the Hanson and Street cases presumptively support the impingement upon associational freedom created by the agency shop here at issue. Thus, insofar as the service charge is used to finance expenditures by the union for the purposes of collecting bargaining, contract administration, and grievance adjustment, those two decisions of this Court appear to require validation of the agency-shop agreement before us.

While recognizing the apparent precedential weight of the Hanson and Street cases, the appellants advance two reasons why those decisions should not control decision of the present case. First, the appellants note that it is *government* employment that is involved here, thus directly implicating constitutional guarantees, in contrast to the private employment that was the subject of the Hanson and Street decisions. Second, the appellants say that in the public sector collective bargaining itself is inherently "political," and that to require them to give financial support to it is to require the "ideological conformity" that the Court expressly found absent in the Hanson case. 351 U.S. at 238. We find neither argument persuasive.

Because it is employment by the State that is here involved, the appellants suggest that this case is governed by a long line of decisions holding that public employment cannot be conditioned upon the surrender of First Amendment rights. But, while the actions of public employers surely constitute "state action," the union shop, as authorized by the Railway Labor Act, also was found to result from governmental action in Hanson. The plaintiffs' claims in Hanson failed, not because there was no governmental action, but because there was no First Amendment violation. The appellants' reliance on the "unconstitutional conditions" doctrine is therefore misplaced.

The appellants' second argument is that in any event collective bargaining in the public sector is inherently "political" and thus requires a different result under the First and Fourteenth Amendments. This contention rests upon the important and often-noted differences in the nature of collective bargaining in the public and private sectors. . . .

Public employees are not basically different from private employees; on the whole, they have the same sort of skills, the same needs, and seek the same advantages. "The uniqueness of public employment is *not in the employees* nor in the work performed; the uniqueness is in the special character of the employer." Summers, Public Sector Bargaining: Problems of Governmental Decisionmaking, 44 Cin. L. Rev. 669, 670 (1976) (emphasis added). The very real differences between exclusive agent collective bargaining in the public and private sectors are not such as to work any geater infringement upon the First Amendment interests of public employees. A public employee who believes that a union representing him is urging a course that is unwise as a matter of public policy is not barred from expressing his viewpoint. Besides voting in accordance with his convictions, every public employee is largely free to express his views, in public or private, orally or in writing. With some exceptions not pertinent here, public employees are free to participate in the full range of political activities open to other citizens. Indeed, just this Term we have held that the First and Fourteenth Amendments protect the right of a public school teacher to oppose, at a public school board meeting, a position advanced by the teacher's union. In so ruling we recognized that the principle of exclusivity cannot constitutionally be used to muzzle a public employee who, like any other citizen, might wish to express his view about governmental decisions concerning labor relations.

There can be no quarrel with the truism that because public employee unions attempt to influence governmental policy-making, their activities — and the views of members who disagree with them — may be properly termed political. But that characterization does not raise the ideas and beliefs of public employees onto a higher plane than the ideas and beliefs of private employees. It is no doubt true that a central purpose of the First Amendment "was to protect the free discussion of governmental affairs," Post, citing Buckley v. Valeo, 424 US. 1, 14, and Mills v. Alabama, 384 U.S. 214, 218. But our cases have never suggested that expression about philosophical, social, artistic, economic, literary, or ethical matters — to take a nonexhaustive list of labels — is not entitled to full First Amendment protection. Union members in both the public and private sector may find that a variety of union activities conflict with their beliefs.... Nothing in the First Amendment or our cases discussing its meaning makes the question whether the adjective "political" can properly be attached to those beliefs the critical constitutional inquiry.

The differences between public and private sector collective bargaining simply do not translate into differences in First Amendment rights. Even those commentators most acutely aware of the distinctive nature of public-sector bargaining and most seriously concerned with its policy implications agree that "[t]he union security issue in the public sector ... is fundamentally the same issue ... as in the private sector.... No special dimension results from the fact that a union represents public rather than private employees." H. Wellington & R. Winter, The Unions and the Cities 95-96 (1971). We conclude that the Michigan Court of Appeals was correct in viewing this Court's decisions in Hanson and Street as controlling in the present case insofar as the service charges are applied to collective bargaining, contract administration, and grievance adjustment purposes.

C

Because the Michigan Court of Appeals ruled that state law "sanctions the use of nonunion members' fees for purposes other than collective bargaining" 60 Mich. App., at 99, 230 N.W.2d, at 326, and because the complaints allege that such expenditures were made, this case presents constitutional issues not decided in Hanson or Street. Indeed, Street embraced an interpretation of the Railway Labor Act not without its difficulties, see 367 U.S., at 784-786 (Black, J., dissenting); id., at 799-803 (Frankfurter, J., dissenting), precisely to avoid facing the constitutional issues presented by the use of union-shop dues for political and ideological purposes unrelated to collective bargaining, id., at 749-750. Since the state court's construction of the Michigan statute is authoritative, however, we must confront those issues in this case.

Our decisions establish with unmistakable clarity that the freedom of an individual to associate for the purpose of advancing beliefs and ideas is protected by the First and Fourteenth Amendments. . . . Equally clear is the proposition that a government may not require an individual to relinquish rights guaranteed him by the First Amendment as a condition of public employment. . . . The appellants argue that they fall within the protection of these cases because they have been prohibited not from actively associating, but rather from refusing to associate. They specifically argue that they may constitutionally prevent the Union's spending a part of their required service fees to contribute to political candidates and to express political views unrelated to its duties as exclusive bargaining representative. We have concluded that this argument is a meritorious one.

One of the principles underlying the Court's decision in Buckley v. Valeo, 424 U.S. 1, was that contributing to an organization for the purpose of spreading a political message is protected by the First Amendment. Because "[m]aking a contribution . . . enables likeminded persons to pool their resources in furtherance of common political goals," id., at 22, the Court reasoned that limitations upon the freedom to contribute "implicate fundamental First Amendment interests," id., at 23.

The fact that the appellants are compelled to make, rather than prohibited from making, contributions for political purposes works no less an infringement or their constitutional rights. For at the heart of the First Amendment is the notion that an individual should be free to believe as he will, and that in a free society one's beliefs should be shaped by his mind and his conscience rather than coerced by the State. . . .

There will, of course, be difficult problems in drawing lines between collective bargaining activities, for which contributions may be compelled, and ideological activities unrelated to collective bargaining, for which such compulsion is prohibited. The Court held in Street, as a matter of statutory construction, that a similar line must be drawn under the Railway Labor Act, but in the public sector the line may be somewhat hazier. The process of establishing a written collective-bargaining agreement prescribing the terms and conditions of public employment may require not merely concord at the bargaining table, but subsequent approval by other public authorities; related budgetary and appropriations decisions might be seen as an integral part of the bargaining process. We have no occasion in this case, however, to try to define such a dividing line.... All that we decide is that the general allegations in the complaint, if proven, establish a cause of action under the First and Fourteenth Amendments.

III

In determining what remedy will be appropriate if the appellants prove their allegations, the objective must be to devise a way of preventing compulsory subsidization of ideological activity by employees who object thereto without restricting the union's ability to require every employee to contribute to the cost of collective-bargaining activities....

The Court in [Brotherhood of Railway & Steamship Clerks v.] Allen [373 U.S. 113] described a "practical decree" that could properly be entered, providing for (1) the refund of a portion of the exacted funds in the proportion that union political expenditures bear to total union expenditures, and (2) the reduction of future exactions by the same proportion. Id., at 122. Recognizing the difficulties posed by judicial administration of such a remedy, the Court also suggested that it would be highly desirable for unions to adopt a "voluntary plan by which dissenters would be afforded an internal union remedy." Ibid. This last suggestion is particularly relevant to the case at bar, for the Union has adopted such a plan since the commencement of this litigation.

Although Street and Allen were concerned with statutory rather than constitutional violations, that difference surely could not justify any lesser relief in this case. Judged by the standards of those cases, the Michigan Court of Appeals' ruling that the appellants were entitled to no relief at this juncture was unduly restrictive. For all the reasons outlined in Street, the court was correct in denying the broad injunctive relief requested. But in holding that as a prerequisite to any relief each appellant must indicate to the Union the *specific* expenditures to which he objects, the Court of Appeals ignored the clear holding of Allen. As in Allen, the employees here indicated in their pleadings that they opposed ideological expenditures of *any* sort that are unrelated to collective bargaining. To require greater specificity would confront an individual employee with the dilemma of relinquishing either his right to withhold his support of ideological causes to which he objects or his freedom to maintain his own beliefs without public disclosure. It would also place on each employee the considerable burden of monitoring all of the numerous and shifting expenditures made by the Union that are unrelated to its duties as exclusive bargaining representative....

[The opinions of Justices Powell (with whom The Chief Justice and Mr. Justice Blackmun join), Rehnquist, and Stevens are omitted.]

NOTE

In Gavett v. Alexander, 477 F. Supp. 1035 (D.D.C. 1979), the district court applied Abood in a nonunion context and held that a statute requiring membership in the National Rifle Association to buy army rifles at a discount violated the purchasers' equal protection rights. Acknowledging that the government may require an individual to pay dues or make contributions to private organizations if there is a compelling government interest, the court found that the legitimate government objective of developing marksmen could be achieved outside the framework of an organization that used dues for political activities.

For discussion, see, Reilly, The Constitutionality of Labor Unions Collection and Use of Forced Dues for Non-Bargaining Purposes, 32 Mercer 561 (1981); After Abood: Public Sector Union Security and the Protection of Individual Employee Rights, 27 Am. L. Rev. 1 (1977); Staudohar, Individual and Collective Rights in Public Employment Appeals Procedures, 26 Lab. L.J. 431 (1975).

(page 1067) [1296]

NOTES

1. [continued] As noted in International Association of Machinists v. Street, main volume, page 1053 [1280] Congress and the Courts have been concerned with safeguarding the First Amendment rights of union members. In Hanneman v. Breier, 528 F.2d 750 (7th Cir. 1976), the court held that where police officers who opposed the chief of police in a pending collective bargaining dispute distributed a letter confirming the existence of an already publicized internal police investigation, and the letter contained no false statements knowingly or recklessly made, the imposition of sanctions against the officers for disobeying the police department confidentiality rule violated the officers' rights to free speech. In a similar case, Holodnak v. Avco Corp., 514 F.2d 285 (2d Cir.), cert. denied, 423 U.S. 892 (1975), the Second Circuit upheld an award of compensatory but not punitive damages to an employee who challenged his employer and his union for his dismissal for publishing an article critical of employer and union practices. The court found state action present because of the close link between the federal government and the employer through defense contracts, and held that the admittedly strong interest of both the government and the employer in averting labor unrest did not warrant interference with the employee's right of free speech. The court noted that the article, while vituperative, neither was defamatory nor suggested wildcat strikes.

See Maxwell v. United Automobile, Aerospace, and Agricultural Implement Workers of America, Local 1306, 489 F. Supp. 745 (C.D. Ill. 1980) (union disciplinary action against members who criticized the local's leadership for not taking disciplinary action against members involved in wildcat strikes and walkouts violated the members' rights to free expression).

(page 1067) [1297]

NOTES

2. [continued] See Notes 6-8 following Farmer v. United Brotherhood, infra.

4. [continued] See McDaniel v. Essex International, Inc., 571 F.2d 338 (6th Cir. 1978) (reversed and remanded to determine whether a reasonable accommodation to plaintiff's religious beliefs could be made without undue hardship to the union and the employer; plaintiff objected to joining a union and paying dues on religious grounds); Anderson v. General Dynamics Convair Aerospace Division, 589 F.2d 397 (9th Cir. 1978) (union and employer were not relieved of duty to accommodate plaintiff's religious beliefs by plaintiff's payment of equivalent amount to charity of his own choice rather than to union for charitable purposes).

(page 1068) [1298]

NOTES

6. [continued] In Local 3489, United Steelworkers of America, AFL-CIO v. Usery, 429 U.S. 305 (1977), the Court held, 6-3, that a union rule restricting candidacy for local union office to members who had attended at least 50 percent of the local meetings during the previous three-year period violates the LMRDA where the effect of the rule is to exclude 96.5 percent of the union members. The Court found a violation of §401(e) of the LMRDA, which permits union office-holding to be conditioned upon "reasonable qualifications." In finding the rule "unreasonable" under that section, Justice Brennan noted that the rule was not consistent with Title IV's goals of free and democratic elections and further held that the restriction could not be justified as encouraging attendance.

See Marshall v. Local 1402, International Longshoreman's Association of Tampa, Florida and Vicinity, 617 F.2d 96 (5th Cir.), cert. denied, 449 U.S. 869 (1980) (invalidated restrictive candidacy rule despite its liberal excuse provisions).

Recent cases discerning the parameters of Title I and Title IV actions include Kupau v. Yamamoto, 622 F.2d 449 (9th Cir. 1980) (discriminatory application of eligibility rules constituted violation under Title I); Laski v. International Organization of Masters, Mates and Pilots, 502 F. Supp. 134 (S.D.N.Y. 1980) (challenge to validity of pre-election requirements constituted Title IV claim and therefore court lacked jurisdiction).

8. In a case concerning union members' right to be free from racial

discrimination, Handy Andy, Inc., 228 N.L.R.B. No. 59 (Mar. 1, 1977), the NLRB overruled Bekins Moving & Storage Co. of Florida, Inc., 211 N.L.R.B. 138 (1974), and held that neither the Fifth Amendment nor the NLRA requires the Board to resolve questions of alleged racial discrimination by a union before the union's certification as bargaining representative. The Board must certify a duly elected union and then conduct an unfair-labor-practice proceeding, in order to afford the charged union due process protections and at the same time to honor the employees' right to be represented by their designated bargaining agent.

9. Under the LMRDA, union officers owe members a fiduciary duty. See Stelling v. International Brotherhood of Electrical Workers, Local 1547, 587 F.2d 1379 (9th Cir. 1978), cert. denied, 442 U.S. 944 (1979) (union president has fiduciary duty to provide access to union membership lists and referendum vote sought by local). See generally Note, The LMRDA, Section 501: A Tool for Developing International Union Democracy, 5 Golden Gate L. Rev. 367 (1975).

10. See Turner v. Air Transport Lodge 1894, 590 F.2d 409 (2d Cir. 1978), cert. denied, 442 U.S. 919 (1979) (free speech provision of the LMRDA prohibited union from expelling non-Communist Party member who espoused "communist" views in violation of the union constitution; there was no evidence that the union member's conduct caused any harm to the union or interfered in any way with its contractual obligations).

11. In Alvey v. General Electric Company, 622 F.2d 1279 (7th Cir. 1980), the court held that a union may generally limit participation in union affairs to members in good standing, but when the effect of such a rule is to preclude laid-off members from voting on matters affecting their recall rights, the provision violates the LMRDA. The rule at issue precluded those on layoff from paying dues, a prerequisite to maintaining goodstanding.

12. In United Steelworkers v. Sadlowski, 50 U.S.L.W. 4626 (1982), the Supreme Court held a union rule prohibiting nonmember campaign contributions did not violate the free speech and right to sue provisions of the LMRDA, 20 U.S.C. §§101(a)(2) and (4). See generally C. Summers and R. Rabin, The Rights of Union Members (American Civil Liberties Union 1979).

(page 1069) [1300]

NOTES

2. [continued] The National Labor Relations Act does not pre-empt a state cause of action for intentional infliction of emotional distress brought by a union member against the union and its officials. Farmer v. United Brotherhood of Carpenters and Joiners of America, Local 25,

430 U.S. 290 (1977). Plaintiff claimed that as a result of a dispute with union officials, he was subjected to a campaign of personal abuse and harrassment in addition to discrimination in referrals from the union hiring hall. The Court found that while the events complained of might form the basis for unfair labor practice charges before the NLRB, the state's interest in protecting citizens from "outrageous conduct" would not threaten undue interference with the federal regulatory scheme. The Court cautioned, however, that something more than mere discrimination in referrals is required for the state tort to escape federal pre-emption. "[I]t is essential that the state tort be either unrelated to employment discrimination or a function of the particularly abusive manner in which the discrimination is accomplished or threatened rather than a function of the actual or threatened discrimination itself." In Finnegan v. Leu, 50 U.S.L.W. 4480 (1982), the Supreme Court held that the retaliatory discharge of union's business agents by union president, following his election over candidate supported by agents, did not violate the voting rights and free speech provisions of the LMRDA, 20 U.S.C. §§101(a) (1) and (2).

In Florida Power & Light Co. v. International Brotherhood of Electrical Workers, Local 641, 417 U.S. 709 (1974), the Court held, 5-4, that the union had not committed an unfair labor practice when it disciplined supervisory members for crossing picket lines and performing rank and file struck work during a lawful economic strike. The discipline involved fines struck work during a lawful economic strike. The discipline involved fines ranging from $100 to $6000 and, in some cases, expulsion from the union. The Court left open the issue of the appropriateness of such discipline where the supervisory members had performed only supervisory work, although, in dicta, the Court indicated that only supervisory work concerning collective bargaining or grievance adjudication would be protected.

In Chicago Typographical Union No. 16 v. NLRB, 539 F.2d 242 (D.C. Cir. 1976), cert. denied, 438 U.S. 914 (1978), the court affirmed an NLRB holding that the union committed an unfair labor practice by fining and expelling from membership two supervisory members who crossed a union picket line and performed supervisory work and a minimal amount of rank and file work.

(page 1069) [1300]

NOTES

4. [continued] See Longshoreman's and Warehouseman's Union, Local 13 v. NLRB, 581 F.2d 1321 (9th Cir. 1978), cert. denied, 440 U.S. 935 (1979) (union's refusal to permit member to work for 10 days as sanction for failure to pay fines and assessments constituted an unfair

labor practice, unaffected by fact that member could have avoided loss of work by resigning from union).

(page 1070) [1300]

NOTES

5. [continued] In International Brotherhood of Electrical Workers v. Foust, 442 U.S. 43 (1979), the Supreme Court, in a 5-4 vote, held that punitive damages could not be assessed against a union that breached its duty of fair representation under the Railway Labor Act by failing properly to pursue a grievance. The majority opinion, written by Justice Marshall, noted that while punitive damages may act as a deterrent, the underlying purpose of the RLA is compensation, not punishment. Moreover, the majority feared that imposing punitive damages would curtail the broad discretion afforded unions in handling grievances and thereby inhibit the proper functioning of the collective bargaining system. In dissent, Justice Blackmun expressed particular concern that the per se rule was announced in a case involving no racial discrimination, no trampling on workers' bill of rights, and not even the contention that the union's conduct was motivated by personal hostility.

For a discussion of IBEW v. Foust, see, Note, Punitive Damages May Not Be Assessed Under Federal Law Against a Union That Breaches Its Duty of Fair Representation by Failing to Pursue an Employee's Grievance Against His Employer, 46 J. Air L. & Com. 201 (1980).

In Dian v. United Steelworkers of America, 486 F. Supp. 700 (E.D. Pa. 1980), the court applied the ruling in Foust to an action brought under the LMRDA and held that punitive damages could not be awarded in fair representation suits. The court noted the consanguity between the RLA and the LMRDA in that they share common policy goals and are essentially remedial in nature.

6. While unions were permitted to discipline errant members, the member's right to procedural due process must be observed. In Tincher v. Piasecki, 520 F.2d 851 (7th Cir. 1975), the court held that, as a matter of fundamental due process, it was inherently improper for a person who had been charged by the accused union member in a collateral proceeding to participate in a disciplinary proceeding against that union member. The court cited Withrow v. Larkin, 421 U.S. 35 (1975), which articulated the principle of an unconstitutional risk of bias.

Similarly, in Rosario v. Amalgamated Ladies' Garment Cutters' Union, Local 10, 605 F.2d 1228 (2d Cir. 1979), cert. denied, 446 U.S. 919 (1980), the court held that where an intraunion appeal resulted in reversal of member's original conviction, retrial could not be held before the same tribunal which had previously convicted him on identical charges.

7. Similar to unconstitutional bias is union discipline based on per-

sonal animosity toward a particular union member. This practice was held to be a violation of the NLRA in NLRB v. International Longshoremen's & Warehousemen's Union, 514 F.2d 481 (9th Cir. 1975). In that case, a joint union-employer committee had deregistered an employee at the request of the union because of a union committee member's personal hostility toward the employee.

8. Due process also requires that the member employee be given notice of proceedings against him. In Cole v. Erie Lackawanna Railway Co., 541 F.2d 528 (6th Cir. 1976), cert. denied, 433 U.S. 914 (1977), the Sixth Circuit held that the notice requirement of the Railway Labor Act (RLA), 45 U.S.C. §153 First (j) (as amended 1966), does apply to proceedings of the special adjustment boards set up to alleviate the backlog of cases before the National Railroad Adjustment Board. The court also held that the district court was empowered to review the award. Concerning the sufficiency of notice, the court stated:

"The union cannot contend that Appellee's right to effective presentation of his claim to the Board, as guaranteed by Section 153 First (j), has been preserved when he was prevented from conveying potentially helpful information to the Board via union officials. Appellee did not receive notice sufficient to obviate the provision to him of formal notice as required by Section 153 First (j). As the district court noted in concluding that the Board's original determination was improper:

"Without a formal notice from the Board, plaintiff was foreclosed from making the very decision [to represent himself or to be represented by counsel or by union representatives] which §9 First (j) empowers him to make; thus, his failure to act affirmatively cannot be held to have been a waiver of his right." 541 F.2d at 535-536. The court affirmed the district court enforcement of the order of reinstatement and award of partial back pay.

See also, Reilly v. Sheet Metal Workers' International Association, 488 F. Supp. 1121 (S.D.N.Y. 1980) (union's failure to take reasonable means to inform member of charges and of a right to and procedure for defending an appeal from an exoneration of charges constituted due process violation under LMRDA).

B. PROFESSIONAL, TRADE, AND BUSINESS ASSOCIATIONS

(page 1080) [1312]

NOTES

2. [continued] See Sloss and Becker, The Organization Affected With a Public Interest and Its Members — Justice Tobriner's Contribution to Evolving Common Law Doctrine, 29 Hastings L.J. 99 (1977).

(page 1081) [1312]

NOTES

3. [continued] Recent cases on the state action/private hospital issue are collected in State Action of Private Hospitals, 42 A.L.R.F. 463.

(page 1082) [1313]

NOTES

6. [continued] In a recent New York case, In re Press, 45 U.S.L.W. 2237 (N.Y. Sup. Ct., N.Y. Cy., Oct. 27, 1976), the court held that a doctoral candidate's allegations that a private university's denial of her degree was arbitrary and capricious and violated institutional rules and procedures stated a cause of action within the subject matter jurisdication of the New York State Supreme Court. The court held that, while judges may not substitute their judgment on academic matters for that of educators, and while academic qualifications are within the competence of the educational institution, a private university is not beyond the law and must accord uniform treatment to all degree candidates. That is, it must follow its own rules and give all candidates an impartial and fair doctoral examination. The judicial task ends upon a determination that the university regulations were reasonable and fairly administered. See generally Comment, The Dwindling Right of Teachers and the Closing Court-house Door, 44 Fordham L. Rev 511 (1975).

In Ettenson v. Dutchess County Medical Society, the New York Supreme Court refused to enjoin a medical society from reviewing a member physician's bill for treatment of a patient. The physician claimed a due process violation in the finding of the medical society's peer review committee that the bill was excessive. The court ruled that judicial review of the claim was premature because the physician had not exhausted remedies available to him outside the courts. New York Law Journal, June 29, 1977, at 1, col. 2.

Although Joe Kapp succeeded in proving that certain National Football League rules violated federal antitrust laws, he did not convince the jury that the illegality of those rules caused the damage suffered when he refused to sign the league's standard player contract and thus was forbidden to play or practice with any NFL team. Kapp v. National Football League, 586 F.2d 644 (9th Cir. 1978), cert. denied, 441 U.S. 907 (1979). The court of appeals upheld both the lower court's ruling that mere violation of the antitrust laws did not result in injury to Kapp and the jury verdict against him.

Charles Finley also failed to overturn Baseball Commissioner Bowie

Kuhn's disapproval of the sale of Joe Rudi and Rollie Fingers to the Boston Red Sox and Vida Blue to the New York Yankees for cash. Charles O. Finley & Co., Inc. v. Kuhn, 569 F.2d 527 (7th Cir.), cert. denied, 439 U.S. 876 (1978). Although the Seventh Circuit upheld the Major League Agreement's "waiver of recourse to the courts" clause, the court did examine the terms of the agreement to determine if Kuhn had the power to overturn the sales as not in the best interests of baseball. The court concluded that Kuhn acted in good faith after investigation, consideration, and deliberation, and that whether he was right or wrong was beyond the competence and jurisdiction of the court to decide.

See also McCourt v. California Sports, Inc., 600 F.2d 1193 (6th Cir. 1979) (National Hockey League's reserve system exempt from Sherman Act as product of good faith collective bargaining).

(page 1083) [1315]

NOTES

9. [continued] The Ninth Circuit recently approved antitrust scrutiny of professional societies' membership policies. In Boddicker v. Arizona State Dental Association, 549 F.2d 626 (1977), cert. denied, 434 U.S. 825 (1978), two licensed Arizona dentists alleged that the American Dental Association (ADA), the Arizona State Dental Association (ASDA) and the Central Arizona Dental Society (CADS) conspired "to require membership in the ADA as a condition precedent to membership in the ASDA and CADS, thus creating an anticompetitive tying arrangment" in violation of Sections 1 and 2 of the Sherman Act. The district court dismissed the complaint for lack of subject matter jurisdiction and for failure to state a claim upon which relief could be granted.

The Ninth Circuit reversed the district court, holding that membership in these professional societies results in great benefits to dentists, and that the nexus between the ADA's conduct and interstate commerce is "unquestionably" adequate. The court developed the following standard: "[T]o survive a Sherman Act challenge, the particular practice, rule, or regulation of the profession, whether rooted in tradition or the pronouncements of its organizations, must serve the purpose for which the profession exists, viz. to serve the public. Those which only suppress competition between practitioners will fail to survive the challenge. This interpretation permits a harmonization of the end that both the professions and the Sherman Act serve."

See generally, Note, Labor Union Subject to Antitrust As Well As Unfair Labor Practice Remedies When Its Unlawful Activity Directly Affects the Marketplace, 1976 Wis. L. Rev. 271.

(page 1084) [1316]

NOTES

12. [continued] See, Tuma v. Idaho Board of Nursing, 593 P.2d 711 (Idaho Sup. Ct. 1979) (overturned suspension of registered nurse who advised leukemia patient undergoing chemotherapy of alternative treatments such as laetrile; in the absence of a legislative or administrative definition of "unprofessional conduct," her suspension violated due process).

13. Consistent with its current policy of restricting federal court jurisdiction, at least where state review exists, the Supreme Court summarily affirmed a lower court holding that the federal court has no jurisdiction to review a state court order to deny mandamus, which would have required the state real estate commission to issue a broker's license to plaintiff. Howard v. Colorado Real Estate Commission, 430 U.S. 934 (1977) (mem.).

14. In his suit against the Los Angeles Lakers for inadequate supervision of their player Kermit Washington, Rudy Tomjanovich was awarded $3.25 million for injuries sustained when, during an NBA basketball game, Washington punched him in the jaw. Natl. L.J., September 3, 1979, p. 2, col. 1. Similarly, the Tenth Circuit found that the intentional striking of an opposing player during a National Football League game in a manner not condoned by league rules gives rise to a cause of action for reckless misconduct. Hackbart v. Cincinnati Bengals, Inc., 601 F.2d 516, cert. denied, 444 U.S. 931 (1979). But barring specific intent to injure or cause an accident on the part of the other jockey, there was no recovery for injuries caused as a result of "jockey error" or "careless riding" in a horse race. Santiago v. Clark, 444 F. Supp. 1077 (N.D.W. Va. 1978).

C. SOCIAL AND ATHLETIC CLUBS, FRATERNITIES, AND RELIGIOUS ORGANIZATIONS

(page 1087) [1319]

In Serbian Eastern Orthodox Diocese for the United States of America and Canada v. Milvojevich, 426 U.S. 696 (1976), the Supreme Court overturned the Illinois Supreme Court's resolution of an internal church dispute on the grounds that it constituted improper judicial interference with decisions of the highest authorities of a hierarchical church in violation of the First and Fourteenth Amendments. The basic dispute was over control of the Archdiocese, its property, and its assets. An ousted bishop claimed that the proceedings that removed him from his

See were procedurally and substantively defective under the internal regulations of the Church itself and, therefore, were arbitrary and invalid.

"The conclusion of the Illinois Supreme Court that the decisions of the Mother Church were 'arbitrary' was grounded upon an inquiry that persuaded the Illinois Supreme Court that the Mother Church had not followed its own laws and procedures in arriving at those decisions. We have concluded that whether or not there is room for 'marginal civil court review' under the narrow rubrics of 'fraud' or 'collusion' when church tribunals act in bad faith for secular purposes, no ' arbitrariness' exception — in the sense of an inquiry whether the decisions of the highest ecclesiastical tribunal of a hierarchical church complied with church laws and regulations — is consistent with the constitutional mandate that civil courts are bound to accept the decisions of the highest judicatories of a religious organization of hierarchical polity on matters of discipline, faith, internal organization, or ecclesiastical rule, custom, or law. For civil courts to analyze whether the ecclesiastical actions of a church judicatory are in that sense 'arbitrary' must inherently entail inquiry into the procedures that canon or ecclesiastical law supposedly requires the church adjudicatory to follow, or else into the substantive criteria by which they are supposedly to decide the ecclesiastical question. But this is exactly the inquiry that the First Amendment prohibits; recognition of such an exception would undermine the general rule that religious controversies are not the proper subject of civil court inquiry, and that a civil court must accept the ecclesiastical decisions of church tribunals as it finds them. . . ."

". . . In short, under the guise of 'minimal' review under the umbrella of 'arbitrariness,' the Illinois Supreme Court has unconstitutionally undertaken the resolution of quintessentially religious controversies whose resolution the First Amendment commits exclusively to the highest ecclesiastical tribunals of this hierarchical church. And although the Diocesan Bishop controls respondent Monastery of St. Sava and is the principal officer of respondent property-holding corporations, the civil courts must accept that consequence as the incidental effect of an ecclesiastical determination that is not subject to judicial abrogation, having been reached by the final church judicatory in which authority to make the decision resides. . . ."

NOTE

The Supreme Court vacated and remanded a dispute over local church property to the Georgia Supreme Court to determine whether under Georgia law the process of identifying the faction that represents a local church involves considerations of religious doctrine and polity.

Jones v. Wolf, 443 U.S. 595 (1979). If it does, the First Amendment requires that the Georgia courts give deference to the presbyterial commission's determination as to which faction represents the true congregation.

In Mills. v. Baldwin, 377 So. 2d 971 (Fla. 1979), cert. denied, 446 U.S. 983 (1980), the Florida Supreme Court held, in light of Jones v. Wolf, that when the majority of a local church withdrew from the national religious organization with which it had been affiliated and which had hierarchial rather than congregational structure, ownership of property of the local church remained with the minority loyal to the national organization.

Chapter Sixteen

The Rights of Groups with Diminished Constitutional Protection: Prisoners, Mental Patients, and Military Personnel

A. PRISONERS' RIGHTS

(1092) [1324]

NOTES

1. [continued] For a Supreme Court decision applying the standard of Haines v. Kerner to dismiss a complaint against a prison doctor for allegedly constitutionally inadequate medical treatment, see, Estelle v. Gamble, 429 U.S. 97 (1976).

(1093) [1325]

At end of Note 3 add:

BOUNDS v. SMITH
430 U.S. 817 (1977)

Mr. JUSTICE MARSHALL delivered the opinion of the Court.

The issue in this case is whether States must protect the right of prisoners to access to the courts by providing them with law libraries or alternative sources of legal knowledge. In Younger v. Gilmore, 404 U.S. 15 (1971), we held per curiam that such services are constitutionally mandated. Petitioners, officials of the State of North Carolina, ask us to overrule that recent case, but for reasons explained below, we decline the invitation and reaffirm our previous decision....

.... [O]ur decisions have consistently required States to shoulder affirmative obligations to assure all prisoners meaningful access to the courts. It is indisputable that indigent inmates must be provided at state expense with paper and pen to draft legal documents, with notarial services to authenticate them, and with stamps to mail them. States must forego collection of docket fees otherwise payable to the treasury and expend funds for transcripts. State expenditures are necessary to pay lawyers for indigent defendants at trial . . . and in appeals as of right. . . . This is not to say that economic factors may not be considered, for example in choosing the methods used to provide meaningful access. But the cost of protecting a constitutional right cannot justify its total denial. Thus, neither the availability of jailhouse lawyers nor the necessity for affirmative state action is dispositive of respondents' claims. The inquiry is rather whether law libraries or other forms of legal assistance are needed to give prisoners a reasonably adequate opportunity to present claimed violations of fundamental constitutional rights to the courts. . . .

We hold . . . that the fundamental constitutional right of access to the courts requires prison authorities to assist inmates in the preparation and filing of meaningful legal papers by providing prisoners with adequate law libraries or adequate assistance from persons trained in the law.

It should be noted that while adequate law libraries are one constitutionally acceptable method to assure meaningful access to the courts, our decision here, as in Gilmore, does not foreclose alternative means to achieve that goal. Nearly half the States and the District of Columbia provide some degree of professional or quasi-professional legal assistance to prisoners. Such programs take many imaginative forms and may have a number of advantages over libraries alone. Among the alternatives are the training of inmates as para-legal assistants to work under lawyers' supervision, the use of paraprofessionals and law students, either as volunteers or in formal clinical programs, the organization of volunteer attorneys through bar associations or other groups, the hiring of lawyers on a part-time consultant basis, and the use of full-time staff attorneys, working either in new prison legal assistance organizations or as part of public defender or legal services offices. Legal services plans not only result in more efficient and skillful handling of prisoner cases, but also avoid the disciplinary problems associated with writ writers. . . . Independent legal advisors can mediate or resolve administratively many prisoner complaints that would otherwise burden the courts, and can convince inmates that other grievances against the prison or the legal system are ill-founded, thereby facilitating rehabilitation by assuring the inmate that he has not been treated unfairly. . . . [A] legal access program need not include any particular element we have discussed, and we encourage local experimentation. Any plan, however, must be evaluated as a whole to ascertain its compliance with constitutional standards.

[The concurring opinion of Justice Powell and the dissenting opinions of Chief Justice Burger and Justices Stewart and Rehnquist are omitted.]

(page 1096) [1328]

NOTES

9. For recent cases dealing with prisoner access to legal materials and assistance, see: Gordon v. Leeke, 574 F.2d 1147 (4th Cir.), cert. denied, 99 S. Ct. 464 (1978) (nature of district court obligation to assist pro se prisoner-litigant); Buise v. Hudkins, 584 F.2d 223 (7th Cir. 1978), cert. denied, 99 S. Ct. 1234 (1979) (punishment of writ-writer); Williams v. Leeke, 584 F.2d 1336 (4th Cir. 1978) (adequacy of inmate legal facilities); Chapman v. Pickett, 586 F.2d 22 (7th Cir. 1978) (access denied by confinement in segregation); Rhodes v. Robinson, 612 F.2d 766 (3d Cir. 1979) (access to and xeroxing of materials); Battle v. Anderson, 614 F.2d 251 (10th Cir. 1980) (adequacy of legal access plan); Spates v. Manson, 619 F.2d 204 (2d Cir. 1980) (same); Harrell v. Keohane, 621 F.2d 1059 (10th Cir. 1980) (no right of access to photocopying facilities); Kelsey v. Minnesota, 622 F.2d 956 (8th Cir. 1980) (outside legal assistance valid substitute for inadequate library); Cruz v. Hauck, 627 F.2d 710 (5th Cir. 1980) (general challenge to legal access plan); Gilespie v. Civiletti, 629 F.2d 637 (9th Cir. 1980) (right to bring John Doe prison suit); Ramos v. Lamm, 639 F.2d 559 (10th Cir. 1980) (general invalidity of legal access plan) Ruiz v. Estelle, 503 F. Supp. 1265 (S.D. Tex. 1980) (general violations of Bounds v. Smith principles); State ex rel. McCamic v. McCoy, 276 S.E.2d 534 (W. Va. 1981) (invalidity of routine prison searches of attorneys visiting clients).

(page 1102) [1334]

NOTES

1. [continued] In Bell v. Wolfish, 441 U.S. 520 (1979), the Court considered a wide-ranging challenge to restrictions imposed upon federal pre-trial detainees. The issues included restrictions on receipt of package mail. The Wolfish opinion is discussed infra at pp. 304-305.

(page 1103) [1334]

NOTES

2. [continued] The question of prison mail censorship was before the Court again in a related context, in Procunier v. Navarette, 434 U.S. 555 (1977). There an inmate filed a civil rights damage action charging prison officials with systematic and wrongful interference with his outgoing mail during a period from September 1971 until December 1972. Applying the qualified official immunity defense recognized in Wood

v. Strickland, 420 U.S. 308 (1975), the Court described the applicable test as whether "the constitutional right allegedly infringed by [the prison officials] was clearly established at the time of their challenged conduct...." 434 U.S. at 563. Surveying the pre-Procunier v. Martinez case law and finding it unsettled, the Court concluded: "Whether the state of the law is evaluated by reference to the opinions of this Court, of the Courts of Appeals, or of the local District Court, there was no 'clearly established' First and Fourteenth Amendment right with respect to the correspondence of convicted prisoners in 1971-1972. As a matter of law, therefore, there was no basis for rejecting the immunity defense on the ground that petitioners knew or should have known that their alleged conduct violated a constitutional right.... [T]hey could not reasonably have been expected to be aware of a constitutional right that had not yet been declared...." Id. at 565. A dissenting opinion by Justice Stevens observed that more was at stake than just the general First Amendment right of inmate correspondence: "In 1971, Navarette had a well-established right of access to the courts and to legal assistance. Cutting off his communications with law students and legal assistance groups violated this right. While the lower echelon employees may have been under no obligation to read advance sheets, a jury might conclude that at least some of these defendants should have known that at least some of Navarette's mail was entitled to constitutional protection." 434 U.S. at 573-574.

One issue raised but not resolved in Procunier v. Navarette was whether the negligent deprivation of constitutional rights would support a claim for relief under Section 1983. In Parratt v. Taylor, — U.S. —, 68 L. Ed. 2d 420 (1981), another prisoner rights case, the Court finally said yes, but that conclusion did not avail the plaintiff of any relief. The prisoner claimed that $23.50 worth of hobby materials that he had ordered by mail were lost by prison officials, thereby depriving him of property without due process of law. Conceding that the negligent deprivation of constitutional rights was actionable, the Court nevertheless concluded that the prisoner had not been deprived of his property "without due process of law." Since the loss occurred in contravention of state procedures designed to protect against loss of such property and could be remedied through an established post-deprivation state tort claim mechanism, there was no lack of due process in connection with the loss of the property.

For further discussion of Parratt, see Chapter XVII, infra.

(page 1106) [1338]

NOTES

3. [continued]
The issues of press access to inmates and inmate access to the press

were considered again in Houchins v. KQED, Inc., 438 U.S. 1 (1978). The question, as stated by Chief Justice Burger in his plurality opinion, was "whether the news media have a constitutional right of access to a county jail, over and above that of other persons, to interview inmates and make sound recordings, films, and photographs for publication and broadcasting, by newspapers, radio and television." Id. at 3. The answer, once again, was generally no. The opinion emphasized that there were a wide variety of means by which information concerning the jail could reach the public, including monthly media tours, albeit limited in scope and supervised by prison officials, and broad correspondence, telephone, and visitation rights for inmates. While conceding the strong public interest in conditions at jails and prisons and the important role of the media in informing the public, the opinion nevertheless reasoned that these factors "afford no basis for reading into the Constitution a right of the public or of the media to enter these institutions with camera equipment and take moving and still pictures of inmates for broadcast purposes. This Court has never intimated a First Amendment guarantee of a right of access to all sources of information within governmental control." Id. at 8-9. Finding the media arguments largely foreclosed by Pell v. Procunier and Saxbe v. Washington Post Co., the opinion concluded by observing that the extent of access to be permitted should generally be left to determination by the policy-making branches of government.

(page 1107) [1339]

NOTES

4. [continued]. The right of pre-trial detainees with respect to receiving periodicals and books were significantly restricted by the Court in its decision in Bell v. Wolfish, discussed infra at pp. 304-305.

(page 1108) [1340]

Insert at end of Note 5:

JONES v. NORTH CAROLINA PRISONERS' LABOR UNION, INC.
433 U.S. 119 (1977)

Mr. JUSTICE REHNQUIST delivered the opinion of the Court....
Appellee, an organization self-denominated as a Prisoners' Labor Union, was incorporated in late 1974, with a stated goal of "the promotion of charitable labor union purposes" and the formation of a "prisoners' labor union at every prison and jail in North Carolina to

seek through collective bargaining . . . to improve . . . working . . . conditions. . . ."[1] It also proposed to work towards the alteration or elimination of practices and policies of the Department of Correction which it did not approve of, and to serve as a vehicle for the presentation and resolution of inmate grievances. By early 1975, the Union had attracted some 2,000 inmate "members" in 40 different prison units throughout North Carolina. The State of North Carolina . . . sought to prohibit inmate solicitation of other inmates, meetings between members of the Union, and bulk mailings concerning the Union from outside sources. . . .

Suit was filed by the Union . . . [claiming that] its rights, and the rights of its members, to engage in protected free speech, association, and assembly activities were being infringed by the no-solicitation and no-meeting rules. . . .

A three-judge District Court, . . . while dismissing the Union's prayers for damages and attorneys' fees, granted it substantial injunctive relief. . . .

The District Court, we believe, got off on the wrong foot in this case by not giving appropriate deference to the decisions of prison administrators and appropriate recognition to the peculiar and restrictive circumstances of penal confinement. . . . The fact of confinement and the needs of the penal institution impose limitations on constitutional rights, including those derived from the First Amendment, which are implicit in incarceration. . . . Perhaps the most obvious of the First Amendment rights that are necessarily curtailed by confinement are those associational rights that the First Amendment protects outside of prison walls. The concept of incarceration itself entails a restriction on the freedom of inmates to associate with those outside of the penal institution. Equally as obviously, the inmate's "status as a prisoner" and the operational realities of a prison dictate restrictions on the associational rights among inmates. . . .

State correctional officials uniformly testified that the concept of a prisoners' labor union was itself fraught with potential dangers, whether or not such a union intended, illegally, to press for collective-bargaining recognition. . . . :

" . . . In a time when the units are already seriously over-crowded, such an element could aggravate already tense conditions. The purpose of the Union may well be worthwhile projects. But it is evident that the inmate organizers could, if recognized as spokesmen for all inmates, make themselves to be powerful figures among the inmates. If the Union is successful, these inmates would be in a position to misuse their influence. After the inmate Union has become established, there would probably be nothing this Department could do to terminate its existence,

---

[1] . . . . Collective bargaining for inmates with respect to pay, hours of employment, and other terms and conditions of incarceration is illegal under N.C. Gen. Stat. §95-98.

even if its activities became overtly subversive to the functioning of the Department. Work stoppages and routines are easily foreseeable. Riots and chaos would almost inevitably result. Thus, even if the purposes of the Union are as stated in this Complaint, the potential for a dangerous situation exists, a situation which would not be brought under control." The District Court did not reject these beliefs as fanciful or erroneous.... Without a showing that these beliefs were unreasonable, it was error for the District Court to conclude that appellants needed to show more. In particular, the burden was not on appellants to show affirmatively that the Union would be "detrimental to proper penological objectives" or would constitute a "present danger to security and order." [409 F. Supp.] at 944-945. Rather "[s]uch considerations are peculiarly within the province and professional expertise of corrections officials, and, in the absence of substantial evidence in the record to indicate that the officials have exaggerated their response to these considerations, courts should ordinarily defer to their expert judgment in such matters." Pell v. Procunier, 417 U.S., at 827. The necessary and correct result of our deference to the informed discretion of prison administrators permits them, and not the courts, to make difficult judgments concerning institutional operations in situations such as this.

... It is clearly not irrational to conclude that individuals may believe what they want, but that concerted group activity, or solicitation therefor, would pose additional and unwarranted problems and frictions in the operation of the State's penal institutions. The ban on inmate solicitation and group meetings, therefore, was rationally related to the reasonable, indeed to the central, objectives of prison administration. . . .

The invocation of the First Amendment, whether the asserted rights are speech or associational, does not change this analysis. . . . In seeking a "mutual accommodation between institutional needs and objectives [of prisons] and the provisions of the Constitution that are of general application," Wolff v. McDonnell, 418 U.S., at 556, this Court has repeatedly recognized the need for major restrictions on a prisoner's rights. . . . These restrictions have applied as well where First Amendment values were implicated. See, e.g., Pell v. Procunier, supra; Procunier v. Martinez, supra; Meachum v. Fano, 427 U.S. 215 (1976).

An examination of the potential restrictions on speech or association that have been imposed by the regulations under challenge, demonstrate that the restrictions imposed are reasonable, and are consistent with the inmates' status as prisoners and with the legitimate operational considerations of the institution. . . .

Appellant prison officials concluded that the presence, perhaps even the objectives, of a prisoners' labor union would be detrimental to order and security in the prisons. It is enough to say that they have not been conclusively shown to be wrong in this view. The interest in preserving order and authority in the prisons is self-evident. Prison life and relations between the inmates themselves and between the inmates and prison officials or staff, contain the ever-present potential for violent confrontation and conflagration.... Responsible prison officials must be permitted to take reasonable steps to forestall such a threat, and they must be permitted to act before the time when they can compile a dossier on the eve of a riot. The case of a prisoners' union, where the focus is on the presentation of grievances to, and encouragement of adversary relations with, institution officials surely would rank high on anyone's list of potential trouble spots. If the appellants' views as to the possible detrimental effects of the organizational activities of the Union are reasonable, as we conclude they are, then the regulations are drafted no more broadly than they need be to meet the perceived threat — which stems directly from group meetings and group organizational activities of the Union.... When weighed against the First Amendment rights asserted, these institutional reasons are sufficiently weighty to prevail.

[The Court also rejected an Equal Protection claim arising from the fact that certain outside groups like the Jaycees were permitted to operate within the prison. The Court reasoned that since a prison "... can no more easily be converted into a public forum than a military base ... appellants need only demonstrate a rational basis for their distinctions between organizational groups."

Chief Justice Burger concurred; Justice Stevens concurred in part, and Justices Marshall and Brennan dissented.]

NOTE

For cases following Jones, see: Pittman v. Hutto, 594 F.2d 407 (4th Cir. 1979) (magazine censorship); Preast v. Cox 628 F.2d 292 (4th Cir. 1980) (prisoner organizations); Ruiz v. Estelle, 503 F. Supp. 1265 (S.D. Tex 1980) (same); Wool v. Hogan, 505 F. Supp. 928 (D. Vt. 1981) (relying on Jones to uphold ban on inmate's marrying woman who had his child).

(page 1108) [1340]

NOTES

6. [continued] For a recent case holding that paralegals, generally entitled to entry into prison facilities, can be barred if the background of the individual seeking access demonstrates a serious threat to stability and security of the installation, see Philips v. Bureau of Prisons, 591 F.2d 966 (D.C. Cir. 1979); See also, Carey v. Beans, 500 F. Supp 580 (E.D. Pa.1980) (upholding exclusion of unlicensed bail bondsman).

(page 1114) [1346]

NOTES

5. [continued] At least three circuits have now held that religious-based claims of inmates to grow hair or wear beards are entitled to constitutional protection. See Burgin v. Henderson, 536 F.2d 501 (2d Cir. 1976) (Sunni Muslims); Teterud v. Burns, 522 F.2d 357 (8th Cir. 1975) (American Indian); Shabazz v. Barnauskas, 598 F.2d 345 (5th Cir. 1979). But see St. Claire v. Cuyler, 634 F.2d 109 (3d cir. 1980) (no right to fashion Muslim headdress). The Shabazz ruling by the Fifth Circuit was strongly influenced by an opinion by Justice Blackmun, dissenting from the denial of certiorari in a case involving the claims of an orthodox Jew. See Goulden v. Oliver, 442 U.S. 922 (1979).

(page 1115) [1347]

NOTES

1. [continued]. See immediately preceding note in this Supplement for discussion of religious-based claims to control personal appearance.

(page 1122) [1354]

Insert before Notes

HUTTO v. FINNEY
437 U.S. 678 (1978)

Mr. JUSTICE STEVENS delivered the opinion of the Court.

After finding that conditions in the Arkansas penal system constituted cruel and unusual punishment, the District Court entered a series of detailed remedial orders. On appeal to the United States Court of Appeals for the Eighth Circuit, petitioners challenged two aspects of that relief: (1) an order placing a maximum limit of 30 days on confinement in punitive isolation; and (2) an award of attorney's fees to be paid out of Department of Correction funds. The Court of Appeals affirmed and assessed an additional attorney's fee to cover services on appeal. . . . We granted certiorari. . . . and now affirm.

This litigation began in 1969; it is a sequel to two earlier cases holding that conditions in the Arkansas prison system violated the Eighth and Fourteenth Amendments. Only a brief summary of the facts is necessary to explain the basis for the remedial order.

The routine conditions that the ordinary Arkansas convict had to endure were characterized by the District Court as "a dark and evil world completely alien to the free world." 309 F. Supp., at 381. That

301

characterization was amply supported by the evidence. The punishments for misconduct not serious enough to result in punitive isolation were cruel, unusual, and unpredictable. It is the discipline known as "punitive isolation" that is most relevant for present purposes.

Confinement in punitive isolation was for an indeterminate period of time. An average of four, and sometimes as many as 10 or 11, prisoners were crowded into windowless 8′ × 10′ cells containing no furniture other than a source of water and a toilet that could only be flushed from outside the cell.... At night the prisoners were given mattresses to spread on the floor. Although some prisoners suffered from infectious diseases such as hepatitis and venereal disease, mattresses were removed and jumbled together each morning, then returned to the cells at random in the evening.... Prisoners in isolation received fewer than 1,000 calories a day; their meals consisted primarily of 4-inch squares of "grue," a substance created by mashing meat, potatoes, oleo, syrup, vegetables, eggs, and seasoning into a paste and baking the mixture in a pan.

... The situation in the punitive isolation cells was particularly disturbing. The [district] court concluded that either it had misjudged conditions in these cells in 1973 or conditions had become much worse since then. 410 F. Supp., at 275. There were still twice as many prisoners as beds in some cells. And because inmates in punitive isolation are often violently antisocial, overcrowding led to persecution of the weaker prisoners. The "grue" diet was still in use, and practically all inmates were losing weight on it. The cells had been vandalized to a "very substantial" extent. Id., at 276. Because of their inadequate numbers, guards assigned to the punitive isolation cells frequently resorted to physical violence, using nightsticks and Mace in their efforts to maintain order. Prisoners were sometimes left in isolation for months, their release depending on "their attitudes as appraised by prison personnel." Id., at 275.

The court concluded that the constitutional violations identified earlier had not been cured. It entered an order that placed limits on the number of men that could be confined in one cell, required that each have a bunk, discontinued the "grue" diet, and set 30 days as the maximum isolation sentence.... The Court of Appeals affirmed.... 548 F.2d, at 743.

The Eighth Amendment's ban on inflicting cruel and unusual punishments, made applicable to the States by the Fourteenth Amendment, "proscribes more than physically barbarous punishments." Estelle v. Gamble, 429 U.S. 97, 102. It prohibits penalties that are grossly disproportionate to the offense, Weems v. United States, 217 U.S. 349, 367, as well as those that transgress today's "broad and idealistic concepts of dignity, civilized standards, humanity, and decency." Estelle v. Gamble, 429 U.S. 97, 102, quoting Jackson v. Bishop, 404 F.2d 571, 579 (C.A.8

1968). Confinement in a prison or in an isolation cell is a form of punishment subject to scrutiny under Eighth Amendment standards....

Read in its entirety, the District Court's opinion makes it abundantly clear that the length of isolation sentences was not considered in a vacuum. In the court's words, punitive isolation "is not necessarily unconstitutional, but it may be, depending on the duration of the confinement and the conditions thereof." 410 F. Supp., at 275. It is perfectly obvious that every decision to remove a particular inmate from the general prison population for an indeterminate period could not be characterized as cruel and unusual. If new conditions of confinement are not materially different from those affecting other prisoners, a transfer for the duration of a prisoner's sentence might be completely unobjectionable and well within the authority of the prison administrator. Cf. Meachum v. Fano, 427 U.S. 215. It is equally plain, however, that the length of confinement cannot be ignored in deciding whether the confinement meets constitutional standards. A filthy, overcrowded cell and a diet of "grue" might be tolerable for a few days and intolerably cruel for weeks or months....

The order is supported by the interdependence of the conditions producing the violation. The vandalized cells and the atmosphere of violence were attributable, in part, to overcrowding and to deep-seated enmities growing out of months of constant friction. The 30-day limit will help to correct these conditions. Moreover, the limit presents little danger of interference with prison administration, for the Commissioner of Correction himself stated that prisoners should not ordinarily be held in punitive isolation for more than 14 days. 410 F. Supp., at 278. Finally, the exercise of discretion in this case is entitled to special deference because of the trial judge's years of experience with the problem at hand and his recognition of the limits on a federal court's authority in a case of this kind. Like the Court of Appeals, we find no error in the inclusion of a 30-day limitation on sentences to punitive isolation as a part of the District Court's comprehensive remedy.

[The remainder of the Court's opinion, holding that the award of attorneys' fees did not violate the Eleventh Amendment, is omitted, as is the concurring opinion of Justice Brennan addressed solely to that issue.]

Mr. JUSTICE POWELL, with whom The CHIEF JUSTICE joins, concurring in part and dissenting in part.

[Mr. JUSTICE REHNQUIST also filed a dissenting opinion.]

NOTE

For cases finding other particular conditions in violation of the Eighth Amendment, see: Bono v. Saxbe, 620 F.2d 609 (7th Cir. 1980); Parker

v. Cook, 474 F. Supp. 350 (S.D. Fla. 1979); Ruiz v. Estelle, 503 F. Supp. 1265 (S.D. Tex. 1980); see also: Sterling v. Cupp, 625 P.2d 123 (Ore. 1981) (using state constitutional ban against "unnecessary vigor" to invalidate patdown frisks of male inmates by female guards in toilets and showers); but see: Sala v. County of Suffolk, 604 F.2d 207 (2d Cir. 1979) (strip search of female by male guards held not unreasonable).

(page 1126) [1358]

Insert before Notes:

In 1979 and again in 1981, the Court decided two very important "conditions" cases.

In Bell v. Wolfish, 441 U.S. 520 (1979), a "jail" case, the Supreme Court for the first time directly addressed the issue of conditions of confinement for persons who have been charged with a crime but who have not yet been tried. The case involved a modern federally-operated short-term custodial facility in New York City designed primarily to house pre-trial detainees. The District Court invalidated more than twenty practices on constitutional and statutory ground, and the Court of Appeals largely affirmed these rulings, holding that under the Due Process clause of the Fifth Amendment, pre-trial detainees may be "subjected to only those 'restrictions and privations' which 'inhere in their confinement itself or which are justified by compelling necessities of jail administration.'" 573 F.2d at 124. Federal officials sought Supreme Court review of five of the practices condemned below — namely, housing two detainees in one room, prohibiting inmates' receipt of books and magazines except those sent directly from the publisher, banning the receipt of packages of food and personal items, requiring inmates to undergo body cavity searches following contact visits, and requiring that detainees remain outside their rooms during "shakedown" searches.

Justice Rehnquist's opinion first addressed the "double-bunking" practice, and in that context he identified the test to be used in assessing conditions challenges by pre-trial detainees. Purporting to agree with the lower court that the Fifth Amendment, rather than the Eighth, supplies the proper constitutional framework, Justice Rehnquist's opinion then proceeded in essentially an Eighth Amendment mode. Thus, the "compelling necessity" standard applied by the Second Circuit was found to be unwarranted under any Fifth Amendment theory, whether based on the presumption of innocence or fundamental liberty interests. Instead, the Court framed the question as follows: "In evaluating the constitutionality of conditions or restrictions of pretrial detention that implicate only the protection against deprivation of liberty without due process of law, we think that the proper inquiry is whether those conditions amount to punishment of the detainee." 441 U.S. at 535. And the conclusion that "punishment" has occurred turns not on how the challenged practice affects the detainee but, rather, on whether the disability is imposed for the purpose of punishment. Moreover, the Court stated, the government's interests must be evaluated not only in light of the government's interest in ensuring a detainee's appearance at trial, but *also* in terms of "the legitimate operational concerns [that] may require administrative measures that go beyond those that are, strictly speaking, necessary to ensure that the detainee shows up at trial.... Restraints that are reasonably related to the institution's interest in maintaining jail security do not, without more, constitute unconstitutional punishment...." 441 U.S. at 540. When applying these principles to judge the particular challenged practices, the court clearly treated "operational concerns" as the central consideration.

Given this highly deferential approach, it was no surprise that the Court upheld the challenged practices. Double-bunking was found not to constitute Fifth Amendment "punishment," with the Court observing that there is no "one man, one cell" principle "lurking" in the Due Process clause. Likewise, having placed a "heavy burden" on the detainees to show that officials had exaggerated their response to security problems, the Court handily upheld the four security rules as "rational" responses to those concerns, not motivated by "punitive" purposes.

Justice Powell concurred with all of these conclusions, except that he felt the body cavity searches a sufficiently serious intrusion on privacy so as to require "at least some level of cause, such as reasonable suspicion" to justify them. 441 U.S. at 563.

Justice Marshall, dissenting, observed that the use of a test focused on "punitive intent," coupled with "virtually unlimited deference" to official justification produced an ineffectual standard that was lacking in content. In his view, the most relevant factor is the impact of a challenged restriction on the detainee, and the inquiry must be "whether the governmental interests served by any given restriction outweigh the individual deprivations suffered." 441 U.S. at 564. From this perspective, Justice Marshall found the body cavity searches an unjustified and "grievous" offense against "personal dignity and common decency." Finally, Justice Stevens, joined by Justice Brennan, reasoned that the presumption of innocence prohibited the unnecessary and indiscriminate imposition of onerous conditions of confinement on pre-trial detainees merely because they are temporarily housed in the same facility as convicted inmates.

Two years after the decision in Bell v. Wolfish, the Supreme Court addressed the question of whether double-celling of convicted inmates constitutes cruel and unusual punishment under the Eighth Amendment. In Rhodes v. Chapman, — U.S. — , 69 L. Ed. 2d 59 (1981), a district court had concluded that, despite generally favorable conditions at a new Ohio prison, the practice of double-celling, which resulted from the almost immediate overcrowding of the facility, constituted cruel and unusual punishment. The Supreme Court, 8-1, reversed, in an opinion by Justice Powell. This was the Court's first major encounter with the question of Eighth Amendment limitations on prison conditions, and the Court concluded that "the Constitution does not mandate comfortable prisons, and prisons of [this] type, which house persons convicted of serious crimes, cannot be free of discomfort." 69 L. Ed. 2d at 70. Justice Powell made clear, however, that judicial review would still be available where conditions are "deplorable" and "sordid."

Justices Brennan, Blackmun, and Stevens, concurring in the judgment, surveyed the lower court decisions detailing deplorable and unconstitutional conditions at a number of prisons, but they concluded that "this prison, crowded though it is, is one of the better, more humane large prisons in the Nation". Id. at 81-82.

Justice Marshall, the only dissenter, observed that the federal courts were the only effective buffer against unconstitutional conditions in prison: "With the rising crime rates of recent years, there has been an alarming tendency toward a simplistic penological philosophy that if we lock the prison doors and throw away the keys, our streets will somehow be safe. In the current climate, it is unrealistic to expect legislators to care whether the prisons are overcrowded or harmful to inmate health. It is at that point — when conditions are deplorable and the political process offers no redress — that the federal courts are required by the Constitution to play a role. I believe that this vital duty was properly discharged by the District Court and the Court of Appeals in this case. The majority today takes a step toward abandoning that role altogether. I dissent." 69 L. Ed. 2d at 88.

For recent cases involving challenges to general or specific prison and jail conditions see: Spain v. Procunier, 600 F.2d 189 (9th Cir. 1979) (use of tear gas held reasonable); Inmates of Allegheny County Jail v. Pierce, 612 F.2d 754 (3d Cir. 1979) (upholding conditions imposed on pre-trial detainees); Jordan v. Wolke, 615 F.2d 749 (7th Cir. 1980) (same); Bono v. Saxbe, 620 F.2d 609 (7th Cir. 1980) (invalidating strip searches after noncontact visits; Bell v. Wolfish distinguished); Cotton v. Lockhart, 620 F.2d 670 (8th Cir. 1980) (permitting ban on inmate's receiving books and magazines); Campbell v. Cauthron, 623 F.2d 503 (8th Cir. 1980) (invalidating conditions imposed on pre-trial detainees because more onerous than for regular inmates); Hayward v. Procunier, 629 F.2d 599 (9th Cir. 1980) (five-month state of emergency "lockdown" of prison upheld); Jones v. Diamond, 636 F.2d 1364 (5th Cir. 1981) (en banc) (remanded in light of Bell v. Wolfish); Davis v. Smith, 638 F.2d 66 (8th Cir. 1981) (damages awarded for unconstitutional pre-trial detention conditions); Putnam v. Gerloff, 639 F.2d 415 (8th Cir. 1981) (remand for jury trial in damage suit against guards who beat pre-trial detainees); Lock v. Jenkins, 641 F.2d 488 (7th Cir. 1981) (finding conditions imposed on pre-trial detainees to be unconstitutional).

(page 1136) (1365)

NOTE

8. In Estelle v. Gamble, 429 U.S. 97 (1976), a state inmate brought a civil rights action under 42 U.S.C. §1983 against petitioners, the state corrections department medical director (Gray) and two correctional officials, claiming that he was subjected to cruel and unusual punishment in violation of the Eighth Amendment for inadequate treatment of a back injury assertedly sustained while he was engaged in prison work. The District Court dismissed the complaint for failure to state a claim upon which relief could be granted. The Court of Appeals held that the alleged insufficiency of the medical treatment required reinstatement of the complaint.

The Supreme Court reversed: Deliberate indifference by prison personnel to a prisoner's serious illness or injury constitutes cruel and unusual punishment contravening the Eighth Amendment. According to the Court, respondent's claims against Gray do not suggest such indifference, the allegations revealing that Gray and other medical personnel saw respondent on seventeen occasions during a three-month span and treated his injury and other problems. The failure to perform an X-ray or to use additional diagnostic techniques does not constitute cruel and unusual punishment but is at most medical malpractice cognizable in the state courts. The question whether respondent has stated a constitutional claim against the other petitioners, the Director of the Department of Corrections and the warden of the prison, was not separately evaluated by the Court of Appeals and should be considered on remand.

Mr. Justice Blackmun concurred in the judgment and Mr. Justice Stevens wrote a dissenting opinion.

The important issue of affording a federal prisoner a remedy for inadequate medical treatment was addressed by the Court in Carlson v. Green, 446 U.S. 14 (1980). The mother of a federal prisoner who died as a result of injuries sustained at the prison filed suit against prison officials alleging that their failure to supply medical care caused the death and violated her son's constitutional rights to due process, equal protection, and freedom from cruel and unusual punishment. The major issue before the Court was whether the allegations of unconstitutional Eighth Amendment wrongdoing gave rise to a direct federal claim for damages under Bivens v. Six Unknown Named Agents of Federal Bureau of Narcotics, 403 U.S. 388 (1971). The Court held that they did, finding "no special factors counselling hesitation in the absence of affirmative action by Congress," and "no explicit congressional declaration that persons injured by federal officers' violation of the Eighth Amendment may not recover money damages from the agents but must be remitted to another remedy. . . ." 446 U.S. at 19. On the latter point, the Court rejected the contention that the availability of a remedy against the United States under the Federal Tort Claims Act, 28 U.S.C. §2680(h) could displace the Bivens damage action against the officials. Indeed, the Court concluded that "... victims of the kind of intentional wrongdoing alleged in this complaint shall have an action under FTCA against the United States as well as a Bivens action against the individual officials alleged to have infringed their constitutional rights." 446 U.S. at 20. For recent lower court cases dealing with medical treatment issues, see Fielder v. Bosshard, 590 F.2d 105 (5th Cir. 1979) (upholding damage award to parents of prisoner who died because of inadequate medical care); Inmates of Allegheny County Jail v. Pierce, 612 F.2d 754 (3d Cir. 1979) (lack of mental health care violative of Eighth Amendment); Hamilton v. Roth, 624 F.2d 1204 (3d Cir. 1980).

(page 1149) [1381]

NOTE

2.a. The principles identified in Wolff v. McDonnell have more recently been considered by the Court in assessing the validity of specific disciplinary actions.

In Baxter v. Palmigiano, 425 U.S. 308 (1976) (decided together with Enonoto v. Clutchette, both of which are noted in the main volume at pp. 1148-1149 [1380], the Court held that, in prison disciplinary proceedings: (1) prisoners were not entitled to state-appointed counsel, (2) the privilege against self-incrimination did not prohibit drawing adverse inferences from their silence, and (3) no written statement of reasons for denying a prisoner the right of confrontation or cross examination of witnesses need be supplied. The Court expressly left open the question of whether minimum due process safeguards were required whenever loss of privileges short of disciplinary punishment was imposed.

The issue in Meachum v. Fano, 427 U.S. 215 (1976), was whether due process requires a hearing prior to a "punitive" transfer of a prisoner to a prison "the conditions of which are substantially less favorable to the prisoner, absent a state law or practice conditioning such transfers on proof of serious misconduct or the occurrence of other events." Id., at 216. The Court held that no hearing was required because no liberty interest was at stake:

"... [W]e cannot agree that *any* change in the conditions of confinement having a substantial adverse impact on the prisoner involved is sufficient to invoke the protections of the Due Process Clause. The Due Process Clause by its own force forbids the State from convicting any person of crime and depriving him of his liberty without complying fully with the requirements of the Clause. But given a valid conviction, the criminal defendant has been constitutionally deprived of his liberty to the extent that the State may confine him and subject him to the rules of its prison system so long as the conditions of confinement do not otherwise violate the Constitution. The Constitution does not require that the State have more than one prison for convicted felons; nor does it guarantee that the convicted prisoner will be placed in any particular prison if, as is likely, the State has more than one correctional institution. The initial decision to assign the convict to a particular institution is not subject to audit under the Due Process Clause, although the degree of confinement in one prison may be quite different from that in another. The conviction has sufficiently extinguished the defendant's liberty interest to empower the State to confine him in *any* of its prisons.

"Neither, in our view, does the Due Process Clause in and of itself protect a duly convicted prisoner against transfer from one institution to another within the state prison system. Confinement in any of the State's institutions is within the normal limits or range of custody which the conviction has authorized the State to impose. That life in one prison is much more disagreeable than in another does not in itself signify that a Fourteenth Amendment liberty interest is implicated when a prisoner is transferred to the institution with the more severe rules.

". . . [T]o hold as we are urged to do that *any* substantial deprivation imposed by prison authorities triggers the procedural protections of the Due Process Clause would subject to judicial review a wide spectrum of discretionary actions that traditionally have been the business of prison administrators rather than of the federal courts."

Justice Stevens' dissenting opinion, joined by Justices Brennan and Marshall, took the position that each inmate retains a continuing liberty interest in his status.

In Montanye v. Haymes, 427 U.S. 236 (1976), decided on the same day as Meachum v. Fano, the Court made it clear that the rule announced in Meachum applies not only to discretionary administrative transfers but to disciplinary transfers as well. Montanye alleged that he had been transferred to a different prison in order to punish him for advising other prisoners of their legal rights. The district court ruled the transfer a legitimate exercise of official discretion, but the court of appeals reversed, holding that procedural due process attached to punitive transfers, and remanded the case for a determination of whether the transfer was sufficiently burdensome to Montanye to require procedural formalities. Justice White, writing the Supreme Court's opinion, reversed the court of appeals and rejected the distinction based on the purpose of the transfer: "We held in Meachum . . . that no Due Process Clause liberty interest of a duly convicted prison inmate is infringed when he is transferred from one prison to another within the State, whether with or without a hearing, absent some right or justifiable expectation rooted in state law that he will not be transferred except for misbehavior or upon the occurrence of other specified events. . . . The [Due Process]

Clause does not require hearings in connection with transfers whether or not they are the result of the inmate's misbehavior or may be labeled as disciplinary or punitive." Justice Stevens, joined by Justices Brennan and Marshall, dissented. Following the remand, the United States Court of Appeals held that there were genuine issues of material fact as to whether the transfer violated the inmate's right to help other prisoners prepare habeas corpus petitions. Haymes v. Montanye, 547 F.2d 188 (2d. Cir. 1976), cert. denied, 431 U.S. 967 (1977).

For two recent cases involving statutory restrictions on the transfer of inmates from prisons in one state to facilities in another, see: Cuyler v. Adams, 66 L. Ed. 2d 641 (1981), and Howe v. Smith, 69 L. Ed. 2d 171 (1981).

For recent lower court cases involving disciplinary actions and transfers within or between prisons, see: Spain v. Procunier, 600 F.2d 189 (9th Cir. 1979) (permissible to place prisoners in segregation without a hearing); Furtado v. Bishop, 604 F.2d 80 (1st Cir. 1979) (damages for segregated confinement possible if confinement arbitrary, grossly disproportionate to offense, and cruel and unusual); Mitchell v. Hicks, 614 F.2d 1016 (5th Cir. 1980) (where transfer to segregation permissible only for reasons specified in prison regulations, hearings required to establish truth of infractions); Pugliese v. Nelson, 617 F.2d 916 (1st Cir. 1980) (prison classifications that deny prisoners certain privileges do not trigger due process requirements); Bills v. Henderson, 631 F.2d 1287 (6th Cir. 1980) (promulgation of prison guidelines on transfer to segregation entitled prisoners to at least minimal due process safeguards before transfer made); Micklus v. Carlson, 632 F.2d 227 (3d Cir. 1980) (youthful federal offender has statutory right to be kept from adult prisoners; damage action available); Chavis v. Rowe, 643 F.2d 1281 (7th Cir. 1981) (prisoner placed by disciplinary committee in segregation and deprived of good time credit, without statement of evidence and reasons and through failure to disclose exculpatory evidence, was denied due process); Cofone v. Manson, 594 F.2d 934 (2d Cir. 1979) (transfer of prisoner from Connecticut State prison to federal prison in Georgia, without a hearing, held permissible); Cobb v. Aytch, 643 F.2d 946 (3d Cir. 1981) (pre-trial detainees may not be transferred to facility out of the community without a prior hearing); Wakinekona v. Olin, 646 F.2d 378 (9th Cir. 1981), cert. granted, 50 U.S.L.W. 3947 (June 1, 1982) (Hawaii regulations specifying procedures before transfer to California prison create liberty interest and trigger due process safeguards).

(page 1150) [1382]

NOTES

3.a. The Court has decided four recent cases involving the procedures required when officials make decisions that vitally affect a prisoner's status. The cases involved the grant of parole, the commutation of a life sentence, the transfer of a prisoner to a mental institution, and the retroactive change of good time credit rules.

In Greenholtz v. Inmates, Nebraska Penal and Correctional Complex, 442 U.S. 1 (1979), the issues were whether due process applies to the discretionary parole release decision and, if so, what procedures are required. By statute, Nebraska provided detailed procedures and standards to govern the discretionary parole decision. The lower courts had found a "conditional liberty" interest in parole so as to require better procedures than those that Nebraska supplied.

The Supreme Court reversed. First, the Court assessed the general nature of the individual's interest in parole:

"There is no constitutional or inherent right of a convicted person to be conditionally released before the expiration of a valid sentence. The natural desire of an individual to be released is indistinguishable from the initial resistance to being confined. But the conviction, with all its procedural safeguards, has extinguished that liberty right: '[G]iven a valid conviction, the criminal defendant has been constitutionally deprived of his liberty.' Meachum v. Fano, 427 U.S. 215, 224 (1977).

"Decisions of the Executive Branch, however serious their impact, do not automatically invoke due process protection; there simply is no constitutional guarantee that all executive decisionmaking must comply with standards that assure error-free determinations. . . . This is especially true with respect to the sensitive choices presented by the administrative decision to grant parole release.

"A state may, as Nebraska has, establish a parole system, but it has no duty to do so. Moreover, to insure that the state-created parole system serves the public interest purposes of rehabilitation and deterrence, the state may be specific or general in defining the conditions for release and the factors that should be considered by the parole authority." 442 U.S. at 8.

Next, the Court addressed the argument that whenever a state provides a parole system and the possibility of parole, it has created a reasonable entitlement to parole so as to require some procedures:

"The fallacy in respondents' position is that parole *release* and parole *revocation* are quite different. There is a crucial distinction between being deprived of a liberty one has, as in parole, and being denied a conditional liberty that one desires. The parolees in Morrissey (and probationers in Gagnon [v. Scarpelli, 411 U.S. 778 (1973)]) were at liberty and as such could 'be gainfully employed and [were] free to be with family and friends and to form the enduring attachments of normal life.' 408 U.S., at 482. The inmates here, on the other hand, are confined and thus subject to all of the necessary restraints that inhere in a prison.

"A second important difference between discretionary parole *release* from confinement and *termination* of parole lies in the nature of the decision that must be made in each case. As we recognized in Morrissey, the parole revocation determination actually requires two decisions: whether the parolee in fact acted in violation of one or more conditions of parole and whether the parolee should be recommitted either for his or society's benefit. Id., at 479-480. 'The first step in a revocation decision thus involves a wholly retrospective factual question.' Id., at 479.

"The parole release 'decision,' however, is more subtle and depends on an amalgam of elements, some of which are factual but many of which are purely subjective appraisals by the Board members based upon their experience with the difficult and sensitive task of evaluating the advisability of parole release. Unlike the revocation decision, there is not set of facts which, if shown, mandate a decision favorable to the individual. . . .

"That the state holds out the *possibility* of parole provides no more than a mere hope that the benefit will be obtained. . . . To that extent the general interest asserted here is not more substantial than the inmates's hope that he will not be transferred to another prison, a hope which is not protected by due process. Meachum v. Fano, supra, at 225 (1977); Montanye v. Haymes, 427 U.S. 227 (1977)." 442 U.S. at 9-10.

Finally, the Court considered the narrow argument that the specific Nebraska statutory scheme — which provided that parole "shall" be granted unless one or more statutory conditions were found to exist — itself created a protectible exception of parole. Here, the Court agreed that the statute's "expectancy of release" did warrant some constitutional protection but cautioned that "this statute has unique structure and language and thus whether any other state statute provides a protectible entitlement must be decided on a case-by-case basis." 442 U.S. at 12. Turning to the procedures constitutionally required, the Court ruled that, in light of the "subjective nature" of the parole decision, the procedures supplied by the statute were adequate, no adversary hearing is required, and no statement of evidence relied upon need be given. Four Justices disagreed, taking the position that the adoption of a parole system did create a constitutionally protected interest in parole, and that the procedures supplied by Nebraska were inadequate to safeguard that interest. As Justice Marshall put it: ". . . the Court nowhere explains why the [subjective] *nature of the decisional process* has even the slightest bearing in assessing the *nature of the interest* this process may terminate." 442 U.S. at 27 (emphasis in original). See also, Evans v. Dillahunty, — F.2d —, 50 U.S.L.W. 2352 (8th Cir. 1981).

(For a recent decision holding that parole board officials are absolutely immune from suits for damages arising out of decisions to grant, deny or revoke parole, see Sellars v. Procunier, 641 F.2d 1295 (9th Cir. 1981)).

Given the approach in Greenholtz, the result two years later in Connecticut Board of Pardons v. Dumschat, — U.S. —, 69 L. Ed. 2d 158

(1981) is not surprising. The issue was "whether the fact that the Connecticut Board of Pardons has granted approximately three-fourths of the applications for commutation of life sentences creates a constitutional 'liberty interest' or 'entitlement' in life-term inmates so as to require that Board to explain its reasons for denial of an application for commutation." 69 L. Ed. 2d at 162. Chief Justice Burger, writing for the Court, held that it did not: "No matter how frequently a particular form of clemency has been granted, the statistical probabilities standing alone generate no constitutional protections; a contrary conclusion would trivialize the Constitution. The ground for a constitutional claim, if any, must be found in statutes or other rules defining the obligations of the authority charged with exercising clemency." Id. at 165. See also, Jago v. Van Curen, — U.S. — , 50 U.S.L.W. 3370 (Nov. 9, 1981) (per curiam).

The Court was far more generous in upholding a claimed liberty interest in Vitek v. Jones, 445 U.S. 480 (1980), involving the transfer of an inmate from a prison to a state mental institution for treatment of a "mental disease or defect." The Court's 5-4 decision rested on two grounds. First, as in Greenholtz, a statute specifically provided that such a transfer was permissible only where a physician certified that the prisoner "suffers from a mental disease or defect" that "cannot be given proper treatment" in prison. The practice accorded with the provision. The Court found that the statute and the practice under it created a right or expectation that required constitutionally determined procedural protections. Second, even apart from this statutorily derived expectation, the Court recognized the independent liberty interest — of inmate or ordinary citizen — in not being involuntarily committed to a mental institution or labelled mentally ill. Both liberty interests were held to require the following procedural safeguards: written notice in advance of the intent to transfer, an adversary hearing, an opportunity to confront and cross-examine, an independent decision maker, a written statement of evidence relied on and reasons for the decision, and timely notice of these various rights. The Court also upheld the requirement that counsel be made available but, because of Justice Powell's decisive concurring opinion, counsel need not be a licensed attorney.

The last decision in the group, Weaver v. Graham, — U.S. — , 67 L. Ed. 2d 17 (1981), was one of those rare cases decided on the basis of the prohibition against ex post facto laws. The case involved a change in the Florida statutory formula for awarding good time credit toward early release, as applied to an inmate whose crime was committed years before the formula change was enacted. The change reduced from 15 to 9 days the amount of good time credit that an inmate could earn each month. Characterizing the change as a retroactive increase in legislative punishment, the Court unanimously concluded that it constituted an invalid ex post facto law.

B. THE RIGHTS OF MENTAL PATIENTS

(PAGE 1168) [1402]

NOTES

4. [continued] The rights of the civilly committed mentally retarded have been the subject of extensive litigation and public attention. Protracted litigation has been aimed at remedying the conditions at New York's notorious Willowbrook School. See New York State Association for Retarded Children v. Carey, 393 F. Supp. 715 (E.D.N.Y. 1975), aff'd, 596 F.2d 27 (2d Cir. 1979); 492 F. Supp. 1099 (E.D.N.Y. 1980), aff'd, 631 F.2d 162 (2d Cir. 1980). The case resulted in the creation of a special panel to fashion elaborate remedial programs, including mandated expenditure of state funds. See also Welsh v. Likens, 550 F.2d 1122 (8th Cir. 1977).

The Supreme Court has had one opportunity to help remedy these problems but declined to do so. The Developmentally Disabled Assistance and Bill of Rights Act of 1975, 42 U.S.C.§6000 et seq., provided financial assistance to states for the care and treatment of the developmentally disabled, on condition that the recipients agree to abide by a patients' "bill of rights," including the right to treatment. In Pennhurst State School v. Halderman, — U.S. —, 67 L. Ed. 2d 694 (1981), the Court held that the Act did not create any "substantive rights" to treatment or any implied cause of action on behalf of persons at a federally funded facility that fell woefully short of meeting the Act's requirements. The Court found that the Act provided only a "funding incentive," not an enforceable obligation by the states to comply with the "bill of rights." The Court had another opportunity to consider the conditions at Pennhurst in Youngberg v. Romeo, 50 U.S.L.W. 4681 (June 18, 1982), and found constitutional violations in the lack of treatment of and the imposition of physical restraints on mentally retarded persons at state institutions. See also, In Re Hop, 623 P.2d 282 (Cal. Sup. Ct. 1981) (indefinite involuntary confinement of developmentally disabled adults in state hospital, without procedural safeguards available to other comparable individuals, violates Equal Protection Clause).

(page 1169) [1403]

For a recent decision applying the right to treatment of the involuntarily committed mentally ill, see Scott v. Plante, 641 F.2d 117 (3d Cir. 1981); see also Flakes v. Percy, 511 F. Supp. 1325 (W.D. Wis. 1981) finding conditions at mental hospital violative of Eighth Amendment and due process).

(page 1174) [1408]

NOTES

1. [continued] In Stump v. Sparkman, 435 U.S. 349 (1978), the Court granted "absolute" immunity from suit under 42 U.S.C. §1983 to a state court judge who had granted a petition to sterilize a "somewhat retarded" minor, because the judge had not acted in the "clear absence of all jurisdiction." This result was reached despite the lack of a specific statute granting the judge jurisdiction and despite gross procedural deficiencies. For recent cases holding that an incompetent person cannot be sterilized involuntarily without careful judicial safeguards, see In re Grady, 426 A.2d 467 (N.J. 1981); KCM v. Alaska, 627 P.2d 607 (Alaska 1981).

(page 1174) [1408]

NOTE

4. An important issue in the area of mental patients rights is whether such individuals have a right to refuse treatment involving the forced use of antipsychotic drugs, except in emergencies. The Supreme Court recently avoided resolving that issue. In Rogers v. Okin, 634 F.2d 650 (1st Cir. 1980), cert. granted sub nom., Mills v. Rogers, 49 U.S.L.W. 3788 (April 20, 1981), the First Circuit held that such drugs may be administered only as a last resort, based on specific findings, following a due process hearing. The Supreme Court remanded the case for reconsideration in light of an intervening state court ruling. See 50 U.S.L.W. 4676 (June 18, 1982); see also: Rennie v. Klein, 653 F.2d 836, 50 U.S.L.W. 2033 (3d Cir. July 9, 1981) (en banc) (drugs may not be administered except as last resort, but due process hearing not required); Davis v. Hubbard, 506 F. Supp. 915 (N.D. Ohio 1980).

(page 1175) [1410]

NOTE

[continued] The Supreme Court has been very active recently in one area directly affecting the rights of mental patients — the procedures required before involuntary civil commitment to a mental institution can occur in the first place.

First, in Addington v. Texas, 441 U.S. 418 (1979), the question was the standard of proof constitutionally required to civilly commit a person, involuntarily and indefinitely, to a state mental institution. Chief

Justice Burger, for a unanimous Court, held that jury instructions requiring findings of mental illness and dangerousness on the basis of "clear, unequivocal and convincing evidence," were constitutionally acceptable. In validating use of this "intermediate" standard — between the milder preponderance of the evidence test used in normal civil litigation and the stringent "beyond a reasonable doubt" standard used in criminal and juvenile delinquincy proceedings — the Court observed that ". . . the individual's interest in the outcome of a civil commitment proceeding is of such weight and gravity that due process requires the state to justify confinement by proof more substantial than a mere preponderance of the evidence." Id. at 427. But the Court refused to require use of the reasonable doubt test in commitment proceedings. The Court reasoned that such proceedings were not "punitive," that the "moral force" of the standard should be limited to criminal cases, that interested persons were continually "reviewing" the patient's condition and the propriety of continued commitment, and, finally, the inherent uncertainties in identifying mental illness might make it impossible for the state ever to discharge the burden of proof required by the reasonable doubt test.

The Court's unanimity in Addington v. Texas faltered over the issue of what procedures must be required before children may be committed to state mental institutions by their parents or guardians, or by the state. Parham v. J. L., 442 U. S. 584 (1979). Once again Chief Justice Burger wrote for the majority. The Court assumed that a child has a protected liberty interest in avoiding the restraints and stigmatization of confinement in a mental institution, but identified, as a limitation on the child's interest, the role of parents recognized by our culture. The Court reconciled the conflicting interests by according to parents the primary role of deciding upon such commitment, but subjecting that decision to the check of a "neutral fact-finder" who will determine whether the statutory criteria for commitment are met initially and periodically thereafter.

In a case decided the same day, the Court applied these principles to sustain the validity of Pennsylvania's procedures for civil commitment of children. See Secretary of Public Welfare of Pennsylvania v. Institutionalized Juveniles, 442 U.S. 640 (1979).

For recent cases involving similar issues, see Dorsey v. Solomon, 604 F.2d 271 (4th Cir. 1979) (invalidating procedures for involuntary commitment of persons found not guilty by reason of insanity); Suzuki v. Yuen, 617 F. 2d 173 (9th Cir. 1980) (invalidating statute authorizing commitment of persons dangerous to property); Chancery Clerk, Chickasaw County v. Wallace, 646 F.2d 151 (5th Cir. 1981) (specifying whether §1983 or habeas corpus should be proper remedy for persons involuntarily committed).

For procedures required when a person is transferred from a prison to a mental institution, see Vitek v. Jones, discussed supra at 313.

C. THE RIGHTS OF MILITARY PERSONNEL

(page 1192) [1426]

NOTES

1.c. Greer v. Spock, 424 U.S. 828 (1976), concerned Fort Dix, a federal military reservation devoted primarily to basic training for newly inducted Army personnel, and over which the Government exercises exclusive jurisdiction, but permits free civilian access to certain unrestricted areas. However, post regulations ban speeches and demonstrations of a partisan polical nature and also prohibit the distribution of literature without prior approval of post headquarters. Pursuant to these regulations the commanding officer of Fort Dix rejected the request of respondent candidates for President and Vice President to distribute campaign literature and hold a political meeting on the post , and the other respondents, who had been evicted on several occasions for distributing literature not previously approved, were barred from re-entering the post. Respondents brought suit to enjoin enforcement of these regulations on the ground that they violated the First and Fifth Amendments. The District Court issued an injunction prohibiting the military authorities from interfering with the making of political speeches or the distribution of leaflets in areas of Fort Dix open to the general public, and the Court of Appeals affirmed.

The Supreme Court reversed. It first held that the regulations were not constitutionally invalid on their face. Since under the Constitution it is the basic function of a military installation like Fort Dix to train soldiers, not to provide a public forum, and since, as a necessary concomitant to this basic function, a commanding officer has the historically unquestioned power to exclude civilians from the area of his command, any notion that federal military installations, like municipal streets and parks have traditionally served as a place for free public assembly and communication of thoughts by private citizens is false, and therefore respondents had no generalized constitutional right to make political speeches or distribute leaflets at Fort Dix.

The Court also held that the regulations were not applied invalidly in the circumstances of this case. The Court said that, as to the regulation banning political speeches and demonstrations, there was no claim that the military authorities discriminated in any way among candidates based upon the candidates' supposed political views; on the contrary it appeared that Fort Dix has a policy, objectively and evenhandedly applied, of keeping official military activities there wholly free of entanglement with any partisan political campaigns, a policy that the post was constitutionally free to pursue.

As to the regulation governing the distribution of literature, a military commander may disapprove only those publications that he perceives clearly endanger the loyalty, discipline, or morale of troops on the base under his command, and, while this regulation might in the future be applied irrationally, invidiously, or arbitrarily, none of the respondents even submitted any material for review, and the noncandidate respondents had been excluded from the post because they had previously distributed literature there without attempting to obtain approval.

The Court took a similar approach in two more recent military free speech cases. Both Brown v. Glines, 444 U.S. 340 (1980), and Secretary of the Navy v. Huff, 444 U.S. 453 (1980), involved efforts by servicemen at military installations to circulate and gather signatures on petitions to members of Congress. Military regulations which required prior command approval of any such activities were challenged under the First Amendment and also under a special statute, 10 U.S.C. 1034, that protects the right of members of the armed forces to communicate with Congress. In Brown v. Glines, the Court, 5-4, rejected both contentions. Adhering to the approach taken in Greer v. Spock and Parker v. Levy, the Court found that the regulations — which permitted approval to be denied when the commanding officer determined that "a clear danger to the loyalty, discipline, or morale of members of the Armed Forces, or material interference with the accomplishment of a military mission, would result" — protected "a substantial governmental interest unrelated to the suppression of free expression," and restricted speech "no more than is reasonably necessary to protect the substantial governmental interest." 444 U.S. at 354. Concluding that the prior approval requirement was necessary to avoid disruption and safeguard discipline, the Court held that the regulations did not violate the First Amendment. The statutory claim was rejected on the ground that the law's purpose was to protect individual communication of grievances to members of Congress, not group petitions: "... Congress enacted §1034 to ensure that an individual member of the armed services could write to his elected representative without sending his communication through official channels." 444 U.S. at 359. By contrast, "the unrestricted circulation of collective petitions could imperil discipline." Id. at 360.

Justice Brennan dissented, objecting that the regulations "plainly establish an essentially discretionary regime of censorship that arbitrarily deprives respondents of precious communicative rights." Id. at 362. In his view, the scheme was an impermissible prior restraint, with no procedural safeguards, and serving no demonstrated compelling military needs. Justices Stewart, Marshall, and Stevens dissented on the basis of the statute.

For a critical comment on this decision, see Dash, Comment, Brown v. Glines, Bowing To The "Shibboleth of Military Necessity," 47 Brooklyn L. Rev. 249 (1980).

(page 1194) [1428]

NOTES

2.a. [continued] The favorable district court decision in Committee for G.I. Rights v. Callaway, 370 F. Supp. 934 (D.D.C. 1974), was subsequently reversed by the court of appeals on grounds of general judicial deference to military judgments. See 518 F.2d 466 (D.C. Cir. 1975).

(page 1195) [1429]

NOTES

2.b. [continued]. In Matlovich v. Secretary of the Air Force. 591 F.2d 852 (D.C. Cir. 1978), and Berg v. Claytor, 591 F.2d 849 (D.C. Cir. 1978), the court of appeals, in reviewing a discharge for admitted homosexual behavior, held that such dismissals could be arbitrary and capricious where the military failed adequately to explain to the reviewing court why the "unusual circumstances" exception to the dismissal regulations was not applied, and where the serviceman's ability to perform his duties had not been compromised. Contra, Beller v. Middendorf, 632 F.2d 788 (9th cir. 1980).

(page 1198) [1432]

NOTES

4. [continued] In Middendorf v. Henry, 425 U.S. 25 (1976), the Supreme Court held that counsel need not be provided at summary court martial proceedings, which the Court found were not "criminal prosecutions" within the meaning of the Sixth Amendment. Justice Rehnquist wrote the Court's opinion; Justices Brennan, Stewart, and Marshall dissented.

Chapter Seventeen

The Constitutional Litigation Process

(page 1200) [1435]

In his book, Democracy and Distrust (1980), John Hart Ely argued that the principal justification for judicial review in a democracy is to assure the proper functioning of the democratic process. His provocative defense of the Warren Court's use of judicial power as an aid to the functioning of democratic political theory has crystallized much academic writing on judicial review. The principal themes are sounded in Symposia in 56 N.Y.U.L. Rev. No. 4 (1981) and 42 Ohio St. L.J. No. 1 (1981).

A. THE DOCTRINE OF STANDING

(page 1240) [1474]

NOTE—SUPREME COURT STANDING CASES SINCE WARTH v. SELDIN

1. In Duke Power Company v. Carolina Environmental Study Group, 438 U.S. 59 (1978), persons residing in the vicinity of a proposed nuclear power plant were given standing to challenge the constitutionality of a federal statute that limited the plant's liability in case of a nuclear accident. Plaintiffs in Duke Power alleged two distinct standing theories. First, they argued that as residents of the area, they were subject to a risk or injury from a nuclear accident without adequate compensation. The Court declined to grant standing to the plaintiffs as prospective victims, holding that the possibility of the plaintiffs actually being injured in a nuclear accident causing damage beyond the liability ceiling was too speculative. Second, plaintiffs argued that as residents of the area, they would suffer environmental and aesthetic injury if the plant were built and that "but for" the limitation on liability it would prove difficult, if

not impossible, to secure financing for the plant. Chief Justice Burger, writing for the Court, recognized plaintiffs' environmental injury as a sufficient injury in fact to confer standing. Moreover, he ruled that since a direct causal relationship existed between the threatened injury-in-fact (environmental damage caused by the plant) and the challenged statute (making it possible to finance and build the plant), plaintiffs were entitled to raise any legal argument which might invalidate the statute and, thus, prevent the injury in fact from occurring.

It is doubtful whether Duke Power signals a genuine relaxation of the Court's standing rules. Rather, Duke Power may be better understood as an example of the Court's reaching for a case in order to remove a cloud on the financing of nuclear power plants. After straining to uphold standing, the Court reversed the District Court and rejected plaintiffs' position on the merits. If plaintiffs' challenge had been rejected on standing grounds, the lower court's decision invalidating the limitation of liability would have stood as a serious impediment to future financing efforts.

2. Somewhat less cynically, Duke Power may also be read as an example of the current Court's preoccupation with causation-in-fact as a significant element of standing. Once the Court found that the challenged statute in Duke Power was a "but for" cause of the plaintiffs' injury-in-fact, it recognized an obligation to entertain plaintiffs' legal challenge. In Warth v. Seldin, 422 U.S. 490 (1976), plaintiff's failure to have established a causal nexus between their injury-in-fact and defendant's actions precluded the grant of standing. In Simon v. Eastern Kentucky Welfare Rights Organization, 426 U.S. 26 (1976), the causation-in-fact test was applied with a vengeance. In Simon v. EKWRO, indigent plaintiffs alleged that tax-exempt private hospitals were failing to provide adequate health care for indigents in violation of a provision of the Internal Revenue Code that, allegedly, required a hospital to provide services to the poor in order to qualify as a tax-exempt organization to which tax deductible gifts could be given. Plaintiffs alleged that the Internal Revenue Service had issued an incorrect ruling that permitted hospitals to qualify as tax-deductible recipients without providing adequate services to the poor. Justice Powell, expanding on his decision in Warth, recognized that plaintiffs who failed to receive adequate health care suffered an injury-in-fact. However, he held that no showing had been made that private hospitals would provide better health care to the plaintiffs if the challenged ruling were revoked. Rather than provide health care to the poor, Justice Powell speculated that the hospitals might elect to forego tax deductibility. Since, in the Court's estimation, no "but for" relationship existed between the plaintiffs' injury-in-fact and the challenged IRS ruling, the Court held that no Article III case or controversy existed. While it is possible that a stronger causal nexus existed in Duke Power than in Simon v. EKWRO, the relative causal consequences of the two cases are far from self-evident. Indeed,

if one were to speculate on the impact of the decisions, a victory for the plaintiffs in EKWRO would have placed private hospitals under severe pressure to conform to IRS guidelines or lose a major funding source; while a victory for the plaintiffs in Duke Power would have rendered financing a nuclear plant more difficult but not impossible. In Orr v. Orr, 440 U.S. 268 (1979), the Court invalidated an alimony statute that imposed obligations on men to support needy spouses but failed to impose a similar obligation on women. The Court noted that plaintiff was not a needy male and, thus, was not likely to secure any tangible benefit from the litigation. However, the Court speculated that it was theoretically possible that Mississippi would abolish alimony entirely (thus relieving plaintiff of any obligation to pay) rather than expand the concept to both men and women. In Village of Arlington Heights v. Metropolitan Housing Corp., 423 U.S. 1030 (1977), litigants situated similarly to the plaintiffs in Warth v. Seldin were permitted to challenge the constitutionality of restrictive zoning practices. Unlike Warth, the Arlington Heights plaintiffs were able to demonstrate a causal nexus between the challenged zoning practice and failure to build a specific housing project. Similar application of the injury-in-fact test took place in Bryant v. Yellin, 447 U.S. 352 (1980) (prospective purchasers have standing to challenge irrigation regulations affecting purchase price of land); Maryland v. Louisiana, 101 S. Ct. 2114 (1981) (state's status as consumer gives it standing to challenge tax affecting price); and Deposit Guaranty Natl. Bank v. Roper, 456 U.S. 326 (1980) (successful named plaintiff has standing to appeal from denial of class certification since it has an interest in spreading cost of litigation over benefitted class); Larson v. Valente, 50 U.S.L.W. 4411 (1982). See also, Lipscomb v. Wise, 643 F.2d 319 (5th Cir. 1981) (attorney has standing to appeal on issue of attorney's fees). In Wright v. Regan, 48 U.S.L.W. 2322 (D.C. Cir. 1981), the Circuit read EKWRO narrowly and ruled that black children in public schools have standing to sue the IRS to obtain more vigorous enforcement of the rule denying tax-exempt status to private schools that discriminate on the basis of race.

3. Traditional applications of the standing doctrine occurred in Friedman v. Rogers, 440 U.S. 1 (1979) (plaintiff lacks standing to challenge makeup of disciplinary board since no charges pending); Babbitt v. United Farm Workers, 442 U.S. 289 (1979) (plaintiffs lack standing to challenge provisions of Arizona Labor Relations Law because not currently being applied against them); New Jersey v. Portash, 440 U.S. 450 (1979) (defendant has standing to challenge ruling on use of immunized Grand Jury testimony for impeachment purposes even though he did not testify and was, therefore, not impeached); and Hodel v. Virginia Surface Mining and Reclamation Association, 101 S. Ct. 2352 (1981) (plaintiffs lack standing to challenge portions of complex regulatory scheme which have not yet been invoked against them). See also: Halperin v. CIA, 629 F.2d 144 (D.C. Cir. 1980) (no standing to challenge

statutes forbidding disclosure of CIA expenditures); Young v. Klutznick, 652 F.2d 617 (6th Cir. 1981) (no standing to challenge census since the state legislature may amend it); Doherty v. Rutgers School of Law, 487 F. Supp. 1291 (D.N.J. 1981) (white student who failed to meet minimum entrance criteria lacks standing to challenge affirmative action admissions program); Winpsinger v. Watson, 628 F.2d 133 (D.C. Cir. 1980) (anti-Carter voters lack standing to challenge indirect use of public funds to support Carter campaign). In Valley Forge Christian Coll. v. Americans United for Separation of Church & State, 50 U.S.L.W. 4103 (1982), the Supreme Court declined to extend the grant of taxpayers' standing in Flast v. Cohen beyond challenges based on the taxing and spending clause. Thus, the Court declined to grant standing to taxpayers challenging a donation of public property to a sectarian college.

4. The standing of a plaintiff with a reasonable apprehension of prosecution to launch a preemptive strike against the statute at issue was reaffirmed in Zablocki v. Redhail, 434 U.S. 374 (1978); Wooley v. Maynard, 430 U.S. 705 (1977); and most recently, in Carey v. Brown, 447 U.S. 455 (1980).

5. The Court's refusal in Rizzo v. Goode, 423 U.S. 362 (1976), to permit a federal judge to order the Mayor of Philadelphia to establish a mechanism for considering complaints of police abuse is another example of the Court's current preoccupation with causation. Since Mayor Rizzo had not "caused" the injuries alleged, the Court ruled that plaintiffs lacked Article III power to sue him, and the District Court lacked Article III power to include him within the remedial decree. Rizzo v. Goode, by introducing Article III constraints into the remedial phase of a conceded case or controversy, severely limits the ability of federal courts to enter prophylactic decrees aimed at preventing the recurrence or continuation of proven abuses. Prior to Rizzo, it had been assumed that once a case or controversy existed, a federal judge possessed inherent equitable power to enter decrees affecting persons who might not have been proper Article III defendants in the initial phase of the litigation. Of course, where a case or controversy exists between plaintiff and the target of the broad remedial decree, federal judges, even after Rizzo, retain broad equitable powers to order corrective or prophylactic action. Thus, in Hills v. Gautreaux, 425 U.S. 284 (1976), the court sustained a broad remedial decree crossing city boundaries where the target of the decree (the Department of Health, Education, & Welfare) was an appropriate Article III defendant at all stages of the litigation. Post-Rizzo cases granting broad relief are Illinois Migrant Council v. Pilliod, 540 F.2d 1062 (7th Cir. 1976); Shifrin v. Wilson, 412 F. Supp. 1282 (D.D.C. 1976); Tucker v. City of Montgomery Board of Commissioners, 410 F. Supp. 494 (M.D. Ala. 1976); Cicero v. Ogliati, 410 F. Supp. 1080 (S.D.N.Y. 1976). After the Supreme Court's reversal of the district court in Rizzo, the Attorney General of the United States conducted an investigation into allegations of systematic brutality by the

Philadelphia police. The investigation culminated in a federal action brought by the Attorney General which sought to impose relief similar to the relief issued by the district court in Rizzo. However, in United States v. Philadelphia, 644 F.2d 187 (3d Cir. 1980), the Third Circuit ruled that the Attorney General lacked power to sue for redress of systematic police abuse. The court rejected arguments that the Attorney General has inherent power to seek to enjoin conduct which would violate 18 U.S.C. §§241 and 242 and that he may exercise parens patriae standing to enforce 42 U.S.C. §1983 and the Fourteenth Amendment. For similarly narrow readings of the power of the Attorney General, see, United States v. Mattson, 600 F.2d 1295 (9th Cir. 1979), and United States v. Solomon, 563 F.2d 1121 (4th Cir. 1977). See Pub. L. 94-435, 90 Stat. 1383, 1394-1395 (granting parens patriae standing to state attorneys general to enforce antitrust acts).

5. In Pennsylvania v. New Jersey, 426 U.S. 660 (1976), the Court clarified the parens patriae standing of a State to sue on behalf of its citizens — an issue that the Court had declined to resolve during the litigation over the legality of the Vietnam War. In Pennsylvania v. New Jersey, Pennsylvania sought to raise the claims of its citizens that New Jersey's income tax statute was unconstitutional as applied to nonresidents. In declining to grant standing, the Supreme Court limited parens patriae standing to situations where a state's sovereign or quasisovereign interests are implicated. Thus, if a parens patriae suit is nothing more than "a collectivity of private suits," 426 U.S. at 666, a state lacks standing as parens patriae. See also: Hawaii v. Standard Oil Co., 405 U.S. 251, 257-260 (1972); Louisiana v. Texas, 176 U.S. 1, 17 (1900). The distinction between a "quasisovereign" interest and "a collectivity of private suits" will doubtless prove difficult to draw. In Alfred L. Snapp & Son, Inc. v. Puerto Rico, 50 U.S.L.W. 5035 (1982), the Court recognized the parens patrial standing of Puerto Rico to challenge alleged discrimination against Puerto Rican migrant laborers. In Hunt v. Washington State Advertising Commn., 423 U.S. 333 (1977), the Court treated a Washington State agency designed to foster its apple industry as a trade association and, thus, granted it standing to assert the claims of a "member." In Maryland v. Louisiana, 101 S. Ct. 2114 (1981), the Court granted Maryland parens patriae standing to challenge a Louisiana tax that increased the price of natural gas to Maryland consumers. See also: Watt v. Energy Action Educational Foundation, 50 U.S.L.W. 4031 (1981) (California has standing to challenge choice of bidding mechanism for offshore oil drilling; Burch v. Goodyear Tire & Rubber Co., 420 F. Supp. 82 (D. Mich. 1976) (parens patriae standing to invoke Clayton Act).

The general power of a governmental entity to act as a plaintiff was at issue in Philadelphia v. Washington Post Corp., 482 F. Supp. 897 (E.D. Pa. 1980) (Philadelphia may not sue for libel); Pennsylvania v. Porter, 480 F. Supp. 686 (E.D. Pa. 1980) (state cannot bring Section

1983 action); and City of Long Beach v. Bozek, 49 U.S.L.W. 2739 (1981) (municipality can sue for malicious prosecution). For the related question of the power of a government official to act as plaintiff, see: Carsten v. Psychologists Examination Committee, 49 U.S.L.W. 2157 (Cal. Sup. Ct. 1980) (board member lacks standing to challenge board's inaction); McClure v. Carter, 513 F. Supp. 265 (D. Idaho 1981) (Senator lacks standing to challenge appointment and confirmation of federal judge); Riegle v. Federal Open Market Committee, — F.2d — (D.C. Cir. 1982) (Senator lacks standing, on prudential grounds, to challenge failure to submit committee members for Senate confirmation).

6. The cases culminating in Warth v. Seldin tended to treat standing primarily as a matter for sound judicial discretion, with only minimal Article III limits on the exercise of that discretion. In Simon v. EKWRO, however, Justice Powell raised the ante by arguing that Article III forbade the courts to entertain the case. If, as Justice Powell suggests, the current view of standing is rooted in separation of powers concepts inherent in Article III, it is subject neither to Congressional modification nor to relaxation by future courts. In Duke Power, however, the Court seemed satisfied that the existence of a genuine injury in fact satisfied Article III concerns, leaving to prudential considerations the question of whether the case was to be entertained. See also, Orr v. Orr, 440 U.S. 268 (1979). Most recently, in United States Parole Commn. v. Geraghty, 445 U.S. 388 (1980), the Court, over Justice Powell's objections, seemed to retreat from a rigid Article III position toward a more flexible prudential view of standing. For a relaxed view of the requirements of an Article III case or controversy, see: Seatrain Shipbuilding Corp. v. Shell Oil Co., 444 U.S. 572 (1980); GTE Sylvania, Inc. v. Consumers Union, Inc. 445 U.S. 375 (1980); Larson v. Valente, 50 U.S.L.W. 4411 (1982).

7. Where Congress has indicated a desire to permit broad judicial review, the current Court has continued to defer to Congressional intent. Thus, in Buckley v. Valeo, 424 U.S. 1 (1976), the Court applied relaxed ripeness and standing rules to permit expeditious review of the Federal Election Campaign Act. In Gladstone Realtors v. Village of Bellwood, 440 U.S. 91 (1979), the Court ruled that residents of an affected subdivision and the subdivision itself had standing to seek injunctive relief under the Fair Housing Act against real estate agents allegedly involved in racial steering. See also, Havens Realty v. Coleman, 50 U.S.L.W. 4232 (1982) (Fair Housing Act testers have standing to challenge violations). A similarly broad view of standing to enforce the Fair Housing Act was announced in Trafficante v. Metropolitan Life Insurance Company, 409 U.S. 205 (1972).

A decision to grant a private cause of action to an individual to enforce a statutory right is often confused analytically with a decision on whether the individual possesses standing. It is possible for an individual to suffer an injury in fact but, nevertheless, be outside the class of persons whom

Congress has authorized to enforce a given statute. While the Warren court was generous in implying private causes of action from statutes, the Burger court has been far more reluctant to do so. E.g., Blue Chip Stamps v. Manor Drug Store Co., 421 U.S. 723 (1975) (Rule 10b-5 applies only to purchasers and sellers of securities); Piper v. Chris-Craft Industries, 430 U.S.1 (1977) (§14(e) provides cause of action only to target of tender offer, not unsuccessful competitor); Illinois Brick Co. v. Illinois, 431 U.S. 720 (1977) (consumers may not sue for harm flowing from antitrust violations); Cort v. Ash, 422 U.S. 66 (1975) (no private cause of action for violation of ban on corporate campaign contributions). See also, Brunswick Corp. v. Pueblo Bowl-O-Mat, 429 U.S. 477 (1977). However, in Cannon v. University of Chicago, 441 U.S. 677 (1979), the Court recognized a private cause of action for violations of Title IX's ban on sex discrimination, and in Davis v. Passman, 442 U.S. 228 (1979), the Court recognized an implied cause of action for violation of the due process clause of the Fifth Amendment. In statutory "standing" cases like Gladstone and Cannon, the debate is rarely over injury-in-fact, which is concededly present, but over whether the putative plaintiff is within the class of persons that Congress intended to enforce the statute in question.

8. In Marathon Pipeline Co. v. Northern Pipeline Constr. Co., 50 U.S.L.W. 4892 (1982) prob. jur. noted, — U.S. — (1981), the District Court invalidated an attempt to delegate Article III powers to bankruptcy judges.

(page 1252) [1486]

NOTES

1. [continued] The current Court has entertained facial challenges to statutes on both vagueness and overbreadth grounds when the statute purports to regulate First Amendment activity. Thus, in Hynes v. Mayor of Oradell, 425 U.S. 610 (1976), the Court invalidated a statute regulating house to house canvassing on facial vagueness grounds despite the statute's apparently clear application to the party before the Court. See also, Smith v. Goguen, 415 U.S. 566 (1974) (invalidating flag desecration statute as facially vague despite its obvious application to conduct before the Court). However, in non-First Amendment contexts the Court remains reluctant to invoke facial review doctrines to assist a "hard core" litigant. Thus, in United States v. Powell, 423 U.S. 87 (1975) the Court declined to entertain a facial vagueness challenge to a firearms control statute despite serious questions of notice. Moreover, in Young v. American Mini Theaters, Inc., 427 U.S. 50 (1976), the Court appeared to establish a hierarchy of First Amendment values, reserving facial overbreadth and vagueness for those situations involving core protected speech. Where, as in Young, sexually explicit (although non-obscene)

material was at stake, the Court declined to invoke facial review techniques to provide maximum protection for First Amendment activities at the margin of the law. See also, New York v. Ferber, 50 U.S.L.W. 5077 (1982) (declining to envoke facial review of statute regulating sale or promotion of material depicting sexual acts by children). In Bates v. State Bar of Arizona, 433 U.S. 350 (1977), the Court indicated that it would decline to apply overbreadth analysis to the commercial speech area.

(page 1253) [1488]

NOTES

4. [continued] The current Court has expanded the standing of litigants to raise the rights of persons with whom they are closely connected. Thus, in Singleton v. Wulff, 428 U.S. 106 (1976), the Court permitted doctors (who possessed independent standing) to raise the rights of their patients in challenging restrictive abortion legislation. See also, Duke Power Co. v. Carolina Environmental Study Group, 438 U.S. 58 (1978).

In addition to permitting doctors to raise the rights of patients, vendors of 3.2 beer have been permitted to raise the rights of purchasers. Craig v. Boren, 429 U.S. 190 (1976); and speakers have been permitted to raise the rights of putative listeners. E.g., Virginia State Board of Pharmacy v. Virginia Citizen's Consumer Council, 425 U.S. 748 (1976); Linmark Associates, Inc. v. Township of Willingboro, 431 U.S. 85 (1977); Carey v. Population Services, Inc. 431 U.S. 678 (1977); First National Bank of Boston v. Bellotti, 435 U.S. 765 (1978). Organizational plaintiffs have been permitted to raise the rights of their members. E.g., Schweiker v. Gray Panthers, 101 S. Ct. 2633 (1981). For representative lower court applications of third party standing, see: Women's Medical Center v. Roberts, 512 F. Supp. 316 (D.R.I. 1981) (medical facility has standing to raise rights of its patients); Neighborhood Development Corp. v. Advisory Committee on Historic Preservation, 632 F.2d 21 (6th Cir. 1981) (organization has standing to raise members' rights).

The limits on third party standing are illustrated by H.L. v. Matheson, 101 S. Ct. 1164 (1981), where the Supreme Court declined to permit an unemancipated minor to raise the rights of emancipated or mature minors in a challenge to a requirement of parental notice prior to the performance of an abortion. See also, Harris v. McRae, 448 U.S. 297 (1980) (named plaintiffs lack standing to raise Free Exercise claim in absence of showing that they are personally affected). In Friedman v. Harold, 638 F.2d 262 (1st Cir. 1981), a trustee in bankruptcy was deemed to lack standing to assert a bankrupt wife's equal protection rights against her will in order to challenge a statute that shielded the wife's interest in a tenancy by the entirety from attachment by her creditors).

Lawyers have not been permitted to raise the Fifth Amendment rights of their clients (although an equivalent result may be reached by invoking lawyer-client privilege) and passengers in a car have not been permitted to raise the Fourth Amendment rights of the car's owner. Fisher v. United States, 425 U.S. 391 (1976); Rakas v. Illinois, 439 U.S. 128 (1978). See also: United States v. Salucci, 448 U.S. 83 (1980) (abandoning automatic standing rule), and United States v. Payner, 447 U.S. 727 (1980).

In Gilmore v. Utah, 429 U.S. 1012 (1976), Gary Gilmore's mother was denied standing to assert his rights once Gilmore had made a knowing and competent waiver of his right to appeal from his death sentence.

In Babbitt v. United Farm Workers, 442 U.S. 289 (1979), plaintiffs challenged a comprehensive Arizona statute regulating agricultural collective bargaining. The statute provided for onerous election machinery, a ban on "deceptive" consumer publicity, insufficient access to agricultural workers on private property and compulsory arbitration. Violation of any of the statute's provisions was criminally punishable. The district court invalidated the statute on its face as unduly restrictive of First Amendment rights. The Supreme Court, in a potentially disturbing retreat from past overbreadth practice, refused to consider the constitutionality of the consumer publicity and limited access provisions of the statute until the Arizona courts were given an opportunity to construe them. Moreover, the Court refused to consider the challenge to the statute's compulsory arbitration and criminal sanction aspects because no live controversy existed between the parties with respect to those provisions. The election procedures were upheld since they did not preclude extra-statutory methods of gaining union recognition. While the Court's refusal to reach the merits of the Arizona statute may be explained under traditional standing and abstention doctrine, the First Amendment overbreadth doctrine had in the past permitted the Court to strike down amorphous statutes which were likely to affect protected activity adversely despite the lack of a classic Marbury plaintiff. In Collautti v. Franklin, 439 U.S. 379 (1978), the Court invalidated a Pennsylvania statute regulating second trimester abortions of fetuses that "may be viable" on void-for-vagueness grounds. Whether the requirement of abstention in Babbitt can be harmonized with the refusal to abstain in Colautti is doubtful.

B. THE DOCTRINES OF RIPENESS AND MOOTNESS

(page 1253) [1493]

FRANKS v. BOWMAN
424 U.S. 747 (1976)

Mr. JUSTICE BRENNAN delivered the opinion of the Court.
This case presents the question whether identifiable applicants who

were denied employment because of race after the effective date and in violation of Title VII of the Civil Rights Act of 1964, 42 U.S.C. §2000e et seq., may be awarded seniority status retroactive to the dates of their employment applications.

Petitioner Franks brought this class action in the United States District Court for the Northern District of Georgia against his former employer, respondent Bowman Transportation Company, and his unions, the International Union of District 50, Allied and Technical Workers of the United States and Canada and its local, No. 13600, alleging various racially discriminatory employment practices in violation of Title VII....

Respondent Bowman raises a threshold issue of mootness. The District Court found that Bowman had hired Petitioner Lee, the sole named representative of class 3, and had subsequently properly discharged him for cause,[4] and the Court of Appeals affirmed. Bowman argues that since Lee will not in any event be eligible for any hiring relief in favor of OTR nonemployee discriminatees, he has no personal stake in the outcome and therefore the question whether nonemployee discriminatees are entitled to an award of seniority when hired in compliance with the District Court order is moot. Bowman relies on Sosna v. Iowa, 419 U.S. 393 (1975), and Board of School Commissioners v. Jacobs, 420 U.S. 128 (1975). That reliance is misplaced.

Sosna involved a challenge to a one-year residency requirement in a state divorce statute. The District Court properly certified the action as a class action. However, before the case reached this Court, the named representative satisfied the state residency requirement (and had in fact obtained a divorce in another State). 419 U.S. at 398 & n.7. Although the named representative no longer had a personal stake in the outcome, we held that "[w]hen the District Court certified the propriety of the class action, the class of unnamed persons described in the certificate acquired a legal status separate from the interest asserted by the [named representative]," id., at 399, and, accordingly the "cases and controversies" requirement of Article III of the Constitution was satisfied. Id., at 402.[5]

It is true as Bowman emphasizes that Sosna was an instance of the

---

4. The District Court determined that Lee first filed his employment application with Bowman on January 13, 1970, and was discriminatorily refused employment at that time. Lee was later hired by Bowman on September 18, 1970, after he had filed a complaint with the Equal Employment Opportunity Commission. The District Court awarded Lee $6,124.58 as backpay for the intervening period of discrimination.

5. "There must not only be a named plaintiff who has such a case or controversy at the time the complaint is filed, and at the time the class action is certified by the District Court pursuant to Rule 23, but there must be a live controversy at the time this Court reviews the case.... The controversy may exist, however, between a named defendant and a member of the class represented by the named plaintiff, even though the claim of the named plaintiff has become moot." Sosna, supra, at 402.

"capable of repetition, yet evading review" aspect of the law of mootness. Id., at 399-401. And that aspect of Sosna was remarked in Board of School Commissioners v. Jacobs, supra, a case which was held to be moot.[6] But nothing in our Sosna or Board of School Commissioners opinions holds or even intimates that the fact the named plaintiff no longer has a personal stake in the outcome of a certified class action renders the class action moot in the absence of an issue "capable of repetition, yet evading review." . . .

. . . There can be no question that this certified class action "clearly presented" the District Court and the Court of Appeals "with a case or controversy in every sense contemplated by Art. III of the Constitution." Sosna, supra, at 398. Those Courts were presented with the seniority question "in an adversary context and in a form historically viewed as capable of resolution through the judicial process." Flast, supra, at 95. The only constitutional mootness question is therefore whether, with regard to the seniority issues presented, "a live controversy [remains] at the time this Court reviews the case." Sosna, supra, at 402.

The unnamed members of the class are entitled to the relief already afforded Lee, hiring and backpay, and thus to the extent have "such a personal stake in the outcome of the controversy [whether they are also entitled to seniority relief] as to assure that concrete adverseness which sharpens the presentation of issues upon which the court so largely depends for illumination of difficult . . . questions." Baker v. Carr, 369 U.S. 186, 204 (1962). Given a properly certified class action, Sosna contemplates that mootness turns on whether, in the specific circumstances of the given case at the time it is before this Court, an adversary relationship sufficient to fulfill this function exists.[8] In this case, that adversary relationship obviously obtained as to unnamed class members with respect to the underlying cause of action and also continues to obtain as respects their assertion that the relief they have received in entitlement to consideration for hiring and backpay is inadequate without further award of entitlement to seniority benefits. . . . No questions are raised concerning the continuing desire of any of these class members for the seniority relief presently in issue. No questions are raised concerning the tenacity and competence of their counsel in pursuing

---

6. In Board of School Commissioners v. Jacobs, supra, the named plaintiffs no longer possessed a personal stake in the outcome at the time the case reached this Court for review. As the action had not been properly certified as a class action by the District Court, we held it moot. 420 U.S., at 129.

8. Thus, the "capable of repetition, yet evading review" dimension of Sosna must be understood in the context of mootness as one of the policy rules often invoked by the Court "to avoid passing prematurely on constitutional questions. Because [such] rules operate in 'cases confessedly within [the Court's] jurisdiction' . . . they find their source in policy, rather than purely constitutional, considerations." Flast v. Cohen, 392 U.S., at 97. See also, id., at 120 n. 8 (Harlan, J., dissenting); Ashwander v. Tennessee Valley Authority, 297 U.S. 288, 345-348 (1936) (Brandeis, J., concurring).

that mode of legal relief before this Court. It follows that there is no meaningful sense in which a "live controversy" reflecting the issues before the Court could be found to be absent.[9] Accordingly, Bowman's mootness argument has no merit.

[The Court upheld the power to grant retroactive seniority.]

(page 1254) [1495]

NOTES

1. [continued] Classic applications of the mootness doctrine occurred in Craig v. Boren, 429 U.S. 190 (1976), where several plaintiffs challenging a minimum drinking age were mooted because they attained the age during the pendency of the appeal; Environmental Protection Agency v. Brown, 431 U.S. 99 (1977), where the government's concession that a challenged regulation was to be amended mooted the challenge; Kremens v. Bartley, 431 U.S. 119 (1977), where the passage of superseding legislation during the pendency of an appeal mooted the litigation and Vitek v. Jones, 436 U.S. 407 (1978), when a plaintiff's acceptance of parole mooted his challenge to prison conditions. In County of Los Angeles v. Davis, 440 U.S. 625 (1979), the Court dismissed a challenge to racially discriminatory hiring practices as moot because the hiring procedures adopted under pressure of the litigation had cured the allegedly racially discriminatory practices. But see, Finberg v. Sullivan, 634 F.2d 50 (3d Cir. 1981) (promulgation of new attachment rules does not moot decision invalidating old ones).

No issue of back pay existed in County of Los Angeles v. Davis, supra. In Memphis Light, Gas & Water Division v. Craft, 436 U.S.1 (1978), an otherwise moot challenge to an improper utility termination was saved from dismissal by a demand for compensatory damages.

In Alabama v. Davis, 446 U.S. 903 (1980), the Court invoked the Munsingwear doctrine, which requires the vacation of lower court opinions when an appeal becomes moot.

The exception to the mootness doctrine for issues that are capable of repetition (between the parties) yet evasive of review was invoked in Nebraska Press Assn. v. Stuart, 427 U.S. 539 (1976), to permit review of a gag order that had expired during the pendency of the litigation. In Scott v. Kentucky Parole Board, 429 U.S. 60 (1976), however, the Court declined to recognize a mootness exception when the likelihood of repetition between the parties was speculative. In First Natl. Bank of

---

9. Nor are there present in the instance case nonconstitutional policy considerations, supra, n.8, mitigating against review by this Court at the present time. Indeed, to "split up" the underlying case and require that the individual class members begin anew litigation on the sole issue of seniority relief would be destructive of the ends of judicial economy as well as postpone indefinitely relief which under the law may already be long overdue.

Boston v. Bellotti, 435 U.S. 765 (1978), the Court applied the "capable of repetition" doctrine to permit review of a Massachusetts statute barring corporate campaign expenditures even though the election was over. See also: Vitek v. Jones, 445 U.S. 480 (1980), (possibility of second transfer from prison population to mental institution sufficient); Reeves, Inc. v. Stake, 447 U.S. 429 (1980). Murphy v. Hunt, 50 U.S.L.W. 4264 (1982) (bail challenge mooted by conviction); Lane v. Williams, 50 U.S.L.W. 4300 (1982) (expiration of sentence moots challenge to sentence).

(page 1254) [1494]

NOTES

2. [continued] As Franks v. Bowman, 424 U.S. 747 (1976), demonstrates, once a class is properly certified, the mooting of the claim of the named plaintiffs will not deprive the court of Article III power to adjudicate the interest of the class. However, Kremens v. Bartley, 431 U.S. 119 (1977), implies that once the claims of the named plaintiffs have been mooted, the Court possesses discretion to dismiss the claim for class relief when appropriate. See also, Pasadena City Board of Education v. Spangler, 427 U.S. 424 (1976). The doctrine of Franks v. Bowman was applied in Zablocki v. Redhail, 434 U.S. 374 (1978), to permit review of a statute impeding marriage despite the fact that the named plaintiff had left the state to be married elsewhere.

In Deposit Guaranty Natl. Bank v. Roper, 445 U.S. 326 (1980), and United States Parole Commn. v. Geraghty, 445 U.S. 388 (1980), the Court explored the mootness problem in the context of an arguably erroneous denial of class certification by the District Court. In Roper, the Court held that a plaintiff who is successful on the merits but who has been denied class certification may appeal from the denial of class certification since he possesses an interest in spreading the cost of the litigation across the class. In Geraghty, however, plaintiff's claim on the merits had been mooted, and, unlike Roper, he possessed no financial interest in the continued prosecution of the case. Nevertheless, the Court held that Geraghty's counsel was authorized to appeal from an erroneous denial of class certification that, if granted, would have precluded mootness under Franks v. Bowman. Thus, the Court held, the class certification "relates back" to the point at which it should have been granted. If, at that point, class certification would have precluded mootness under Franks v. Bowman, the case may continue. Justice Powell vigorously dissented from Geraghty, arguing that the Court's relation-back doctrine ignores Article III constraints on its authority.

3. [continued] Classic applications of the ripeness doctrine occurred in Baxter v. Palmigiano, 425 U.S. 308 (1976) (deferring challenges to

prison regulations) and Clark v. Valeo, 559 F.2d 642 (D.D.C), aff'd, 431 U.S. 950 (1977) (declining to review the constitutionality of single house veto of Federal Election Commission regulations prior to actual exercise of the veto). In Buckley v. Valeo, 424 U.S. 1 (1976), on the other hand, the Court relaxed its traditional aversion to abstract adjudication to provide a virtual advisory opinion on the constitutionality of the Federal Election Campaign Act. In Nader v. Allegheny Airlines, 426 U.S. 290 (1976), the Court decined to invoke primary jurisdiction as a bar to reviewing the legality of airline bumping practices. The analytical similarities among ripeness, primary jurisdiction and Pullman abstention as decision deferral techniques have not yet been explored.

It may be more appropriate to view Babbitt v. United Farm Workers, 442 U.S. 289 (1979), as a discretionary ripeness case in which the Court was reluctant to provide a review of a complex statutory scheme in the absence of a clear factual record. Buckley v. Valeo, supra, is an example of the pitfalls that the Court risks when it relaxes its prudential ripeness concerns. In Hodel v. Virginia Surface Mining & Reclamation Assn., 101 S. Ct. 2352 (1981), the Court invoked traditional notions of ripeness to avoid being drawn into a facial review of a complex regulatory scheme.

C. THE DOCTRINES OF IMMUNITY

(page 1256) [1498]

NOTES

1. [continued] In Stump v. Sparkman, 435 U.S. 349 (1978), the doctrine of judicial immunity was applied to a judge who had issued an ex parte order of sterilization for a fourteen-year-old girl without notice, hearing, or the appointment of a guardian ad litem. Justice Powell dissented, arguing that the power to order ex parte sterilization was so clearly beyond the court's power as to fall outside the judicial function. The majority disagreed.

In Rankin v. Howard, 633 F.2d 844 (9th Cir. 1981), however, the court declined to grant judicial immunity to a probate judge who knowingly acted beyond his jurisdiction in issuing a collusive ex parte order of guardianship.

In Dennis v. Sparks, 101 S. Ct. 183 (1980), the Court declined to clothe a judge's co-conspirators with derivative judicial immunity. In Supreme Court of Virginia v. Consumers Union, 446 U.S. 719 (1980), the Court ruled that judges enjoy legislative immunity in connection with the promulgation of disciplinary rules. However, the Court noted that when judges act as enforcers of the rules, they are not entitled to absolute immunity and, thus, may be liable for attorneys fees awarded pursuant to 42 U.S.C. §1988. The issue of judicial immunity in connection with actions seeking prospective relief was left open. In Morrison v. Ayoob, 627 F.2d 669 (3d Cir. 1980), the court granted fees against judges in a case seeking prospective relief. In Turner v. Raynes, 611 F.2d 92 (5th Cir. 1980), the Circuit ruled that nonlawyer Justices of the Peace enjoy judicial immunity. See also, Finley v. Murry, 50 U.S.L.W. 4525 (1982) (dismissing issue of immunity of court clerks as improvidently granted).

In Butz v. Economou, 438 U.S. 478 (1978), the Court applied a functional analysis in recognizing that certain executive officials perform adjudicative functions which warrant absolute immunity. In Sellars v. Procunier, 641 F.2d 1295 (9th Cir. 1981), parole board members were deemed absolutely immune from suit. However, in Payton v. United States, 636 F.2d 132 (5th Cir. 1981), a suit for negligent release of a parolee was not deemed barred by the discretionary act exception of the Federal Tort Claims Act.

(page 1257) [1498]

NOTES

2. [continued] In Imbler v. Pachtman, 424 U.S. 409 (1976), the Court held that a state prosecutor is absolutely immune from §1983 liability for acts within the scope of his duties in initiating and pursuing a criminal prosecution. The absolute immunity granted in Imbler appears to cover only courtroom connected activity and does not insulate a prosecutor from suit for investigative abuses. See generally: Martin v. Merola 532 F.2d 191 (2d Cir. 1976); Palermo v. Warden, Green Haven State Prison, 545 F.2d 286 (2d Cir. 1976). See also: Dellums v. Powell, 660 F.2d 802 (D.C. Cir. 1981) (Attorney General absolutely immune from suit for malicious prosecution); and Briscoe v. LaHue, 663 F.2d 713 (7th Cir. 1981) (witnesses in state criminal proceedings absolutely immune from §1983 suit alleging perjury).

Similar absolute immunity for prosecutorial activity was recognized in Gaskill v. Specter, 503 F. Supp. 120 (C.D. Cal. 1980) (EEOC lawyer absolutely immune from suit by putative class members); Taylor v. Kavanaugh, 640 F.2d 450 (2d Cir. 1981) (district attorney immune from claim that he falsely induced plea bargain); Simons v. Bellinger, 643 F.2d 774 (9th Cir. 1980) (Committee on Unauthorized Practice immune from damage claim); James v. Benton, 373 So. 2d 307 (Ala. 1979) (district attorney immune from claim that failed to prosecute vigorously enough); Burke v. Miller, 580 F.2d 108 (4th Cir. 1979) (witness called by DA entitled to immunity); and George v. Kay, 632 F.2d 1103 (4th Cir. 1981) (postal inspectors immune from defamation action for statements made in course of investigation). See also, Butz v. Economou, 438 U.S. 478 (1978) (recognizing prosecutorial immunity for certain administrative officials). However, in Doe v. County of Suffolk, 494 F. Supp. 179

(E.D.N.Y. 1979), a social worker who commenced a child custody petition was afforded only a qualified good faith immunity.

(page 1258) [1499]

NOTES

3. [continued] In Ferri v. Ackerman, 449 U.S. 193 (1980), the Court ruled that court-appointed defense cousel is not entitled to an absolute federal immunity against state malpractice actions, leaving the states discretion to set their own immunity standards. Prior to Ferri, courts had tended to provide public defenders and prosecutors with an equivalent immunity. E.g., Robinson v. Bergstrom, 579 F.2d 401 (7th Cir. 1978). However, the more recent cases tend to provide public defenders with only a qualified good faith immunity. E.g., Reese v. Danforth, 406 A.2d 735 (Pa. 1979); Dodson v. Polk County, 628 F.2d 1104 (8th Cir. 1980). See also, Polk v. Dodson, 50 U.S.L.W. 4071 (1982) (public defenders do not act under color of law).

(page 1264) [1506]

NOTES

1. [continued] In United States v. Helstoski, 442 U.S. 477 (1979), the Court held that legislative acts, such as votes and speeches on the floor of Congress, could not be introduced as evidence in a legislator's trial for bribery. The Court reasoned that the Speech or Debate clause immunized such legislative acts from subsequent scrutiny in any forum. However, in United States v. Gillock, 445 U.S. 360 (1980), the Court declined to afford a similar immunity to state legislators facing similar charges in federal court. Moreover, in Hutchinson v. Proxmire, 443 U.S. 111 (1979), the Court ruled that press releases were not governed by Speech or Debate protection and, thus, could be found the basis for a suit for libel.

(page 1265) [1506]

NOTES

2. [continued] In Lake County Estates v. Tahoe Regional Planning Agency, 440 U.S. 391 (1979), and Supreme Court of Virginia v. Consumers Union, 446 U.S. 719 (1980), the Supreme Court suggested that local law-making bodies enjoy broad legislative immunity covering the promulgation, as opposed to the implementation, of regulations. In Gorman Towers v. Bogoslavsky, 626 F.2d 607 (8th Cir. 1980), and Bruce v. Riddle, 631 F.2d 272 (4th Cir. 1980), courts recognized broad legislative immunity in connection with the enactment of zoning ordinances.

(page 1265) [1507]

NOTES

3. [continued] While, under Gillock, state legislators receive less immunity from criminal prosecution than members of Congress, courts have continued to afford broad legislative immunity in connection with facially legitimate state legislative activity. E.g., Star Distributors, Ltd. v. Marino, 613 F.2d 4 (2d Cir. 1980) (prospective challenge to validity of state legislative committee subpoena blocked by legislative immunity).

(page 1277) [1518]

NOTES

1. [continued] In Butz v. Economou, 438 U.S. 478 (1978), the Supreme Court ruled that high-ranking federal officials were not entitled to absolute immunity for acts taken within their official sphere. Rather, applying an analysis similar to that in Scheuer v. Rhodes, 416 U.S. 232 (1974), the Court recognized a "qualified" immunity that requires an official to establish a good faith reasonable belief that his actions are lawful before invoking immunity. The Butz court recognized that certain Executive officials, such as hearing examiners and prosecutors in administrative proceedings, perform functions analagous to those performed by judges and prosecutors. Such "quasi-judicial" Executive officials enjoy absolute immunity.

In Kissinger v. Halperin, 101 S. Ct. 3132 (1981) (per curiam), the Supreme Court affirmed by an equally divided Court (Justice Rehnquist not participating) a Circuit Court ruling that had declined to recognize an absolute Presidential immunity for illegal wire-taps. However, in Nixon v. Fitzgerald, 50 U.S.L.W. 4799 (1982), the Supreme Court recognized absolute Presidential immunity. In Harlow v. Fitzgerald, 50 U.S.L.W. 4815 (1982), the Court recognized that absolute immunity was available to Presidential aides, if functionally necessary to protect the President's freedom to act. Moreover the Court redefined the qualified immunity available to executive officials, by imposing an objective standard keyed to reasonable knowledge of the law.

In Gomez v. Toledo, 446 U.S. 635 (1980), the Court recognized that the burden of pleading good faith lies with the defendant. The placement of the burden of persuasion on the issue of good faith has not yet been resolved. See generally, Cruz v. Beto, 603 F.2d 1178 (5th Cir. 1979). The effect of Gomez on Cruz is unclear.

Finally, when an executive official is sued in his official, as opposed to his individual, capacity, no good faith immunity is available since the suit is really aimed at a governmental entity. See generally: Owen v. City of Independence, 445 U.S. 622 (1980); Universal Amusement Co. v. Hofheinz, 646 F.2d 996 (5th Cir. 1981) (no qualified immunity for of ficial capacity; not entitled to good faith immunity from award of attorneys fees). See generally, Familias Unidas v. Briscoe, 619 F.2d 391 (5th Cir. 1980).

(page 1283) [1524]

FITZPATRICK v. BITZER
427 U.S. 445 (1976)

Mr. JUSTICE REHNQUIST delivered the opinion of the Court.

In the 1972 Amendments to Title VII of the Civil Rights Act of 1964, Congress, acting under §5 of the Fourteenth Amendment, authorized federal courts to award money damages in favor of a private individual against a state government found to have subjected that person to employment discrimination on the basis of "race, color, religion, sex, or national origin." The principal question presented by these cases is whether, as against the shield of sovereign immunity afforded the State by the Eleventh Amendment, Edelman v. Jordan, 415 U.S. 651 (1974), Congress has the power to authorize federal courts to enter such an award against the State as a means of enforcing substantive guarantees of tthe Fourteenth Amendment....

Both parties in the instant case agree with the Court of Appeals that the suit for retroactive benefits by these parties is in fact indistinguishable from that sought to be maintained in Edelman, since what is sought here is a damage award payable to a private party from the state treasury.

Our analysis begins where Edelman ended, for in this Title VII case the "threshold fact of congressional authorization," 415 U.S., at 672, to sue the State as employer is clearly present....

As ratified by the States after the Civil War, [the Fourteenth] Amendment quite clearly contemplates limitations on their authority. In relevant part, it provides:

"Section 1.... No State shall make or enforce any law which shall abridge the privileges or immunities of citizens of the United States; nor shall any State deprive any person of life, liberty, or property, without due process of law; nor deny to any person within its jurisdiction the equal protection of the laws....

"Section 5. The Congress shall have power to enforce, by appropriate legislation, the provisions of this article."

The substantive provisions are by express terms directed at the States. Impressed upon them by those provisions are duties with respect to their treatment of private individuals. Standing behind the imperatives is Congress' power to "enforce" them "by appropriate legislation."

The impact of the Fourteenth Amendment upon the relationship between the Federal Government and the States, and the reach of congressional power under §5, were examined at length by this Court in Ex parte Virginia, 100 U.S. 339 (1880). A state judge had been arrested and indicted under a federal criminal statute prohibiting the exclusion on the basis of race of any citizen from service as a juror in a state court. The judge claimed that the statute was beyond Congress' power to enact under either the Thirteenth or the Fourteenth Amendments. The Court first observed that these Amendments "were intended to be, what they really are, limitations of the power of the States and enlargements of the power of the Congress." 100 U.S., at 345. It then addressed the relationship between the language of §5 and the substantive provisions of the Fourteenth Amendment:

"The prohibitions of the Fourteenth Amendment are directed to the States, and they are to a degree restrictions of State power. It is these which Congress is empowered to enforce, and to enforce against State action, however put forth, whether that action be executive, legislative, or judicial. Such enforcement is no invasion of State sovereignty. No law can be, which the people of the States have, by the Constitution of the United States, empowered Congress to enact. . . . It is said the selection of jurors for her courts and the administration of her laws belong to each State; that they are her rights. This is true in the general. But in exercising her rights, a State cannot disregard the limitations which the Federal Constitution has applied to her power. Her rights do not reach to that extent. Nor can she deny to the general government the right to exercise all its granted powers, though they may interfere with the full enjoyment of rights she would have if those powers had not been thus granted. Indeed, every addition of power to the general government involves a corresponding diminution of the governmental powers of the States. It is carved out of them. . . .

"The argument in support of the petition for a habeas corpus ignores entirely the power conferred upon Congress by the Fourteenth Amendment. Were it not for the fifth section of that amendment, there might be room for argument that the first section is only declaratory of the moral duty of the State. . . . But the Constitution now expressly gives authority for congressional interference and compulsion in the cases embraced within the Fourteenth Amendment. It is but a limited authority, true, extending only to a single class of cases; but within its limits it is complete." 100 U.S., at 345-348.

Ex parte Virginia's contemporaneous recognition of this shift in the federal-state balance has been carried forward by more recent decisions of this Court. See, e.g., South Carolina v. Katzenbach, 383 U.S. 301, 308 (1966); Mitchum v. Foster, 407 U.S. 225, 238-239 (1972).

There can be no doubt that this line of cases has sanctioned intrusions by Congress, acting under the Civil War amendments, into the judicial, executive, and legislative spheres of autonomy previously reserved to the States. The legislation considered in each case was grounded on the expansion of Congress' powers — with the corresponding diminution of state sovereignty — found to be intended by the Framers and made part of the Constitution upon the States' ratification of those Amendments, a phenomenon aptly described as a "car[ving] out" in Ex parte Virginia, 100 U.S., at 346.

It is true that none of these previous cases presented the question of the relationship between the Eleventh Amendment and the enforcement power granted to Congress under §5 of the Fourteenth Amendment. But we think that the Eleventh Amendment, and the principle of state sovereignty which it embodies, see Hans v. Louisiana, 134 U. S. 1 (1890), are necessarily limited by the enforcement provisions of §5 of the Fourteenth Amendment. In that section Congress is expressly granted authority to enforce "by appropriate legislation" the substantive provisions of the Fourteenth Amendment, which themselves embody significant limitations on state authority. When Congress acts pursuant to §5, not only is it exercising legislative authority that is plenary within the terms of the constitutional grant, it is exercising that authority under one section of a constitutional Amendment whose other sections by their own terms embody limitations on state authority. We think that Congress may, in determining what is "appropriate legislation" for the purpose of enforcing the provisions of the Fourteenth Amendment, provide for private suits against States or state officials which are constitutionally impermissible in other contexts. See Edelman v. Jordan, supra; Ford Motor Co. v. Department of Treasury, supra.

III

In No. 75-283, the state officials contest the Court of Appeals' conclusion that an award of attorney's fees in this case would under Edelman have only an "ancillary effect" on the state treasury and could therefore be permitted as falling outside the Eleventh Amendment under the doctrine of Ex parte Young, supra. 415 U.S., at 667-668. We need not address this question, since, given the express congressional authority for such an award in a case brought under Title VII, it follows necessarily from our holding in No. 75-251 that Congress' exercise of power in this respect is also not barred by the Eleventh Amendment.

[The concurring opinions of Justices Brennan and Stevens are omitted.]

(page 1285) [1526]

NOTES

1. [continued] In Hutto v. Finney, 437 U.S. 678 (1978), the Supreme Court ruled that the Attorneys Fee Awards Act of 1976, which authorizes an award of attorney fees to counsel for successful plaintiffs in actions

brought under 42 U.S.C. §§1981, 1982, 1983, and 1985(3), acted to override the Eleventh Amendment within the meaning of Fitzpatrick v. Bitzer. Thus, after Hutto, attorneys' fees may be awarded in civil rights actions against Eleventh Amendment entities. In Gates v. Collier, 616 F.2d 1268 (5th Cir. 1980), the Fifth Circuit ruled that a state statute which forbade the payment of attorneys fees was superseded by the Congressional action.

In Quern v. Jordan, 440 U.S. 332 (1979), a majority of the Court ruled that §1983 was not intended to override the Eleventh Amendment. Thus, the Eleventh Amendment continues to bar retrospective relief against a state. See also, Alaska v. Green, — P.2d — (Alaska Sup. Ct. 1981) (state not person for §1983 purposes, even if has waived Eleventh Amendment immunity). In Quern v. Jordan, 440 U.S. 332 (1979), the Court ruled that an injunction requiring state officials to notify members of the plaintiff class of the state administrative machinery available to collect retrospective payments due the class was not a violation of the Eleventh Amendment since it was merely ancillary to the grant of prospective relief. See, Laskarus v. Thornburgh, 661 F.2d 23 (3d Cir. 1981) (state officials not immune from injunctive relief ordering employee's reinstatement). In Cary v. White, 407 F. Supp. 121 (D. Del. 1976), the continued operation of a state mental health facility after the enactment in 1974 of FLSA provisions authorizing suit by state employees was deemed a waiver of Eleventh Amendment immunity. In Marrapese v. Rhode Island, 500 F. Supp. 1207 (D.R.I. 1980), Judge Pettine ruled that Rhode Island's complete waiver of sovereign immunity operated as a waiver of the Eleventh Amendment as well.

Courts have continued to experience difficulty in determining whether school boards are local entities or state entities for Eleventh Amendment purposes. In Mt. Healthy City School District Board of Education v. Doyle, 429 U.S. 274 (1977), the Court ruled that a school board with local taxing power and the power to issue bonds was a "local" entity outside the protection of the Eleventh Amendment. In Jagnandan v. Giles, 538 F.2d 1166 (5th Cir. 1976), The Fifth Circuit recognized the Eleventh Amendment status of a state university system.

2. [continued] In Hutto v. Finney, supra, the Court ruled that costs and fees incurred as a consequence of bad faith or unreasonable conduct by an Eleventh Amendment defendant could be assessed against a state pursuant to the familiar rule that actions by the United States against state entities to enforce federal rights are not barred by the Eleventh Amendment.

3. [continued] In Lake Country Estates, Inc. v. Tahoe Regional Planning Agency, 440 U.S. 391 (1979), the Court ruled that an entity created by interstate compact was not entitled to Eleventh Amendment immunity since it was not established to act as an arm of the state. However, the Court ruled that the individual Commissioners performed essentially

legislative tasks and were, thus, entitled to absolute immunity. In Carey v. White, 50 U.S.L.W. 4621 (1982), the Court declined to permit a taxpayer to interplead states asserting conflicting claims to estate taxes based on domicile. See also, Florida Dept. of State v. Treasure Salvors, Inc., 50 U.S.L.W. 5056 (1982) (11th Amendment does not bar replevin).

(page 1286) [1527]

NOTES

5. [continued] Under Quern v. Jordan, it is clear that a cause of action sounding in 42 U.S.C. §1983 is subject to Eleventh Amendment constraints. It remains unclear whether a cause of action based directly on Section 1 of the Fourteenth Amendment may be said to override an immunity based on the Eleventh Amendment.

(page 1286) [1527]

NOTES

6. [continued] In Nevada v. Hall, 440 U.S. 410 (1979), the Court ruled that a resident of California (which had waived sovereign immunity) was entitled to sue Nevada (which had only partially waived immunity) in a California court for damages caused by a Nevada employee while driving in California. The Court ruled that as long as California no longer recognized sovereign immunity for tort, it was not obliged by comity or notions of Full Faith and Credit to respect Nevada's retention of the doctrine. How such a judgment would be enforced, assuming Nevada has no assets in California, raises a host of difficult problems. Would Nevada be obliged to open its courts under the Full Faith and Credit clause to the enforcement of a judgment against itself, which was obtained only by declining to give comity to Nevada's immunity policy? In State of California v. State of Arizona, 440 U.S. 59 (1979), the Supreme Court discussed the impact of United States sovereign immunity on the original jurisdiction of the Supreme Court. California invoked the original jurisdiction of the Supreme Court to settle a dispute with Arizona over the ownership of riparian lands. The United States, as owner of the riverbed, was an indispensible party. However, the Court ruled, the sovereign immunity of the United States might well preclude the assertion of jurisdiction. The Court found a waiver of sovereign immunity in the grant to the district courts of jurisdiction to determine boundary claims involving the United States. Accordingly, it declined to accept original jurisdiction, remanding the proceeding to district court. For examples of state court approaches to sovereign immunity, see Mayle v. Pennsylvania Dept. of Highways, 479 Pa. 2d. 1394, (1978), (abolishing sovereign immunity in Pennsylvania);

Worthington v. Wyoming, — P.2d — (Wyo. 1979) (courts lack power to abrogate sovereign immunity); Figueroa v. State, 604 P.2d 1198 (Haw. 1979) (state sovereign immunity bars action based on state constitution).

In Martinez v. California, 444 U.S. 277 (1980), the Court reminded states that federal rules govern the scope of immunity in a Section 1983 action in state court.

(page 1286) [1528]

NOTES

6. [continued] The sovereign immunity of foreign states is discussed in Letelier v. Republic of Chile, 488 F. Supp. 665 (D.D.C. 1981) (sovereign immunity does not bar case arising out of political assassination in United States); Filartiga v. Pena-Irala, 630 F.2d 786 (2d Cir. 1980) (federal Courts have subject matter jurisdiction under the Alien Tort Act of wrongful death claim alleging torture by Paraguayan police as a violation of the law of nations); Sugarman v. Aero-Mexico, 626 F.2d 270 (3d Cir. 1980) (business activity by foreign sovereigns not entitled to sovereign immunity). However, in Machinists v. OPEC, 649 F.2d 1354 (9th Cir. 1981), the court ruled that the oil producers' cartel was shielded from U.S. antitrust laws by sovereign immunity. See also, Williams v. Shipping Corp. of India, 653 F.2d 875 (4th Cir. 1981) (Foreign Sovereign Immunities Act bars Section 1332 suit against agency of foreign government).

(page 1287) [1528]

NOTES

9. [continued] In Santa Clara Pueblo v. Martinez, 436 U.S. 49 (1978), the Court ruled that tribal immunity barred a suit challenging discriminatory practices in recognizing tribal membership.

(page 1287) [1528]

NOTES

10. In 1974 Congress amended the Federal Tort Claims Act to permit suits against the United States for a series of intentional torts generally associated with police abuse, such as false imprisonment and assault. 28 U.S.C. §2680(h). Thus, from and after 1974, sovereign immunity no longer bars suits against the United States for many tortious acts of federal law enforcement officials.

11. Suits under the Federal Tort Claims Act require the presentation of an administrative demand prior to instituting suit. Neither punitive damages nor jury trials are available in a Tort Claims action, although

an advisory jury may be empanelled to assist in valuing the rights at issue. Finally, in a Tort Claims action, plaintiff must demonstrate that the challenged action constitutes a tort under the law of the State where the act took place (or, perhaps, the law of the forum State). Once tortious conduct is demonstrated, the United States becomes liable in the same manner as would a private party. The major exception to the Tort Claims Act is its exception for "discretionary acts" 28 U.S.C. §2680(a); e.g., Dalehite v. United States, 346 U.S. 15 (1953). Since most Tort Claims actions in a civil liberties context involve unconstitutional activity, the discretionary act exception should exert little influence in the area. Thus in Dale v. Cruikshank, 76 Civ. 9362 (D. Haw. 1976), and Birnbaum et al. v. United States, 76 Civ. 1837 (E.D.N.Y. 1979) courts declined to dismiss Tort Claims Actions seeking damages for unlawful mail opening by the CIA, ruling that unlawful action could not fall within the discretionary act exception. An award of $1,000 to each plaintiff whose mail was unlawfully opened was affirmed in Birnbaum v. United States, 436 F. Supp. 967 (E.D.N.Y. 1977), aff'd, 588 F.2d 319 (2d Cir. 1978).

12. In United States v. Testan, 424 U.S. 392 (1976), the Court ruled that the Tucker Act did not constitute an independent cause of action or a waiver of sovereign immunity. In United States v. Orleans, 425 U.S. 807 (1976), the Court ruled that OEO antipoverty agencies were not instrumentalities of the Federal government for the purposes of federal Tort Claims Act liability. In Stencel Aero Engineering Corporation v. United States, 431 U.S. 666 (1977), the Court ruled that a defendant cannot implead the United States in an action against it by a serviceman, since the plaintiff-serviceman could not have sued the United States directly. In Griffin v. Harris, 480 F. Supp. 1072 (E.D. Pa. 1980), the court recognized that sovereign immunity would not bar an order requiring HEW to refund rent overcharges. See also, Bertot v. School District, 613 F.2d 245 (10th Cir. 1980) (no good faith defense to award of back pay in Section 1983 case).

D. THE POLITICAL QUESTION DOCTRINE

(page 1292) [1533]

NOTES

1. [continued] In Elrod v. Burns, 427 U.S. 347 (1976), the Court rejected a political question challenge to its power to rule on the constitutionality of patronage dismissals. In Delaware Tribal Business Committee v. Weeks, 430 U.S. 73 (1977), the Court rejected a political question challenge to its authority to review a statute governing the distribution of Indian tribal funds. However, in the Serbian Eastern Orthodox Diocese v. Milivojevich, 426 U.S. 696 (1976), the Court's inability to ascertain criteria for decision making that would not involve it in religious doctrinal issues caused the Court to decline to adjudicate

the matter. See also, Jones v. Wolf, 443 U.S. 595 (1979) (remanding dispute over church property to determine whether issues of religious doctrine present).

In Goldwater v. Carter, 444 U.S. 996 (1979), a majority of the Court, acting presumably on political question grounds, dismissed without opinion a challenge to President Carter's termination of an international agreement with Taiwan. Challenges to the abatement of private claims against Iran as part of the negotiations leading to the release of U.S. hostages were rejected in, e.g., Unidyne Corp. v. Government of Iran, 512 F. Supp. 705 (E.D. Va. 1981); American Intl. Group v. Islamic Republic of Iran, 49 U.S.L.W. 2786 (D.C. Cir. 1981); Chas. T. Main Intl., Inc. v. Khuzestan Water & Power Authority, 651 F.2d 800 (1st Cir. 1981).

In Halperin v. CIA, 629 F.2d 144 (D.C. Cir. 1980), the court suggested that close judicial scrutiny of the CIA would be barred by the political question doctrine. However, in Abu Eain v. Wilkes, 641 F.2d 504 (7th Cir. 1981), the court reaffirmed the responsibility of the judiciary to decide whether a defendant has committed a political offense in connection with a request for extradition under the Foreign Extradition Treaty.

E. PROBLEMS OF FEDERAL JURISDICTION AND FEDERALISM: FEDERAL JURISDICTION OVER STATE OFFICIALS ALLEGED TO BE VIOLATING FEDERAL CONSTITUTIONAL RIGHTS

(page 1294) [1535]

See generally, Developments in the Law, Federalism, 90 Harv. L. Rev. (1977); Symposium, State Courts and Federalism in the 1980's, 22 William & Mary L. Rev. No. 4 (1981).

(page 1298) [1540]

INTRODUCTORY NOTE

With the recognition of the critical role played by 42 U.S.C. §1983 and 28 U.S.C. §1343(3) in providing federal judicial review over state and local actions, the statutes have been subjected to conflicting pressures by forces seeking to expand or contract the federal judicial presence in local affairs. The civil rights bar has sought to expand Section 1983 to permit suits against governmental entities, while defendants have urged a narrow reading of the cause of action provided by Section 1983.

MONELL v. DEPARTMENT OF SOCIAL SERVICES
436 U.S. 658 (1978)

Mr. JUSTICE BRENNAN delivered the opinion of the Court.
Petitioners, a class of female employees of the Department of Social

Services and the Board of Education of the City of New York, commenced this action under 42 U.S.C. §1983 in July 1971. The gravamen of the complaint was that the Board and the Department had as a matter of official policy compelled pregnant employees to take unpaid leaves of absence before such leaves were required for medical reasons. Cf. Cleveland Board of Education v. LaFleur, 414 U.S. 632 (1974). The suit brought injunctive relief and back pay for periods of unlawful forced leave. Named as defendants in the action were the Department and its Commissioner, the Board and its Chancellor, and the city of New York and its Mayor. In each case, the individual defendants were sued solely in their official capacities.

On cross-motions for summary judgment, the District Court for the Southern District of New York held moot petitioners' claims for injunctive and declaratory relief since the city of New York and the Board, after the filing of the complaint, had changed their policies relating to maternity leaves so that no pregnant employee would have to take leave unless she was medically unable to continue to perform her job. 394 F. Supp. 853, 855. No one now challenges this conclusion. The court did conclude, however, that the acts complained of were unconstitutional under LaFleur, supra. 394 F. Supp. at 855. Nonetheless plaintiff's prayers for back pay were denied because any such damages would come ultimately from the City of New York and, therefore, to hold otherwise would be to "circumvent" the immunity conferred on municipalities by Monroe v. Pape, 365 U.S. 167 (1961). See 394 F. Supp., at 855. . . .

In Monroe v. Pape, we held that "Congress did not undertake to bring municipal corporations within the ambit of [§1983]." 365 U.S., at 187. The sole basis for this conclusion was an inference drawn from Congress' rejection of the "Sherman amendment" to the bill which became Civil Rights Act of 1871, 17 Stat. 13 — the precursor of §1983 — which would have held a municipal corporation liable for damage done to the person or property of its inhabitants by *private* persons "riotously and tumultuously assembled." Cong. Globe, 42d Cong., 1st Sess., 749 (1871) (hereinafter "Globe"). Although the Sherman amendment did not seek to amend §1 of the Act, which is now §1983, and although the nature of the obligation created by that amendment was vastly different from that created by §1, the Court nonetheless concluded in Monroe that Congress must have meant to exclude municipal corporations from the coverage of §1 because " 'the House [in voting against the Sherman amendment] had solemnly decided that in their judgment Congress had no constitutional power to impose any *obligation* upon county and town organizations, the mere instrumentality for the administration of state law.' " 365 U.S., at 190 (emphasis added), quoting Globe, at 804 (Rep. Poland). This statement, we thought, showed that Congress doubted its "constitutional power . . . to impose *civil liability* on municipalities," 365

U.S., at 190 (emphasis added), and that such doubt would have extended to any type of civil liability.

A fresh analysis of debate on the Civil Rights Act of 1871, and particularly of the case law which each side mustered in its support, shows, however, that Monroe incorrectly equated the "obligation" of which Representative Poland spoke with "civil liability."

[Mr. Justice Brennan's exhaustive canvass of the legislative history of §1983 is omitted.]

Our analysis of the legislative history of the Civil Rights Act of 1871 compels the conclusion that Congress *did* intend municipalities and other local government units to be included among those persons to whom §1983 applies. Local governing bodies, therefore, can be sued directly under §1983 for monetary, declaratory, or injunctive relief where, as here, the action that is alleged to be unconstitutional implements or executes a policy statement, ordinance, regulation, or decision officially adopted and promulgated by that body's officers. Moreover, although the touchstone of the §1983 action against a government body is an allegation that official policy is responsible for a deprivation of rights protected by the Constitution, local governments, like every other §1983 "person," by the very terms of the statute, may be sued for constitutional deprivations visited pursuant to governmental "custom" even though such a custom has not received formal approval through the body's official decisionmaking channels. As Mr. Justice Harlan, writing for the Court, said in Adickes v. S. H. Kress & Co., 398 U.S. 144, 167-168 (1970): "Congress included custom and usage [in §1983] because of persistent and widespread discriminatory practices of State officials. . . . Although not authorized by written law, such practices of state officials could well be so permanent and well settled as to constitute a 'custom or usage' with the force of law."

On the other hand, the language of §1983, read against the background of the same legislative history, compels the conclusion that Congress did not intend municipalities to be held liable unless action pursuant to official municipal policy of some nature caused a constitutional tort. In particular, we conclude that a municipality cannot be held liable *solely* because it employs a tortfeasor — or, in other words, a municipality cannot be held liable under §1983 on a respondent superior theory.

We begin with the language of §1983 as passed:

"*[A]ny person who,* under color of any law, statute, ordinance, regulation, custom, or usage of any State, *shall subject, or cause to be subjected,* any person . . . to the deprivation of any rights, privileges, or immunities secured by the Constitution of the United States, shall, any such law, statute, ordinance, regulation, custom, or usage of the State to the contrary notwithstanding, be liable to the party injured in any action at law, suit in equity, or other proper proceeding for redress...." Globe App., at 335 (emphasis added). The italicized language plainly imposes liability on a government that, under color of some official policy, "causes" an employee to violate another's constitutional rights. At the same time, that language cannot be easily read to impose liability vicariously on governing bodies solely on the basis of an employer-employee relationship with a tortfeasor. Indeed, the fact that Congress did specifically provide that *A*'s tort became *B*'s liability if *B* "caused" *A* to subject another to a tort suggests that Congress did not intend §1983 liability to attach where such causation was absent. See Rizzo v. Goode, 423 U.S. 362, 370-371 (1976).

Equally important, creation of a federal law of respondeat superior would have raised all the constitutional problems associated with the obligation to keep the peace, an obligation Congress chose not to impose because it thought imposition of such an obligation unconstitutional. To this day, there is disagreement about the basis for imposing liability on an employer for the torts of an employee when the sole nexus between the employer and the tort is the fact of the employer-employee relationship. See W. Prosser, Law of Torts, §69, at 569 (4th ed. 1971). Nonetheless, two justifications tend to stand out. First is the commonsense notion that no matter how blameless an employer appears to be in an individual case, accidents might nonetheless be reduced if employers had to bear the costs of accidents. See, e.g., ibid.; 2 F. Harper & F. James, The Law of Torts, §26.3, at 1368-1369 (1956). Second is the argument that the cost of accidents should be spread to the community as a whole on an insurance theory. See, e.g., id., §26.5; W. Prosser, supra, at 459.

The first justification is of the same sort that was offered for statutes like the Sherman amendment: "The obligation to make compensation for injury resulting from riot is, by arbitrary enactment of statutes; affirmatory law, and the reason of passing the statute is to secure a more perfect police regulation." Globe, at 777 (Sen. Frelinghuysen). This justification was obviously insufficient to sustain the amendment against perceived constitutional difficulties and there is no reason to suppose that a more general liability imposed for a similar reason would have been thought less constitutionally objectionable. The second justification was similarly put forward as a justification for the Sherman amendment: "we do not look upon [the Sherman amendment] as a punishment.... It is a mutual insurance." Id., at 792 (Rep. Butler). Again, this justification was insufficient to sustain the amendment.

We conclude, therefore, that a local government may not be sued for an injury inflicted solely by its employees or agents. Instead, it is when execution of a government's policy or custom, whether made by its lawmakers or by those whose edicts or acts may fairly be said to represent official policy, inflicts the injury that the government as an entity is responsible under §1983. Since this case unquestionably involves official policy as the moving force of the constitutional violation found by the District Court, see pp.1-2, and n.2, supra, we must reverse the judgment below. In so doing, we have no occasion to address, and do not address, what the full contours of municipal liability under §1983 may be. We have attempted only to sketch so much of the §1983 cause of action against a local government as is apparent from the history of the 1871 Act and our prior cases and we expressly leave further development of this action to another day. . . .

Mr. JUSTICE POWELL, concurring. . . .

[I]f we continued to adhere to a rule of absolute municipal immunity under §1983, we could not long avoid the question of whether "we should, by analogy to our decision in Bivens v. Six Unknown Fed. Narcotics Agents, 403 U.S. 388 (1971), imply a cause of action directly from the Fourteenth Amendment which would not be subject to the limitations contained in §1983. . . ." Mt. Healthy City Board of Ed. v. Doyle, 429 U.S. 274, 278 (1977). One aspect of that inquiry would be whether there are any "special factors counselling hesitation in the absence of affirmative action by Congress," Bivens, supra, at 396, such as an "explicit congressional declaration that persons injured by a [municipality] may not recover money damages . . . , but must instead be remitted to another remedy, equally effective in the view of Congress," id., at 397. In light of the Court's persuasive re-examination in today's decision of the 1871 debates, I would have difficulty inferring from §1983 "an explicit congressional declaration" against municipal liability for the implementation of official policies in violation of the Constitution. Rather than constitutionalize a cause of action against local government that Congress intended to create in 1871, the better course is to confess error and set the record straight, as the Court does today.

Difficult questions nevertheless remain for another day. There are substantial line-drawing problems in determining "when execution of a government's policy or custom" can be said to inflict constitutional injury such that "government as an entity is responsible under §1983." This case, however, involves formal, written policies of a municipal department and school board; it is the clear case. The Court also reserves decision on the availability of a qualified municipal immunity. Initial resolution of the question whether the protection available at common law for municipal corporations, see dissenting opinion of Mr. Justice Rehnquist, or other principles support a qualified municipal immunity in the context of the §1983 damages action, is left to the lower federal courts.

Mr. JUSTICE REHNQUIST, with whom The CHIEF JUSTICE joins, dissenting. . . .

Whatever the merits of the constitutional arguments raised against it, the fact remains that Congress rejected the concept of municipal tort liability on the only occasion in which the question was explicitly presented. Admittedly this fact is not conclusive as to whether Congress intended §1 to embrace a municipal corporation within the meaning of "person," and thus the reasoning of Monroe on this point is subject to challenge. The meaning of §1 of the Act of 1871 has been subjected in this case to a more searching and careful analysis than it was in Monroe, and it may well be that on the basis of this closer analysis of the legislative debates a conclusion contrary to the Monroe holding could have been reached when that case was decided 17 years ago. But the rejection of the Sherman Amendment remains instructive in that here alone did the legislative debates squarely focus on the liability of municipal corporations, and that liability was rejected. Any inference which might be drawn from the Dictionary Act or from general expressions of benevolence in the debate on §1 that the word "person" was intended to include municipal corporations falls far short of showing "beyond doubt" that this Court in Monroe "misapprehended the meaning of the controlling provision." Errors such as the Court may have fallen into in Monroe do not end the inquiry as to stare decisis; they merely begin it. I would adhere to the holding of Monroe as to the liability of a municipal corporation under §1983.

The decision in Monroe v. Pape, was the fountainhead of the torrent of civil rights litigation of the last 17 years. Using §1983 as a vehicle, the courts have articulated new and previously unforeseeable interpretations of the Fourteenth Amendments. At the same time, the doctrine of municipal immunity enunciated in Monroe has protected municipalities and their limited treasures from the consequences of their officials' failure to predict the course of this Court's constitutional jurisprudence. None of the Members of this Court can foresee the practical consequences of today's removal of that protection. Only the Congress, which has the benefit of the advice of every segment of this diverse Nation, is equipped to consider the results of such a drastic change in the law. It seems all but inevitable that it will find it necessary to do so after today's decision.

NOTES

1. [continued] Prior to the Supreme Court's surprising turnabout in Monell, the civil rights bar had expended substantial energy unsuccessfully in seeking to assert Section 1983 claims against governmental entities. E.g., Aldinger v. Howard, 427 U.S. 1 (1976) (pendent jurisdiction improper over municipality not a "person" under Section 1983); Moor v. Alameda County, 411 U.S. 693 (1973) (county not a "person" even though fully suable under state law); City of Kenosha v. Bruno, 412 U.S. 507 (1973) (city not a person for purposes of prospective equitable

relief). As Justice Powell's concurrence suggests, the Court's discovery that municipalities were "persons" was aided by the increasing propensity of courts to imply causes of action sounding directly in the Constitution against governmental entities. See generally, Mt. Healthy City School Dist. Board of Ed. v. Doyle, 429 U.S. 274 (1977). One day, before the Supreme Court's decision in Monell, the Second Circuit, en banc, ruled that municipalities were subject to suit on constitutionally based causes of action regardless of their liability under Section 1983. Turpin v. Mailet, 579 F.2d 152 (2d Cir.), vacated and remanded, 439 U.S. 977 (1978), vacated, 591 F.2d 426 (2d Cir. 1979). After Monell, the Circuit vacated Turpin as no longer necessary. See Note, Damage Remedies Against Municipalities for Constitutional Violations, 90 Harv. L. Rev. 922 (1976).

In Aiello v. City of Wilmington, 470 F. Supp. 414 (D. Del. 1979), Monell was held retroactive. See also, CCC v. City of Boulder, 50 U.S. 4144 (1982) (localities not immune from antitrust laws unless executing explicit state policy).

In order to establish governmental liability under Monell, a Section 1983 plaintiff must demonstrate that the challenged act may fairly be attributed to the entity as its policy or custom. Custom need not be embodied in a written law or regulation. E.g., Knight v. Carlson, 478 F. Supp. 55 (E.D. Cal. 1979); Woody v. City of West Miami, 477 F. Supp. 1073 (S.D. Fla. 1979). In Smith v. Ambrogio, 456 F. Supp. 1130 (D. Conn. 1978), the court held that official policy giving rise to Section 1983 liability may be found in a pattern of "persistent practices" sufficiently known to and approved by city officials to constitute a custom of "equivalent though unofficial authoritativeness." 456 F. Supp. at 1134. In N.A. Cold Storage Co. v. County of Cook, 468 F. Supp. 424 (N.D. Ill. 1979), the court found an allegation that policymaking officials engaged in systematic and widespread tax assessment discrimination sufficient to state a Section 1983 cause of action against the governmental unit, reasoning that if the actions of the government officials are, in actuality, the actions of the government, the government may be held liable for those actions. See also, State of Missouri ex rel. Gore v. Woehner, 475 F. Supp. 274 (E.D. Mo. 1979). But see, Fair Assessment in Real Estate v. McNarry, 50 U.S.L.W. 4017 (1982) (comity bars damage action in federal court for unconstitutional tax assessments). Neglect or refusal to enforce laws already on the books, or a systematic maladminstration of those laws, was held to qualify as a custom in Mayes v. Elrod, 470 F. Supp. 1188 (N.D. Ill. 1979). See generally: Schnapper, Civil Rights Litigation after Monell, 79 Colum. L. Rev. 213 (1979); Note Municipal Liability under Section 1983: The Meaning of "Policy or Custom," 79 Colum. L. Rev. 304 (1979). See also, Echols v. Strickland, 92 F.R.D. 75, (S.D. Tex. 1981) (act of agent with final authoriy may bind entity for purposes of Monell); Familias Unidas v. Briscoe, 619 F.2d 391 (5th Cir.

1980) (same); Turpin v. Mailet, 619 F.2d 196 (2d Cir. 1980) (tacit approval of police misconduct may render municipality liable, but single incident not sufficient to establish policy or custom); Owens v. Haas, 601 F.2d 1242 (2d Cir. 1979) (gross negligence in training and supervision of employees renders government defendant liable under Section 1983); Salinas v. Breier, 517 F. Supp. 1272 (E.D. Wisc. 1981) (police chief liable for unconstitutional custom); Branden v. Allen, 516 F. Supp. 1355 (1981) (police chief's failure to inform himself of known dangerous propensity of officer renders him liable under Section 1983).

Respondeat superior liability is not recognized under Section 1983. E.g., Baskin v. Parker, 588 F.2d 965 (5th Cir. 1979). See generally: Note, Section 1983 Municipal Liability and the Doctrine of Respondeat Superior, 46 U. Chi. L. Rev. 935 (1979); Comment, Respondeat Superior Liability of Municipalities for Constitutional Torts After Monell: New Remedies to Pursue? 44 Mo. L. Rev. 514 (1979). See also: Popow v. City of Margate, 476 F. Supp. 1237 (D.N.J. 1979); Ellis v. City of Chicago, 478 F. Supp. 333 (N.D. Ill. 1979). In Leite v. City of Providence, 463 F. Supp. 585 (D.R.I. 1978), simple negligence was held insufficient to trigger municipal liability under Section 1983. See generally, Note, Section 1983 Liability for Negligence, 58 Neb. L. Rev. 271 (1979). When back pay is at issue, several courts have treated it as an "equitable" remedy to avoid immunity and good-faith defense problems. E.g., Shuman v. City of Philadelphia, 470 F. Supp. 499 (E.D. Pa. 1979). Since, after Owen, municipalities cannot invoke a derivative good-faith defense, it should no longer be necessary to characterize back pay as "equitable" in order to award relief against a municipality. In Hartford Accident and Indemnity Co. v. Village of Hempstead, 48 N.Y.2d 218, 422 N.Y.S.2d 47 (1979), the New York Court of Appeals ruled that it was against public policy to permit municipalities to insure against punitive damage awards in Section 1983 cases. Official defendants who retain private counsel in Section 1983 actions are not entitled to reimbursement from the governmental entity, even if they win. Corning v. Village of Laurel Hollow, 48 N.Y.2d 348, 422 N.Y.S.2d 932 (1979).

The Monell court declined to decide whether a governmental entity is entitled to a derivative good faith defense. However, in Owen v. City of Independence, 445 U.S. 622 (1980), the Court ruled that municipalities are not entitled to a qualified good faith immunity in Section 1983 cases. Thus, as long as the criteria of Monell are satisfied, the good faith defense available to individual defendants will not block compensatory relief against the governmental defendant. In Newport v. Fact Concerts, Inc., 101 S. Ct. 2748 (1981), the Court ruled that Section 1983 did not authorize the award of punitive damages against a municipality.

The recognition that an entity may be a defendant in a Section 1983 action may alleviate problems caused by Rizzo v. Goode, 423 U.S. 352 (discussed supra). As long as a government entity is available to serve as an Article III defendant, the doctrinal problems of formulating broad prophylactic relief against a mayor or a police commissioner are eased.

(page 1311) [1552]

PARRATT v. TAYLOR
101 S. Ct. 1908 (1981)

JUSTICE REHNQUIST delivered the opinion of the Court.

The respondent is an inmate at the Nebraska Penal and Correctional Complex who ordered by mail certain hobby materials valued at $23.50. The hobby materials were lost and respondent brought suit under 42 U.S.C. §1983 to recover their value. At first blush one might well inquire why respondent brought an action in federal court to recover damages of such a small amount for negligent loss of property, but because 28 U.S.C. §1343, the predicate for the jurisdiction of the United States District Court, contains no minimum dollar limitation, he was authorized by Congress to bring his action under that section if he met its requirements and if he stated a claim for relief under 42 U.S.C. §1983. Respondent claimed that his property was negligently lost by prison officials in violation of his rights under the Fourteenth Amendment to the United States Constitution. More specifically, he claimed that he had been deprived of property without due process of law. . . .

The facts underlying this dispute are not seriously contested. Respondent paid for the hobby materials he ordered with two drafts drawn on his inmate account by prison officials. The packages arrived at the complex and were signed for by two employees who worked in the prison hobby center. One of the employees was a civilian and the other was an inmate. Respondent was in segregation at the time and was not permitted to have the hobby materials. Normal prison procedures for the handling of mail packages is that upon arrival they are either delivered to the prisoner who signs a receipt for the package or the prisoner is notified to pick up the package and to sign a receipt. No inmate other than the one to whom the package is addressed is supposed to sign for a package. After being released from segregation, respondent contacted several prison officials regarding the whereabouts of his packages. The officials were never able to locate the packages or to determine what caused their disappearance.

In 1976, respondent commenced this action against the petitioners, the Warden and Hobby Manager of the prison, in the District Court seeking to recover the value of the hobby materials which he claimed had been lost as a result of the petitioners' negligence. Respondent alleged that petitioners' conduct deprived him of property without due process of law in violation of the Fourteenth Amendment of the United

States Constitution. Respondent chose to proceed in the United States District Court under 28 U.S.C. §1343 and 42 U.S.C. §1983, even though the State of Nebraska had a tort claims procedure which provided a remedy to persons who suffered tortious losses at the hands of the State....

While we have twice granted certiorari in cases to decide whether mere negligence will support a claim for relief under §1983, see Procunier v. Navarette, 434 U.S. 555 (1978), and Baker v. McCollan, 443 U.S. 137 (1979), we have in each of those cases found it unnecessary to decide the issue. In Procunier, supra, we held that regardless of whether the §1983 complaint framed in terms of negligence stated a claim for relief, the defendants would clearly have been entitled to qualified immunity and therefore not liable for damages. In Baker, supra, we held that no deprivation of any rights, privileges or immunities secured by the Constitution and laws of the United States had occurred, and therefore it was unnecessary to decide whether mere negligence on the part of the actor would have rendered him liable had there been such a deprivation. These two decisions, however, have not aided the various courts of appeals and district courts in their struggle to determine the correct manner in which to analyze claims such as the present one which allege facts that are commonly thought to state a claim for a common-law tort normally dealt with by state courts, but instead are couched in terms of a constitutional deprivation and relief is sought under §1983....

... We, therefore, once more put our shoulder to the wheel hoping to be of greater assistance to courts confronting such a fact situation than it appears we have been in the past.

Nothing in the language of §1983 or its legislative history limits the statute solely to intentional deprivations of constitutional rights. In Baker v. McCollan, supra, we suggested that simply because a wrong was negligently as opposed to intentionally committed did not foreclose the possibility that such action could be brought under §1983. We explained: "[T]he question whether an allegation of simple negligence is sufficient to state a cause of action under §1983 is more elusive than it appears at first blush. It may well not be susceptible of a uniform answer across the entire spectrum of conceivable constitutional violations which might be the subject of a §1983 action." 443 U.S., at 139, 140. Section 1983, unlike its criminal counterpart, 18 U.S.C. §242, has never been found by this Court to contain a state of mind requirement....

Both Baker v. McCollan and Monroe v. Pape suggest that §1983 affords a "civil remedy" for deprivations of federally protected rights caused by persons acting under color of state law without any express requirement of a particular state of mind. Accordingly, in any §1983 action the initial inquiry must focus on whether the two essential elements to a §1983 action are present: (1) whether the conduct complained of was committed by a person acting under color of state law; and (2) whether this conduct deprived a person of rights, privileges, or immunities secured by the Constitution or laws of the United States. . . .

Unquestionably, respondent's claim satisfies three prerequisites of a valid due process claim: the petitioners acted under color of state law; the hobby kit falls within the definition of property; and the alleged loss, even though negligently caused, amounted to a deprivation. Standing alone, however, these three elements do not establish a violation of the Fourteenth Amendment. Nothing in that amendment protects against all deprivations of life, liberty or property by the State. The Fourteenth Amendment protects only against deprivations "without due process of law." Baker v. McCollan, supra, 443 U.S., at 145. Our inquiry therefore must focus on whether the respondent has suffered a deprivation of property without due process of law. In particular, we must decide whether the tort remedies which the State of Nebraska provides as a means of redress for property deprivations satisfies the requirements of procedural due process.

This Court has never directly addressed the question of what process is due a person when an employee of a State negligently takes his property. In some cases this Court has held that due process requires a predeprivation hearing before the State interferes with any liberty or property interest enjoyed by its citizens. In most of these cases, however, the deprivation of property was pursuant to some established state procedure and "process" could be offered before any actual deprivation took place. For example, in Mullane v. Central Hanover Tr. Co., 339 U.S. 306 (1950), the Court struck down on due process grounds a New York statute that allowed a trust company, when it sought a judicial settlement of its trust accounts, to give notice by publication to all beneficiaries even if the whereabouts of the beneficiaries were known. The Court held that personal notice in such situations was required and stated, "when notice is a person's due, process which is a mere gesture is not due process.'" Id., at 315. More recently, in Bell v. Burson, 402 U.S. 535 (1971), we reviewed a state statute which provided for the taking of the drivers license and registration of an uninsured motorist who had been involved in an accident. We recognized that a drivers license is often involved in the livelihood of a person and as such could not be summarily taken without a prior hearing. In Fuentes v. Shevin, 407 U.S. 67 (1972), we struck down the Florida prejudgment replevin statute which allowed secured creditors to obtain writs in ex parte proceedings. We held that due process required a prior hearing before the State authorized its agents to seize property in a debtor's possession. See also Boddie v. Connecticut, 401 U.S. 371 (1971); Goldberg v. Kelly, 397 U.S. 254 (1970); and Sniadach v. Family Finance Corp., 395 U.S. 337 (1969). In all these cases, deprivations of property were authorized by an established state procedure and due process was held to require predeprivation notice and hearing in order to serve as a check on the possibility that a wrongful deprivation would occur.

We have, however, recognized that postdeprivation remedies made available by the State can satisfy the Due Process Clause. In such cases, the normal predeprivation notice and opportunity to be heard is pretermitted if the State provides a postdeprivation remedy. In North American Cold Storage Co. v. Chicago, 211 U.S. 306 (1908), we upheld the right of a State to seize and destroy unwholesome food without a preseizure hearing. The possibility of erroneous destruction of property was outweighed by the fact that the public health emergency justified immediate action and the owner of the property could recover his damages in an action at law after the incident. In Ewing v. Mytinger & Casselberry, 339 U.S. 594 (1950), we upheld under the Fifth Amendment Due Process Clause the summary seizure and destruction of drugs without a preseizure hearing. Similarly, in Fahey v. Mallonee, 332 U.S. 245 (1947), we recognized that the protection of the public interest against economic harm can justify the immediate seizure of property without a prior hearing when substantial questions are raised about the competence of a bank's management. In Bowles v. Willingham, 321 U.S. 503 (1944), we upheld in the face of a due process challenge the authority of the Administrator of the Office of Price Administration to issue rent control orders without providing a hearing to landlords before the order or regulation fixing rents became effective. See also Corn Exchange Bank v. Coler, 280 U.S. 218 (1918); McKay v. McInnes, 279 U.S. 820 (1929); Coffin Brothers v. Bennett, 277 U.S. 29 (1928); and Ownbey v. Morgan, 256 U.S. 94 (1921). These cases recognize that either the necessity of quick action by the State or the impracticality of providing any meaningful predeprivation process can, when coupled with the availability of some meaningful means by which to assess the propriety of the State's action at some time after the initial taking, satisfy the requirements of procedural due process. As we stated in Mitchell v. W. T. Grant Co., 416 U.S. 600 (1974):

"Petitioner asserts that his right to a hearing before his possession is in any way disturbed is nonetheless mandated by a long line of cases in this Court culminating in Sniadach v. Family Finance Corp., 395 U.S. 337 (1969), and Fuentes v. Shevin, 407 U.S. 67 (1972). The pre-Sniadach cases are said by petitioner to hold that 'the opportunity to be heard must precede any actual deprivation of private property.' Their import, however, is not so clear as petitioner would have it: they merely stand for the proposition that a hearing must be had before one is finally deprived of his property and do not deal at all with the need for a pretermination hearing where a full and immediate post-termination hearing is provided. The usual rule has been '[w]here only property rights are involved, mere postponement of the judicial enquiry is not a denial of due process, if the opportunity given for ultimate judicial determination of liability is adequate.' Phillips v. Commissioner, 283 U.S. 589, 596-597 (1931)." Id., at 611.

Our past cases mandate that some kind of hearing is required at some time before a State finally deprives a person of his property interests. The fundamental requirement of due process is the opportunity to be heard and it is an "opportunity which must be granted at a meaningful time and in a meaningful manner." Armstrong v. Manzo, 380 U.S. 545, 552 (1965). However, as many of the above cases recognize, we have rejected the proposition that "at a meaningful time and in a meaningful manner" *always* requires the State to provide a hearing prior to the initial deprivation of property. This rejection is based in part on the impracticability in some cases of providing any preseizure hearing under a State authorized procedure, and the assumption that at some time a full and meaningful hearing will be available.

The justifications which we have found sufficient to uphold takings of property without any predeprivation process are applicable to a situation such as the present one involving a tortious loss of a prisoner's property as a result of a random and unauthorized act by a state employee. In such a case, the loss is not a result of some established state procedure and the State cannot predict precisely when the loss will occur. It is difficult to conceive of how the State could provide a meaningful hearing before the deprivation takes place. The loss of property, although attributable to the State as action under "color of law," is in almost all cases beyond the control of the State. Indeed, in most cases it is not only impracticable, but impossible to provide a meaningful hearing before the deprivation. That does not mean, of course, that the State can take property without providing a meaningful postdeprivation hearing. The prior cases which have excused the prior hearing requirement have rested in part on the availability of some meaningful opportunity subsequent to the initial taking for a determination of rights and liabilities. . . .

. . . This analysis is also quite consistent with the approach taken by this Court in Ingraham v. Wright, 430 U.S. 651 (1977), where the Court was confronted with the claim that corporal punishment in public schools violated due process. Arguably, the facts presented to the Court in Ingraham were more egregious than those presented here inasmuch as the Court was faced with both an intentional act (as opposed to negligent conduct) and a deprivation of liberty. However, we reasoned: " 'At some point the benefit of an additional safeguard to the individual affected . . . and to society in terms of increased assurance that the action is just may be out-weighed by the cost.' Mathews v. Eldridge, 432 U.S., at 348. We think that point has been reached in this case. In view of the low incidence of abuse, the openness of our schools, *and the common-law safeguards that already exist*, the risk of error that may result in violation of a school child's subsequent rights can only be regarded as minimal.

Imposing additional administrative safeguards as a constitutional requirement might reduce that risk marginally, but would also entail a significant intrusion into an area of primary educational responsibility." Id., at 682. (Emphasis supplied.)

IV

Application of the principles recited above to this case leads us to conclude the respondent has not alleged a violation of the Due Process Clause of the Fourteenth Amendment. Although he has been deprived of property under color of state law, the deprivation did not occur as a result of some established state procedure. Indeed, the deprivation occurred as a result of the unauthorized failure of agents of the State to follow established state procedure. There is no contention that the procedures themselves are inadequate nor is there any contention that it was practicable for the State to provide a predeprivation hearing. Moreover, the State of Nebraska has provided respondent with the means by which he can receive redress for the deprivation. The State provides a remedy to persons who believe they have suffered a tortious loss at the hands of the State. See Neb. Rev. Stat. § 81-8,209 et seq. (Reissue 1976). Through this tort claims procedure the state hears and pays claims of prisoners housed in its penal institutions. This procedure was in existence at the time of the loss here in question but respondent did not use it. It is argued that the State does not adequately protect the respondent's interests because it provides only for an action against the State as opposed to its individual employees, it contains no provisions for punitive damages, and there is no right to a trial by jury. Although the state remedies may not provide the respondent with all the relief which may have been available if he could have proceeded under § 1983, that does not mean that the state remedies are not adequate to satisfy the requirements of due process. The remedies provided could have fully compensated the respondent for the property loss he suffered, and we hold that they are sufficient to satisfy the requirements of due process.

Our decision today is fully consistent with our prior cases. To accept respondent's argument that the conduct of the state officials in this case constituted a violation of the Fourteenth Amendment would almost necessarily result in turning every alleged injury whch may have been inflicted by a state official acting under "color of law" into a violation of the Fourteenth Amendment cognizable under § 1983. It is hard to perceive any logical stopping place to such a line of reasoning. Presumably, under this rationale any party who is involved in nothing more than an automobile accident with a state official could allege a constitutional violation under § 1983. Such reasoning "would make the Fourteenth Amendment a font of tort law to be superimposed upon whatever systems may already be administered by the states." Paul v. Davis, 424 U.S. 693, 701. We do not think that the drafters of the Fourteenth Amendment intended the amendment to play such a role in our society.

Accordingly, the judgment of the Court of Appeals is

Reversed.

JUSTICE WHITE, concurring.

I join the opinion of the Court but with the reservations stated by my Brother Blackmun in his concurring opinion.

JUSTICE BLACKMUN, concurring.

While I join the Court's opinion in this case, I write separately to emphasize my understanding of its narrow reach. This suit concerns the deprivation only of property and was brought only against supervisory personnel, whose simple "negligence" was assumed but, on this record, not actually proved. I do not read the Court's opinion as applicable to a case concerning deprivation of life or of liberty. Cf. Moore v. City of East Cleveland, 431 U.S. 494 (1977). I also do not understand the Court to intimate that the sole content of the Due Process Clause is procedural regularity. I continue to believe that there are certain governmental actions that, even if undertaken with a full panoply of procedural protection, are, in and of themselves, antithetical to fundamental notions of due process. See, e.g., Boddie v. Connecticut, 401 U.S. 371 (1971); Roe v. Wade, 410 U.S. 113 (1973).

Most importantly, I do not understand the Court to suggest that the provision of "postdeprivation remedies," within a state system would cure the unconstitutional nature of a state official's intentional act that deprives a person of property. While the "random and unauthorized" nature of negligent acts by state employees makes it difficult for the State to "provide a meaningful hearing before the deprivation takes place," it is rare that the same can be said of intentional acts by state employees. When it is possible for a State to institute procedures to contain and direct the intentional actions of its officials, it should be required, as a matter of due process, to do so. See Sniadach v. Family Finance Corp., 395 U.S. 337 (1969); Fuentes v. Shevin, 407 U.S. 67 (1972); Goldberg v. Kelly, 397 U.S. 254 (1970). In the majority of such cases, the failure to provide adequate process prior to inflicting the harm would violate the Due Process Clause. The mere availability of a subsequent tort remedy before tribunals of the same authority that, through its employees, deliberately inflicted the harm complained of, might well not provide the due process of which the Fourteenth Amendment speaks.

JUSTICE POWELL, concurring in the result.

This case presents the question whether a state prisoner may sue to recover damages under 42 U.S.C. §1983, alleging that a violation of the Due Process Clause of the Fourteenth Amendment occurred when two shipments mailed to him were lost due to the negligence of the prison's warden and "hobby manager." Unlike the Court, I do not believe that such negligent acts by state officials constitute a deprivation of property within the meaning of the Fourteenth Amendment, regardless of whatever subsequent procedure a State may or may not provide. I therefore concur only in the result. . . .

The central question in this case is whether *unintentional* but negligent acts by state officials, causing respondent's loss of property, are actionable under the Due Process Clause. In my view, this question requires the Court to determine whether intent is an essential element of a due process claim, just as we have done in cases applying the Equal Protection Clause and the Eighth Amendment's prohibition of "cruel and unusual punishment." The intent question cannot be given "a uniform answer across the entire spectrum of conceivable constitutional violations which might be the subject of a §1983 action." Baker v. McCollan, 443 U.S. 137, 139-140 (1979). Rather, we must give close attention to the nature of the particular constitutional violation asserted, in determining whether intent is a necessary element of such a violation.

In the due process area, the question is whether intent is required before there can be a "deprivation" of life, liberty or property. In this case, for example, the negligence of the prison officials caused respondent to lose his property. Nevertheless, I would not hold that such a negligent act, causing unintended loss of or injury to property, works a deprivation in the *constitutional sense*. Thus, no procedure for compensation is constitutionally required.

JUSTICE MARSHALL, concurring in part and dissenting in part.

I join the opinion of the Court insofar as it holds that negligent conduct by persons acting under color of state law may be actionable under 42 U.S.C. §1983. I also agree with the majority that in cases involving claims of *negligent* deprivation of property without due process of law, the availability of an adequate post-deprivation cause of action for damages under state law may preclude a finding of a violation of the Fourteenth Amendment. I part company with the majority, however, over its conclusion that there was an adequate state law remedy available to respondent it this case. My disagreement with the majority is not because of any shortcomings in the Nebraska tort claims procedure. Rather, my problem is with the majority's application of its legal analysis to the facts of this case.

It is significant, in my view, that respondent is a state prisoner whose access to information about his legal rights is necessarily limited by his confinement. Furthermore, there is no claim that either petitioners or any other officials informed respondent that he could seek redress for the alleged deprivation of his property by filing an action under the Nebraska tort claims procedure. This apparent failure takes on additional significance in light of the fact that respondent pursued his complaint about the missing hobby kit through the prison's grievance procedure. In cases such as this, I believe prison officials have an affirmative obligation to inform a prisoner who claims that he is aggrieved by official action about the remedies available under state law. If they fail to do so, then they should not be permitted to rely on the existence of such remedies as adequate alternatives to §1983 action for wrongful deprivation of property. Since these prison officials do not represent that respondent was informed about his rights under state law, I cannot join in the judgment of the Court in this case.

Thus, although I agree with much of the majority's reasoning, I would affirm the judgment of the Court of Appeals.

[The concurring statement of Justice Stewart is omitted.]

PAUL v. DAVIS
424 U.S. 693 (1976)

Mr. JUSTICE REHNQUIST delivered the opinion of the Court.

We granted certiorari, 421 U.S. 909 (1975), in this case to consider whether respondent's charge that petitioners' defamation of him, standing alone and apart from any other governmental action with respect to him, stated a claim for relief under 42 U.S.C. §1983 and the Fourteenth Amendment. For the reasons hereinafter stated, we conclude that it does not.

Petitioner Paul is the Chief of Police of the Louisville, Ky., Division of Police, while petitioner McDaniel occupies the same position in the Jefferson County, Ky., Division of Police. In late 1972 they agreed to combine their efforts for the purpose of alerting local area merchants to possible shoplifters who might be operating during the Christmas season. In early December petitioners distributed to approximately 800 merchants in the Louisville metropolitan area a flyer, which began as follows:

"TO: BUSINESS MEN IN THE METROPOLITAN AREA

"The Chiefs of The Jefferson County and City of Louisville Police Departments, in an effort to keep their officers advised on shoplifting activity, have approved the attached alphabetically arranged flyer of subjects known to be active in this criminal field.

"This flyer is being distributed to you, the business man, so that you may inform your security personnel to watch for these subjects. These persons have been arrested during 1971 and 1972 or have been active in various criminal fields in high density shopping areas.

"Only the photograph and name of the subject is shown on this flyer, if additional information is desired, please forward a request in writing...."

The flyer consisted of five pages of "mug shot" photos, arranged alphabetically. Each page was headed:

"NOVEMBER 1972
CITY OF LOUISVILLE
JEFFERSON COUNTY
POLICE DEPARTMENTS
ACTIVE SHOPLIFTERS"

In approximately the center of page 2 there appeared photos and the name of the respondent, Edward Charles Davis III.

Respondent appeared on the flyer because on June 14, 1971, he had been arrested in Louisville on a charge of shoplifting. He had been arraigned on this charge in September 1971, and, upon his plea of not guilty, the charge had been "filed away with leave [to reinstate]," a disposition which left the charge outstanding. Thus, at the time petitioners caused the flyer to be prepared and circulated respondent had been charged with shoplifting but his guilt or innocence of that offense had never been resolved. Shortly after circulation of the flyer the charge against respondent was finally dismissed by a judge of the Louisville Police Court.

At the time the flyer was circulated respondent was employed as a photographer by the Louisville Courier-Journal and Times. The flyer, and respondent's inclusion therein, soon came to the attention of respondent's supervisor, the Executive Director of Photography for the two newspapers. This individual called respondent in to hear his version of the events leading to his appearing in the flyer. Following this discussion, the supervisor informed respondent that although he would not be fired, he "had best not find himself in a similar situation" in the future.

Respondent thereupon brought this §1983 action in the District Court for the Western District of Kentucky, seeking redress for the alleged violation of rights guaranteed to him by the Constitution of the United States. Claiming jurisdiction under 28 U.S.C. §1343(3), respondent sought damages as well as declaratory and injunctive relief. Petitioners moved to dismiss this complaint. . . .

Respondent's due process claim is grounded upon his assertion that the flier, and in particular the phrase "Active Shoplifters" appearing at the head of the page upon which his name and photograph appear, impermissibly deprived him of some "liberty" protected by the Fourteenth Amendment. His complaint asserted that the "active shoplifter" designation would inhibit him from entering business establishments for fear of being suspected of shoplifting and possibly apprehended, and would seriously impair his future employment opportunities. Accepting that such consequences may flow from the flier in question, respondent's complaint would appear to state a classical claim for defamation actionable in the courts of virtually every State. Imputing criminal behavior to an individual is generally considered defamatory per se, and actionable without proof of special damages.

Respondent brought his action, however, not in the state courts of Kentucky but in a United States District Court for that State. He asserted not a claim for defamation under the laws of Kentucky, but a claim that he had been deprived of rights secured to him by the Fourteenth Amendment of the United States Constitution. Concededly if the same allegations had been made about respondent by a private individual, he would have nothing more than a claim for defamation under state law. But, he contends, since petitioners are respectively an official of city and of county government, his action is thereby transmuted into one for deprivation by the State of rights secured under the Fourteenth Amendment.

In Greenwood v. Peacock, 384 U.S. 808, in the course of considering an important and not wholly dissimilar question of the relationship between the national and the state governments, the Court said that "it is worth contemplating what the result would be if the strained interpretation of §1443(1) urged by the individual petitioners were to prevail." 384 U.S. 808, 832. We, too, pause to consider the result should respondent's interpretation §1983 and of the Fourteenth Amendment be accepted.

If respondent's view is to prevail, a person arrested by law enforcement officers who announce that they believe such person to be responsible for a particular crime in order to calm the fears of an aroused populace, presumably obtains a claim against such officers under §1983. And since it is surely far more clear from the language of the Fourteenth Amendment that "life" is protected against state deprivation than it is that reputation is protected against state injury, it would be difficult to see why the survivors of an innocent bystander mistakenly shot by a policeman or negligently killed by a sheriff driving a government vehicle, would not have claims equally cognizable under §1983.

It is hard to perceive any logical stopping place to such a line of reasoning. Respondent's construction would seem almost necessarily to result in every legally cognizable injury which may have been inflicted by a state official acting under "color of law" establishing a violation of the Fourteenth Amendment. We think it would come as a great surprise to those who drafted and shepherded the adoption of that Amendment to learn that it worked such a result, and a study of our decisions convinces us they do not support the construction urged by respondent.

II

The result reached by the Court of Appeals which respondent seeks to sustain here, must be bottomed on one of two premises. The first is that the Due Process Clause of the Fourteenth Amendment and §1983 make actionable many wrongs inflicted by government employees which had heretofore been thought to give rise only to state law tort claims. The second premise is that the infliction by state officials of a "stigma" to one's reputation is somehow different in kind from the infliction by the same official of harm or injury to other interests protected by state law, so that an injury to reputation is actionable under §1983 and the Fourteenth Amendment even if other such harms are not. We examine each of these premises in turn.

A

The first premise would be contrary to pronouncements in our cases on more than one occasion with respect to the scope of §1983 and of the Fourteenth Amendment. In the leading case of Screws v. United States, 325 U.S. 91 (1945), the Court considered the proper application of the criminal counterpart of §1983, likewise intended by Congress to enforce the guarantees of the Fourteenth Amendment. In his opinion for the Court plurality in that case, Mr. Justice Douglas observed that: "Violation of local law does not necessarily mean that federal rights have been invaded. The fact that a prisoner is assaulted, injured, or even murdered by state officials does not necessarily mean that he is deprived of any right protected and secured by the Constitution or laws of the United States." 325 U.S. at 108-109.

After recognizing that Congress' power to criminalize the conduct of state officials under the aegis of the Fourteenth Amendment was not unlimited because that Amendment "did not alter the basic relation between the States and the national government," the plurality opinion observed that Congress should not be understood to have attempted "to make all torts of state officials federal crimes. It brought within [the criminal provision] only specified acts 'under color' of law and then only those acts which deprived a person of some rights secured by the Constitution or laws of the United States." Id., at 109.

This understanding of the limited effect of the Fourteenth Amendment was not lost in the Court's decision in Monroe v. Pape, 365 U.S. 167 (1961). There the Court was careful to point out that the complaint stated a cause of action under the Fourteenth Amendment because it alleged an unreasonable search and seizure violative of the guarantee "contained in the Fourth Amendment [and] made applicable to the States by reason of the Due Process Clause of the Fourteenth Amendment." 365 U.S., at 171. Respondent, however has pointed to no specific constitutional guarantee safeguarding the interest he asserts has been invaded. Rather he apparently believes that the Fourteenth Amendment's Due Process Clause should ex proprio vigore extend to him a right to be free of injury wherever the State may be characterized as the tortfeasor. But such a reading would make of the Fourteenth Amendment a font of tort law to be superimposed upon whatever systems may already be administered by the States. We have noted the "constitutional shoals" that confront any attempt to derive from congressional civil rights statutes a body of general federal tort law, Griffin v. Breckenridge, 403 U.S. 88, 101-102 (1971); a fortiori the procedural guarantees of the Due Process Clause cannot be the source for such law.

B

The second premise upon which the result reached by the Court of Appeals could be rested — that the infliction by state officials of a "stigma" to one's reputation is somehow different in kind from infliction by a state official of harm to other interests protected by state law — is equally unattainable. The words "liberty" and "property" as used in the Fourteenth Amendment do not in terms single out reputation as a candidate for special protection over and above other interests that may be protected by state law. While we have in a number of our prior cases pointed out the frequently drastic effect of the "stigma" which may result from defamation by the government in a variety of contexts, this line of cases does not establish the proposition that reputation alone, apart from some more tangible interests such as employment, is either "liberty" or "property" by itself sufficient to invoke the procedural protection of the Due Process Clause. . . .

It is apparent from our decisions that there exist a variety of interests which are difficult of definition but are nevertheless comprehended within the meaning of either "liberty" or "property" as meant in the Due Process Clause. These interests attain this constitutional status by virtue of the fact that they have been initially recognized and protected by state law,[5] and we have repeatedly ruled that the procedural guarantees of the Fourteenth Amendment apply whenever the State seeks to remove or significantly alter that protected status. In Bell v. Burson, 402 U.S. 535 (1971), for example, the State by issuing drivers' licenses recognized in its citizens a right to operate a vehicle on the highways of the State. The Court held that the State could not withdraw this right without giving petitioner due process. In Morrissey v. Brewer, 408 U.S. 471 (1972), the State afforded parolees the right to remain at liberty as long

---

5. There are other interests, of course, protected not by virtue of their recognition by the law of a particular State, but because they are guaranteed in one of the provisions of the Bill of Rights which has been "incorporated" into the Fourteenth Amendment. Section 1983 makes a deprivation of such rights actionable independently of state law. See Monroe v. Pape, 365 U.S. 167 (1961).

Our discussion in Part III is limited to consideration of the procedural guarantees of the Due Process Clause and is not intended to describe those substantive limitations upon state action which may be encompassed within the concept of "liberty" expressed in the Fourteenth Amendment.

as the conditions of their parole were not violated. Before the State could alter the status of a parolee because of alleged violations of these conditions, we held that the Fourteenth Amendment's guarantee of due process of law required certain procedural safeguards.

In each of these cases, as a result of the state action complained of, a right or status previously recognized by state law was distinctly altered or extinguished. It was this alteration, officially removing the interest from the recognition and protection previously afforded by the State, which we found sufficient to invoke the procedural guarantees contained in the Due Process Clause of the Fourteenth Amendment. But in the interest in reputation alone which respondent seeks to vindicate in this action in federal court is quite different from the "liberty" or "property" recognized in those decisions. Kentucky law does not extend to respondent any legal guarantee of present enjoyment of reputation which has been altered as a result of petitioners' actions. Rather his interest in reputation is simply one of a number which the State may protect against injury by virtue of its tort law, providing a forum for vindication of those interests by means of damages actions. And any harm or injury to that interest, even where as here inflicted by an officer of the State, does not result in a deprivation of any "liberty" or "property" recognized by state or federal law, nor has it worked any change of respondent's status as theretofore recognized under the State's laws. For these reasons we hold that the interest in reputation asserted in this case is neither "liberty" or "property" guaranteed against state deprivation without due process of law.

Respondent in this case cannot assert denial of any right vouchsafed to him by the State and thereby protected under the Fourteenth Amendment. That being the case, petitioners' defamatory publications, however seriously they may have harmed respondent's reputation, did not deprive him of any "liberty" or "property" interests protected by the Due Process Clause.

IV

Respondent's complaint also alleged a violation of a "right to privacy guaranteed by the First, Fourth, Fifth, Ninth, and Fourteenth Amendments." The Court of Appeals did not pass upon this claim since it found the allegations of a due process violation sufficient to require reversal of the District Court's order. As we have disagreed with the District Court on the due process issue, we find it necessary to pass upon respondent's other theory in order to determine whether there is any support for the litigation he seeks to pursue.

While there is no "right of privacy" found in any specific guarantee of the Constitution, the Court has recognized that "zones of privacy" may be created by more specific constitutional guarantees and thereby impose limits upon government power. See Roe v. Wade, 410 U.S. 113, 152-153 (1973). Respondent's case, however, comes within none of these areas. He does not seek to suppress evidence seized in the course of an unreasonable search. See Katz v. United States, 389 U.S. 347, 351 (1967); Terry v. Ohio, 392 U.S. 1, 8-9 (1968). And our other "right of privacy" cases, while defying categorical description, deal generally with substantive aspects of the Fourteenth Amendment. In Roe the Court point out that the personal rights found in this guarantee of personal privacy must be limited to those which are "fundamental" or "implicit in the concept of ordered liberty" as described in Palko v. Connecticut, 301 U.S. 319, 325 (1937). The activities detailed as being within this definition were ones very different from that for which respondent claims constitutional protection — matters relating to marriage, procreation, contraception, family relationships, and child rearing and education. In these areas it has been held that there are limitations on the States' power to substantively regulate conduct.

Respondent's claim is far afield from this line of decisions. He claims constitutional protection against the disclosure of the fact of his arrest on a shoplifting charge. His claim is based not upon any challenge to the State's ability to restrict his freedom of action in a sphere contended to be "private," but instead on a claim that the State may not publicize a record of an official act such as an arrest. None of our substantive privacy decisions hold this or anything like this, and we decline to enlarge them in this manner.

None of respondent's theories of recovery were based upon rights secured to him by the Fourteenth Amendment. Petitioners therefore were not liable to him under §1983. The judgment of the Court of Appeals holding otherwise is reversed.

Mr. Justice Stevens took no part in the consideration or decision of this case.

Mr. JUSTICE BRENNAN, with whom Mr. JUSTICE WHITE, and Mr. JUSTICE MARSHALL concur, dissenting.

I dissent. The Court today holds that police officials, acting in their official capacities as law enforcers, may on their own initiative and without trial constitutionally condemn innocent individuals as criminals and thereby brand them with one of the most stigmatizing and debilitating labels in our society. If there are no constitutional restraints on such oppressive behavior, the safeguards constitutionally accorded an accused in a criminal trial are rendered a sham, and no individual can feel secure that he will not be arbitrarily singled but for similar ex parte punishment by those primarily charged with fair enforcement of the law. The Court accomplishes this result by excluding a person's interest in his good name and reputation from all constitutional protection, regardless of the character of or necessity for the Government's actions. The result, which is demonstrably inconsistent with our prior case law and unduly restrictive in its construction of our precious Bill of Rights, is one in which I cannot concur.

To clarify what is at issue in this case, it is first necessary to dispel some misconceptions apparent in the Court's opinion. 42 U.S.C. §1983 provides:

"Every person who, under color of any statute, ordinance, regulation, custom, or usage, of any State or Territory, subjects, or causes to be subjected, any citizen of the United States or other person within the jurisdiction thereof to the deprivation of any rights, privileges, or immunities secured by the Constitution and laws, shall be liable to the party injured in an action at law, suit in equity, or other proper proceeding for redress."

Thus, as the Court indicates, respondent's complaint, to be cognizable under §1983, must allege both a deprivation of a constitutional right and the effectuation of that deprivation under color of law. See, e.g., Adickes v. S. H. Kress & Co., 398 U.S. 144, 150 (1970). But the implication that the existence vel non of a state remedy — for example, a cause of action for defamation — is relevant to the determination whether there is a cause of action under §1983, is wholly unfounded. "It is no answer that the State has a law which if enforced would give relief. The federal remedy is supplementary to the state remedy, and the latter need not be first sought and refused before the federal one is invoked." Monroe v. Pape, 365 U.S. 167, 183 (1961). See also, e.g., McNeese v. Board of Education, 373 U.S. 668, 671-672 (1963). Indeed, even if the Court were creating a novel doctrine that state law is in any way relevant, it would be incumbent upon the Court to inquire whether respondent has an adequate remedy under Kentucky law or whether petitioners would be immunized by state doctrines of official or sovereign immunity. The Court, however, undertakes no such inquiry.

Equally irrelevant is the Court's statement that "Concededly if the same allegations had been made about respondent by a private individual, he would have nothing more than a claim for defamation under state law." The action complained of here is "state action" allegedly in violation of the Fourteenth Amendment and that Amendment, which is *only* designed to prohibit "state" action, clearly renders unconstitutional actions taken by state officials that would merely be criminal or tortious if engaged in by those acting in their private capacities. Of course, if a private citizen enters the home of another, manacles and threatens the owner, and searches the house in the course of a robbery, he would be criminally and civilly liable under state law, but no constitutional rights of the owner would be implicated. However, if state police officials engage in the same acts in the course of a narcotics investigation, the owner may maintain a damage action against the police under §1983 for deprivation of constitutional rights "under color of" state law. Cf. Bivens v. Six Unknown Named Agents of Federal Bureau of Narcotics,

403 U.S. 388, 390-392 (1971). See also, e.g., Monroe v. Pape, supra. In short, it is difficult to believe that the Court seriously suggests that there is some anomaly in the distinction, for constitutional purposes, between tortious conduct committed by a private citizen and the same conduct committed by state officials under color of state law. . . .

"In a Constitution for a free people, there can be no doubt that the meaning of 'liberty' must be broad indeed. See, e.g., Bolling v. Sharpe, 347 U.S. 497, 499-500; Stanley v. Illinois, 405 U.S. 645." Board of Regents v. Roth, 408 U.S. 564, 572 (1972). "Without doubt, it denotes not merely freedom from bodily restraint but also the right of the individual . . . generally to enjoy those privileges long recognized . . . as essential to the orderly pursuit of happiness by free men." Meyer v. Nebraska, 262 U.S. 390, 399 (1923). Certainly the enjoyment of one's good name and reputation has been recognized repeatedly in our cases as being among the most cherished of rights enjoyed by a free people, and therefore as falling within the concept of personal "liberty." . . .

I had always thought that one of this Court's most important roles is to provide a formidable bulwark against governmental violation of the constitutional safeguards securing in our free society the legitimate expectations of every person to innate human dignity and sense of worth. It is a regrettable abdication of that role and a saddening denigration of our majestic Bill of Rights when the Court tolerates arbitrary and capricious official conduct branding an individual as a criminal without compliance with constitutional procedures designed to ensure the fair and impartial ascertainment of criminal culpability. Today's decision must surely be a short-lived aberration.[18]

18. In light of my conviction that the State may not condemn an individual as a criminal without following the mandates of the trial process, I need not address the question whether there is an independent right of privacy which would yield the same result. Indeed, privacy notions appear to be inextricably interwoven with the considerations which require that a State not single an individual out for punishment outside the judicial process. Essentially, the core concept would be that a State cannot broadcast even such factual events as the occurrence of an arrest that does not culminate in a conviction when there are no legitimate law enforcement justifications for doing so, since the State is chargeable with the knowledge that many employers will treat an arrest the same as a conviction and deny the individual employment or other opportunities on the basis of a fact that has no probative value with respect to actual criminal culpability. See, e.g., Michelson v. United States, 335 U.S. 469, 482 (1948). Schware v. Board of Bar Examiners, 353 U.S. 232, 241 (1957). A host of state and federal courts, relying on both privacy notions and the presumption of innocence, have begun to develop a line of cases holding that there are substantive limits on the power of the Government to disseminate unresolved arrest records outside the law enforcement system, see, e.g., Utz v. Cullinane, — U.S. App. D.C. — , 520 F.2d 467 (1975): Tarlton v. Saxbe, 165 U.S. App. D.C. 293, 507 F.2d 1116 (1974); United States v. Dooley, 364 F. Supp. 75 (E.D. Pa. 1973); Menard V. Mitchell, 328 F. Supp. 718, 725-726 (D.C. 1971), reversed on other grounds, Menard v. Saxbe, 162 U.S. App. D.C. 284, 498 F.2d 1017 (1974); United States v. Kalish, 271 F. Supp. 968 (D.P.R. 1967); Davidson v. Dill, 503 P.2d 157 (Colo. 1972); Eddy v. Moore, 5 Wash. App. 334, 487 P.2d 211 (1971): I fear that after today's decision, these nascent doctrines will never have the

NOTES

1. Since Section 1983 provides a federal cause of action for the deprivation of constitutional rights, opponents of broad federal judicial review of local governmental activity have advanced a sub-constitutional tort analysis designed to shift the responsibility for policing certain forms of governmental abuse to state courts. The sub-constitutional tort analysis has operated on four levels.

   a. *The requirement of intent — negligence as a constitutional tort.* As Justice Powell argued in his concurrence in Parratt v. Taylor, it is possible to read Section 1983 as requiring a degree of scienter, at least in certain settings. The argument was often summarized by asserting that mere negligence could not found a Section 1983 cause of action. The Court inconclusively explored the scienter path in Baker v. McCollan, 443 U.S. 137 (1979), Procunier v. Navarette, 434 U.S. 555 (1978), and Estelle v. Gamble, 429 U.S. 97 (1976). However, in Parratt v. Taylor, 101 S. Ct. 1908 (1981), the Court abandoned the attempt and ruled that Section 1983 does not require any particular state of mind. As long as the other requirements of a Section 1983 claim are satisfied, negligent deprivation of constitutional rights may give rise to a Section 1983 claim. The Court's apparent willingness to recognize that negligent behavior may give rise to a Section 1983 claim should be contrasted with the Court's reluctance to permit recovery for negligent governmental behavior having a disparate impact on racial minorities. E.g., Washington v. Davis, 426 U.S. 229 (1976). It may be possible to resolve the apparent conflict by treating negligence as a species of scienter for the purposes of constitutional analysis. See, Harper v. Creer, 544 F.2d 1121 (1st Cir. 1976), and Doe v. Swinton, — F. Supp. — (E.D. Va. 1978) ($50,000 verdict for negligence leading to homosexual rape in prison); Watson v. McGee, 527 F. Supp. 234 (S.D. Ohio 1982) (prisoners may sue under Section 1983 for negligence causing fire).

   b. *The requirement of a cognizable constitutional interest.* In order to make out a Section 1983 claim, a plaintiff must establish the deprivation of a right, privilege, or immunity secured by the Constitution or laws of the United States. Unless a plaintiff can identify a cognizable constitutional interest, the challenged governmental activity may be tortious, but it will not fall under Section 1983 and cannot be found to be the basis

---

opportunity for full growth and analysis. Since the Court of Appeals did not address respondent's privacy claims, and since there has not been substantial briefing or oral argument on that point, the Court's pronouncements are certainly unncessary. Of course, States that are more sensitive than is this Court to the privacy and other interests of individuals erroneously caught up in the criminal justice system are certainly free to adopt or adhere to higher standards under state law. See, e.g., Michigan v. Mosley, 423 U.S. 96, 120-121 (1975) (Brennan, J., dissenting).

Mr. Justice White does not concur in this fototnote.

for federal jurisdiction. For example, in Paul v. Davis, 424 U.S. 693 (1976), and Ingraham v. Wright [reproduced in Chapter X], plaintiffs, challenging defamation by a police chief and excessive corporal punishment by a school principal, sought to anchor their claims in the constitution in order to invoke federal jurisdiction. The defamation plaintiff in Paul v. Davis, alleged a deprivation of Ninth Amendment privacy rights and a deprivation of a Fourteenth Amendment interest in liberty caused by the damage to his reputation. The assault plaintiff in Ingraham v. Wright alleged a violation of the Eighth Amendment ban on cruel and unusual punishment as well as a deprivation of a Fourteenth Amendment liberty interest caused by the beating.

The Court rejected both the Ninth Amendment claim in Paul v. Davis and the Eighth Amendment claim in Ingraham, driving both plaintiffs back to a pure Fourteenth Amendment Due Process claim. In order to establish a Due Process claim, the plaintiff's deprivation must be characterized as a loss of life, liberty or property. Life is relatively easy to define. But see, Harman v. Daniels, 525 F. Supp. 798 (D.W. Va. 1981) (fetus cannot sue for Section 1983 damages). However, as Paul v. Davis and Bishop v. Wood, 426 U.S. 341 (1976), illustrate, it is considerably more difficult to determine whether a given governmental act has deprived anyone of liberty or property.

In Paul v. Davis, Justice Rehnquist ruled that an individual's interest in reputation was not a liberty interest protected by the Fourteenth Amendment. Justice Rehnquist challenged the plaintiffs to suggest a principled stopping point between recognizing defamation by a police chief as a Section 1983 violation and recognizing negligent driving by a fireman as a violation of the Constitution. Unless such a principled stopping point exists, Justice Rehnquist's position is difficult to rebut. One possible stopping point, suggested by Justice Brennan's opinion in Bivens v. Six Unknown Agents, 401 U.S. 388 (1971), would be to differentiate between injuries that are within the peculiar power of the state to inflict and injuries that may be equally inflicted by state or private individuals. As applied to Paul v. Davis, the defamation at stake in that case could only have been carried out by a law enforcement official. A private person would not have access to the necessary information and, more importantly, would not have commanded the same attention and credibility. In Paul v. Davis, it was the imprimatur of the state that caused the communication to be intensely damaging. If, on the other hand, one is hit by a firetruck, the nature of the injury is unaffected by its status as a government vehicle. When the harm inflicted is dependent upon the government status of the actor, Justice Brennan's reasoning in Bivens suggests that the relationship between the government and the individual should be governed by principles of constitutional, as opposed to tort, law.

In Bishop v. Wood, 426 U.S. 341 (1976), the Court ruled that unless local law recognizes a property interest in the item at issue, its loss cannot give rise to a deprivation of property within the meaning of the Fourteenth Amendment. Justice Brennan dissented, arguing that local law should not finally define the concept of property for Fourteenth Amendment purposes. See also, Prune Yard Shopping Center v. Robbins, 447 U.S. 74 (1980). For limits on the ability of states to define away traditional property interests, see Loretto v. Teleprompter Manhattan CATV Corp., 50 U.S.L.W. 4988 (1982).

c. *The absence of due process of law.* Even if a plaintiff succeeds in establishing the existence of a liberty or property interest, he must demonstrate that it has been denied without due process of law. Putting aside the thorny question of whether the Due Process clause imposes substantive limitations on the government, the garden variety procedural due process claim will generally argue that some form of deliberative activity must precede the deprivation. Thus, in Ingraham v. Wright, plaintiffs argued that the liberty interest at stake could be denied only after a hearing. Similarly, in Parratt v. Taylor, the plaintiff argued that his property interest could be denied only after a hearing. In both cases, the Court rejected the argument that the Fourteenth Amendment required a pre-event hearing, ruling that the availability of prompt post-event remedies constituted "due process of law." Of course, taken to its extreme, the notion that post-event hearings satisfy due process requirements would vitiate most procedural due process claims and would deprive the federal courts of much of their jurisdiction over Fourteenth Amendment claims. However, as Justice Blackmun's cautious concurrence in Parratt demonstrates, the post-event hearing technique is likely to be used only in property contexts and only when the deprivation is unintentional. While the technique was used in Ingraham in a liberty context involving excessive corporal punishment of a student, the Ingraham court declined to pass on the substantive due process claim and lower federal courts have recognized that allegations of severe corporal punishment of students violate substantive due process. Hall v. Tawney, 621 F.2d 607 (4th Cir. 1980). See also, Doe v. Renfrow, 631 F.2d 91 (7th Cir. 1980) (nude search of 13-year-old girl creates Section 1983 claim).

d. *State action and action under color of law.* Finally, even if a constitutionally cognizable interest has been denied, the defendants must have engaged in state action and acted under color of state law to transform a tort into a constitutional violation. In Belcher v. Stengel, 429 U.S. 118 (1976), the Court dismissed certiorari as improvidently granted on the issue of whether a shooting by an off-duty patrolman constituted action under color of law within the meaning of Section 1983. In Flagg Bros., Inc. v. Brooks, 436 U.S. 149 (1978), the Court ruled that when a warehouseman engaged in a summary sale of a debtor's property to satisfy his lien pursuant to a New York Statutory authorization, he acted under color of state law but did not engage in state action. However, in Lugar v. Edmondson Oil Co., 50 U.S.L.W. 4850 (1982), the Court ruled that a creditor invoking state pre-judgement attachment procedure engages in state action and acts under color of law for purposes of a challenge to the constitutionality of the procedure. In Polk County v. Dodson, — U.S. — (1981), the Court ruled that a public defender does not act under a color of law within the meaning of Section 1983. In Blum v. Yarestsky, 50 U.S.L.W. 4859 (1982), the Court ruled that a private nursing home that received most of its funding from the state did not engage in state action when it discharged patients. In Rendall v. Baker-Kohn, 50 U.S.L.W. 4825 (1982), the Court ruled that a private school funded by the state did not engage in state action when it dismissed teachers.

Lower courts have found the requisite action under color of state law in Golden Rule Ins. Co. v. Mathias, 408 N.E.2d 310 (Ill. App. Ct. 1980), private persons grading state brokerage exams act under color of state law); Ross v. Allen, 515 F. Supp. 972 (S.D.N.Y. 1981) (state-funded school for handicapped state action for purposes of retaliatory dismissal of teacher for informing students of rights); Janusaitis v. Middlebury Vol. Fire Dept., 607 F.2d 17 (2d Cir. 1979) (volunteer fire department state action for purposes of First Amendment analysis under public function doctrine).

Private persons who act jointly with public officials have been deemed to act under color of state law. E.g., Fitzgerald v. Mountain Laurel Racing, Inc., 607 F.2d 589 (3d Cir. 1979) (participation of public officials in the decision-making process of private group renders it state action); Holman v. Central Ark. Broadcasting Co., 610 F.2d 542 (8th Cir. 1980) (reporter present at behest of police may act under color of law). See also, Safeguard Mutual Ins. Co. v. Miller, 477 F. Supp. 299 (E.D. Pa. 1979). Similarly, joint state/federal activity has been deemed to make out a Section 1983 cause of action. E.g., Rowe v. Tennessee, 609 F.2d 259 (6th Cir. 1979); Peck v. United States, 470 F. Supp. 1003 (S.D.N.Y. 1979).

2. In Martinez v. California, 444 U.S. 277 (1980), the Supreme Court ruled that a parolee who committed murder six months after his release did not act under the color of state law. The Court's analysis appears to import notions of proximate cause from the area of tort into the definition of §1983 liability.

3. The scope of the Section 1983 cause of action was dramatically broadened by the Supreme Court in Maine v. Thiboutot, 448 U.S. 1 (1980), when the Court ruled that the phrase "and laws" in Section 1983 was intended to provide a cause of action for the violation of federal statutory rights flowing from the Social Security Act. However, in Pennhurst State School v. Halderman, 101 S. Ct. 1531 (1981), the Court ruled that Congress had intended to confine the plaintiffs to the cause of action established by the underlying statute. See also, First Natl. Bank

of Omaha v. Marquette Natl. Bank, 636 F.2d 195 (8th Cir. 1980) (no Section 1983 cause of action for violation of banking statute); Tatro v. Texas, 481 F. Supp. 1224 (N.D. Tex. 1981) (no Section 1983 cause of action for violation of Education for All Handicapped Children Act); Garrity v. Gallen, 522 F. Supp. 171 (D.N.H. 1981) (no Section 1983 cause of action for violation of Developmentally Disabled Act). In Middlesex County Sewage Auth. v. National Sea Clammers Assn., 101 S. Ct. 2615 (1981), the Court held that Section 1983 did not establish a cause of action for the violation of federal common law. See also, City of Milwaukee v. Illinois, 101 S. Ct. 1784 (1981).

With the abolition of the jurisdictional amount in federal question cases, the principal practical difference between asserting Section 1983 or asserting a cause of action based on the underlying statute is the potential for an award of attorney fees in a Section 1983 case. See generally, Maine v. Thiboutot, 448 U.S. 1 (1980) (awarding attorney fees in Social Security Act case brought in state court as a Section 1983 claim).

4. In Owen v. City of Independence, 445 U.S. 622 (1980), the Court answered the question reserved in Monell and held that government defendants are not entitled to a derivative immunity based on the good faith of their agents. Thus, as long as the challenged act may be fairly charged to a government entity as its custom or policy, good faith belief in its legality will not preclude an award of compensatory damages payable by the government. In Gomez v. Toledo, 446 U.S. 635 (1980), the Court placed the burden of pleading good faith on the defendant in a Section 1983 case, since good faith is an affirmative defense. Presumably, the customary rule which places the persuasion burden on the party asserting a good faith defense will operate as well, although Justice Rehnquist considers the issue an open one. See generally, Doe v. Renfrow, 631 F.2d 91 (8th Cir. 1980), (no good faith defense available for nude search of 13-year-old school girl).

(page 1306) [1547]

NOTES

8. [continued] In Carey v. Piphus, 435 U.S. 247 (1977), the Court held that in order to recover more than nominal damages for a deprivation of procedural due process, a plaintiff must demonstrate actual injury flowing from defendant's acts. If the same result would have occurred even with a hearing; or, if no serious harm was inflicted upon the plaintiff, only nominal damages are available. The Court explicitly authorized an award of attorney fees in connection with an award of nominal damages. In Carey, the Court reserved judgment on whether violations of other constitutional rights, such as First Amendment rights,

were compensible in the absence of actual harm. In Newport v. Fact Concerts, 101 S. Ct. 2748 (1981), the Court held that Section 1983 does not authorize an award of punitive damages against a municipality. Presumably, punitive damages may be assessed against individual Section 1983 defendants. In Boyd v. Shawnee Mission Public Schools, 552 F. Supp. 1115 (D. Kan. 1981), punitive damages were awarded against a school district under 42 U.S.C. §1981. In Hartford Accident Co. v. Hempstead, 422 N.Y.S.2d 47 (1979), the New York Court of Appeals ruled that insurance contracts covering punitive damages in Section 1983 cases were against public policy. Finally, in Gurmankin v. Costanzo, 626 F.2d 1115 (3d Cir. 1980), the court ruled that back pay was a presumptive remedy in a Section 1983 case.

(page 1308) [1549]

NOTES

10. [continued] Congressional reaction to Alyeska Pipeline was swift, culminating in passage of the Attorneys Fee Act of 1976, 42 U.S.C. §1988, which authorizes the award of fees to a "prevailing party" in actions brought under the Reconstruction civil rights statutes. In Christiansburg Garment Co. v. EEOC, 434 U.S. 412 (1977), the Court, construing analogous provisions of Title VII, ruled that fees should be routinely awarded to prevailing plaintiffs but should be awarded to prevailing defendants only if the claim were frivolous. In Hutto v. Finney, 437 U.S. 678 (1978), the Court ruled that the Eleventh Amendment did not bar an award of fees against a state defendant because Congress intended to override the Eleventh Amendment when it enacted 42 U.S.C. Section 1988. See generally, Fitzpatrick v. Bitzer, 427 U.S. 445 (1976) (reproduced supra). In Gates v. Collier, 616 F.2d 1268 (5th Cir. 1980), the Fifth Circuit ruled that a state statute forbidding the payment of fees could not preclude the enforcement of a fee award.

The Court has consistently construed statutes authorizing attorneys fees in civil rights cases liberally. Thus, in New York Gaslight Club v. Carey, 447 U.S. 54 (1980), the Court authorized the award of fees for time spent in administrative proceedings prior to litigation. In Maher v. Gagne, 448 U.S. 122 (1980), fees for negotiating a favorable settlement were upheld. See also, Sullivan v. Pennsylvania Dept. of Labor & Industry, 663 F.2d 443 (3d Cir. 1982) (fee for prevailing in arbitration upheld). In Maine v. Thiboutot, 448 U.S. 1 (1980), the Court ruled that fees in connection with Section 1983 cases in state courts were authorized under Section 1988, regardless of the prevailing local rule. In Supreme Court of Virginia v. Consumers Union, 446 U.S. 719 (1980), the Court authorized an award of fees against judges acting in an administrative capacity. See also: Roberts v. S. S. Kryiakovla D. Lemos, 651 F.2d 201

(3d Cir. 1981) (authorizing award of costs for indispensible experts); Bagby v. Beal, 606 F.2d 411 (3d Cir. 1979) (fees may be awarded for time spent in obtaining fees); Staten v. Pittsburgh Housing Auth., 638 F.2d 599 (3d Cir. 1980) (fees may be awarded for simple cases); Harradine v. Board of Supervisors, — N.Y.S.2d — (4th Dept. 1980) (fees authorized in state case, even though Section 1983 not explicitly raised). Courts have, however, consistently denied fees to pro se litigants. Crooker v. Department of Justice, 632 F.2d 916 (1st Cir. 1980) (no pro se fees in FOIA case); Lovell v. Snow, 637 F.2d 170 (1st Cir. 1981) (no fees for pro se Section 1983 plaintiff).

In order to be eligible for a fee, a civil rights plaintiff must be a "prevailing party." In Hanrahan v. Hampton, 446 U.S. 754 (1980), the Court ruled that merely securing a reversal of a directed verdict and a new trial did not render a plaintiff a prevailing party for fee purposes. See also: Bly v. McLeod, 605 F.2d 134 (4th Cir. 1979) (securing of preliminary injunction followed by loss on merits does not entitle plaintiff to fees); Swietlowich v. County of Buck, 620 F.2d 33 (3d Cir. 1980) (securing new trial does not justify fee award); Blow v. Lascaris, 523 F. Supp. 913 (N.D.N.Y. 1981) (prevailing plaintiff in state administrative proceeding not entitled to Section 1988 fee award). In Familias Unidas v. Briscoe, 619 F.2d 391 (5th Cir. 1980), the Court ruled that fees were authorized only in connection with issues on which the plaintiff had prevailed. The court noted, however, that work relevant to both winning and losing issues qualified fully for fees. In Baker v. Detroit, 504 F. Supp. 841 (E.D. Mich. 1980), a successful defendant-intervenor was treated as though he were a prevailing plaintiff for the purpose of an award of fees. In Kirkland v. New York State Dept. of Correctional Servs., 524 F. Supp. 1214 (S.D.N.Y. 1981), intervening defendants raising good faith claims were deemed immune from a fee award since their claims were not frivolous.

In White v. New Hampshire Dept. of Social Services, 50 U.S.L.W. 4255 (1982), the Court ruled that applications for attorneys fees do not fall within the 10-day period established by Rule 59(e).

The fact that a prevailing party is represented by Legal Services or a pro bono attorney should not affect the fee award. E.g.: Maryland Crystal v. Ramsden, 635 F.2d 590 (7th Cir. 1980) (fees cannot be lower because plaintiff represented by Legal Services or pro bono attorney); Kessler v. Associates Financing Service, 639 F.2d 498 (9th Cir. 1981) (Legal Services office entitled to fee); Oldham v. Ehrlich, 617 F.2d 163 (8th Cir. 1980) (cannot reduce fees because lawyer works for Legal Services office); Lamphere v. Brown Univ., 610 F.2d 46 (1st Cir. 1979) (receipt of contributions by plaintiff should not diminish fee award). See also: Furtado v. Bishop, 635 F.2d 915 (1st Cir. 1981) (imposition of ceiling on fees equal to 50 percent of recovery invalid); Lipscomb v.

Wise, 643 F.2d 319, 49 U.S.L.W. 2701 (5th Cir. 1981) (attorney has standing to appeal from fee decision); Memphis Sheraton Corp. v. Kirkley, 614 F.2d 131 (4th Cir. 1979) (award of fees appealable even though amount not set). However, in National Treasury Employees Union v. Department of Treasury, 49 U.S.L.W. 2815 (D.C. Cir. 1981), the court ruled that when fees are payable to an attorney's employer and are not ploughed back into a litigation program, they must be calculated with reference to the lawyers' salary rather than on the basis of the fair market value of the services.

Awards of attorney fees in Section 1983 cases may not be made against the United States. Knights of Ku Klux Klan v. East Baton Rouge School Board, 643 F.2d 1034 (5th Cir. 1981), NAACP v. Civiletti, 609 F.2d 514 (D.C. Cir. 1979); Shannon v. HUD, 577 F.2d 84 (3d Cir. 1978). See also, McNamara v. Moody, 606 F.2d 621 (5th Cir. 1979) (no Section 1983 fees against government officials personally unless bad faith involved); Brown v. Stackler, 612 F.2d 1057, 48 U.S.L.W. 2502 (7th Cir. 1980) (excessive fee demand may result in no award).

Defendants may not recoup their fees unless the Section 1983 action meets the "groundless" standard established by Christianburg Garment Co. v. EEOC, 434 U.S. 412 (1978). However, if plaintiff's counsel acts improperly, even in connection with a plausible claim, fees may be awarded against counsel personally. Roadway Exp. v. Piper, 447 U.S. 752 (1980) (fees may be awarded under Rule 37 and pursuant to inherent power of court). See also, Corning v. Village of Laurel Hollow, 442 N.Y.S.2d 932 (N.Y. 1979) (officials who hire private counsel not entitled to reimbursement from town even if they win).

In a related area, the Court upheld the right of pro bono lawyers for organizations like the ACLU and NAACP to approach prospective clients in order to offer free legal representation. In re Primus, 436 U.S. 412 (1978). However, where the solicitation is fee generating in a garden variety private tort case, the Court has sustained disciplinary action. Ohralik v. Ohio, 436 U.S. 447 (1978). The Court has not yet considered whether so-called "cause" lawyers hoping to receive court awarded fees may approach prospective clients to offer free legal representation.

See ACLU v. Tennessee, 496 F. Supp. 218 (M.D. Tenn. 1980) (statute barring ACLU from paying litigation expenses invalid).

11. [continued] In Lorillard v. Pons, 434 U.S. 575 (1978), the Court ruled that claims for back pay under the Age Discrimination Act are within the guarantee of a jury trial provided by the Seventh Amendment. However, in Atlas Roofing Co. v. Occupational Safety and Health Review Commission, 430 U.S. 442 (1977), the Court ruled that newly created statutory rights may be enforced in an administrative proceeding, thereby avoiding a jury trial. However, to the extent newly created statutory rights are enforced in federal court, a jury trial is required by

the Seventh Amendment. Thus, Congress might, if it wished, provide for administrative enforcement of open-housing legislation and, thus, avoid Curtis v. Loether, 415 U.S. 189 (1974).

14. [continued] The intimate relationship between state procedure and Section 1983 was explored in Robertson v. Wegmann, 436 U.S. 584 (1978), where the Court upheld a Louisiana statute providing that Section 1983 actions fail to survive the original plaintiff. Although Louisiana is, apparently one of the few states in which a Section 1983 claim will not survive, the Court ruled that Section 1983 was subject to state procedures so long as they are nondiscriminatory and do not frustrate the effectiveness of Section 1983. See also, Jones v. Hildebrant, 432 U.S. 182 (1977). However, in Carlson v. Green, 446 U.S. 14 (1980), the Court ruled that when the cause of death was related to the constitutional claim, a federal rule permitting survivorship would apply.

Similar issues arise in connection with defining the appropriate statute of limitations for a Section 1983 action. Congress has not enacted a uniform period, leaving the courts free to adopt the most appropriate state statute. In Board of Regents v. Tomanio, 446 U.S. 478 (1980), the Court refused to permit the Second Circuit to toll the running of the applicable New York statute while state remedies were exhausted, holding that New York tolling rules must govern. Compare, Walker v. Armco Steel Corp, 446 U.S. 740 (1980) (state tolling rules govern in diversity litigation). For a representative case, see Regan v. Sullivan, 557 F.2d 300 (2d Cir. 1977) (Section 1983 limitation period three years in New York; unclear whether Bivens period is three or six years).

12. [continued] In Great American Fed. Sav. & Loan Assn. v. Novotny, 442 U.S. 366 (1979), the Supreme Court ruled that Section1985(3) did not provide a cause of action for private acts in violation of Title VII. Instead, plaintiffs alleging activity that violates Title VII must seek relief pursuant to the more limited administrative and legal procedures available directly under Title VII. In Novotny, the Court reasoned that Section 1985(3) was not designed to create new rights but merely to provide a remedy for preexisting rights. Novotny, thus, casts doubt on whether Section 1985(3) may be used against private conspiracies to deny constitutional rights which are protected only against "state action." Entirely apart from the power of Congress to authorize such relief, Novotny reads Section 1985(3) narrowly as a statute that was not designed to create new substantive rights. Of course, even after Novotny, it can be argued that in enacting Section 1985(3) Congress must have intended to prevent private persons from frustrating the enjoyment of rights carefully protected against state interference. See, e.g., Fantroy v. Greater St. Louis Labor Council, 478 F. Supp. 355 (E.D. Mo. 1979). However, in Weiss v. Willow Tree Civic Association, 467 F. Supp. 803 (S.D.N.Y. 1979), Judge Weinfeld read Novotny as forbidding the use of Section 1985(3) against private action in derogation of rights pro-

tected solely against "state action." Some tension appears to exist between Novotny, holding that Section 1985(3) does not provide a cause of action for private violations of Title VII, and Main v. Thiboutot, 448 U.S. 1 (1980), holding that Section 1983 was intended to provide a cause of action for any violation of a federal statute committed under color of state law. See also, Chapman v. Houston Welfare Rights Org., 441 U.S. 600 (1979), and United States v. Johnson, 390 U.S. 563 (1968) (private interference with Title II subject to Section 241 prosecution).

Recent cases recognizing a Section 1985(3) cause of action include, Fisher v. Shamburg, 624 F.2d 156 (10th Cir. 1980) (Section 1985(3) establishes cause of action for damages against persons who beat a black because he patronized a segregated restaurant); New York v. 11 Cornwell Co., 508 F. Supp. 273 (E.D.N.Y. 1981) (neighbors' actions in buying house to prevent its use as a home for the retarded creates Section 1985(3) claim); Ward v. Connor, 657 F.2d 45 (4th Cir. 1981) (religious groups may invoke Section 1985(3) against deprogrammers who kidnap adherents). But see, Murphy v. Mt. Carmel High School, 543 F.2d 1189 (7th Cir. 1976) (private activity in violation of free speech does not establish Section 1985(3) cause of action).

Courts have continued to experience difficulty in defining the "victim classes" which may trigger Section 1985(3) protection. In Peacock v. Guaranty Fed. Sav. & Loan Assn., 48 U.S.L.W. 2434 (M.D. Fla. 1979), the court declined to recognize persons who refused to take lie detectors as a Section 1985(3) victim class. Similarly, in Carchman v. Korman Corp., 594 F.2d 354 (3d Cir. 1979), the Third Circuit declined to recognize tenant organizers as an eligible class. But see, Ackley v. Maple Woodman Associates, 47 U.S.L.W. 2647 (Ohio C.P. Ct. 1979) (recognizing Section 1985(3) claim on behalf of person denied apartment because of organizing efforts). In Phaby v. KSD, 476 F. Supp. 1051 (E.D. Mo. 1979), and Fantroy v. Greater St. Louis Labor Council, 478 F. Supp. 355 (E.D. Mo. 1979), the court recognized political belief and affiliation as an appropriate class-based trait justifying Section 1985(3) protection.

In Peck v. United States, 470 F. Supp. 1003 (S.D.N.Y. 1979) and Paton v. LaPrade, 471 F. Supp. 166 (D.N.J. 1979), the court ruled that Sections 1985(3) and 1986 (failure to prevent deprivations of constitutional rights) were available against federal defendants acting under color of federal law.

(page 1312) [1553]

NOTE — JURISDICTION OVER SUPREMACY CLAUSE CASES

[continued] In Chapman v. Houston Welfare Rights Organization, 441 U.S. 600 (1979), the Court ruled that violations of the Supremacy clause do not give rise to a cause of action under Section 1983 and are not cognizable under 28 U.S.C. Section 1343(3). Moreover, the Court ruled, the Social Security Act is not a statute for the protection of civil or equal rights. Accordingly, its violation does not give rise to Section 1343 jurisdiction. However, with the abolition of the jurisdictional amount in federal question cases, it is unnecessary to seek to assert Section 1343 jurisdiction, since jurisdiction is available in statutory cases under Section 1331(a). In Eikenberry v. Callahan, 49 U.S.L.W. 2704 (D.C. Cir. 1981), the court ruled that the abolition of the jurisdictional amount applied retroactively to all pending cases.

(page 1315) [1556]

CARLSON v. GREEN
446 U.S. 14 (1980)

Mr. JUSTICE BRENNAN delivered the opinion of the Court.

Respondent brought this suit in the District Court for the Southern District of Indiana on behalf of the estate of her deceased son, Joseph Jones, Jr., alleging that he suffered personal injuries from which he died because the petitioners, federal prison officials, violated his due process, equal protection, and Eighth Amendment rights.[1] Asserting jurisdiction under 28 U.S.C. §1331(a), she claimed compensatory and punitive damages for the constitutional violations. Two questions are presented for decision: (1) Is a remedy available directly under the Constitution given that respondent's allegations could also support a suit against the United States under the Federal Tort Claims Act? and (2) If so, is survival of the cause of action governed by federal common law or by state statutes?

I

The District Court held that under Estelle v. Gamble, 429 U.S. 97 (1976), the allegations set out in note 1, supra, pleaded a violation of the Eight Amendment's proscription against infliction of cruel and unusual punishment giving rise to a cause of action for damages under Bivens v. Six Unknown Named Agents of Federal Bureau of Narcotics,

---

1. More specifically, respondent alleged that petitioners, being fully apprised of the gross inadequacy of medical facilities and staff at the Federal Correction Center in Terre Haute, Indiana, and of the seriousness of Jones' chronic asthmatic condition, nonetheless, kept him in that facility against the advice of doctors, failed to give him competent medical attention for some eight hours after he had an asthmatic attack, administered contraindicated drugs which made his attack more severe, attempted to use a respirator known to be inoperative which further impeded his breathing, and delayed for too long a time his transfer to an outside hospital. The complaint further alleges that Jones' death resulted from these acts and omissions, that petitioners were deliberately indifferent to Jones' serious medical needs, and that their indifference was in part attributable to racial prejudice.

403 U.S. 388 (1971). The court recognized that the decedent could have maintained this action if he had survived, but dismissed the complaint because in its view the damages remedy as a matter of federal law was limited to that provided by Indiana's survivorship and wrongful death laws and, as the court construed those laws, the damages available to Jones' estate failed to meet §1331(a)'s $10,000 jurisdictional amount requirement....

II

Bivens established that the victims of a constitutional violation by a federal agent have a right to recover damages against the official in federal court despite the absence of any statute conferring such a right. Such a cause of action may be defeated in a particular case, however, in two situations. The first is when defendants demonstrate "special factors counselling hesitation in the absence of affirmative action by Congress." Id., 403 U.S., at 396; Davis v. Passman, 442 U.S. 228, 245 (1979). The second is when defendants show that Congress has provided an alternative remedy which it explicitly declared to be a *substitute* for recovery directly under the Constitution and viewed as equally effective. Bivens, 403 U.S., at 397; Davis v. Passman, 442 U.S., at 245-247.

Neither situation obtains in this case. First, the case involves no special factors counselling hesitation in the absence of affirmative action by Congress. Petitioners do not enjoy such independent status in our constitutional scheme as to suggest that judicially created remedies against them might be inappropriate. Davis v. Passman, 442 U.S., at 246. Moreover, even if requiring them to defend respondent's suit might inhibit their efforts to perform their official duties, the qualified immunity accorded them under Butz v. Economou, 438 U.S. 478 (1978), provides adequate protection. See Davis v. Passman, 442 U.S., at 246.

Second, we have here no explicit congressional declaration that persons injured by federal officers' violations of the Eighth Amendment may not recover money damages from the agents but must be remitted to another remedy, equally effective in the view of Congress. Petitioners point to nothing in the Federal Tort Claims Act (FTCA) or its legislative history to show that Congress meant to pre-empt a Bivens remedy or to create an equally effective remedy for constitutional violations. FTCA was enacted long before Bivens was decided, but when Congress amended FTCA in 1974 to create a cause of action against the United States for intentional torts committed by federal law enforcement officers, 28 U.S.C. §2680(h), the congressional comments accompanying that amendment made it crystal clear that Congress views FTCA and Bivens as parallel, complementary causes of action:

"[A]fter the date of enactment of this measure, innocent individuals who are subjected to raids [like that in Bivens] will have a cause of action against the individual Federal agents *and* the Federal Government. Furthermore, this provision should be viewed as a *counterpart* to the Bivens case and its progenty [sic], in that it waives the defense of sovereign immunity so as to make the Government independently liable in damages for the same type of conduct that is alleged to have occurred in Bivens (and for which that case imposes liability upon the individual Government officials involved.)" S. Rep. No. 93-588, 93d Cong., 1st Sess., 3 (1973) (emphasis supplied).

In the absence of a contrary expression from Congress, §2680(h) thus contemplates that victims of the kind of intentional wrongdoing alleged in this complaint shall have an action under FTCA against the United States as well as a Bivens action against the individual officials alleged to have infringed their constitutional rights. . . .

Four additional factors, each suggesting that the Bivens remedy is more effective than the FTCA remedy, also support our conclusion that Congress did not intend to limit respondent to an FTCA action. First, the Bivens remedy, in addition to compensating victims, serves a deterrent purpose. See Butz v. Economou, 438 U.S. 478, 505 (1978). Because the Bivens remedy is recoverable against individuals, it is a more effective deterrent than the FTCA remedy against the United States. It is almost axiomatic that the threat of damages has a deterrent effect, Imbler v. Pachtman, 424 U.S. 409, 442 (1976) (White, J., concurring in the judgment), surely particularly so when the individual official faces personal financial liability. . . .

Second, our decision, although not expressly addressing and deciding the question, indicate that punitive damages may be awarded in a Bivens suit. . . . But punitive damages in a FTCA suit are statutorily prohibited. 28 U.S.C. §2674. Thus FTCA is that much less effective than a Bivens action as a deterrent to unconstitutional acts.

Third, a plaintiff cannot opt for a jury in an FTCA action, 28 U.S.C. §2402, as he may in a Bivens suit. . . .

Fourth, an action under FTCA exists only if the State in which the alleged misconduct occurred would permit a cause of action for that misconduct to go forward. 28 U.S.C. §1346(b) (United States liable "in accordance with the law of the place where the act or omission occurred."). Yet it is obvious that the liability of federal officials for violations of citizens' constitutional rights should be governed by uniform rules. . . .

Plainly FTCA is not a sufficient protector of the citizens' constitutional rights, and without a clear congressional mandate we cannot hold that Congress relegated respondent exclusively to the FTCA remedy.

III

Bivens actions are a creation of federal law and, therefore, the question whether respondent's action survived Jones' death is a question of federal law. See Burks v. Lasker, 441 U.S. 471, 476 (1979). Petitioners, however, would have us fashion a federal rule of survivorship that incorporates the survivorship laws of the forum State, at least where the state law is not inconsistent with federal law. Respondent argues, on the other hand, that only a uniform federal rule of survivorship is compatible with the goal of deterring federal officials from infringing federal constitutional rights in the manner alleged in respondent's complaint. We agree with respondent. Whatever difficulty we might have resolving the question were the federal involvement less clear, we hold that only a uniform federal rule of survivorship will suffice to redress the constitutional deprivation here alleged and to protect against repetition of such conduct. . . .

Robertson v. Wegmann, supra, holding that a §1983 action would abate in accordance with Louisiana survivorship law is not to the contrary. There the plaintiff's death was not caused by the acts of the defendants upon which the suit was based. Moreover, Robertson expressly recognized that to prevent frustration of the deterrence goals of §1983 (which in part also underlie Bivens actions, see Part II, supra) "[a] state official contemplating illegal activity must always be prepared to face the prospect of a §1983 action being filed against him." 436 U.S., at 592. A federal official contemplating unconstitutional conduct similarly must be prepared to face the prospect of a Bivens action. A uniform rule that claims such as respondent's survive the decedent's death is essential if we are not to "frustrate in [an] important way the achievement" of the goals of Bivens actions. Auto Workers v. Hoosier Cardinal Corp., 383 U.S. 696, 702 (1966).

Affirmed.

Mr. JUSTICE POWELL, with whom Mr. JUSTICE STEWART joins, concurring in the judgment.

Although I join the judgment, I do not agree with much of the language in the Court's opinion. The Court states the principles governing Bivens actions as follows:

"Bivens established that the victims of a constitutional violation . . . have a right to recover damages. . . . Such a cause of action may be defeated . . . in two situations. The first is when defendants demonstrate 'special factors counselling hesitation in the absence of affirmative action by Congress.' . . . The second is when defendants show that Congress has provided an alternative remedy which it explicitly declared to be a *substitute* for recovery directly under the Constitution and viewed as equally effective. . . ." (emphasis in original).

The foregoing statement contains dicta that go well beyond the prior holdings of this Court. . . .

The Court's absolute language is all the more puzzling because it comes in a case where the implied remedy is plainly appropriate under any measure of discretion. The Federal Tort Claims Act, on which petitioners rely, simply is not an adequate remedy. And there are reasonably clear indications that Congress did not intend that statute to displace Bivens claims. No substantial contrary policy has been identified, and I am aware of none. I therefore agree that a private damages remedy properly is inferred from the Constitution in this case. But I do not agree that Bivens plaintiffs have a "right" to such a remedy whenever the defendant fails to show that Congress has "provided an [equally effective] alternative remedy which it explicitly declared to be a *substitute.* . . ." In my view, the Court's willingness to infer federal causes of action that cannot be found in the Constitution or in a statute denigrates the doctrine of separation of powers and hardly comports with a rational system of justice. Cf. Cannon v. University of Chicago, 441 U.S. 677, 730-749 (1979) (Powell, J., dissenting).

II

In Part III of its opinion, the Court holds that " 'whenever the relevant state survival statute would abate a Bivens-type action brought against defendants whose conduct results in death, the federal common law allows survival of the action.' " Ante, quoting 581 F.2d 699, 674-675 (C.A. 7 1978). I agree that the relevant policies require the application of federal common law to allow survival in this case.

It is not "obvious" to me, however, that "the liability of federal officials for violations of citizens' constitutional rights should be governed by uniform rules" in every case. On the contrary, federal courts routinely refer to state law to fill the procedural gaps in national remedial schemes. The policy against invoking the federal common law except where necessary to the vitality of a federal claim is codified in 42 U.S.C. §1988, which directs that state law ordinarily will govern those aspects of §1983 actions not covered by the "laws of the United States."

The Court's opinion in this case does stop short of mandating uniform rules to govern all aspects of Bivens actions. But the Court also says that the preference for state law embodied in §1988 is irrelevant to the selection of rules that will govern actions against federal officers under Bivens. Ibid. I see no basis for this view. In Butz v. Economou, 438 U.S. 478, 498-504, and n.25 (1978), the Court thought it unseemly that different rules should govern the liability of federal and state officers for similar constitutional wrongs. I would not disturb that understanding today.

Mr. CHIEF JUSTICE BURGER, dissenting.

Although I would be prepared to join an opinion giving effect to Bivens v. Six Unknown Federal Narcotics Agents, 403 U.S. 388 (1971), — which I thought wrongly decided — I cannot join today's unwarranted expansion of that decision. The Federal Tort Claims Act provides an adequate remedy for prisoners' claim of medical mistreatment. For me, that is the end of the matter. . . .

Mr. JUSTICE REHNQUIST, dissenting.

The Court today adopts a fomalistic procedural approach for inferring private damage remedies from constitutional provisions that in my view still further highlights the wrong turn this Court took in Bivens v. Six Unknown Federal Narcotics Agents, 403 U.S. 388 (1971). Although ordinarily this Court should exercise judicial restraint in attempting to attain a wise accommodation between liberty and order under the Constitution, to dispose of this case as if Bivens were rightly decided would in the words of Mr. Justice Frankfurter be to start with an "unreality." Kovacs v. Cooper, 336 U.S. 77, 89 (1949) (Frankfurter, J., concurring). Bivens is a decision "by a closely divided court, unsupported by the confirmation of time," and, as a result of its weak precedential and doctrinal foundation, it cannot be viewed as a check on "the living process of striking a wise balance between liberty and order as new cases come here for adjudication." Cf id.; B. & W. Taxi Co. v. B. & Y. Taxi Co., 276 U.S. 518, 532-533 (1927) (Holmes, J., dissenting); Hudgens v. National Labor Relations Board, 424 U.S. 507 (1975), overruling Amalgamated Food Employees Union v. Logan Valley Plaza, 391 U.S. 308 (1968).

The Court concludes that Congress intended a Bivens action under the Eighth Amendment to exist concurrently with actions under the Federal Tort Claims Act (FTCA) because Congress did not indicate that it meant the FTCA "to preempt a Bivens remedy or to create an equally effective remedy for constitutional violations," ante, nor are there any "special factors counselling [judicial] hesitation." Id. The Court's opinion otherwise lacks even an arguably principled basis for deciding in what circumstances an inferred constitutional damage remedy is appropriate and for defining the contours of such a remedy. And its "practical" conclusion is all the more anomalous in that Congress in 1974 amended the FTCA to permit private damage recoveries for intentional torts committed by federal law enforcement officers, thereby enabling persons injured by such officers' violations of their federal constitutional rights in many cases to obtain redress for their injuries.

In my view, it is "an exercise of power that the Constitution does not give us" for this Court to infer a private civil damage remedy from the Eighth Amendment or any other constitutional provision. Id., at 428 (Black, J., dissenting). The creation of such remedies is a task that is more appropriately viewed as falling within the legislative sphere of authority. Ibid. . . .

(page 1316) [1557]

NOTES

3. The Supreme Court's decisions in Davis v. Passman, 442 U.S. 228 (1979), and Carlson v. Green appear to hold that private causes of action

for damages may be inferred from most, if not all, of the substantive provisions of the Constitution, at least when a government official is the defendant. When, however, the constitutional provisions at issue govern the relationship between private persons, the recognition of an implied cause of action would constitutionalize areas of state tort law which are generally deemed adequate in the context of private relationships. Thus, in Turner v. Unification Church, 473 F. Supp. 367 (D.R.I 1978), aff'd, 602 F.2d 458 (1st Cir. 1979), Judge Pettine declined to imply a cause of action from the Thirteenth Amendment against a private defendant, noting that state tort law provided adequate relief.

See also, Ellis v. Blum, 643 F.2d 68 (2d Cir. 1981) (emotional distress caused by due process violation actionable under Bivens); Citizens Savings v. Califano, 480 F. Supp. 843 (D.D.C. 1979) (failure to process reimbursement claims does not give rise to Bivens claim).

4. The Supreme Courts' decisions in Monell and Owen v. City of Independence have rendered it unnecessary to seek to imply a Bivens cause of action against a municipality. The precise relationship between the expanded version of Section 1983 in Monell and a Bivens cause of action remains largely unexplored, especially in those situations where the Bivens claim is procedurally more advantageous. In Turpin v. Mailet, 579 F.2d 152 (2d Cir. 1978) (en banc), the Second Circuit recognized a Bivens claim against a municipality. However, after Monell was decided, the Circuit vacated its decision as unnecessary, since full relief was available under Section 1983. Turpin v. Mailet, 591 F.2d 426 (2d Cir. 1979). In Molina v. Richardson, 578 F.2d 846 (9th Cir. 1978), the Ninth Circuit declined to infer a Bivens claim against a municipality.

In Butz v. Economou, 438 U.S. 478 (1978) and G. M. Leasing Co. v. United States, 429 U.S. 338 (1977), the Court held that individual Bivens defendants are entitled to a good faith defense. Presumably given Owen v. City of Independence, 445 U.S. 622 (1980), the United States may not claim a derivative good faith defense in connection with an action under the federal Tort Claims Act. In Universal Amusement Co., Inc. v. Hofheinz, 646 F.2d 996 (5th Cir. 1981), the court declined to permit a Bivens defendant sued in his official capacity to assert a qualified good faith immunity. But see, Harlow v. Fitzgerald, 50 U.S.L.W. 4815 (1982). In Rhodes v. City of Wichita, 516 F. Supp. 501 (D. Kan. 1981), the court ruled that respondeat superior liability existed in Bivens claims against municipalities. In Jaffee v. United States, 592 F.2d 712 (3d Cir.), cert. denied, 441 U.S. 961, Judge Gibbons, writing for a panel of the Third Circuit, ruled that military superiors who ordered plaintiffs to remain dangerously close to experimental atomic explosions were entitled to a qualifed, rather than an absolute, immunity in connection with a Bivens claim for damages. The panel opinion has reversed after a rehearing en banc. 663 F.2d 1226 (3d Cir. 1981). In view of the resolution of the identical issue in the context of Section 1983, good faith must be pleaded by the defendant as an affirmative defense. Presumably, the persuasion burden on the issue will rest with the defendant. See, Gomez v. Toledo, 446 U.S. 635 (1980). In Nixon v. Fitzgerald, 50 U.S.L.W. 4799 (1982), the President was granted absolute immunity from Bivens claims. See also, Harlow v. Fitzgerald, 50 U.S.L.W. 4815 (1982) (Presidential aides entitled to absolute immunity if functionally necessary; otherwise entitled to qualified immunity). The general area of immunity is discussed infra in connection with Section 1983 liability.

5. In Stafford v. Briggs, 444 U.S. 527 (1980), the Court ruled that the nationwide service of process and liberal venue rules of 28 U.S.C. §§1391(e), 1362 applied only to actions seeking prospective equitable relief. Actions for damages must satisfy the traditional venue requirements of Section 1391(b). Service of process will be governed by state long-arm practice. See generally, Worldwide VW v. Woodson, 444 U.S. 286 (1980) and Rush v. Savchuck, 444 U.S. 320 (1980) for the limits of long-arm jurisdiction. For a discussion of jurisdictional as well as other obstacles to successful recovery in Bivens actions, see Note, Damages or Nothing — the Efficacy of the Bivens-Type Remedy, 64 Cornell L. Rev. 667 (1979).

6. Given Carlson v. Green, the existence of a federal Tort Claims Act remedy does not foreclose a Bivens claim. Whether a plaintiff can assert both a Bivens and an FTCA claim, either simultaneously or serially, has not yet been explored. In Birnbaum v. United States, 588 F.2d 319 (2d Cir. 1978), the Circuit affirmed a Tort Claims award of $1,000 for illegal opening of mail by the CIA.

7. In Figueroa v. State, 604 P.2d 1198 (Haw. 1979), state sovereign immunity was held to preclude a Bivens-type claim for damages based on violations of the Hawaii State Constitution.

8. The $10,000 jurisdictional amount in cases asserting federal question jurisdiction under 28 U.S.C. §1331(a) has been abolished. Thus, Bivens claims no longer need satisfy a jurisdictional amount.

(page 1327) [1568]

The abolition of the $10,000 jurisdictional amount in suits against federal officials removed the pressure to use the APA as an independent basis of federal jurisdiction. Not surprisingly, therefore, in Califano v. Sanders, 430 U.S. 99 (1977), the Court ruled that the APA is not an independent base of jurisdiction.

(page 1331) [1572]

NOTES

1. [continued] In United States v. Testan, 424 U.S. 392 (1976), the Court narrowly construed the Tucker Act, holding that it neither waived sovereign immunity nor provided an independent cause of action.

(page 1332) [1573]

9. Jurisdiction over employment discrimination claims sounding in Title VII is provided by 42 U.S.C. §2000e-16. In Brown v. General Services Administration, 425 U.S. 820 (1976), and Chandler v. Roudebush, 425 U.S. 840 (1976), the Court ruled that the administrative exhaustion requirements and the limitations on time provided by Section 717 are mandatory, but that, once complied with, a Title VII claimant is entitled to a de novo hearing in federal court.

Jurisdiction over Social Security Act Claims is provided by 42 U.S.C §405(h). In Weinberger v. Salfi, 422 U.S. 749 (1975), the Court ruled that the administrative exhaustion requirements of Section 405(g) were mandatory. However, in Matthews v. Diaz, 426 U.S. 67 (1976), and Matthews v. Eldridge, 424 U.S. 219 (1976), the court recognized that administrative exhaustion in Social Security cases was waivable and subject to traditional futility doctrine. In Matthews v. Weber, 423 U.S. 261 (1976), the Court sustained the practice of routing Social Security Act cases to federal magistrates for an advisory determination subject to review by a federal district judge. See also, Califano v. Sanders, 430 U.S. 99 (1977) (narrowly defining jurisdiction to review failure to re-open denial of social security claim). In Maine v. Thiboutot, 448 U.S. 1 (1980), the Court recognized that Section 1983 established a cause of action for the violation of the Social Security Act.

In Farmer v. Carpenter's Local, 430 U.S. 290 (1977), the Court recognized concurrent jurisdiction in state court over torts arising out of the employment relationship, which do not implicate the basic policies of the National Labor Relations Act. Thus, a union member was permitted to sue his union in state court for defamation and intentional infliction of emotional distress.

In Themtron Products, Inc. v. Hermansdorfer, 423 U.S. 336 (1976), the Court ruled that a District Court could not decline to accept a properly removed case merely because its dockets were overcrowded.

In Commissioner of Internal Revenue v. Shapiro, 424 U.S. 800 (1976), the Court reiterated the traditional view that the Federal Tax Anti-Injunction Act did not deprive the federal courts of jurisdiction to enjoin an IRS collection attempt when (a) no possibility existed that the government would prevail, and (b) irreparable injury would be created by permitting the collection precedures to go forward. In Tully v. Griffin, 429 U.S. 68 (1976), the Court rigorously applied the State Tax Anti-Injunction Act (28 U.S.C. §1341) to reverse an injunction against New York's attempt to collect sales tax from a Vermont retailer because a "plain, speedy and efficient" remedy existed (allegedly) in New York state courts. In California v. Grace Brethan Church, 50 U.S.L.W. 4703 (1982), the Court applied the state Anti-Injunction Act to action for declaratory judgements as well. See also, Moe v. The Confederated

Salish and Kootenai Tribes, 425 U.S. 463 (1976) (holding 28 U.S.C. § 1341 inapplicable to suit by Indians to enjoin state taxes); Rosewell v. LaSalle Natl. Bank, 101 S. Ct. 1221 (1981) (state procedure requiring two-year wait without interest is adequate). In Fair Assessment v. McNary, 50 U.S.L.W. 4017 (1981), the Court adopted a broad reading of comity, which barred federal judicial scrutiny of allegedly discriminatory administration of a state tax system. In Mobil Oil v. Tully, 499 F. Supp. 888 (N.D.N.Y. 1980), the court held that a provision forbidding a taxpayer to pass along the tax was not subject to the Tax Anti-Injunction Act.

(page 1333) [1574]

1. [continued] Congress virtually abolished three-judge courts in August 1976 by amending 28 U.S.C. 2284. Certain election cases arising under the Voting Rights Act and reapportionment litigation appear to be the principal areas in which three-judge courts will continue to play a significant role. Pub. L. 94-381.

(page 1336) [1577]

NOTES

11. [continued] In Mandel v. Bradley, 432 U.S. 173 (1977), the Court, once again, altered its view on the binding effect of a Supreme Court summary affirmance. After Mandel, a summary affirmance is deemed binding only as to the result of a given case and is not deemed to adopt the reasoning of the lower courts. In effect, Mandel reduces the precedential value of summary affirmances to the narrowest possible basis for the Court's order.

(page 1344) [1585]

NOTES

2. [continued] In Burrell v. McCray, 426 U.S. 471 (1976), the Court dismissed a writ of certiorari as improvidently granted on the issue of whether exhaustion of administrative remedies could be required of Section 1983 plaintiffs challenging prison conditions under the Eighth Amendment. Justice Brennan, dissenting from the dismissal, indicated that five Justices favored affirming the comprehensive decision of the Fourth Circuit, which had declined to order administrative exhaustion. 516 F.2d 357 (4th Cir. 1975). In 1980 Congress amended Section 1983 to require exhaustion of administrative remedies in prisoner's rights suits. In Patsy v. Florida State Board of Regents, 50 U.S.L.W. 4731

(1982), the Court held that the exhaustion of administrative remedies was not required in §1983 cases unless specifically required by Congress.

(page 1345) [1586]

NOTES

3. [continued] In Swain v. Pressley, 430 U.S. 372 (1977), the Court upheld a requirement that a habeas corpus petitioner exhaust available remedies in the Article I courts created for the District of Columbia. See, e.g., Tully v. Griffin, 429 U.S. 68 (1976) (federal court lacks jurisdiction under 28 U.S.C. §1341 to interfere with state tax process when "plain, speedy and efficient remedy" exists in state courts). See also, Rosewell v. LaSalle Natl. Bank, 101 S. Ct. 1221 (1981); Fair Assessment v. McNary, 50 U.S.L.W. 4017 (1981); and California v. Grace Brethren Church, 50 U.S.L.W. 4703 (1982).

(page 1364) [1605]

NOTES

2. [continued] In Trainor v. Hernandez, 431 U.S. 434 (1977), Juidice v. Vail, 430 U.S. 327 (1977), and Moore v. Sims, 442 U.S. 415 (1979), the Court continued to expand the Younger doctrine into the civil area. In Trainor, the pendency of a civil fraud action brought by the state to recoup allegedly improper welfare payments was deemed to preclude a federal challenge to the attachment procedures utilized in the state lawsuit. In Juidice, the pendency of a civil contempt proceeding in aid of the collection of a money judgment was deemed to preclude a challenge to the failure of the contempt proceeding to provide counsel. In Moore, the pendency of a Texas proceeding for the removal of children from their parents was deemed to preclude a challenge to the constitutionality of the procedures governing the state proceeding. Finally, in Middlesex Ethics Committee v. Garden State Bar Assn., 50 U.S.L.W. 4712 (1982), the Court ruled that comity precluded interference with pending attorney disciplinary proceedings. Although the Court has expanded Younger to certain civil contexts in which the state is a party and in which the state has a strong interest, the Court has studiously declined to decide whether Younger applies to private litigation between private parties. Compare, Louisville Area Inter-Faith Committee v. Nottingham Liquors, 542 F.2d 652 (6th Cir. 1976) (comity bars federal court review of state anti-picketing injunction obtained by private party) with Puerto Rico International Airlines, Inc. v. Recio, 520 F.2d 1342 (1st Cir. 1975) (Younger does not apply to private litigation). The authorities are collected in Johnson v. Kelly, 583 F.2d 1242 (3d Cir. 1978). The incon-

sistent application of Younger in the lower courts is illustrated by Rucker v. Wilson, 475 F. Supp. 1164 (E.D. Mich. 1979) (Younger requires abstention when administrative proceeding pending); Schuman v. Muller, 484 F. Supp. 1334 (M.D. Pa. 1978) (state court retention of jurisdiction to oversee consent decree bars prospective federal challenge); New Jersey-Philadelphia Presbytery v. New Jersey, 654 F.2d 868 (3d Cir. 1981) (pending state enforcement proceeding does not bar nonparties from challenging licensing scheme on First Amendment grounds).

(page 1367) [1608]

EXAMINING BOARD OF ENGINEERS, ARCHITECTS, AND SURVEYORS v. FLORES DE OTERO
426 U.S. 572 (1976)

Mr. JUSTICE BLACKMUN delivered the opinion of the Court.

This case presents the issue whether the United States District Court for the District of Puerto Rico possesses jurisdiction, under 28 U.S.C. §1343(3), to entertain a suit based upon 42 U.S.C. §1983, and, if the answer is in the affirmative, the further issue whether Puerto Rico's restriction, by statute, of licenses for civil engineers to United States citizens is constitutional. The first issue, phrased another way, is whether Puerto Rico is a "State," for purposes of §1343(3), insofar as that statute speaks of deprivation "under color of any State law"; the resolution of that question was reserved in Calero-Toledo v. Pearson Yacht Leasing Co., 415 U.S. 663 n.11 (1974)....

III

Appellants, ... argue that the District Court should have abstained from reaching the merits of the constitutional claim. Fornaris v. Ridge Tool Co., 400 U.S. 41 (1970), is cited as an example of abstention in a Puerto Rico context. We conclude that the District Court correctly determined that abstention was unnecessary. The case presents no novel question concerning the judicially created abstention doctrine; it requires instead, only the application of settled principles reviewed just last Term in Harris County Commrs. Court v. Moore, 420 U.S. 77 (1975).

Appellants urge that abstention was appropriate for two reasons. First, it is said that §689 should be construed by the Commonwealth courts in the light of §1483 of the Civil Code, P.R. Laws Ann., Tit. 31, §4124 (1968). This provision imposes liability on a contractor for defective construction of a building. We fail to see, however, how §4124 in any way could affect the interpretation of §689 which imposes, with the exceptions that have been noted, a requirement of citizenship for the licensing of an engineer.

Appellants' second argument is that the Commonwealth courts should be permitted to adjudicate the validity of the citizenship requirement in the light of §§1 and 7 of Art. II of the Puerto Rico Constitution, 1 P.R. Laws Ann., Const., Art. II, §§1, 7 (1965). Section 1 provides: "No discrimination shall be made on account of race, color, sex, birth, social origin or condition, or political or religious ideas." Section 7 provides: "No person in Puerto Rico shall be denied the equal protection of the laws." These constitutional provisions are not so interrelated with §689 that it may be said, as in Harris County, that the law of the Commonwealth is ambiguous. Rather, the abstention issue seems clearly controlled by Wisconsin v. Constantineau, 400 U.S. 433 (1971), where, as it was said in Harris County, 420 U.S., at 84-85, n.8, "we declined to order abstention where the federal due process claim was not complicated by an unresolved state law question, even though the plaintiffs might have sought relief under a similar provision of the state constitution." Indeed, to hold that abstention is required because §689 might conflict with the cited broad and sweeping constitutional provisions, would convert abstention from an exception into a general rule.

[The Court also ruled that Puerto Rico was a state within the meaning of §1983 and that the regulation was unconstitutional.]

NOTES

1. Otero firmly rejects the position initially urged by Chief Justice Burger in his dissent in Wisconsin v. Constantineau, 400 U.S. 433 (1971) that the possible existence of a state constitutional remedy requires a federal court to abstain from adjudicating a federal constitutional claim. The uneasy truce between Monroe v. Pape and the Pullman abstention doctrine is described in Neuborne, The Procedural Assault on the Warren Legacy, 5 Hofstra L. Rev. 545, 560 (1977).

2. Bellotti v. Baird, 428 U.S. 132 (1976), and Carey v. Bert Randolph Sugar, 425 U.S. 73 (1976), constitute classic applications of Pullman abstention, under which facial challenges to ambiguous state statutes are routed initially to state court to determine the true meaning of the challenged statute. The appropriate role of Pullman abstention in an "as applied" challenge to an ambiguous statute is less clear. Arguably, "as applied" challenges should be no more subject to abstention than was the claim in Otero. While the desire to avoid unnecessary constitutional adjudication militates strongly in favor of abstention in such cases, it is difficult to understand why the desire to avoid unnecessary federal constitutional adjudication is stronger in an "as applied" case than in Otero.

3. In United States v. Texas, 45 U.S.L.W. 2482 (S.D. Tex. 1977), the court refused to apply the abstention doctrine to a voting rights case

brought by the United States. In The Herald Co. v. McNeal, 553 F.2d 1125 (8th Cir. 1977), the 8th Circuit declined to abstain when it would unduly delay a decision on the merits. In Goldberg v. Carey, 601 F.2d 653 (2d Cir. 1979), the Circuit held that an abstention order was appealable as of right as a denial of a request for a preliminary injunction.

4. In Babbitt v. United Farm Workers, 442 U.S. 289 (1979), the Court abstained from deciding the constitutionality of several provisions of the Arizona Agricultural Labor Relations Act, despite the fact that the vagueness and overbreadth of the statute appeared to inhibit persons from engaging in First Amendment activity. Is the Court's decision to abstain in Babbitt consistent with Justice Powell's refusal to order abstention in Procunier v. Martinez, 416 U.S. 396 (1974)? Does the suggestion in Babbitt that the district court provide interim relief against enforcement pending state court clarification of the statute's meaning provide a practical accommodation of the interest in encouraging protected activity while respecting state competence to construe its own laws?

(page 1375) [1616]

ALLEN v. McCURRY
449 U.S. 90 (1980)

JUSTICE STEWART delivered the opinion of the Court.

At a hearing before his criminal trial in a Missouri court, the respondent, Willie McCurry, invoked the Fourth and Fourteenth Amendments to suppress evidence that had been seized by the police. The trial court denied the suppression motion in part, and McCurry was subsequently convicted after a jury trial. The conviction was later affirmed on appeal. State v. McCurry, 587 S.W.2d 337 (Mo. Ct. App.). Because he did not assert that the state courts had denied him a "full and fair opportunity" to litigate his search and seizure claim, McCurry was barred by this Court's decision in Stone v. Powell, 428 U.S. 465, 96 S. Ct. 3037, 49L. Ed. 2d 1067, from seeking a writ of habeas corpus in a federal district court. Nevertheless, he sought federal court redress for the alleged constitutional violation by bringing a damage suit under 42 U.S.C. §1983 against the officers who had entered his home and seized the evidence in question. We granted certiorari to consider whether the unavailability of federal habeas corpus prevented the police officers from raising the state courts' partial rejection of McCurry's constitutional claim as a collateral estoppel defense to the §1983 suit against them for damages.

I

In April 1977, several undercover police officers, following an informant's tip that McCurry was dealing in heroin, went to his house in

St. Louis, Mo., to attempt a purchase. Two officers, petitioners Allen and Jacobsmeyer, knocked on the front door, while the other officers hid nearby. When McCurry opened the door, the two officers asked to buy some heroin "caps." McCurry went back into the house and returned soon thereafter, firing a pistol at and seriously wounding Allen and Jacobsmeyer. After a gun battle with the other officers and their reinforcements, McCurry retreated into the house; he emerged again when the police demanded that he surrender. Several officers then entered the house without a warrant, purportedly to search for other persons inside. One of the officers seized drugs and other contraband that lay in plain view, as well as additional contraband he found in dresser drawers and in auto tires on the porch.

McCurry was charged with possession of heroin and assault with intent to kill. At the pretrial suppression hearing, the trial judge excluded the evidence seized from the dresser drawers and tires, but denied suppression of the evidence found in plain view. McCurry was convicted of both the heroin and assault offenses.

McCurry subsequently filed the present §1983 action for $1 million in damages against petitioners Allen and Jacobsmeyer, other unnamed individual police officers, and the city of St. Louis and its police department. The complaint alleged a conspiracy to violate McCurry's Fourth Amendment rights, an unconstitutional search and seizure of his house, and an assault on him by unknown police officers after he had been arrested and handcuffed.

II

The federal courts have traditionally adhered to the related doctrines of res judicata and collateral estoppel. Under res judicata, a final judgment on the merits of an action precludes the parties or their privies from relitigating issues that were or could have been raised in that action. Cromwell v. County of Sac., 94 U.S. 351, 352, 24 L. Ed. 195. Under collateral estoppel, once a court has decided an issue of fact or law necessary to its judgment, that decision may preclude relitigation of the issue in a suit on a different cause of action involving a party to the first case. Montana v. United States, 440 U.S. 147, 153, 99 S.Ct. 970, 973, 59 L. Ed. 2d 210. As this Court and other courts have often recognized, res judicata and collateral estoppel relieve parties of the cost and vexation of multiple lawsuits, conserve judicial resources, and, by preventing inconsistent decisions, encourage reliance on adjudication. Id., at 153-154.

III

This Court has never directly decided whether the rules of res judicata and collateral estoppel are generally applicable to §1983 actions. But in

Preiser v. Rodriguez, 411 U.S. 475, 497, 93 S. Ct. 1827, 1840, 36 L. Ed. 2d 439, the Court noted with implicit approval the view of other federal courts that res judicata principles fully apply to civil rights suits brought under that statute. See also Huffman v. Pursue, 420 U.S. 592, 606, n.18, 95 S. Ct. 1200, 1209, n.18, 43 L. Ed. 2d 482; Wolff v. McDonnell, 418 U.S. 539, 554, n.12, 94 S. Ct. 2963, 2974, n.12, 41 L. Ed. 2d 935. And the virtually unanimous view of the Courts of Appeals since Preiser has been that §1983 presents no categorical bar to the application of res judicata and collateral estoppel concepts. These federal appellate court decisions have spoken with little explanation or citation in assuming the compatibility of §1983 and rules of preclusion, but the statute and its legislative history clearly support the courts' decisions.

As the Court has understood the history of the legislation, Congress realized that in enacting §1983 it was altering the balance of judicial power between the state and federal courts. See Mitchum v. Foster, supra, 407 U.S., at 241, 92 S. Ct., at 2161. But in doing so, Congress was adding to the jurisdiction of the federal courts, not subtracting from that of the state courts. See Monroe v. Pape, supra, 365 U.S., at 183, 81 S. Ct., at 481 ("The federal remedy is supplementary to the state remedy...."). The debates contain several references to the concurrent jurisdiction of the state courts over federal questions, and numerous suggestions that the state courts would retain their established jurisdiction so that they could, when the then current political passions abated, demonstrate a new sensitivity to federal rights.

To the extent that it did intend to change the balance of power over federal questions between the state and federal courts, the 42d Congress was acting in a way thoroughly consistent with the doctrines of preclusion. In reviewing the legislative history of §1983 in Monroe v. Pape, supra, the Court inferred that Congress had intended a federal remedy in three circumstances: where state substantive law was facially unconstitutional, where state procedural law was inadequate to allow full litigation of a constitutional claim, and where state procedural law, though adequate in theory, was inadequate in practice. 365 U.S., at 173-174. In short, the federal courts could step in where the state courts were unable or unwilling to protect federal rights. Id., at 176. This understanding of §1983 might well support an exception to res judicata and collateral estoppel where state law did not provide fair procedures for the litigation of constitutional claims, or where a state court failed to even acknowledge the existence of the constitutional principle on which a litigant based his claim. Such an exception, however, would be essentially the same as the important general limit on rules of preclusion that already exists: Collateral estoppel does not apply where the party against whom an earlier court decision is asserted did not have a full and fair opportunity to litigate the claim or issue decided by the first court. But the Court's view of §1983 in Monroe lends no strength to any argument that Congress intended to allow relitigation of federal issues decided after a full and fair hearing in a state court simply because the state court's decision may have been erroneous.

The actual basis of the Court of Appeals' holding appears to be a generally framed principle that every person asserting a federal right is entitled to one unencumbered opportunity to litigate that right in a federal district court, regardless of the legal posture in which the federal claim arises. But the authority for this principle is difficult to discern. It cannot lie in the Constitution, which makes no such guarantee, but leaves the scope of the jurisdiction of the federal district courts to the wisdom of Congress. And no such authority is to be found in §1983 itself. For reasons already discussed at length, nothing in the language or legislative history of §1983 proves any congressional intent to deny binding effect to a state court judgment or decision when the state court, acting within its proper jurisdiction, has given the parties a full and fair opportunity to litigate federal claims, and thereby has shown itself willing and able to protect federal rights. And nothing in the legislative history of §1983 reveals any purpose to afford less deference to judgments in state criminal proceedings than to those in state civil proceedings. There is, in short, no reason to believe that Congress intended to provide a person claiming a federal right an unrestricted opportunity to relitigate an issue already decided in state court simply because the issue arose in a state proceeding in which he would rather not have been engaged at all.

The only other conceivable basis for finding a universal right to litigate a federal claim in a federal district court is hardly a legal basis at all, but rather a general distrust of the capacity of the state courts to render correct decisions on constitutional issues. It is ironic that Stone v. Powell provided the occasion for the expression of such an attitude in the present litigation, in view of this Court's emphatic reaffirmation in that case of the constitutional obligation of the state courts to uphold federal law, and its expression of confidence in their ability to do so. 428 U.S., at 493-494, n.35, see Robb v. Connolly, 111 U.S. 624, 637, (Harlan, J.).

The Court of Appeals erred in holding that McCurry's inability to obtain federal habeas corpus relief upon his Fourth Amendment claim renders the doctrine of collateral estoppel inapplicable to his §1983 suit. Accordingly, the judgment is reversed, and the case is remanded to the Court of Appeals for proceedings consistent with this opinion.

It is so ordered.

JUSTICE BLACKMUN, with whom JUSTICE BRENNAN and JUSTICE MARSHALL join, dissenting.

The legal principles with which the Court is concerned in this civil case obviously far transcend the ugly facts of respondent's criminal convictions in the courts of Missouri for heroin possession and assault.

The Court today holds that notions of collateral estoppel apply with full force to this suit brought under 42 U.S.C. §1983. In my view, the Court, in so ruling, ignores the clear import of the legislative history of that statute and disregards the important federal policies that underlie its enforcement. It also shows itself insensitive both to the significant differences between the §1983 remedy and the exclusionary rule, and to the pressures upon a criminal defendant that make a free choice of forum illusory. I do not doubt that principles of preclusion are to be given such effect as is appropriate in a §1983 action. In many cases, the denial of res judicata or collateral estoppel effect would serve no purpose and would harm relations between federal and state tribunals. Nonetheless, the Court's analysis in this particular case is unacceptable to me. It works injustice on this §1983 plaintiff, and it makes more difficult the consistent protection of constitutional rights, a consideration that was at the core of the enacters' intent. Accordingly, I dissent.

The following factors persuade me to conclude that this respondent should not be precluded from asserting his claim in federal court. First, at the time §1983 was passed, a nonparty's ability, as a practical matter, to invoke collateral estoppel was nonexistent. One could not preclude an opponent from relitigating an issue in a new cause of action, though that issue had been determined conclusively in a prior proceeding, unless there was "mutuality." Additionally, the definitions of "cause of action" and "issue" were narrow. As a result, and obviously, no preclusive effect could arise out of a criminal proceeding that would affect subsequent *civil* litigation. Thus, the 42d Congress could not have anticipated or approved that a criminal defendant, tried and convicted in state court, would be precluded from raising against police officers a constitutional claim arising out of his arrest.

Also, the process of deciding in a state criminal trial whether to exclude or admit evidence is not at all the equivalent of a §1983 proceeding. The remedy sought in the latter is utterly different. In bringing the civil suit the criminal defendant does not seek to challenge his conviction collaterally. At most, he wins damages. In contrast, the exclusion of evidence may prevent a criminal conviction. A trial court, faced with the decision whether to exclude relevant evidence, confronts institutional pressures that may cause it to give a different shape to the Fourth Amendment right from what would result in civil litigation of a damages claim. Also, the issue whether to exclude evidence is subsidiary to the purpose of a criminal trial, which is to determine the guilt or innocence of the defendant, and a trial court, at least subconsciously, must weigh the potential damage to the truth-seeking process caused by excluding relevant evidence. See Stone v. Powell, 428 U.S. 465, 489-495 (1976). Cf. Bivens v. Six Unknown Federal Narcotics Agents, 403 U.S. 388, 411-424 (dissenting opinion).

A state criminal defendant cannot be held to have chosen "voluntarily" to litigate his Fourth Amendment claim in the state court. The risk of conviction puts pressure upon him to raise all possible defenses. He also faces uncertainty about the wisdom of forgoing litigation on any issue, for there is the possibility that he will be held to have waived his right to appeal on that issue. The "deliberate by-pass" of state procedures, which the imposition of collateral estoppel under these circumstances encourages, surely is not a preferred goal. To hold that a criminal defendant who raises a Fourth Amendment claim at his criminal trial "freely and without reservation submits his federal claims for decision by the state courts," see England v. Medical Examiners, 375 U.S., at 419, 84 S. Ct., at 466, is to deny reality. The criminal defendant is an involuntary litigant in the state tribunal, and against him all the forces of the State are arrayed. To force him to a choice between forgoing either a potential defense or a federal forum for hearing his constitutional civil claim is fundamentally unfair.

I would affirm the judgment of the Court of Appeals.

NOTES

1. In Stone v. Powell, 428 U.S. 465 (1976), the Supreme Court held that if a state provided a full and fair consideration of defendants' Fourth Amendment exclusionary rule claim, habeas corpus review in a federal District Court was unavailable. The Court's reasoning turned on the marginal deterrent effect which the existence of habeas corpus review was likely to have on unconstitutional police conduct. In Allen v. McCurry, 449 U.S. 90 (1980), the Court declined to permit relitigation of a Fourth Amendment issue in the context of a Section 1983 claim. See also, Waste Mgmt. v. Fokakis, 614 F.2d 138 (7th Cir. 1980) (collateral estoppel bars corporation from challenging state criminal conviction under Section 1983); Hanson v. Circuit Court, 591 F.2d 404 (4th Cir. 1979).

In Jackson v. Virginia, 447 U.S. 307 (1979), the Court declined to extend Stone v. Powell to habeas corpus petitions alleging racial discrimination in the selection of the grand jury. Where a "fundamental" value (such as racial fairness) of our judicial system is at stake, a petitioner may seek habeas corpus review even after losing in state court. Thus far, exclusionary rule claims appear to be the sole constitutional claims ineligible for relitigation under habeas corpus. However, in Sumner v. Mata, 101 S. Ct. 761 (1980), the Court admonished that state findings of fact should be presumed correct in a federal habeas corpus proceeding.

In Rose v. Mitchell, 443 U.S. 545 (1979), the Court expanded the scope of habeas corpus to permit challenges to the sufficiency of the evidence, as well as to legal deficiencies. In Browder v. Director, Dept. of Corrections, 434 U.S. 257 (1978), the Court ruled that habeas corpus petitions were subject to the mandatory time constraints contained in Rules 52(b) and 59 of the Federal Rules of Civil Procedure.

2. Stone v. Powell, 428 U.S. 465 (1976), may be read as imposing a res judicata bar on the relitigation of Fourth Amendment issues determined by state courts. A similar bar has been imposed in the relitigation of Section 1981 claims that had been adversely determined in state court. Mitchell v. NBC, Inc., 553 F.2d 265 (2d Cir. 1977). See also, Kremer v. Chemical Construction Corp., 50 U.S.L.W. 4487 (1982) (applying §1738 to preclude relitigation of Title VII claim rejected by State court). In Gates v. Henderson, 568 F.2d 830 (2d Cir. 1977), the Second Circuit read the preclusive effect of Stone narrowly and required an explicit state rejection of the Fourth Amendment claim before precluding its consideration in federal court. In his dissent in Stone, Justice Brennan attacked the misuse of a congressionally mandated exhaustion requirement as the basis of a preclusion doctrine. Civil rights lawyers, faced with the spread of the Younger doctrine into the civil area, fear a similar progression from exhaustion to preclusion in Section 1983 cases. Specifically, lawyers fear that litigants who become locked into state forums by the operation of the comity doctrine will find themselves precluded from subsequent resort to federal court at the completion of the state proceedings. Such a result is now a reality in the child custody area. Lehman v. Lycoming County Children's Services Agency, 50 U.S.L.W. 5010 (1982) (habeas corpus unavailable to challenge state deprivation of parental rights). In Wooley v. Maynard, 430 U.S. 705 (1977), the Court appeared to retreat from the imposition of a comity based preclusion doctrine. In Maynard, a Jehovah's Witness had been twice convicted in state court of violating a New Hampshire motor vehicle regulation requiring the display of the motto "Live Free or Die" on his license plates. After paying his fines and serving a brief sentence, Maynard, instead of appealing from his state convictions, challenged the prospective application of the regulation to him pursuant to a Section 1983 action in federal court. The Supreme Court, rejecting the contention that Maynard's failure to have appealed deprived the federal court of power to rule on the prospective application of the statute, upheld the grant of a permanent injunction against its enforcement. Thus, while the failure to appeal probably precluded a collateral attack on the state convictions, neither the state convictions nor the failure to appeal precluded federal judicial review over the statute's constitutionality as prospectively applied. Whether Maynard would apply in a situation where the state forum gave serious attention to a clearly articulated position is unclear, since Maynard was unrepresented by counsel in the state proceedings, and the Justice of the Peace who imposed the traffic convictions was not legally trained. But see, Bennum v. Board of Governors of Rutgers, 413 F. Supp. 1274 (D.N.J. 1977) (state judgment rejecting claim for negligent tenure denial precludes subsequent Title VII action

based on some facts). The Court's application of collateral estoppel to the plaintiff's claim in Allen v. McCurry renders the possibility of pyramiding the exhaustion and preclusion doctrines a real one.

In Chancery Court v. Wallace, 646 F.2d 151 (5th Cir. 1981) a challenge to the procedures used in a civil commitment statute was successfully couched as a Section 1983 claim, thus avoiding the requirement that habeas corpus petitioners exhaust state judicial remedies. See generally Rose v. Lundy, 50 U.S.L.W. 4267 (1982) (habeas corpus petition containing exhausted and nonexhausted claims must be dismissed).

3. In non-civil rights contexts the Supreme Court has vigorously championed preclusion in order to conserve judicial energy. Thus, in Parklane Hosiery Company v. Shore, 439 U.S. 322 (1979), the Court abandoned mutuality as a requirement for collateral estoppel and in Montana v. United States, 440 U.S. 147 (1979), the Court imposed preclusion on the United States because it had financed and directed an earlier unsuccessful case in the name of a private party. See also, County of Imperial v. Munoz, 101 S. Ct. 289 (1980) (anti-injunction act bars relitigation of a state injunction except by genuine "strangers" to the state litigation); Federated Dept. Stores v. Moite, 101 S. Ct. 526 (1981) (res judicata applies to party who failed to appeal from adverse judgment despite success of other persons on appeal). However, in Barrantine v. Arkansas Best Freight System, 101 S. Ct. 1437 (1981), the Court declined to invest an administrative proceeding with preclusive effect. See also, United States v. Sioux Nation of Indians, 448 U.S. 371 (1980) (United States may elect to waive res judicata effect of prior decision).

4. Representative lower court applications of the preclusion doctrine include, Society Hill Civic Assn. v. Harris, 632 F.2d 1035 (3d Cir. 1980) (nonparties may attack prospective application of state consent decree); United States v. ITT Rayonier, 627 F.2d 996 (9th Cir. 1980) (state judgment in case involving state EPA binds federal EPA under doctrine of "virtual representations"); General Foods Corp. v. Mass Dept. of Public Health, 648 F.2d 784 (1st Cir. 1981) (member of trade association may be bound by decree if participated in litigation); Walsh v. International Longshoremen's Assn., 630 F.2d 864 (1st Cir. 1980) (claim I bars claim III, even though claim II was decided differently); Harrington v. Vandalia — Butler Board of Ed., 649 F.2d 434 (6th Cir. 1981) (earlier Title VII dismissal of claim for compensatory relief bars Section 1983 claim). For cases declining to apply preclusion, see, Johnson v. General Motors Corporation, 598 F.2d 432 (5th Cir. 1979) (Section 23(b)(2) class members who did not receive notice not barred from asserting Section 23(b)(3) claims); Gunther v. Iowa State Men's Reformatory, 612 F.2d 1079 (8th Cir. 1979) (state decision reversing state administrative ruling favorable to plaintiff not preclusive in federal Title VII claim). But see Sinicropi v. Nassau County, 601 F.2d 60 (2d Cir. 1979) (contra) and Kremer v. Chemical Construction Corp., 50 U.S.L.W.

4487 (1982) (§1738 requires preclusive effect be given state judgement affirming state administrative rejection of Title VII claims).

NOTE — SECTION 1983 CLAIMS IN STATE COURT

1. In Martinez v. California, 444 U.S. 277 (1980), the Supreme Court ruled that state courts may entertain Section 1983 claims. Even prior to Martinez, however, most state courts had welcomed Section 1983 claims. E.g., New Times, Inc. v. Arizona Bd. of Regents, 519 P.2d 169 (Ariz. 1974); Brown v. Pritchess, 531 P.2d 772 (Cal. 1975); Silverman v. University of Colo., 541 P.2d 93 (Colo. 1975); Bohacs v. Reid, 379 N.E.2d 1372 (Ill. 1978); Alberty v. Daniel, 323 N.E.2d 110 (Ill. 1974); Hirych v. State, 136 N.W.2d 910 (Mich. 1965); Dudley v. Bell, 213 N.W.2d 805 (Mich. 1973); Brody v. Leamy, 90 Misc. 2d 1, 393 N.Y.S. 2d 243 (Sup. Ct. 1977); Commonwealth ex rel. Saunders v. Creamer, 345 A.2d 702, 703 n.3 (Pa. 1975); Terry v. Kolski, 254 N.W.2d 704 (Wis. 1977).

See also Tobeluk v. Lind, 589 P.2d 873 (Alaska 1979); Thorpe v. Durango School Dist., 591 P.2d 1329 (1978), aff'd, 614 P.2d 880 (Colo. 1980); Ramirez v. County of Hudson, 404 A.2d 1271 (N.J. Ch. Div. 1979); James v. Board of Ed., 340 N.E.2d 735,737 (N.Y. 1975) (Fuchsberg, J., dissenting); Young v. Toia, 66 A.D.2d 377, 413 N.Y.S.2d 530 (1979); Lange v. Nature Conservancy, Inc., 601 P.2d 963 (Wash. 1979); Board of Trustees v. Holso, 584 P.2d 1009 (Wyo. 1978); Shapiro v. Columbia Union Natl. Bank, 576 S.W.2d 310 (Mo. 1979).

Two state courts have declined to exercise jurisdiction over Section 1983 claims. Backus v. Chilivis, 224 S.E.2d 370 (1976) (partial); Chamberlain v. Brown, 442 S.W.2d 248 (Tenn. 1969). However, the rationale of the Tennessee Supreme Court in Chamberlain, which turned on a presumed grant of exclusive jurisdiction to the federal courts, seems to have been undercut by the Supreme Court's recognition that federal jurisdiction over Section 1983 claims is not exclusive.

2. Although the Martinez court reserved the question of whether a state court must entertain a Section 1983 claim, prior case law appears to render the jurisdiction mandatory. In Mondou v. New York, N.H. & H.R.R., 223 U.S.1 (1912), and Testa v. Katt, 330 U.S. 386 (1947), the Supreme Court ruled that states may not discriminate against federal causes of action. If a state court would entertain a similar state-based claim, it may not decline to entertain a federal cause of action. Since state courts are unlikely to refuse to entertain state constitutional claims, the anti-discrimination principle imposes a de facto obligation on state courts to entertain Section 1983 claims.

3. In Maine v. Thiboutot, 448 U.S. 1 (1980), the Supreme Court required Maine to apply federal attorney's fee rules to a Section 1983 claim in state court despite contrary local practice. The extent to which

Section 1983 claims in state court should trigger an "obverse Erie" analysis requiring state judges to apply federal collateral rules to federal claims is discussed in Neuborne, Toward Procedural Parity in Constitutional Litigation, 22 William & Mary L. Rev. 725 (1981).